FRIEDRICH NIETZSCHE

Human, All-Too-Human
Parts 1 and 2
Beyond Good and Evil

*Translated by Helen Zimmern
and Paul V. Cohn*

*With an Introduction by
Ray Furness*

**WORDSWORTH CLASSICS
OF WORLD LITERATURE**

For my husband
ANTHONY JOHN RANSON
with love from your wife, the publisher
Eternally grateful for your
unconditional love

Readers who are interested in other titles from
Wordsworth Editions are invited to visit our
website at www.wordsworth-editions.com

This edition published 2008 by Wordsworth Editions Limited
8B East Street, Ware, Hertfordshire SG12 9HJ

ISBN 978 1 84022 591 4

This edition © Wordsworth Editions Limited 2014
Introduction © Ray Furness 2008

Wordsworth® is a registered trademark of
Wordsworth Editions Limited

Wordsworth Editions is
the company founded in 1987 by
MICHAEL TRAYLER

Typeset in Great Britain by Roperford Editorial
Printed and bound by Clays Ltd, St Ives plc

CONTENTS

INTRODUCTION   VII

FURTHER READING   XXIV

HUMAN, ALL-TOO-HUMAN, PART 1

Preface   3

First Division: *First and Last Things*   11

Second Division: *The History of the Moral Sentiments*   36

Third Division: *The Religious Life*   72

Fourth Division: *Concerning the Soul of Artists and Authors*   98

Fifth Division: *The Signs of Higher and Lower Culture*   132

Sixth Division: *Man in Society*   169

Seventh Division: *Wife and Child*   187

Eighth Division: *A Glance at the State*   202

Ninth Division: *Man Alone by Himself*   226

An Epode: *Among Friends*   260

HUMAN, ALL-TOO-HUMAN, PART 2

Preface   263

Part One: *Miscellaneous Maxims and Opinions*   271

Part Two: *The Wanderer and his Shadow*   387

Preface   515
First Chapter: *Prejudices of Philosophers*   517
Second Chapter: *The Free Spirit*   537
Third Chapter: *The Religious Mood*   555
Fourth Chapter: *Apophthegms and Interludes*   570
Fifth Chapter: *The Natural History of Morals*   584
Sixth Chapter: *We Scholars*   603
Seventh Chapter: *Our Virtues*   620
Eighth Chapter: *Peoples and Countries*   642
Ninth Chapter: *What is Noble?*   662
From the Heights   691

INTRODUCTION

On Thursday 25 April 1878, towards midday, the Wagners received a copy of Nietzsche's latest work; Cosima records a feeling of oppression, of apprehension when looking cursorily at it. Wagner himself remarked that he was doing the author a favour by not reading it, for which Nietzsche would later show gratitude. Wagner glanced at certain passages whilst cutting the pages; Cosima detected 'much ire and doggedness' in it and aroused her husband's humour by pointing out that the dedicatee, one Voltaire, would have been precisely the man *not* to have understood *The Birth of Tragedy*, whose 1871 preface had been a glorious tribute to her husband. She and Wagner would likewise, had they seen section 37 and its praise of Paul Rée, author of *On the Origin of Moral Sensations,* disciple of Auguste Comte, positivist and Jew to boot, have been united in their scornful disapprobation. One month later, in a letter to Franz Overbeck, Protestant theologian, professor at Basle and lifelong friend of Nietzsche, Wagner will refer to Nietzsche's apostasy and comment that 'There is no doubt that very *striking* changes have taken place in him [Nietzsche]; but anyone who observed him in his *psychic spasms* years ago could almost be justified in saying that a long-dreaded and not entirely unpredictable catastrophe had now overtaken him.' He refers again to Nietzsche's book which he had no intention of reading, having gained an inkling of its drift. The book was entitled *Human, All-Too-Human. A Book for Free Spirits.**

* A note on this work's genealogy. The first part, Volume I, was published in 1878 and was dedicated to Voltaire; it consisted of 638 numbered sections in nine chapters. The second edition appeared in 1886 with the dedication removed and a newly written preface and a poetic postlude added. Volume II consists of two sequels, *Miscellaneous Maxims and Opinions,* published in 1879 and consisting of 408 sections, and *The Wanderer and his Shadow,* published in 1880 and containing 350 sections and a dialogue. The second edition, 1886, combines these two sequels as Volume II of *Human, All-Too-Human,* the only change being the addition of a newly written preface. References hereafter will be to *HH* plus volume and section number.

In his *Ecce Homo* (see *Twilight of the idols*, Wordsworth Classics of World Literature, 2007), Nietzsche's most extraordinary, extravagant and imaginative autobiography, in the chapter 'Why I Write such Excellent Books', *HH* is described as the memorial of a crisis and the expression of a triumph. Here, Nietzsche explains, he comes to terms with, and succeeds in expunging, those tendencies within himself which he had overcome: Wagner, Christianity, idealism and Romantic excesses. The name of Voltaire on the title page shows the new master whom Nietzsche now admires, this *grand seigneur* of the intellect, the centenary of whose death, in 1878, Nietzsche sought to commemorate. Nietzsche now wishes to appear as a pitiless spirit, seeking out those secret hiding places in which ideals are wont to skulk. 'With a torch in my hand, the light of which is not by any means a flickering one, I illuminate this nether world with beams that are like blades. It is war [. . .] One error after the other is quietly laid upon ice; the ideal is not refuted – it freezes . . . ' The 'genius', the 'saint', the 'hero', 'faith', he writes, are subjected to merciless scrutiny – and found wanting; a 'free spirit' upturns every stone and looks into the darkest corner of the human psyche. It is not the erstwhile acolyte of Wagner who now speaks to us but an admirer of the French *lumières*, of La Rochefoucauld and Voltaire, witty, acerbic and sophisticated. Nietzsche now adopts the pose of dandy, a man affecting fine raiment (to Jakob Burckhardt's annoyance in Basle), a man wielding (in his intellect at least) an elegant rapier. And he is unable to resist, in *Ecce Homo*, the claim that *HH* crossed in the post with the text of Richard Wagner's *Parsifal* which the composer had sent him; it seemed to him that two swords were clashing here (although, in truth, some four months elapsed between his receipt of Wagner's text in the January of 1878 and his initially reluctant dispatch of his new book to Bayreuth in the April).

It is as a disciple of the Enlightenment, then, that Nietzsche wishes to appear, one who has set aside the dark blandishments of myth, of Dionysus, of Wagner. Voltaire and the French will be his guides – but we are justified in casting doubts on this emancipation, this apparent conversion: Voltaire's wit and literary elegance could never triumph over Nietzsche's 'spiritual intoxications' (Heller). Is there really to be a new '*Réalisme*' in his writing? He had certainly worked closely with Paul Rée in the winter of 1876-7 and had admired the Jewish psychologist's demolition of traditional assessments of altruism and conscience in this 'boldest and coldest thinker' (*HH* I, 37), as we have noticed. (Rée would later, with Nietzsche, form part of that remarkable *ménage à trois* with Lou Salomé, and the two men would pose for a notorious photograph taken on May 13, 1882 in Lucerne where they are both pulling a cart on which Lou Salomé squats, brandishing a rudimentary whip). Does Nietzsche, then, have new mentors? His enthusiasm for Rée's writing would cool, however (a letter to Heinrich von Stein, 15 October 1885 rejects Rée's comments on the conscience as empty, boring and wrong), and Voltaire, we know, is simply a stick with which to beat Wagner; he is dropped from the second edition of *HH* (1886) and is, significantly, nowhere to be found in the last pages of 'Miscellaneous Maxims and Opinions' (*HH* II, 408, 'The Journey to Hades') where, in stately German prose, Nietzsche writes of his descent to the underworld where he sacrifices not only sheep but his own blood to commune with the great thinkers and writers of the past who have accompanied him on his intellectual journey.

The reader of *HH* is confronted by a plethora of scintillating aphorisms, of maxims, discursive miniatures, chiselled contradictions, personified antitheses; our thinker, despising the straitjacket of systems of thought, may now attack from different angles, illuminate from different directions. (For want of a better term I shall follow Michael Tanner and call those utterances sections, however inappropriate this term may be to the very short entities.) Are Nietzsche's perspectives not highly subjective? Indeed they are, and he will wear many masks to worry and tease us. *HH* begins with a cluster of penetrating sections which insist on the need for a new, scientific, psychological approach to such concepts as goodness, morality, metaphysics and religion, and insists that historical philosophy can no longer be separated from the natural sciences (*HH* I, 2). Following in Rée's footsteps he insists (*HH* I, 1) that metaphysical philosophy, in insisting that goodness derives from a higher reality, is false; goodness and beauty may simply be sublimations of what has traditionally been called evil. In section 9 Nietzsche admits that there *might* be a metaphysical world; we look at everything through the human head and cannot cut this off. These suppositions may have been *valuable*, *terrible*, *delightful*, but they must now be refuted, are no longer needed. What *are* needed are what Nietzsche calls ecumenical goals or aims (section 25) to replace outdated notions of morality, a scientific approach to understand the preconditions of culture – and it is the evaluations and analysis of cultures which will become Nietzsche's most urgent preoccupation. It seems, then, that a rationalist is speaking to us here, a man seeking to sweep away illusions and imposing rigorous intellectual standards, but the issues are never quite as simple as this; if this is positivism then it is positivism of a very peculiar kind.

HH I, section 29 is of great interest now. The deep thinker, Nietzsche writes, seeks to approach the real essence of the world through his science (that is, through reason and logic). But he *means* to do so still more through his religion and arts. These latter are the 'blossoms of the world' rather than its stalk, the 'representation' rather than ultimate reality itself. But this 'representation', or *error*, has made man so deep, sensitive and inventive that he has put forth such glorious manifestations as religion, painting, music and literature. Pure knowledge, Nietzsche writes, would not have been capable of it. It may also seem that error is more life-enhancing than its opposite, and hence to be welcomed in the creation of beauty. It is these meditations on art and culture which make *HH* and subsequent writings such fascinating books. For art in its highest achievements can be a manifestation of the will to power, and the future philosopher with the hammer must needs respect it.

Could the 'scientific man' be seen as a further development of the 'artistic man'? (section 220). Art may be based on illusions but ultimately teaches us that 'Whatever it may be, life is good'; we may renounce it, but not the ability it has taught us, the ability to affirm, 'just as we have given up religion,' Nietzsche continues, 'but not the exalting and intensifying temperament acquired through religion.' Could the 'intensity and multiplicity of the joy of life' be guaranteed by science? Or would a higher culture 'give man two brain-chambers,' a double brain, as it were, to deal with science and non-science (section 251). And if science gives less pleasure in herself by throwing suspicion on the consolations of religion, metaphysics and art, those greatest of all sources of pleasure to which mankind owes almost its whole humanity, then a vast impoverishment ensues. *HH* I, section 278 uses the simile of the dance to portray what a great culture can be: sufficient strength and flexibility are needed to give poetry, religion and metaphysics 'a hundred paces start' – and then feel their force and beauty! Can science do this? Can there be a dance between science and non-science, a bold dance, not 'dull reeling to and fro' but a Bacchic dance such as Dionysus exemplified? Yet Nietzsche, unable to rest, continues to worry, fret, probe. *Why* does man need art? *Beyond Good and Evil* (hereafter *BGE*), in section 291, tells us that man is a complex, mendacious, artful and inscrutable animal who has invented audacious falsifications for self-aggrandisement and pleasure: 'there is, perhaps, much more in the conception of "art" than is generally believed.' But then, as we have noted, art, great art, is driven by the need to weave a veil of illusions to keep us in life; section 16 of *HH* II ('Miscellaneous Maxims and Opinions') states unequivocally, under the heading 'The good seduces to life', that 'All good things, even all good books that are written against life, are strong means of attraction to life'. The blooms of art and metaphysics, we know, may be illusory, but they transfigure the barren wastes of life and give man more satisfying pabulum than the aridities of science; we, mankind, give the world, that mass of errors and fantasies, meaning by bestowing on it the accumulated treasure of the past, and it *is* a treasure, for the value of our humanity depends upon it. We do not hear a desiccated scholar talking here but a man alert to the glories of what the human imagination can achieve: we are the colourists who bestow a glorious motley on the world (*HH* I, 16).

And yet (and how often is there not an 'and yet' in Nietzsche's thinking?) – has not a belief in some transcendental reality, remote, absolute, eternal, caused irreparable harm by devaluing the here and now? Has not Christianity brought morbidity and harmful self-castigation in its wake? The 1886 preface to *HH* II portrays Wagner as a man brought low by Christianity; this all-conquering hero, Nietzsche writes, is no more, and is, composing *Parsifal*, nothing more than a decayed and despairing Romantic, collapsing helpless and broken before the Christian cross. How can *Parsifal*, Nietzsche implies, be taken seriously in the modern age, the age of science, reason, psychology? How could Christianity be taken as ultimate truth? Section 113 in *HH* I paints an almost nostalgic picture of a time of faith with Sunday bells tolling in honour of a crucified Jew who claimed to be the Son of God. Nietzsche lists the main tenets of Christianity: is it possible, he asks, that such things were once believed? Is there a feeling of regret at its passing? Its antiquity is revered, but the son of the Protestant pastor at Röcken now checks himself and remembers his French mentors: he, remembering La Rochfoucauld, dismisses pity (for it weakens and debilitates) and agrees with Mérimée that evil is mostly committed for sheer pleasure (*HH* I, 50). Section 57 'improves' St Luke's 'he that humbleth himself shall be exalted' to 'he that humbleth himself wishes to be exalted': the mob finds pleasure in self-abasement and seeks thereby to undermine the self-confidence of the strong (this will be dealt with at much greater length in *Towards a Genealogy of Morals*). Section 137 discusses ascetic morality and sees that the tyranny over the self is a neurotic form of the will to power; a further cluster of sections attempt to see Christianity not as a religion of universal peace and love but as a religion of resentment, introversion and sickness where gratitude is a form of revenge (44) and the suffering of the weak is a desire to arouse sympathy and thereby demonstrate a power to hurt (50). In Christianity it is the herd which comes to the top, destroying the aristocratic values of the strong; it is a vindictive religion which emasculates and seeks domination through cunning and manipulation. In section 142 Nietzsche quotes the German Romantic poet Novalis on the strange and disturbing association of lust, religion and cruelty – how is it, Novalis wondered, that their close relationship and common tendency had not long ago been recognised? Those Sunday bells, tolling peacefully, seem now to serve a religion not of love but of neurosis, cruelty, sickness and morbidity.

Are artists necessarily irreligious? Nietzsche could have quoted Novalis again here who wrote: 'The artist is totally irreligious – he can work in religion as he does in bronze.' (He does tell us something similar in *HH* I, 125 in a reference to Homer and his gods, for artists use beliefs as mere material: Goethe did this, as did Shakespeare). Most telling is section 150. Here Nietzsche writes that art emerges most powerfully when religions recede. 'It takes over a number of feelings and moods produced by religion, clasps them to its heart, and then becomes itself deeper, more soulful, so that it is able to communicate exaltation and enthusiasm, which it could not yet do before.' If the Enlightenment has shaken the dogmas of religion then religious feeling will throw itself upon art, sometimes, even, into political life or even science. Wherever, Nietzsche concludes, human endeavour wears a loftier, more gloomy aspect, there, indeed the remains of religion may still be found, in incense, shadows, spirits. (The messianic zeal of the fanatical dictators of the twentieth century and their arrogation of quasi-divine status are surely adumbrated here). A most moving section is *HH* I, 220, which acknowledges that, in their loftiest soarings, the artists of all ages have exalted and divinely transfigured these concepts which the modern thinker (that is, Nietzsche) recognises as false: they 'glorify mankind's religious and philosophical errors'. If 'the rainbow colours around the outer edges of human knowledge and imagination fade', then this kind of art, the art of Dante, Raphael and Michelangelo, and the glories of Gothic cathedrals, can never be repeated, indicating as they do a cosmic as well as a metaphysical meaning in the work of art. Out of this, Nietzsche writes (having, seemingly, put aside thoughts on art's irreligiosity), a touching legend will grow, a legend that such an art and such a faith once existed. There is an elegiac note in this writing, far removed from the slickness of Rée and the acerbic witticisms of the French. This is a Nietzsche who admits (*HH* II, 153) how strong a 'free spirit's' metaphysical need is, when listening to Beethoven; he feels himself floating above the earth in a starry dome with the dream of *immortality* (Nietzsche's emphasis) in his heart, with the stars shining around him and the earth sinking further and further away. If, Nietzsche claims, this 'free thinker' feels 'a deep pain in his heart' and sighs for the one who will lead him back to his 'lost darling' – be it called religion or metaphysics – then indeed his intellectual character (that is, his scepticism) is certainly put to the test. And this thinker (and surely we recognise him) is the one who can extol the glories (*HH* II, 238: 'Miscellaneous Maxims and Opinions') of German music and also (270) the 'Eternal Child' in man who is never able to forget the fairy-tales of his youth.

In *HH* II, 224 ('Miscellaneous Maxims and Opinions') our future anti-Christ (or anti-Christian) honours Christianity, that 'silent Christian community' in ancient Rome, for its having stifled and conquered the Rome of Juvenal, 'that poisonous toad with the eye of Venus'. This Christianity, with its 'cracked, weary yet melodious bell' is balm to the ears of tired, dissipated souls. But for the 'heroic, child-like, animal' soul of the younger races Christianity was a poison, implanting the doctrines of sinfulness and damnation. A more belligerent tone becomes noticeable now and anticipates the strident truculence of much of Nietzsche's later writing. *HH* I, 246 speaks of those terrible energies – Evil – which are like the glaciers that have furrowed and gouged the landscapes but which were necessary for the later formation of woods, meadows and streams. Wild and destructive forces are needed in order that the milder civilisations might make their dwellings there. Amoral forces are adumbrated, and Nietzsche's provocative imagery, describing the need of 'such a highly cultivated, and therefore necessarily weary humanity as that of present-day Europe, [for] not only wars but the greatest and most terrible wars (that is, occasional relapses into barbarism)', lest its culture be destroyed by – culture (*HH* I, 477), necessarily sends a *frisson* through the modern reader. 'Good blood' is needed (*HH* I, 440): the art of being able to command and the art of proud obedience. That '*Pathos der Distanz*' is touched upon here, the concepts of rank and hierarchy which we shall notice later. Is life then strife and turmoil, preparing the way for that superior being who can bless and affirm? Perhaps, but there is calmness too, passages of quietness in Nietzsche's writing (*HH* II, 'The Wanderer and his Shadow', 8) where gentle night is extolled, the dim, red lamplight and the weary soul who awaits the injunction 'Rest awhile, poor troubled spirit.' And in *HH* II, 192 our thinker flees discord and uproar to find his joy in Arcadia: 'A garden, figs, a little cheese and three or four good friends – that was the luxury of Epicurus', and Nietzsche can find no fault with it.

In *Human, All-Too-Human* a fascinating and unsettling thinker overwhelms the reader with brilliant and frequently provocative ideas, forcing him to *think* above all and assess his own intellectual, moral and religious standpoint. In *The Gay Science* (1882) section 345 Nietzsche will explain that all great problems demand great love, and of that only the strong who have a firm grip on themselves are capable. It makes the most telling difference, he avers, whether a thinker has a personal relationship with his problems, finding in them his destiny, his distress and his greatest happiness, or an 'impersonal' one, merely touching them with the antennae of cold, curious thought; we can have no doubt in which category Nietzsche would have placed himself. Love and serenity are not often associated with Nietzsche, but it is the last section in the fifth chapter of *HH* I, 292, ('Signs of Higher and Lower Culture') which contains the fondest of admonitions: that we should go forth upon the path of wisdom, throwing off displeasure and never regretting that we had once been religious, for religion gave us a genuine and precious access to art; having loved religion and art, these glorious fruits of older civilisations, loved them as a mother and a nurse, we must now outgrow them. No honey is sweeter than that of knowledge, and mellowness will come with wisdom − it was thus intended by nature. Ironic indeed that our philosopher who preaches a quiet acceptance of existence and awaits with calmness and dignity 'the mists of death' should be seen above all as the one who is endlessly torn, buffeted and crucified upon the agonies and splendour of his own mind.

Beyond Good and Evil: Prelude to a Philosophy of the Future

To turn again to *Ecce Homo* (not 'reliable' in any mundane sense, as we know, but highly enlightening nevertheless, and entertaining): *Beyond Good and Evil* (hereafter *BGE*) is described as a work of critique, a necessary adjunct to *Thus Spake Zarathustra*, that paean of grandiloquent affirmation. (The full title insists that it is a 'Prelude to a Philosophy of the Future': this philosophy was, in fact, never completed, but remained a mass of unfinished material, to parts of which the tentative title *The Will to Power* was given. Nietzsche wisely abandoned the project, but unscrupulous commentators, such as his sister, published a so-called work bearing that title in 1901, after Nietzsche's death: see Hollingdale for a succinct account of the unpublished *Nachlaß* and Nietzsche's concept of the *Transvaluation of all Values*.) As God chose to rest after his great task of creation, Nietzsche writes, and coiled himself as a serpent around the foot of the tree of knowledge, our author leaves the prophet and mountain world of Zarathustra and looks at the contemporary world around him. Does he have peers to help him in his attack on morality, on the immense task of transvaluation? As a skilful angler he cast out his fishhooks, his baits − but is it his fault that nothing was caught? '*There were no fish to come and bite . . .*'

In all its essential points this book (*BGE*) is 'a criticism of modernity'. It is an enormously stimulating book, invigorating, startling, witty and, like much of Nietzsche, disorientating. It was published in 1886 with a preface written the year before, a preface which, in a light-hearted manner, suggests that truth is a woman and that those dogmatic souls afflicted with a terrible seriousness will not be able to woo her. A light, more elegant path is needed, a fresh and sparkling approach; this most brilliant of stylists had chided (in *The Gay Science*) the great majority of men for whom the intellect is 'a clumsy, gloomy, creaking machine' and sought to emulate a writer such as Heine whose divine malice was 'a guarantee of perfection itself'. Dogmatic philosophy, the preface continues, is likened to an enormous, awe-inspiring caricature, as is Platonism with its invention of 'pure spirit', as is Christianity, this 'Platonism for the "people"'. Such edifices of thought and belief, once admired, are now redundant, but a 'tension of soul' has been created by them which could now be put to better use. It is we 'good Europeans', we free, very free spirits who are now ready to approach the concept of truth in different ways and not waste our energies on a chimera. The reader's attention is immediately seized and those, it must be stated, who found *Thus Spake Zarathustra* a garish aberration, a monstrous excrescence on the German literary and philosophical landscape (and the notion of the *Übermensch* likewise) will relish Nietzsche's return to an intellectually more familiar, less extravagant setting.

A thinker 'beyond good and evil' is one who has accepted the death of God, a momentous, monstrous event, and one announced in *The Gay Science* (most memorably in the outburst of the madman with his lantern on the marketplace) and elaborated upon in *Thus Spake Zarathustra*. This thinker must also accept the resultant repercussions in the world of morality: there is no divine ground of being, no absolute standard of truth or order, no 'heavenly Father'. Man has freed himself from metaphysical sanctions and elects to stand alone. Nineteenth-century atheism, then? The triumph of truth, of intellectual honesty over superstition? But the issues are considerably more complex and interesting, as they were in *HH*, and our free, our 'very free' spirit has some very unsettling things to say about the notion of truth itself.

The opening of *BGE* teases the reader with the witty assertion that the will to truth may not be the highest good, and this putative reader is asked to think about the *value* of the will to truth. Why not rather untruth? Uncertainty? Ignorance? 'The problem of the value of truth stepped before us . . . ' (*BGE* 1) Does the philosopher not seek the truth? Indeed he does, but he must also question the value of truth. If appearance were to have a higher and more fundamental value for life, then why deplore it? (*BGE* 2) If a truth were harmful to life, why applaud it? (*BGE* 39). Nietzsche delights in worrying and teasing, pouncing and harrying. 'The falseness of an opinion is not for us any objection to it: it is here, perhaps, that our new language sounds most strangely . . . To recognise untruth *as a condition of life*: this is certainly to impugn the traditional ideas of value in a dangerous manner, and a philosophy which ventures to do so thereby alone places itself beyond good and evil' (*BGE* 4). The reader is certainly in unfamiliar territory here, but it becomes apparent that philosophy now must in some way be a means to achieve power and not primarily a means to truth. It is section 211 (in the chapter 'We Scholars') that states this quite clearly. We must not, we are told, confound 'philosophical workers' and 'scientific men in general' with genuine philosophers. The real philosopher may indeed have been a critic, dogmatist, historian, poet, collector, traveller, riddle-reader, moralist, seer, free spirit; he may have travelled the whole range of human values and estimations, able to gaze upwards as well as down. 'But these are only preliminary conditions for this task; this task itself demands something else – it requires him to *create values* . . . The *real philosophers* [. . .] are *commanders and law-givers*; they say "Thus *shall* it be! . . . " Their knowing is *creating*, their creating is law-giving, their will to truth is – *Will to Power*.' And the final rhetorical question is a flourish indeed: 'Are there at present such philosophers? Have there ever been such philosophers? *Must* there not be such philosophers some day . . . ?'

In *Towards a Genealogy of Morality* (*GM*), a work which appeared shortly after *BGE* and may be seen very much as a companion to it Nietzsche states quite clearly that 'All science must, from now on, prepare the way for the future work of the philosopher: this work being understood to mean that the philosopher has to solve the *problem* of values and that he has to decide upon a *hierarchy* of values'. Truth is not a metaphysical absolute (for since the death of God these no longer exist); it must now be seen as a 'part of a human economy of living' (Pearson/Large), and questions of truth are to be 'situated in the context of a thinking of life, of nature, of history and culture' (ibid). Such questions must now be incorporated into life, embedded in life and, above all, enhance life. The new philosophy will insist that our thinking is fundamentally informed by a multiplicity of warring instincts (*BGE* 6), and the primary desire of a living thing is to discharge and release its strength (*BGE* 13); that which inhibits or stunts life must be expunged. A bracing and unsettling element enters into Nietzsche's writing when he describes his detestation of complacency, normality and happiness as understood by the common man: section 44 of chapter two, 'The Free Spirit', is meant to shake and appal his readers – and succeeds. He launches a spirited attack on levellers, on democrats, on those who seek 'the green-meadow happiness of the herd', who long for security, safety, comfort, equality, sympathy. 'We opposite ones', he writes, believe that 'severity, violence, slavery, danger in the street and in the heart, secrecy, stoicism, temptations to devilry of every kind, everything wicked, terrible, tyrannical, predatory and serpentine in man' will be equally favourable to the furtherance of the plant 'man', helping him grow more vigorously, more rampant, more powerful. The chapter ends with an exuberant panegyric of 'the new philosophers' who are full of malice against the seduction of money, honours, position; they will be grateful for distress and to the vicissitudes of illness, inquisitive to a fault, inventive in scheming, hiding under the mantles of light – they will be night-owls of work even in the brightest day, scarecrows even, and jealous of their solitude. Such are the free thinkers as Nietzsche sees them, and he asks the philosophers of the future if they can emulate this. The impact of the headlong, rushing rhetoric on the readers of Nietzsche's day can well be imagined.

Beyond Good and Evil astonishes and appals in equal measure, for Nietzsche has the courage to confront the moralistic assumptions of his age and finds them moribund and decadent, weakened by an enfeebled and moribund Christianity, by its offshoot socialism, and an inability to find and create *greatness*. Chapter nine ('What is noble?') immediately insists on a pathos of distance, upon the need for a hierarchy, an aristocracy which can impose its values upon the herd (needless to say, this aristocracy would never be found in the *Almanac de Gotha*, for whose scions Nietzsche had nothing but contempt). The higher civilisations, we read (257), arise when men with natural instincts, barbarians in every sense of the word, men of prey possessing unbridled strength of will and an unquenchable thirst for power, throw themselves upon weaker, more peaceful races or upon older, more mellow civilisations 'in which the final, vital force would flicker out in brilliant fireworks of wit and depravity'. The barbarian caste enjoys physical superiority but also 'psychical' – they are more *complete* men, and therefore 'more complex beasts'. The modern reader may well find this repugnant, as he will section 259. To refrain mutually from injury and violence, Nietzsche writes, is all very well, but is a *denial* of life, a principle of dissolution and decay. For life is essentially appropriation, injury, conquest, suppression, severity; exploitation does not belong to the depraved but to the very nature of life, life as a manifestation of the will to power. And the following section, 260, continues and intensifies ideas put forward in *HH* (I, 45) and which will later be amplified in *GM*, that there is a master-morality and a slave-morality. What the master race calls 'good' is that which is creative, ruthless, honourable and proud, and 'bad' is the opposite, that is meekness, submissiveness, passivity and timid egalitarianism. These virtues of the slaves and the oppressed are heralded by them as 'good', whilst pride, arrogance, imperiousness and cruelty are called 'evil'. Christianity is now exposed for sapping the strength of the 'good' (i.e. strong and aristocratic) by attacking life itself and denying the will to power, or rather, through '*ressentiment*' seeking to bring down the hierarchical structure of life and bringing 'to nought things that are'. Christianity will move centre-stage in Nietzsche's thinking as the arch-enemy of life, of procreation (a very witty *aperçu* in *BGE* 168 explains that 'Christianity gave Eros poison to drink: he did not die of it, certainly, but degenerated into Vice'), in its belief in original sin, its contempt for the body, its promulgation of such doctrines as the Immaculate Conception of Mary which defiles natural conception (see *The Antichrist;* section 34), and its emphasis on a Beyond which cannot but debase the here and now. In *BGE* our Antichrist lays about himself with vigour and panache. A transvaluation of values is heralded (203) in which the values of the herd are rejected, corrupted as they are by 'modern ideas' (equality etc), and Christo-European morality, yet a tremendous force will be created with a 'new pressure and hammer of which a conscience shall be steeled and a heart transformed into brass'. The world of Zarathustra is not far, the prophet who sought to 'press his hand upon the wax of millennia', and his disciple, exulting, foresees the new law-givers, ruthless, inviolate and creative.

Let us pause here. A brilliant writer puts opinions before us which may be truly shocking, but he who reads Nietzsche, this 'melodramatist of the inner life' (Tanner), as he would any other philosopher is a poor reader indeed. Nietzsche delights in overwhelming the reader with a fusillade of reckless suggestions and propositions in order to unsettle him, and he seeks to find those who can affirm after the death of the absolute and the resulting threat of nihilism. Truth, as has been suggested, must be a coordinate in life, and it is man who must create values and seek a fulfilled and even joyous existence without guidance from some extraneous force. In ever-increasing loneliness (and worsening health) Nietzsche frequently overstates his case, shrilly sometimes, sometimes with mordant wit. In *BGE* 292 he tells us that a philosopher is constantly experiencing, seeing, hearing, suspecting, hoping and dreaming extraordinary things; he is struck by his own thoughts as though they came from without, from above and below, like lightning bolts; he may even himself be a thunderstorm, going about pregnant with new lightning, an ominous person, ringed around by roaring and rumbling, gaping and sinister. This philosopher often runs away from himself, is often afraid of himself – but he cannot disown himself completely. He knows the dangers of what he is saying, but feels that it is necessary to extol the man of prey, Cesare Borgia (*BGE* 197) at the expense of the 'temperate man, the mediocre . . . ' We in the twenty-first century, with knowledge of barbarism, master-races, blonde beasts and monstrous dictators may wince, but Nietzsche's daring apostasy and thrilling provocations were certainly a salutary shock to nineteenth-century readers, a lightning bolt indeed and an exposure to the shocks of recently discovered dynamite detonated by the one who, in *Ecce Homo*, identified himself with this explosive. To castigate flabby humanism and limp velleity Nietzsche frequently assumes a mask of ferocity, knowing full well the dangers of his stance: 'He who fights with monsters,' he tells us (*BGE* 146), 'should be careful lest he thereby becomes a monster himself. And if you gaze long into the abyss, the abyss will also gaze into you.'

Nietzsche's refusal to tie himself to a rigid, constricting system of thought, his preference for a darting perspectivism allows him to use dazzling contradictions to disorientate the reader and force him, as it were, to do the necessary work of weighing, sifting and evaluating. The preface to the second part of *HH* told us that Nietzsche takes sides *against* himself and *for* everything that hurts him (II, 6). Perhaps Voltaire's precepts were, after all, '*Blödsinn*', stupidity? (a modern translation has suggested 'Hogwash'!) Does man really 'only search for truth to do good'? Then, Nietzsche writes, 'I wager he finds nothing!' (*BGE* 35) And must we not, after all, admire, esteem and respect the one who stammered that we should love mankind *for God's sake*? This has so far been 'the noblest and remotest sentiment to which mankind has attained'. Love for mankind, we read (*BGE* 60), without any redeeming intention in the background, is folly and brutishness and such a love, even though it may be an aberration, receives its 'grain of salt and sprinkling of ambergris'; this is one of the highest flights that man has achieved. The chapter 'What is noble?' praises the respect given to the bible throughout the centuries: this is 'perhaps the best example of discipline and refinement of manners which Europe owes to Christianity'. Such a respect, Nietzsche continues, is still to be found among the lower classes, but the 'cultured', the believers in 'modern ideas', are repulsive in their lack of shame, their easy insolence. The faith of the humble, then, is to be praised, whereas the glib enlightenment of the chattering classes is denigrated (*BGE* 263); religion, metaphysics and art constitute a glorious treasure, the treasure of a tradition, and the man of rank and nobility of spirit bows before them.

Nietzsche's 'genetic-reductive' approach to intellectual problems, his 'penchant for personified antitheses' (Martin) led him, as we have often noted, to dedicate that first edition of *HH* to Voltaire, knowing full well that it would rouse Wagner's wrath. But Voltaire has been pushed from his pedestal, and Wagner's greatness acknowledged. The first section, a paragraph, of chapter eight of *BGE* ('People and Countries'), is the best analysis ever written of Wagner's overture to *Die Meistersinger von Nürnberg*, a work which is one of the glories of nineteenth-century German music. He heard, Nietzsche explains, 'once again for the first time' Wagner's masterpiece, a piece of 'gorgeous, heavy, latter-day art, proud of presupposing that two centuries of music are still living' – and it is an honour to the Germans that such a proud assertion was not displaced. Nietzsche has very few good things to say about the Germans (and those who hold him responsible for encouraging the Germans to regard themselves as a 'master race' show a deplorable ignorance of his work), but here he sees the music of Wagner as portraying, as none other, the German style, manifold, formless, inexhaustible, as well as a German plenitude and potency of soul. Yet he also detects the *raffinements* of decadence in this music, for the German soul, he explains, is too young, and yet too ripe; the Germans belong to the day before yesterday and the day after tomorrow – 'they have, as yet, no today' (*BGE* 241). There is, it seems, great potential in the German soul, for both triumphs and triumphalism – but then Nietzsche checks himself and in *BGE* 244 he lambasts his fellow countrymen and reminds them it was not for nothing that they were called the '*tiusche Volk*', the 'deceptive people'. The English are rejected for their cant, their lack of music and philosophy, whilst the French are praised, as are the Jews (a riposte here, surely, to Wagner's anti-Semitism). And so the iridescence of Nietzsche's thought, trenchant and darting, outrageous, brilliant, illuminating and subversive, endlessly plays before us.

The penultimate section of the book (*BGE* 295) invokes the god Dionysus, that dark deity who had been introduced in *The Birth of Tragedy* and who would accompany Nietzsche to the very end of his lucid mental life (*The Dionysus Dithyrambs*) and beyond. The god is now presented in a tone which is both earnest and mischievous: he, Nietzsche, has learned 'far too much' about him, from mouth to mouth, for he is the god's last disciple and initiate. In *The Birth of Tragedy* Dionysus has been exalted as the amoral principle of life-affirmation; here he is praised as the 'genius of the heart', a god of allurement who scents the 'drop of goodness and sweet spirituality' under thick dark ice, the divining rod who seeks the gold hidden in mud and who is drawn to mankind, this brave, inventive animal who can find his way through every labyrinth. Yet man must learn to be stronger, more evil and more profound – also more beautiful. Nietzsche then tells us of the tempter-god's halcyon smile, a smile which hinted that a 'charming compliment' had been made. It seems that the storm and stress of the earlier acolyte of Dionysus has learned to appreciate a more coquettish flirtation – for Truth, as we know, is a woman who does not seek the plodding advances of a professor but a more skilful and appreciative suitor. The very last words of the book, before the poetic postlude, speak once more of those 'evil thoughts', red and garish, which were the 'sudden sparks and marvels' of the philosopher's solitude, but they also tell of more muted colours, the mellow colours of afternoon with which the transient things of the world may be immortalised. The final poem, somewhat awkwardly, brings Zarathustra back from his high mountains and announces the feast of festivals and the nuptials of night and day.

RAY FURNESS

FURTHER READING

Aschheim, Steven, *The Nietzsche Legacy in Germany 1890–1990*, Berkeley 1992

Blackham, Harold, *Six Existentialist Thinkers*, London 1956, 1961

Bridgwater, Patrick, *Nietzsche in Anglosaxony*, Leicester 1972

Deleuze, Gilles, *Nietzsche and Philosophy* (tr. Tomlinson), London 1983

Heller, Erich, *The Disinherited Mind*, London 1952

Heller, Erich, *The Importance of Nietzsche*, Chicago 1988

Hollingdale, R. J., *Nietzsche: The Man and his Philosophy*, London 1965

Kaufmann, Walter, *Nietzsche: Philosopher, Psychologist, Antichrist* (4th edition), Princeton 1974

Martin, Nicholas (ed.), *Nietzsche and the German Tradition*, Oxford and Berne 2003

Nietzsche, F., *Daybreak: Thoughts on the Prejudices of Morality* (tr. Hollingdale), Cambridge 1972

Nietzsche, F., *Beyond Good and Evil: Prelude to a Philosophy of the Future* (tr. Hollingdale), London 1973, 1990

Pasley, Malcolm (ed.), *Nietzsche: Imagery and Thought*, London 1978

Pearson, Keith Ansell and Large, Duncan (eds.), *The Nietzsche Reader*, Oxford 2006

Tanner, Michael, *Nietzsche*, Oxford 1994

HUMAN, ALL-TOO-HUMAN
PART ONE

PREFACE

I

I have been told frequently, and always with great surprise, that there is something common and distinctive in all my writings, from the *Birth of Tragedy* to the latest published *Prelude to a Philosophy of the Future*. They all contain, I have been told, snares and nets for unwary birds, and an almost perpetual unconscious demand for the inversion of customary valuations and valued customs. What? *Everything* only – human – all–too–human? People lay down my writings with this sigh, not without a certain dread and distrust of morality itself, indeed almost tempted and encouraged to become advocates of the *worst* things: as being perhaps only the *best* disparaged? My writings have been called a school of suspicion and especially of disdain, more happily, also, a school of courage and even of audacity. Indeed, I myself do not think that any one has ever looked at the world with such a profound suspicion; and not only as occasional Devil's Advocate, but equally also, to speak theologically, as enemy and impeacher of God; and he who realises something of the consequences involved, in every profound suspicion, something of the chills and anxieties of loneliness to which every uncompromising *difference of outlook* condemns him who is affected therewith, will also understand how often I sought shelter in some kind of reverence or hostility, or scientificality or levity or stupidity, in order to recover from myself, and, as it were, to obtain temporary self-forgetfulness; also why, when I did not find what I *needed*, I was obliged to manufacture it, to counterfeit and to imagine it in a suitable manner (and what else have poets ever done? And for what purpose has all the art in the world existed?). What I always required most, however, for my cure and self-recovery, was the belief that I was *not* isolated in such circumstances, that I did not *see* in an isolated manner – a magic suspicion of relationship and similarity to others in outlook and desire, repose in the confidence of friendship, a blindness in both parties without suspicion or note of interrogation, an enjoyment of foregrounds, and surfaces of the near and the nearest, of all that has colour, epidermis, and outside appearance. Perhaps I might be reproached in this respect for much 'art' and fine false coinage; for instance, for voluntarily and knowingly shutting my eyes to Schopenhauer's blind will to morality at a time when I had become sufficiently clear-sighted about morality; also for deceiving myself about Richard Wagner's incurable romanticism, as if it were a beginning and not an end; also about the Greeks, also about the Germans and their future and there would still probably be quite a long list of such alsos? Supposing however, that this were all true and that I were reproached with good reason, what do *you* know, what *could* you know as to how much artifice of self-preservation, how much rationality and higher protection there is in such self-deception – and how much falseness I still *require* in order to allow myself again and again the luxury of *my* sincerity? . . . In short, I still live; and life, in spite of ourselves, is not devised by morality; it *demands* illusion, it *lives* by illusion . . . but – There! I am already beginning again and doing what I have always done, old immoralist and bird-catcher that I am – I am talking un-morally, ultra-morally, 'beyond good and evil'? . . .

2

Thus then, when I found it necessary, I *invented* once on a time the 'free spirits', to whom this discouragingly encouraging book with the title *Human, all-too-Human*, is dedicated. There are no such 'free spirits' nor have there been such, but, as already said, I then required them for company to keep me cheerful in the midst of evils (sickness, loneliness, foreignness – *acedia*, inactivity) as brave companions and ghosts with whom I could laugh and gossip when so inclined and send to the devil when they became bores – as compensation for the lack of friends. That such free spirits *will be possible* some day, that our Europe *will* have such bold and cheerful wights amongst her sons of tomorrow and the day after tomorrow, actually and bodily, and not merely, as in my case, as the shadows of a hermit's phantasmagoria – I should be the last to doubt thereof. Already I see them *coming*, slowly, slowly; and perhaps I am doing something to hasten their coming when I describe in advance under what auspices I *see* them originate, and upon what paths I *see* them come.

3

One may suppose that a spirit in which the type 'free spirit' is to become fully mature and sweet, has had its decisive event in a *great emancipation*, and that it was all the more fettered previously and apparently bound for ever to its corner and pillar. What is it that binds most strongly? What cords are almost unrendable? In men of a lofty and select type it will be their duties; the reverence which is suitable to youth, respect and tenderness for all that is time-honoured and worthy, gratitude to the land which bore them, to the hand which led them, to the sanctuary where they learnt to adore – their most exalted moments themselves will bind them most effectively, will lay upon them the most enduring obligations. For those who are thus bound the great emancipation comes suddenly, like an earthquake; the young soul is all at once convulsed, unloosened and extricated – it does not itself know what is happening. An impulsion and compulsion sway and over-master it like a command; a will and a wish awaken, to go forth on their course, anywhere, at any cost; a violent, dangerous curiosity about an undiscovered world flames and flares in every sense. 'Better to die than live *here*' – says the imperious voice and seduction, and this 'here', this 'at home' is all that the soul has hitherto loved! A sudden fear and suspicion of that which it loved, a flash of disdain for what was called its 'duty', a rebellious, arbitrary, volcanically throbbing longing for travel, foreignness, estrangement, coldness, disenchantment, glaciation, a hatred of love, perhaps a sacrilegious clutch and look *backwards*, to where it hitherto adored and loved, perhaps a glow of shame at what it was just doing, and at the same time a rejoicing *that* it was doing it, an intoxicated, internal, exulting thrill which betrays a triumph – a triumph? Over what? Over whom? An enigmatical, questionable, doubtful triumph, but the *first* triumph nevertheless; – such evil and painful incidents belong to the history of the great emancipation. It is, at the same time, a disease which may destroy the man, this first outbreak of power and will to self-decision, self-valuation, this will to *free* will; and how much disease is manifested in the

wild attempts and eccentricities by which the liberated and emancipated one now seeks to demonstrate his mastery over things! He
roves about raging with unsatisfied longing; whatever he captures
has to suffer for the dangerous tension of his pride; he tears to
pieces whatever attracts him. With a malicious laugh he twirls
round whatever he finds veiled or guarded by a sense of shame;
he tries how these things look when turned upside down. It is a
matter of arbitrariness with him, and pleasure in arbitrariness, if
he now perhaps bestow his favour on what had hitherto a bad
repute – if he inquisitively and temptingly haunt what is specially
forbidden. In the background of his activities and wanderings –
for he is restless and aimless in his course as in a desert – stands
the note of interrogation of an increasingly dangerous curiosity.
'Cannot *all* valuations be reversed? And is good perhaps evil? And
God only an invention and artifice of the devil? Is everything,
perhaps, radically false? And if we are the deceived, are we
not thereby also deceivers? *Must* we not also be deceivers?' –
Such thoughts lead and mislead him more and more, onward
and away. Solitude encircles and engirdles him, always more
threatening, more throttling, more heart-oppressing, that terrible
goddess and *mater saeva cupidinum* – but who knows nowadays
what *solitude* is? . . .

4

From this morbid solitariness, from the desert of such years of
experiment, it is still a long way to the copious, overflowing
safety and soundness which does not care to dispense with disease
itself as an instrument and angling-hook of knowledge; – to
that *mature* freedom of spirit which is equally self-control and
discipline of the heart, and gives access to many and opposed
modes of thought; – to that inward comprehensiveness and
daintiness of superabundance, which excludes any danger of the
spirit's becoming enamoured and lost in its own paths, and lying
intoxicated in some corner or other; to that excess of plastic,
healing, formative, and restorative powers, which is exactly the
sign of *splendid* health, that excess which gives the free spirit the
dangerous prerogative of being entitled to live by *experiments* and
offer itself to adventure; the free spirit's prerogative of mastership!
Long years of convalescence may lie in between, years full of

many-coloured, painfully-enchanting magical transformations, curbed and led by a tough *will to health*, which often dares to dress and disguise itself as actual health. There is a middle condition therein, which a man of such a fate never calls to mind later on without emotion; a pale, delicate light and a sunshine-happiness are peculiar to him, a feeling of bird-like freedom, prospect, and haughtiness, a *tertium quid* in which curiosity and gentle disdain are combined. A 'free spirit' – this cool expression does good in every condition, it almost warms. One no longer lives, in the fetters of love and hatred, without Yea, without Nay, voluntarily near, voluntarily distant, preferring to escape, to turn aside, to flutter forth, to fly up and away; one is fastidious like every one who has once seen an immense variety *beneath* him – and one has become the opposite of those who trouble themselves about things which do not concern them. In fact, it is nothing but things which now concern the free spirit – and how many things! – which no longer *trouble* him!

5

A step further towards recovery, and the free spirit again draws near to life; slowly, it is true, and almost stubbornly, almost distrustfully. Again it grows warmer around him, and, as it were, yellower; feeling and sympathy gain depth, thawing winds of every kind pass lightly over him. He almost feels as if his eyes were now first opened to what is *near*. He marvels and is still; where has he been? The near and nearest things, how changed they appear to him! What a bloom and magic they have acquired meanwhile! He looks back gratefully – grateful to his wandering, his austerity and self-estrangement, his far-sightedness and his bird-like flights in cold heights. What a good thing that he did not always stay 'at home', 'by himself', like a sensitive, stupid tenderling. He has been *beside himself*, there is no doubt. He now sees himself for the first time – and what surprises he feels thereby! What thrills unexperienced hitherto! What joy even in the weariness, in the old illness, in the relapses of the convalescent! How he likes to sit still and suffer, to practise patience, to lie in the sun! Who is as familiar as he with the joy of winter, with the patch of sunshine upon the wall! They are the most grateful animals in the world, and also the most unassuming, these lizards of convalescents with their faces half-turned towards life once more: – there are those amongst them who never let a day pass without hanging a little hymn of praise on its trailing fringe. And, speaking seriously, it is a radical *cure* for all pessimism (the well-known disease of old idealists and falsehood-mongers) to become ill after the manner of these free spirits, to remain ill a good while, and then grow well (I mean 'better') for a still longer period. It is wisdom, practical wisdom, to prescribe even health for one's self for a long time only in small doses.

6

About this time it may at last happen, under the sudden illuminations of still disturbed and changing health, that the enigma of that great emancipation begins to reveal itself to the free, and ever freer, spirit – that enigma which had hitherto lain obscure, questionable, and almost intangible, in his memory. If for a long time he scarcely dared to ask himself, 'Why so apart? so alone? denying everything that I revered? denying reverence itself? Why this hatred, this suspicion, this severity towards my own virtues?' – he now dares and asks the questions aloud, and already hears something like an answer to them – 'Thou shouldst become master over thyself and master also of thine own virtues. Formerly *they* were thy masters; but they are only entitled to be thy tools amongst other tools. Thou shouldst obtain power over thy pro and contra, and learn how to put them forth and withdraw them again in accordance with thy higher purpose. Thou shouldst learn how to take the proper perspective of every valuation – the shifting, distortion, and apparent teleology of the horizons and everything that belongs to perspective; also the amount of stupidity which opposite values involve, and all the intellectual loss with which every pro and every contra has to be paid for. Thou shouldst learn how much *necessary* injustice there is in every for and against, injustice as inseparable from life, and life itself as *conditioned* by the perspective and its injustice. Above all thou shouldst see clearly where the injustice is always greatest: – namely, where life has developed most punily, restrictedly, necessitously, and incipiently, and yet cannot help regarding *itself* as the purpose and standard of things, and for the sake of self-preservation, secretly, basely, and continuously wasting away and calling in question the higher, greater, and richer – thou shouldst see clearly the problem of gradation of rank, and how power and right and amplitude of perspective grow up together. Thou shouldst – But enough; the free spirit *knows* henceforth which 'thou shalt' he has obeyed, and also what he *can* now *do*, what he only now – *may do*. . . .

7

Thus doth the free spirit answer himself with regard to the riddle of emancipation, and ends therewith, while he generalises his case, in order thus to decide with regard to his experience. 'As it has happened to *me!*' he says to himself, 'so must it happen to every one in whom a *mission* seeks to embody itself and to "come into the world".' The secret power and necessity of this mission will operate in and upon the destined individuals like an unconscious pregnancy – long before they have had the mission itself in view and have known its name. Our destiny rules over us, even when we are not yet aware of it; it is the future that makes laws for our today. Granted that it is *the problem of the gradations of rank*, of which we may say that it is *our* problem, we free spirits; now only in the midday of our life do we first understand what preparations, detours, tests, experiments, and disguises the problem needed, before it *was permitted* to rise before us, and how we had first to experience the most manifold and opposing conditions of distress and happiness in soul and body, as adventurers and circum-navigators of the inner world called 'man', as surveyors of all the 'higher' and the 'one-above-another', also called 'man' – penetrating everywhere, almost without fear, rejecting nothing, losing nothing, tasting everything, cleansing everything from all that is accidental, and, as it were, sifting it out – until at last we could say, we free spirits, 'Here – a *new* problem! Here a long ladder, the rungs of which we ourselves have sat upon and mounted – which we ourselves at some time have *been*! Here a higher place, a lower place, an under-us, an immeasurably long order, a hierarchy which we *see*; here – *our* problem!'

8

No psychologist or augur will be in doubt for a moment as to what stage of the development just described the following book belongs (or is assigned) to. But where are these psychologists nowadays? In France, certainly; perhaps in Russia; assuredly not in Germany. Reasons are not lacking why the present-day Germans could still even count this as an honour to them – bad enough, surely, for one who in this respect is un-German in disposition and constitution! This *German* book, which has been able to find readers in a wide circle of countries and nations – it has been about ten years going its rounds – and must understand some sort of music and piping art, by means of which even coy foreign ears are seduced into listening – it is precisely in Germany that this book has been most negligently read, and worst *listened to*; what is the reason? 'It demands too much,' I have been told, 'it appeals to men free from the pressure of coarse duties, it wants refined and fastidious senses, it needs superfluity – superfluity of time, of clearness of sky and heart, of *otium* in the boldest sense of the term: – purely good things, which we Germans of today do not possess and therefore cannot give.' After such a polite answer my philosophy advises me to be silent and not to question further; besides, in certain cases, as the proverb points out, one only *remains* a philosopher by being – silent.*

Nice, Spring 1886

---

* An allusion to the mediaeval Latin distich:
    O si tacuisses,
    Philosophus mansisses, – J. M. K.

First Division – *First And Last Things*

I

Chemistry of Ideas and Sensations – Philosophical problems adopt in almost all matters the same form of question as they did two thousand years ago; how can anything spring from its opposite? for instance, reason out of unreason, the sentient out of the dead, logic out of unlogic, disinterested contemplation out of covetous willing, life for others out of egoism, truth out of error? Metaphysical philosophy has helped itself over those difficulties hitherto by denying the origin of one thing in another, and assuming a miraculous origin for more highly valued things, immediately out of the kernel and essence of the 'thing in itself'. Historical philosophy, on the contrary, which is no longer to be thought of as separate from physical science, the youngest of all philosophical methods, has ascertained in single cases (and presumably this will happen in everything) that there are no opposites except in the usual exaggeration of the popular or metaphysical point of view, and that an error of reason lies at the bottom of the opposition: according to this explanation, strictly understood, there is neither an unegoistical action nor an entirely disinterested point of view, they are both only sublimations in which the fundamental element appears almost evaporated, and is only to be discovered by the closest observation. All that we require, and which can only be given us by the present advance of the single sciences, is a *chemistry* of the moral, religious, aesthetic ideas and sentiments, as also of those emotions which we experience in ourselves both in the great and in the small phases of social and intellectual intercourse, and even in solitude; but what if this chemistry should result in the fact that also in this case the most beautiful colours have been obtained from base, even despised materials? Would many be inclined to pursue such examinations? Humanity likes to put all questions as to origin and beginning out of its mind; must one not be almost dehumanised to feel a contrary tendency in one's self?

2

Inherited faults of philosophers – All philosophers have the common fault that they start from man in his present state and hope to attain their end by an analysis of him. Unconsciously they look upon 'man' as an *aeterna veritas*, as a thing unchangeable in all commotion, as a sure measure of things. Everything the philosopher has declared about man is, however, at bottom no more than a testimony as to the man of a *very limited* period of time. Lack of historical sense is the family failing of all philosophers; many, without being aware of it, even take the most recent manifestation of man, such as has arisen under the impress of certain religions, even certain political events, as the fixed form from which one has to start out. They will not learn that man has become, that the faculty of cognition has become; while some of them would have it that the whole world is spun out of this faculty of cognition. Now, everything *essential* in the development of mankind took place in primeval times, long before the four thousand years we more or less know about; during these years mankind may well not have altered very much. But the philosopher here sees 'instincts' in man as he now is and assumes that these belong to the unalterable facts of mankind and to that extent could provide a key to the understanding of the world in general: the whole of teleology is constructed by speaking of the man of the last four millennia as of an eternal man towards whom all things in the world have had a natural relationship from the time he began. But everything has become: there are *no eternal facts*, just as there are no absolute truths. Consequently what is needed from now on is *historical philosophising*, and with it the virtue of modesty.

3

Estimation of unpretentious truths – It is the mark of a higher culture to value the little unpretentious truths which have been discovered by means of rigorous method more highly than the errors handed down by metaphysical ages and men, which blind us and make us happy. At first, one has scorn on his lips for unpretentious truths, as if they could offer no match for the others: they stand so modest, simple, sober, even apparently discouraging, while the other truths are so beautiful, splendid, enchanting, or even enrapturing. But truths that are hard won, certain, enduring, and therefore still of consequence for all further knowledge are the higher; to keep to them is manly, and shows bravery, simplicity, restraint. Eventually, not only the individual, but all mankind will be elevated to this manliness, when men finally grow accustomed to the greater esteem for durable, lasting knowledge and have lost all belief in inspiration and a seemingly miraculous communication of truths.

The admirers of *forms*, with their standard of beauty and sublimity, will, to be sure, have good reason to mock at first, when esteem for unpretentious truths and the scientific spirit first comes to rule, but only because either their eye has not yet been opened to the charm of the *simplest* form, or because men raised in that spirit have not yet been fully and inwardly permeated by it, so that they continue thoughtlessly to imitate old forms (and poorly, too, like someone who no longer really cares about the matter). Previously, the mind was not obliged to think rigorously; its importance lay in spinning out symbols and forms. That has changed; that earnestness in the symbolical has become the mark of a lower culture. As our arts themselves grow evermore intellectual, our senses more spiritual, and as, for instance, people now judge concerning what sounds well to the senses quite differently from how they did a hundred years ago, so the forms of our life grow ever more *spiritual*, to the eye of older ages perhaps *uglier*, but only because it is incapable of perceiving how the kingdom of the inward, spiritual beauty constantly grows deeper and wider, and to what extent the inner intellectual look may be of more importance to us all than the most beautiful bodily frame and the noblest architectural structure.

4

Astrology and the like – It is probable that the objects of religious, moral, aesthetic and logical sentiment likewise belong only to the surface of things, while man willingly believes that here, at least, he has touched the heart of the world; he deceives himself, because those things enrapture him so profoundly, and make him so profoundly unhappy, and he therefore shows the same pride here as in astrology. For astrology believes that the firmament moves round the destiny of man; the moral man, however, takes it for granted that what he has essentially at heart must also be the essence and heart of things.

5

Misunderstanding of dreams – In the ages of a rude and primitive civilisation man believed that in dreams he became acquainted with a *second actual world*; herein lies the origin of all metaphysics. Without dreams there could have been found no reason for a division of the world. The distinction, too, between soul and body is connected with the most ancient comprehension of dreams, also the supposition of an imaginary soul-body, therefore the origin of all belief in spirits, and probably also the belief in gods. 'The dead continues to live, *for* he appears to the living in a dream': thus men reasoned of old for thousands and thousands of years.

6

The scientific spirit partially but not wholly powerful – The *smallest* subdivisions of science taken separately are dealt with purely in relation to themselves – the general, great sciences, on the contrary, regarded as a whole, call up the question – certainly a very non-objective one – 'Wherefore? To what end?' It is this utilitarian consideration which causes them to be dealt with less impersonally when taken as a whole than when considered in their various parts. In philosophy, above all, as the apex of the entire pyramid of science, the question as to the utility of knowledge is involuntarily brought forward, and every philosophy has the unconscious intention of ascribing to it the *greatest* usefulness. For this reason there is so much high-flying metaphysics in all philosophies and such a shyness of the apparently unimportant solutions of physics; for the importance of knowledge for life *must* appear as great as possible. Here is the antagonism between the separate provinces of science and philosophy. The latter desires, what art does, to give the greatest possible depth and meaning to life and actions; in the former one seeks knowledge and nothing further, whatever may emerge thereby. So far there has been no philosopher in whose hands philosophy has not grown into an apology for knowledge;

on this point, at least, every one is an optimist, that the greatest usefulness must be ascribed to knowledge. They are all tyrannised over by logic, and this is optimism – in its essence.

7

The kill-joy in science – Philosophy separated from science when it asked the question, 'Which is the knowledge of the world and of life which enables man to live most happily?' This happened in the Socratic schools; the veins of scientific investigation were bound up by the point of view of *happiness* – and are so still.

8

Pneumatic explanation of nature – Metaphysics explains the writing of Nature, so to speak, *pneumatically*, as the Church and her learned men formerly did with the Bible. A great deal of understanding is required to apply to Nature the same method of strict interpretation as the philologists have now established for all books with the intention of clearly understanding what the text means, but not suspecting a *double* sense or even taking it for granted. Just, however, as with regard to books, the bad art of interpretation is by no means overcome, and in the most cultivated society one still constantly comes across the remains of allegorical and mystic interpretation, so it is also with regard to Nature, indeed it is even much worse.

9

The metaphysical world – It is true that there *might* be a metaphysical world; the absolute possibility of it is hardly to be disputed. We look at everything through the human head and cannot cut this head off; while the question remains, What would be left of the world if it had been cut off? This is a purely scientific problem, and one not very likely to trouble mankind; but everything which has hitherto made metaphysical suppositions *valuable, terrible, delightful* for man, what has produced them, is passion, error, and self-deception; the very worst methods of knowledge, not the best, have taught belief therein. When these methods have been discovered as the foundation of all existing religions and metaphysics, they have been refuted. Then there still always remains that possibility; but there is nothing to be done with it, much less is it possible to let happiness, salvation, and life depend on the spider-thread of such a possibility. For nothing could be said of the metaphysical world but that it would be a different condition, a condition inaccessible and incomprehensible to us; it would be a thing of negative qualities. Were the existence of such a world ever so well proved, the fact would nevertheless remain that it would be precisely the most irrelevant of all forms of knowledge: more irrelevant than the knowledge of the chemical analysis of water to the sailor in danger in a storm.

10

The harmlessness of metaphysics in the future – Directly the origins of religion, art, and morals have been so described that one can perfectly explain them without having recourse to metaphysical concepts at the beginning and in the course of the path, the strongest interest in the purely theoretical problem of the 'thing-in-itself' and the 'phenomenon' ceases. For however it may be here, with religion, art, and morals we do not touch the 'essence of the world in itself'; we are in the domain of representation, no 'intuition' can carry us further. With the greatest calmness we shall leave the question as to how our own conception of the world can differ so widely from the revealed essence of the world, to physiology and the history of the evolution of organisms and ideas.

11

Language as a presumptive science – The importance of language for the development of culture lies in the fact that in language man has placed a world of his own beside the other, a position which he deemed so fixed that he might therefrom lift the rest of the world off its hinges, and make himself master of it. Inasmuch as man has believed in the ideas and names of things as *aeternae veritates* for a great length of time, he has acquired that pride by which he has raised himself above the animal; he really thought that in language he possessed the knowledge of the world. The maker of language was not modest enough to think that he only gave designations to things, he believed rather that with his words he expressed the widest knowledge of the things; in reality language is the first step in the endeavour after science. Here also it is belief in ascertained truth, from which the mightiest sources of strength have flowed. Much later – only now – it is dawning upon men that they have propagated a tremendous error in their belief in language. Fortunately it is now too late to reverse the development of reason, which is founded upon that belief. *Logic*, also, is founded upon suppositions to which nothing in the actual world corresponds – for instance, on the supposition of the equality of things, and the identity of the same thing at different points of time – but that particular science arose out of the contrary belief (that such things really existed in the actual world). It is the same with mathematics, which would certainly not have arisen if it had been known from the beginning that in Nature there are no exactly straight lines, no real circle, no absolute standard of size.

12

Dream and culture – The function of the brain which is most influenced by sleep is the memory; not that it entirely ceases; but it is brought back to a condition of imperfection, such as everyone may have experienced in pre-historic times, whether asleep or awake. Arbitrary and confused as it is, it constantly confounds things on the ground of the most fleeting resemblances; but with the same arbitrariness and confusion the ancients invented their mythologies, and even at the present day travellers are accustomed to remark how prone the savage is to forgetfulness, how, after a short tension of memory, his mind begins to sway here and there from sheer weariness and gives forth lies and nonsense. But in dreams we all resemble the savage; bad recognition and erroneous comparisons are the reasons of the bad conclusions, of which we are guilty in dreams: so that, when we clearly recollect what we have dreamt, we are alarmed at ourselves at harbouring so much foolishness within us. The perfect distinctness of all dream-representations, which pre-suppose absolute faith in their reality, recall the conditions that appertain to primitive man, in whom hallucination was extraordinarily frequent, and sometimes simultaneously seized entire communities, entire nations. Therefore, in sleep and in dreams we once more carry out the task of early humanity.

13

The logic of dreams – In sleep our nervous system is perpetually excited by numerous inner occurrences; nearly all the organs are disjointed and in a state of activity, the blood runs its turbulent course, the position of the sleeper causes pressure on certain limbs, his coverings influence his sensations in various ways, the stomach digests and by its movements it disturbs other organs, the intestines writhe, the position of the head occasions unaccustomed play of muscles, the feet, unshod, not pressing upon the floor with the soles, occasion the feeling of the unaccustomed just as does the different clothing of the whole body: all this, according to its daily change and extent, excites by its extraordinariness the entire system to the very functions of the brain, and thus there are a hundred occasions for the spirit to be surprised and to seek for the *reasons* of this excitation; – the dream, however, is *the seeking and representing of the causes* of those excited sensations – that is, of the supposed causes. A person who, for instance, binds his feet with two straps will perhaps dream that two serpents are coiling round his feet; this is first hypothesis, then a belief, with an accompanying *mental* picture and interpretation – 'These serpents must be the *causa* of those sensations which I, the sleeper, experience,' – so decides the mind of the sleeper. The immediate past, so disclosed, becomes to him the present through his excited imagination. Thus every one knows from experience how quickly the dreamer weaves into his dream a loud sound that he hears, such as the ringing of bells or the firing of cannon, that is to say, explains it from *afterwards* so that he first *thinks* he experiences the producing circumstances and then that sound. But how does it happen that the mind of the dreamer is always so mistaken, while the same mind when awake is accustomed to be so temperate, careful, and sceptical with regard to its hypotheses? so that the first random hypothesis for the explanation of a feeling suffices for him to believe immediately in its truth? (For in dreaming we believe in the dream as if it were a reality, *i.e.* we think our hypothesis completely proved.) I hold, that as man now still reasons in dreams, so men reasoned also *when awake* through thousands of years; the first *causa* which occurred to the mind to explain anything that required an explanation, was sufficient and stood for truth. (Thus, according to travellers' tales, savages still do to this very day.) This ancient element in human nature still manifests itself in our dreams, for it is the foundation upon which the higher reason has developed and still develops in every individual; the dream carries us back into remote conditions of human culture, and provides a ready means of understanding them better. Dream-thinking is now so easy to us because during immense periods of human development we have been so well drilled in this form of fantastic and cheap explanation, by means of the first agreeable notions. In so far, dreaming is a recreation for the brain, which by day has to satisfy the stern demands of thought, as they are laid down by the higher culture. We can at once discern an allied process even in our awakened state, as the door and ante-room of the dream. If we shut our eyes, the brain produces a number of impressions of light and colour, probably as a kind of after-play and echo of all those effects of light which crowd in upon it by day. Now, however, the understanding, together with the imagination, instantly works up this play of colour, shapeless in itself, into definite figures, forms, landscapes, and animated groups. The actual accompanying process thereby is again a kind of conclusion from the effect to the cause: since the mind asks, 'Whence come these impressions of light and colour?' it supposes those figures and forms as causes; it takes them for the origin of those colours and lights, because in the daytime, with open eyes, it is accustomed to find a producing cause for every colour, every effect of light. Here, therefore, the imagination constantly places pictures before the mind, since it supports itself on the visual impressions of the day in their production, and the dream-imagination does just the same thing – that is, the supposed cause is deduced from the effect and represented after the effect; all this happens with extraordinary rapidity, so that here, as with the conjuror, a confusion of judgment may arise and a sequence may look like something simultaneous, or even like a reversed sequence. From these circumstances we may gather *how lately* the more acute logical thinking, the strict discrimination of cause and effect has been developed, when our reasoning and understanding faculties *still* involuntarily hark back to those primitive forms of deduction, and when we pass about half our life in this condition. The poet, too, and the artist assign causes for their moods and conditions which are by no means the true ones; in this they recall an older humanity and can assist us to the understanding of it.

14

Co-echoing – All *stronger* moods bring with them a co-echoing of kindred sensations and moods, they grub up the memory, so to speak. Along with them something within us remembers and becomes conscious of similar conditions and their origin. Thus there are formed quick habitual connections of feelings and thoughts, which eventually, when they follow each other with lightning speed, are no longer felt as complexes but as *unities*. In this sense one speaks of the moral feeling, of the religious feeling, as if they were absolute unities: in reality they are streams with a hundred sources and tributaries. Here also, as so often happens, the unity of the word is no security for the unity of the thing.

15

No internal and external in the world – As Democritus transferred the concepts 'above' and 'below' to endless space where they have no sense, so philosophers in general have transferred the concepts 'Internal' and 'External' to the essence and appearance of the world; they think that with deep feelings one can penetrate deeply into the internal and approach the heart of Nature. But these feelings are only deep in so far as along with them, barely noticeable, certain complicated groups of thoughts, which we call deep, are regularly excited; a feeling is deep because we think that the accompanying thought is deep. But the 'deep' thought can nevertheless be very far from the truth, as, for instance, every metaphysical one; if one take away from the deep feeling the commingled elements of thought, then the *strong* feeling remains, and this guarantees nothing for knowledge but itself, just as strong faith proves only its strength and not the truth of what is believed in.

16

Phenomenon and thing-in-itself – Philosophers are in the habit of setting themselves before life and experience – before that which they call the world of appearance – as before a picture that is once for all unrolled and exhibits unchangeably fixed the same process –

this process, they think, must be rightly interpreted in order to come to a conclusion about the being that produced the picture: about the thing-in-itself, therefore, which is always accustomed to be regarded as sufficient ground for the world of phenomenon. On the other hand, since one always makes the idea of the metaphysical stand definitely as that of the unconditioned, *consequently* also unconditioning, one must directly disown all connection between the unconditioned (the metaphysical world) and the world which is known to us; so that the thing-in-itself should most certainly *not* appear in the phenomenon, and every conclusion from the former as regards the latter is to be rejected. Both sides overlook the fact that that picture – that which we now call human life and experience – has gradually evolved – nay, is still in the full process of evolving – and therefore should not be regarded as a fixed magnitude from which a conclusion about its originator might be deduced (the sufficing cause) or even merely neglected. It is because for thousands of years we have looked into the world with moral, aesthetic, and religious pretensions, with blind inclination, passion, or fear, and have surfeited ourselves in the vices of illogical thought, that this world has gradually *become* so marvellously motley, terrible, full of meaning and of soul, it has acquired colour – but we were the colourists; the human intellect, on the basis of human needs, of human emotions, has caused this 'phenomenon' to appear and has carried its erroneous fundamental conceptions into things. Late, very late, it takes to thinking, and now the world of experience and the thing-in-itself seem to it so extraordinarily different and separated, that it gives up drawing conclusions from the former to the latter – or in a terribly mysterious manner demands the renunciation of our intellect, of our personal will, in order *thereby* to reach the essential, that one may *become essential*. Again, others have collected all the characteristic features of our world of phenomenon – that is, the idea of the world spun out of intellectual errors and inherited by us – and *instead of accusing the intellect* as the offenders, they have laid the blame on the nature of things as being the cause of the hard fact of this very sinister character of the world, and have preached the deliverance from Being. With all these conceptions the constant and laborious process of science (which at last celebrates its greatest triumph in a *history of the origin of thought*) becomes completed in various ways, the result of which might perhaps run as follows – 'That which we now call the world is the result of a mass of errors and fantasies which arose gradually in the general development of organic being, which are inter-grown with each other, and are now inherited by us as the accumulated treasure of all the past – as a treasure, for the value of our humanity depends upon it. From this world of representation strict science is really only able to liberate us to a very slight extent – as it is also not at all desirable – inasmuch as it cannot essentially break the power of primitive habits of feeling; but it can gradually elucidate the history of the rise of that world as representation – and lift us, at least for moments, above and beyond the whole process. Perhaps we shall then recognise that the thing in itself is worth a Homeric laugh; that it *seemed* so much, indeed everything, and *is* really empty, namely, empty of meaning.'

17

Metaphysical explanations – The young man values metaphysical explanations, because they show him something highly significant in things which he found unpleasant or despicable, and if he is dissatisfied with himself, the feeling becomes lighter when he recognises the innermost world-puzzle or world-misery in that which he so strongly disapproves of in himself. To feel himself less responsible and at the same time to find things more interesting – that seems to him a double benefit for which he has to thank metaphysics. Later on, certainly, he gets distrustful of the whole metaphysical method of explanation; then perhaps it grows clear to him that those results can be obtained equally well and more scientifically in another way: that physical and historical explan-ations produce the feeling of personal relief to at least the same extent, and that the interest in life and its problems is perhaps still more aroused thereby.

18

Fundamental questions of metaphysics – When the history of the rise of thought comes to be written, a new light will be thrown on the following statement of a distinguished logician: – 'The primordial general law of the cognisant subject consists in the inner necessity of recognising every object in itself in its own nature, as a thing identical with itself, consequently self-existing and at bottom remaining ever the same and unchangeable: in short, in recognising everything as a substance.' Even this law, which is here called 'primordial', has evolved: it will some day be shown how gradually this tendency arises in the lower organisms, how the feeble mole-eyes of their organisations at first see only the same thing – how then, when the various awakenings of pleasure and displeasure become noticeable, various substances are gradually distinguished, but each with one attribute, *i.e.* one single relation to such an organism. The first step in logic is the judgment – the nature of which, according to the decision of the best logicians, consists in belief. At the bottom of all belief lies *the sensation of the pleasant or the painful* in relation to the *sentient subject*. A new third sensation as the result of two previous single sensations is the judgment in its simplest form. We organic beings have originally no interest in anything but its relation to *us* in connection with pleasure and pain. Between the moments (the states of feeling) when we become conscious of this connection, lie moments of rest, of non-feeling; the world and everything is then without interest for us, we notice no change in it (as even now a deeply interested person does not notice when any one passes him). To the plant, things are as a rule tranquil and eternal, everything like itself. From the period of the lower organisms man has inherited the belief that *similar things* exist (this theory is only contradicted by the matured experience of the most advanced science). The primordial belief of everything organic from the beginning is perhaps even this, that all the rest of the world is one and immovable. The point furthest removed from those early beginnings of logic is the idea of *Causality* – indeed we still really think that all sensations and activities are acts of the free will; when the sentient individual contemplates himself, he regards every sensation, every alteration as something *isolated*, that is to say, unconditioned and disconnected – it rises up in us without connection with anything foregoing or following. We are hungry, but do not originally think that the organism must be nourished; the feeling seems to make itself felt *without cause and purpose*, it isolates itself and regards itself as arbitrary. Therefore, belief in the freedom of the will is an original error of everything organic, as old as the existence of the awakenings of logic in it; the belief in unconditioned substances and similar things is equally a primordial as well as an old error of everything organic. But inasmuch as all metaphysics has concerned itself chiefly with substance and the freedom of will, it may be designated as the science which treats of the fundamental errors of mankind, but treats of them as if they were fundamental truths.

19

Number – The discovery of the laws of numbers is made upon the ground of the original, already prevailing error, that there are many similar things (but in reality there is nothing similar), at least, that there are things (but there is no 'thing'). The supposition of plurality always presumes that there is something which appears frequently – but here already error reigns, already we imagine beings, unities, which do not exist. Our sensations of space and time are false, for they lead – examined in sequence – to logical contradictions. In all scientific determinations we always reckon inevitably with certain false quantities, but as these quantities are at least constant, as, for instance, our sensation of time and space, the conclusions of science have still perfect accuracy and certainty in their connection with one another; one may continue to build upon them – until that final limit where the erroneous original suppositions, those constant faults, come into conflict with the conclusions, for instance in the doctrine of atoms. There still we always feel ourselves compelled to the acceptance of a 'thing' or material 'substratum' that is moved, whilst the whole scientific procedure has pursued the very task of resolving everything substantial (material) into motion; here, too, we still separate with our sensation the mover and the moved and cannot get out of this circle, because the belief in things has from immemorial times been bound up with our being. When Kant says, 'The understanding does not derive its laws from Nature, but dictates them to her,' it is perfectly true with regard to the idea of Nature which we are compelled to associate with her (Nature = World as representation, that is to say as error), but which is the summing up of a number of errors of the understanding. The laws of numbers are entirely inapplicable to a world which is not our representation – these laws obtain only in the human world.

20

A few steps back – A degree of culture, and assuredly a very high one, is attained when man rises above superstitious and religious notions and fears, and, for instance, no longer believes in guardian angels or in original sin, and has also ceased to talk of the salvation of his soul – if he has attained to this degree of freedom, he has still also to overcome metaphysics with the greatest exertion of his intelligence. Then, however, a *retrogressive movement* is necessary; he must understand the historical justification as well as the psychological in such representations, he must recognise how the greatest advancement of humanity has come therefrom, and how, without such a retrocursive movement, we should have been robbed of the best products of hitherto existing mankind. With regard to philosophical metaphysics, I always see increasing numbers who have attained to the negative goal (that all positive metaphysics is error), but as yet few who climb a few rungs backwards; one ought to look out, perhaps, over the last steps of the ladder, but not try to stand upon them. The most enlightened only succeed so far as to free themselves from metaphysics and look back upon it with superiority, while it is necessary here, too, as in the hippodrome, to turn round the end of the course.

21

Conjectural victory of scepticism – For once let the sceptical starting-point be accepted – granted that there were no other metaphysical world, and all explanations drawn from metaphysics about the only world we know were useless to us, in what light should we then look upon men and things? We can think this out for ourselves, it is useful, even though the question whether anything metaphysical has been scientifically proved by Kant and Schopenhauer were altogether set aside. For it is quite possible, according to historical probability, that some time or other man, as a general rule, may grow *sceptical*; the question will then be this: What form will human society take under the influence of such a mode of thought? Perhaps the *scientific proof* of some metaphysical world or other is already so *difficult* that mankind will never get rid of a certain distrust of it. And when there is distrust of metaphysics, there are on the whole the same results as if it had been directly

refuted and *could* no longer be believed in. The historical question
with regard to an unmetaphysical frame of mind in mankind
remains the same in both cases.

22

Unbelief in the 'monumentum aere perennius' – An actual drawback
which accompanies the cessation of metaphysical views lies in the
fact that the individual looks upon his short span of life too
exclusively and receives no stronger incentives to build durable
institutions intended to last for centuries – he himself wishes to
pluck the fruit from the tree which he plants, and therefore he no
longer plants those trees which require regular care for centuries,
and which are destined to afford shade to a long series of generations. For metaphysical views furnish the belief that in them
the last conclusive foundation has been given, upon which henceforth all the future of mankind is compelled to settle down and
establish itself; the individual furthers his salvation, when, for
instance, he founds a church or convent, he thinks it will be
reckoned to him and recompensed to him in the eternal life of
the soul, it is work for the soul's eternal salvation. Can science
also arouse such faith in its results? As a matter of fact, it needs
doubt and distrust as its most faithful auxiliaries; nevertheless
in the course of time, the sum of inviolable truths – those,
namely, which have weathered all the storms of scepticism, and
all destructive analysis – may have become so great (in the
regimen of health, for instance), that one may determine to found
thereupon 'eternal' works. For the present the *contrast* between
our excited ephemeral existence and the long-winded repose of
metaphysical ages still operates too strongly, because the two ages
still stand too closely together; the individual man himself now
goes through too many inward and outward developments for
him to venture to arrange his own lifetime permanently, and
once and for all. An entirely modern man, for instance, who is
going to build himself a house, has a feeling as if he were going
to immure himself alive in a mausoleum.

23

The age of comparison – The less men are fettered by tradition, the
greater becomes the inward activity of their motives; the greater,

again, in proportion thereto, the outward restlessness, the confused flux of mankind, the polyphony of strivings. For whom is there still an absolute compulsion to bind himself and his descendants to one place? For whom is there still anything strictly compulsory? As all styles of arts are imitated simultaneously, so also are all grades and kinds of morality, of customs, of cultures. Such an age obtains its importance because in it the various views of the world, customs, and cultures can be compared and experienced simultaneously – which was formerly not possible with the always localised sway of every culture, corresponding to the rooting of all artistic styles in place and time. An increased aesthetic feeling will now at last decide amongst so many forms presenting themselves for comparison; it will allow the greater number, that is to say all those rejected by it, to die out. In the same way a selection amongst the forms and customs of the higher moralities is taking place, of which the aim can be nothing else than the downfall of the lower moralities. It is the age of comparison! That is its pride, but more justly also its grief. Let us not be afraid of this grief! Rather will we comprehend as adequately as possible the task our age sets us: posterity will bless us for doing so – a posterity which knows itself to be as much above the terminated original national cultures as above the culture of comparison, but which looks back with gratitude on both kinds of culture as upon antiquities worthy of veneration.

24

The possibility of progress – When a scholar of the ancient culture forswears the company of men who believe in progress, he does quite right. For the greatness and goodness of ancient culture lie behind it, and historical education compels one to admit that they can never be fresh again; an unbearable stupidity or an equally insufferable fanaticism would be necessary to deny this. But men can *consciously* resolve to develop themselves towards a new culture; whilst formerly they only developed unconsciously and by chance, they can now create better conditions for the rise of human beings, for their nourishment, education and instruction; they can administer the earth economically as a whole, and can generally weigh and restrain the powers of man. This new, conscious culture kills the old, which, regarded as a whole, has led an unconscious animal and plant life; it also kills distrust in progress – progress is *possible*. I must say that it is over-hasty and almost nonsensical to believe that progress must *necessarily* follow; but how could one deny that it is possible? On the other hand, progress in the sense and on the path of the old culture is not even thinkable. Even if romantic fantasy has also constantly used the word 'progress' to denote its aims (for instance, circumscribed primitive national cultures), it borrows the picture of it in any case from the past; its thoughts and ideas on this subject are entirely without originality.

25

Private and ecumenical morality – Since the belief has ceased that a God directs in general the fate of the world and, in spite of all apparent crookedness in the path of humanity, leads it on gloriously, men themselves must set themselves ecumenical aims embracing the whole earth. The older morality, especially that of Kant, required from the individual actions which were desired from all men – that was a delightfully naïve thing, as if each one knew off-hand what course of action was beneficial to the whole of humanity, and consequently which actions in general were desirable; it is a theory like that of free trade, taking for granted that the general harmony *must* result of itself according to innate laws of amelioration. Perhaps a future contemplation of the needs of humanity will show that it is by no means desirable that all men should act alike; in the interest of ecumenical aims it might rather be that for whole sections of mankind, special, and perhaps under certain circumstances even evil, tasks would have to be set. In any case, if mankind is not to destroy itself by such a conscious universal rule, there must previously be found, as a scientific standard for ecumenical aims, a *knowledge of the conditions of culture* superior to what has hitherto been attained. Herein lies the enormous task of the great minds of the next century.

26

Reaction as progress – Now and again there appear rugged, powerful, impetuous, but nevertheless backward-lagging minds which conjure up once more a past phase of mankind; they serve to prove that the new tendencies against which they are working are not yet sufficiently strong, that they still lack something, otherwise they would show better opposition to those exorcisers. Thus, for example, Luther's Reformation bears witness to the fact that in his century all the movements of the freedom of the spirit were still uncertain, tender, and youthful; science could not yet lift up its head. Indeed the whole Renaissance seems like an early spring which is almost snowed under again. But in this century also, Schopenhauer's metaphysics showed that even now the scientific spirit is not yet strong enough; thus the whole mediaeval Christian view of the world and human feeling could celebrate its resurrection in Schopenhauer's doctrine, in spite of the long-achieved destruction of all Christian dogmas. There is much science in his doctrine, but it does not dominate it: it is rather the old well-known 'metaphysical requirement' that does so. It is certainly one of the greatest and quite invaluable advantages which we gain from Schopenhauer, that he occasionally forces our sensations back into older, mightier modes of contemplating the world and man, to which no other path would so easily lead us. The gain to history and justice is very great – I do not think that any one would so easily succeed now in doing justice to Christianity and its Asiatic relations without Schopenhauer's assistance, which is specially impossible from the basis of still existing Christianity. Only after this great *success of justice*, only after we have corrected so essential a point as the historical mode of contemplation which the age of enlightenment brought with it, may we again bear onward the banner of enlightenment, the banner with the three names, Petrarch, Erasmus, Voltaire. We have turned reaction into progress.

27

A substitute for religion – It is believed that something good is said of philosophy when it is put forward as a substitute for religion for the people. As a matter of fact, in the spiritual economy there is need, at times, of an *intermediary* order of thought: the transition from religion to scientific contemplation is a violent, dangerous leap, which is not to be recommended. To this extent the recommendation is justifiable. But one should eventually learn that the needs which have been satisfied by religion and are now to be satisfied by philosophy are not unchangeable; these

themselves can be *weakened* and *eradicated*. Think, for instance, of
the Christian's distress of soul, his sighing over inward corruption,
his anxiety for salvation – all notions which originate only in errors
of reason and deserve not satisfaction but destruction. A philosophy can serve either to *satisfy* those needs or to *set them aside*; for
they are acquired, temporally limited needs, which are based upon
suppositions contradictory to those of science. Here, in order to
make a transition, *art* is far rather to be employed to relieve the
mind over-burdened with emotions; for those notions receive
much less support from it than from a metaphysical philosophy.
It is easier, then, to pass over from art to a really liberating
philosophical science.

28

Ill-famed words – Away with those wearisomely hackneyed terms
Optimism and Pessimism! For the occasion for using them
becomes less and less from day to day; only the chatterboxes still
find them so absolutely necessary. For why in all the world should
any one wish to be an optimist unless he had a God to defend who
must have created the best of worlds if he himself be goodness and
perfection – what thinker, however, still needs the hypothesis
of a God? But every occasion for a pessimistic confession of faith is
also lacking when one has no interest in being annoyed at the
advocates of God (the theologians, or the theologising philosophers), and in energetically defending the opposite view, that
evil reigns, that pain is greater than pleasure, that the world is
a bungled piece of work, the manifestation of an ill-will to life.
But who still bothers about the theologians now – except the
theologians? Apart from all theology and its contentions, it is quite
clear that the world is not good and not bad (to say nothing of its
being the best or the worst), and that the terms 'good' and 'bad'
have only significance with respect to man, and indeed, perhaps,
they are not justified even here in the way they are usually
employed; in any case we must get rid of both the calumniating
and the glorifying conception of the world.

29

Intoxicated by the scent of the blossoms – It is supposed that the ship of
humanity has always a deeper draught, the heavier it is laden; it is

believed that the deeper a man thinks, the more delicately he feels, the higher he values himself, the greater his distance from the other animals – the more he appears as a genius amongst the animals – all the nearer will he approach the real essence of the world and its knowledge; this he actually does too, through science, but he *means* to do so still more through his religions and arts. These certainly are blossoms of the world, but by no means any *nearer to the root of the world* than the stalk; it is not possible to understand the nature of things better through them, although almost every one believes he can. *Error* has made man so deep, sensitive, and inventive that he has put forth such blossoms as religions and arts. Pure knowledge could not have been capable of it. Whoever were to unveil for us the essence of the world would give us all the most disagreeable disillusionment. Not the world as thing–in–itself, but the world as representation (as error) is so full of meaning, so deep, so wonderful, bearing happiness and unhappiness in its bosom. This result leads to a philosophy of the logical denial of the world, which, however, can be combined with a practical world–affirming just as well as with its opposite.

30

Bad habits in reasoning – The usual false conclusions of mankind are these: a thing exists, therefore it has a right to exist. Here there is inference from the ability to live to its suitability; from its suitability to its rightfulness. Then: an opinion brings happiness; therefore it is the true opinion. Its effect is good; therefore it is itself good and true. To the effect is here assigned the predicate beneficent, good, in the sense of the useful, and the cause is then furnished with the same predicate good, but here in the sense of the logically valid. The inversion of the sentences would read thus: an affair cannot be carried through, or maintained, therefore it is wrong; an opinion causes pain or excites, therefore it is false. The free spirit who learns only too often the faultiness of this mode of reasoning, and has to suffer from its consequences, frequently gives way to the temptation to draw the very opposite conclusions, which, in general, are naturally just as false: an affair cannot be carried through, therefore it is good; an opinion is distressing and disturbing, therefore it is true.

31

The illogical necessary – One of those things that may drive a thinker into despair is the recognition of the fact that the illogical is necessary for man, and that out of the illogical comes much that is good. It is so firmly rooted in the passions, in language, in art, in religion, and generally in everything that gives value to life, that it cannot be withdrawn without thereby hopelessly injuring these beautiful things. It is only the all-too-naïve people who can believe that the nature of man can be changed into a purely logical one; but if there were degrees of proximity to this goal, how many things would not have to be lost on this course! Even the most rational man has need of nature again from time to time, *i.e.* his *illogical* fundamental attitude *towards all things*.

32

Injustice necessary – All judgments on the value of life are illogically developed, and therefore unjust. The inexactitude of the judgment lies, firstly, in the manner in which the material is presented, namely very imperfectly; secondly, in the manner in which the conclusion is formed out of it; and thirdly, in the fact that every separate element of the material is again the result of vitiated recognition, and this, too, of necessity. For instance, no experience of an individual, however near he may stand to us, can be perfect, so that we could have a logical right to make a complete estimate of him; all estimates are rash, and must be so. Finally, the standard by which we measure, our nature, is not of unalterable dimensions – we have moods and vacillations, and yet we should have to recognise ourselves as a fixed standard in order to estimate correctly the relation of any thing whatever to ourselves. From this it will, perhaps, follow that we should make no judgments at all; if one could only live without making estimations, without having likes and dislikes! For all dislike is connected with an estimation, as well as all inclination. An impulse towards or away from anything without a feeling that something advantageous is desired, something injurious avoided, an impulse without any kind of conscious valuation of the worth of the aim does not exist in man. We are from the beginning illogical, and therefore unjust beings, *and can recognise this*; it is one of the greatest and most inexplicable discords of existence.

33

Error about life necessary for life – Every belief in the value and worthiness of life is based on vitiated thought; it is only possible through the fact that sympathy for the general life and suffering of mankind is very weakly developed in the individual. Even the rarer people who think outside themselves do not contemplate this general life, but only a limited part of it. If one understands how to direct one's attention chiefly to the exceptions – I mean to the highly gifted and the rich souls – if one regards the production of these as the aim of the whole world-development and rejoices in its operation, then one may believe in the value of life, because one thereby *overlooks* the other men – one consequently thinks fallaciously. So too, when one directs one's attention to all mankind, but only considers *one* species of impulses in them, the less egoistical ones, and excuses them with regard to the other instincts, one may then again entertain hopes of mankind in general and believe so far in the value of life, consequently in this case also through fallaciousness of thought. Let one, however, behave in this or that manner: with such behaviour one is an *exception* amongst men. Now, most people bear life without any considerable grumbling, and consequently *believe* in the value of existence, but precisely because each one is solely self-seeking and self-affirming, and does not step out of himself like those exceptions; everything extra-personal is imperceptible to them, or at most seems only a faint shadow. Therefore on this alone is based the value of life for the ordinary everyday man, that he regards himself as more important than the world. The great lack of imagination from which he suffers is the reason why he cannot enter into the feelings of other beings, and therefore sympathises as little as possible with their fate and suffering. He, on the other hand, who really *could* sympathise therewith, would have to despair of the value of life; were he to succeed in comprehending and feeling in himself the general consciousness of mankind, he would collapse with a curse on existence; for mankind as a whole has *no* goals, consequently man, in considering his whole course, cannot find in it his comfort and support, but his despair. If, in all that he does, he considers the final aimlessness of man, his own activity assumes in his eyes the character of wastefulness. But to feel one's self just as much wasted as humanity (and not only as an individual) as we see the single blossom of nature wasted, is a feeling above all other feelings. But who is capable of it? Assuredly only a poet, and poets always know how to console themselves.

34

For tranquillity — But does not our philosophy thus become a tragedy? Does not truth become hostile to life, to improvement? A question seems to weigh upon our tongue and yet hesitate to make itself heard: whether one *can* consciously remain in untruthfulness? or, supposing one were *obliged* to do this, would not death be preferable? For there is no longer any 'must' ; morality, in so far as it had any 'must' or 'shalt', has been destroyed by our mode of contemplation, just as religion has been destroyed. Knowledge can only allow pleasure and pain, benefit and injury to subsist as motives; but how will these motives agree with the sense of truth? They also contain errors (for, as already said, inclination and aversion, and their very incorrect determinations, practically regulate our pleasure and pain). The whole of human life is deeply immersed in untruthfulness; the individual cannot draw it up out of this well, without thereby taking a deep dislike to his whole past, without finding his present motives — those of honour, for instance — inconsistent, and without opposing scorn and disdain to the passions which conduce to happiness in the future. Is it true that there remains but one sole way of thinking which brings after it despair as a personal experience, as a theoretical result, a philosophy of dissolution, disintegration, and self-destruction? I believe that the decision with regard to the after-effects of the knowledge will be given through the *temperament* of a man; I could imagine another after-effect, just as well as that one described, which is possible in certain natures, by means of which a life would arise much simpler, freer from emotions than is the present one, so that though at first, indeed, the old motives of passionate desire might still have strength from old hereditary habit, they would gradually become weaker under the influence of purifying knowledge. One would live at last amongst men, and with one's self as with *Nature* without praise, reproach, or agitation, feasting one's eyes, as if it were a *play*, upon much of which one was formerly afraid. One would be free from the emphasis, and would no longer feel the goading, of the thought that one is not only nature or more than nature. Certainly, as already remarked, a good temperament would be necessary for this, an even, mild, and naturally joyous soul, a disposition which would not always need to be on its guard against spite and sudden outbreaks, and would not convey in its utterances anything of a grumbling or sudden nature – those well-known vexatious qualities of old dogs and men who have been long chained up. On the contrary, a man from whom the ordinary fetters of life have so far fallen that he continues to live only for the sake of ever better knowledge must be able to renounce without envy and regret: much, indeed almost everything that is precious to other men, he must regard as the *all-sufficing* and the most desirable condition; the free, fearless soaring over men, customs, laws, and the traditional valuations of things. The joy of this condition he imparts willingly, and he *has* perhaps nothing else to impart – wherein, to be sure, there is more privation and renunciation. If, nevertheless, more is demanded from him, he will point with a friendly shake of his head to his brother, the free man of action, and will perhaps not conceal a little derision, for as regards this 'freedom' it is a very peculiar case.

Second Division – *The History of the Moral Sentiments*

35

Advantages of psychological observation – That reflection on the human, all-too-human – or, according to the learned expression, psychological observation – is one of the means by which one may lighten the burden of life, that exercise in this art produces presence of mind in difficult circumstances, in the midst of tiresome surroundings, even that from the most thorny and unpleasant periods of one's own life one may gather maxims and thereby feel a little better: all this was believed, was known in former centuries. Why was it forgotten by our century, when in Germany at least, even in all Europe, the poverty of psychological observation betrays itself by many signs? Not exactly in novels, tales, and philosophical treatises – they are the work of exceptional individuals – rather in the judgments on public events and personalities; but above all there is a lack of the art of psychological analysis and summing-up in every rank of society, in which a great deal is talked about men, but nothing about *man*. Why do we allow the richest and most harmless subject of conversation to escape us? Why are not the great masters of psychological maxims more read? For, without any exaggeration, the educated man in Europe who has read La Rochefoucauld and his kindred in mind and art, is rarely found, and still more rare is he who knows them and does not blame them. It is probable, however, that even this exceptional reader will find much less pleasure in them than the form of this artist should afford him; for even the clearest head is not capable of rightly estimating the art of shaping and polishing maxims unless he has really been brought up to it and has competed in it. Without this practical teaching one deems this shaping and polishing to be easier than it is; one has not a sufficient perception of fitness and charm. For this reason the present readers of maxims find in them a comparatively small pleasure, hardly a mouthful of pleasantness, so that they resemble the people who generally look at cameos, who praise because they cannot love, and are very ready to admire, but still more ready to run away.

36

Objection – Or should there be a counter-reckoning to that theory that places psychological observation amongst the means of charming, curing, and relieving existence? Should one have sufficiently convinced one's self of the unpleasant consequences of this art to divert from it designedly the attention of him who is educating himself in it? As a matter of fact, a certain blind belief in the goodness of human nature, an innate aversion to the analysis of human actions, a kind of shamefacedness with respect to the nakedness of the soul may really be more desirable for the general well-being of a man than that quality, useful in isolated cases, of psychological sharp-sightedness; and perhaps the belief in goodness, in virtuous men and deeds, in an abundance of impersonal good-will in the world, has made men better inasmuch as it has made them less distrustful. When one imitates Plutarch's heroes with enthusiasm, and turns with disgust from a suspicious examination of the motives for their actions, it is not truth which benefits thereby, but the welfare of human society; the psychological mistake and, generally speaking, the insensibility on this matter helps humanity forwards, while the recognition of truth gains more through the stimulating power of hypothesis than La Rochefoucauld has said in his preface to the first edition of his '*Sentences et maximes morales*'. . . '*Ce que le monde nomme vertu n'est d'ordinaire qu'un fantôme formé par nos passions, à qui on donne un nom honnête pour faire impunément ce qu'on veut.*' La Rochefoucauld and those other French masters of soul-examination (who have lately been joined by a German, the author of *Psychological Observations**) resemble good marksmen who again and again hit the bull's-eye; but it is the bull's-eye of human nature. Their art arouses astonishment; but in the end a spectator who is not led by the spirit of science, but by humane intentions, will probably execrate an art which appears to implant in the soul the sense of the disparagement and suspicion of mankind.

* Dr Paul Rée. – J. M. K.

37

Nevertheless – However it may be with reckoning and counter-reckoning, in the present condition of philosophy the awakening of moral observation is necessary. Humanity can no longer be spared the cruel sight of the psychological dissecting-table with its knives and forceps. For here rules that science which inquires into the origin and history of the so-called moral sentiments, and which, in its progress, has to draw up and solve complicated sociological problems: – the older philosophy knows the latter one not at all, and has always avoided the examination of the origin and history of moral sentiments on any feeble pretext. With what consequences it is now very easy to see, after it has been shown by many examples how the mistakes of the greatest philosophers generally have their starting-point in a wrong explanation of certain human actions and sensations, just as on the ground of an erroneous analysis – for instance, that of the so-called unselfish actions – a false ethic is built up; then, to harmonise with this again, religion and mythological confusion are brought in to assist, and finally the shades of these dismal spirits fall also over physics and the general mode of regarding the world. If it is certain, however, that superficiality in psychological observation has laid, and still lays, the most dangerous snares for human judgments and conclusions, then there is need now of that endurance of work which does not grow weary of piling stone upon stone, pebble on pebble; there is need of courage not to be ashamed of such humble work and to turn a deaf ear to scorn. And this is also true – numberless single observations on the human and all-too-human have first been discovered, and given utterance to, in circles of society which were accustomed to offer sacrifice therewith to a clever desire to please, and not to scientific knowledge – and the odour of that old home of the moral maxim, a very seductive odour, has attached itself almost inseparably to the whole species, so that on its account the scientific man involuntarily betrays a certain distrust of this species and its earnestness. But it is sufficient to point to the consequences, for already it begins to be seen what results of a serious kind spring from the ground of psychological observation. What, after all, is the principal axiom to which the boldest and coldest thinker, the author of the book *On the Origin of Moral Sensations*,* has attained by means of his incisive and decisive analyses of human actions? 'The moral man,' he says, 'is no nearer to the intelligible (metaphysical) world than is the physical man.' This theory, hardened and sharpened under the hammer-blow of historical knowledge, may some time or other, perhaps in some future period, serve as the axe which is applied to the root of the 'metaphysical need' of man – whether *more* as a blessing than a curse to the general welfare it is not easy to say, but in any case as a theory with the most important consequences, at once fruitful and terrible, and looking into the world with that Janus-face which all great knowledge possesses.

38

How far useful – It must remain for ever undecided whether psychological observation is advantageous or disadvantageous to man; but it is certain that it is necessary, because science cannot do without it. Science, however, has no consideration for ultimate purposes, any more than Nature has, but just as the latter occasionally achieves things of the greatest suitableness without intending to do so, so also true science, as the *imitator of nature in ideas*, will occasionally and in many ways further the usefulness and welfare of man – *but also without intending to do so.*

But whoever feels too chilled by the breath of such a reflection has perhaps too little fire in himself; let him look around him meanwhile and he will become aware of illnesses which have need of ice-poultices, and of men who are so 'kneaded together' of heat and spirit that they can hardly find an atmosphere that is cold and biting enough. Moreover, as individuals and nations that are too serious have need of frivolities, as others too mobile and excitable have need occasionally of heavily oppressing burdens for the sake of their health, should not we, the more *intellectual* people of this age, that grows visibly more and more inflamed, seize all quenching and cooling means that exist, in order that we may at least remain as constant, harmless, and moderate as we still are, and thus, perhaps, serve some time or other as mirror and self-contemplation for this age?

39

The fable of intelligible freedom – The history of the sentiments by means of which we make a person responsible consists of the following principal phases. First, all single actions are called good or bad without any regard to their motives, but only on account of the useful or injurious consequences which result for the community. But soon the origin of these distinctions is forgotten, and it is deemed that the qualities 'good' or 'bad' are contained in the action itself without regard to its consequences, by the same error according to which language describes the stone as hard, the tree as green – with which, in short, the result is regarded as the cause. Then the goodness or badness is implanted in the motive, and the action in itself is looked upon as morally ambiguous. Mankind even goes further, and applies the predicate good or bad no longer to single motives, but to the whole nature of an individual, out of whom the motive grows as the plant grows out of the earth. Thus, in turn, man is made responsible for his operations, then for his actions, then for his motives, and finally for his nature. Eventually it is discovered that even this nature cannot be responsible, inasmuch as it is an absolutely necessary consequence concreted out of the elements and influences of past and present things – that man, therefore, cannot be made responsible for anything, neither for his nature, nor his motives, nor his actions, nor his effects. It has therewith come to be recognised that the history of moral valuations is at the same time the history of an error, the error of responsibility, which is based upon the error of the freedom of will. Schopenhauer thus decided against it: because certain actions bring ill humour ('consciousness of guilt') in their train, there must be a responsibility; for there would be *no reason* for this ill humour if not only all human actions were not done of necessity – which is actually the case and also the belief of this philosopher – but man himself from the same necessity is precisely the *being* that he is – which Schopenhauer denies. From the fact of that ill humour Schopenhauer thinks he can prove a liberty which man must somehow have had, not with regard to actions, but with regard to nature; liberty, therefore, to *be* thus or otherwise, not to *act* thus or otherwise. From the *esse*, the sphere of freedom and responsibility, there results, in his opinion, the *operari*, the sphere of strict causality, necessity, and irresponsibility. This ill humour is apparently directed to the *operari* – in so far it is erroneous – but in reality it is directed to the *esse*, which is the deed of a free will, the fundamental cause of the existence of an individual, man becomes that which he *wishes* to be, his will is anterior to his existence. Here the mistaken conclusion is drawn that from the fact of the ill humour, the justification, the reasonable *admissableness* of this ill humour is presupposed; and starting from this mistaken conclusion, Schopenhauer arrives at his fantastic sequence of the so-called intelligible freedom. But the ill humour after the deed is not necessarily reasonable, indeed it is assuredly not reasonable, for it is based upon the erroneous presumption that the action need *not* have inevitably followed. Therefore, it is only because man *believes* himself to be free, not because he is free, that he experiences remorse and pricks of conscience. Moreover, this ill humour is a habit that can be broken off; in many people it is entirely absent in connection with actions where others experience it. It is a very changeable thing, and one which is connected with the development of customs and culture, and probably only existing during a comparatively short period of the world's history. Nobody is responsible for his actions, nobody for his nature; to judge is identical with being unjust. This also applies when an individual judges himself. The theory is as clear as sunlight, and yet every one prefers to go back into the shadow and the untruth, for fear of the consequences.

40

The super-animal – The beast in us wishes to be deceived; morality is a lie of necessity in order that we may not be torn in pieces by it. Without the errors which lie in the assumption of morality, man would have remained an animal. Thus, however, he has considered himself as something higher and has laid strict laws upon himself. Therefore he hates the grades which have remained nearer to animalness, whereby the former scorn of the slave, as a not-yet-man, is to be explained as a fact.

41

The unchangeable character – That the character is unchangeable is not true in a strict sense; this favourite theory means, rather, that during the short lifetime of an individual the new influencing motives cannot penetrate deeply enough to destroy the ingrained marks of many thousands of years. But if one were to imagine a man of eighty thousand years, one would have in him an absolutely changeable character, so that a number of different individuals would gradually develop out of him. The shortness of human life misleads us into forming many erroneous ideas about the qualities of man.

42

The order of possessions and morality – The once-accepted hierarchy of possessions, according as this or the other is coveted by a lower, higher, or highest egoism, now decides what is moral or immoral. To prefer a lesser good (for instance, the gratification of the senses) to a more highly valued good (for instance, health) is accounted immoral, and also to prefer luxury to liberty. The hierarchy of possessions, however, is not fixed and equal at all times; if any one prefers vengeance to justice he is moral according to the standard of an earlier civilisation, but immoral according to the present one. To be 'immoral', therefore, denotes that an individual has not felt, or not felt sufficiently strongly, the higher, finer, spiritual motives which have come in with a new culture; it marks one who has remained behind, but only according to the difference of degrees. The order of possessions itself is *not* raised and lowered according to a moral point of view; but each time that it is fixed it supplies the decision as to whether an action is moral or immoral.

43

Cruel people as those who have remained behind – People who are cruel nowadays must be accounted for by us as the grades of earlier civilisations which have survived; here are exposed those deeper formations in the mountain of humanity which usually remain concealed. They are backward people whose brains, through all manner of accidents in the course of inheritance, have not been developed in so delicate and manifold a way. They show us what we all *were* and horrify us, but they themselves are as little responsible as is a block of granite for being granite. There must, too, be grooves and twists in our brains which answer to that condition of mind, as in the form of certain human organs there are supposed to be traces of a fish-state. But these grooves and twists are no longer the bed through which the stream of our sensation flows.

44

Gratitude and revenge – The reason why the powerful man is grateful is this: his benefactor, through the benefit he confers, has mistaken and intruded into the sphere of the powerful man – now the latter, in return, penetrates into the sphere of the benefactor by the act of gratitude. It is a milder form of revenge. Without the satisfaction of gratitude, the powerful man would have shown himself powerless, and would have been reckoned as such ever after. Therefore every society of the good, which originally meant the powerful, places gratitude amongst the first duties – Swift propounded the maxim that men were grateful in the same proportion as they were revengeful.

45

The twofold early history of good and evil – The conception of good and evil has a twofold early history, namely, *once* in the soul of the ruling tribes and castes. Whoever has the power of returning good for good, evil for evil, and really practises requital, and who is, therefore, grateful and revengeful, is called good; whoever is powerless, and unable to requite, is reckoned as bad. As a good man one is reckoned among the 'good', a community which has common feelings because the single individuals are bound to one another by the sense of requital. As a bad man one belongs to the 'bad', to a party of subordinate, powerless people who have no common feeling. The good are a caste, the bad are a mass like dust. Good and bad have for a long time meant the same thing as noble and base, master and slave. On the other hand, the enemy is not looked upon as evil, he can requite. In Homer the Trojan and the Greek are both good. It is not the one who injures us, but the one who is despicable, who is called bad. Good is inherited in the community of the good; it is impossible that a bad man could spring from such good soil. If, nevertheless, one of the good ones does something which is unworthy of the good, refuge is sought in excuses; the guilt is thrown upon a god, for instance; it is said that he has struck the good man with blindness and madness –

Then in the soul of the oppressed and powerless. Here every *other* man is looked upon as hostile, inconsiderate, rapacious, cruel, cunning, be he noble or base; evil is the distinguishing word for man, even for every conceivable living creature, *e.g.* for a god; human, divine, is the same thing as devilish, evil. The signs of goodness, helpfulness, pity, are looked upon with fear as spite, the prelude to a terrible result, stupefaction and out-witting – in short, as refined malice. With such a disposition in the individual a community could hardly exist, or at most it could exist only in its crudest form, so that in all places where this conception of good and evil obtains, the downfall of the single individuals, of their tribes and races, is at hand – Our present civilisation has grown up on the soil of the *ruling* tribes and castes.

46

Sympathy stronger than suffering – There are cases when sympathy is stronger than actual suffering. For instance, we are more pained when one of our friends is guilty of something shameful than when we do it ourselves. For one thing, we have more faith in the purity of his character than he has himself; then our love for him, probably on account of this very faith, is stronger than his love for himself. And even if his egoism suffers more thereby than our egoism, inasmuch as it has to bear more of the bad consequences of his fault, the un-egoistic in us – this word is not to be taken too seriously, but only as a modification of the expression – is more deeply wounded by his guilt than is the un-egoistic in him.

47

Hypochondria – There are people who become hypochondriacal through their sympathy and concern for another person; the kind of sympathy which results therefrom is nothing but a disease. Thus there is also a Christian hypochondria, which afflicts those solitary, religiously-minded people who keep constantly before their eyes the sufferings and death of Christ.

48

Economy of goodness – Goodness and love, as the most healing herbs and powers in human intercourse, are such costly discoveries that one would wish as much economy as possible to be exercised in the employment of these balsamic means; but this is impossible. The economy of goodness is the dream of the most daring Utopians.

49

Goodwill – Amongst the small, but countlessly frequent and therefore very effective, things to which science should pay more attention than to the great, rare things, is to be reckoned goodwill; I mean that exhibition of a friendly disposition in intercourse, that smiling eye, that clasp of the hand, that cheerfulness with which almost all human actions are usually accompanied. Every teacher, every official, adds this to whatever is his duty; it is the perpetual occupation of humanity, and at the same time the waves of its light, in which everything grows; in the narrowest circle, namely, within the family, life blooms and flourishes only through that goodwill. Kindliness, friendliness, the courtesy of the heart, are ever-flowing streams of un-egoistic impulses, and have given far more powerful assistance to culture than even those much more famous demonstrations which are called pity, mercy, and self-sacrifice. But they are thought little of, and, as a matter of fact, there is not much that is un-egoistic in them. The *sum* of these small doses is nevertheless mighty, their united force is amongst the strongest forces. Thus one finds much more happiness in the world than sad eyes see, if one only reckons rightly, and does not forget all those moments of comfort in which every day is rich, even in the most harried of human lives.

50

The wish to arouse pity – In the most remarkable passage of his auto-portrait (first printed in 1658), La Rochefoucauld assuredly hits the nail on the head when he warns all sensible people against pity, when he advises them to leave that to those orders of the people who have need of passion (because it is not ruled by reason), and to reach the point of helping the suffering and acting energetically in an accident; while pity, according to his judgment, weakens the soul. Certainly we should *exhibit* pity, but take good care not to *feel* it, for the unfortunate are so *stupid* that to them the exhibition of pity is the greatest good in the world. One can, perhaps, give a more forcible warning against this feeling of pity if one looks upon that need of the unfortunate not exactly as stupidity and lack of intellect, a kind of mental derangement which misfortune brings with it (and as such, indeed, La Rochefoucauld appears to regard it), but as something quite different and more serious. Observe children, who cry and scream *in order* to be pitied, and therefore wait for the moment when they will be noticed; live in intercourse with the sick and mentally oppressed, and ask yourself whether that ready complaining and whimpering, that making a show of misfortune, does not, at bottom, aim at *making the spectators miserable*; the pity which the spectators then exhibit is in so far a consolation for the weak and suffering in that the latter recognise therein that they *possess still one power*, in spite of their weakness, *the power of giving pain*. The unfortunate derives a sort of pleasure from this feeling of superiority, of which the exhibition of pity makes him conscious; his imagination is exalted, he is still powerful enough to give the world pain. Thus the thirst for pity is the thirst for self-gratification, and that, moreover, at the expense of his fellow-men; it shows man in the whole inconsiderateness of his own dear self, but not exactly in his 'stupidity', as La Roche-foucauld thinks. In society-talk three-fourths of all questions asked and of all answers given are intended to cause the interlocutor a little pain; for this reason so many people pine for company; it enables them to feel their power. There is a powerful charm of life in such countless but very small doses in which malice makes itself felt, just as goodwill, spread in the same way throughout the world, is the ever-ready means of healing. But are there many honest people who will admit that it is pleasing to give pain? that one not infrequently amuses one's self – and amuses one's self very well – in causing mortifications to others, at least in thought, and firing off at them the grape-shot of petty malice? Most people are too dishonest, and a few are too good, to know anything of this *pudendum*; these will always deny that Prosper Mérimée is right when he says, '*Sachez aussi qu'il n'y a rien de plus commun que de faire le mal pour le plaisir de le faire.*'

51

How appearance bcomes actuality – The actor finally reaches such a point that even in the deepest sorrow he cannot cease from thinking about the impression made by his own person and the general scenic effect; for instance, even at the funeral of his child, he will weep over his own sorrow and its expression like one of his own audience. The hypocrite, who always plays one and the same part, ceases at last to be a hypocrite; for instance, priests, who as young men are generally conscious or unconscious hypocrites, become at last natural, and are then really without any affectation, just priests; or if the father does not succeed so far, perhaps the son does, who makes use of his father's progress and inherits his habits. If any one long and obstinately desires to *appear* something, he finds it difficult at last to *be* anything else. The profession of almost every individual, even of the artist, begins with hypocrisy, with an imitating from without, with a copying of the effective. He who always wears the mask of a friendly expression must eventually obtain a power over well-meaning dispositions without which the expression of friendliness is not to be compelled – and finally, these, again, obtain a power over him, he *is* well-meaning.

52

The point of honour in deception – In all great deceivers one thing is noteworthy, to which they owe their power. In the actual act of deception, with all their preparations, the dreadful voice, expression, and mien, in the midst of their effective scenery they are overcome by their *belief in themselves*; it is this, then, which speaks so wonderfully and persuasively to the spectators. The founders of religions are distinguished from those great deceivers in that they never awake from their condition of self-deception; or at times, but very rarely, they have an enlightened moment when doubt overpowers them; they generally console themselves, however, by ascribing these enlightened moments to the influence of the Evil One. There must be self-deception in order that this and that may *produce* great *effects*. For men believe in the truth of everything that is visibly, strongly believed in.

53

The nominal degrees of truth – One of the commonest mistakes is this: because some one is truthful and honest towards us, he must speak the truth. Thus the child believes in its parents' judgment, the Christian in the assertions of the Founder of the Church. In the same way men refuse to admit that all those things which men defended in former ages with the sacrifice of life and happiness were nothing but errors; it is even said, perhaps, that they were degrees of the truth. But what is really meant is that when a man has honestly believed in something, and has fought and died for his faith, it would really be too *unjust* if he had only been inspired by an error. Such a thing seems a contradiction of eternal justice; therefore the heart of sensitive man ever enunciates against his head the axiom: between moral action and intellectual insight there must absolutely be a necessary connection. It is unfortunately otherwise; for there is no eternal justice.

54

Falsehood – Why do people mostly speak the truth in daily life? – Assuredly not because a god has forbidden falsehood. But, firstly, because it is more convenient, as falsehood requires invention, deceit, and memory. (As Swift says, he who tells a lie is not sensible how great a task he undertakes; for in order to uphold one lie he must invent twenty others.) Therefore, because it is advantageous in upright circumstances to say straight out, 'I want this, I have done that,' and so on; because, in other words, the path of compulsion and authority is surer than that of cunning. But if a child has been brought up in complicated domestic circumstances, he employs falsehood, naturally and unconsciously says whatever best suits his interests; a sense of truth and a hatred of falsehood are quite foreign and unknown to him, and so he lies in all innocence.

55

Throwing suspicion on morality for faith's sake – No power can be maintained when it is only represented by hypocrites; no matter how many 'worldly' elements the Catholic Church possesses, its strength lies in those still numerous priestly natures who render life hard and full of meaning for themselves, and whose glance and worn bodies speak of nocturnal vigils, hunger, burning prayers, and perhaps even of scourging; these move men and inspire them with fear. What if it were *necessary* to live thus? This is the terrible question which their aspect brings to the lips. Whilst they spread this doubt they always uprear another pillar of their power; even the free-thinker does not dare to withstand such unselfishness with hard words of truth, and to say, 'Thyself deceived, deceive not others!' Only the difference of views divides them from him, certainly no difference of goodness or badness; but men generally treat unjustly that which they do not like. Thus we speak of the cunning and the infamous art of the Jesuits, but overlook the self-control which every individual Jesuit practises, and the fact that the lightened manner of life preached by Jesuit books is by no means for their benefit, but for that of the laity. We may even ask whether, with precisely similar tactics and organisation, we enlightened ones would make equally good tools, equally admirable through self-conquest, indefatigableness, and renunciation.

56

Victory of knowledge over radical evil – It is of great advantage to him who desires to be wise to have witnessed for a time the spectacle of a thoroughly evil and degenerate man; it is false, like the contrary spectacle, but for whole long periods it held the mastery, and its roots have even extended and ramified themselves to us and our world. In order to understand *ourselves* we must understand *it*; but then, in order to mount higher we must rise above it. We recognise, then, that there exist no sins in the metaphysical sense; but, in the same sense, also no virtues; we recognise that the entire domain of ethical ideas is perpetually tottering, that there are higher and deeper conceptions of good and evil, of moral and immoral. He who does not desire much more from things than a knowledge of them easily makes peace with his soul, and will make a mistake (or commit a sin, as the world calls it) at the most from ignorance, but hardly from covetousness. He will no longer wish to excommunicate and exterminate desires; but his only, his wholly dominating ambition, to *know* as well as possible at all times, will make him cool and will soften all the savageness in his disposition. Moreover, he has been freed from a number of tormenting conceptions, he has no more feeling at the mention of the words 'punishments of hell', 'sinfulness', 'incapacity for good', he recognises in them only the vanishing shadow-pictures of false views of the world and of life.

57

Morality as the self-disintegration of man – A good author, who really has his heart in his work, wishes that some one could come and annihilate him by representing the same thing in a clearer way and answering without more ado the problems therein proposed. The loving girl wishes she could prove the self-sacrificing faithfulness of her love by the unfaithfulness of her beloved. The soldier hopes to die on the field of battle for his victorious fatherland; for his loftiest desires triumph in the victory of his country. The mother gives to the child that of which she deprives herself – sleep, the best food, sometimes her health and fortune. But are all these un-egoistic conditions? Are these deeds of morality *miracles*, because, to use Schopenhauer's expression, they are 'impossible and yet performed'? Is it not clear that in all four cases the individual loves *something of himself*, a thought, a desire, a production, better than *anything else of himself*, that he therefore divides his nature and to one part sacrifices all the rest? Is it something *entirely* different when an obstinate man says, 'I would rather be shot than move a step out of my way for this man'? The *desire for something* (wish, inclination, longing) is present in all the instances mentioned; to give way to it, with all its consequences, is certainly not 'un-egoistic'. – In ethics man does not consider himself as *individuum* but as *dividuum*.

58

What one may promise – One may promise actions, but no senti-ments, for these are involuntary. Whoever promises to love or hate a person, or be faithful to him for ever, promises something which is not within his power; he can certainly promise such actions as are usually the results of love, hate, or fidelity, but which may also spring from other motives; for many ways and motives lead to one and the same action. The promise to love some one for ever is, therefore, really: So long as I love you I will act towards you in a loving way; if I cease to love you, you will still receive the same treatment from me, although inspired by other motives, so that our fellow-men will still be deluded into the belief that our love is unchanged and ever the same. One promises therefore, the continuation of the semblance of love, when, without self-deception, one speaks vows of eternal love.

59

Intellect and morality – One must have a good memory to be able to keep a given promise. One must have a strong power of imagination to be able to feel pity. So closely is morality bound to the goodness of the intellect.

60

To wish for revenge and to take revenge – To have a revengeful thought and to carry it into effect is to have a violent attack of fever, which passes off, however – but to have a revengeful thought without the strength and courage to carry it out is a chronic disease, a poisoning of body and soul which we have to bear about with us. Morality, which only takes intentions into account, considers the two cases as equal; usually the former case is regarded as the worse (because of the evil consequences which may perhaps result from the deed of revenge). Both estimates are short-sighted.

61

The power of waiting – Waiting is so difficult that even great poets have not disdained to take incapability of waiting as the motive for their works. Thus Shakespeare in *Othello* or Sophocles in *Ajax*, to whom suicide, had he been able to let his feelings cool down for one day, would no longer have seemed necessary, as the oracle intimated; he would probably have snapped his fingers at the terrible whisperings of wounded vanity, and said to himself, 'Who has not already, in my circumstances, mistaken a fool for a hero? Is it something so very extraordinary?' On the contrary, it is something very commonly human; Ajax might allow himself that consolation. Passion will not wait; the tragedy in the lives of great men frequently lies *not* in their conflict with the times and the baseness of their fellow-men, but in their incapacity of postponing their work for a year or two; they cannot wait. In all duels advising friends have one thing to decide, namely whether the parties concerned can still wait awhile; if this is not the case, then a duel is advisable, inasmuch as each of the two says, 'Either I continue to live and that other man must die immediately, or *vice versa*.' In such case waiting would mean a prolonged suffering of the terrible martyrdom of wounded honour in the face of the insulter, and this may entail more suffering than life is worth.

62

Revelling in vengeance – Coarser individuals who feel themselves insulted, make out the insult to be as great as possible, and relate the affair in greatly exaggerated language, in order to be able to revel thoroughly in the rarely awakened feelings of hatred and revenge.

63

The value of disparagement – In order to maintain their self-respect in their own eyes and a certain thoroughness of action, not a few men, perhaps even the majority, find it absolutely necessary to run down and disparage all their acquaintances. But as mean natures are numerous, and since it is very important whether they possess that thoroughness or lose it, hence –

64

The man in a passion – We must beware of one who is in a passion against us as of one who has once sought our life; for the fact that we still live is due to the absence of power to kill – if looks would suffice, we should have been dead long ago. It is a piece of rough civilisation to force some one into silence by the exhibition of physical savageness and the inspiring of fear. That cold glance which exalted persons employ towards their servants is also a relic of that caste division between man and man, a piece of rough antiquity; women, the preservers of ancient things, have also faithfully retained this *survival* of an ancient habit.

65

Whither honesty can lead – Somebody had the bad habit of occasionally talking quite frankly about the motives of his actions, which were as good and as bad as the motives of most men. He first gave offence, then aroused suspicion, was then gradually excluded from society and declared a social outlaw, until at last justice remembered such an abandoned creature, on occasions when it would otherwise have had no eyes, or would have closed them. The lack of power to hold his tongue concerning the common secret, and the irresponsible tendency to see what no one wishes to see – himself – brought him to a prison and an early death.

66

Punishable, but never punished – Our crime against criminals lies in the fact that we treat them like rascals.

67

Sancta simplicitas of virtue – Every virtue has its privileges; for example, that of contributing its own little faggot to the scaffold of every condemned man.

68

Morality and consequences – It is not only the spectators of a deed who frequently judge of its morality or immorality according to its consequences, but the doer of the deed himself does so. For the motives and intentions are seldom sufficiently clear and simple, and sometimes memory itself seems clouded by the consequences of the deed, so that one ascribes the deed to false motives or looks upon unessential motives as essential. Success often gives an action the whole honest glamour of a good conscience; failure casts the shadow of remorse over the most estimable deed. Hence arises the well-known practice of the politician, who thinks, 'Only grant me success, with that I bring all honest souls over to my side and make myself honest in my own eyes.' In the same way success must replace a better argument. Many educated people still believe that the triumph of Christianity over Greek philosophy is a proof of the greater truthfulness of the former – although in this case it is only the coarser and more powerful that has triumphed over the more spiritual and delicate. Which possesses the greater truth may be seen from the fact that the awakening sciences have agreed with Epicurus' philosophy on point after point, but on point after point have rejected Christianity.

69

Love and justice – Why do we over-estimate love to the disadvantage of justice, and say the most beautiful things about it, as if it were something very much higher than the latter? Is it not visibly more stupid than justice? Certainly, but precisely for that reason all the *pleasanter* for every one. It is blind, and possesses an abundant cornucopia, out of which it distributes its gifts to all, even if they do not deserve them, even if they express no thanks for them. It is as impartial as the rain, which, according to the Bible and experience, makes not only the unjust, but also occasionally the just wet through to the skin.

70

Execution – How is it that every execution offends us more than does a murder? It is the coldness of the judges, the painful preparations, the conviction that a human being is here being used as a warning to scare others. For the guilt is not punished, even if it existed – it lies with educators, parents, surroundings, in ourselves, not in the murderer – I mean the determining circumstances.

71

Hope – Pandora brought the box of ills and opened it. It was the gift of the gods to men, outwardly a beautiful and seductive gift, and called the Casket of Happiness. Out of it flew all the evils, living winged creatures, thence they now circulate and do men injury day and night. One single evil had not yet escaped from the box, and by the will of Zeus Pandora closed the lid and it remained within. Now for ever man has the casket of happiness in his house and thinks he holds a great treasure; it is at his disposal, he stretches out his hand for it whenever he desires; for he does not know the box which Pandora brought was the casket of evil, and he believes the ill which remains within to be the greatest blessing – it is hope. Zeus did not wish man, however much he might be tormented by the other evils, to fling away his life, but to go on letting himself be tormented again and again. Therefore he gives man hope – in reality it is the worst of all evils, because it prolongs the torments of man.

72

The degree of moral inflammability unknown – According to whether we have or have not had certain disturbing views and impressions – for instance, an unjustly executed, killed, or martyred father; a faithless wife; a cruel hostile attack – it depends whether our passions reach fever heat and influence our whole life or not. No one knows to what he may be driven by circumstances, pity, or indignation; he does not know the degree of his own inflammability. Miserable little circumstances make us miserable; it is generally not the quantity of experiences, but their quality, on which lower and higher man depends, in good and evil.

73

The martyr in spite of himself – There was a man belonging to a party who was too nervous and cowardly ever to contradict his comrades; they made use of him for everything, they demanded everything from him, because he was more afraid of the bad opinion of his companions than of death itself; his was a miserable, feeble soul. They recognised this, and on the ground of these qualities they made a hero of him, and finally even a martyr. Although the coward inwardly always said No, with his lips he always said Yes, even on the scaffold, when he was about to die for the opinions of his party; for beside him stood one of his old companions, who so tyrannised over him by word and look that he really suffered death in the most respectable manner, and has ever since been celebrated as a martyr and a great character.

74

The every-day standard – One will seldom go wrong if one attributes extreme actions to vanity, average ones to habit, and petty ones to fear.

75

Misunderstanding concerning virtue – Whoever has known immorality in connection with pleasure, as is the case with a man who has a pleasure-seeking youth behind him, imagines that virtue must be connected with absence of pleasure – Whoever, on the contrary, has been much plagued by his passions and vices, longs to find in virtue peace and the soul's happiness. Hence it is possible for two virtuous persons not to understand each other at all.

76

The ascetic – The ascetic makes a necessity of virtue.

77

Transferring honour from the person to the thing – Deeds of love and sacrifice for the benefit of one's neighbour are generally honoured, wherever they are manifested. Thereby we multiply the valuation of things which are thus loved, or for which we sacrifice ourselves, although perhaps they are not worth much in themselves. A brave army is convinced of the cause for which it fights.

78

Ambition a substitute for the moral sense – The moral sense must not be lacking in those natures which have no ambition. The ambitious manage without it, with almost the same results. For this reason the sons of unpretentious, unambitious families, when once they lose the moral sense, generally degenerate very quickly into complete scamps.

79

Vanity enriches – How poor would be the human mind without vanity! Thus, however, it resembles a well-stocked and constantly replenished bazaar which attracts buyers of every kind. There they can find almost everything, obtain almost everything, provided that they bring the right sort of coin, namely admiration.

80

Old age and death – Apart from the commands of religion, the question may well be asked, Why is it more worthy for an old man who feels his powers decline, to await his slow exhaustion and extinction than with full consciousness to set a limit to his life? Suicide in this case is a perfectly natural, obvious action, which should justly arouse respect as a triumph of reason, and did arouse it in those times when the heads of Greek philosophy and the sturdiest patriots used to seek death through suicide. The seeking, on the contrary, to prolong existence from day to day, with anxious consultation of doctors and painful mode of living, without the power of drawing nearer to the actual aim of life, is far less worthy. Religion is rich in excuses to reply to the demand for suicide, and thus it ingratiates itself with those who wish to cling to life.

81

Errors of the sufferer and the doer – When a rich man deprives a poor man of a possession (for instance, a prince taking the sweetheart of a plebeian), an error arises in the mind of the poor man; he thinks that the rich man must be utterly infamous to take away from him the little that he has. But the rich man does not estimate so highly the value of a *single* possession, because he is accustomed to have many; hence he cannot imagine himself in the poor man's place, and does not commit nearly so great a wrong as the latter supposes. They each have a mistaken idea of the other. The injustice of the powerful, which, more than anything else, rouses indignation in history, is by no means so great as it appears. Alone the mere inherited consciousness of being a higher creation, with higher claims, produces a cold temperament, and leaves the conscience quiet; we all of us feel no injustice when the difference is very great between ourselves and another creature, and kill a fly, for instance, without any pricks of conscience. Therefore it was no sign of badness in Xerxes (whom even all Greeks describe as superlatively noble) when he took a son away from his father and had him cut in pieces, because he had expressed a nervous, ominous distrust of the whole campaign; in this case the individual is put out of the way like an unpleasant insect; he is too lowly to be allowed any longer to cause annoyance to a ruler of the world. Yes, every cruel man is not so cruel as the ill-treated one imagines; the idea of pain is not the same as its endurance. It is the same thing in the case of unjust judges, of the journalist who leads public opinion astray by small dishonesties. In all these cases cause and effect are surrounded by entirely different groups of feelings and thoughts; yet one unconsciously takes it for granted that doer and sufferer think and feel alike, and according to this supposition we measure the guilt of the one by the pain of the other.

82

The skin of the soul – As the bones, flesh, entrails, and blood-vessels are enclosed within a skin, which makes the aspect of man endurable, so the emotions and passions of the soul are enwrapped with vanity – it is the skin of the soul.

83

The sleep of virtue – When virtue has slept, it will arise again all the fresher.

84

The refinement of shame – People are not ashamed to think something foul, but they are ashamed when they think these foul thoughts are attributed to them.

85

Malice is rare – Most people are far too much occupied with themselves to be malicious.

86

The tongue in the balance – We praise or blame according as the one or the other affords more opportunity for exhibiting our power of judgment.

87

St Luke xviii.14, *improved* – He that humbleth himself wishes to be exalted.

88

The prevention of suicide – There is a certain right by which we may deprive a man of life, but none by which we may deprive him of death; this is mere cruelty.

89

Vanity – We care for the good opinion of men, firstly because they are useful to us, and then because we wish to please them (children their parents, pupils their teachers, and well-meaning people generally their fellow-men). Only where the good opinion of men is of importance to some one, apart from the advantage thereof or his wish to please, can we speak of vanity. In this case the man wishes to please himself, but at the expense of his fellow-men, either by misleading them into holding a false opinion about him, or by aiming at a degree of 'good opinion' which must be painful to every one else (by arousing envy). The individual usually wishes to corroborate the opinion he holds of himself by the opinion of others, and to strengthen it in his own eyes; but the strong habit of authority – a habit as old as man himself – induces many to support by authority their belief in themselves: that is to say, they accept it first from others; they trust the judgment of others more than their own. The interest in himself, the wish to please himself, attains to such a height in a vain man that he misleads others into having a false, all too elevated estimation of him, and yet nevertheless sets store by their authority – thus causing an error and yet believing in it. It must be confessed, therefore, that vain people do not wish to please others so much as themselves, and that they go so far therein as to neglect their advantage, for they often endeavour to prejudice their fellow-men unfavourably, inimicably, enviously, consequently injuriously against themselves, merely in order to have pleasure in themselves, personal pleasure.

90

The limits of human love – A man who has declared that another is an idiot and a bad companion, is angry when the latter eventually proves himself to be otherwise.

91

Moralité larmoyante – What a great deal of pleasure morality gives! Only think what a sea of pleasant tears has been shed over descriptions of noble and unselfish deeds! This charm of life would vanish if the belief in absolute irresponsibility were to obtain supremacy.

92

The origin of justice – Justice (equity) has its origin amongst powers which are fairly equal, as Thucydides (in the terrible dialogue between the Athenian and Melian ambassadors) rightly comprehended: that is to say, where there is no clearly recognisable supremacy, and where a conflict would be useless and would injure both sides, there arises the thought of coming to an understanding and settling the opposing claims; the character of *exchange* is the primary character of justice. Each party satisfies the other, as each obtains what he values more than the other. Each one receives that which he desires, as his own henceforth, and whatever is desired is received in return. Justice, therefore, is recompense and exchange based on the hypothesis of a fairly equal degree of power – thus, originally, revenge belongs to the province of justice, it is an exchange. Also gratitude – Justice naturally is based on the point of view of a judicious self-preservation, on the egoism, therefore, of that reflection, 'Why should I injure myself uselessly and perhaps not attain my aim after all?' So much about the *origin* of justice. Because man, according to his intellectual custom, has *forgotten* the original purpose of so-called just and reasonable actions, and particularly because for hundreds of years children have been taught to admire and imitate such actions, the idea has gradually arisen that such an action is un-egoistic; upon this idea, however, is based the high estimation in which it is held: which, moreover, like all valuations, is constantly growing, for something that is valued highly is striven after, imitated, multiplied, and increases, because the value of the output of toil and enthusiasm of each individual is added to the value of the thing itself. How little moral would the world look without this forgetfulness! A poet might say that God had placed forgetfulness as door-keeper in the temple of human dignity.

93

The right of the weaker – When any one submits under certain conditions to a greater power, as a besieged town for instance, the counter-condition is that one can destroy one's self, burn the town, and so cause the mighty one a great loss. Therefore there is a kind of *equalisation* here, on the basis of which rights may be determined. The enemy has his advantage in maintaining it. In so far there are also rights between slaves and masters, that is, precisely so far as the possession of the slave is useful and important to his master. The *right* originally extends *so far as* one *appears* to be valuable to the other, essentially unlosable, unconquerable, and so forth. In so far the weaker one also has rights, but lesser ones. Hence the famous *unusquisque tantum juris habet, quantum potentia valet* (or more exactly, *quantum potentia valere creditur*).

94

The three phases of hitherto existing morality – It is the first sign that the animal has become man when its actions no longer have regard only to momentary welfare, but to what is enduring, when it grows *useful* and *practical*; here the free rule of reason first breaks out. A still higher step is reached when he acts according to the principle of *honour*; by this means he brings himself into order, submits to common feelings and that exalts him still higher over the phase in which he was led only by the idea of usefulness from a personal point of view; he respects and wishes to be respected, i.e. he understands usefulness as dependent upon what he thinks of others and what others think of him. Eventually he acts, on the highest step of the *hitherto* existing morality, according to *his* standard of things and men; he himself decides for himself and others what is honourable, what is useful; he has become the law-giver of opinions, in accordance with the ever more highly developed idea of what is useful and honourable. Knowledge enables him to place that which is most useful, that is to say the general, enduring usefulness, above the personal, the honourable recognition of general, enduring validity above the momentary; he lives and acts as a collective individual.

95

The morality of the mature individual – The impersonal has hitherto been looked upon as the actual distinguishing mark of moral action; and it has been pointed out that in the beginning it was in consideration of the common good that all impersonal actions were praised and distinguished. Is not an important change in these views impending, now when it is more and more recognised that it is precisely in the most *personal* possible considerations that the common good is the greatest, so that a *strictly personal* action now best illustrates the present idea of morality, as utility for the mass? To make a whole *personality* out of ourselves, and in all that we do to keep that personality's *highest good* in view, carries us further than those sympathetic emotions and actions for the benefit of others. We all still suffer, certainly, from the too small consideration of the personal in us; it is badly developed – let us admit it; rather has our mind been forcibly drawn away from it and offered as a sacrifice to the State, to science, or to those who stand in need of help, as if it were the bad part which must be sacrificed. We are still willing to work for our fellow-men, but only so far as we find our own greatest advantage in this work, no more and no less. It is only a question of what we understand as *our advantage*; the unripe, undeveloped, crude individual will understand it in the crudest way.

96

Custom and morality – To be moral, correct, and virtuous is to be obedient to an old-established law and custom. Whether we submit with difficulty or willingly is immaterial, enough that we do so. He is called 'good' who, as if naturally, after long precedent, easily and willingly, therefore, does what is right, according to whatever this may be (as, for instance, taking revenge, if to take revenge be considered as right, as amongst the ancient Greeks). He is called good because he is good 'for something'; but as goodwill, pity, consideration, moderation, and such like, have come, with the change in manners, to be looked upon as 'good for something', as useful, the good-natured and helpful have, later on, come to be distinguished specially as 'good'. (In the beginning other and more important kinds of usefulness stood in the foreground.) To be evil is to be 'not moral' (immoral), to be immoral is to be in opposition to tradition, however sensible or stupid it may be; injury to the community (the 'neighbour' being understood thereby) has, however, been looked upon by the social laws of all different ages as being eminently the actual 'immorality', so that now at the word 'evil' we immediately think of voluntary injury to one's neighbour. The fundamental antithesis which has taught man the distinction between moral and immoral, between good and evil, is not the 'egoistic' and 'un-egoistic', but the being bound to the tradition, law, and solution thereof. How the tradition has *arisen* is immaterial, at all events without regard to good and evil or any immanent categorical imperative, but above all for the purpose of preserving a *community*, a generation, an association, a people; every superstitious custom that has arisen on account of some falsely explained accident, creates a tradition, which it is moral to follow; to separate one's self from it is dangerous, but more dangerous for the *community* than for the individual (because the Godhead punishes the community for every outrage and every violation of its rights, and the individual only in proportion). Now every tradition grows continually more venerable, the farther off lies its origin, the more this is lost sight of; the veneration paid it accumulates from generation to generation, the tradition at last becomes holy and excites awe; and thus in any case the morality of piety is a much older morality than that which requires un-egoistic actions.

97

Pleasure in traditional custom – An important species of pleasure, and therewith the source of morality, arises out of habit. Man does what is habitual to him more easily, better, and therefore more willingly; he feels a pleasure therein, and knows from experience that the habitual has been tested, and is therefore useful; a custom that we can live with is proved to be wholesome and advantageous in contrast to all new and not yet tested experiments. According to this, morality is the union of the pleasant and the useful; moreover, it requires no reflection. As soon as man can use compulsion, he uses it to introduce and enforce his *customs*; for in his eyes they are proved as the wisdom of life. In the same way a company of individuals compels each single one to adopt the same customs. Here the inference is wrong; because we feel at ease with a morality, or at least because we are able to carry on existence with it, therefore this morality is necessary, for it seems to be the *only* possibility of feeling at ease; the ease of life seems to grow out of it alone. This comprehension of the habitual as a necessity of existence is pursued even to the smallest details of custom – as insight into genuine causality is very small with lower peoples and civilisations, they take precautions with superstitious fear that everything should go in its same groove; even where custom is difficult, hard, and burdensome, it is preserved on account of its apparent highest usefulness. It is not known that the same degree of well-being can also exist with other customs, and that even higher degrees may be attained. We become aware, however, that all customs, even the hardest, grow pleasanter and milder with time, and that the severest way of life may become a habit and therefore a pleasure.

98

Pleasure and social instinct – Out of his relations with other men, man obtains a new species of *pleasure* in addition to those pleasurable sensations which he derives from himself; whereby he greatly increases the scope of enjoyment. Perhaps he has already taken too many of the pleasures of this sphere from animals, which visibly feel pleasure when they play with each other, especially the mother with her young. Then consider the sexual relations, which make almost every female interesting to a male with regard to pleasure, and *vice versa*. The feeling of pleasure on the basis of human relations generally makes man better; joy in common, pleasure enjoyed together is increased, it gives the individual security, makes him good-tempered, and dispels mistrust and envy, for we feel ourselves at ease and see others at ease. *Similar manifestations of pleasure* awaken the idea of the same sensations, the feeling of being like something; a like effect is produced by common sufferings, the same bad weather, dangers, enemies. Upon this foundation is based the oldest alliance, the object of which is the mutual obviating and averting of a threatening danger for the benefit of each individual. And thus the social instinct grows out of pleasure.

99

The innocent side of so-called evil actions – All 'evil' actions are prompted by the instinct of preservation, or, more exactly, by the desire for pleasure and the avoidance of pain on the part of the individual; thus prompted, but not evil. 'To cause pain *per se*' *does not exist*, except in the brains of philosophers, neither does 'to give pleasure *per se*' (pity in Schopenhauer's meaning). In the social condition *before* the State we kill the creature, be it ape or man, who tries to take from us the fruit of a tree when we are hungry and approach the tree, as we should still do with animals in inhospitable countries. The evil actions which now most rouse our indignation, are based upon the error that he who causes them has a free will, that he had the option, therefore, of not doing us this injury. This belief in option arouses hatred, desire for revenge, spite, and the deterioration of the whole imagination, while we are much less angry with an animal because we consider it irresponsible. To do injury, not from the instinct of preservation, but as *requital*, is the consequence of a false judgment and therefore equally innocent. The individual can in the condition which lies before the State, act sternly and cruelly towards other creatures for the purpose of *terrifying*, to establish his existence firmly by such terrifying proofs of his power. Thus act the violent, the mighty, the original founders of States, who subdue the weaker to themselves. They have the right to do so, such as the State still takes for itself; or rather, there is no right that can hinder this. The ground for all morality can only be made ready when a stronger individual or a collective individual, for instance society or the State, subdues the single individuals, draws them out of their singleness, and forms them into an association. *Compulsion* precedes morality, indeed morality itself is compulsion for a time, to which one submits for the avoidance of pain. Later on it becomes custom – later still, free obedience, and finally almost instinct, then, like everything long accustomed and natural, it is connected with pleasure – and is henceforth called virtue.

100

Shame – Shame exists everywhere where there is a 'mystery'; this, however, is a religious idea, which was widely extended in the older times of human civilisation. Everywhere were found bounded domains to which access was forbidden by divine right, except under certain conditions; at first locally, as, for example, certain spots that ought not to be trodden by the feet of the uninitiated, in the neighbourhood of which these latter experienced horror and fear. This feeling was a good deal carried over into other relations, for instance, the sex relations, which, as a privilege and *aduton* of riper years, had to be withheld from the knowledge of the young for their advantage, relations for the protection and sanctification of which many gods were invented and were set up as guardians in the nuptial chamber. (In Turkish this room is on this account called harem, 'sanctuary', and is distinguished with the same name, therefore, that is used for the entrance courts of the mosques.) Thus the kingdom is as a centre from which radiate power and glory, to the subjects a mystery full of secrecy and shame, of which many after-effects may still be felt among nations which otherwise do not by any means belong to the bashful type. Similarly, the whole world of inner conditions, the so-called 'soul', is still a mystery for all who are not philosophers, after it has been looked upon for endless ages as of divine origin and as worthy of divine intercourse; according to this it is an *aduton* and arouses shame.

101

Judge not – In considering earlier periods, care must be taken not to fall into unjust abuse. The injustice in slavery, the cruelty in the suppression of persons and nations, is not to be measured by our standard. For the instinct of justice was not then so far developed. Who dares to reproach the Genevese Calvin with the burning of the physician Servetus? It was an action following and resulting from his convictions, and in the same way the Inquisition had a good right; only the ruling views were false, and produced a result which seems hard to us because those views have now grown strange to us. Besides, what is the burning of a single individual compared with eternal pains of hell for almost all! And yet this idea was universal at that time, without essentially injuring by its dreadfulness the conception of a God. With us, too, political sectarians are hardly and cruelly treated, but because one is accustomed to believe in the necessity of the State, the cruelty is not so deeply felt here as it is where we repudiate the views. Cruelty to animals in children and Italians is due to ignorance, i.e. the animal, through the interests of Church teaching, has been placed too far behind man. Much that is dreadful and inhuman in history, much that one hardly likes to believe, is mitigated by the reflection that the one who commands and the one who carries out are different persons, the former does not behold the right and therefore does not experience the strong impression on the imagination; the latter obeys a superior and therefore feels no responsibility. Most princes and military heads, through lack of imagination, easily appear hard and cruel without really being so. *Egoism is not evil* because the idea of the 'neighbour' – the word is of Christian origin and does not represent the truth – is very weak in us; and we feel ourselves almost as free and irresponsible towards him as towards plants and stones. We have yet to *learn* that others suffer, and this can never be completely learnt.

102

'Man always acts rightly' – We do not complain of nature as immoral because it sends a thunderstorm and makes us wet – why do we call those who injure us immoral? Because in the latter case we take for granted a free will functioning voluntarily; in the former we see necessity. But this distinction is an error. Thus we do not call even intentional injury immoral in all circumstances; for instance, we kill a fly unhesitatingly and intentionally, only because its buzzing annoys us; we punish a criminal intentionally and hurt him in order to protect ourselves and society. In

the first case it is the individual who, in order to preserve himself, or even to protect himself from worry, does intentional injury; in the second case it is the State. All morals allow intentional injury *in the case of necessity*, that is, when it is a matter of *self-preservation!* But these two points of view suffice to explain all evil actions committed by men against men, we are desirous of obtaining pleasure or avoiding pain; in any case it is always a question of self-preservation. Socrates and Plato are right: whatever man does he always does well, that is, he does that which seems to him good (useful) according to the degree of his intellect, the particular standard of his reasonableness.

103

The harmlessness of malice – The aim of malice is *not* the suffering of others in itself, but our own enjoyment; for instance, as the feeling of revenge, or stronger nervous excitement. All teasing, even, shows the pleasure it gives to exercise our power on others and bring it to an enjoyable feeling of preponderance. Is it *immoral* to taste pleasure at the expense of another's pain? Is malicious joy* devilish, as Schopenhauer says? We give ourselves pleasure in nature by breaking off twigs, loosening stones, fighting with wild animals, and do this in order to become thereby conscious of our strength. Is the knowledge, therefore, that another suffers through us, the same thing concerning which we otherwise feel irresponsible, supposed to make us immoral? But if we did not know this we would not thereby have the enjoyment of our own superiority, which can only *manifest* itself by the suffering of others, for instance, in teasing. All pleasure *per se* is neither good nor evil; whence should come the decision that in order to have pleasure ourselves we may not cause displeasure to others? From the point of view of usefulness alone, that is, out of consideration for the *consequences*, for *possible* displeasure, when the injured one or the replacing State gives the expectation of resentment and revenge: this only can have been the original reason for denying ourselves such actions. *Pity* aims just as little at the pleasure of others as malice at the pain of others *per se*. For it contains at least two (perhaps many more) elements of a personal pleasure, and is so

* This is the untranslatable word *Schadenfreude*, which means joy at the misfortune of others. – J. M. K.

far self-gratification; in the first place as the pleasure of emotion, which is the kind of pity that exists in tragedy, and then, when it impels to action, as the pleasure of satisfaction in the exercise of power. If, besides this, a suffering person is very dear to us, we lift a sorrow from ourselves by the exercise of sympathetic actions. Except by a few philosophers, pity has always been placed very low in the scale of moral feelings, and rightly so.

104

Self-defence – If self-defence is allowed to pass as moral, then almost all manifestations of the so-called immoral egoism must also stand; men injure, rob, or kill in order to preserve or defend themselves, to prevent personal injury, they lie where cunning and dissimulation are the right means of self-preservation. *Intentional injury*, when our existence or safety (preservation of our comfort) is concerned, is conceded to be moral; the State itself injures, according to this point of view, when it punishes. In unintentional injury, of course, there can be nothing immoral, that is ruled by chance. Is there, then, a kind of intentional injury where our existence or the preservation of our comfort is *not* concerned? Is there an injuring out of pure *malice*, for instance in cruelty? If one does not know how much an action hurts, it is no deed of malice; thus the child is not malicious towards the animal, not evil; he examines and destroys it like a toy. But *do* we ever know entirely how an action hurts another? As far as our nervous system extends we protect ourselves from pain; if it extended farther, to our fellow-men, namely, we should do no one an injury (except in such cases as we injure ourselves, where we cut ourselves for the sake of cure, tire and exert ourselves for the sake of health). We *conclude* by analogy that something hurts somebody, and through memory and the strength of imagination we may suffer from it ourselves. But still what a difference there is between toothache and the pain (pity) that the sight of toothache calls forth! Therefore, in injury out of so-called malice the *degree* of pain produced is always unknown to us; but inasmuch as there is *pleasure* in the action (the feeling of one's own power, one's own strong excitement), the action is committed, in order to preserve the comfort of the individual, and is regarded, therefore, from a similar point of view as defence and falsehood in necessity. No life without pleasure; the struggle for pleasure is the struggle for life. Whether the individual so fights this fight that men call him good, or so that they call him evil, is determined by the measure and the constitution of his *intellect*.

105

Recompensing justice – Whoever has completely comprehended the doctrine of absolute irresponsibility can no longer include the so-called punishing and recompensing justice in the idea of justice, should this consist of giving to each man his due. For he who is punished does not deserve the punishment, he is only used as a means of henceforth warning away from certain actions; equally so, he who is rewarded does not merit this reward, he could not act otherwise than he did. Therefore the reward is meant only as an encouragement to him and others, to provide a motive for subsequent actions; words of praise are flung to the runners on the course, not to the one who has reached the goal. Neither punishment nor reward is anything that comes to one as *one's own*; they are given from motives of usefulness, without one having a right to claim them. Hence we must say, 'The wise man gives no reward because the deed has been well done,' just as we have said, 'The wise man does not punish because evil has been committed, but in order that evil shall not be committed'. If punishment and reward no longer existed, then the strongest motives which deter men from certain actions and impel them to certain other actions, would also no longer exist; the needs of mankind require their continuance; and inasmuch as punishment and reward, blame and praise, work most sensibly on vanity, the same need requires the continuance of vanity.

106

At the waterfall – In looking at a waterfall we imagine that there is freedom of will and fancy in the countless turnings, twistings, and breakings of the waves; but everything is compulsory, every movement can be mathematically calculated. So it is also with human actions; one would have to be able to calculate every single action beforehand if one were all-knowing; equally so all progress of knowledge, every error, all malice. The one who acts certainly labours under the illusion of voluntariness; if the world's wheel were to stand still for a moment and an all-knowing, calculating reason were there to make use of this pause, it could foretell the future of every creature to the remotest times, and mark out every track upon which that wheel would continue to roll. The delusion of the acting agent about himself, the supposition of a free will, belongs to this mechanism which still remains to be calculated.

107

Irresponsibility and innocence – The complete irresponsibility of man for his actions and his nature is the bitterest drop which he who understands must swallow if he was accustomed to see the patent of nobility of his humanity in responsibility and duty. All his valuations, distinctions, disinclinations, are thereby deprived of value and become false – his deepest feeling for the sufferer and the hero was based on an error; he may no longer either praise or blame, for it is absurd to praise and blame nature and necessity. In the same way as he loves a fine work of art, but does not praise it, because it can do nothing for itself; in the same way as he regards plants, so must he regard his own actions and those of mankind. He can admire strength, beauty, abundance, in themselves; but must find no merit therein – the chemical progress and the strife of the elements, the torments of the sick person who thirsts after recovery, are all equally as little merits as those struggles of the soul and states of distress in which we are torn hither and thither by different impulses until we finally decide for the strongest – as we say (but in reality it is the strongest motive which decides for us). All these motives, however, whatever fine names we may give them, have all grown out of the same root, in which we believe the evil poisons to be situated; between good and evil actions there is no difference of species, but at most of degree. Good actions are sublimated evil ones; evil actions are vulgarised and stupefied good ones. The single longing of the individual for self-gratification (together with the fear of losing it) satisfies itself in all circumstances: man may act as he can, that is as he must, be it in deeds of vanity, revenge, pleasure, usefulness, malice, cunning; be it in deeds of sacrifice, of pity, of knowledge. The degrees of the power of judgment determine whither any one lets himself be drawn through this longing; to every society, to every individual, a scale of possessions is continually present, according to which he determines his actions and judges those of others. But this standard changes constantly; many actions are called evil and are only stupid, because the degree of intelligence which decided for them was very low. In a certain sense, even, all actions are still stupid; for the highest degree of human intelligence which can now be attained will assuredly be yet surpassed, and then, in a retrospect, all our actions and judgments will appear as limited and hasty as the actions and judgments of primitive wild peoples now appear limited and hasty to us. To recognise all this may be deeply painful, but consolation comes after: such pains are the pangs of birth. The butterfly wants to break through its chrysalis: it rends and tears it, and is then blinded and confused by the unaccustomed light, the kingdom of liberty. In such people as are *capable* of such sadness – and how few are! – the first experiment made is to see whether *mankind can change itself* from a *moral* into a *wise* mankind. The sun of a new gospel throws its rays upon the highest point in the soul of each single individual, then the mists gather thicker than ever, and the brightest light and the dreariest shadow lie side by side. Everything is necessity – so says the new knowledge, and this knowledge itself is necessity. Everything is innocence, and knowledge is the road to insight into this innocence. Are pleasure, egoism, vanity *necessary* for the production of the moral phenomena and their highest result, the sense for truth and justice in knowledge; were error and the con- fusion of the imagination the only means through which mankind could raise itself gradually to this degree of self-enlightenment and self-liberation – who would dare to undervalue these means? Who would dare to be sad if he perceived the goal to which those roads led? Everything in the domain of morality has evolved, is change- able, unstable, everything is dissolved, it is true; but *everything is also streaming towards one goal.* Even if the inherited habit of erroneous valuation, love and hatred, continue to reign in us, yet under the influence of growing knowledge it will become weaker; a new habit, that of comprehension, of not loving, not hating, of over- looking, is gradually implanting itself in us upon the same ground, and in thousands of years will perhaps be powerful enough to give humanity the strength to produce wise, innocent (consciously innocent) men, as it now produces unwise, guilt-conscious men – *that is the necessary preliminary step, not its opposite.*

108

The double fight against evil – When misfortune overtakes us we can either pass over it so lightly that its cause is removed, or so that the result which it has on our temperament is altered, through a changing, therefore, of the evil into a good, the utility of which is perhaps not visible until later on. Religion and art (also metaphysical philosophy) work upon the changing of the temperament, partly through the changing of our judgment on events (for instance, with the help of the phrase 'whom the Lord loveth He chasteneth'), partly through the awakening of a pleasure in pain, in emotion generally (whence the tragic art takes its starting-point). The more a man is inclined to twist and arrange meanings the less he will grasp the causes of evil and disperse them; the momentary mitigation and influence of a narcotic, as for example in toothache, suffices him even in more serious sufferings. The more the dominion of creeds and all arts dispense with narcotics, the more strictly men attend to the actual removing of the evil, which is certainly bad for writers of tragedy; for the material for tragedy is growing scarcer because the domain of pitiless, inexorable fate is growing ever narrower – but worse still for the priests, for they have hitherto lived on the narcotisation of human woes.

109

Sorrow is knowledge – How greatly we should like to exchange the false assertions of the priests, that there is a god who desires good from us, a guardian and witness of every action, every moment, every thought, who loves us and seeks our welfare in all misfortune – how greatly we would like to exchange these ideas for truths which would be just as healing, pacifying and beneficial as those errors! But there are no such truths; at most philosophy can oppose to them metaphysical appearances (at bottom also un-truths). The tragedy consists in the fact that we cannot *believe* those dogmas of religion and metaphysics, if we have strict methods of truth in heart and brain: on the other hand, mankind has, through development, become so delicate, irritable and suffering, that it has need of the highest means of healing and consolation; whence also the danger arises that man would bleed to death from recognised truth, or, more correctly, from discovered error. Byron has expressed this in the immortal lines: –

> Sorrow is knowledge: they who know the most
> Must mourn the deepest o'er the fatal truth,
> The Tree of Knowledge is not that of Life.

For such troubles there is no better help than to recall the stately levity of Horace, at least for the worst hours and eclipses of the soul, and to say with him:

> . . . quid aeternis minorem
> consiliis animum fatigas?
>
> cur non sub alta vel platano vel hac
> pinu jacentes . . . *

But assuredly frivolity or melancholy of every degree is better than a romantic retrospection and desertion of the flag, an approach to Christianity in any form; for according to the present condition of knowledge it is absolutely impossible to approach it without hopelessly soiling our *intellectual conscience* and giving ourselves away to ourselves and others. Those pains may be unpleasant enough, but we cannot become leaders and educators of mankind without pain; and woe to him who would wish to attempt this and no longer have that clear conscience!

110

The truth in religion – In the period of rationalism justice was not done to the importance of religion, of that there is no doubt, but equally there is no doubt that in the reaction that followed this

---

* Why harass with eternal designs a mind too weak to compass them ? Why not, as we lie beneath a lofty plane-tree or this pine . . . [drink while we may] ? Hor., *Odes* II. ii. 11-14. – J. M. K.

rationalism justice was far overstepped; for religions were treated lovingly, even amorously, and, for instance, a deeper, even the very deepest, understanding of the world was ascribed to them; which science has only to strip of its dogmatic garment in order to possess the 'truth' in unmythical form. Religions should, there-fore – this was the opinion of all opposers of rationalism – *sensu allegorico*, with all consideration for the understanding of the masses, give utterance to that ancient wisdom which is wisdom itself, inasmuch as all true science of later times has always led up to it instead of away from it, so that between the oldest wisdom of mankind and all later harmonies similarity of discernment and a progress of knowledge – in case one should wish to speak of such a thing – rests not upon the nature but upon the way of com-municating it. This whole conception of religion and science is thoroughly erroneous, and none would still dare to profess it if Schopenhauer's eloquence had not taken it under its protection; this resonant eloquence which, however, only reached its hearers a generation later. As surely as from Schopenhauer's religious-moral interpretations of men and the world much may be gained for the understanding of the Christian and other religions, so surely also is he mistaken about the *value of religion for knowledge*. Therein he himself was only a too docile pupil of the scientific teachers of his time, who all worshipped romanticism and had forsworn the spirit of enlightenment; had he been born in our present age he could not possibly have talked about the *sensus allegoricus* of religion; he would much rather have given honour to truth, as he used to do, with the words, *'no religion, direct or indirect, either as dogma or as allegory, has ever contained a truth'*. For each has been born of fear and necessity, through the byways of reason did it slip into existence; once, perhaps, when imperilled by science, some philo-sophic doctrine has lied itself into its system in order that it may be found there later, but this is a theological trick of the time when a religion already doubts itself. These tricks of theology (which certainly were practised in the early days of Christianity, as the religion of a scholarly period steeped in philosophy) have led to that superstition of the *sensus allegoricus*, but yet more the habits of the philosophers (especially the half-natures, the poetical philo-sophers and the philosophising artists), to treat all the sensations which they discovered in *themselves* as the fundamental nature of man in general, and hence to allow their own religious feelings an important influence in the building up of their systems. As philosophers frequently philosophised under the custom of religious habits, or at least under the anciently inherited power of that 'metaphysical need', they developed doctrinal opinions which really bore a great resemblance to the Jewish or Christian or Indian religious views – a resemblance, namely, such as children usually bear to their mothers, only that in this case the fathers were not clear about that motherhood, as happens sometimes – but in their innocence romanced about a family likeness between all religion and science. In reality, between religions and real science there exists neither relationship nor friendship, nor even enmity; they live on different planets. Every philosophy which shows a religious comet's tail shining in the darkness of its last prospects makes all the science it contains suspicious; all this is presumably also religion, even though in the guise of science. Moreover, if all nations were to agree about certain religious matters, for instance the existence of a God (which, it may be remarked, is not the case with regard to this point), this would only be an argument *against* those affirmed matters, for instance the existence of a God; the *consensus gentium* and *hominum* in general can only take place in case of a huge folly. On the other hand, there is no *consensus omnium sapientium*, with regard to any single thing; with that exception mentioned in Goethe's lines:

> *Alle die Weisesten aller der Zeiten*
> *Lacheln und winken und stimmen mit ein:*
> *Thoricht, auf Bess'rung der Thoren zu harren!*
> *Kinder der Klugheit, o habet die Narren*
> *Eben zum Narren auch, wie sich's gehort!**

Spoken without verse and rhyme and applied to our case, the *consensus sapientium* consists in this: that the *consensus gentium* counts as a folly.

---

* All greatest sages of all latest ages
    Will chuckle and slily agree,
  'Tis folly to wait till a fool's empty pate
    Has learnt to be knowing and free:
  So children of wisdom, make use of the fools
  And use them whenever you can as your tools. – J.M.K

III

The origin of the religious cult – If we go back to the times in which the religious life flourished to the greatest extent, we find a fundamental conviction, which we now no longer share, and whereby the doors leading to a religious life are closed to us once for all – it concerns Nature and intercourse with her. In those times people knew nothing of natural laws; neither for earth nor for heaven is there a 'must' ; a season, the sunshine, the rain may come or may not come. In short, every idea of natural causality is lacking. When one rows, it is not the rowing that moves the boat, but rowing is only a magical ceremony by which one compels a *daemon* to move the boat. All maladies, even death itself, are the result of magical influences. Illness and death never happen naturally; the whole conception of 'natural sequence' is lacking – it dawned first amongst the older Greeks, that is, in a very late phase of humanity, in the conception of *Moira*, enthroned above the gods. When a man shoots with a bow, there is still always present an irrational hand and strength; if the wells suddenly dry up, men think first of subterranean *daemons* and their tricks; it must be the arrow of a god beneath whose invisible blow a man suddenly sinks down. In India (says Lubbock) a carpenter is accustomed to offer sacrifice to his hammer, his hatchet, and the rest of his tools; in the same way a Brahmin treats the pen with which he writes, a soldier the weapons he requires in the field of battle, a mason his trowel, a labourer his plough. In the imagination of religious people all nature is a summary of the actions of conscious and voluntary creatures, an enormous complex of *arbitrariness*. No conclusion may be drawn with regard to everything that is outside of us, that anything will *be* so and so, *must* be so and so; the approximately sure, reliable are *we*, man is the *rule*, nature is *irregularity*, this theory contains the fundamental conviction which obtains in rude, religiously productive primitive civilisations. We latter-day men feel just the contrary – the richer man now feels himself inwardly, the more polyphonous is the music and the noise of his soul, the more powerfully the symmetry of nature works upon him; we all recognise with Goethe the great means in nature for the appeasing of the modern soul; we listen to the pendulum swing of this greatest of clocks with a longing for rest, for home and tranquillity, as if we could absorb this symmetry into ourselves and could only thereby arrive at the enjoyment of ourselves. Formerly it was otherwise; if we consider the rude, early condition of nations, or contemplate present-day savages at close quarters, we find them most strongly influenced by *law* and by *tradition*: the individual is almost automatically bound to them, and moves with the uniformity of a pendulum. To him Nature – uncomprehended, terrible, mysterious Nature must appear as the *sphere of liberty*, of voluntariness, of the higher power, even as a superhuman degree of existence, as God. In those times and conditions, however, every individual felt that his existence, his happiness, and that of the family and the State, and the success of all undertakings, depended on those spontaneities of nature; certain natural events must appear at the right time, others be absent at the right time. How can one have any influence on these terrible unknown things, how can one bind the sphere of liberty? Thus he asks himself, thus he inquires anxiously; is there, then, no means of making those powers as regular through tradition and law as you are yourself? The aim of those who believe in magic and miracles is to *impose a law on nature* – and, briefly, the religious cult is a result of this aim. The problem which those people have set themselves is closely related to this: how can the *weaker* race dictate laws to the *stronger*, rule it, and guide its actions (in relation to the weaker)? One would first remember the most harmless sort of compulsion, that compulsion which one exercises when one has gained any one's affection. By imploring and praying, by submission, by the obligation of regular taxes and gifts, by flattering glorifications, it is also possible to exercise an influence upon the powers of nature, inasmuch as one gains the affections; love binds and becomes bound. Then one can make compacts by which one is mutually bound to a certain behaviour, where one gives pledges and exchanges vows. But far more important is a species of more forcible compulsion, by magic and witchcraft. As with the sorcerer's help man is able to injure a more powerful enemy and keep him in fear, as the love-charm works at a distance, so the weaker man believes he can influence the mightier spirits of nature. The principal thing in all witchcraft is that we must get into our possession something that belongs to some one, hair, nails, food from their table, even their portrait, their name. With such apparatus we can then practise sorcery; for the fundamental rule is, to everything spiritual there belongs something corporeal; with the help of this we are able to bind the spirit, to injure it, and destroy it; the corporeal furnishes the handles with which we can grasp the spiritual. As man controls man, so he controls some natural spirit or other; for this has also its corporeal part by which it may be grasped. The tree and, compared with it, the seed from which it sprang – this enigmatical contrast seems to prove that the same spirit embodied itself in both forms, now small, now large. A stone that begins to roll suddenly is the body in which a spirit operates; if there is an enormous rock lying on a lonely heath it seems impossible to conceive human strength sufficient to have brought it there, consequently the stone must have moved there by itself, that is, it must be possessed by a spirit. Everything that has a body is susceptible to witchcraft, therefore also the natural spirits. If a god is bound to his image we can use the most direct compulsion against him (through refusal of sacrificial food, scourging, binding in fetters, and so on). In order to obtain by force the missing favour of their god the lower classes in China wind cords round the image of the one who has left them in the lurch, pull it down and drag it through the streets in the dust and the dirt: 'You dog of a spirit,' they say, 'we gave you a magnificent temple to live in, we gilded you prettily, we fed you well, we offered you sacrifice, and yet you are so ungrateful.' Similar forcible measures against pictures of the Saints and Virgin when they refused to do their duty in pestilence or drought, have been witnessed even during the present century in Catholic countries. Through all these magic relations to nature, countless ceremonies have been called into life; and at last, when the confusion has grown too great, an endeavour has been made to order and systematise them, in order that the favourable course of the whole progress of nature, i.e. of the great succession of the seasons, may seem to be guaranteed by a corresponding course of a system of procedure. The essence of the religious cult is to determine and confine nature to human advantage, *to impress it with a legality, therefore, which it did not originally possess*; while at the present time we wish to recognise the legality of nature in order to adapt ourselves to it. In short, then, the religious cult is based upon the representations of sorcery between man and man – and the sorcerer is older than the priest. But it is likewise based upon other and nobler representations; it premises the sympathetic relation of man to man, the presence of goodwill, gratitude, the hearing of pleaders, of treaties between enemies, the granting of pledges, and the claim to the protection of property. In very low stages of civilisation man does not stand in the relation of a helpless slave to nature, he is *not* necessarily its involuntary bondsman. In the *Greek* grade of religion, particularly in relation to the Olympian gods, there may even be imagined a common life between two castes, a nobler and more powerful one, and one less noble; but in their origin both belong to each other somehow, and are of one kind; they need not be ashamed of each other. That is the nobility of the Greek religion.

112

At the sight of certain antique sacrificial instruments – The fact of how many feelings are lost to us may be seen, for instance, in the mingling of the *droll*, even of the *obscene*, with the religious feeling. The sensation of the possibility of this mixture vanishes, we only comprehend historically that it existed in the feasts of Demeter and Dionysus, in the Christian Easter-plays and Mysteries. But we also know that which is noble in alliance with burlesque and such like, the touching mingled with the laughable, which perhaps a later age will not be able to understand.

113

Christianity as antiquity – When on a Sunday morning we hear the old bells ring out, we ask ourselves, 'Is it possible! This is done on account of a Jew crucified two thousand years ago who said he was the Son of God. The proof of such an assertion is wanting.' Certainly in our times the Christian religion is an antiquity that dates from very early ages, and the fact that its assertions are still believed, when otherwise all claims are subjected to such strict examination, is perhaps the oldest part of this heritage. A God who creates a son from a mortal woman; a sage who requires that man should no longer work, no longer judge, but should pay attention to the signs of the approaching end of the world; a justice that accepts an innocent being as a substitute in sacrifice; one who commands his disciples to drink his blood; prayers for miraculous intervention; sins committed against a God and atoned for through a God; the fear of a future to which death is the portal; the form of the cross in an age which no longer knows the signification and the shame of the cross,* how terrible all this appears to us, as if risen from the grave of the ancient past! Is it credible that such things are still believed?

114

What is un-Greek in Christianity – The Greeks did not regard the Homeric gods as raised above them like masters, nor themselves as being under them like servants, as the Jews did. They only saw, as in a mirror, the most perfect examples of their own caste; an ideal, therefore, and not an opposite of their own nature. There is a feeling of relationship, a mutual interest arises, a kind of symmachy. Man thinks highly of himself when he gives himself such gods, and places himself in a relation like that of the lower nobility towards the higher; while the Italian nations hold a genuine peasant-faith, with perpetual fear of evil and mischievous powers and tormenting spirits. Wherever the Olympian gods retreated into the background, Greek life was more sombre and more anxious. Christianity, on the contrary, oppressed man and crushed him utterly, sinking him as if in deep mire; then into the feeling of absolute depravity it suddenly threw the light of divine mercy, so that the surprised man, dazzled by forgiveness, gave a cry of joy and for a moment believed that he bore all heaven within himself. All psychological feelings of Christianity work upon this unhealthy excess of sentiment, and upon the deep corruption of head and heart it necessitates; it desires to destroy, break, stupefy, confuse – only one thing it does not desire, namely *moderation*, and therefore it is in the deepest sense barbaric, Asiatic, ignoble and un-Greek.

115

To be religious with advantage – There are sober and industrious people on whom religion is embroidered like a hem of higher humanity; these do well to remain religious, it beautifies them. All people who do not understand some kind of trade in weapons –

* It may be remembered that the cross was the gallows of the ancient world. – J. M. K.

tongue and pen included as weapons – become servile; for such the Christian religion is very useful, for then servility assumes the appearance of Christian virtues and is surprisingly beautified. People to whom their daily life appears too empty and monotonous easily grow religious; this is comprehensible and excusable, only they have no right to demand religious sentiments from those whose daily life is not empty and monotonous.*

116

The commonplace Christian – If Christianity were right, with its theories of an avenging God, of general sinfulness, of redemption, and the danger of eternal damnation, it would be a sign of weak intellect and lack of character not to become a priest, apostle or hermit, and to work only with fear and trembling for one's own salvation; it would be senseless thus to neglect eternal benefits for temporary comfort. Taking it for granted that there is *belief*, the commonplace Christian is a miserable figure, a man that really cannot add two and two together, and who, moreover, just because of his mental incapacity for responsibility, did not deserve to be so severely punished as Christianity has decreed.

117

Of the wisdom of Christianity – It is a clever stroke on the part of Christianity to teach the utter unworthiness, sinfulness, and despicableness of mankind so loudly that the disdain of their fellow-men is no longer possible. 'He may sin as much as he likes, he is not essentially different from me – it is I who am unworthy and despicable in every way,' says the Christian to himself. But even this feeling has lost its sharpest sting, because the Christian no longer believes in his individual despicableness; he is bad as men are generally, and comforts himself a little with the axiom, 'We are all of one kind'.

118

Change of front – As soon as a religion triumphs it has for its enemies all those who would have been its first disciples.

---

* This may give us one of the reasons for the religiosity still happily prevailing in England and the United States. – J. M. K.

119

The fate of Christianity – Christianity arose for the purpose of lightening the heart; but now it must first make the heart heavy in order afterwards to lighten it. Consequently it will perish.

120

The proof of pleasure – The agreeable opinion is accepted as true – this is the proof of the pleasure (or, as the Church says, the proof of the strength), of which all religions are so proud when they ought to be ashamed of it. If Faith did not make blessed it would not be believed in; of how little value must it be, then!

121

A dangerous game – Whoever now allows scope to his religious feelings must also let them increase, he cannot do otherwise. His nature then gradually changes; it favours whatever is connected with and near to the religious element, the whole extent of judgment and feeling becomes clouded, overcast with religious shadows. Sensation cannot stand still; one must therefore take care.

122

The blind disciples – So long as one knows well the strength and weakness of one's doctrine, one's art, one's religion, its power is still small. The disciple and apostle who has no eyes for the weaknesses of the doctrine, the religion, and so forth, dazzled by the aspect of the master and by his reverence for him, has on that account usually more power than the master himself. Without blind disciples the influence of a man and his work has never yet become great. To help a doctrine to victory often means only so to mix it with stupidity that the weight of the latter carries off also the victory for the former.

123

Church disestablishment – There is not enough religion in the world even to destroy religions.

124

The sinlessness of Man – If it is understood how 'sin came into the world', namely through errors of reason by which men held each other, even the single individual held himself, to be much blacker and much worse than was actually the case, the whole sensation will be much lightened, and man and the world will appear in a blaze of innocence which it will do one good to contemplate. In the midst of nature man is always the child *per se*. This child sometimes has a heavy and terrifying dream, but when it opens its eyes it always finds itself back again in Paradise.

125

The irreligiousness of artists – Homer is so much at home amongst his gods, and is so familiar with them as a poet, that he must have been deeply irreligious; that which the popular faith gave him – a meagre, rude, partly terrible superstition – he treated as freely as the sculptor does his clay, with the same unconcern, therefore, which Aeschylus and Aristophanes possessed, and by which in later times the great artists of the Renaissance distinguished themselves, as also did Shakespeare and Goethe.

126

The art and power of false interpretations – All the visions, terrors, torpors, and ecstasies of saints are well-known forms of disease, which are only, by reason of deep-rooted religious and psycho-logical errors, differently *explained* by him, namely not as diseases. Thus, perhaps, the *daimonion* of Socrates was only an affection of the ear, which he, in accordance with his ruling moral mode of thought, *expounded* differently from what would be the case now. It is the same thing with the madness and ravings of the prophets and soothsayers; it is always the degree of knowledge, fantasy, effort, morality in the head and heart of the *interpreters* which has *made* so much of it. For the greatest achievements of the people who are called geniuses and saints it is necessary that they should secure interpreters by force, who *misunderstand* them for the good of mankind.

127

The veneration of insanity – Because it was remarked that excitement frequently made the mind clearer and produced happy inspirations it was believed that the happiest inspirations and suggestions were called forth by the greatest excitement; and so the insane were revered as wise and oracular. This is based on a false conclusion.

128

The promises of Science – The aim of modern science is: as little pain as possible, as long a life as possible – a kind of eternal blessedness, therefore; but certainly a very modest one as compared with the promises of religions.

129

Forbidden generosity – There is not sufficient love and goodness in the world to permit us to give some of it away to imaginary beings.

130

The continuance of the religious cult in the feelings – The Roman Catholic Church, and before that all antique cults, dominated the entire range of means by which man was put into unaccustomed moods and rendered incapable of the cold calculation of judgment or the clear thinking of reason. A church quivering with deep tones; the dull, regular, arresting appeals of a priestly throng, unconsciously communicates its tension to the congregation and makes it listen almost fearfully, as if a miracle were in preparation; the influence of the architecture, which, as the dwelling of a Godhead, extends into the uncertain and makes its apparition to be feared in all its sombre spaces – who would wish to bring such things back to mankind if the necessary suppositions are no longer believed? But the *results* of all this are not lost, nevertheless; the inner world of noble, emotional, deeply contrite dispositions, full of presentiments, blessed with hope, is inborn in mankind mainly through this cult; what exists of it now in the soul was then cultivated on a large scale as it germinated, grew up and blossomed.

131

The painful consequences of religion – However much we may think we have weaned ourselves from religion, it has nevertheless not been done so thoroughly as to deprive us of pleasure in encountering religious sensations and moods in music, for instance; and if a philosophy shows us the justification of metaphysical hopes and the deep peace of soul to be thence acquired, and speaks, for instance, of the 'whole, certain gospel in the gaze of Raphael's

Madonnas', we receive such statements and expositions particularly warmly; here the philosopher finds it easier to prove; that which
he desires to give corresponds to a heart that desires to receive.
Hence it may be observed how the less thoughtful free spirits really
only take offence at the dogmas, but are well acquainted with the
charm of religious sensations; they are sorry to lose hold of the
latter for the sake of the former. Scientific philosophy must be very
careful not to smuggle in errors on the ground of that need – a
need which has grown up and is consequently temporary, even
logicians speak of 'presentiments' of truth in ethics and in art (for
instance, of the suspicion that 'the nature of things is one'), which
should be forbidden to them Between the carefully established
truths and such 'presaged' things there remains the unbridgable
chasm that those are due to intellect and these to requirement.
Hunger does not prove that food *exists* to satisfy it, but that it
desires food. To 'presage' does not mean the acknowledgment of
the existence of a thing in any one degree, but its possibility, in
so far as it is desired or feared; 'presage' does not advance one
step into the land of certainty. We believe involuntarily that the
portions of a philosophy which are tinged with religion are better
proved than others; but actually it is the contrary, but we have the
inward desire that it *may* be so, that that which makes blessed,
therefore, may be also the true. This desire misleads us to accept
bad reasons for good ones.

132

Of the Christian need of redemption – With careful reflection it must
be possible to obtain an explanation free from mythology of that
process in the soul of a Christian which is called the need of
redemption, consequently a purely psychological explanation.
Up to the present, the psychological explanations of religious
conditions and processes have certainly been held in some disrepute, inasmuch as a theology which called itself free carried on its
unprofitable practice in this domain; for here from the beginning
(as the mind of its founder, Schleiermacher, gives us reason to
suppose) the preservation of the Christian religion and the continuance of Christian theology was kept in view; a theology which
was to find a new anchorage in the psychological analyses of
religious 'facts', and above all a new occupation. Unconcerned

about such predecessors we hazard the following interpretation of
the phenomenon in question. Man is conscious of certain actions
which stand far down in the customary rank of actions; he even
discovers in himself a tendency towards similar actions, a tendency which appears to him almost as unchangeable as his whole
nature. How willingly would he try himself in that other species
of actions which in the general valuation are recognised as the
loftiest and highest, how gladly would he feel himself to be full of
the good consciousness which should follow an unselfish mode of
thought! But unfortunately he stops short at this wish, and the
discontent at not being able to satisfy it is added to all the other
discontents which his lot in life or the consequences of those
above-mentioned evil actions have aroused in him; so that a deep
ill-humour is the result, with the search for a physician who could
remove this and all its causes. This condition would not be felt so
bitterly if man would only compare himself frankly with other
men – then he would have no reason for being dissatisfied with
himself to a particular extent, he would only bear his share of
the common burden of human dissatisfaction and imperfection.
But he compares himself with a being who is said to be capable
only of those actions which are called unegoistic, and to live in
the perpetual consciousness of an unselfish mode of thought, *i.e.*
with God; it is because he gazes into this clear mirror that his
image appears to him so dark, so unusually warped. Then he is
alarmed by the thought of that same creature, in so far as it floats
before his imagination as a retributive justice; in all possible small
and great events he thinks he recognises its anger and menaces,
that he even feels its scourge-strokes as judge and executioner.
Who will help him in this danger, which, by the prospect of an
immeasurable duration of punishment, exceeds in horror all the
other terrors of the idea?

133

Before we examine the further consequences of this mental state,
let us acknowledge that it is not through his 'guilt' and 'sin' that
man has got into this condition, but through a series of errors of
reason; that it was the fault of the mirror if his image appeared
so dark and hateful to him, and that that mirror was *his* work,
the very imperfect work of human imagination and power of

judgment. In the first place, a nature that is only capable of purely unegoistic actions is more fabulous than the phoenix; it cannot even be clearly imagined, just because, when closely examined, the whole idea 'unegoistic action' vanishes into air. No man *ever* did a thing which was done only for others and without any personal motive; how should he be *able* to do anything which had no relation to himself, and therefore without inward obligation (which must always have its foundation in a personal need)? How could the *ego* act without *ego*? A God who, on the contrary, is *all* love, as such a one is often represented, would not be capable of a single unegoistic action, whereby one is reminded of a saying of Lichtenberg's which is certainly taken from a lower sphere: 'We cannot possibly *feel* for others, as the saying is; we feel only for ourselves. This sounds hard, but it is not so really if it be rightly understood. We do not love father or mother or wife or child, but the pleasant sensations they cause us;' or, as Rochefoucauld says: *'Si on croit aimer sa maîtresse pour l'amour d'elle, on est bien trompé.'* To know the reason why actions of love are valued more than others, not on account of their nature, namely, but of their *usefulness*, we should compare the examinations already mentioned, *On the Origin of Moral Sentiments*. But should a man desire to be entirely like that God of Love, to do and wish everything for others and nothing for himself, the latter is impossible for the reason that he must do *very much* for himself to be able to do something for the love of others. Then it is taken for granted that the other is sufficiently egoistic to accept that sacrifice again and again, that living for him – so that the people of love and sacrifice have an interest in the continuance of those who are loveless and incapable of sacrifice, and, in order to exist, the highest morality would be obliged positively to *compel* the existence of un-morality (whereby it would certainly annihilate itself). Further: the conception of a God disturbs and humbles so long as it is believed in; but as to how it arose there can no longer be any doubt in the present state of the science of comparative ethnology; and with a comprehension of this origin all belief falls to the ground. The Christian who compares his nature with God's is like Don Quixote, who undervalued his own bravery because his head was full of the marvellous deeds of the heroes of the chivalric romances – the standard of measurement in both cases belongs to the domain of fable. But if the idea of God is removed, so is also the feeling of 'sin' as a trespass against divine laws, as a stain in a creature vowed to God. Then, perhaps, there still remains that dejection which is inter-grown and connected with the fear of the punishment of worldly justice or of the scorn of men; the dejection of the pricks of conscience, the sharpest thorn in the consciousness of sin, is always removed if we recognise that though by our own deed we have sinned against human descent, human laws and ordinances, still that we have not imperilled the 'eternal salvation of the Soul' and its relation to the Godhead. And if man succeeds in gaining philosophic conviction of the absolute necessity of all actions and their entire irresponsibility, and absorbing this into his flesh and blood, even those remains of the pricks of conscience vanish.

134

Now if the Christian, as we have said, has fallen into the way of self-contempt in consequence of certain errors through a false, unscientific interpretation of his actions and sensations, he must notice with great surprise how that state of contempt, the pricks of conscience and displeasure generally, does not endure, how some-times there come hours when all this is wafted away from his soul and he feels himself once more free and courageous. In truth, the pleasure in himself, the comfort of his own strength, together with the necessary weakening through time of every deep emotion, has usually been victorious; man loves himself once again, he feels it – but precisely this new love, this self-esteem, seems to him incredible, he can only see in it the wholly undeserved descent of a stream of mercy from on high. If he formerly believed that in every event he could recognise warnings, menaces, punishments, and every kind of manifestation of divine anger, he now finds divine goodness in all his experiences – this event appears to him to be full of love, that one a helpful hint, a third, and, indeed, his whole happy mood, a proof that God is merciful. As formerly, in his state of pain, he interpreted his actions falsely, so now he misinterprets his experiences; his mood of comfort he believes to be the working of a power operating outside of himself, the love with which he really loves himself seems to him to be divine love; that which he calls mercy, and the prologue to redemption, is actually self-forgiveness, self-redemption.

135

Therefore: A certain false psychology, a certain kind of imaginative interpretation of motives and experiences, is the necessary preliminary for one to become a Christian and to feel the need of redemption. When this error of reason and imagination is recognised, one ceases to be a Christian.

136

Of Christian asceticism and holiness – As greatly as isolated thinkers have endeavoured to depict as a miracle the rare manifestations of morality, which are generally called asceticism and holiness, miracles which it would be almost an outrage and sacrilege to explain by the light of common sense, as strong also is the inclination towards this outrage. A mighty impulse of nature has at all times led to a protest against those manifestations; science, in so far as it is an imitation of nature, at least allows itself to rise against the supposed inexplicableness and unapproachableness of these objections. So far it has certainly not succeeded: those appearances are still unexplained, to the great joy of the above-mentioned worshippers of the morally marvellous. For, speaking generally, the unexplained *must* be absolutely inexplicable, the inexplicable absolutely unnatural, supernatural, wonderful – thus runs the demand in the souls of all religious and metaphysical people (also of artists, if they should happen to be thinkers at the same time); whilst the scientist sees in this demand the 'evil principle' in itself. The general, first probability upon which one lights in the contemplation of holiness and asceticism is this, that their nature is a *complicated* one, for almost everywhere, within the physical world as well as in the moral, the apparently marvellous has been successfully traced back to the complicated, the many-conditioned. Let us venture, therefore, to isolate separate impulses from the soul of saints and ascetics, and finally to imagine them as inter-grown.

137

There is a *defiance of self*, to the sublimest manifestation of which belong many forms of asceticism. Certain individuals have such great need of exercising their power and love of ruling that, in default of other objects, or because they have never succeeded otherwise, they finally excogitate the idea of tyrannising over certain parts of their own nature, portions or degrees of themselves. Thus many a thinker confesses to views which evidently do not serve either to increase or improve his reputation; many a one deliberately calls down the scorn of others when by keeping silence he could easily have remained respected; others contradict former opinions and do not hesitate to be called inconsistent – on the contrary, they strive after this, and behave like reckless riders who like a horse best when it has grown wild, unmanageable, and covered with sweat. Thus man climbs dangerous paths up the highest mountains in order that he may laugh to scorn his own fear and his trembling knees; thus the philosopher owns to views on asceticism, humility, holiness, in the brightness of which his own picture shows to the worst possible disadvantage. This crushing of one's self, this scorn of one's own nature, this *spernere se sperni*, of which religion has made so much, is really a very high degree of vanity. The whole moral of the Sermon on the Mount belongs here; man takes a genuine delight in doing violence to himself by these exaggerated claims, and afterwards idolising these tyrannical demands of his soul. In every ascetic morality man worships one part of himself as a God, and is obliged, therefore, to diabolise the other parts.

138

Man is not equally moral at all hours, this is well known. If his morality is judged to be the capability for great self-sacrificing resolutions and self-denial (which, when continuous and grown habitual, are called holiness), he is most moral in the *passions*; the higher emotion provides him with entirely new motives, of which he, sober and cold as usual, perhaps does not even believe himself capable. How does this happen? Probably because of the proximity of everything great and highly exciting; if man is once wrought up to a state of extraordinary suspense, he is as capable of carrying out a terrible revenge as of a terrible crushing of his need for revenge. Under the influence of powerful emotion, he desires in any case the great, the powerful, the immense; and if he happens to notice that the sacrifice of himself satisfies him as well as, or better than, the sacrifice of others, he chooses that. Actually, therefore, he only cares about discharging his emotion; in order to ease his tension he seizes the enemy's spears and buries them in his breast. That there was something great in self-denial and not in revenge had to be taught to mankind by long habit; a Godhead that sacrificed itself was the strongest, most effective symbol of this kind of greatness. As the conquest of the most difficult enemy, the sudden mastering of an affection – thus this denial *appears*; and so far it passes for the summit of morality. In reality it is a question of the confusion of one idea with another, while the temperament maintains an equal height, an equal level. Temperate men who are resting from their passions no longer understand the morality of those moments; but the general admiration of those who had the same experiences upholds them; pride is their consolation when affection and the understanding of their deed vanish. Therefore, at bottom even those actions of self-denial are not moral, inasmuch as they are not done strictly with regard to others; rather the other only provides the highly-strung temperament with an opportunity of relieving itself through that denial.

139

In many respects the ascetic seeks to make life easy for himself, usually by complete subordination to a strange will or a comprehensive law and ritual; something like the way a Brahmin leaves nothing whatever to his own decision but refers every moment to holy precepts. This submission is a powerful means of attaining self-mastery: man is occupied and is therefore not bored, and yet has no incitement to self-will or passion; after a completed deed there is no feeling of responsibility and with it no tortures of remorse. We have renounced our own will once and for ever, and this is easier than only renouncing it occasionally; as it is also easier to give up a desire entirely than to keep it within bounds. When we remember the present relation of man to the State, we find that, even here, unconditional obedience is more convenient than conditional. The saint, therefore, makes his life easier by absolute renunciation of his personality, and we are mistaken if in that phenomenon we admire the loftiest heroism of morality. In any case it is more difficult to carry one's person-ality through without vacillation and unclearness than to liberate one's self from it in the above-mentioned manner; moreover, it requires far more spirit and consideration.

140

After having found in many of the less easily explicable actions manifestations of that pleasure in *emotion per se*, I should like to recognise also in self-contempt, which is one of the signs of holiness, and likewise in the deeds of self-torture (through hunger and scourging, mutilation of limbs, feigning of madness) a means by which those natures fight against the general weariness of their life-will (their nerves); they employ the most painful irritants and cruelties in order to emerge for a time, at all events, from that dulness and boredom into which they so frequently sink through their great mental indolence and that submission to a strange will already described.

141

The commonest means which the ascetic and saint employs to render life still endurable and amusing consists in occasional warfare with alternate victory and defeat. For this he requires an opponent, and finds it in the so-called 'inward enemy'. He principally makes use of his inclination to vanity, love of honour and rule, and of his sensual desires, that he may be permitted to regard his life as a perpetual battle and himself as a battlefield upon which good and evil spirits strive with alternating success. It is well known that sensual imagination is moderated, indeed almost dispelled, by regular sexual intercourse, whereas, on the contrary, it is rendered unfettered and wild by abstinence or irregularity. The imagination of many Christian saints was filthy to an extraordinary degree; by virtue of those theories that these desires were actual demons raging within them they did not feel themselves to be too responsible; to this feeling we owe the very instructive frankness of their self-confessions. It was to their interest that this strife should always be maintained in one degree or another, because, as we have already said, their empty life was thereby entertained. But in order that the strife might seem sufficiently important and arouse the enduring sympathy and admiration of non-saints, it was necessary that sensuality should be ever more reviled and branded, the danger of eternal damnation was so tightly bound up with these things that it is highly probable that for whole centuries Christians generated children with a bad conscience, wherewith humanity has certainly suffered a great injury. And yet here truth is all topsy-turvy, which is particularly unsuitable for truth. Certainly Christianity had said that every man is conceived and born in sin, and in the insupportable superlative-Christianity of Calderon this thought again appears, tied up and twisted, as the most distorted paradox there is, in the well-known lines –

> The greatest sin of man
> Is that he was ever born.

In all pessimistic religions the act of generation was looked upon as evil in itself. This is by no means the verdict of all mankind, not even of all pessimists. For instance, Empedocles saw in all erotic things nothing shameful, diabolical, or, sinful; but rather, in the great plain of disaster he saw only one hopeful and redeeming figure, that of Aphrodite; she appeared to him as a guarantee that the strife should not endure eternally, but that the sceptre should one day be given over to a gentler *daemon*. The actual Christian pessimists had, as has been said, an interest in the dominance of a diverse opinion; for the solitude and spiritual wilderness of their lives they required an ever living enemy, and a generally recognised enemy, through whose fighting and overcoming they could constantly represent themselves to the non-saints as incomprehensible, half-supernatural beings. But when at last this enemy took to flight for ever in consequence of their mode of life and their impaired health, they immediately understood how to populate their interior with new daemons. The rising and falling of the scales of pride and humility sustained their brooding minds as well as the alternations of desire and peace of soul. At that time psychology served not only to cast suspicion upon everything human, but to oppress, to scourge, to crucify; people *wished* to find themselves as bad and wicked as possible, they *sought* anxiety for the salvation of their souls, despair of their own strength. Everything natural with which man has connected the idea of evil and sin (as, for instance, he is still accustomed to do with regard to the erotic) troubles and clouds the imagination, causes a frightened glance, makes man quarrel with himself and uncertain and distrustful of himself. Even his dreams have the flavour of a restless conscience. And yet in the reality of things this suffering from what is natural is entirely without foundation, it is only the consequence of opinions *about* things. It is easily seen how men grow worse by considering the inevitably-natural as bad, and afterwards always feeling themselves made thus. It is the trump-card of religion and metaphysics, which wish to have man evil and sinful by nature, to cast suspicion on nature and thus really to *make* him bad, for he learns to feel himself evil since he cannot divest himself of the clothing of nature. After living for long a natural life, he gradually comes to feel himself weighed down by such a burden of sin that supernatural powers are necessary to lift this burden, and therewith arises the so-called need of redemption, which corresponds to no real but only to an imaginary sinfulness. If we survey the separate moral demands of the earliest times of Christianity it will everywhere be found that requirements are exaggerated in order that man *cannot* satisfy them; the intention is not that he should become more moral, but that he should feel himself as *sinful as possible*. If man had not found this feeling *agreeable* – why would he have thought out such an idea and stuck to it so long? As in the antique world an immeasurable power of intellect and inventiveness was expended in multiplying the pleasure of life by festive cults, so also in the age of Christianity an immeasurable amount of intellect has been sacrificed to another endeavour – man must by all means be made to feel himself sinful and thereby be excited, *enlivened, en-souled*. To excite, enliven, en-soul at all costs – is not that the watchword of a relaxed, over-ripe, over-cultured age? The range of all natural sensations had been gone over a hundred times, the soul had grown weary, whereupon the saint and the ascetic invented a new species of stimulants for life. They presented themselves before the public eye, not exactly as an example for the many, but as a terrible and yet ravishing spectacle, which took place on that border-land between world and over-world, wherein at that time all people believed they saw now rays of heavenly light and now unholy tongues of flame glowing in the depths. The saint's eye, fixed upon the terrible meaning of this short earthly life, upon the nearness of the last decision concerning endless new spans of existence, this burning eye in a half-wasted body made men of the old world tremble to

their very depths; to gaze, to turn shudderingly away, to feel anew
the attraction of the spectacle and to give way to it, to drink deep
of it till the soul quivered with fire and ague – that was the last
pleasure that antiquity invented after it had grown blunted even at the
sight of beast-baitings and human combats.

142

Now to sum up. That condition of soul in which the saint or
embryo saint rejoiced, was composed of elements which we all
know well, only that under the influence of other than religious
conceptions they exhibit themselves in other colours and are then
accustomed to encounter man's blame as fully as, with that
decoration of religion and the ultimate meaning of existence,
they may reckon on receiving admiration and even worship –
might reckon, at least, in former ages. Sometimes the saint
practises that defiance of himself which is a near relative of
domination at any cost and gives a feeling of power even to the
most lonely; sometimes his swollen sensibility leaps from the
desire to let his passions have full play into the desire to
overthrow them like wild horses under the mighty pressure of a
proud spirit; sometimes he desires a complete cessation of all
disturbing, tormenting, irritating sensations, a waking sleep, a
lasting rest in the lap of a dull, animal, and plant-like indolence;
sometimes he seeks strife and arouses it within himself, because
boredom has shown him its yawning countenance. He scourges
his self-adoration with self-contempt and cruelty, he rejoices in
the wild tumult of his desires and the sharp pain of sin, even in the
idea of being lost; he understands how to lay a trap for his
emotions, for instance even for his keen love of ruling, so that he
sinks into the most utter abasement and his tormented soul is
thrown out of joint by this contrast; and finally, if he longs for
visions, conversations with the dead or with divine beings, it is at
bottom a rare kind of delight that he covets, perhaps that delight
in which all others are united. Novalis, an authority on questions
of holiness through experience and instinct, tells the whole secret
with naïve joy: 'It is strange enough that the association of lust,
religion, and cruelty did not long ago draw men's attention to
their close relationship and common tendency.'

143

That which gives the saint his historical value is not the thing he *is*, but the thing he *represents* in the eyes of the unsaintly. It was through the fact that errors were made about him, that the state of his soul was *falsely interpreted*, that men separated themselves from him as much as possible, as from something incomparable and strangely superhuman, that he acquired the extraordinary power which he exercised over the imagination of whole nations and whole ages. He did not know himself; he himself interpreted the writing of his moods, inclinations, and actions according to an art of interpretation which was as exaggerated and artificial as the spiritual interpretation of the Bible. The distorted and diseased in his nature, with its combination of intellectual poverty, evil knowledge, ruined health, and over-excited nerves, remained hidden from his own sight as well as from that of his spectators. He was not a particularly good man, and still less was he a particularly wise one; but he *represented* something that exceeded the human standard in goodness and wisdom. The belief in him supported the belief in the divine and miraculous, in a religious meaning of all existence, in an impending day of judgment. In the evening glory of the world's sunset, which glowed over the Christian nations, the shadowy form of the saint grew to vast dimensions, it grew to such a height that even in our own age, which no longer believes in God, there are still thinkers who believe in the saint.

144

It need not be said that to this description of the saint which has been made from an average of the whole species, there may be opposed many a description which could give a more agreeable impression. Certain exceptions stand out from among this species, it may be through great mildness and philanthropy, it may be through the magic of unusual energy; others are attractive in the highest degree, because certain wild ravings have poured streams of light on their whole being, as is the case, for instance, with the famous founder of Christianity, who thought he was the Son of God and therefore felt himself sinless – so that through this idea – which we must not judge too hardly because the whole antique world swarms with sons of God – he reached that same goal, that feeling of complete sinlessness, complete irresponsibility, which every one can now acquire by means of science. Neither have I mentioned the Indian saints, who stand midway between the Christian saint and the Greek philosopher, and in so far represent no pure type. Knowledge, science — such as existed then — the uplifting above other men through logical discipline and training of thought, were as much fostered by the Buddhists as distinguishing signs of holiness as the same qualities in the Christian world are repressed and branded as signs of unholiness.

Fourth Division – *Concerning the Soul of Artists and Authors*

145

The perfect should not have grown – With regard to everything that is perfect we are accustomed to omit the question as to how perfection has been acquired, and we only rejoice in the present as if it had sprung out of the ground by magic. Probably with regard to this matter we are still under the effects of an ancient mythological feeling. It still *almost* seems to us (in such a Greek temple, for instance, as that of Paestum) as if one morning a god in sport had built his dwelling of such enormous masses, at other times it seems as if his spirit had suddenly entered into a stone and now desired to speak through it. The artist knows that his work is only fully effective if it arouses the belief in an improvisation, in a marvellous instantaneousness of origin; and thus he assists this illusion and introduces into art those elements of inspired unrest, of blindly groping disorder, of listening dreaming at the beginning of creation, as a means of deception, in order so to influence the soul of the spectator or hearer that it may believe in the sudden appearance of the perfect. It is the business of the science of art to contradict this illusion most decidedly, and to show up the mistakes and pampering of the intellect, by means of which it falls into the artist's trap.

146

The artist's sense of truth – With regard to recognition of truths, the artist has a weaker morality than the thinker; he will on no account let himself be deprived of brilliant and profound interpretations of life, and defends himself against temperate and simple methods and results. He is apparently fighting for the higher worthiness and meaning of mankind; in reality he will not renounce the *most effective* suppositions for his art, the fantastical, mythical, uncertain, extreme, the sense of the symbolical, the over-valuation of person-ality, the belief that genius is something miraculous; he considers, therefore, the continuance of his art of creation as more important than the scientific devotion to truth in every shape, however simple this may appear.

147

Art as raiser of the dead – Art also fulfils the task of preservation and even of brightening up extinguished and faded memories; when it accomplishes this task it weaves a rope round the ages and causes their spirits to return. It is, certainly, only a phantom-life that results therefrom, as out of graves, or like the return in dreams of our beloved dead, but for some moments, at least, the old sensation lives again and the heart beats to an almost forgotten time. Hence, for the sake of the general usefulness of art, the artist himself must be excused if he does not stand in the front rank of the enlightenment and progressive civilisation of humanity; all his life long he has remained a child or a youth, and has stood still at the point where he was overcome by his artistic impulse; the feelings of the first years of life, however, are acknowledged to be nearer to those of earlier times than to those of the present century. Unconsciously it becomes his mission to make mankind more childlike; this is his glory and his limitation.

148

Poets as the lighteners of life – Poets, inasmuch as they desire to lighten the life of man, either divert his gaze from the wearisome present, or assist the present to acquire new colours by means of a life which they cause to shine out of the past. To be able to do this, they must in many respects themselves be beings who are turned towards the past, so that they can be used as bridges to far distant times and ideas, to dying or dead religions and cultures. Actually they are always and of necessity *epigoni*. There are, however, certain drawbacks to their means of lightening life – they appease and heal only temporarily, only for the moment; they even prevent men from labouring towards a genuine improvement in their conditions, inasmuch as they remove and apply palliatives to precisely that passion of discontent that induces to action.

149

The slow arrow of beauty — The noblest kind of beauty is that which does not transport us suddenly, which does not make stormy and intoxicating impressions (such a kind easily arouses disgust), but that which slowly filters into our minds, which we take away with us almost unnoticed, and which we encounter again in our dreams; but which, however, after having long lain modestly on our hearts, takes entire possession of us, fills our eyes with tears and our hearts with longing. What is it that we long for at the sight of beauty? We long to be beautiful, we fancy it must bring much happiness with it. But that is a mistake.

150

The animation of art — Art raises its head where creeds relax. It takes over many feelings and moods engendered by religion, lays them to its heart, and itself becomes deeper, more full of soul, so that it is capable of transmitting exultation and enthusiasm, which it previously was not able to do. The abundance of religious feelings which have grown into a stream are always breaking forth again and desire to conquer new kingdoms, but the growth of the Enlightenment undermined the dogmas of religion and inspired a fundamental mistrust of them — so that the feelings, thrust by the Enlightenment out of the religious sphere, throw themselves into art, in a few cases into political life, even straight into science. Everywhere where human endeavour wears a loftier, gloomier aspect, it may be assumed that the fear of spirits, incense, and church-shadows have remained attached to it.

151

How metre beautifies — Rhythm casts a veil over reality; it causes various artificialities of speech and obscurities of thought; by the shadow it throws upon thought it sometimes conceals it, and sometimes brings it into prominence. As shadow is necessary to beauty, so the 'dull' is necessary to lucidity. Art makes the aspect of life endurable by throwing over it the veil of obscure thought.

152

The art of the ugly soul — Art is confined within too narrow limits if it be required that only the orderly, respectable, well-behaved soul should be allowed to express itself therein. As in the plastic arts, so also in music and poetry: there is an art of the ugly soul side by side with the art of the beautiful soul; and the mightiest effects of art, the crushing of souls, moving of stones and humanising of beasts, have perhaps been best achieved precisely by that art.

153

Art makes heavy the heart of the thinker — How strong metaphysical need is and how difficult nature renders our departure from it may be seen from the fact that even in the free spirit, when he has cast off everything metaphysical, the loftiest effects of art can easily produce a resounding of the long silent, even broken, metaphysical string — it may be, for instance, that at a passage in Beethoven's Ninth Symphony he feels himself floating above the earth in a starry dome with the dream of immortality in his heart; all the stars seem to shine round him, and the earth to sink farther and farther away — If he becomes conscious of this state, he feels a deep pain at his heart, and sighs for the man who will lead back to him his lost darling, be it called religion or metaphysics. In such moments his intellectual character is put to the test.

154

Playing with life — The lightness and frivolity of the Homeric imagination was necessary to calm and occasionally to raise the immoderately passionate temperament and acute intellect of the Greeks. If their intellect speaks, how harsh and cruel does life then appear! They do not deceive themselves, but they intentionally weave lies round life. Simonides advised his countrymen to look upon life as a game; earnestness was too well-known to them as pain (the gods so gladly hear the misery of mankind made the theme of song), and they knew that through art alone misery might be turned into pleasure. As a punishment for this insight, however, they were so plagued with the love of romancing that it was difficult for them in everyday life to keep themselves free from falsehood and deceit; for all poetic nations have such a love of falsehood, and yet are innocent withal. Probably this occasionally drove the neighboring nations to desperation.

155

The belief in inspiration – It is to the interest of the artist that there should be a belief in sudden suggestions, so-called inspirations; as if the idea of a work of art, of poetry, the fundamental thought of a philosophy shone down from heaven like a ray of grace. In reality the imagination of the good artist or thinker constantly produces good, mediocre, and bad, but his power of judgment, most clear and practised, rejects and chooses and joins together, just as we now learn from Beethoven's notebooks that he gradually composed the most beautiful melodies, and in a manner selected them, from many different attempts. He who makes less severe distinctions, and willingly abandons himself to imitative memories, may under certain circumstances become a great *improvisatore*; but artistic improvisation ranks low in comparison with serious and laboriously chosen artistic thoughts. All great men were great workers, unwearied not only in invention but also in rejection, reviewing, transforming, and arranging.

156

Inspiration again – If the productive power has been suspended for a length of time, and has been hindered in its outflow by some obstacle, there comes at last such a sudden outpouring, as if an immediate inspiration were taking place without previous inward working, consequently a miracle. This constitutes the familiar deception, in the continuance of which, as we have said, the interest of all artists is rather too much concerned. The capital has only *accumulated*, it has not suddenly fallen down from heaven. Moreover, such apparent inspirations are seen elsewhere, for instance in the realm of goodness, of virtue and of vice.

157

The sufferings of genius and their value – The artistic genius desires to give pleasure, but if his mind is on a very high plane he does not easily find any one to share his pleasure; he offers entertainment but nobody accepts it. This gives him, in certain circumstances, a comically touching pathos; for he has really no right to force pleasure on men. He pipes, but none will dance: can that be tragic? Perhaps – As compensation for this deprivation, however, he finds more pleasure in creating than the rest of mankind experiences in all other species of activity. His sufferings are considered as exaggerated, because the sound of his complaints is louder and his tongue more eloquent; and yet sometimes his sufferings are really very great; but only because his ambition and his envy are so great. The learned genius, like Kepler and Spinoza, is usually not so covetous and does not make such an exhibition of his really greater sufferings and deprivations. He can reckon with greater certainty on future fame and can afford to do without the present, whilst an artist who does this always plays a desperate game that makes his heart ache. In very rare cases, when in one and the same individual are combined the genius of power and of knowledge and the moral genius, there is added to the above-mentioned pains that species of pain which must be regarded as the most curious exception in the world; an extra- and supra-personal sensibility attuned to a nation, to humanity, to all civilisation, to all suffering existence, which acquires its value through its connection with particularly difficult and remote perceptions (pity in itself is worth but little). But by what standard, on what scales can we measure whether or not it is genuine? Is it not almost imperative to be mistrustful of all who *talk* of possessing sensiblities of this sort?

158

The destiny of greatness – Every great phenomenon is succeeded by degeneration, especially in the domain of art. The example of the great tempts vainer natures to superficial imitation or exaggeration; all great talents have the fatality of crushing many weaker forces and germs, and of laying nature waste all nature around them. The happiest arrangement in the development of an art is for several geniuses mutually to hold one another within bounds; in this strife it generally happens that light and air are also granted to the weaker and more delicate natures.

159

Art dangerous for the artist – When art takes strong hold of an individual it draws him back to the contemplation of those times when art flourished best, and it has then a retrograde effects. The artist grows more and more to reverence sudden inspirations; he believes in gods and daemons, he spiritualises all nature, hates science, is changeable in his moods like the ancients, and longs for an overthrow of all existing conditions which are not favourable to art, and does this with the impetuosity and unreasonableness of a child. Now, in himself, the artist is already a backward nature, because he halts at a game that belongs properly to youth and childhood; to this is added the fact that he is educated back into former times. Thus there gradually arises a fierce antagonism between him and his contemporaries, and a sad ending; according to the accounts of the ancients, Homer and Aeschylus spent their last years, and died, in melancholy.

160

Created people – When it is said that the dramatist (and the artist above all) *creates* real characters, it is a fine deception and exaggeration, in the existence and propagation of which art celebrates one of its unconscious but at the same time abundant triumphs. As a matter of fact, we do not understand much about a real, living man, and we generalise very superficially when we ascribe to him this and that character; this *very imperfect* attitude of ours towards man is represented by the poet, inasmuch as he makes into men (in this sense 'creates') outlines as *superficial* as our knowledge of man is superficial. There is a great deal of delusion about these created characters of artists; they are by no means living productions of nature, but are like painted men, somewhat too thin, they will not bear close inspection. And when it is said that the character of the ordinary living being contradicts itself frequently, and that the one created by the dramatist is the original model conceived by nature, this is quite wrong. A genuine man is something absolutely *necessary* (even in those so-called contradictions), but we do not always recognise this necessity. The imaginary man, the phantasm, signifies something necessary, but only to those who understand a real man only in a crude, unnatural simplification, so that a few strong, oft-repeated traits, with a great deal of light and shade and half-light about them, amply satisfy their notions. They are, therefore, ready to treat the phantasm as as a genuine, necessary man, because with real men they are accustomed to regard a phantasm, an outline, an intentional abbreviation as the whole. That the painter and the sculptor express the 'idea' of man is a vain imagination and delusion: whoever says this is in subjection to the eye, for this sees only the surface, the epidermis of the human body – the inward body, however, is equally a part of the idea. Plastic art wishes to make character visible on the surface; histrionic art employs speech for the same purpose, it reflects character in sounds. Art starts from the natural *ignorance* of man about his interior condition (in body and character); it is not meant for philosophers or natural scientists.

161

The over-valuation of self in the belief in artists and philosophers – We are all prone to think that the excellence of a work of art or of an artist is proved when it moves and touches us. But there *our own excellence* in judgment and sensibility must have been proved first, which is not the case. In all plastic art, who had greater power to effect a charm than Bernini, who made a greater effect than the orator that appeared after Demosthenes introduced the Asiatic style and gave it a predominance which lasted throughout two centuries? This predominance during whole centuries is not a proof of the excellence and enduring validity of a style; therefore we must not be too certain in our good opinion of any artist – this is not only belief in the truthfulness of our sensations but also in the infallibility of our judgment, whereas judgment or sensation, or even both, may be too coarse or too fine, exaggerated or crude. Neither are the blessings and blissfulness of a philosophy or of a religion proofs of its truth: just as little as the happiness which an insane person derives from his fixed idea is a proof of the reasonableness of this idea.

162

The cult of genius for the sake of vanity – Because we think well of ourselves, but nevertheless do not imagine that we are capable of the conception of one of Raphael's pictures or of a scene such as those of one of Shakespeare's dramas, we persuade ourselves that the faculty for doing this is quite extraordinarily wonderful, a very rare case, or, if we are religiously inclined, a grace from above. Thus the cult of genius fosters our vanity, our self-love, for it is only when we think of it as very far removed from us, as a *miraculum*, that it does not wound us (even Goethe, who was free from envy, called Shakespeare a star of the farthest heavens, whereby we are reminded of the line '*die Sterne, die begehrt man nicht*'.*) But, apart from those suggestions of our vanity, the activity of a genius does not seem so radically different from the activity of a mechanical inventor, of an astronomer or historian or strategist. All these forms of activity are explicable if we realise men whose minds are active in one special direction, who make use of everything as material, who always eagerly study their own inward life and that of others, who find types and incitements everywhere, who never weary in the employment of their means. Genius does nothing but learn how to lay stones, then to build, always to seek for material and always to work upon it. Every human activity is marvellously complicated, and not only that of genius, but it is no 'miracle'. Now whence comes the belief that genius is found only in artists, orators, and philosophers, that they alone have 'intuition' (by which we credit them with a kind of magic glass by means of which they see straight into one's 'being')? It is clear that men only speak of genius where the workings of a great intellect are most agreeable to them and they have no desire to feel envious. To call any one 'divine' is as much as saying 'here we have no occasion for rivalry'. Thus it is that everything completed and perfect is stared at, and everything incomplete is undervalued. Now nobody can see how the work of an artist has *developed*; that is its advantage, for everything of which the development is seen is looked on coldly. The perfected art of representation precludes all thought of its development, it tyrannises as a present perfection. For this reason artists of representation are especially held to be possessed of genius, but not scientific men. In reality, however, the former valuation and the latter under-valuation are only puerilities of reason.

---

* The allusion is to Goethe's lines:
    Die Sterne, die begehrt man nicht,
    Man freut sick ihrer Pracht.

    We do not want the stars themselves,
    Their brilliancy delights our hearts. – J. M. K.

163

The earnestness of handicraft – Do not talk of gifts, of inborn talents! We could mention great men of all kinds who were but little gifted. But they *obtained* greatness, became 'geniuses' (as they are called), through qualities of the lack of which nobody who is conscious of them likes to speak. They all had that thorough earnestness for work which learns first how to form the different parts perfectly before it ventures to make a great whole; they gave themselves time for this, because they took more pleasure in doing small, accessory things well than in the effect of a dazzling whole. For instance, the recipe for becoming a good novelist is easily given, but the carrying out of the recipe presupposes qualities which we are in the habit of overlooking when we say, 'I have not sufficient talent.' Make a hundred or more sketches of novel-plots, none more than two pages long, but of such clearness that every word in them is necessary; write down anecdotes every day until you learn to find the most pregnant, most effective form; never weary of collecting and delineating human types and characters; above all, narrate things as often as possible and listen to narrations with a sharp eye and ear for the effect upon other people present; travel like a landscape painter and a designer of costumes; take from different sciences everything that is artistically effective, if it be well represented; finally, meditate on the motives for human actions, scorn not even the smallest point of instruction on this subject, and collect similar matters by day and night. Spend some ten years in these various exercises: then the creations of your study may be allowed to see the light of day. But what do most people do, on the contrary? They do not begin with the part, but with the whole. Perhaps they make one good stroke, excite attention, and ever afterwards their work grows worse and worse, for good, natural reasons. But sometimes, when intellect and character are lacking for the formation of such an artistic career, fate and necessity take the place of these qualities and lead the future master step by step through all the phases of his craft.

164

The danger and the gain in the cult of genius – The belief in great, superior, fertile minds is not necessarily, but still very frequently, connected with that wholly or partly religious superstition that those spirits are of superhuman origin and possess certain marvellous faculties, by means of which they obtained their knowledge in ways quite different from the rest of mankind. They are credited with having an immediate insight into the nature of the world, through a peep-hole in the mantle of the phenomenon as it were, and it is believed that, without the trouble and severity of science, by virtue of this marvellous prophetic sight, they could impart something final and decisive about mankind and the world. So long as there are still believers in miracles in the world of knowledge it may perhaps be admitted that the believers themselves derive a benefit therefrom, inasmuch as by their absolute subjection to great minds they obtain the best discipline and schooling for their own minds during the period of development. On the other hand, it may at least be questioned whether the superstition of genius, of its privileges and special faculties, is useful for a genius himself when it implants itself in him. In any case it is a dangerous sign when man shudders at his own self, be it that famous Caesarian shudder or the shudder of genius which applies to this case, when the incense of sacrifice, which by rights is offered to a God alone, penetrates into the brain of the genius, so that he begins to waver and to look upon himself as something superhuman. The slow consequences are: the feeling of irresponsibility, the exceptional rights, the belief that mere intercourse with him confers a favour, and frantic rage at any attempt to compare him with others or even to place him below them and to bring into prominence whatever is unsuccessful in his work. Through the fact that he ceases to criticise himself one pinion after another falls out of his plumage – that superstition undermines the foundation of his strength and even makes him a hypocrite after his power has failed him. For great minds it is, therefore, perhaps better when they come to an understanding about their strength and its source, when they comprehend what purely human qualities are mingled in them, what a combination they are of fortunate conditions: thus once it was continual energy, a decided application to individual aims, great personal courage, and then the good fortune of an education, which at an early period provided the best teachers, examples, and methods. Assuredly, if its aim is to make the

greatest possible *effect*, abstruseness has always done much for itself
and that gift of partial insanity; for at all times that power has been
admired and envied by means of which men were deprived of will
and imbued with the fancy that they were preceded by supernatural leaders. Truly, men are exalted and inspired by the belief
that some one among them is endowed with supernatural powers,
and in this respect insanity, as Plato says, has brought the greatest
blessings to mankind In a few rare cases this form of insanity may
also have been the means by which an all-round exuberant nature
was kept within bounds; in individual life the imaginings of frenzy
frequently exert the virtue of remedies which are poisons in
themselves; but in every 'genius' that believes in his own divinity
the poison shows itself at last in the same proportion as the 'genius'
grows old; we need but recollect the example of Napoleon, for it
was most assuredly through his faith in himself and his star, and
through his scorn of mankind, that he grew to that mighty unity
which distinguished him from all modern men, until at last, however, this faith developed into an almost insane fatalism, robbed
him of his quickness of comprehension and penetration, and was
the cause of his downfall.

165

Genius and nullity – It is precisely the *original* artists, those who
create out of their own heads, who in certain circumstances
can bring forth complete *emptiness* and husk, whilst the more
dependent natures, the so-called talented ones, are full of memories of all manner of goodness, and even in a state of weakness
produce something tolerable. But if the original ones are abandoned by themselves, memory renders them no assistance; they
become empty.

166

The public – The people really demands nothing more from tragedy
than to be deeply affected, in order to have a good cry occasionally;
the artist, on the contrary, who sees the new tragedy, takes pleasure
in the clever technical inventions and tricks, in the management and
distribution of the material, in the novel arrangement of old motives
and old ideas. His attitude is the aesthetic attitude towards a work of
art, that of the creator; the one first described, with regard solely to

the material, is that of the people. Of the individual who stands between the two nothing need be said: he is neither 'people' nor artist, and does not know what he wants – therefore his pleasure is also clouded and insignificant.

167

The artistic education of the public – If the same *motif* is not employed in a hundred ways by different masters, the public never learns to get beyond their interest in the subject; but at last, when it is well acquainted with the *motif* through countless different treatments, and no longer finds in it any charm of novelty or excitement, it will then begin to grasp and enjoy the various shades and delicate new inventions in its treatment.

168

The artist and his followers must keep in step – The progress from one grade of style to another must be so slow that not only the artists but also the auditors and spectators can follow it and know exactly what is going on. Otherwise there will suddenly appear that great chasm between the artist, who creates his work upon a height apart, and the public, who cannot rise up to that height and finally sinks discontentedly deeper. For when the artist no longer raises his public it rapidly sinks downwards, and its fall is the deeper and more dangerous in proportion to the height to which genius has carried it, like the eagle, out of whose talons a tortoise that has been borne up into the clouds falls to its destruction.

169

The source of the comic element – If we consider that for many thousands of years man was an animal that was susceptible in the highest degree to fear, and that everything sudden and unexpected had to find him ready for battle, perhaps even ready for death; that even later, in social relations, all security was based on the expected, on custom in thought and action, we need not be surprised that at everything sudden and unexpected in word and deed, if it occurs without danger or injury, man becomes exuberant and passes over into the very opposite of fear – the terrified, trembling, crouching being shoots upward, stretches itself: man laughs. This transition from momentary fear into short-lived exhilaration is called the *Comic*. On the other hand, in the tragic phenomenon, man passes swiftly from great, enduring exuberance into great fear and anguish; but as amongst mortals great and lasting exuberance is much rarer than the cause for fear, there is far more comedy than tragedy in the world; we laugh much more often than we are agitated.

170

The artist's ambition – The Greek artists, the tragedians for instance, composed in order to conquer; their whole art cannot be imagined without rivalry – the good Hesiodan Eris, Ambition, gave wings to their genius. This ambition further demanded that their work should achieve the greatest excellence *in their own eyes*, as they understood excellence, *without any regard* for the reigning taste and the general opinion about excellence in a work of art; and thus it was long before Aeschylus and Euripides achieved any success, until at last they *educated* judges of art, who valued their work according to the standards which they themselves appointed. Hence they strove for victory over rivals according to their own valuation, they really wished to *be* more excellent; they demanded assent from without to this self-valuation, the confirmation of this verdict. To achieve honour means in this case: 'to make oneself superior to others, and to desire that this should be recognised publicly.' Should the former condition be wanting, and the latter nevertheless desired, it is then called *vanity*. Should the latter be lacking and not missed, then it is named pride.

171

What is needful to a work of art – Those who talk so much about the needful factors of a work of art exaggerate, if they are artists they do so *in majorem artis gloriam*, if they are laymen, from ignorance. The form of a work of art, which gives speech to their thoughts and is, therefore, their mode of talking, is always somewhat uncertain, like all kinds of speech. The sculptor can add or omit many little traits, as can also the exponent, be he an actor or, in music, a performer or conductor. These many little traits and finishing touches today afford him pleasure one day and none the next; they exist more for the sake of the artist than the art; for he also has occasional need of sweetmeats and playthings to prevent him becoming morose with the severity and self-restraint which the representation of the dominant idea demands of him.

172

To cause the master to be forgotten – The pianoforte player who executes the work of a master will have played best if he has made his audience forget the master, and if it seemed as if he were relating a story from his own life or just passing through some experience. Assuredly, if he is of no importance, every one will abhor the garrulity with which he talks us about his own life. Therefore he must know how to influence his hearer's imagination favourably towards himself. Hereby are explained all the weaknesses and follies of 'the virtuoso'.

173

Corriger la fortune. – There are unfortunate accidents in the lives of great artists, which compel the painter, for instance, to sketch out his most important picture only as a passing thought, or such as obliged Beethoven to leave behind him only the insufficient pianoforte score of many great sonatas (as in the great B flat). In these cases the artist of a later day must endeavour to fill out the life of the great man – what, for instance, he would do who, as master of all orchestral effects, would call into life that symphony which has fallen into the piano-trance.

174

Reducing – Many things, events or persons, cannot bear treatment on a small scale. The Laocoön group cannot be reduced to a knick-knack; great size is necessary to it. But more seldom still does anything that is naturally small bear enlargement; for which reason biographers succeed far oftener in representing a great man as small than a small one as great.

175

Sensuousness in present-day art – Artists nowadays frequently miscalculate when they count on the sensuous effect of their works, for their spectators or hearers have no longer a fully sensuous nature, and quite contrary to the artist's intention, his work produces in them a 'holiness' of feeling which is closely related to boredom – Their sensuousness begins, perhaps, just where that of the artist ceases; they meet, therefore, only at one point at the most.

176

Shakespeare as a moralist – Shakespeare meditated much on the passions, and on account of his temperament had probably a close acquaintance with many of them (dramatists are in general rather wicked men). He could, however, not talk on the subject, like Montaigne, but put his observations thereon into the mouths of impassioned figures, which is contrary to nature, certainly, but makes his dramas so rich in thought that they cause all others to seem poor in comparison and readily arouse a general aversion to them. Schiller's reflections (which are almost always based on erroneous or trivial fancies) are just theatrical reflections, and as such are very effective: whereas Shakespeare's reflections do honour to his model, Montaigne, and contain quite serious thoughts in polished form, but on that account are too remote and refined for the eyes of the theatrical public, and are consequently ineffective.

177

Securing a good hearing – It is not sufficient to know how to play well; one must also know how to secure a good hearing. A violin in the hands of the greatest master gives only a little sqeak when the place where it is heard is too large; the master may then be mistaken for any bungler.

178

The incomplete as the effective – Just as figures in relief make such a strong impression on the imagination because they seem in the act of emerging from the wall and only stopped by some sudden hindrance; so the relief-like, incomplete presentation of a thought, or a whole philosophy, is sometimes more effective than its exhaustive amplification – more is left for the investigation of the onlooker, he is incited to the further study of that which stands out before him in such strong light and shade; he is prompted to think out the subject, and even to overcome the hindrance which hitherto prevented it from emerging clearly.

179

Against the eccentric – When art arrays itself in the most shabby material it is most easily recognised as art.

180

Collective intellect – A good author possesses not only his own intellect but also that of his friends.

181

Different kinds of mistakes – The misfortune of acute and clear authors is that people consider them shallow and therefore do not devote any effort to them: and the good fortune of obscure writers is that the reader makes an effort to understand them and places the delight in his own zeal to their credit.

182

Relation to science – None of the people have any real interest in a science, who only begin to be enthusiastic about it when they themselves have made discoveries in it.

183

The key – The single thought on which an eminent man sets a great value, arousing the derision and laughter of the masses, is for him a key to hidden treasures; for them. however, it is nothing *more* than a piece of old iron.

184

Untranslatable – It is neither the best nor the worst parts of a book which are untranslatable.

185

Author's paradoxes – The so-called paradoxes of an author to which a reader objects are often not in the author's book at all, but in the reader's head.

186

Wit – The wittiest authors produce a scarcely noticeable smile.

187

Antithesis – Antithesis is the narrow gate through which error is fondest of sneaking to the truth.

188

Thinkers as stylists – Most thinkers write badly because they communicate not only their thoughts, but also the thinking of them.

189

Thoughts in poetry – The poet conveys his thoughts ceremoniously in the vehicle of rhythm, usually because they are not able to go on foot.

190

The sin against the reader's intellect – If the author renounces his talent in order merely to put himself on a level with the reader, he commits the only deadly sin which the latter will never forgive, should he notice anything of it. One may say everything that is bad about a person, but in the manner *in which* it is said one must know how to resvive his vanity anew.

191

The limits of uprightness – Even the most upright author lets fall a word too much when he wishes to round off a period.

192

The best author – The best author will be he who is ashamed to become one.

193

Draconian law against authors – One should regard authors as criminals who only obtain acquittal or mercy in the rarest cases – that would be a remedy for books becoming too rife.

194

The fools of modern culture – The fools of medieval courts correspond to our *feuilleton* writers: they are the same kind of mem, semi-rational, witty, extravagant, foolish, sometimes there only for the purpose of lessening the pathos of the outlook with fancies and

chatter, and of drowning with their clamour the far too deep and
solemn chimes of great events; they were formerly in the service of
princes and nobles, now they are in the service of parties (since a
large portion of the old obsequiousness in the intercourse of the
people with their prince still survives in party-feeling and party-
discipline). Modern literary men, however, are generally very
similar to the *feuilleton* writers, they are the 'fools of modern
culture', whom one judges more leniently when one does not
regard them as fully responsible beings. To look upon writing as a
regular profession should justly be regarded as a form of madness.

195

After the example of the Greeks – It is a great hindrance to knowledge
at present that, owing to centuries of exaggeration of feeling, all
words have become vague and inflated. The higher stage of
culture, which is under the sway (though not under the tyranny)
of knowledge, requires great sobriety of feeling and thorough concentration of words – on which points the Greeks in the time of
Demosthenes set an example to us. Exaggeration is a distinguishing mark of all modern writings, and even when they are simply
written the expressions therein are still *felt* as too eccentric. Careful
reflection, conciseness, coldness, plainness, even carried intentionally to the farthest limits – in a word, suppression of feeling and
taciturnity – these are the only remedies. For the rest, this cold
manner of writing and feeling is now very attractive, as a contrast;
and to be sure, there is a new danger therein. For intense cold is as
good a stimulus as a high degree of warmth.

196

Good narrators, bad explainers – In good narrators there is often found
an admirable psychological sureness and logicalness, as far as these
qualities can be observed in the actions of their personages, in
positively ludicrous contrast to their inexperienced psychological
reasoning, so that their culture appears to be as extraordinarily high
one moment as it seems regrettably defective the next. It happens far
too frequently that they are give an evidently false explanation of
their own heroes and their actions – of this there is no doubt,
however improbable the thing may appear. It is quite likely that the
greatest pianoforte player has thought but little about the technical

conditions and the special virtues, drawbacks, usefulness and tract-
ability of each finger (dactylic ethics), and makes big mistakes
whenever he speaks of such things.

197

The writings of acquaintances and their readers – We read the writings of
our acquaintances (friends and enemies) in a double sense, inasmuch
as our perception constantly whispers, 'That is something of
himself, a remembrance of his inward being, his experiences, his
talents,' and at the same time another kind of perception endeavours
to estimate the profit of the work itself, what valuation it merits
apart from its author, how far it will enrich knowledge. These two
manners of reading and estimating interfere with each other, as may
naturally be supposed. And a conversation with a friend will only
bear good fruit of knowledge when both think only of the matter
under consideration and forget that they are friends.

198

Rhythmical sacrifice – Good writers alter the rhythm of many a period
merely because they do not credit the general reader with the ability
to comprehend the measure followed by the period in its first
version; thus they make it easier for the reader, by giving the
preference to the better known rhythms. This regard for the
rhythmical incapacity of the modern reader has already called forth
many a sigh, for much has been sacrificed to it – Does not the same
thing happen to good musicians?

199

The incomplete as an artistic stimulant – The incomplete is often more
effective than perfection, and this is the case with eulogies. To
effect their purpose a stimulating incompleteness is necessary, as an
irrational element, which calls up a sea before the hearer's imagination, and, like a mist, conceals the opposite coast, i.e. the limits of
the object of praise. If the well-known merits of a person are
referred to and described at length and in detail, it always gives rise
to the suspicion that these are his only merits. The perfect eulogist
takes his stand above the person praised, he appears to *overlook* him.
Therefore complete praise has a weakening effect.

200

Precautions in writing and teaching – Whoever has once written and has been seized with the passion for writing learns from almost all that he does and experiences that which is literally communicable. He thinks no longer of himself, but of the author and his public; he desires insight into things; but not for his own use. He who teaches is mostly incapable of doing anything for his own good: he is always thinking of the good of his scholars, and all knowledge delights him only insofar as he is able to teach it. He comes at last to regard himself in the end as a medium of knowledge, and above all as a means thereto, so that he has lost all serious consideration for himself.

201

The necessity for bad authors – There will always be a need of bad authors; for they meet the taste of readers of an undeveloped, immature age – these have their requirements as well as mature readers. If human life were of greater length, the number of mature individuals would be greater than that of the immature, or at least equally great; but as it is, by far the greater number die too young: i.e. there are always many more undeveloped intellects with bad taste. These demand, with the greater impetuosity of youth, the satisfaction of their needs, and they *insist* on having bad authors.

202

Too near and too far – The reader and the author very often do not understand each other, because the author knows his theme too well and finds it almost slow, so that he omits the examples, of which he knows hundreds; the reader, however, is interested in the subject, and is liable to find it poorly proved if examples are lacking.

203

A vanished preparation for art – Of everything that was practised in public schools, the thing of greatest value was the exercise in Latin style – this was an exercise in art, whilst all other occupations aimed only at the acquirement of knowledge. It is a barbarism to put German composition before it, for there is no typical German style developed by public oratory; but if there is a desire to advance

practice in thought by means of German composition, then it is
certainly better for the time being to pay no attention to style, to
separate the practice in thought, therefore, and the practice in
reproduction. The latter should confine itself to the various modes
of presenting a given subject, and should not concern itself with
the independent finding of a subject. The mere presentment
of a given subject was the task of the Latin style, for which the
old teachers possessed a long-vanished delicacy of ear. Formerly,
whoever learned to write well in a modern language had to thank
this practice for the acquirement (now we are obliged to go to
school to the older French teachers). But yet more: he obtained an
idea of the loftiness and difficulty of form, and was prepared for art
in the only right way: by practice.

204

Dark and over-brightness side by side – Authors who, in general, do
not understand how to express their thoughts clearly are fond of
choosing, in detail, the strongest, most exaggerated distinctions
and superlatives – thereby is produced an effect of light, which is
like torchlight in intricate forest paths.

205

Literary painting – An important object will be best described if the
colours for the painting are taken out of the object itself, as a
chemist does, and then employed like an artist, so that the drawing
develops from the outlines and transitions of the colours. Thus the
painting acquires something of the entrancing natural element
which gives such importance to the object itself.

206

Books which teach one to dance – There are writers who, by portraying the impossible as possible, and by speaking of morality and
genius as if both were merely a mood or a whim, elicit a feeling
of high-spirited freedom, as if man were rising up on tiptoe and
simply had to dance out of inner pleasure.

207

Unfinished thoughts – Just as not only manhood, but also youth and
childhood have value *per se*, and are not to be looked upon merely as

passages and bridges, so also unfinished thoughts have their value. For this reason we must not torment a poet with subtle explanations, but must take pleasure in the uncertainty of his horizon, as if the way to further thoughts were still open. We stand on the threshold; we wait as for the digging up of a treasure, it is as if a well of profundity were about to be discovered. The poet anticipates something of the thinker's pleasure in the discovery of a leading thought, and makes us covetous, so that we give chase to it; but it flutters past our head and exhibits the loveliest butterfly wings – and yet it escapes us.

208

The book grown almost into a human being – Every author is surprised anew at the way in which his book, as soon he has sent it out, continues to have a life of its own; it seems to him as if one part of an insect had been cut off and now went on its own way. Perhaps he forgets it almost entirely; perhaps he rises above the view expressed therein; perhaps he understands it no longer, and has lost that impulse upon which he soared at the time he conceived the book; meanwhile it seeks its readers, inflames life, pleases, horrifies, inspires new works, becomes the soul of designs and actions – in short, it lives like a creature endowed with mind and soul, and yet is no human being. The happiest fate is that of the author who, as an old man, is able to say that all there was in him of life-inspiring, strengthening, exalting, enlightening thoughts and feelings still lives on in his writings, and that he himself now only represents the gray ashes, whilst the fire has been kept alive and spread out. And if we consider that every human action, not only a book, is in some way or other the cause of other actions, decisions and thoughts; that everything that happens is inseparably connected with everything that is going to happen, we recognise the real *immortality*; that of movement – that which has once moved is enclosed and immortalised in the general union of all existence, like an insect within a piece of amber.

209

Joy in old age – The thinker, as likewise the artist, who has put his best self into his works, feels an almost malicious joy when he sees how mind and body aare being slowly damaged and destroyed by time, as if from a dark corner he were spying a thief at his money-chest, knowing all the time that it was empty and his treasures in safety.

210

Quiet fruitfulness – The born aristocrats of the mind are not in too much of a hurry: their creations appear and fall from the tree on some quiet autumn evening, without being rashly desired, instigated, or pushed aside by new matter. The unceasing desire to create is vulgar, and betrays envy, jealousy, and ambition. If a man is something, it is not really necessary for him to do anything – and yet he does a great deal. There is a human species higher even than the 'productive' man.

211

Achilles and Homer – It is always like the case of Achilles and Homer – the one *has* the experience and sensations, the other *describes* them. A genuine author only puts into words the feelings and adventures of others, he is an artist, and divines much from the little he has experienced. Artists are by no means creatures of great passion; but they frequesntly *represent* themselves as such with the unconscious feeling that their depicted passions will be better believed if their own life gives credence to their experience in these affairs. The need only let themselves go, not control themselves, and give free play to their anger and their desires, and everyone will immediately cry out, 'How passionate he is!' But the deeply stirring passion that consumes and often destroys the individual is another matter: those who have really experienced it do not describe it in dramas, harmonies or romances. Artists are frequently *unbridled* individuals in so far as they are not artists, but that is a different thing.

212

Old doubts about the effect of art – Should pity and fear really be unburdened through tragedy, as Aristotle would have it, so that the hearers return home colder and quieter? Should ghost-stories really make us less fearful and superstitious? In the case of certain physical processes, in the satisfaction of love, for instance, it is true that with the fulfilment of a need there follows an alleviation and temporary decrease in the impulse. But fear and pity are not in this sense the needs of particular organs which require to be relieved. And in time every instinct is even *strengthened* by practice in its satisfaction, in spite of that periodical mitigation. It might be possible that in each single case pity and fear would be soothed and relieved by tragedy: nevertheless, they might, on the whole, be increased by tragic influences, and Plato would be right in saying that tragedy makes us altogether more timid and susceptible. The tragic poet himself would then of necessity acquire a gloomy and fearful view of the world, and a yielding, irritable, tearful soul; it would also agree with Plato's view if the tragic poets, and likewise the entire part of the community that derived particular pleasure from them. degenerated into ever greater licentiousness and intemperance. But what right, indeed, has our age to give an answer to that great question of Plato's as to the moral influence of art? If we even had art – where have we an influence, any kind of an art-influence?

213

Pleasure in nonsense – How can we take pleasure in nonsense? But wherever there is laughter in the world this is the case: it may even be said that almost everywhere where there is happiness, there is found pleasure in nonsense. The transformation of experience into its opposite, of the suitable into the unsuitable, the obligatory into the optional (but in such a manner that this process causes no injury and is only imagined in jest), is a pleasure; for it temporarily liberates us from the yoke of the obligatory, suitable and experienced, in which we usually find our pitiless masters; we play and laugh when the expected (which generally causes fear and expectancy) happens without bringing any injury. It is the pleasure felt by slaves in the Saturnalian feasts.

214

The ennobling of reality – Through the fact that in the aphrodisiac impulse men discerned a godhead and with adoring gratitude felt it working within themselves, this emotion has in the course of time become imbued with higher conceptions, and has thereby been materially ennobled. Thus certain nations, by virtue of this art of idealisation, have created great aids to culture out of diseases – the Greeks, for instance, who in earlier centuries suffered from great nervous epidemics (like epilepsy and the St Vitus' Dance), and developed out of them the splendid type of the Bacchante. The Greeks, however, enjoyed an astonishingly high degree of health – their secret was, to revere even disease as a god, if it only possessed power.

215

Music – Music by and for itself is not so portentous for our inward nature, so deeply moving, that it ought to be looked upon as the *direct* language of the feelings; but its ancient union with poetry has infused so much symbolism into rhythmical movement, into loudness and softness of tone, that we now *imagine* it speaks directly *to* and comes *from* the inward nature. Dramatic music is only possible when the art of harmony has acquired an immense range of symbolical means, through song, opera and a hundred attempts at description by sound. 'Absolute music' is either form *per se*, in the rude condition of music, when playing in time and with varying degrees of strength gives pleasure, or the symbolism of form which speaks to the understanding even without poetry, after the two arts were joined finally together after long development and the musical form had been woven about with threads of meaning and feeling. People who are backward in musical development can appreciate a piece of harmony merely as execution, whilst those who are advanced will comprehend it symbolically. No music is deep and full of meaning in itself, it does not speak of 'will', of the 'thing-in-itself'; that could be imagined by the intellect only in an age which had conquered for musical symbolism the entire range of inner life. It was the intellect itself that first *gave* this meaning to sound, just as it also gave meaningto the relation between lines and masses in architecture, but which in itself is quite foreign to mechanical laws.

216

Gesture and speech – Older than speech is the imitation of gestures, which is carried on unconsciously and which, in the general repression of the language of gesture and trained control of the muscles, is still so great that we cannot lokk at a face moved by emotion without feeling an agitation of our own face (it may be remarked that feigned yawning excites real yawning in the any one

who sees it). The imitated gesture leads the one who imitates back
to the sensation it expressed in the face or body of the one
imitated. Thus men learned to understand one another; thus the
child still learns to understand the mother. Generally speaking,
painful sensations may also have been expressed by gestures, and
the pain that caused them (for instance, tearing the hair, beating
the breast, forcible distortion and straining of the muscles of
the face). On the other hand, gestures of joy were themselves
joyful and lent themselves easily to the communication of the
understanding; (laughter, as the expression of the feeling when
being tickled, which is pleasurable, serves also for the expression
of other pleasurable sensations). As soon as men understood
each other by gestures, there could be established a *symbolism* of
gesture; I mean, an understanding could be arrived at respecting
the language of accents, so that first *accent* and gesture (to which
it was symbolically added) were produced, and later only the the
accent alone. In former times there happened very frequently that
which now happens in the development of music, especially of
dramatic music – while music, without explanatory dance and
pantomime (language of gesture), is at first only empty sound, but
by long familiarity with the combination of music and movement
the ear becomes schooled into instant interpretation of the figures
of sound, and finally attains a height of quick understanding,
where it has no longer any need of visible movement, and *understands* the sound-poet without it. It is then called absolute music,
that is, music in which, without further help, everything is
symbolically understood.

217

The spiritualising of higher art – By virtue of extraordinary intellectual
exercise through the art-development of the new music, our ears
have been growing more intellectual. For this reason we can now
endure a much greater volume of sound, much more 'noise',
because we are far better practised in listening for the *sense* in it than
were our ancestors. As a matter of fact, all our senses have been
somewhat blunted, because they immediately look for the sense;
that is, they ask what 'it means' and not what 'it is' – such a blunting
betrays itself, for instance, in the absolute dominion of the
tempature of sounds; for ears which still make the finer distinctions,

between *cis* and *des*, for instance, are now amongst the exceptions. In this respect our ear has grown coarser. And then the ugly side of the world, the one originally hostile to the senses, has been conquered for music; its power has been immensely widened, especially in the expression of the noble, the terrible, and the mysterious: our music now gives utterance to things which had formerly no tongue. In the same way certain painters have rendered the eye more intellectual, and have gone far beyond that which was formerly called pleasure in colour and form. Here, too, that side of the world originally considered as ugly has been conquered by the artistic intellect. What results from all this? The more capable of thought that eye and ear become, the more they approach the limit where they become senseless, the seat of pleasure is moved into the brain, the organs of the senses themselves become dulled and weak, the symbolical takes more and more the place of the actual – and thus we arrive at barbarism in this way as surely as in any other. In the meantime we may say: the world is uglier than ever, but it *represents* a more beautiful world than has ever existed. But the more the amber-scent of meaning is dispersed and evaporated, the rarer become those who perceive it, and the remainder halt at what is ugly and endeavour to enjoy it direct, an aim, however, which they never succeed in attaining. Thus, in Germany there is a twofold direction of musical development, here a throng of ten thousand with ever higher, finer demands, ever listening more and more for the 'it means', and there the immense countless mass which yearly grows more incapable of understanding what is important even in the form of sensual ugliness, and which therefore turns ever more willingly to what in music is ugly and foul in itself, that is, to the basely sensual.

218

A stone is more of a stone than formerly – As a general rule we no longer understand architecture, at least by no means in the same way as we understand music. We have outgrown the symbolism of lines and figures, just as we are no longer accustomed to the sound-effects of rhetoric, and have not absorbed this kind of mother's milk of culture since our first moment of life. Everything in a Greek or Christian building originally had a meaning, and referred to a higher order of things; this feeling of inexhaustible meaning enveloped the edifice like a mystic veil. Beauty was only a secondary consideration in the system, without in any way materially injuring the fundamental sentiment of the mysteriously-exalted, the divinely and magically consecrated; at the most, beauty *tempered horror* – but this horror was everywhere presupposed. What is the beauty of a building now? The same thing as the beautiful face of a stupid woman, a kind of mask.

219

The religious source of the newer music – Soulful music arose out of the Catholicism re-established after the Council of Trent, through Palestrina, who endowed the newly-awakened, earnest, and deeply moved spirit with sound; later on, in Bach, it appeared also in Protestantism, as far as this had been deepened by the Pietists and released from its originally dogmatic character. The supposition and necessary preparation for both origins is the familiarity with music, which existed during and before the Renaissance, namely that learned occupation with music, which was really scientific pleasure in the masterpieces of harmony and voice-training. On the other hand, the opera must have preceded it, wherein the layman made his protest against a music that had grown too learned and cold, and endeavoured to re-endow Polyhymnia with a soul. Without the change to that deeply religious sentiment, without the dying away of the inwardly moved temperament, music would have remained learned or operatic; the spirit of the counter-reformation is the spirit of modern music (for that pietism in Bach's music is also a kind of counter-reformation). So deeply are we indebted to the religious life. Music was the counter-reformation in the field of art; to this belongs also the later painting of the Caracci and Caravaggi, per-haps also the baroque style, in any case more than the architecture of the Renaissance or of antiquity. And we might still ask: if our newer music could move stones, would it build them up into antique architecture? I very much doubt it. For that which predominates in this music, affections, pleasure in exalted, highly-strained senti-ments, the desire to be alive at any cost, the quick change of feeling, the strong relief-effects of light and shade, the combination of the ecstatic and the naïve – all this has already reigned in the plastic arts and created new laws of style – but it was neither in the time of antiquity nor of the Renaissance.

220

The beyond in art – It is not without deep pain that we acknowledge the fact that in their loftiest soarings, artists of all ages have exalted and divinely transfigured precisely those ideas which we now recognise as false; they are the glorifiers of humanity's religious and philosophical errors, and they could not have been this without belief in the absolute truth of these errors. But if the belief in such truth diminishes at all, if the rainbow colours at the farthest ends of human knowledge and imagination fade, then this kind of art can never re-flourish, for, like the *Divina Commedia,* Raphael's paintings, Michelangelo's frescoes, and Gothic cathedrals, they indicate not only a cosmic but also a metaphysical meaning in the work of art. Out of all this will grow a touching legend that such an art and such an artistic faith once existed.

221

Revolution in poetry – The strict limit which the French dramatists marked out with regard to unity of action, time and place, construction of style, verse and sentence, selection of words and ideas, was a school as important as that of counterpoint and fugue in the development of modern music or that of the Gorgianic figures in Greek oratory. Such a restriction may appear absurd; nevertheless there is no means of getting out of naturalism except by confining ourselves at first to the strongest (perhaps most arbitrary) means. Thus we gradually learn to walk gracefully on the narrow paths that bridge giddy abysses, and acquire great suppleness of movement as a result, as the history of music proves to our living eyes. Here we see how, step by step, the fetters get looser, until at last they may appear to be altogether thrown off; this *appearance* is the highest achievement of a necessary development in art. In the art of modern poetry there existed no such fortunate, gradual emerging from self-imposed fetters. Lessing held up to scorn in Germany the French form, the only modern form of art, and pointed to Shakespeare; and thus the steadiness of that unfettering was lost and a spring was made into naturalism – that is, back into the beginnings of art. From this Goethe endeavoured to save himself, by always trying to limit himself anew in different ways; but even the most gifted only succeeds by continuously experimenting, if the thread of development has once been broken. It is to the unconsciously revered, if also repudiated, model of French tragedy that Schiller owes his comparative sureness of form, and he remained fairly independent of Lessing (whose dramatic attempts he is well known to have rejected). But after Voltaire the French themselves suddenly lacked the great talents which would have led the development of tragedy out of constraint to that apparent freedom; later on they followed the German example and made a spring into a sort of Rousseau-like state of nature and experiments. It is only necessary to read Voltaire's 'Mahomet' from time to time in order to perceive clearly what European culture has lost through that breaking down of tradition. Once for all, Voltaire was the last of the great dramatists who with Greek proportion controlled his manifold soul, equal even to the greatest storms of tragedy – he was able to do what no German could, because the French nature is much nearer akin to the Greek than is the German; he was also the last great writer who in the wielding of prose possessed the Greek ear, Greek artistic conscientiousness, and Greek simplicity and grace; he was, also, one of the last men able to combine in himself the greatest freedom of mind and an absolutely unrevolutionary way of thinking without being inconsistent and cowardly. Since that time the modern spirit, with its restlessness and its hatred of moderation and restrictions, has obtained the mastery on all sides, let loose at first by the fever of revolution, and then once more putting a bridle on itself when it became filled with fear and horror at itself – but it was the bridle of rigid logic, no longer that of artistic moderation. It is true that through that unfettering for a time we are able to enjoy the poetry of all nations, everything that has sprung up in hidden places, original, wild, wonderfully beautiful and gigantically irregular, from folk-songs up to the 'great barbarian' Shakespeare; we taste the joys of local colour and costume, hitherto unknown to all artistic nations; we make liberal use of the 'barbaric advantages' of our time, which Goethe accentuated against Schiller in order to place the formlessness of his *Faust* in the most favourable light. But for how much longer? The encroaching flood of poetry of all styles and all nations must gradually sweep away that magic garden upon which a quiet and hidden growth would still have been possible; all poets *must* become experimenting imitators, daring copyists, however great their primary strength may be. Eventually, the public, which has lost the habit of seeing the actual artistic fact in the *controlling* of depicting power, in the organising mastery over all art-means, *must* come ever more and more to value power for power's sake, colour for colour's sake, idea for idea's sake, inspiration for inspiration's sake; accordingly it will not enjoy the elements and conditions of the work of art, unless *isolated*, and finally will make the very natural demand that the artist *must* deliver it to them isolated. True, the 'senseless' fetters of Franco-Greek art have been thrown off, but unconsciously we have grown accustomed to consider all fetters, all restrictions as senseless; and so art moves towards its liberation, but, in so doing, it touches – which is certainly highly edifying – upon all the phases of its beginning, its childhood, its incompleteness, its sometime boldness and excesses, in perishing it interprets its origin and growth. One of the great ones, whose instinct may be relied on and whose theory lacked nothing but thirty years *more* of practice, Lord Byron, once said: that with regard to poetry in general, the more he thought about it the more convinced he was that one and all we are entirely on a wrong track, that we are following an inwardly false revolutionary system, and that either our own generation or the next will yet arrive at this same conviction. It is the same Lord Byron who said that he 'looked upon Shakespeare as the very worst model, although the most extraordinary poet.' And does not Goethe's mature artistic insight in the second half of his life say practically the same thing? – that insight by means of which he made such a bound in advance of whole generations that, generally speaking, it may be said that Goethe's influence has not yet begun, that his time has still to come. Just because his nature held him fast for a long time in the path of the poetical revolution, just because he drank to the dregs of whatsoever new sources, views and expedients had been indirectly discovered through that breaking down of tradition, of all that had been unearthed from under the ruins of art, his later transformation and conversion carries so much weight; it shows that he felt the deepest longing to win back the traditions of art, and to give in fancy the ancient perfection and completeness to the abandoned ruins and colonnades of the temple, with the imagination of the eye at least, should the strength of the arm be found too weak to build where such tremendous powers were needed even to destroy. Thus he lived in art as in the remembrance of the true art, his poetry had become an aid to remembrance, to the understanding of old and long-departed ages of art. With respect to the strength of the new age, his demands could not be satisfied; but the pain this occasioned was amply balanced by the joy that they have been satisfied once, and that we ourselves can still participate in this satisfaction. Not individuals, but more or less ideal masks; no reality, but an allegorical generality; topical characters, local colours toned down and rendered mythical almost to the point of invisibility; contemporary feeling and the problems of contemporary society reduced to the simplest forms, stripped of their attractive, interesting pathological qualities, made *ineffective* in every other but the artistic sense; no new materials and characters, but the old, long-accustomed ones in constant new animation and transformation; that is art, as Goethe *understood* it later, as the Greeks and even the French *practised* it.

222

What remains of art. It is true that art has a much greater value in the case of certain metaphysical hypotheses, for instance when the belief obtains that the character is unchangeable and that the essence of the world manifests itself continually in all character and action; thus the artist's work becomes the symbol of the *eternally constant*, while according to our views the artist can only endow his picture with temporary value, because man on the whole has developed and is mutable, and even the individual man has nothing fixed and constant. The same thing holds good with another metaphysical hypothesis: assuming that our visible world were only a delusion, as metaphysicians declare, then art would come very close to the real world; for there would then be far too much similarity between the world of appearance and the dream-world of the artist; and the remaining difference would place the meaning of art higher even than the meaning of nature, because art would represent the same forms, the types and models of nature. But those suppositions are false; and what position does art retain after this acknowledgment? Above all, for centuries it has taught us to look upon life in every shape with interest and pleasure, and to carry our feelings so far that at last we exclaim, 'Whatever it may be, life is good.' This teaching of art, to take pleasure in existence and to regard human life as a piece of nature, without too vigorous movement, as an object of regular development – this teaching has grown into us; it reappears as an all-powerful need for knowledge. We could renounce art, but we should not therewith forfeit the ability it has taught us – just as we have given up religion, but not the exalting and intensifying of temperament acquired through religion. As the plastic arts and music are the standards of that wealth of feeling really acquired and obtained through religion, so also, after a disappearance of art, the intensity and multiplicity of the joys of life which it had implanted in us would still demand satisfaction. The scientific man is the further development of the artistic man.

223

The after-glow of art – Just as in an old age ee remember our youth and celebrate festivals of memory, so in a short time mankind will stand towards art: its relation will be that of a *touching memory* of the joys of youth. Never, perhaps, in former ages was art dealt with so seriouly and thoughtfully as now when it appears to be surrounded by the magic influence of death. We call to mind that Greek city in southern Italy, which once a year still celebrates its Greek feasts , amidst tears and mourning, that foreign barbarism triumphs ever more and more over the customs its people brought with them into the land; and never has Hellenism been so much appreciated, nowhere has this golden nectar been drunk with so great delight, as amongst these fast disappearing Hellenes. The artist will soon come to be regarded as a splendid relic; and to him, as a to a wonderful stranger on whose power and beauty depended the happiness of former ages, there will be paid such honour as is not often enjoyed by one of our race. The best in us is perhaps inherited from the sentiments of former times, to which it is hardly possible for us now to return by direct ways; the sun has already disappeared, but the heavens of our life are still glowing and illuminated by it, although we can behold it no longer.

224

Ennoblement through degeneration – History teaches that a race of
people is best preserved where the greater number hold one
common spirit in consequence of the similarity of their accustomed
and indisputable principles: in consequence, therefore, of their
common faith. Thus strength is afforded by good and thorough
customs, thus is learnt the subjection of the individual, and stren-
uousness of character becomes a birth gift and afterwards is fostered
as a habit. The danger to these communities founded on individuals
of strong and similar character is that gradually increasing stupidity
through transmission, which follows all stability like its shadow. It
is on the more unrestricted, more uncertain and morally weaker
individuals that depends the *intellectual progress* of such communities,
it is they who attempt all that is new and manifold. Numbers of
these perish on account of their weakness, without having achieved
any specially visible effect; but generally, particularly when they
have descendants, they flare up and from time to time inflict a
wound on the stable element of the community. Precisely in this
sore and weakened place the community is *inoculated* with something new; but its general strength must be great enough to absorb
and assimilate this new thing into its blood. Deviating natures are
of the utmost importance wherever there is to be progress. Every
wholesale progress must be preceded by a partial weakening. The
strongest natures *retain* the type, the weaker ones help it to *develop*.
Something similar happens in the case of individuals; a deterioration, a mutilation, even a vice and, above all, a physical or moral
loss is seldom without its advantage. For instance, a sickly man
in the midst of a warlike and restless race will perhaps have more
chance of being alone and thereby growing quieter and wiser, the
one-eyed man will possess a stronger eye, the blind man will have

a deeper inward sight and will certainly have a keener sense of hearing. In so far it appears to me that the famous Struggle for Existence is not the only point of view from which an explanation can be given of the progress or strengthening of an individual or a race. Rather must two different things converge: firstly, the multiplying of stable strength through mental binding in faith and common feeling; secondly, the possibility of attaining to higher aims, through the fact that there are deviating natures and, in consequence, partial weakening and wounding of the stable strength; it is precisely the weaker nature, as the more delicate and free, that makes all progress at all possible. A people that is crumbling and weak in any one part, but as a whole still strong and healthy, is able to absorb the infection of what is new and incorporate it to its advantage. The task of education in a single individual is this: to plant him so firmly and surely that, as a whole, he can no longer be diverted from his path. Then, however, the educator must wound him, or else make use of the wounds which fate inflicts, and when pain and need have thus arisen, something new and noble can be inoculated into the wounded places. With regard to the State, Machiavelli says that, 'the form of Government is of very small importance, although half-educated people think otherwise. The great aim of State-craft should be duration, which outweighs all else, inasmuch as it is more valuable than liberty.' It is only with securely founded and guaranteed duration that continual development and ennobling inoculation are at all possible. As a rule, however, authority, the dangerous companion of all duration, will rise in opposition to this.

225

Free-thinker a relative term – We call that man a free-thinker who thinks otherwise than is expected of him in consideration of his origin, surroundings, position, and office, or by reason of the prevailing contemporary views. He is the exception, fettered minds are the rule; these latter reproach him, saying that his free principles either have their origin in a desire to be remarkable or else cause free actions to be inferred – that is to say, actions which are not compatible with fettered morality. Sometimes it is also said that the cause of such and such free principles may be traced to mental perversity and extravagance; but only malice speaks thus, nor does it believe what it says, but wishes thereby to do an injury, for the free-thinker usually bears the proof of his greater goodness and keenness of intellect written in his face so plainly that the fettered spirits understand it well enough. But the two other derivations of free-thought are honestly intended; as a matter of fact, many free-thinkers are created in one or other of these ways. For this reason, however, the tenets to which they attain in this manner might be truer and more reliable than those of the fettered spirits. In the knowledge of truth, what really matters is the *possession* of it, not the impulse under which it was sought, the way in which it was found. If the free-thinkers are right then the fettered spirits are wrong, and it is a matter of indifference whether the former have reached truth through immorality or the latter hitherto retained hold of untruths through morality. Moreover, it is not essential to the free-thinker that he should hold more correct views, but that he should have liberated himself from what was customary, be it successfully or disastrously. As a rule, however, he will have truth, or at least the spirit of truth-investigation, on his side; he demands reasons, the others demand faith.

226

The origin of faith – The fettered spirit does not take up his position from conviction, but from habit; he is a Christian, for instance, not because he had a comprehension of different creeds and could take his choice; he is an Englishman, not because he decided for England, but he found Christianity and England ready-made and accepted them without any reason, just as one who is born in a wine-country becomes a wine-drinker. Later on, perhaps, as he was a Christian and an Englishman, he discovered a few reasons in favour of his habit; these reasons may be upset, but he is not therefore upset in his whole position. For instance, let a fettered spirit be obliged to bring forward his reasons against bigamy and then it will be seen whether his holy zeal in favour of monogamy is based upon reason or upon custom. The adoption of guiding principles without reasons is called *faith*.

227

Conclusions drawn from the consequences and traced back to reason and un-reason – All states and orders of society, professions, matrimony, education, law: all these find strength and duration only in the faith which the fettered spirits repose in them – that is, in the absence of reasons, or at least in the averting of inquiries as to reasons. The restricted spirits do not willingly acknowledge this, and feel that it is a *pudendum*. Christianity, however, which was very simple in its intellectual ideas, remarked nothing of this *pudendum*, required faith and nothing but faith, and passionately repulsed the demand for reasons; it pointed to the success of faith: 'You will soon feel the advantages of faith,' it suggested, 'and through faith shall ye be saved.' As an actual fact, the State pursues the same course, and every father brings up his son in the same way: 'Only believe this,' he says, 'and you will soon feel the good it does.' This implies, however, that the truth of an opinion is proved by its personal usefulness; the wholesomeness of a doctrine must be a guarantee for its intellectual surety and solidity. It is exactly as if an accused person in a court of law were to say, 'My counsel speaks the whole truth, for only see what is the result of his speech: I shall be acquitted.' Because the fettered spirits retain their principles on account of their usefulness, they suppose that the free spirit also seeks his own advantage in his views and only holds that to be true which is profitable to him. But as he appears to find profitable just the contrary of that which his compatriots or equals find profitable, these latter assume that his principles are dangerous to them; they say or feel, 'He must not be right, for he is injurious to us.'

228

The strong, good character – The restriction of views, which habit has made instinct, leads to what is called strength of character. When any one acts from few but always from the same motives, his actions acquire great energy; if these actions accord with the principles of the fettered spirits, they are recognised, and they produce, moreover, in those who perform them the sensation of a good conscience. Few motives, energetic action, and a good conscience compose what is called strength of character. The man of strong character lacks a knowledge of the many possibilities and directions of action; his intellect is fettered and restricted, because in a given case it shows him, perhaps, only two possibilities; between these two he must now of necessity choose, in accordance with his whole nature, and he does this easily and quickly because he has not to choose between fifty possibilities. The educating surroundings aim at fettering every individual, by always placing before him the smallest number of possibilities. The individual is always treated by his educators as if he were, indeed, something new, but should become a *duplicate*. If he makes his first appearance as something unknown, unprecedented, he must be turned into something known and precedented. In a child, the familiar manifestation of restriction is called a good character; in placing itself on the side of the fettered spirits the child first discloses its awakening common feeling; with this foundation of common sentiment, he will eventually become useful to his State or rank.

229

The standards and values of the fettered spirits – There are four species of things concerning which the restricted spirits say they are in the right. Firstly: all things that last are right; secondly: all things that are not burdens to us are right; thirdly: all things that are advantageous for us are right; fourthly: all things for which we have made sacrifices are right. The last sentence, for instance, explains why a war that was begun in opposition to popular feeling is carried on with enthusiasm directly a sacrifice has been made for it. The free spirits, who bring their case before the forum of the fettered spirits, must prove that free spirits always existed, that free-spiritism is therefore enduring, that it will not become a burden, and, finally, that on the whole they are an advantage to the fettered spirits. It is because they cannot convince the restricted spirits on this last point that they profit nothing by having proved the first and second propositions.

230

Esprit fort – Compared with him who has tradition on his side and requires no reasons for his actions, the free spirit is always weak, especially in action; for he is acquainted with too many motives and points of view, and has, therefore, an uncertain and unpractised hand. What means exist of making him *strong in spite of this*, so that he will, at least, manage to survive, and will not perish ineffectually? What is the source of the strong spirit (*esprit fort*)? This is especially the question as to the production of genius. Whence comes the energy, the unbending strength, the endurance with which the one, in opposition to accepted ideas, endeavours to obtain an entirely individual knowledge of the world?

231

The rise of genius – The ingenuity with which a prisoner seeks the means of freedom, the most cold-blooded and patient employment of every smallest advantage, can teach us of what tools Nature sometimes makes use in order to produce Genius – a word which I beg will be understood without any mythological and religious flavour; she, Nature, begins it in a dungeon and excites to the utmost its desire to free itself. Or to give another picture: some one who has completely *lost his way* in a wood, but who with unusual energy strives to reach the open in one direction or another, will sometimes discover a new path which nobody knew previously – thus arise geniuses, who are credited with originality. It has already been said that mutilation, crippling, or the loss of some important organ, is frequently the cause of the unusual development of another organ, because this one has to fulfil its own and also another function. This explains the source of many a brilliant talent. These general remarks on the origin of genius may be applied to the special case, the origin of the perfect free spirit.

232

Conjecture as to the origin of free-spiritism – Just as the glaciers increase when in equatorial regions the sun shines upon the seas with greater force than hitherto, so may a very strong and spreading free-spiritism be a proof that somewhere or other the force of feeling has grown extraordinarily.

233

The voice of history – In general, history *appears* to teach the following about the production of genius: it ill-treats and torments mankind – calls to the passions of envy, hatred, and rivalry – drives them to desperation, people against people, throughout whole centuries! Then, perhaps, like a stray spark from the terrible energy thereby aroused, there flames up suddenly the light of genius; the will, like a horse maddened by the rider's spur, thereupon breaks out and leaps over into another domain. He who could attain to a comprehension of the production of genius, and desires to carry out practically the manner in which Nature usually goes to work, would have to be just as evil and regardless as Nature itself. But perhaps we have not heard rightly.

234

The value of the middle of the road – It is possible that the production of genius is reserved to a limited period of mankind's history. For we must not expect from the future everything that very defined conditions were able to produce; for instance, not the astounding effects of religious feeling. This has had its day, and much that is very good can never grow again, because it could grow out of that alone. There will never again be a horizon of life and culture that is bounded by religion. Perhaps even the type of the saint is only possible with that certain narrowness of intellect, which apparently has completely disappeared. And thus the greatest height of intelligence has perhaps been reserved for a single age; it appeared – and appears, for we are still in that age when an extraordinary, long-accumulated energy of will concentrates itself, as an exceptional case, upon *intellectual* aims. That height will no longer exist when this wildness and energy cease to be cultivated. Mankind probably approaches nearer to its actual aim in the middle of its road, in the middle time of its existence, than at the end. It may be that powers with which, for instance, art is a condition, die out altogether; the pleasure in lying, in the undefined, the symbolical, in intoxication, in ecstasy might fall into disrepute. For certainly, when life is ordered in the perfect State, the present will provide no more motive for poetry, and it would only be those persons who had remained behind who would ask for poetical unreality. These, then, would assuredly look longingly backwards to the times of the imperfect State, of half-barbaric society, to our times.

235

Genius and the ideal state in conflict – The Socialists demand a comfortable life for the greatest possible number. If the lasting house of this life of comfort, the perfect State, had really been attained, then this life of comfort would have destroyed the ground out of which grow the great intellect and the mighty individual generally, I mean powerful energy. Were this State reached, mankind would have grown too weary to be still capable of producing genius. Must we not hence wish that life should retain its forcible character, and that wild forces and energies should continue to be called forth afresh? But warm and sympathetic hearts desire precisely the *removal* of that wild and forcible character, and the warmest hearts we can imagine desire it the most passionately of all, whilst all the time its passion derived its fire, its warmth, its very existence precisely from that wild and forcible character; the warmest heart, therefore, desires the removal of its own foundation, the destruction of itself – that is, it desires something illogical, it is not intelligent. The highest intelligence and the warmest heart cannot exist together in one person, and the wise man who passes judgment upon life looks beyond goodness and only regards it as something which is not without value in the general summing-up of life. The wise man must *oppose* those digressive wishes of unintelligent goodness, because he has an interest in the continuance of his type and in the eventual appearance of the highest intellect; at least, he will not advance the founding of the 'perfect State', inasmuch as there is only room in it for wearied individuals. Christ, on the contrary, he whom we may consider to have had the warmest heart, advanced the process of making man stupid, placed himself on the side of the intellectually poor, and retarded the production of the greatest intellect, and this was consistent. His opposite, the man of perfect wisdom – this may be safely prophesied – will just as necessarily hinder the production of a Christ. The State is a wise arrangement for the protection of one individual against another; if its ennobling is exaggerated the individual will at last be weakened by it, even effaced – thus the original purpose of the State will be most completely frustrated.

236

The zones of culture – It may be figuratively said that the ages of culture correspond to the zones of the various climates, only that they lie one behind another and not beside each other like the geographical zones. In comparison with the temperate zone of culture, which it is our object to enter, the past, speaking generally, gives the impression of a *tropical climate*. Violent contrasts, sudden changes between day and night, heat and colour-splendour, the reverence of all that was sudden, mysterious, terrible, the rapidity with which storms broke: everywhere that lavish abundance of the provisions of nature; and opposed to this, in our culture, a clear but by no means bright sky, pure but fairly unchanging air, sharpness, even cold at times; thus the two zones are contrasts to each other. When we see how in that former zone the most raging passions are suppressed and broken down with mysterious force by metaphysical representations, we feel as if wild tigers were being crushed before our very eyes in the coils of mighty serpents; our mental climate lacks such episodes, our imagination is temperate, even in dreams there does not happen to us what former peoples saw waking. But should we not rejoice at this change, even granted that artists are essentially spoiled by the disappearance of the tropical culture and find us non-artists a little too timid? In so far artists are certainly right to deny 'progress', for indeed it is doubtful whether the last three thousand years show an advance in the arts. In the same way, a metaphysical philosopher like Schopenhauer would have no cause to acknowledge progress with a regard to metaphysical philosophy and religion if he glanced back over the last four thousand years. For us, however, the *existence* even of the temperate zones of culture is progress.

237

Renaissance and Reformation – The Italian Renaissance contained within itself all the positive forces to which we owe modern culture. Such were the liberation of thought, the disregard of authorities, the triumph of education over the darkness of tradition, enthusiasm for science and the scientific past of mankind, the unfettering of the Individual, an ardour for truthfulness and a dislike of delusion and mere effect (which ardour blazed forth in an entire company of artistic characters, who with the greatest moral purity required from themselves perfection in their works, and nothing but perfection); yes, the Renaissance had positive forces, which have, *as yet*, never become so mighty again in our modern culture. It was the Golden Age of the last thousand years, in spite of all its blemishes and vices. On the other hand, the German Reformation stands out as an energetic protest of antiquated spirits, who were by

no means tired of mediaeval views of life, and who received the
signs of its dissolution, the extraordinary flatness and alienation of
the religious life, with deep dejection instead of with the rejoicing
that would have been seemly. With their northern strength and
stiff-neckedness they threw mankind back again, brought about
the counter-reformation, that is, a Catholic Christianity of self-
defence, with all the violences of a state of siege, and delayed for
two or three centuries the complete awakening and mastery of the
sciences; just as they probably made for ever impossible the
complete inter-growth of the antique and the modern spirit. The
great task of the Renaissance could not be brought to a termination, this was prevented by the protest of the contemporary
backward German spirit (which, for its salvation, had had sufficient
sense in the Middle Ages to cross the Alps again and again). It
was the chance of an extraordinary constellation of politics
that Luther was preserved, and that his protest gained strength,
for the Emperor protected him in order to employ him as a
weapon against the Pope, and in the same way he was secretly
favoured by the Pope in order to use the Protestant princes as a
counter-weight against the Emperor. Without this curious
counter-play of intentions, Luther would have been burnt like
Huss – and the morning sun of enlightenment would probably
have risen somewhat earlier, and with a splendour more beauteous
than we can now imagine.

238

Justice against the becoming god – When the entire history of culture
unfolds itself to our gaze, as a confusion of evil and noble, of true
and false ideas, and we feel almost seasick at the sight of these
tumultuous waves, we then understand what comfort resides
in the conception of a *becoming God*. This Deity is unveiled
ever more and more throughout the changes and fortunes of
mankind; it is not all blind mechanism, a senseless and aimless
confusion of forces. The deification of the process of being is a
metaphysical outlook, seen as from a lighthouse overlooking the
sea of history, in which a far too historical generation of scholars
found their comfort. This must not arouse anger, however
erroneous the view may be. Only those who, like Schopenhauer,
deny development also feel none of the misery of this historical

wave, and therefore, because they know nothing of that becoming God and the need of His supposition, they should in
justice withhold their scorn.

239

The fruits according to their seasons – Every better future that is
desired for mankind is necessarily in many respects also a worse
future, for it is foolishness to suppose that a new, higher grade of
humanity will combine in itself all the good points of former
grades, and must produce, for instance, the highest form of art.
Rather has every season its own advantages and charms, which
exclude those of the other seasons. That which has grown out of
religion and in its neighbourhood cannot grow again if this has
been destroyed; at the most, straggling and belated off-shoots may
lead to deception on that point, like the occasional outbreaks of
remembrance of the old art, a condition that probably betrays the
feeling of loss and deprivation, but which is no proof of the power
from which a new art might be born.

240

The increasing severity of the world – The higher culture an individual
attains, the less field there is left for mockery and scorn. Voltaire
thanked Heaven from his heart for the invention of marriage and
the Church, by which it had so well provided for our cheer. But he
and his time, and before him the sixteenth century, had exhausted
their ridicule on this theme; everything that is now made fun of
on this theme is out of date, and above all too cheap to tempt a
purchaser. Causes are now inquired after; ours is an age of seriousness. Who cares now to discern, laughingly, the difference between
reality and pretentious sham, between that which man *is* and that
which he wishes to represent; the feeling of this contrast has quite a
different effect if we seek reasons. The more thoroughly any one
understands life, the less he will mock, though finally, perhaps, he
will mock at the 'thoroughness of his understanding'.

241

The genius of culture – If any one wished to imagine a genius of
culture, what would it be like? It handles as its tools falsehood,
force, and thoughtless selfishness so surely that it could only be

called an evil, demoniacal being; but its aims, which are occasionally transparent, are great and good. It is a centaur, half-beast,
half-man, and, in addition, has angel's wings upon its head.

242

The miracle-education – Interest in Education will acquire great
strength only from the moment when belief in a God and His
care is renounced, just as the art of healing could only flourish
when the belief in miracle-cures ceased. So far, however, there is
universal belief in the miracle-education; out of the greatest
disorder and confusion of aims and unfavourableness of conditions, the most fertile and mighty men have been seen to grow;
could this happen naturally? Soon these cases will be more closely
looked into, more carefully examined; but miracles will never be
discovered. In similar circumstances countless persons perish
constantly; the few saved have, therefore, usually grown stronger,
because they endured these bad conditions by virtue of an inexhaustible inborn strength, and this strength they had also exercised
and increased by fighting against these circumstances; thus the
miracle is explained. An education that no longer believes in
miracles must pay attention to three things: first, how much
energy is inherited? Secondly, by what means can new energy be
aroused? Thirdly, how can the individual be adapted to so many
and manifold claims of culture without being disquieted and
destroying his personality – in short, how can the individual be
initiated into the counterpoint of private and public culture, how
can he lead the melody and at the same time accompany it?

243

The future of the physician – There is now no profession which
would admit of such an enhancement as that of the physician;
that is, after the spiritual physicians the so-called pastors, are no
longer allowed to practise their conjuring tricks to public applause,
and a cultured person gets out of their way. The highest mental
development of a physician has not yet been reached, even if he
understands the best and newest methods, is practised in them, and
knows how to draw those rapid conclusions from effects to causes
for which the diagnostics are celebrated; besides this, he must
possess a gift of eloquence that adapts itself to every individual and

draws his heart out of his body; a manliness, the sight of which alone drives away all despondency (the canker of all sick people), the tact and suppleness of a diplomatist in negotiations between such as have need of joy for their recovery and such as, for reasons of health, must (and can) give joy; the acuteness of a detective and an attorney to divine the secrets of a soul without betraying them – in short, a good physician now has need of all the artifices and artistic privileges of every other professional class. Thus equipped, he is then ready to be a benefactor to the whole of society, by increasing good works, mental joys and fertility, by preventing evil thoughts, projects and villainies (the evil source of which is so often the belly), by the restoration of a mental and physical aristocracy (as a maker and hinderer of marriages), by judiciously checking all so-called soul-torments and pricks of conscience. Thus from a 'medicine man' he becomes a saviour, and yet need work no miracle, neither is he obliged to let himself be crucified.

244

In the neighbourhood of insanity – The sum of sensations, knowledge and experiences, the whole burden of culture, therefore, has become so great that an overstraining of nerves and powers of thought is a common danger, indeed the cultivated classes of European countries are throughout neurotic, and almost every one of their great families is on the verge of insanity in one of their branches. True, health is now sought in every possible way; but in the main a diminution of that tension of feeling, of that oppressive burden of culture, is needful, which, even though it might be bought at a heavy sacrifice, would at least give us room for the great hope of a *new Renaissance*. To Christianity, to the philosophers, poets, and musicians we owe an abundance of deeply emotional sensations; in order that these may not get beyond our control we must invoke the spirit of science, which on the whole makes us somewhat colder and more sceptical, and in particular cools the faith in final and absolute truths; it is chiefly through Christianity that it has grown so wild.

245

The bell-founding of culture – Culture has been made like a bell, within a covering of coarser, commoner material, falsehood, violence, the boundless extension of every individual 'I', of every separate people – this was the covering. Is it time to take it off? Has the liquid set, have the good and useful impulses, the habits of the nobler nature become so certain and so general that they no longer require to lean on metaphysics and the errors of religion, no longer have need of hardnesses and violence as powerful bonds between man and man, people and people? No sign from any God can any longer help us to answer this question; our own insight must decide. The earthly rule of man must be taken in hand by man himself, his 'omniscience' must watch over the further fate of culture with a sharp eye.

246

The cyclopes of culture – Whoever has seen those furrowed basins which once contained glaciers, will hardly deem it possible that a time will come when the same spot will be a valley of woods and meadows and streams. It is the same in the history of mankind; the wildest forces break the way, destructively at first, but their activity was nevertheless necessary in order that later on a milder civilisation might build up its house. These terrible energies – that which is called Evil – are the cyclopic architects and road-makers of humanity.

247

The circulation of humanity – It is possible that all humanity is only a phase of development of a certain species of animal of limited duration. Man may have grown out of the ape and will return to the ape again,* without anybody taking an interest in the ending of this curious comedy. Just as with the decline of Roman civilisation and its most important cause, the spread of Christianity, there was a general uglification of man within the Roman Empire, so, through the eventual decline of general culture, there might result a far greater uglification and finally an animalising of man till he reached the ape. But just because we are able to face this prospect, we shall perhaps be able to avert such an end.

* This may remind one of Gobineau's more jocular saying: '*Nous ne descendons pas du singe, mais nous y allons?*' – J. M. K.

248

The consoling speech of a desperate advance – Our age gives the impression of an intermediate condition; the old ways of regarding the world, the old cultures still partially exist, the new are not yet sure and customary and hence are without decision and consistency. It appears as if everything would become chaotic, as if the old were being lost, the new worthless and ever becoming weaker. But this is what the soldier feels who is learning to march; for a time he is more uncertain and awkward, because his muscles are moved sometimes according to the old system and sometimes according to the new, and neither gains a decisive victory. We waver, but it is necessary not to lose courage and give up what we have newly gained. Moreover, we *cannot* go back to the old, we *have* burnt our boats; there remains nothing but to be brave whatever happen – *March ahead*, only get forward! Perhaps our behaviour looks like *progress*; but if not, then the words of Frederick the Great may also be applied to us, and indeed as a consolation: '*Ah, mon cher Sulzer, vous ne connaissez pas assez cette race maudite à laquelle nous appartenons?*'

249

Suffering from past culture – Whoever has solved the problem of culture suffers from a feeling similar to that of one who has inherited unjustly-gotten riches, or of a prince who reigns thanks to the violence of his ancestors. He thinks of their origin with grief and is often ashamed, often irritable. The whole sum of strength, joy, vigour, which he devotes to his possessions, is often balanced by a deep weariness, he cannot forget their origin. He looks despondingly at the future; he knows well that his successors will suffer from the past as he does.

250

Manners – Good manners disappear in proportion as the influence of a Court and an exclusive aristocracy lessens; this decrease can be plainly observed from decade to decade by those who have an eye for public behaviour, which grows visibly more vulgar. No one any longer knows how to court and flatter intelligently; hence arises the ludicrous fact that in cases where we *must* render actual homage (to a great statesman or artist, for instance), the words of deepest feeling, of simple, peasant-like honesty, have to be borrowed, owing to the embarrassment resulting from the lack of grace and wit. Thus the public ceremonious meeting of men appears ever more clumsy, but more full of feeling and honesty without really being so. But must there always be a decline in manners? It appears to me, rather, that manners take a deep curve and that we are approaching their lowest point. When society has become sure of its intentions and principles, so that they have a moulding effect (the manners we have learnt from former moulding conditions are now inherited and always more weakly learnt), there will then be company manners, gestures and social expressions, which must appear as necessary and simply natural because they are intentions and principles. The better division of time and work, the gymnastic exercise transformed into the accompaniment of all beautiful leisure, increased and severer meditation, which brings wisdom and suppleness even to the body, will bring all this in its train. Here, indeed, we might think with a smile of our scholars, and consider whether, as a matter of fact, they who wish to be regarded as the forerunners of that new culture are distinguished by their better manners? This is hardly the case; although their spirit may be willing enough their flesh is weak. The past of culture is still too powerful in their muscles, they still stand in a fettered position, and are half worldly priests and half dependent educators of the upper classes, and besides this they have been rendered crippled and lifeless by the pedantry of science and by antiquated, spiritless methods. In any case, therefore, they are physically, and often three-fourths mentally, still the courtiers of an old, even antiquated culture, and as such are themselves antiquated; the new spirit that occasionally inhabits these old dwellings often serves only to make them more uncertain and frightened. In them there dwell the ghosts of the past as well as the ghosts of the future; what wonder if they do not wear the best expression or show the most pleasing behaviour?

251

The future of science – To him who works and seeks in her, Science gives much pleasure – to him who *learns* her facts, very little. But as all important truths of science must gradually become common-place and everyday matters, even this small amount of pleasure ceases, just as we have long ceased to take pleasure in learning the admirable multiplication table. Now if Science goes on giving less pleasure in herself, and always takes more pleasure in throwing suspicion on the consolations of metaphysics, religion and art, that greatest of all sources of pleasure, to which mankind owes almost its whole humanity, becomes impoverished. Therefore a higher culture must give man a double brain, two brain-chambers, so to speak, one to feel science and the other to feel non-science, which can lie side by side, without con-fusion, divisible, exclusive; this is a necessity of health. In one part lies the source of strength, in the other lies the regulator; it must be heated with illusions, onesidednesses, passions; and the malicious and dangerous consequences of over-heating must be averted by the help of conscious Science. If this necessity of the higher culture is not satisfied, the further course of human development can almost certainly be foretold: the interest in what is true ceases as it guarantees less pleasure; illusion, error, and imagination reconquer step by step the ancient territory, because they are united to pleasure; the ruin of science: the relapse into barbarism is the next result; mankind must begin to weave its web afresh after having, like Penelope, destroyed it during the night. But who will assure us that it will always find the necessary strength for this?

252

The pleasure in discernment – Why is discernment, that essence of the searcher and the philosopher, connected with pleasure? Firstly, and above all, because thereby we become conscious of our strength, for the same reason that gymnastic exercises, even without spectators, are enjoyable. Secondly, because in the course of knowledge we surpass older ideas and their representatives, and become, or believe ourselves to be, conquerors. Thirdly, because even a very little new knowledge exalts us above *every one*, and makes us feel we are the only ones who know the subject aright. These are the three most important reasons of the pleasure, but there are many others, according to the nature of the discerner. A not inconsiderable index of such is given, where no one would look for it, in a passage of my parenetic work on Schopenhauer,* with the arrangement of which every experienced servant of knowledge may be satisfied, even though he might wish to dispense with the ironical touch that seems to pervade those pages. For if it be true that for the making of a scholar 'a number of very human impulses and desires must be thrown together', that the scholar is indeed a very noble but not a pure metal, and 'consists of a confused blending of very different impulses and attractions,' the same thing may be said equally of the making and nature of the artist, the philosopher and the moral genius and whatever glorified great names there may be in that list. *Everything* human deserves ironical consideration with respect to its origin, therefore irony is so *superfluous* in the world.

253

Fidelity as a proof of validity – It is a perfect sign of a sound theory if during *forty years* its originator does not mistrust it; but I maintain that there has never yet been a philosopher who has not eventually deprecated the philosophy of his youth. Perhaps, however, he has not spoken publicly of this change of opinion, for reasons of ambition, or, what is more probable in noble natures, out of delicate consideration for his adherents.

254

The increase of what is interesting – In the course of higher education everything becomes interesting to man, he knows how to find the instructive side of a thing quickly and to put his finger on the place where it can fill up a gap in his ideas, or where it may verify a thought. Through this boredom disappears more and more, and so does excessive excitability of temperament. Finally he moves among men like a botanist among plants, and looks upon himself as a phenomenon, which only greatly excites his discerning instinct.

255

The superstition of the simultaneous – Simultaneous things hold together, it is said. A relative dies far away, and at the same time we

* This refers to his essay, 'Schopenhauer as Educator', in *Thoughts Out of Season*, vol. ii. of the English edition. – J. M. K.

dream about him – Consequently! But countless relatives die and we do not dream about them. It is like shipwrecked people who make vows; afterwards, in the temples, we do not see the votive tablets of those who perished. A man dies, an owl hoots, a clock stops, all at one hour of the night – must there not be some connection? Such an intimacy with nature as this supposition implies is flattering to mankind. This species of superstition is found again in a refined form in historians and delineators of culture, who usually have a kind of hydrophobic horror of all that senseless mixture in which individual and national life is so rich.

256

Action and not knowledge exercised by science – The value of strictly pursuing science for a time does not lie precisely in its results, for these, in proportion to the ocean of what is worth knowing, are but an infinitesimally small drop. But it gives an additional energy, decisiveness, and toughness of endurance; it teaches how to attain an *aim suitably*. In so far it is very valuable, with a view to all that is done later on, to have once been a scientific man.

257

The youthful charm of science – The search for truth still retains the charm of being in strong contrast to gray and now tiresome error; but this charm is gradually disappearing. It is true we still live in the youthful age of science and are accustomed to follow truth as a lovely girl; but how will it be when one day she becomes an elderly, ill-tempered looking woman? In almost all sciences the fundamental knowledge is either found in earliest times or is still being sought; what a different attraction this exerts compared to that time when everything essential has been found and there only remains for the seeker a scanty gleaning (which sensation may be learnt in several historical disciplines).

258

The statue of humanity – The genius of culture fares as did Cellini when his statue of Perseus was being cast; the molten mass threatened to run short, but it *had* to suffice, so he flung in his plates and dishes, and whatever else his hands fell upon. In the same way genius flings in errors, vices, hopes, ravings, and other things of

5. THE SIGNS OF HIGHER AND LOWER CULTURE 151

baser as well as of nobler metal, for the statue of humanity must emerge and be finished; what does it matter if commoner material is used here and there?

259

A male culture – The Greek culture of the classic age is a male culture. As far as women are concerned, Pericles expresses everything in the funeral speech: 'They are best when they are as little spoken of as possible amongst men.' The erotic relation of men to youths was the necessary and sole preparation, to a degree unattainable to our comprehension, of all manly education (pretty much as for a long time all higher education of women was only attainable through love and marriage). All idealism of the strength of the Greek nature threw itself into that relation, and it is probable that never since have young men been treated so attentively, so lovingly, so entirely with a view to their welfare (*virtus*) as in the fifth and sixth centuries B.C. according to the beautiful saying of Hölderlin: '*denn liebend giebt der Sterbliche vom Besten.*'* The higher the light in which this relation was regarded, the lower sank intercourse with woman; nothing else was taken into consideration than the production of children and lust; there was no intellectual intercourse, not even real love-making. If it be further remembered that women were even excluded from contests and spectacles of every description, there only remain the religious cults as their sole higher occupation. For although in the tragedies Electra and Antigone were represented, this was only *tolerated* in art, but not liked in real life – just as now we cannot endure anything pathetic in *life* but like it in art. The women had no other mission than to produce beautiful, strong bodies, in which the father's character lived on as unbrokenly as possible, and therewith to counteract the increasing nerve-tension of such a highly developed culture. This kept the Greek culture young for a relatively long time; for in the Greek mothers the Greek genius always returned to nature.

260

The prejudice in favour of greatness – It is clear that men overvalue everything great and prominent. This arises from the conscious or unconscious idea that they deem it very useful when one

* For it is when loving that mortal man gives of his best. – J. M. K.

person throws all his strength into one thing and makes himself into a monstrous organ. Assuredly, an *equal* development of all his powers is more useful and happier for man; for every talent is a vampire which sucks blood and strength from other powers, and an exaggerated production can drive the most gifted almost to madness. Within the circle of the arts, too, extreme natures excite far too much attention; but a much lower culture is necessary to be captivated by them. Men submit from habit to everything that seeks power.

261

The tyrants of the mind – It is only where the ray of myth falls that the life of the Greeks shines; otherwise it is gloomy. The Greek philosophers are now robbing themselves of this myth; is it not as if they wished to quit the sunshine for shadow and gloom? Yet no plant avoids the light; and, as a matter of fact, those philosophers were only seeking a *brighter* sun; the myth was not pure enough, not shining enough for them. They found this light in their knowledge, in that which each of them called his 'truth'. But in those times knowledge shone with a greater glory; it was still young and knew but little of all the difficulties and dangers of its path; it could still hope to reach in one single bound the central point of all being, and from thence to solve the riddle of the world. These philosophers had a firm belief in themselves and their 'truth', and with it they over-threw all their neighbours and predecessors; each one was a warlike, violent *tyrant*. The happiness in believing themselves the possessors of truth was perhaps never greater in the world, but neither were the hardness, the arrogance, and the tyranny and evil of such a belief. They were tyrants, they were that, therefore, which every Greek wanted to be, and which every one was if he *was able*. Perhaps Solon alone is an exception; he tells in his poems how he disdained personal tyranny. But he did it for love of his works, of his law-giving; and to be a law-giver is a sublimated form of tyranny. Parmenides also made laws. Pythagoras and Empedocles probably did the same; Anaximander founded a city. Plato was the incarnate wish to become the greatest philosophic law-giver and founder of States; he appears to have suffered terribly over the non-fulfilment of his nature, and towards his end his soul was filled with the bitterest gall. The more the

Greek philosophers lost in power the more they suffered inwardly from this bitterness and malice; when the various sects fought for their truths in the street, then first were the souls of these wooers of truth completely clogged through envy and spleen; the tyrannical element then raged like poison within their bodies. These many petty tyrants would have liked to devour each other; there survived not a single spark of love and very little joy in their own knowledge. The saying that tyrants are generally murdered and that their descendants are short-lived, is true also of the tyrants of the mind. Their history is short and violent, and their after-effects break off suddenly. It may be said of almost all great Hellenes that they appear to have come too late: it was thus with Aeschylus, with Pindar, with Demosthenes, with Thucydides: one generation – and then it is passed for ever. That is the stormy and dismal element in Greek history. We now, it is true, admire the gospel of the tortoises. To think historically is almost the same thing now as if in all ages history had been made according to the theory 'The smallest possible amount in the longest possible time!' Oh! how quickly Greek history runs on! Since then life has never been so extravagant – so unbounded. I cannot persuade myself that the history of the Greeks followed that *natural* course for which it is so celebrated. They were much too variously gifted to be *gradual* in the orderly manner of the tortoise when running a race with Achilles, and that is called natural development. The Greeks went rapidly forward, but equally rapidly downwards; the movement of the whole machine is so intensified that a single stone thrown amid its wheels was sufficient to break it. Such a stone, for instance, was Socrates; the hitherto so wonderfully regular, although certainly too rapid, development of the philosophical science was destroyed in one night. It is no idle question whether Plato, had he remained free from the Socratic charm, would not have discovered a still higher type of the philosophic man, which type is for ever lost to us. We look into the ages before him as into a sculptor's work-shop of such types. The fifth and sixth centuries B.C. seemed to promise something more and higher even than they produced; they stopped short at promising and announcing. And yet there is hardly a greater loss than the loss of a type, of a new, hitherto undiscovered highest *possibility of the philosophic life*. Even of the older type the greater number are badly transmitted; it seems to me that all philosophers, from Thales to Democritus, are remarkably difficult to recognise, but whoever succeeds in imitating these figures walks amongst specimens of the mightiest and purest type. This ability is certainly rare, it was even absent in those later Greeks who occupied themselves with the knowledge of the older philosophy; Aristotle, especially, hardly seems to have had eyes in his head when he stands before these great ones. And thus it appears as if these splendid philosophers had lived in vain, or as if they had only been intended to prepare the quarrelsome and talkative followers of the Socratic schools. As I have said, here is a gap, a break in development; some great misfortune must have happened, and the only statue which might have revealed the meaning and purpose of that great artistic training was either broken or unsuccessful; what actually happened has remained for ever a secret of the workshop.

That which happened amongst the Greeks – namely, that every great thinker who believed himself to be in possession of the absolute truth became a tyrant, so that even the mental history of the Greeks acquired that violent, hasty and dangerous character shown by their political history – this type of event was not therewith exhausted, much that is similar has happened even in more modern times, although gradually becoming rarer and now but seldom showing the pure, naïve conscience of the Greek philosophers. For on the whole, opposition doctrines and scepticism now speak too powerfully, too loudly. The period of mental tyranny is past. It is true that in the spheres of higher culture there must always be a supremacy, but henceforth this supremacy lies in the hands of the *oligarchs of the mind*. In spite of local and political separation they form a cohesive society, whose members *recognise and acknowledge* each other, whatever public opinion and the verdicts of review and newspaper writers who influence the masses may circulate in favour of or against them. Mental superiority, which formerly divided and embittered, nowadays generally *unites*; how could the separate individuals assert themselves and swim through life on their own course, against all currents, if they did not see others like them living here and there under similar conditions, and grasp their hands in the struggle as much against the ochlocratic character of the half mind and half culture as against the occasional attempts to establish a tyranny with the help of the masses? Oligarchs are necessary to each other, they are each other's best joy, they understand their signs, but each is nevertheless free, he fights and conquers in *his* place and perishes rather than submit.

262

Homer – The greatest fact in Greek culture remains this, that Homer became so early Pan-Hellenic. All mental and human freedom to which the Greeks attained is traceable to this fact. At the same time it has actually been fatal to Greek culture, for Homer levelled, inasmuch as he centralised and dissolved the more serious instincts of independence. From time to time there arose from the depths of Hellenism an opposition to Homer; but he always remained victorious. All great mental powers have an oppressing effect as well as a liberating one; but it certainly makes a difference whether it is Homer or the Bible or Science that tyrannises over mankind.

263

Talents – In such a highly developed humanity as the present, each individual naturally has access to many talents. Each has an *inborn talent*, but only in a few is that degree of toughness, endurance, and energy born and trained that he really becomes a talent, *becomes* what he *is* – that is, that he discharges it in works and actions.

264

The witty person either overvalued or undervalued – Unscientific but talented people value every mark of intelligence, whether it be on a true or a false track; above all, they want the person with whom they have intercourse to entertain them with his wit, to spur them on, to inflame them, to carry them away in seriousness and play, and in any case to be a powerful amulet to protect them against boredom. Scientific natures, on the other hand, know that the gift of possessing all manner of notions should be strictly controlled by the scientific spirit: it is not that which shines, deludes and excites, but the often insignificant truth that is the fruit which he knows how to shake down from the tree of knowledge. Like Aristotle, he is not permitted to make any distinction between the 'bores' and the 'wits', his *daemon* leads him through the desert as well as through tropical vegetation, in order that he may only take pleasure in the really actual, tangible, true. In insignificant scholars this produces a general disdain and suspicion of cleverness, and, on the other hand, clever people frequently have an aversion to science, as have, for instance, almost all artists.

265

Sense in school – School has no task more important than to teach strict thought, cautious judgment, and logical conclusions, hence it must pay no attention to what hinders these operations, such as religion, for instance. It can count on the fact that human vagueness, custom, and need will later on unstring the bow of all-too-severe thought. But so long as its influence lasts it should enforce that which is the essential and distinguishing point in man: 'Sense and Science, the *very highest* power of man' – as Goethe judges. The great natural philosopher, Von Baer, thinks that the superiority of all Europeans, when compared to Asiatics, lies in the trained capability of giving reasons for that which they believe, of which the latter are utterly incapable. Europe went to the school of logical and critical thought, Asia still fails to know how to distinguish between truth and fiction, and is not conscious whether its convictions spring from individual observation and systematic thought or from imagination. Sense in the school has made Europe what it is; in the Middle Ages it was on the road to become once more a part and dependent of Asia – forfeiting, therefore, the scientific mind which it owed to the Greeks.

266

The undervalued effect of public-school teaching – The value of a public school is seldom sought in those things which are really learnt there and are carried away never to be lost, but in those things which are learnt and which the pupil only acquires against his will, in order to get rid of them again as soon as possible. Every educated person acknowledges that the reading of the classics, as now practised, is a monstrous proceeding carried on before young people are ripe enough for it by teachers who with every word, often by their appearance alone, throw a mildew on a good author. But therein lies the value, generally unrecognised, of these teachers who speak *the abstract language of the higher culture*, which, though dry and difficult to understand, is yet a sort of higher gymnastics of the brain: and there is value in the constant recurrence in their language of ideas, artistic expressions, methods and allusions which the young people hardly ever hear in the conversations of their relatives and in the street. Even if the pupils only *hear*, their intellect is involuntarily trained to a scientific mode of regarding things. It is not possible to emerge from this discipline entirely untouched by its abstract character, and to remain a simple child of nature.

267

Learning many languages – The learning of many languages fills the memory with words instead of with facts and thoughts, and this is a vessel which, with every person, can only contain a certain limited amount of contents. Therefore the learning of many languages is injurious, inasmuch as it arouses a belief in possessing dexterity and, as a matter of fact, it lends a kind of delusive importance to social intercourse. It is also indirectly injurious in that it opposes the acquirement of solid knowledge and the intention to win the respect of men in an honest way. Finally, it is the axe which is laid to the root of a delicate sense of language in our mother-tongue, which thereby is incurably injured and destroyed. The two nations which produced the greatest stylists, the Greeks and the French, learned no foreign languages. But as human intercourse must always grow more cosmopolitan, and as, for instance, a good merchant in London must now be able to read and write eight languages, the learning of many tongues has certainly become a necessary evil; but which, when finally carried to an extreme, will compel mankind to find a remedy, and in some far-off future there will be a new language, used at first as a language of commerce, then as a language of intellectual intercourse generally, then for all, as surely as some time or other there will be aviation. Why else should philology have studied the laws of languages for a whole century, and have estimated the necessary, the valuable, and the successful portion of each separate language?

268

The war history of the individual – In a single human life that passes through many styles of culture we find that struggle condensed which would otherwise have been played out between two generations, between father and son; the closeness of the relationship *sharpens* this struggle, because each party ruthlessly drags in the familiar inward nature of the other party; and thus this struggle in the single individual becomes most *embittered*; here every new phase disregards the earlier ones with cruel injustice and misunderstanding of their means and aims.

269

A quarter of an hour earlier – A man is found occasionally whose views are beyond his time, but only to such an extent that he anticipates the common views of the next decade. He possesses public opinion before it is public; that is, he has fallen into the arms of a view that deserves to be trivial a quarter of an hour sooner than other people. But his fame is usually far noisier than the fame of those who are really great and prominent.

270

The art of reading – Every strong tendency is one-sided; it approaches the aim of the straight line and, like this, is exclusive, that is, it does not touch many other aims, as do weak parties and natures in their wave-like rolling to-and-fro; it must also be forgiven to philologists that they are one-sided. The restoration and keeping pure of texts, besides their explanation, carried on in common for hundreds of years, has finally enabled the right methods to be found; the whole of the Middle Ages was absolutely incapable of a strictly philological explanation, that is, of the simple desire to comprehend what an author says – it was an achievement, finding these methods, let it not be under-valued! Through this all science first acquired continuity and steadiness, so that the art of reading rightly, which is called philology, attained its summit.

271

The art of reasoning – The greatest advance that men have made lies in their acquisition of the art to *reason rightly*. It is not so very natural, as Schopenhauer supposes when he says, 'All are capable of reasoning, but few of judging,' it is learnt late and has not yet attained supremacy. False conclusions are the rule in older ages; and the mythologies of all peoples, their magic and their superstition, their religious cult and their law are the inexhaustible sources of proof of this theory.

272

Phases of individual culture – The strength and weakness of mental productiveness depend far less on inherited talents than on the accompanying amount of *elasticity*. Most educated young people of thirty turn round at this solstice of their lives and are afterwards disinclined for new mental turnings. Therefore, for the salvation of a constantly increasing culture, a new generation is immediately necessary, which will not do very much either, for in order to come up with the father's culture the son must exhaust almost all the inherited energy which the father himself possessed at that stage of life when his son was born; with the little addition he gets further on (for as here the road is being traversed for the second time progress is a little quicker; in order to learn that which the father knew, the son does not consume quite so much strength). Men of great elasticity, like Goethe, for instance, get through almost more than four generations in succession would be capable of; but then they advance too quickly, so that the rest of mankind only comes up with them in the next century, and even then perhaps not completely, because the exclusiveness of culture and the consecutiveness of development have been weakened by the frequent interruptions. Men catch up more quickly with the ordinary phases of intellectual culture which has been acquired in the course of history. Nowadays they begin to acquire culture as religiously inclined children, and perhaps about their tenth year these sentiments attain to their highest point, and are then changed into weakened forms (pantheism), whilst they draw near to science; they entirely pass by God, immortality, and such-like things, but are overcome by the witchcraft of a metaphysical philosophy. Eventually they find even this unworthy of belief; art, on the contrary, seems to vouchsafe more and more, so that for a time metaphysics is metamorphosed and continues to exist either as a transition to art or as an artistically transfiguring temperament. But the scientific sense grows more imperious and conducts man to natural sciences and history, and particularly to the severest methods of knowledge, whilst art has always a milder and less exacting meaning. All this usually happens within the first thirty years of a man's life. It is the recapitulation of *pensum* for which humanity had laboured perhaps thirty thousand years.

273

Retrograded, not left behind – Whoever, in the present day, still derives his development from religious sentiments, and perhaps lives for some length of time afterwards in metaphysics and art, has assuredly gone back a considerable distance and begins his race with other modern men under unfavourable conditions; he apparently loses time and space. But because he stays in those domains where ardour and energy are liberated and force flows continuously as a volcanic stream out of an inexhaustible source, he goes forward all the more quickly as soon as he has freed himself at the right moment from those dominators; his feet are winged, his breast has learned quieter, longer, and more enduring breathing. He has only retreated in order to have sufficient room to leap; thus something terrible and threatening may lie in this retrograde movement.

274

A portion of our ego as an artistic object – It is a sign of superior culture consciously to retain and present a true picture of certain phases of development which commoner men live through almost thought-lessly and then efface from the tablets of their souls: this is a higher species of the painter's art which only the few understand. For this it is necessary to isolate those phases artificially. Historical studies form the qualification for this painting, for they constantly incite us in regard to a portion of history, a people, or a human life, to imagine for ourselves a quite distinct horizon of thoughts, a certain strength of feelings, the prominence of this or the obscurity of that. Herein consists the historic sense, that out of given instances we can quickly reconstruct such systems of thoughts and feelings, just as we can mentally reconstruct a temple out of a few pillars and remains of walls accidentally left standing. The next result is that we understand our fellow-men as belonging to distinct systems and representatives of different cultures – that is, as necessary, but as changeable; and, again, that we can separate portions of our own development and put them down independently.

275

Cynics and Epicureans – The cynic recognises the connection between the multiplied and stronger pains of the more highly cultivated man and the abundance of requirements; he comprehends, therefore, that the multitude of opinions about what is beautiful, suitable, seemly and pleasing, must also produce very rich sources of enjoyment, but also of displeasure. In accordance with this view he educates himself backwards, by giving up many of these opinions and withdrawing from certain demands of culture; he thereby gains a feeling of freedom and strength; and gradually, when habit has made his manner of life endurable, his sensations of displeasure are, as a matter of fact, rarer and weaker than those of cultivated people, and approach those of the domestic animal; moreover, he experiences everything with the charm of contrast, and – he can also scold to his heart's content; so that thereby he again rises high above the sensation-range of the animal. The Epicurean has the same point of view as the cynic; there is usually only a difference of temperament between them. Then the Epicurean makes use of his higher culture to render himself independent of prevailing opinions, he raises himself above them, whilst the cynic only remains negative. He walks, as it were, in wind-protected, well-sheltered, half-dark paths, whilst over him, in the wind, the tops of the trees rustle and show him how violently agitated is the world out there. The cynic, on the contrary, goes, as it were, naked into the rushing of the wind and hardens himself to the point of insensibility.

276

Microcosm and macrocosm of culture – The best discoveries about culture man makes within himself when he finds two heterogeneous powers ruling therein. Supposing some one were living as much in love for the plastic arts or for music as he was carried away by the spirit of science, and that he were to regard it as impossible for him to end this contradiction by the destruction of one and complete liberation of the other power, there would therefore remain nothing for him to do but to erect around himself such a large edifice of culture that those two powers might both dwell within it, although at different ends, whilst between them there dwelt reconciling, intermediary powers, with predominant strength to quell, in case of need, the rising conflict. But such an edifice of culture in the single individual will bear a great resemblance to the culture of entire periods, and will afford consecutive analogical teaching concerning it. For wherever the great architecture of culture manifested itself it was its mission to compel opposing powers to agree, by means of an overwhelming accumulation of other less unbearable powers, without thereby oppressing and fettering them.

277

Happiness and culture – We are moved at the sight of our childhood's surroundings – the arbour, the church with its graves, the pond and the wood, all this we see again with pain. We are seized with pity for ourselves; for what have we not passed through since then! And everything here is so silent, so eternal, only we are so changed, so moved; we even find a few human beings, on whom Time has sharpened his teeth no more than on an oak tree – peasants, fishermen, woodmen – they are unchanged. Emotion and self-pity at the sight of lower culture is the sign of higher culture; from which the conclusion may be drawn that happiness has certainly not been increased by it. Whoever wishes to reap happiness and comfort in life should always avoid higher culture.

278

The simile of the dance – It must now be regarded as a decisive sign of great culture if some one possesses sufficient strength and flexibility to be as pure and strict in discernment as, in other moments, to be capable of giving poetry, religion, and metaphysics a hundred paces' start and then feeling their force and beauty. Such a position amid two such different demands is very difficult, for science urges the absolute supremacy of its methods, and if this insistence is not yielded to, there arises the other danger of a weak wavering between different impulses. Meanwhile, to cast a glance, in simile at least, on a solution of this difficulty, it may be remembered that *dancing* is not the same as a dull reeling to and fro between different impulses. High culture will resemble a bold dance – wherefore, as has been said, there is need of much strength and suppleness.

279

Of the relieving of life – A primary way of lightening life is the idealisation of all its occurrences; and with the help of painting we should make it quite clear to ourselves what idealising means. The painter requires that the spectator should not observe too closely or too sharply, he forces him back to a certain distance from whence to make his observations; he is obliged to take for granted a fixed distance of the spectator from the picture – he must even suppose an equally certain amount of sharpness of eye in his spectator; in such things he must on no account waver. Every one, therefore, who desires to idealise his life must not look at it too closely, and must always keep his gaze at a certain distance. This was a trick that Goethe, for instance, understood.

280

Aggravation as relief, and vice versa – Much that makes life more difficult in certain grades of mankind serves to lighten it in a higher grade, because such people have become familiar with greater aggravations of life. The contrary also happens; for instance, religion has a double face, according to whether a man looks up to it to relieve him of his burden and need, or looks down upon it as upon fetters laid on him to prevent him from soaring too high into the air.

281

The higher culture is necessarily misunderstood – He who has strung his instrument with only two strings, like the scholars (who, besides the *instinct of knowledge* possess only an acquired *religious* instinct), does not understand people who can play upon more strings. It lies in the nature of the higher, *many-stringed* culture that it should always be falsely interpreted by the lower; an example of this is when art appears as a disguised form of the religious. People who are only religious understand even science as a searching after the religious sentiment, just as deaf mutes do not know what music is, unless it be visible movement.

282

Lamentation – It is, perhaps, the advantages of our epoch that bring with them a backward movement and an occasional undervaluing of the *vita contemplativa*. But it must be acknowledged that our time is poor in the matter of great moralists, that Pascal, Epictetus, Seneca, and Plutarch are now but little read, that work and industry – formerly in the following of the great goddess Health – sometimes appear to rage like a disease. Because time to think and tranquillity in thought are lacking, we no longer ponder over different views, but content ourselves with hating them. With the enormous acceleration of life, mind and eye grow accustomed to a partial and false sight and judgment, and all people are like travellers whose only acquaintance with countries and nations is derived from the railway. An independent and cautious attitude of knowledge is looked upon almost as a kind of madness; the free spirit is brought into disrepute, chiefly through scholars, who miss their thoroughness and ant-like industry in his art of regarding things and would gladly banish him into one single corner of science, while it has the different and higher mission of commanding the battalion rearguard of scientific and learned men from an isolated position, and showing them the ways and aims of culture. A song of lamentation such as that which has just been sung will probably have its own period, and will cease of its own accord on a forcible return of the genius of meditation.

283

The chief deficiency of active people – Active people are usually deficient in the higher activity, I mean individual activity. They are active as officials, merchants, scholars, that is as a species, but not as quite distinct separate and *single* individuals; in this respect they are idle. It is the misfortune of the active that their activity is almost always a little senseless. For instance, we must not ask the money-making banker the reason of his restless activity, it is foolish. The active roll as the stone rolls, according to the stupidity of mechanics. All mankind is divided, as it was at all times and is still, into slaves and freemen; for whoever has not two-thirds of his day for himself is a slave, be he otherwise whatever he likes, statesman, merchant, official, or scholar.

284

In favour of the idle – As a sign that the value of a contemplative life has decreased, scholars now vie with active people in a sort of hurried enjoyment, so that they appear to value this mode of enjoying more than that which really pertains to them, and which, as a matter of fact, is a far greater enjoyment. Scholars are ashamed of *otium*. But there is one noble thing about idleness and idlers. If idleness is really the *beginning* of all vice, it finds itself, therefore, at least in near neighbourhood of all the virtues; the idle man is still a better man than the active. You do not suppose that in speaking of idleness and idlers I am alluding to you, you sluggards?

285

Modern unrest – Modern restlessness increases towards the west, so that Americans look upon the inhabitants of Europe as altogether peace-loving and enjoying beings, whilst in reality they swarm about like wasps and bees. This restlessness is so great that the higher culture cannot mature its fruits, it is as if the seasons followed each other too quickly. For lack of rest our civilisation is turning into a new barbarism. At no period have the active, that is, the restless, been of *more* importance. One of the necessary corrections, therefore, which must be undertaken in the character of humanity is to strengthen the contemplative element on a large scale. But every individual who is quiet and steady in heart and head already has the right to believe that he possesses not only a good temperament, but also a generally useful virtue, and even fulfils a higher mission by the preservation of this virtue.

286

To what extent the active man is lazy – I believe that every one must have his own opinion about everything concerning which opinions are possible, because he himself is a peculiar, unique thing, which assumes towards all other things a new and never hitherto existing attitude. But idleness, which lies at the bottom of the active man's soul, prevents him from drawing water out of his own well. Freedom of opinion is like health; both are individual, and no good general conception can be set up of either of them. That which is necessary for the health of one individual is the cause of disease in another, and many means and ways to the freedom of the spirit are for more highly developed natures the ways and means to confinement.

287

Censor vitae – Alternations of love and hatred for a long period distinguish the inward condition of a man who desires to be free in his judgment of life; he does not forget, and bears everything a grudge, for good and evil. At last, when the whole tablet of his soul is written full of experiences, he will not hate and despise existence, neither will he love it, but will regard it sometimes with a joyful, sometimes with a sorrowful eye, and, like nature, will be now in a summer and now in an autumn mood.

288

The secondary result – Whoever earnestly desires to be free will therewith and without any compulsion lose all inclination for faults and vices; he will also be more rarely overcome by anger and vexation. His will desires nothing more urgently than to discern, and the means to do this, that is, the permanent condition in which he is best able to discern.

289

The value of disease – The man who is bed-ridden often perceives that he is usually ill of his position, business, or society, and through them has lost all self-possession. He gains this piece of knowledge from the idleness to which his illness condemns him.

290

Sensitiveness in the country – If there are no firm, quiet lines on the horizon of his life, a species of mountain and forest line, man's inmost will itself becomes restless, inattentive, and covetous, as is the nature of a dweller in towns; he has no happiness and confers no happiness.

291

Prudence of the free spirits – Free-thinkers, those who live by knowledge alone, will soon attain the supreme aim of their life and their ultimate position towards society and State, and will gladly content themselves, for instance, with a small post or an income that is just sufficient to enable them to live; for they will arrange to live in such a manner that a great change of outward prosperity, even an overthrow of the political order, would not cause an overthrow of their life. To all these things they devote as little energy as possible in order that with their whole accumulated strength, and with a long breath, they may dive into the element of knowledge. Thus they can hope to dive deep and be able to see the bottom. Such a spirit seizes only the point of an event, he does not care for things in the whole breadth and prolixity of their folds, for he does not wish to entangle himself in them. He, too, knows the weekdays of restraint, of dependence and servitude. But from time to time there must dawn for him a Sunday of liberty, otherwise he could not endure life. It is probable that even his love for humanity will be prudent and somewhat short-winded, for he desires to meddle with the world of inclinations and of blindness only as far as is necessary for the purpose of knowledge. He must trust that the genius of justice will say something for its disciple and protégé if accusing voices were to call him poor in love. In his mode of life and thought there is a *refined heroism*, which scorns to offer itself to the great mob-reverence, as its coarser brother does, and passes quietly through and out of the world. Whatever labyrinths it traverses, beneath whatever rocks its stream has occasionally worked its way – when it reaches the light it goes clearly, easily, and almost noiselessly on its way, and lets the sunshine strike down to its very bottom.

292

Forward – And thus forward upon the path of wisdom, with a firm step and good confidence! However you may be situated, serve yourself as a source of experience! Throw off the displeasure at your nature, forgive yourself your own individuality, for in any case you have in yourself a ladder with a hundred steps upon which you can mount to knowledge. The age into which with grief you feel yourself thrown thinks you happy because of this good fortune; it calls out to you that you shall still have experiences which men of later ages will perhaps be obliged to forego. Do not despise the fact of having been religious; consider fully how you have had a genuine access to art. Can you not, with the help of these experiences, follow immense stretches of former humanity with a clearer understanding? Is not that ground which sometimes displeases you so greatly, that ground of clouded thought, precisely the one upon which have grown many of the most glorious fruits of older civilisations? You must have loved religion and art as you loved mother and nurse – otherwise you cannot be wise. But you must be able to see beyond them, to outgrow them; if you remain under their ban you do not understand them. You must also be familiar with history and that cautious play with the balances: 'On the one hand – on the other hand.' Go back, treading in the footsteps made by mankind in its great and painful journey through the desert of the past, and you will learn most surely whither it is that all later humanity never can or may go again. And inasmuch as you wish with all your strength to see in advance how the knots of the future are tied, your own life acquires the value of an instrument and means of knowledge. It is within your power to see that all you have experienced, trials, errors, faults, deceptions, passions, your love and your hope, shall be merged wholly in your aim. This aim is to become a necessary chain of culture-links yourself, and from this necessity to draw a conclusion as to the necessity in the progress of general culture. When your sight has become strong enough to see to the bottom of the dark well of your nature and your knowledge, it is possible that in its mirror you may also behold the far-away visions of future civilisations. Do you think that such a life with such an aim is too wearisome, too empty of all that is agreeable? Then you have still to learn that no honey is sweeter than that of knowledge, and that the overhanging clouds of trouble must be to you as an udder from which you shall draw milk for your refreshment. And only when old age approaches will you rightly perceive how you listened to the voice of nature, that nature which rules the whole world through pleasure; the same life which has its zenith in age has also its zenith in wisdom, in that mild sunshine of a constant mental joyfulness; you meet them both, old age and wisdom, upon one ridge of life – it was thus intended by Nature. Then it is time, and no cause for anger, that the mists of death approach. Towards the light is your last movement; a joyful cry of knowledge is your last sound.

Sixth Division – *Man In Society*

293

Well-meant dissimulation – In intercourse with men a well-meant dissimulation is often necessary, as if we did not see through the motives of their actions.

294

Copies – We not unfrequently meet with copies of prominent persons; and as in the case of pictures, so also here, the copies please more than the originals.

295

The public speaker – One may speak with the greatest appropriateness, and yet so that everybody cries out to the contrary, that is to say, when one does not speak to everybody.

296

Want of confidence – Want of confidence among friends is a fault that cannot be censured without becoming incurable.

297

The art of giving – To have to refuse a gift, merely because it has not been offered in the right way, provokes animosity against the giver.

298

The most dangerous partisan – In every party there is one who, by his far too dogmatic expression of the party-principles, excites defection among the others.

299

Advisers of the sick – Whoever gives advice to a sick person acquires a feeling of superiority over him, whether the advice be accepted or rejected. Hence proud and sensitive sick persons hate advisers more than their sickness.

300

Double nature of equality – The rage for equality may so manifest itself that we seek either to draw all others down to ourselves (by belittling, disregarding, and tripping up), or ourselves and all others upwards (by recognition, assistance, and congratulation).

301

Against embarrassment – The best way to relieve and calm very embarrassed people is to give them decided praise.

302

Preference for certain virtues – We set no special value on the possession of a virtue until we perceive that it is entirely lacking in our adversary.

303

Why we contradict – We often contradict an opinion when it is really only the tone in which it is expressed that is unsympathetic to us.

304

Confidence and intimacy – Whoever proposes to command the intimacy of a person is usually uncertain of possessing his confidence. Whoever is sure of a person's confidence attaches little value to intimacy with him.

305

The equilibrium of friendship – The right equilibrium of friendship in our relation to other men is sometimes restored when we put a few grains of wrong on our own side of the scales.

306

The most dangerous physicians – The most dangerous physicians are those who, like born actors, imitate the born physician with the perfect art of imposture,

307

When paradoxes are permissible – In order to interest clever persons in a theory, it is sometimes only necessary to put it before them in the form of a prodigious paradox.

308

How courageous people are won over – Courageous people are persuaded to a course of action by representing it as more dangerous than it really is.

309

Courtesies – We regard the courtesies shown us by unpopular persons as offences.

310

Keeping people waiting – A sure way of exasperating people and of putting bad thoughts into their heads is to keep them waiting long. That makes them immoral.

311

Against the confidential – Persons who give us their full confidence think they have thereby a right to ours. That is a mistake; people acquire no right through gifts.

312

A mode of settlement – It often suffices to give a person whom we have injured an opportunity to make a joke about us to give him personal satisfaction, and even to make him favourably disposed to us.

313

The vanity of the tongue – Whether man conceals his bad qualities and vices, or frankly acknowledges them, his vanity in either case seeks its advantage thereby, only let it be observed how nicely he distinguishes those from whom he conceals such qualities from those with whom he is frank and honest.

314

Considerate – To have no wish to offend or injure any one may as well be the sign of a just as of a timid nature.

315

Requisite for disputation – He who cannot put his thoughts on ice should not enter into the heat of dispute.

316

Intercourse and pretension – We forget our pretensions when we are always conscious of being amongst meritorious people; being alone implants presumption in us. The young are pretentious, for they associate with their equals, who are all ciphers but would fain have a great significance.

317

Motives of an attack – One does not attack a person merely to hurt and conquer him, but perhaps merely to become conscious of one's own strength.

318

Flattery – Persons who try by means of flattery to put us off our guard in intercourse with them, employ a dangerous expedient, like a sleeping-draught, which, when it does not send the patient to sleep, keeps him all the wider awake.

319

A good letter-writer – A person who does not write books, thinks much, and lives in unsatisfying society, will usually be a good letter-writer.

320

The ugliest of all – It may be doubted whether a person who has travelled much has found anywhere in the world uglier places than those to be met with in the human face.

321

The sympathetic ones – Sympathetic natures, ever ready to help in misfortune, are seldom those that participate in joy; in the happiness of others they have nothing to occupy them, they are superfluous, they do not feel themselves in possession of their superiority, and hence readily show their displeasure.

322

The relatives of a suicide – The relatives of a suicide take it in ill part that he did not remain alive out of consideration for their reputation.

323

Ingratitude foreseen – He who makes a large gift gets no gratitude; for the recipient is already overburdened by the acceptance of the gift.

324

In dull society – Nobody thanks a witty man for politeness when he puts himself on a par with a society in which it would not be polite to show one's wit.

325

The presence of witnesses – We are doubly willing to jump into the water after some one who has fallen in, if there are people present who have not the courage to do so.

326

Being silent – For both parties in a controversy, the most disagreeable way of retaliating is to be vexed and silent; for the aggressor usually regards the silence as a sign of contempt.

327

Friends' secrets – Few people will not expose the private affairs of their friends when at a loss for a subject of conversation.

328

Humanity – The humanity of intellectual celebrities consists in courteously submitting to unfairness in intercourse with those who are not celebrated.

329

The embarrassed – People who do not feel sure of themselves in society seize every opportunity of publicly showing their superiority to close friends, for instance by teasing them.

330

Thanks – A refined nature is vexed by knowing that some one owes it thanks, a coarse nature by knowing that it owes thanks to some one.

331

A sign of estrangement – The surest sign of the estrangement of the opinions of two persons is when they both say something ironical to each other and neither of them feels the irony.

332

Presumption in connection withe merit – Presumption in connection with merit offends us even more than presumption in persons devoid of merit, for merit in itself offends us.

333

Danger in the voice – In conversation we are sometimes confused by the tone of our own voice, and misled to make assertions that do not at all correspond to our opinions.

334

In conversation – Whether in conversation with others we mostly agree or mostly disagree with them is a matter of habit; there is sense in both cases.

335

Fear of our neighbour – We are afraid of the animosity of our neighbour, because we are apprehensive that he may thereby discover our secrets.

336

Distinguishing by blaming – Highly respected persons distribute even their blame in such fashion that they try to distinguish us there-with. It is intended to remind us of their serious interest in us. We misunderstand them entirely when we take their blame literally and protest against it; we thereby offend them and estrange our-selves from them.

337

Indignation at the goodwill of others – We are mistaken as to the extent to which we think we are hated or feared; because, though we ourselves know very well the extent of our divergence from a person, tendency, or party, those others know us only super-ficially, and can, therefore, only hate us superficially. We often meet with goodwill which is inexplicable to us; but when we comprehend it, it shocks us, because it shows that we are not considered with sufficient seriousness or importance.

338

Thwarting vanities – When two persons meet whose vanity is equally great, they have afterwards a bad impression of each other, because each has been so occupied with the impression he wished to produce on the other that the other has made no impression upon him; at last it becomes clear to them both that their efforts have been in vain, and each puts the blame on the other.

339

Improper behaviour as a good sign – A superior mind takes pleasure in the tactlessness, pretentiousness, and even hostility of ambitious youths; it is the vicious habit of fiery horses which have not yet carried a rider, but, in a short time, will be so proud to carry one.

340

When it is advisable to suffer wrong – It is well to put up with accusations without refutation, even when they injure us, when the accuser would see a still greater fault on our part if we contradicted and perhaps even refuted him. In this way, certainly, a person may always be wronged and always have right on his side, and may eventually, with the best conscience in the world, become the most intolerable tyrant and tormentor; and what happens in the individual may also take place in whole classes of society.

341

Too little honoured – Very conceited persons, who have received less consideration than they expected, attempt for a long time to deceive themselves and others with regard to it, and become subtle psychologists in order to make out that they have been amply honoured. Should they not attain their aim, should the veil of deception be torn, they give way to all the greater fury.

342

Primitive conditions re-echoing in speech – By the manner in which people make assertions in their intercourse we often recognise an echo of the times when they were more conversant with weapons than anything else; sometimes they handle their assertions like sharp-shooters using their arms, sometimes we think we hear the whizz and clash of swords, and with some men an assertion crashes down like a stout cudgel. Women, on the contrary, speak like beings who for thousands of years have sat at the loom, plied the needle, or played the child with children.

343

The narrator – He who gives an account of something readily betrays whether it is because the fact interests him, or because he wishes to excite interest by the narration. In the latter case he will exaggerate, employ superlatives, and such like. He then does not usually tell his story so well, because he does not think so much about his subject as about himself.

344

The reciter – He who recites dramatic works makes discoveries about his own character; he finds his voice more natural in certain moods and scenes than in others, say in the pathetic or in the scurrilous, while in ordinary life, perhaps, he has not had the opportunity to exhibit pathos or scurrility.

345

A comedy scene in real life – Some one conceives an ingenious idea on a theme in order to express it in society. Now in a comedy we should hear and see how he sets all sail for that point, and tries to land the company at the place where he can make his remark, how he continuously pushes the conversation towards the one goal, sometimes losing the way, finding it again, and finally arriving at the moment: he is almost breathless – and then one of the company takes the remark itself out of his mouth! What will he do? Oppose his own opinion?

346

Unintentionally discourteous – When a person treats another with unintentional discourtesy – for instance, not greeting him because not recognising him – he is vexed by it, although he cannot reproach his own sentiments; he is hurt by the bad opinion which he has produced in the other person, or fears the consequences of his bad humour, or is pained by the thought of having injured him – vanity, fear, or pity may therefore be aroused; perhaps all three together.

347

A masterpiece of treachery – To express a tantalising distrust of a fellow-conspirator, lest he should betray one, and this at the very moment when one is practising treachery one's self, is a master-piece of wickedness; because it absorbs the other's attention and compels him for a time to act very unsuspiciously and openly, so that the real traitor has thus acquired a free hand.

348

To injure and to be injured – It is far pleasanter to injure and afterwards beg for forgiveness than to be injured and grant for-giveness. He who does the former gives evidence of power and afterwards of kindness of character. The person injured, however, if he does not wish to be considered inhuman, *must* forgive; his enjoyment of the other's humiliation is insignificant on account of this constraint.

349

In a dispute – When we contradict another's opinion and at the same time develop our own, the constant consideration of the other opinion usually disturbs the natural attitude of our own which appears more intentional, more distinct, and perhaps some-what exaggerated.

350

An artifice – He who wants to get another to do something difficult must on no account treat the matter as a problem, but must set forth his plan plainly as the only one possible; and when the adversary's eye betrays objection and opposition he must understand how to break off quickly, and allow him no time to put in a word.

351

Pricks of conscience after social gatherings – Why does our conscience prick us after ordinary social gatherings? Because we have treated serious things lightly, because in talking of persons we have not spoken quite justly or have been silent when we should have spoken, because, sometimes, we have not jumped up and run away – in short, because we have behaved in society as if we belonged to it.

352

We are misjudged – He who always listens to hear how he is judged is always vexed. For we are misjudged even by those who are nearest to us ('who know us best'). Even good friends sometimes vent their ill-humour in a spiteful word; and would they be our friends if they knew us rightly? The judgments of the indifferent wound us deeply, because they sound so impartial, so objective almost. But when we see that some one hostile to us knows us in a concealed point as well as we know ourselves, how great is then our vexation!

353

The tyranny of the portrait – Artists and statesmen, who out of particular features quickly construct the whole picture of a man or an event, are mostly unjust in demanding that the event or person should afterwards be actually as they have painted it; they demand straightway that a man should be just as gifted, cunning, and unjust as he is in their representation of him.

354

Relatives as the best friends – The Greeks, who knew so well what a friend was, they alone of all peoples have a profound and largely philosophical discussion of friendship; so that it is by them firstly (and as yet lastly) that the problem of the friend has been recognised as worthy of solution – these same Greeks have designated *relatives* by an expression which is the superlative of the word 'friend'. This is inexplicable to me.

355

Misunderstood honesty – When any one quotes himself in conversation ('I then said', 'I am accustomed to say'), it gives the impression of presumption; whereas it often proceeds from quite an opposite source; or at least from honesty, which does not wish to deck and adorn the present moment with wit which belongs to an earlier moment.

356

The parasite – It denotes entire absence of a noble disposition when a person prefers to live in dependence at the expense of others, usually with a secret bitterness against them, in order only that he may not be obliged to work. Such a disposition is far more frequent in women than in men, also far more pardonable (for historical reasons).

357

On the altar of reconciliation – There are circumstances under which one can only gain a point from a person by wounding him and becoming hostile; the feeling of having a foe torments him so much that he gladly seizes the first indication of a milder disposition to effect a reconciliation, and offers on the altar of this reconciliation what was formerly of such importance to him that he would not give it up at any price.

358

Presumption in demanding pity – There are people who, when they have been in a rage and have insulted others, demand, firstly, that it shall all be taken in good part; and, secondly, that they shall be pitied because they are subject to such violent paroxysms. So far does human presumption extend.

359

Bait – 'Every man has his price' – that is not true. But perhaps every one can be found a bait of one kind or other at which he will snap. Thus, in order to gain some supporters for a cause, it is only necessary to give it the glamour of being philanthropic, noble, charitable, and self-denying – and to what cause could this glamour not be given! It is the sweetmeat and dainty of *their* soul; others have different ones.

360

The attitude in praising – When good friends praise a gifted person he often appears to be delighted with them out of politeness and goodwill, but in reality he feels indifferent. His real nature is quite unmoved towards them, and will not budge a step on that account out of the sun or shade in which it lies; but people wish to please by praise, and it would grieve them if one did not rejoice when they praise a person.

361

The experience of Socrates – If one has become a master in one thing, one has generally remained, precisely thereby, a complete dunce in most other things; but one forms the very reverse opinion, as was already experienced by Socrates. This is the annoyance which makes association with masters disagreeable.

362

A means of defence – In warring against stupidity, the most just and gentle of men at last become brutal. They are thereby, perhaps, taking the proper course for defence; for the most appropriate argument for a stupid brain is the clenched fist. But because, as has been said, their character is just and gentle, they suffer more by this means of protection than they injure their opponents by it.

363

Curiosity – If curiosity did not exist, very little would be done for the good of our neighbour. But curiosity creeps into the houses of the unfortunate and the needy under the name of duty or of pity. Perhaps there is a good deal of curiosity even in the much-vaunted maternal love.

364

Disappointment in Society – One man wishes to be interesting for his opinions, another for his likes and dislikes, a third for his acquaintances, and a fourth for his solitariness – and they all meet with disappointment. For he before whom the play is performed thinks himself the only play that is to be taken into account.

365

The duel – It may be said in favour of duels and all affairs of honour that if a man has such susceptible feelings that he does not care to live when So-and-so says or thinks this or that about him, he has a right to make it a question of the death of the one or the other. With regard to the fact that he is so susceptible, it is not at all to be remonstrated with; in that matter we are the heirs of the past, of its greatness as well as of its exaggerations, without which no greatness ever existed. So when there exists a code of honour which lets blood stand in place of death, so that the mind is relieved after a regular duel it is a great blessing, because otherwise many human lives would be in danger. Such an institution, moreover, teaches men to be cautious in their utterances and makes intercourse with them possible.

366

Nobleness and gratitude – A noble soul will be pleased to owe gratitude, and will not anxiously avoid opportunities of coming under obligation; it will also be moderate afterwards in the expression of its gratitude; baser souls, on the other hand, are unwilling to be under any obligation, or are afterwards immoderate in their expressions of thanks and altogether too devoted. The latter is, moreover, also the case with persons of mean origin or depressed circumstances; to show *them* a favour seems to them a miracle of grace.

367

Occasions of eloquence – In order to talk well one man needs a person who is decidedly and avowedly his superior to talk to, while another can only find absolute freedom of speech and happy turns of eloquence before one who is his inferior. In both cases the cause is the same; each of them talks well only when he talks *sans gêne* – the one because in the presence of something higher he does not feel the impulse of rivalry and competition, the other because he also lacks the same impulse in the presence of something lower. Now there is quite another type of men, who talk well only when debating, with the intention of conquering. Which of the two types is the more aspiring: the one that talks well from excited ambition, or the one that talks badly or not at all from precisely the same motive?

368

The talent for friendship – Two types are distinguished amongst people who have a special faculty for friendship. The one is ever on the ascent, and for every phase of his development he finds a friend exactly suited to him. The series of friends which he thus acquires is seldom a consistent one, and is sometimes at variance and in contradiction, entirely in accordance with the fact that the later phases of his development neutralise or prejudice the earlier phases. Such a man may jestingly be called a *ladder*. The other type is represented by him who exercises an attractive influence on very different characters and endowments, so that he wins a whole circle of friends; these, however, are thereby brought voluntarily into friendly relations with one another in spite of all differences. Such a man may be called a *circle*, for this homogeneousness of such different temperaments and natures must somehow be typified in him. Furthermore, the faculty for having good friends is greater in many people than the faculty for being a good friend.

369

Tactics in conversation – After a conversation with a person one is best pleased with him when one has had an opportunity of exhibiting one's intelligence and amiability in all its glory. Shrewd people who wish to impress a person favourably make use of this circumstance, they provide him with the best opportunities for making a good joke, and so on in conversation. An amusing conversation might be imagined between two very shrewd persons, each wishing to impress the other favourably, and therefore each throwing to the other the finest chances in conversation, which neither of them accepted, so that the conversation on the whole might turn out spiritless and unattractive because each assigned to the other the opportunity of being witty and charming.

370

Discharge of indignation – The man who meets with a failure attributes this failure rather to the ill-will of another than to fate. His irritated feelings are alleviated by thinking that a person and not a thing is the cause of his failure; for he can revenge himself on persons, but is obliged to swallow down the injuries of fate. Therefore when anything has miscarried with a prince, those about him are accustomed to point out some individual as the ostensible cause, who is sacrificed in the interests of all the courtiers; for otherwise the prince's indignation would vent itself on them all, as he can take no revenge on the Goddess of Destiny herself.

371

Assuming the colours of the environment – Why are likes and dislikes so contagious that we can hardly live near a very sensitive person without being filled, like a hogshead, with his *fors* and *againsts*? In the first place, complete forbearance of judgment is very difficult, and sometimes absolutely intolerable to our vanity; it has the same appearance as poverty of thought and sentiment, or as timidity and unmanliness; and so we are, at least, driven on to take a side, perhaps contrary to our environment, if this attitude gives greater pleasure to our pride. As a rule, however – and this is the second point – we are not conscious of the transition from indifference to liking or disliking, but we gradually accustom ourselves to the sentiments of our environment, and because sympathetic agreement and acquiescence are so agreeable, we soon wear all the signs and party-colours of our surroundings.

372

Irony – Irony is only permissible as a pedagogic expedient, on the part of a teacher when dealing with his pupils; its purpose is to humble and to shame, but in the wholesome way that causes good resolutions to spring up and teaches people to show honour and gratitude, as they would to a doctor, to him who has so treated them. The ironical man pretends to be ignorant, and does it so well that the pupils conversing with him are deceived, and in their firm belief in their own superior knowledge they grow bold and expose all their weak points; they lose their cautiousness and reveal themselves as they are – until all of a sudden the light which they have held up to the teacher's face casts its rays back very humiliatingly upon themselves. Where such a relation as that between teacher and pupil, does not exist, irony is a rudeness and a vulgar conceit. All ironical writers count on the silly species of human beings, who like to feel themselves superior to all others in common with the author himself, whom they look upon as the mouthpiece of their arrogance. Moreover, the habit of irony, like that of sarcasm, spoils the character; it gradually fosters the quality of a malicious superiority; one finally grows like a snappy dog, that has learnt to laugh as well as to bite.

373

Arrogance – There is nothing one should so guard against as the growth of the weed called arrogance, which spoils all one's good harvest; for there is arrogance in cordiality, in showing honour, in kindly familiarity, in caressing, in friendly counsel, in acknowledgment of faults, in sympathy for others – and all these fine things arouse aversion when the weed in question grows up among them. The arrogant man – that is to say, he who desires to appear more than he is *or passes for* – always miscalculates. It is true that he obtains a momentary success, inasmuch as those with whom he is arrogant generally give him the amount of honour that he demands, owing to fear or for the sake of convenience; but they take a bad revenge for it inasmuch as they subtract from the value which they hitherto attached to him just as much as he demands above that amount. There is nothing for which men ask to be paid dearer than for humiliation. The arrogant man can make his really great merit so suspicious and small in the eyes of others that they tread on it with dusty feet. If at all, we should only allow ourselves a *proud* manner where we are quite sure of not being misunderstood and considered as arrogant; as, for instance, with friends and wives. For in social intercourse there is no greater folly than to acquire a reputation for arrogance; it is still worse than not having learnt to deceive politely.

374

Tête-à-tête – Private conversation is the perfect conversation, because everything the one person says receives its particular colouring, its tone, and its accompanying gestures *out of strict consideration for the other person* engaged in the conversation; it therefore corresponds to what takes place in intercourse by letter, viz., that one and the same person exhibits ten kinds of psychical expression, according as he writes now to this individual and now to that one. In duologue there is only a single refraction of thought; the person conversed with produces it, as the mirror in whom we want to behold our thoughts anew in their finest form. But how is it when there are two or three, or even more persons conversing with one? Conversation then necessarily loses something of its individualising subtlety, different considerations thwart and neutralise each other; the style which pleases one does not suit the taste of another. In intercourse with several individuals a person is therefore to withdraw within himself and represent facts as they are; but he has also to remove from the subjects the pulsating ether of humanity which makes conversation one of the pleasantest things in the world. Listen only to the tone in which those who mingle with whole groups of men are in the habit of speaking; it is as if the fundamental base of all speech were, 'It is *myself*, *I* say this, so make what you will of it!' That is the reason why clever ladies usually leave a singular, painful, and forbidding impression on those who have met them in society; it is the talking to many people, before many people, that robs them of all intellectual amiability and shows only their conscious dependence on themselves, their tactics, and their intention of gaining a public victory in full light; whilst in a private conversation the same ladies become womanly again, and recover their intellectual grace and charm.

375

Posthumous fame – There is sense in hoping for recognition in a distant future only when we take it for granted that mankind will remain essentially unchanged, and that whatever is great is not for one age only but will be looked upon as great for all time. But this is an error. In all their sentiments and judgments concerning what is good and beautiful mankind have greatly changed; it is mere fantasy to imagine one's self to be a mile ahead, and that the whole of mankind is coming our way. Besides, a scholar who is misjudged may at present reckon with certainty that his discovery will be made by others, and that, at best, it will be allowed to him later on by some historian that he also already knew this or that but was not in a position to secure the recognition of his knowledge. Not to be recognised is always interpreted by posterity as lack of power. In short, one should not so readily speak in favour of haughty solitude. There are, however, exceptional cases; but it is chiefly our faults, weakness, and follies that hinder the recognition of our great qualities.

376

Of friends – Just consider with thyself how different are the feelings, how divided are the opinions of even the nearest acquaintances;

how even the same opinions in thy friend's mind have quite a different aspect and strength from what they have in thine own; and how manifold are the occasions which arise for misunderstanding and hostile severance. After all this thou wilt say to thyself, 'How insecure is the ground upon which all our alliances and friendships rest, how liable to cold downpours and bad weather, how lonely is every creature!' When a person recognises this fact, and, in addition, that all opinions and the nature and strength of them in his fellow-men are just as necessary and irresponsible as their actions; when his eye learns to see this internal necessity of opinions, owing to the indissoluble interweaving of character, occupation, talent, and environment – he will perhaps get rid of the bitterness and sharpness of the feeling with which the sage exclaimed, 'Friends, there are no friends!' Much rather will he make the confession to himself: – Yes, there are friends, but they were drawn towards thee by error and deception concerning thy character; and they must have learnt to be silent in order to remain thy friends; for such human relationships almost always rest on the fact that some few things are never said, are never, indeed, alluded to; but if these pebbles are set rolling friendship follows afterwards and is broken. Are there any who would not be mortally injured if they were to learn what their most intimate friends really knew about them? By getting a knowledge of ourselves, and by looking upon our nature as a changing sphere of opinions and moods, and thereby learning to despise ourselves a little, we recover once more our equilibrium with the rest of mankind. It is true that we have good reason to despise each of our acquaintances, even the greatest of them; but just as good reason to turn this feeling against ourselves. And so we will bear with each other, since we bear with ourselves; and perhaps there will come to each a happier hour, when he will exclaim:

'Friends, there are really no friends!' thus cried th' expiring old
    sophist;
'Foes, there is really no foe!' – thus shout I, the incarnate fool.

377

The perfect woman – The perfect woman is a higher type of humanity than the perfect man, and also something much rarer. The natural history of animals furnishes grounds in support of this theory.

378

Friendship and marriage – The best friend will probably get the best wife, because a good marriage is based on talent for friendship.

379

The survival of the parents – The undissolved dissonances in the relation of the character and sentiments of the parents survive in the nature of the child and make up the history of its inner sufferings.

380

Inherited from the mother – Every one bears within him an image of woman, inherited from his mother: it determines his attitude towards women as a whole, whether to honour, despise, or remain generally indifferent to them.

381

Correcting nature – Whoever has not got a good father should procure one.

382

Fathers and sons – Fathers have much to do to make amends for having sons.

383

The error of gentlewomen – Gentlewomen think that a thing does not really exist when it is not possible to talk of it in society.

384

A male disease – The surest remedy for the male disease of self-contempt is to be loved by a sensible woman.

385

A species of jealousy – Mothers are readily jealous of the friends of sons who are particularly successful. As a rule a mother loves *herself* in her son more than the son.

386

Rational irrationality – In the maturity of life and intelligence the feeling comes over a man that his father did wrong in begetting him.

387

Maternal excellence – Some mothers need happy and honoured children, some need unhappy ones – otherwise they cannot exhibit their maternal excellence.

388

Different sighs – Some husbands have sighed over the elopement of their wives, the greater number, however, have sighed because nobody would elope with theirs.

389

Love matches – Marriages which are contracted for love (so-called love-matches) have error for their father and need (necessity) for their mother.

390

Women's friendships – Women can enter into friendship with a man perfectly well; but in order to maintain it the aid of a little physical antipathy is perhaps required.

391

Ennui – Many people, especially women, never feel ennui because they have never learnt to work properly.

392

An element of love – In all feminine love something of maternal love also comes to light.

393

Unity of place and drama – If married couples did not live together, happy marriages would be more frequent.

394

The usual consequences of marriage – All intercourse which does not elevate a person, debases him, and *vice versa*; hence men usually sink a little when they marry, while women are somewhat elevated. Over-intellectual men require marriage in proportion as they are opposed to it as to a repugnant medicine.

395

Learning to command – Children of unpretentious families must be taught to command, just as much as other children must be taught to obey.

396

Wanting to be in love – Betrothed couples who have been matched by convenience often exert themselves *to fall in love*, to avoid the reproach of cold, calculating expediency. In the same manner those who become converts to Christianity for their advantage exert themselves to become genuinely pious, because the religious cast of countenance then becomes easier to them.

397

No standing still in love – A musician who *loves* the slow *tempo* will play the same pieces ever more slowly. There is thus no standing still in any love.

398

Modesty – Women's modesty usually increases with their beauty.*

399

Marriage on a good basis – A marriage in which each wishes to realise an individual aim by means of the other will stand well; for

* The opposite of this aphorism also holds good. – J. M. K.

instance, when the woman wishes to become famous through the man and the man beloved through the woman.

400

Proteus-nature – Through love women actually become what they appear to be in the imagination of their lovers.

401

To love and to possess – As a rule women love a distinguished man to the extent that they wish to possess him exclusively. They would gladly keep him under lock and key, if their vanity did not forbid, but vanity demands that he should also appear distinguished before others.

402

The test of a good marriage – The goodness of a marriage is proved by the fact that it can stand an 'exception'.

403

Bringing anyone round to anything – One may make any person so weak and weary by disquietude, anxiety, and excess of work or thought that he no longer resists anything that appears complicated, but gives way to it – diplomatists and women know this.

404

Propriety and honesty – Those girls who mean to trust exclusively to their youthful charms for their provision in life, and whose cunning is further prompted by worldly mothers, have just the same aims as courtesans, only they are wiser and less honest.

405

Masks – There are women who, wherever one examines them, have no inside, but are mere masks. A man is to be pitied who has connection with such almost spectre-like and necessarily unsatisfactory creatures, but it is precisely such women who know how to excite a man's desire most strongly; he seeks for their soul, and seeks evermore.

406

Marriage as a long talk – In entering on a marriage one should ask one's self the question, 'Do you think you will pass your time well with this woman till your old age?' All else in marriage is transitory; talk, however, occupies most of the time of the association.

407

Girlish dreams – Inexperienced girls flatter themselves with the notion that it is in their power to make a man happy; later on they learn that it is equivalent to underrating a man to suppose that he needs only a girl to make him happy. Women's vanity requires a man to be something more than merely a happy husband.

408

The dying-out of Faust and Marguerite – According to the very intelligent remark of a scholar, the educated men of modern Germany resemble somewhat a mixture of Mephistopheles and Wagner, but are not at all like Faust, whom our grandfathers (in their youth at least) felt agitating within them. To them, therefore – to continue the remark – Marguerites are not suited, for two reasons. And because the latter are no longer desired they seem to be dying out.

409

Classical education for girls – For goodness sake let us not give our classical education to girls! An education which, out of ingenious, inquisitive, ardent youths, so frequently makes – copies of their teacher!

410

Without rivals – Women readily perceive in a man whether his soul has already been taken possession of; they wish to be loved without rivals, and find fault with the objects of his ambition, his political tasks, his sciences and arts, if he have a passion for such things. Unless he be distinguished thereby – then, in the case of a love-relationship between them, women look at the same time for an increase of *their own* distinction; under such circumstances, they favour the lover.

411

The feminine intellect – The intellect of women manifests itself as perfect mastery, presence of mind, and utilisation of all advantages. They transmit it as a fundamental quality to their children, and the father adds thereto the darker background of the will. His influence determines as it were the rhythm and harmony with which the new life is to be performed; but its melody is derived from the mother. For those who know how to put a thing properly: women have intelligence, men have character and passion. This does not contradict the fact that men actually achieve so much more with their intelligence: they have deeper and more powerful impulses; and it is these which carry their understanding (in itself something passive) to such an extent. Women are often silently surprised at the great respect men pay to their character. When, therefore, in the choice of a partner men seek specially for a being of deep and strong character, and women for a being of intelligence, brilliancy, and presence of mind, it is plain that at bottom men seek for the ideal man, and women for the ideal woman – consequently not for the complement but for the completion of their own excellence.

412

Hesiod's opinion confirmed – It is a sign of women's wisdom that they have almost always known how to get themselves supported, like drones in a bee-hive. Let us just consider what this meant originally, and why men do not depend upon women for their support. Of a truth it is because masculine vanity and reverence are greater than feminine wisdom; for women have known how to secure for themselves by their subordination the greatest advantage, in fact, the upper hand. Even the care of children may originally have been used by the wisdom of women as an excuse for withdrawing themselves as much as possible from work. And at present they still understand when they are really active (as housekeepers, for instance) how to make a bewildering fuss about it, so that the merit of their activity is usually ten times over-estimated by men.

413

Lovers as short-sighted people — A pair of powerful spectacles has sometimes sufficed to cure a person in love; and whoever has had sufficient imagination to represent a face or form twenty years older, has probably gone through life not much disturbed.

414

Women in hatred — In a state of hatred women are more dangerous than men; for one thing, because they are hampered by no regard for fairness when their hostile feelings have been aroused, but let their hatred develop unchecked to its utmost consequences; then also, because they are expert in finding sore spots (which every man and every party possess), and pouncing upon them: for which purpose their dagger-pointed intelligence is of good service (whilst men, hesitating at the sight of wounds, are often generously and conciliatorily inclined).

415

Love — The love idolatry which women practise is fundamentally and originally an intelligent device, inasmuch as they increase their power by all the idealisings of love and exhibit themselves as so much the more desirable in the eyes of men. But by being accustomed for centuries to this exaggerated appreciation of love, it has come to pass that they have been caught in their own net and have forgotten the origin of the device. They themselves are now still more deceived than the men, and on that account also suffer more from the disillusionment which, almost necessarily, enters into the life of every woman — so far, at any rate, as she has sufficient imagination and intelligence to be able to be deceived and undeceived.

416

The emancipation of women — Can women be at all just, when they are so accustomed to love and to be immediately biased for or against? For that reason they are also less interested in things and more in individuals: but when they are interested in things they immediately become their partisans, and thereby spoil their pure, innocent effect. Thus there arises a danger, by no means small, in entrusting politics and certain portions of science to them (history, for instance). For what is rarer than a woman who really knows what science is? Indeed the best of them cherish in their breasts a secret scorn for science, as if they were somehow superior to it. Perhaps all this can be changed in time; but meanwhile it is so.

417

The inspiration in women's judgments – The sudden decisions, for or against, which women are in the habit of making, the flashing illumination of personal relations caused by their spasmodic inclinations and aversions, in short, the proofs of feminine injustice have been invested with a lustre by men who are in love, as if all women had inspirations of wisdom, even without the Delphic cauldron and the laurel wreaths; and their utterances are interpreted and duly set forth as Sibylline oracles for long afterwards. When one considers, however, that for every person and for every cause something can be said in favour of it but equally also something against it, that things are not only two-sided, but also three- and four-sided, it is almost difficult to be entirely at fault in such sudden decisions; indeed, it might be said that the nature of things has been so arranged that women should always carry their point.*

418

Being loved – As one of every two persons in love is usually the one who loves, the other the one who is loved, the belief has arisen that in every love-affair there is a constant amount of love; and that the more of it the one person monopolises the less is left for the other. Exceptionally it happens that the vanity of each of the parties persuades him or her that it is *he* or *she* who must be loved; so that both of them wish to be loved: from which cause many half funny, half absurd scenes take place, especially in married life.

419

Contradictions in feminine minds – Owing to the fact that women are so much more personal than objective, there are tendencies

* It may be remarked that Nietzsche changed his view on this subject later on, and ascribed more importance to woman's intuition. cf. also Disraeli's reference to the 'High Priestesses of predestination'. – J. M. K.

included in the range of their ideas which are logically in contradiction to one another; they are accustomed in turn to become enthusiastically fond just of the representatives of these tendencies and accept their systems in the lump; but in such wise that a dead place originates wherever a new personality afterwards gets the ascendancy. It may happen that the whole philosophy in the mind of an old lady consists of nothing but such dead places.

420

Who suffers the more? – After a personal dissension and quarrel between a woman and a man the latter party suffers chiefly from the idea of having wounded the other, whilst the former suffers chiefly from the idea of not having wounded the other sufficiently; so she subsequently endeavours by tears, sobs, and discomposed mien, to make his heart heavier.

421

An opportunity for feminine magnanimity – If we could disregard the claims of custom in our thinking we might consider whether nature and reason do not suggest several marriages for men, one after another: perhaps that, at the age of twenty-two, he should first marry an older girl who is mentally and morally his superior, and can be his leader through all the dangers of the twenties (ambition, hatred, self-contempt, and passions of all kinds). This woman's affection would subsequently change entirely into maternal love, and she would not only submit to it but would encourage the man in the most salutary manner, if in his thirties he contracted an alliance with quite a young girl whose education he himself should take in hand. Marriage is a necessary institution for the twenties; a useful, but not necessary, institution for the thirties; for later life it is often harmful, and promotes the mental deterioration of the man.

422

The tragedy of childhood – Perhaps it not infrequently happens that noble men with lofty aims have to fight their hardest battle in childhood; by having perchance to carry out their principles in opposition to a base-minded father addicted to feigning and falsehood, or living, like Lord Byron, in constant warfare with a childish and passionate mother. He who has had such an experience will never be able to forget all his life who has been his greatest and most dangerous enemy.

423

Parental folly – The grossest mistakes in judging a man are made by his parents; this is a fact, but how is it to be explained? Have the parents too much experience of the child and cannot any longer arrange this experience into a unity? It has been noticed that it is only in the earlier period of their sojourn in foreign countries that travellers rightly grasp the general distinguishing features of a people; the better they come to know it, they are the less able to see what is typical and distinguishing in a people. As soon as they grow short-sighted their eyes cease to be long-sighted. Do parents, therefore, judge their children falsely because they have never stood far enough away from them? The following is quite another explanation: people are no longer accustomed to reflect on what is close at hand and surrounds them, but just accept it. Perhaps the usual thoughtlessness of parents is the reason why they judge so wrongly when once they are compelled to judge their children.

424

The future of marriage – The noble and liberal-minded women who take as their mission the education and elevation of the female sex, should not overlook one point of view: marriage regarded in its highest aspect, as the spiritual friendship of two persons of opposite sexes, and accordingly such as is hoped for in future, contracted for the purpose of producing and educating a new generation – such marriage, which only makes use of the sensual, so to speak, as a rare and occasional means to a higher purpose, will, it is to be feared, probably need a natural auxiliary, namely, *concubinage*. For if, on the grounds of his health, the wife is also to serve for the sole satisfaction of the man's sexual needs, a wrong perspective, opposed to the aims indicated, will have most influence in the choice of a wife. The aims referred to, the production of descendants, will be accidental, and their successful education highly improbable. A good wife, who has to be friend, helper, child-bearer, mother, family-head and manager, and has even perhaps to conduct her own business and affairs separately from those of the husband, cannot at the same time be a concubine; it would, in general, be asking too much of her. In the future, therefore, a state of things might take place the opposite of what existed at Athens in the time of Pericles; the men, whose wives were then little more to them than concubines, turned besides to the Aspasias, because they longed for the charms of a companion-ship gratifying both to head and heart, such as the grace and intellectual suppleness of women could alone provide. All human institutions, just like marriage, allow only a moderate amount of practical idealising, failing which coarse remedies immediately become necessary.

425

The 'Storm and Stress' period of women – In the three or four civilised countries of Europe, it is possible, by several centuries of educ-ation, to make out of women anything we like – even men, not in a sexual sense, of course, but in every other. Under such influences they will acquire all the masculine virtues and forces; at the same time, of course, they must also have taken all the masculine weaknesses and vices into the bargain: so much, as has been said, we can command. But how shall we endure the inter-mediate state thereby induced, which may even last two or three centuries, during which feminine follies and injustices, woman's original birthday endowment, will still maintain the ascendancy over all that has been otherwise gained and acquired? This will be the time when indignation will be the peculiar masculine passion; indignation, because all arts and sciences have been overflowed and choked by an unprecedented dilettanteism, philosophy talked to death by brain-bewildering chatter, politics more fantastic and partisan than ever, and society in complete disorganisation, because the conservatrices of ancient customs have become ridiculous to themselves, and have endeavoured in every way to place themselves outside the pale of custom. If indeed women had their greatest power in custom, where will they have to look in order to reacquire a similar plenitude of power after having renounced custom?

426

Free-spirit and marriage – Will free thinkers live with women? In general, I think that, like the prophesying birds of old, like the truth-thinkers and truth-speakers of the present, they must prefer to *fly alone*.

427

The happiness of marriage – Everything to which we are accustomed draws an ever-tightening cobweb-net around us; and presently we notice that the threads have become cords, and that we ourselves sit in the middle like a spider that has here got itself caught and must feed on its own blood. Hence the free spirit hates all rules and customs, all that is permanent and definitive, hence he painfully tears asunder again and again the net around him, though in consequence thereof he will suffer from numerous wounds, slight and severe; for he must break off every thread *from himself*, from his body and soul. He must learn to love where he has hitherto hated, and *vice versa*. Indeed, it must not be a thing impossible for him to sow dragon's teeth in the same field in which he formerly scattered the abundance of his bounty. From this it can be inferred whether he is suited for the happiness of marriage.

428

Too intimate – When we live on too intimate terms with a person it is as if we were again and again handling a good engraving with our fingers; the time comes when we have soiled and damaged paper in our hands, and nothing more. A man's soul also gets worn out by constant handling; at least, it eventually *appears* so to us – never again do we see its original design and beauty. We always lose through too familiar association with women and friends; and some times we lose the pearl of our life thereby.

429

The golden cradle – The free spirit will always feel relieved when he has finally resolved to shake off the motherly care and guardianship with which women surround him. What harm will a rough wind, from which he has been so anxiously protected, do him? Of what consequence is a genuine disadvantage, loss, misfortune, sickness, illness, fault, or folly more or less in his life, compared with the bondage of the golden cradle, the peacock's-feather fan, and the oppressive feeling that he must, in addition, be grateful because he is waited on and spoiled like a baby? Hence it is that the milk which is offered him by the motherly disposition of the women about him can so readily turn into gall.

430

A voluntary victim – There is nothing by which able women can so alleviate the lives of their husbands, should these be great and famous, as by becoming, so to speak, the receptacle for the general disfavour and occasional ill-humour of the rest of mankind. Contemporaries are usually accustomed to overlook many mistakes, follies, and even flagrant injustices in their great men if only they can find some one to maltreat and kill, as a proper victim for the relief of their feelings. A wife not infrequently has the ambition to present herself for this sacrifice, and then the husband may indeed feel satisfied – he being enough of an egoist to have such a voluntary storm-, rain-, and lightning-conductor beside him.

431

Agreeable adversaries – The natural inclination of women towards quiet, regular, happily tuned existences and intercourse, the oil-like and calming effect of their influence upon the sea of life, operates unconsciously against the heroic inner impulse of the free spirit. Without knowing it, women act as if they were taking away the stones from the path of the wandering mineralogist in order that he might not strike his foot against them – when he has gone out for the very purpose of striking against them.

432

The discord of two concords – Woman wants to serve, and finds her happiness therein; the free spirit does not want to be served, and therein finds his happiness.

433

Xantippe – Socrates found a wife such as he required – but he would not have sought her had he known her sufficiently well; even the heroism of his free spirit would not have gone so far. As a matter of fact, Xantippe forced him more and more into his peculiar profession, inasmuch as she made house and home doleful and dismal to him; she taught him to live in the streets and wherever gossiping and idling went on, and thereby made him the greatest Athenian street-dialectician, who had, at last, to compare himself to a gad-fly which a god had set on the neck of the beautiful horse Athens to prevent it from resting.

434

Blind to the future – Just as mothers have senses and eye only for those pains of their children that are evident to the senses and eye, so the wives of men of high aspirations cannot accustom themselves to see their husbands suffering, starving, or slighted – although all this is, perhaps, not only the proof that they have rightly chosen their attitude in life, but even the guarantee that their great aims *must* be achieved some time. Women always intrigue privately against the higher souls of their husbands; they want to cheat them out of their future for the sake of a painless and comfortable present.

435

Authority and freedom – However highly women may honour their husbands, they honour still more the powers and ideas recognised by society; they have been accustomed for millennia to go along with their hands folded on their breasts, and their heads bent before every thing dominant, disapproving of all resistance to public authority. They therefore unintentionally, and as if from instinct, hang themselves as a drag on the wheels of free-spirited, independent endeavour, and in certain circumstances make their husbands highly impatient, especially when the latter persuade themselves that it is really love which prompts the action of their wives. To disapprove of women's methods and generously to honour the motives that prompt them – that is man's nature and often enough his despair.

436

Ceterum censeo – It is laughable when a company of paupers decree the abolition of the right of inheritance, and it is not less laughable when childless persons labour for the practical lawgiving of a country: they have not enough ballast in their ship to sail safely over the ocean of the future. But it seems equally senseless if a man who has chosen for his mission the widest knowledge and estimation of universal existence, burdens himself with personal considerations for a family, with the support, protection, and care of wife and child, and in front of his telescope hangs that gloomy veil through which hardly a ray from the distant firmament can penetrate. Thus I, too, agree with the opinion that in matters of the highest philosophy all married men are to be suspected.

437

Finally – There are many kinds of hemlock, and fate generally finds an opportunity to put a cup of this poison to the lips of the free spirit – in order to 'punish' him, as every one then says. What do the women do about him then? They cry and lament, and perhaps disturb the sunset-calm of the thinker, as they did in the prison at Athens. 'Oh Crito, bid some one take those women away!' said Socrates at last.

438

Asking to be heard – The demagogic disposition and the intention of working upon the masses is at present common to all political parties; on this account they are all obliged to change their principles into great *al fresco* follies and thus make a show of them. In this matter there is no further alteration to be made: indeed, it is superfluous even to raise a finger against it; for here Voltaire's saying applies: '*Quand la populace se mêle de raisonner, tout est perdu.*' Since this has happened we have to accommodate ourselves to the new conditions, as we have to accommodate ourselves when an earthquake has displaced the old boundaries and the contour of the land and altered the value of property. Moreover, when it is once for all a question in the politics of all parties to make life endurable to the greatest possible majority, this majority may always decide what they understand by an endurable life; if they believe their intellect capable of finding the right means to this end, why should we doubt about it? They *want*, once for all, to be the architects of their own good or ill fortune; and if their feeling of free choice and their pride in the five or six ideas that their brain conceals and brings to light, really makes life so agreeable to them that they gladly put up with the fatal consequences of their narrow-mindedness, there is little to object to, provided that their narrow-mindedness does not go so far as to demand that *everything* shall become politics in this sense, that *all* shall live and act according to this standard. For, in the first place, it must be more than ever permissible for some people to keep aloof from politics and to stand somewhat aside. To this they are also impelled by the pleasure of free choice, and connected with this there may even be some little pride in keeping silence when too many, and only the many, are speaking. Then this small group must be excused if they do not attach such great importance to the happiness of the majority (nations or strata of population may be understood thereby), and are occasionally guilty of an ironical grimace; for their seriousness lies elsewhere, their conception of happiness is quite different, and their aim cannot be encompassed by every clumsy hand that has just five fingers. Finally, there comes from time to time – what is certainly most difficult to concede to them, but must also be conceded – a moment when they emerge from their silent solitariness and try once more the strength of their lungs; they then call to each other like people lost in a wood, to make themselves known and for mutual encouragement; whereby, to be sure, much becomes audible that sounds evil to ears for which it is not intended. Soon, however, silence again prevails in the wood, such silence that the buzzing, humming, and fluttering of the countless insects that live in, above, and beneath it, are again plainly heard.

439

Culture and caste – A higher culture can only originate where there are two distinct castes of society: that of the working class, and that of the leisured class who are capable of true leisure; or, more strongly expressed, the caste of compulsory labour and the caste of free labour. The point of view of the division of happiness is not essential when it is a question of the production of a higher culture; in any case, however, the leisured caste is more susceptible to suffering and suffer more, their pleasure in existence is less and their task is greater. Now supposing there should be quite an interchange between the two castes, so that on the one hand the duller and less intelligent families and individuals are lowered from the higher caste into the lower, and, on the other hand, the freer men of the lower caste obtain access to the higher, a condition of things would be attained beyond which one can only perceive the open sea of vague wishes. Thus speaks to us the vanishing voice of the olden time; but where are there still ears to hear it?

440

Of good blood – That which men and women of good blood poss-ess much more than others, and which gives them an undoubted right to be more highly appreciated, are two arts which are always increased by inheritance: the art of being able to command, and the art of proud obedience. Now wherever commanding is the business of the day (as in the great world of commerce and industry), there results something similar to these families of good blood, only the noble bearing in obedience is lacking which is an inheritance from feudal conditions and hardly grows any longer in the climate of our culture.

441

Subordination – The subordination which is so highly valued in military and official ranks will soon become as incredible to us as the secret tactics of the Jesuits have already become; and when this subordination is no longer possible a multitude of astonishing results will no longer be attained, and the world will be all the poorer. It must disappear, for its foundation is disappearing, the belief in unconditional authority, in ultimate truth; even in military ranks physical compulsion is not sufficient to produce it, but only the inherited adoration of the princely as of something superhuman. In *freer* circumstances people subordinate themselves only on conditions, in compliance with a mutual contract, consequently with all the provisos of self-interest.

442

The national army – The greatest disadvantage of the national army, now so much glorified, lies in the squandering of men of the highest civilisation; it is only by the favourableness of all circumstances that there are such men at all; how carefully and anxiously should we deal with them, since long periods are required to create the chance conditions for the production of such delicately organised brains! But as the Greeks wallowed in the blood of Greeks, so do Europeans now in the blood of Europeans: and indeed, taken relatively, it is mostly the highly cultivated who are sacrificed, those who promise an abundant and excellent posterity; for such stand in the front of the battle as commanders, and also expose themselves to most danger, by reason of their higher ambition. At present, when quite other and higher tasks are assigned than *patria* and *honor*, the rough Roman patriotism is either something dishonourable or a sign of being behind the times.

443

Hope as presumption – Our social order will slowly melt away, as all former orders have done, as soon as the suns of new opinions have shone upon mankind with a new glow. We can only wish this melting away in the hope thereof, and we are only reasonably entitled to hope when we believe that we and our equals have more strength in heart and head than the representatives of the existing state of things. As a rule, therefore, this hope will be a presumption, an *over-estimation*.

444

War – Against war it may be said that it makes the victor stupid and the vanquished revengeful. In favour of war it may be said that it barbarises in both its above-named results, and thereby makes more natural; it is the sleep or the winter period of culture; man emerges from it with greater strength for good and for evil.

445

In the prince's service – To be able to act quite regardlessly it is best for a statesman to carry out his work not for himself but for a prince. The eye of the spectator is dazzled by the splendour of this general disinterestedness, so that it does not see the malignancy and severity which the work of a statesman brings with it.*

446

A question of power, not of right – As regards Socialism, in the eyes of those who always consider higher utility, if it is *really* a rising against their oppressors of those who for centuries have been oppressed and downtrodden, there is no problem of *right* involved (notwithstanding the ridiculous, effeminate question, 'How far *ought* we to grant its demands?') but only a problem of *power* ('How far *can* we make use of its demands?'); the same, therefore, as in the case of a natural force – steam, for instance – which is either forced by man into his service, as a machine-god, or which, in case of defects of the machine, that is to say, defects of human calculation in its

---

* This aphorism may have been suggested by Nietzsche's observing the behaviour of his great contemporary, Bismarck, towards the dynasty. – J. M. K.

construction, destroys it and man together. In order to solve this question of power we must know how strong Socialism is, in what modification it may yet be employed as a powerful lever in the present mechanism of political forces; under certain circumstances we should do all we can to strengthen it. With every great force – be it the most dangerous – men have to think how they can make of it an instrument for their purposes. Socialism acquires a *right* only if war seems to have taken place between the two powers, the representatives of the old and the new, when, however, a wise calculation of the greatest possible preservation and advantageousness to both sides gives rise to a desire for a treaty. Without treaty no right. So far, however, there is neither war nor treaty on the ground in question, therefore no rights, no 'ought'.

447

Utilising the most trivial dishonesty – The power of the press consists in the fact that every individual who ministers to it only feels himself bound and constrained to a very small extent. He usually expresses *his* opinion, but sometimes also does *not* express it in order to serve his party or the politics of his country, or even himself. Such little faults of dishonesty, or perhaps only of a dishonest silence, are not hard to bear by the individual, but the consequences are extraordinary, because these little faults are committed by many at the same time. Each one says to himself: 'For such small concessions I live better and can make my income; by the want of such little compliances I make myself impossible.' Because it seems almost morally indifferent to write a line more (perhaps even without signature), or not to write it, a person who has money and influence can make any opinion a public one. He who knows that most people are weak in trifles, and wishes to attain his own ends thereby, is always dangerous.

448

Too loud a tone in grievances – Through the fact that an account of a bad state of things (for instance, the crimes of an administration, bribery and arbitrary favour in political or learned bodies) is greatly exaggerated, it fails in its effect on intelligent people, but has all the greater effect on the unintelligent (who would have remained indifferent to an accurate and moderate account). But as these latter are considerably in the majority, and harbour in themselves stronger will-power and more impatient desire for action, the exaggeration becomes the cause of investigations, punishments, promises, and reorganisations. In so far it is useful to exaggerate the accounts of bad states of things.

449

The apparent weather-makers of politics – Just as people tacitly assume that he who understands the weather, and foretells it about a day in advance, makes the weather, so even the educated and learned, with a display of superstitious faith, ascribe to great statesmen as their most special work all the important changes and conjunctures that have taken place during their administration, when it is only evident that they knew something thereof a little earlier than other people and made their calculations accordingly – thus they are also looked upon as weather-makers – and this belief is not the least important instrument of their power.

450

New and old conceptions of government – To draw such a distinction between Government and people as if two separate spheres of power, a stronger and higher, and a weaker and lower, negotiated and came to terms with each other, is a remnant of transmitted political sentiment, which still accurately represents the historic establishment of the conditions of power in *most* States. When Bismarck, for instance, describes the constitutional system as a compromise between Government and people, he speaks in accordance with a principle which has its reason in history (from whence, to be sure, it also derives its admixture of folly, without which nothing human can exist). On the other hand, we must now learn – in accordance with a principle which has originated only in the *brain* and has still to *make* history – that Government is nothing but an organ of the people, not an attentive, honourable 'higher' in relation to a 'lower' accustomed to modesty. Before we accept this hitherto unhistorical and arbitrary, although logical, formulation of the conception of Government, let us but consider its consequences, for the relation between people and Government is the strongest typical relation, after the pattern of which the relationship between teacher and pupil, master and servants, father and family, leader and soldier, master and apprentice, is unconsciously formed. At present, under the influence of the prevailing constitutional system of government, all these relationships are changing a little – they are becoming compromises. But how they will have to be reversed and shifted, and change name and nature, when that newest of all conceptions has got the upper hand everywhere in people's minds! – to achieve which, however, a century may yet be required. In this matter there is nothing further to be wished for except caution and slow development.

451

Justice as the decoy-cry of parties – Well may noble (if not exactly very intelligent) representatives of the governing classes asseverate: 'We will treat men equally and grant them equal rights'; so far a socialistic mode of thought which is based on *justice* is possible; but, as has been said, only within the ranks of the governing class, which in this case *practises* justice with sacrifices and abnegations. On the other hand, to *demand* equality of rights, as do the Socialists of the subject caste, is by no means the outcome of justice, but of covetousness. If you expose bloody pieces of flesh to a beast, and withdraw them again, until it finally begins to roar, do you think that roaring implies justice?

452

Possession and justice – When the Socialists point out that the division of property at the present day is the consequence of countless deeds of injustice and violence, and, *in summa*, repudiate obligation to anything with so unrighteous a basis, they only perceive something isolated. The entire past of ancient civilisation is built up on violence, slavery, deception, and error; we, however, cannot annul ourselves, the heirs of all these conditions, nay, the concrescences of all this past, and are not entitled to demand the withdrawal of a single fragment thereof. The unjust disposition lurks also in the souls of non-possessors; they are not better than the possessors and have no moral prerogative; for at one time or another their ancestors have been possessors. Not forcible new distributions, but gradual transformations of opinion are necessary; justice in all matters must become greater, the instinct of violence weaker.

453

The helmsman of the passions – The statesman excites public passions in order to have the advantage of the counter-passions thereby aroused. To give an example: a German statesman knows quite well that the Catholic Church will never have the same plans as Russia; indeed, that it would far rather be allied with the Turks than with the former country; he likewise knows that Germany is threatened with great danger from an alliance between France and Russia. If he can succeed, therefore, in making France the focus and fortress of the Catholic Church, he has averted this danger for a lengthy period. He has, accordingly, an interest in showing hatred against the Catholics in transforming, by all kinds of hostility, the supporters of the Pope's authority into an impassioned political power which is opposed to German politics, and must, as a matter of course, coalesce with France as the adversary of Germany; his aim is the catholicising of France, just as necessarily as Mirabeau saw the salvation of his native land in de-catholicising it. The one State, therefore, desires to muddle millions of minds of another State in order to gain advantage thereby. It is the same disposition which supports the republican form of government of a neighbouring State – *le désordre organisé*, as Mérimée says – for the sole reason that it assumes that this form of government makes the nation weaker, more distracted, less fit for war.

454

The dangerous revolutionary spirits – Those who are bent on revolutionising society may be divided into those who seek something for themselves thereby and those who seek something for their children and grandchildren. The latter are the more dangerous, for they have the belief and the good conscience of disinterestedness. The others can be appeased by favours: those in power are still sufficiently rich and wise to adopt that expedient. The danger begins as soon as the aims become impersonal; revolutionists seeking impersonal interests may consider all defenders of the present state of things as personally interested, and may therefore feel themselves superior to their opponents.

455

The political value of paternity – When a man has no sons he has not a full right to join in a discussion concerning the needs of a particular community. A person must himself have staked his dearest object along with the others: that alone binds him fast to the State; he must have in view the well-being of his descendants, and must, therefore, above all, have descendants in order to take a right and natural share in all institutions and the changes thereof. The development of higher morality depends on a person's having sons; it disposes him to be unegoistic, or, more correctly, it extends his egoism in its duration and permits him earnestly to strive after goals which lie beyond his individual lifetime.

456

Pride of descent – A man may be justly proud of an unbroken line of *good* ancestors down to his father – not however of the line itself, for every one has that. Descent from good ancestors constitutes the real nobility of birth; a single break in the chain, one bad ancestor, therefore, destroys the nobility of birth. Every one who talks about his nobility should be asked: 'Have you no violent, avaricious, dissolute, wicked, cruel man amongst your ancestors?' If with good cognisance and conscience he can answer No, then let his friendship be sought.

457

Slaves and labourers – The fact that we regard the gratification of vanity as of more account than all other forms of well-being (security, position, and pleasures of all sorts), is shown to a ludicrous extent by every one wishing for the abolition of slavery and utterly abhorring to put any one into this position (apart altogether from political reasons), while every one must acknowledge to himself that in all respects slaves live more securely and more happily than modern labourers, and that slave labour is very easy labour compared with that of the 'labourer'. We protest in the name of the 'dignity of man' ; but, expressed more simply, that is just our darling vanity which feels non-equality, and inferiority in public estimation, to be the hardest lot of all. The cynic thinks differently concerning the matter, because he despises honour – and so Diogenes was for some time a slave and tutor.

458

Leading minds and their instruments – We see that great statesmen, and in general all who have to employ many people to carry out their plans, sometimes proceed one way and sometimes another; they either choose with great skill and care the people suitable for their plans, and then leave them a comparatively large amount of liberty, because they know that the nature of the persons selected impels them precisely to the point where they themselves would have them go; or else they choose badly, in fact take whatever comes to hand, but out of every piece of clay they form something useful for their purpose. These latter minds are the more high-handed; they also desire more submissive instruments; their knowledge of mankind is usually much smaller, their contempt of mankind greater than in the case of the first mentioned class, but the machines they construct generally work better than the machines from the workshops of the former.

459

Arbitrary law necessary – Jurists dispute whether the most perfectly thought-out law or that which is most easily understood should prevail in a nation. The former, the best model of which is Roman Law, seems incomprehensible to the layman, and is therefore not the expression of his sense of justice. Popular laws, the Germanic, for instance, have been rude, superstitious, illogical, and in part idiotic, but they represented very definite, inherited national morals and sentiments. But where, as with us, law is no longer custom, it can only *command* and be compulsion; none of us any longer possesses a traditional sense of justice; we must therefore content ourselves with *arbitrary laws* which are the expressions of the necessity that there *must be* law. The most logical is then in any case the most acceptable, because it is the most *impartial*, granting even that in every case the smallest unit of measure in the relation of crime and punishment is arbitrarily fixed.

460

The great man of the masses – The recipe for what the masses call a great man is easily given. In all circumstances let a person provide them with something very pleasant, or first let him put it into their heads that this or that would be very pleasant, and then let him give it to them. On no account give it *immediately*, however: but let him acquire it by the greatest exertions, or seem thus to acquire it. The masses must have the impression that there is a powerful, nay indomitable strength of will operating; at least it must seem to be there operating. Everybody admires a strong will, because nobody possesses it, and everybody says to himself that if he did possess it there would no longer be any bounds for him and his egoism. If, then, it becomes evident that such a strong will effects something very agreeable to the masses, instead of hearkening to the wishes of covetousness, people admire once more, and wish good luck to themselves. Moreover, if he has all the qualities of the masses, they are the less ashamed before him, and he is all the more popular. Consequently, he may be violent, envious, rapacious, intriguing, flattering, fawning, inflated, and, according to circumstances, anything whatsoever.

461

Prince and God – People frequently commune with their princes in the same way as with their God, as indeed the prince himself was frequently the Deity's representative, or at least His high priest. This almost uncanny disposition of veneration, disquiet, and shame, grew, and has grown, much weaker, but occasionally it flares up again, and fastens upon powerful persons generally. The cult of genius is an echo of this veneration of Gods and Princes. Wherever an effort is made to exalt particular men to the superhuman, there is also a tendency to regard whole grades of the population as coarser and baser than they really are.

462

My utopia – In a better arranged society the heavy work and trouble of life will be assigned to those who suffer least through it, to the most obtuse, therefore; and so step by step up to those who are most sensitive to the highest and sublimest kinds of suffering, and who therefore still suffer notwithstanding the greatest alleviations of life.

463

A delusion in subversive doctrines – There are political and social dreamers who ardently and eloquently call for the overthrow of all order, in the belief that the proudest fane of beautiful humanity will then rear itself immediately, almost of its own accord. In these dangerous dreams there is still an echo of Rousseau's superstition, which believes in a marvellous primordial goodness of human nature, buried up, as it were; and lays all the blame of that burying-up on the institutions of civilisation, on society, State, and education. Unfortunately, it is well known by historical experiences that every such overthrow reawakens into new life the wildest energies, the long-buried horrors and extravagances of remotest ages; that an overthrow, therefore, may possibly be a source of strength to a deteriorated humanity, but never a regulator, architect, artist, or perfecter of human nature. It was not *Voltaire's* moderate nature, inclined towards regulating, purifying, and reconstructing, but *Rousseau's* passionate follies and half-lies that aroused the optimistic spirit of the Revolution, against which I cry, '*Ecrasez l'infâme!*' Owing to this *the Spirit of enlightenment and progressive development* has been long scared away; let us see – each of us individually – if it is not possible to recall it!

464

Moderation – When perfect resoluteness in thinking and investigating, that is to say, freedom of spirit, has become a feature of character, it produces moderation of conduct; for it weakens avidity, attracts much extant energy for the furtherance of intellectual aims, and shows the semi-usefulness, or uselessness and danger, of all sudden changes.

465

The resurrection of the spirit – A nation usually renews its youth on a political sick-bed, and there finds again the spirit which it had gradually lost in seeking and maintaining power. Culture is indebted most of all to politically weakened periods

466

New opinions in the old home – The overthrow of opinions is not immediately followed by the overthrow of institutions; on the contrary, the new opinions dwell for a long time in the desolate and haunted house of their predecessors, and conserve it even for want of a habitation.

467

Public education – In large States public education will always be extremely mediocre, for the same reason that in large kitchens the cooking is at best only mediocre.

468

Innocent corruption – In all institutions into which the sharp breeze of public criticism does not penetrate an innocent corruption grows up like a fungus (for instance, in learned bodies and senates).

469

Scholars as politicians – To scholars who become politicians the comic role is usually assigned; they have to be the good conscience of a state policy.

470

The wolf hidden behind the sheep – Almost every politician, in certain circumstances, has such need of an honest man that he breaks into the sheep-fold like a famished wolf; not, however, to devour a stolen sheep, but to hide himself behind its woolly back.

471

Happy times – A happy age is no longer possible, because men only wish for it but do not desire to have it; and each individual, when good days come for him, learns positively to pray for disquiet and misery. The destiny of mankind is arranged for *happy moments* – every life has such – but not for happy times. Nevertheless, such times will continue to exist in man's imagination as 'over the hills and far away', an heirloom of his earliest ancestors; for the idea of the happy age, from the earliest times to the present, has no doubt been derived from the state in which man, after violent exertions in hunting and warfare, gives himself over to repose, stretches out his limbs, and hears the wings of sleep rustle around him. It is a false conclusion when, in accordance with that old habit, man imagines that after *whole periods* of distress and trouble he will be able also to enjoy the state of happiness in *proportionate increase and duration*.

472

Religion and government – So long as the State, or, more properly, the Government, regards itself as the appointed guardian of a number of minors, and on their account considers the question whether religion should be preserved or abolished, it is highly probable that it will always decide for the preservation thereof. For religion satisfies the nature of the individual in times of loss, destitution, terror, and distrust, in cases, therefore, where the Government feels itself incapable of doing anything directly for the mitigation of the spiritual sufferings of the individual; indeed, even in general unavoidable and next to inevitable evils (famines, financial crises, and wars) religion gives to the masses an attitude of tranquillity and confiding expectancy. Whenever the necessary or accidental deficiencies of the State Government, or the dangerous consequences of dynastic interests, strike the eyes of the intelligent and make them refractory, the unintelligent will only think they see the finger of God therein and will submit with patience to the dispensations from *on high* (a conception in which divine and human modes of government usually coalesce); thus internal civil peace and continuity of development will be preserved. The power which lies in the unity of popular feeling, in the existence of the same opinions and aims for all, is protected and confirmed by religion – the rare cases excepted in which a priesthood cannot agree with the State about the price, and therefore comes into conflict with it. As a rule the State will know how to win over the priests, because it needs their most private and secret system for educating souls, and knows how to value servants who apparently, and outwardly, represent quite other interests. Even at present no power can become 'legitimate' without the assistance of the priests; a fact which Napoleon understood. Thus, absolutely paternal government and the careful preservation of religion necessarily go hand-in-hand. In this connection it must be taken for granted that the rulers and governing classes are enlightened concerning the advantages which religion affords, and consequently feel themselves to a certain extent superior to it, inasmuch as they use it as a means; thus freedom of spirit has its origin here. But how will it be when the totally different interpretation of the idea of Government, such as is taught in *democratic* States, begins to prevail? When one sees in it nothing but the instrument of the popular will, no 'upper' in contrast to an 'under', but merely a function of the sole sovereign, the people? Here also only the same attitude which the people assume towards religion can be assumed by the Government; every diffusion of enlightenment will have to find an echo even in the representatives, and the utilising and exploiting of religious impulses and consolations for State purposes will not be so easy (unless powerful party leaders occasionally exercise an influence resembling that of enlightened despotism). When, however, the State is not permitted to derive any further advantage from religion, or when people think far too variously on religious matters to allow the State to adopt a consistent and uniform procedure with respect to them, the way out of the difficulty will necessarily present itself, namely to treat religion as a private affair and leave it to the conscience and custom of each single individual. The first result of all is that religious feeling seems to be strengthened, inasmuch as hidden and suppressed impulses thereof, which the State had unintentionally or intentionally stifled, now break forth and rush to extremes; later on, however, it is found that religion is overgrown with sects, and that an abundance of dragon's teeth were sown as soon as religion was made a private affair. The spectacle of strife, and the hostile laying bare of all the weaknesses of religious confessions, admit finally of no other expedient except that every better and more talented person should make irreligiousness his private affair, a sentiment which now obtains the upper hand even in the minds of the governing classes, and, almost against their will, gives an anti-religious character to their measures. As soon as this happens, the sentiment of persons still religiously disposed, who formerly adored the State as something half sacred or wholly sacred, changes into decided *hostility to the State*; they lie in wait for governmental measures, seeking to hinder, thwart, and disturb as much as they can, and, by the fury of their contradiction, drive the opposing parties, the irreligious ones, into an almost fanatical enthusiasm *for* the State; in connection with which there is also the silently co-operating influence, that since their separation from religion the hearts of persons in these circles are conscious of a void, and seek by devotion to the State to provide themselves provisionally with a substitute for religion, a kind of stuffing for the void. After these perhaps lengthy transitional struggles, it is finally decided whether the religious parties are still strong enough to revive an old condition of things, and turn the wheel backwards: in which case enlightened despotism (perhaps less enlightened and more timorous than formerly), inevitably gets the State into its hands, or whether the non-religious parties achieve their purpose, and, possibly through schools and education, check the increase of their opponents during several generations, and finally make them no longer possible. Then, however, their enthusiasm for the State also abates: it always becomes more obvious that along with the religious adoration which regards the State as a mystery and a supernatural institution, the reverent and pious relation to it has also been convulsed. Henceforth individuals see only that side of the State which may be useful or injurious to them, and press forward by all means to obtain an influence over it. But this rivalry soon becomes too great; men and parties change too rapidly, and throw each other down again too furiously from the mountain when they have only just succeeded in getting aloft. All the measures which such a Government carries out lack the guarantee of permanence; people then fight shy of undertakings which would require the silent growth of future decades or centuries to produce ripe fruit. Nobody henceforth feels any other obligation to a law than to submit for the moment to the power which introduced the law; people immediately set to work, however, to undermine it by a new power, a newly-formed majority. Finally – it may be confidently asserted – the distrust of all government, the insight into the useless and harassing nature of these short-winded struggles, must drive men to an entirely new resolution: to the abrogation of the conception of the State and the abolition of the contrast of 'private and public'. Private concerns gradually absorb the business of the State; even the toughest residue which is left over from the old work of governing (the business, for instance, which is meant to protect private persons from private persons) will at last some day be managed by private enterprise. The neglect, decline, and *death of the State*, the liberation of the private person (I am careful not to say the individual), are the consequences of the democratic conception of the State; that is its mission. When it has accomplished its task – which, like everything human, involves much rationality and irrationality – and when all relapses into the old malady have been overcome, then a new leaf in the story-book of humanity will be unrolled, on which readers will find all kinds of strange tales and perhaps also some amount of good. To repeat shortly what has been said: the interests of the tutelary Government and the interests of religion go hand-in-hand, so that when the latter begins to decay the foundations of the State are also shaken. The belief in a divine regulation of political affairs, in a mystery in the existence of the State, is of religious origin: if religion disappears, the State will inevitably lose its old veil of Isis, and will no longer arouse veneration. The sovereignty of the people, looked at closely, serves also to dispel the final fascination and superstition in the realm of these sentiments; modern democracy is the historical form of the *decay of the State*. The outlook which results from this certain decay is not, however, unfortunate in every respect; the wisdom and the selfishness of men are the best developed of all their qualities; when the State no longer meets the demands of these impulses, chaos will least of all result, but a still more appropriate expedient than the State will get the mastery over the State. How many organising forces have already been seen to die out! For example, that of the *gens* or clan which for millennia was far mightier than the power of the family, and indeed already ruled and regulated long before the latter existed. We ourselves see the important notions of the right and might of the family, which once possessed the supremacy as far as the Roman system extended, always becoming paler and feebler. In the same way a later generation will also see the State become meaningless in certain parts of the world – an idea which many contemporaries can hardly contemplate without alarm and horror. To *labour* for the propagation and realisation of this idea is, certainly, another thing; one must think very presumptuously of one's reason, and only half understand history, to set one's hand to the plough at present – when as yet no one can show us the seeds that are afterwards to be sown upon the broken soil. Let us, therefore, trust to the 'wisdom and selfishness of men' that the State may *yet* exist a good while longer, and that the destructive attempts of over-zealous, too hasty socialists may be in vain!

473

Socialism, with regard to its means – Socialism is the fantastic younger brother of almost decrepit despotism, which it wants to succeed; its efforts are, therefore, in the deepest sense reactionary. For it desires such an amount of State power as only despotism has possessed – indeed, it outdoes all the past, in that it aims at the complete annihilation of the individual, whom it deems an un-authorised luxury of nature, which is to be improved by it into an appropriate *organ of the general community*. Owing to its relation-ship, it always appears in proximity to excessive developments of power, like the old typical socialist, Plato, at the court of the Sicilian tyrant; it desires (and under certain circumstances furthers) the Caesarian despotism of this century, because, as has been said, it would like to become its heir. But even this inheritance would not suffice for its objects, it requires the most submissive prostration of all citizens before the absolute State, such as has never yet been realised; and as it can no longer even count upon the old religious piety towards the State, but must rather strive involuntarily and continuously for the abolition thereof – because it strives for the abolition of all existing *States* – it can only hope for existence occasionally, here and there for short periods, by means of the extremest terrorism. It is therefore silently preparing itself for reigns of terror, and drives the word 'justice' like a nail into the heads of the half-cultured masses in order to deprive them completely of their understanding (after they had already suffered seriously from the half-culture), and to provide them with a good conscience for the bad game they are to play. Socialism may serve to teach, very brutally and impressively, the danger of all accum-ulations of State power, and may serve so far to inspire distrust of the State itself. When its rough voice strikes up the war-cry '*as much State as possible*' the shout at first becomes louder than ever – but soon the opposition cry also breaks forth, with so much greater force: '*as little State as possible*'.

474

The development of the mind feared by the state – The Greek *polis* was, like every organising political power, exclusive and distrustful of the growth of culture; its powerful fundamental impulse seemed almost solely to have a paralysing and obstructive effect thereon. It did not want to let any history or any becoming have a place in culture; the education laid down in the State laws was meant to be obligatory on all generations to keep them at *one* stage of development. Plato also, later on, did not desire it to be otherwise in his ideal State. *In spite of* the *polis* culture developed itself in this manner; indirectly to be sure, and against its will, the *polis* furnished assistance because the ambition of individuals therein was stimulated to the utmost, so that, having once found the path of intellectual development, they followed it to its farthest extremity. On the other hand, appeal should not be made to the panegyric of Pericles, for it is only a great optimistic dream about the alleged necessary connection between the *Polis* and Athenian culture; immediately before the night fell over Athens (the plague and the breakdown of tradition), Thucydides makes this culture flash up once more like a transfiguring afterglow, to efface the remembrance of the evil day that had preceded.

475

European man and the destruction of nationalities – Commerce and industry, interchange of books and letters, the universality of all higher culture, the rapid changing of locality and landscape, and the present nomadic life of all who are not landowners – these circumstances necessarily bring with them a weakening, and finally a destruction of nationalities, at least of European nationalities; so that, in consequence of perpetual crossings, there must arise out of them all a mixed race, that of the European man. At present the isolation of nations, through the rise of *national* enmities, consciously or unconsciously counteracts this tendency; but nevertheless the process of fusing advances slowly, in spite of those occasional counter-currents. This artificial nationalism is, however, as dangerous as was artificial Catholicism, for it is essentially an unnatural condition of extremity and martial law, which has been proclaimed by the few over the many, and requires artifice, lying, and force to maintain its reputation. It is not the interests of the many (of the peoples), as they probably say, but it is first of all the interests of certain princely dynasties, and then of certain commercial and social classes, which impel to this nationalism; once we have recognised this fact, we should just fearlessly style ourselves *good Europeans* and labour actively for the amalgamation of nations; in which efforts Germans may assist by virtue of their hereditary position as *interpreters and intermediaries between nations*. By the way, the great problem of the *Jews* only exists within the national States, inasmuch as their energy and higher intelligence, their intellectual and volitional capital, accumulated from generation to generation in tedious schools of suffering, must necessarily attain to universal supremacy here to an extent provocative of envy and hatred; so that the literary misconduct is becoming prevalent in almost all modern nations – and all the more so as they again set up to be national – of sacrificing the Jews as the scapegoats of all possible public and private abuses. So soon as it is no longer a question of the preservation or establishment of nations, but of the production and training of a European mixed-race of the greatest possible strength, the Jew is just as useful and desirable an ingredient as any other national remnant Every nation, every individual, has unpleasant and even dangerous qualities – it is cruel to require that the Jew should be an exception. Those qualities may even be dangerous and frightful in a special degree in his case; and perhaps the young Stock-Exchange Jew is in general the most repulsive invention of the human species. Nevertheless, in a general summing up, I should like to know how much must be excused in a nation which, not without blame on the part of all of us, has had the most mournful history of all nations, and to which we owe the most loving of men (Christ), the most upright of sages (Spinoza), the mightiest book, and the most effective moral law in the world? Moreover, in the darkest times of the Middle Ages, when Asiatic clouds had gathered darkly over Europe, it was Jewish free-thinkers, scholars, and physicians who upheld the banner of enlightenment and of intellectual independence under the severest personal sufferings, and defended Europe against Asia; we owe it not least to their efforts that a more natural, more reasonable, at all events un-mythical, explanation of the world was finally able to get the upper hand once more, and that the link of culture which now unites us with the enlightenment of Greco-Roman antiquity has remained unbroken. If Christianity has done everything to orientalise the Occident, Judaism has assisted essentially in occidentalising it anew; which, in a certain sense, is equivalent to making Europe's mission and history a *continuation of that of Greece*.

476

Apparent superiority of the Middle Ages – The Middle Ages present in the Church an institution with an absolutely universal aim, involving the whole of humanity – an aim, moreover, which – presumedly – concerned man's highest interests; in comparison therewith the aims of the States and nations which modern history exhibits make a painful impression; they seem petty, base, material, and restricted in extent. But this different impression on our imagination should certainly not determine our judgment; for that universal institution corresponded to feigned and fictitiously fostered needs, such as the need of salvation, which, wherever they did not already exist, it had first of all to create: the new institutions, however, relieve actual distresses; and the time is coming when institutions will arise to minister to the common, genuine needs of all men, and to cast that fantastic prototype, the Catholic Church, into shade and oblivion.

477

War indispensable – It is nothing but fanaticism and beautiful soulism to expect very much (or even, much only) from humanity when it has forgotten how to wage war. For the present we know of no other means whereby the rough energy of the camp, the deep impersonal hatred, the cold-bloodedness of murder with a good conscience, the general ardour of the system in the destruction of the enemy, the proud indifference to great losses, to one's own existence and that of one's friends, the hollow, earthquake-like convulsion of the soul, can be as forcibly and certainly communicated to enervated nations as is done by every great war: owing to the brooks and streams that here break forth, which, certainly, sweep stones and rubbish of all sorts along with them and destroy the meadows of delicate cultures, the mechanism, in the workshops of the mind is afterwards, in favourable circumstances, rotated by new power. Culture can by no means dispense with passions, vices, and malignities. When the Romans, after having become Imperial, had grown rather tired of war, they attempted to gain new strength by beast-baitings, gladiatoral combats, and Christian persecutions. The English of today, who appear on the whole to have also renounced war, adopt other means in order to generate anew those vanishing forces; namely, the dangerous exploring expeditions, sea voyages and mountaineerings, nominally undertaken for scientific purposes, but in reality to bring home surplus strength from adventures and dangers of all kinds. Many other such substitutes for war will be discovered, but perhaps precisely thereby it will become more and more obvious that such a highly cultivated and therefore necessarily enfeebled humanity as that of modern Europe not only needs wars, but the greatest and most terrible wars, consequently occasional relapses into barbarism, lest, by the means of culture, it should lose its culture and its very existence.

478

Industry in the south and the north — Industry arises in two entirely different ways. The artisans of the South are not industrious because of acquisitiveness but because of the constant needs of others. The smith is industrious because some one is always coming who wants a horse shod or a carriage mended. If nobody came he would loiter about in the market-place. In a fruitful land he has little trouble in supporting himself, for that purpose he requires only a very small amount of work, certainly no industry; eventually he would beg and be contented. The industry of English workmen, on the contrary, has acquisitiveness behind it; it is conscious of itself and its aims; with property it wants power, and with power the greatest possible liberty and individual distinction.

479

Wealth as the origin of a nobility of race — Wealth necessarily creates an aristocracy of race, for it permits the choice of the most beautiful women and the engagement of the best teachers; it allows a man cleanliness, time for physical exercises, and, above all, immunity from dulling physical labour. So far it provides all the conditions for making man, after a few generations, move and even act nobly and handsomely: greater freedom of character and absence of niggardliness, of wretchedly petty matters, and of abasement before bread-givers. It is precisely these negative qualities which are the most profitable birthday gift, that of happiness, for the young man; a person who is quite poor usually comes to grief through nobility of disposition, he does not get on, and acquires nothing, his race is not capable of living. In this connection, however, it must be remembered that wealth produces almost the same effects whether one have three hundred or thirty thousand thalers a year; there is no further essential progression of the favourable conditions afterwards. But to have less, to beg in boyhood and to abase one's self is terrible, although it may be the proper starting-point for such as seek their happiness in the splendour of courts, in subordination to the mighty and influential, or for such as wish to be heads of the Church. (It teaches how to slink crouching into the underground passages to favour.)

480

Envy and inertia in different courses – The two opposing parties, the socialist and the national – or whatever they may be called in the different countries of Europe – are worthy of each other; envy and laziness are the motive powers in each of them. In the one camp they desire to work as little as possible with their hands, in the other as little as possible with their heads; in the latter they hate and envy prominent, self-evolving individuals, who do not willingly allow themselves to be drawn up in rank and file for the purpose of a collective effect; in the former they hate and envy the better social caste, which is more favourably circumstanced outwardly, whose peculiar mission, the production of the highest blessings of culture, makes life inwardly all the harder and more painful. Certainly, if it be possible to make the spirit of the collective effect the spirit of the higher classes of society, the socialist crowds are quite right, when they also seek outward equalisation between themselves and these classes, since they are certainly internally equalised with one another already in head and heart. Live as higher men, and always do the deeds of higher culture – thus everything that lives will acknowledge your right, and the order of society, whose summit ye are, will be safe from every evil glance and attack!

481

High politics and their detriments – Just as a nation does not suffer the greatest losses that war and readiness for war involve through the expenses of the war, or the stoppage of trade and traffic, or through the maintenance of a standing army, however great these losses may now be, when eight European States expend yearly the sum of five milliards of marks thereon – but owing to the fact that year after year its ablest, strongest, and most industrious men are withdrawn in extraordinary numbers from their proper occupations and callings to be turned into soldiers: in the same way, a nation that sets about practising high politics and securing a decisive voice among the great Powers does not suffer its greatest losses where they are usually supposed to be. In fact, from this time onward it constantly sacrifices a number of its most conspicuous talents upon the 'Altar of the Fatherland' or of national ambition, whilst formerly other spheres of activity were open to those talents which are now swallowed up by politics. But apart from these public hecatombs, and in reality much more horrible, there is a drama which is constantly being performed simultaneously in a hundred thousand acts; every able, industrious, intellectually striving man of a nation that thus covets political laurels, is swayed by this covetousness, and no longer belongs entirely to himself alone as he did formerly; the new daily questions and cares of the public welfare devour a daily tribute of the intellectual and emotional capital of every citizen; the sum of all these sacrifices and losses of individual energy and labour is so enormous, that the political growth of a nation almost necessarily entails an intellectual impoverishment and lassitude, a diminished capacity for the performance of works that require great concentration and specialisation. The question may finally be asked: 'Does it then *pay*, all this bloom and magnificence of the total (which indeed only manifests itself as the fear of the new Colossus in other nations, and as the compulsory favouring by them of national trade and commerce) when all the nobler, finer, and more intellectual plants and products, in which its soil was hitherto so rich, must be sacrificed to this coarse and opalescent flower of the nation?*

482

Repeated once more – Public opinion – private laziness.

* This is once more an allusion to modern Germany. – J. M. K.

483

The enemies of truth – Convictions are more dangerous enemies of truth than lies.

484

A topsy-turvy world – We criticise a thinker more severely when he puts an unpleasant statement before us; and yet it would be more reasonable to do so when we find his statement pleasant.

485

Decided character – A man far oftener appears to have a decided character from persistently following his temperament than from persistently following his principles.

486

The one thing needful – One thing a man must have: either a naturally light disposition or a disposition *lightened* by art and knowledge.

487

The passion for things – Whoever sets his passion on things (sciences, arts, the common weal, the interests of culture) withdraws much fervour from his passion for persons (even when they are the representatives of those things; as statesmen, philosophers, and artists are the representatives of their creations).

488

Calmness in action – As a cascade in its descent becomes more deliberate and suspended, so the great man of action usually acts with *more* calmness than his strong passions previous to action would lead one to expect.

489

Not too deep – Persons who grasp a matter in all its depth seldom remain permanently true to it. They have just brought the depth up into the light, and there is always much evil to be seen there.

490

The illusion of idealists – All idealists imagine that the cause which they serve is essentially better than all other causes, and will not believe that if their cause is really to flourish it requires precisely the same evil-smelling manure which all other human undertakings have need of.

491

Self-observation – Man is exceedingly well protected from himself and guarded against his self-exploring and self-besieging; as a rule he can perceive nothing of himself but his outworks. The actual fortress is inaccessible, and even invisible, to him, unless friends and enemies become traitors and lead him inside by secret paths.

492

The right calling – Men can seldom hold on to a calling unless they believe or persuade themselves that it is really more important than any other. Women are the same with their lovers.

493

Nobility of disposition – Nobility of disposition consists largely in good-nature and absence of distrust, and therefore contains precisely that upon which money-grabbing and successful men take a pleasure in walking with superiority and scorn.

494

Goal and path – Many are obstinate with regard to the once-chosen path, few with regard to the goal.

495

The offensiveness in an individual way of life – All specially individual lines of conduct excite irritation against him who adopts them;

people feel themselves reduced to the level of commonplace creatures by the extra ordinary treatment he bestows on himself.

496

The privilege of greatness – It is the privilege of greatness to confer intense happiness with insignificant gifts.

497

Unintentionally noble – A person behaves with unintentional noble-ness when he has accustomed himself to seek naught from others and always to give to them.

498

A condition of heroism – When a person wishes to become a hero, the serpent must previously have become a dragon, otherwise he lacks his proper enemy.

499

Friends – Fellowship in joy, and not sympathy in sorrow, makes people friends.

500

Making use of ebb and flow – For the purpose of knowledge we must know how to make use of the inward current which draws us towards a thing, and also of the current which after a time draws us away from it.

501

Joy in itself – 'Joy in the Thing'; people say; but in reality it is joy in itself by means of the thing.

502

The unassuming man – He who is unassuming towards persons manifests his presumption all the more with regard to things (town, State, society, time, humanity). That is his revenge.

503

Envy and jealousy – Envy and jealousy are the pudenda of the human soul. The comparison may perhaps be carried further.

504

The noblest hypocrite – It is a very noble hypocrisy not to talk of one's self at all.

505

Vexation – Vexation is a physical disease, which is not by any means cured when its cause is subsequently removed.

506

The champions of truth – Truth does not find fewest champions when it is dangerous to speak it, but when it is dull.

507

More troublesome even than enemies – Persons of whose sympathetic attitude we are not, in all circumstances, convinced, while for some reason or other (gratitude, for instance) we are obliged to maintain the appearance of unqualified sympathy with them, trouble our imagination far more than our enemies do.

508

Free nature – We are so fond of being out among Nature, because it has no opinions about us.

509

Each superior in one thing – In civilised intercourse every one feels himself superior to all others in at least one thing; kindly feelings generally are based thereon, inasmuch as every one can, in certain circumstances, render help, and is therefore entitled to accept help without shame.

510

Consolatory arguments – In the case of a death we mostly use consolatory arguments not so much to alleviate the grief as to make excuses for feeling so easily consoled.

511

Persons loyal to their convictions – Whoever is very busy retains his general views and opinions almost unchanged. So also does every one who labours in the service of an idea; he will nevermore examine the idea itself, he no longer has any time to do so; indeed, it is against his interests to consider it as still admitting of discussion.

512

Morality and quantity – The higher morality of one man as compared with that of another, often lies merely in the fact that his aims are quantitively greater. The other, living in a circumscribed sphere, is dragged down by petty occupations.

513

'The life' as the proceeds of life – A man may stretch himself out ever so far with his knowledge; he may seem to himself ever so objective, but eventually he realises nothing therefrom but his own biography.

514

Iron necessity – Iron necessity is a thing which has been found, in the course of history, to be neither iron nor necessary.

515

Experience – The unreasonableness of a thing is no argument against its existence, but rather a condition thereof.

516

Truth – Nobody dies nowadays of fatal truths, there are too many antidotes to them.

517

A fundamental insight – There is no pre-established harmony between the promotion of truth and the welfare of mankind.

518

Man's lot – He who thinks most deeply knows that he is always in the wrong, however he may act and decide.

519

Truth as Circe – Error has made animals into men; is truth perhaps capable of making man into an animal again?

520

The danger of our culture – We belong to a period of which the culture is in danger of being destroyed by the appliances of culture.

521

Greatness means leading the way – No stream is large and copious of itself, but becomes great by receiving and leading on so many tributary streams. It is so, also, with all intellectual greatnesses. It is only a question of some one indicating the direction to be followed by so many affluents; not whether he was richly or poorly gifted originally.

522

A feeble conscience – People who talk about their importance to mankind have a feeble conscience for common bourgeois rectitude, keeping of contracts, promises, etc.

523

Desiring to be loved – The demand to be loved is the greatest of presumptions.

524

Contempt for men – The most unequivocal sign of contempt for man is to regard everybody merely as a means to *one's own* ends, or of no account whatever.

525

Partisans through contradiction – Whoever has driven men to fury against himself has also gained a party in his favour.

526

Forgetting experiences – Whoever thinks much and to good purpose easily forgets his own experiences, but not the thoughts which these experiences have called forth.

527

Sticking to an opinion – One person sticks to an opinion because he takes pride in having acquired it himself – another sticks to it because he has learnt it with difficulty and is proud of having understood it; both of them, therefore, out of vanity.

528

Avoiding the light – Good deeds avoid the light just as anxiously as evil deeds; the latter fear that pain will result from publicity (as punishment), the former fear that pleasure will vanish with publicity (the pure pleasure *per se*, which ceases as soon as satisfaction of vanity is added to it).

529

The length of the day – When one has much to put into them, a day has a hundred pockets.

530

The genius of tyranny – When an invincible desire to obtain tyrannical power has been awakened in the soul, and constantly keeps up its fervour, even a very mediocre talent (in politicians, artists, etc.) gradually becomes an almost irresistible natural force.

531

The enemy's life – He who lives by fighting with an enemy has an interest in the preservation of the enemy's life.*

532

More important – Unexplained, obscure matters are regarded as more important than explained, clear ones.

533

Valuation of services rendered – We estimate services rendered to us according to the value set on them by those who render them, not according to the value they have for us.

---

* This is why Nietzsche pointed out later on that he had an interest in the preservation of Christianity, and that he was sure his teaching would not undermine this faith – just as little as anarchists have undermined kings – but have left them seated all the more firmly on their thrones. – J. M. K.

534

Unhappiness – The distinction associated with unhappiness (as if it were a sign of stupidity, unambitiousness, or commonplaceness to feel happy) is so great that when any one says to us, 'How happy you are!' we usually protest.

535

Imagination in anguish – When one is afraid of anything, one's imagination plays the part of that evil spirit which springs on one's back just when one has the heaviest load to bear.

536

The value of insipid opponents – We sometimes remain faithful to a cause merely because its opponents never cease to be insipid.

537

The value of a profession – A profession makes us thoughtless; that is its greatest blessing. For it is a bulwark behind which we are permitted to withdraw when commonplace doubts and cares assail us.

538

Talent – Many a man's talent appears less than it is, because he has always set himself too heavy tasks.

539

Youth – Youth is an unpleasant period; for then it is not possible or not prudent to be productive in any sense whatsoever.

540

Too great aims – Whoever aims publicly at great things and at length perceives secretly that he is too weak to achieve them, has usually also insufficient strength to renounce his aims publicly, and then inevitably becomes a hypocrite.

541

In the current – Mighty waters sweep many stones and shrubs away with them; mighty spirits many foolish and confused minds.

542

The dangers of intellectual emancipation – In a seriously intended intellectual emancipation a person's mute passions and cravings also hope to find their advantage.

543

The incarnation of the mind – When any one thinks much and to good purpose, not only his face but also his body acquires a sage look.

544

Seeing badly and hearing badly – The man who sees little always sees less than there is to see; the man who hears badly always hears something more than there is to hear.

545

Self-enjoyment in vanity – The vain man does not wish so much to be prominent as to feel himself prominent; he therefore disdains none of the expedients for self-deception and self-outwitting. It is not the opinion of others that he sets his heart on, but his opinion of their opinion.

546

Exceptionally vain – He who is usually self-sufficient becomes exceptionally vain, and keenly alive to fame and praise when he is physically ill. The more he loses himself the more he has to endeavour to regain his position by means of the opinion of others.

547

The 'witty' – Those who seek wit do not possess it.

548

A hint to the heads of parties – When one can make people publicly support a cause they have also generally been brought to the point of inwardly declaring themselves in its favour, because they wish to be regarded as consistent.

549

Contempt – Man is more sensitive to the contempt of others than to self-contempt.

550

The tie of gratitude – There are servile souls who carry so far their sense of obligation for benefits received that they strangle themselves with the tie of gratitude.

551

The prophet's knack – In predicting beforehand the procedure of ordinary individuals, it must be taken for granted that they always make use of the smallest intellectual expenditure in freeing themselves from disagreeable situations.

552

Man's sole right – He who swerves from the traditional is a victim of the unusual; he who keeps to the traditional is its slave. The man is ruined in either case.

553

Below the beast – When a man roars with laughter he surpasses all the animals by his vulgarity.

554

Partial knowledge – He who speaks a foreign language imperfectly has more enjoyment therein than he who speaks it well. The enjoyment is with the partially initiated.

555

Dangerous helpfulness – There are people who wish to make human life harder for no other reason than to be able afterwards to offer men their life-alleviating recipes – their Christianity, for example.

556

Industriousness and conscientiousness – Industriousness and conscientiousness are often antagonists, owing to the fact that industriousness wants to pluck the fruit sour from the tree while conscientiousness wants to let it hang too long, until it falls and is bruised.

557

Casting suspicion – We endeavour to cast suspicion on persons whom we cannot endure.

558

The conditions are lacking – Many people wait all their lives for the opportunity to be good in *their own way*.

559

Lack of friends – Lack of friends leads to the inference that a person is envious or presumptuous. Many a man owes his friends merely to the fortunate circumstance that he has no occasion for envy.

560

Danger in manifoldness – With one talent more we often stand less firmly than with one less; just as a table stands better on three feet than on four.

561

An exemplar for others – Whoever wants to set a good example must add a grain of folly to his virtue; people then imitate their exemplar and at the same time raise themselves above him, a thing they love to do.

562

Being a target – The bad things others say about us are often not really aimed at us, but are the manifestations of spite or ill-humour occasioned by quite different causes.

563

Easily resigned – We suffer but little on account of ungratified wishes if we have exercised our imagination in distorting the past.

564

In danger – One is in greatest danger of being run over when one has just got out of the way of a carriage.

565

The role according to the voice – Whoever is obliged to speak louder than he naturally does (say, to a partially deaf person or before a large audience), usually exaggerates what he has to communicate. Many a one becomes a conspirator, malevolent gossip, or intriguer, merely because his voice is best suited for whispering,

566

Love and hatred – Love and hatred are not blind, but are dazzled by the fire which they carry about with them.

567

Advantageously persecuted – People who cannot make their merits perfectly obvious to the world endeavour to awaken a strong hostility against themselves. They have then the consolation of thinking that this hostility stands between their merits and the acknowledgment thereof – and that many others think the same thing, which is very advantageous for their recognition.

568

Confession – We forget our fault when we have confessed it to another person, but he does not generally forget it.

569

Self-sufficiency – The Golden Fleece of self-sufficiency is a protection against blows, but not against needle-pricks.

570

Shadows in the flame – The flame is not so bright to itself as to those whom it illuminates – so also the wise man.

571

Our own opinions – The first opinion that occurs to us when we are suddenly asked about anything is not usually our own, but only the current opinion belonging to our caste, position, or family; our own opinions seldom float on the surface.

572

The origin of courage – The ordinary man is as courageous and invulnerable as a hero when he does not see the danger, when he has no eyes for it. Reversely, the hero has his one vulnerable spot upon the back, where he has no eyes.

573

The danger in the physician – One must be born for one's physician, otherwise one comes to grief through him.

574

Marvellous vanity – Whoever has courageously prophesied the weather three times and has been successful in his hits, acquires a certain amount of inward confidence in his prophetic gift. We give credence to the marvellous and irrational when it flatters our self-esteem.

575

A profession – A profession is the backbone of life.

576

The danger of personal influence – Whoever feels that he exercises a great inward influence over another person must give him a perfectly free rein, must, in fact, welcome and even induce occasional opposition, otherwise he will inevitably make an enemy.

577

Recognition of the heir – Whoever has founded something great in an unselfish spirit is careful to rear heirs for his work. It is the sign of a tyrannical and ignoble nature to see opponents in all possible heirs, and to live in a state of self-defence against them.

578

Partial knowledge – Partial knowledge is more triumphant than complete knowledge; it takes things to be simpler than they are, and so makes its theory more popular and convincing.

579

Unsuitable for a party-man – Whoever thinks much is unsuitable for a party-man; his thinking leads him too quickly beyond the party.

580

A bad memory – The advantage of a bad memory is that one enjoys several times the same good things for the first time.

581

Self-affliction – Want of consideration is often the sign of a discordant inner nature, which craves for stupefaction.

582

Martyrs – The disciples of a martyr suffer more than the martyr.

583

Arrears of vanity – The vanity of many people who have no occasion to be vain is the inveterate habit, still surviving from the time when people had no right to the belief in themselves and only begged it in small sums from others.

584

Punctum saliens of passion – A person falling into a rage or into a violent passion of love reaches a point when the soul is full like a hogshead, but nevertheless a drop of water has still to be added, the good will for the passion (which is also generally called the evil will). This item only is necessary, and then the hogshead overflows.

585

A gloomy thought – It is with men as with the charcoal fires in the forest. It is only when young men have cooled down and have got charred, like these piles, that they become *useful*. As long as they fume and smoke they are perhaps more interesting, but they are useless and too often uncomfortable. Humanity ruthlessly uses every individual as material for the heating of its great machines; but what then is the purpose of the machines, when all individuals (that is, the human race) are useful only to maintain them? Machines that are ends in themselves: is that the *umana commedia*?

586

The hour-hand of life – Life consists of rare single moments of the greatest importance, and of countless intervals during which, at best, the phantoms of those moments hover around us. Love, the spring, every fine melody, the mountains, the moon, the sea – all speak but once fully to the heart, if, indeed, they ever do quite attain to speech. For many people have not those moments at all, and are themselves intervals and pauses in the symphony of actual life.

587

Attack or compromise – We often make the mistake of showing violent enmity towards a tendency, party, or period, because we happen only to get a sight of its most exposed side, its stuntedness, or the inevitable 'faults of its virtues' – perhaps because we ourselves have taken a prominent part in them. We then turn our backs on them and seek a diametrically opposite course; but the better way would be to seek out their strong good sides, or to develop them in ourselves. To be sure, a keener glance and a better will are needed to improve the becoming and the imperfect than are required to see through it in its imperfection and to deny it.

588

Modesty – There is true modesty (that is the knowledge that we are not the works we create); and it is especially becoming in a great mind, because such a mind can well grasp the thought of absolute irresponsibility (even for the good it creates). People do not hate a great man's presumptuousness in so far as he feels his strength, but because he wishes to prove it by injuring others, by dominating them, and seeing how long they will stand it. This, as a rule, is even a proof of the absence of a secure sense of power, and makes people doubt his greatness. We must therefore beware of presumption from the standpoint of wisdom.

589

The day's first thought – The best way to begin a day well is to think, on awakening, whether we cannot give pleasure during the day to at least one person. If this could become a substitute for the religious habit of prayer our fellow-men would benefit by the change.

590

Presumption as the last consolation – When we so interpret a misfortune, an intellectual defect, or a disease that we see therein our predestined fate, our trial, or the mysterious punishment of our former misdeeds, we thereby make our nature interesting and exalt ourselves in imagination above our fellows. The proud sinner is a well-known figure in all religious sects.

591

The vegetation of happiness – Close beside the world's woe, and often upon its volcanic soil, man has laid out his little garden of happiness. Whether one regard life with the eyes of him who only seeks knowledge therefrom, or of him who submits and is resigned, or of him who rejoices over surmounted difficulties – everywhere one will find some happiness springing up beside the evil – and in fact always the more happiness the more volcanic the soil has been, only it would be absurd to say that suffering itself is justified by this happiness.

592

The path of our ancestors – It is sensible when a person develops still further in himself the talent upon which his father or grandfather spent much trouble, and does not shift to some thing entirely new; otherwise he deprives himself of the possibility of attaining perfection in any one craft. That is why the proverb says, 'Which road shouldst thou ride? – That of thine ancestors.'

593

Vanity and ambition as educators – As long as a person has not become an instrument of general utility, ambition may torment him; if, however, that point has been reached, if he necessarily works like a machine for the good of all, then vanity may result; it will humanise him in small matters and make him more sociable, endurable, and considerate, when ambition has completed the coarser work of making him useful.

594

Philosophical novices. Immediately we have comprehended the wisdom of a philosopher, we go through the streets with a feeling as if we had been re-created and had become great men; for we encounter only those who are ignorant of this wisdom, and have therefore to deliver new and unknown verdicts concerning everything. Because we now recognise a law-book we think we must also comport ourselves as judges.

595

Pleasing by displeasing – People who prefer to attract attention, and thereby to displease, desire the same thing as those who neither wish to please nor to attract attention, only they seek it more ardently and indirectly by means of a step by which they apparently move away from their goal. They desire influence and power, and therefore show their superiority, even to such an extent that it becomes disagreeable; for they know that he who has finally attained power pleases in almost all he says and does, and that even when he displeases he still seems to please. The free spirit also, and in like manner the believer, desire power, in order some day to please thereby; when, on account of their doctrine, evil fate, persecution, dungeon, or execution threaten them, they rejoice in the thought that their teaching will thus be engraved and branded on the heart of mankind; though its effect is remote they accept their fate as a painful but powerful means of still attaining to power.

596

Casus belli and the like – The prince who, for his determination to make war against his neighbour, invents a *casus belli*, is like a father who foists on his child a mother who is henceforth to be regarded as such. And are not almost all publicly avowed motives of action just such spurious mothers?

597

Passion and right – Nobody talks more passionately of his rights than he who, in the depths of his soul, is doubtful about them. By getting passion on his side he seeks to confound his understanding and its doubts – he thus obtains a good conscience, and along with it success with his fellow-men.

598

The trick of the resigning one – He who protests against marriage, after the manner of Catholic priests, will conceive of it in its lowest and vulgarest form. In the same way he who disavows the honour of his contemporaries will have a mean opinion of it; he can thus dispense with it and struggle against it more easily. Moreover, he who denies himself much in great matters will readily indulge himself in small things. It might be possible that he who is superior to the approbation of his contemporaries would nevertheless not deny himself the gratification of small vanities.

599

The years of presumption – The proper period of presumption in gifted people is between their twenty-sixth and thirtieth years; it is the time of early ripeness, with a large residue of sourness. On the ground of what we feel within ourselves we demand honour and humility from men who see little or nothing of it, and because this tribute is not immediately forthcoming we revenge ourselves by the look, the gesture of arrogance, and the tone of voice, which a keen ear and eye recognise in every product of those years, whether it be poetry, philosophy, or pictures and music. Older men of experience smile thereat, and think with emotion of those beautiful years in which one resents the fate of *being* so much and *seeming* so little. Later on one really *seems* more – but one has lost the good belief in *being* much – unless one remain for life an incorrigible fool of vanity.

600

Deceptive and yet defensible – Just as in order to pass by an abyss or to cross a deep stream on a plank we require a railing, not to hold fast by, for it would instantly break down with us, but to give the notion of security to the eye, so in youth we require persons who unconsciously render us the service of that railing. It is true they would not help us if we really wished to lean upon them in great danger, but they afford the tranquillising sensation of protection close to one (for instance, fathers, teachers, friends, as all three usually are).

601

Learning to love – One must learn to love, one must learn to be kind, and this from childhood onwards; when education and chance give us no opportunity for the exercise of these feelings our soul becomes dried up, and even incapable of understanding the fine devices of loving men. In the same way hatred must be learnt and fostered, when one wants to become a proficient hater – otherwise the germ of it will gradually die out.

602

Ruin as ornament – Persons who pass through numerous mental phases retain certain sentiments and habits of their earlier states, which then project like a piece of inexplicable antiquity and grey stonework into their new thought and action, often to the embellishment of the whole surroundings.

603

Love and honour – Love desires, fear avoids. That is why one cannot be both loved and honoured by the same person, at least not at the same time.* For he who honours recognises power – that is to say, he fears it, he is in a state of reverential fear (*Ehr-furcht*). But love recognises no power, nothing that divides, detaches, superordinates, or subordinates. Because it does not honour them, ambitious people secretly or openly resent being loved.

604

A prejudice in favour of cold natures – People who quickly take fire grow cold quickly, and therefore are, on the whole, unreliable. For those, therefore, who are always cold, or pretend to be so, there is the favourable prejudice that they are particularly trustworthy, reliable persons; they are confounded with those who take fire slowly and retain it long.

605

The danger in free opinions – Frivolous occupation with free opinions has a charm, like a kind of itching; if one yields to it further, one begins to chafe the places; until at last an open, painful wound results; that is to say, until the free opinion begins to disturb and torment us in our position in life and in our human relations.

606

Desire for sore affliction – When passion is over it leaves behind an obscure longing for it, and even in disappearing it casts a seductive glance at us. It must have afforded a kind of pleasure to have been beaten with this scourge. Compared with it, the more moderate

* Women never understand this. – J. M. K.

sensations appear insipid; we still prefer, apparently, the more violent displeasure to languid delight.

607

Dissatisfaction with others and with the world – When, as so frequently happens, we vent our dissatisfaction on others when we are really dissatisfied with ourselves, we are in fact attempting to mystify and deceive our judgment; we desire to find a motive *a posteriori* for this dissatisfaction, in the mistakes or deficiencies of others, and so lose sight of ourselves. Strictly religious people, who have been relentless judges of themselves, have at the same time spoken most ill of humanity generally; there has never been a saint who reserved sin for himself and virtue for others, any more than a man who, according to Buddha's rule, hides his good qualities from people and only shows his bad ones.

608

Confusion of cause and effect – Unconsciously we seek the principles and opinions which are suited to our temperament, so that at last it seems as if these principles and opinions had formed our character and given it support and stability, whereas exactly the contrary has taken place. Our thoughts and judgments are, apparently, to be taken subsequently as the causes of our nature, but as a matter of fact *our* nature is the cause of our so thinking and judging. And what induces us to play this almost unconscious comedy? Inertness and convenience, and to a large extent also the vain desire to be regarded as thoroughly consistent and homogeneous in nature and thought; for this wins respect and gives confidence and power.

609

Age in relation to truth – Young people love what is interesting and exceptional, indifferent whether it is truth or falsehood. Riper minds love what is interesting and extraordinary when it is truth. Matured minds, finally, love truth even in those in whom it appears plain and simple and is found tiresome by ordinary people, because they have observed that truth is in the habit of giving utterance to its highest intellectual verities with all the appearance of simplicity.

610

Men as bad poets – Just as bad poets seek a thought to fit the rhyme in the second half of the verse, so men in the second half of life, having become more scrupulous, are in the habit of seeking pursuits, positions, and conditions which suit those of their earlier life, so that outwardly all sounds well, but their life is no longer ruled and continuously determined anew by a powerful thought: in place thereof there is merely the intention of finding a rhyme.

611

Ennui and play – Necessity compels us to work, with the product of which the necessity is appeased; the ever new awakening of necessity, however, accustoms us to work. But in the intervals in which necessity is appeased and asleep, as it were, we are attacked by ennui. What is this? In a word it is the habituation to work, which now makes itself felt as a new and additional necessity; it will be all the stronger the more a person has been accustomed to work, perhaps, even, the more a person has suffered from necessities. In order to escape ennui, a man either works beyond the extent of his former necessities, or he invents play, that is to say, work that is only intended to appease the general necessity for work. He who has become satiated with play, and has no new necessities impelling him to work, is sometime attacked by the longing for a third state, which is related to play as gliding is to dancing, as dancing is to walking, a blessed, tranquil movement; it is the artists' and philosophers' vision of happiness.

612

Lessons from pictures – If we look at a series of pictures of ourselves, from the time of later childhood to the time of mature manhood, we discover with pleased surprise that the man bears more resemblance to the child than to the youth: that probably, therefore, in accordance with this fact, there has been in the interval a temporary alienation of the fundamental character, over which the collected, concentrated force of the man has again become master. With this observation this other is also in accordance, namely, that all strong influences of passions, teachers, and political events, which in our youthful years draw us hither and thither, seem later on to be referred back again to a fixed standard; of course they still continue to exist and operate within us, but our fundamental sentiments and opinions have now the upper hand, and use their influence perhaps as a source of strength, but are no longer merely regulative, as was perhaps the case in our twenties. Thus even the thoughts and sentiments of the man appear more in accordance with those of his childish years, and this objective fact expresses itself in the above-mentioned subjective fact.

613

The tone of voice of different ages – The tone in which youths speak, praise, blame, and versify, displeases an older person because it is too loud, and yet at the same time dull and confused like a sound in a vault, which acquires such a loud ring owing to the emptiness; for most of the thought of youths does not gush forth out of the fullness of their own nature, but is the accord and the echo of what has been thought, said, praised or blamed around them. As their sentiments, however (their inclinations and aversions), resound much more forcibly than the reasons thereof, there is heard, whenever they divulge these sentiments, the dull, clanging tone which is a sign of the absence or scarcity of reasons. The tone of riper age is rigorous, abruptly concise, moderately loud, but, like everything distinctly articulated, is heard very far off. Old age, finally, often brings a certain mildness and consideration into the tone of the voice, and as it were, sweetens it; in many cases, to be sure, it also sours it.

614

The atavist and the forerunner – The man of unpleasant character, full of distrust, envious of the success of fellow-competitors and neighbours, violent and enraged at divergent opinions, shows that he belongs to an earlier grade of culture, and is, therefore, an atavism; for the way in which he behaves to people was right and suitable only for an age of club-law; he is an *atavist*. The man of a different character, rich in sympathy, winning friends everywhere, finding all that is growing and becoming amiable, rejoicing at the honours and successes of others and claiming no privilege of solely knowing the truth, but full of a modest distrust – he is a forerunner who presses upward towards a higher human culture. The man of unpleasant character dates from the times when the rude basis of human intercourse had yet to be laid, the other lives on the upper floor of the edifice of culture, removed as far as possible from the howling and raging wild beast imprisoned in the cellars.

615

Consolation for hypochondriacs – When a great thinker is temporarily subjected to hypochondriacal self-torture he can say to himself, by way of consolation: 'It is thine own great strength on which this parasite feeds and grows; if thy strength were smaller thou wouldst have less to suffer.' The statesman may say just the same thing when jealousy and vengeful feeling, or, in a word, the tone of the *bellum omnium contra omnes*, for which, as the representative of a nation, he must necessarily have a great capacity, occasionally intrudes into his personal relations and makes his life hard.

616

Estranged from the present – There are great advantages in estranging one's self for once to a large extent from one's age, and being as it were driven back from its shores into the ocean of past views of things. Looking thence towards the coast one commands a view, perhaps for the first time, of its aggregate formation, and when one again approaches the land one has the advantage of understanding it better, on the whole, than those who have never left it.

617

Sowing and reaping on the field of personal defects – Men like Rousseau understand how to use their weaknesses, defects, and vices as manure for their talent. When Rousseau bewails the corruption and degeneration of society as the evil results of culture, there is a personal experience at the bottom of it, the bitterness which gives sharpness to his general condemnation and poisons the arrows with which he shoots; he unburdens himself first as an individual, and thinks of getting a remedy which, while benefiting society directly, will also benefit himself indirectly by means of society.

618

Philosophically minded – We usually endeavour to acquire *one* attitude of mind, *one* set of opinions for all situations and events of life – it is mostly called being philosophically minded. But for the acquisition of knowledge it may be of greater importance not to make ourselves thus uniform, but to hearken to the low voice of the different situations in life; these bring their own opinions with them. We thus take an intelligent interest in the life and nature of many persons by not treating ourselves as rigid, persistent single individuals.

619

In the fire of contempt – It is a fresh step towards independence when one first dares to give utterance to opinions which it is considered as disgraceful for a person to entertain; even friends and acquaintances are then accustomed to grow anxious. The gifted nature must also pass through this fire; it afterwards belongs far more to itself.

620

Self-sacrifice – In the event of choice, a great sacrifice is preferred to a small one, because we compensate ourselves for the great sacrifice by self-admiration, which is not possible in the case of a small one.

621

Love as an artifice – Whoever really wishes to *become acquainted* with something new (whether it be a person, an event, or a book), does well to take up the matter with all possible love, and to avert his eye quickly from all that seems hostile, objectionable, and false therein – in fact to forget such things; so that, for instance, he gives the author of a book the best start possible, and straightway, just as in a race, longs with beating heart that he may reach the goal. In this manner one penetrates to the heart of the new thing, to its moving point, and this is called becoming acquainted with it. This stage having been arrived at, the understanding afterwards makes its restrictions; the over-estimation and the temporary suspension of the critical pendulum were only artifices to lure forth the soul of the matter.

622

Thinking too well and too ill of the world – Whether we think too well or too ill of things, we always have the advantage of deriving therefrom a greater pleasure, for with a too good preconception we usually put more sweetness into things (experiences) than they actually contain. A too bad preconception causes a pleasant disappointment, the pleasantness that lay in the things themselves is increased by the pleasantness of the surprise. A gloomy temperament, however, will have the reverse experience in both cases.

623

Profound people – Those whose strength lies in the deepening of impressions – they are usually called profound people – are relatively self-possessed and decided in all sudden emergencies, for in the first moment the impression is still shallow, it only then *becomes* deep. Long foreseen, long expected events or persons, however, excite such natures most, and make them almost incapable of eventually having presence of mind on the arrival thereof.

624

Intercourse with the higher self – Every one has his good day, when he finds his higher self; and true humanity demands that a person shall be estimated according to this state and not according to his work-days of constraint and bondage. A painter, for instance, should be appraised and honoured according to the most exalted vision he could see and represent. But men themselves commune very differently with this their higher self, and are frequently their own play-actors, in so far as they repeatedly imitate what they are in those moments. Some stand in awe and humility before their ideal, and would fain deny it; they are afraid of their higher self because, when it speaks, it speaks pretentiously. Besides, it has a ghost-like freedom of coming and staying away just as it pleases; on that account it is often called a gift of the gods, while in fact everything else is a gift of the gods (of chance); this, however, is the man himself.

625

Lonely people – Some people are so much accustomed to being alone in self-communion that they do not at all compare themselves with others, but spin out their soliloquising life in a quiet, happy mood, conversing pleasantly, and even hilariously, with themselves. If, however, they are brought to the point of comparing themselves with others, they are inclined to a brooding under-estimation of their own worth, so that they have first to be compelled by others *to form* once more a good and just opinion of themselves, and even from this acquired opinion they will always want to subtract and abate something. We must not, therefore, grudge certain persons their loneliness or foolishly commiserate them on that account, as is so often done.

626

Without melody – There are persons to whom a constant repose in themselves and the harmonious ordering of all their capacities is so natural that every definite activity is repugnant to them. They resemble music which consists of nothing but prolonged, harmonious accords, without even the tendency to an organised and animated melody showing itself. All external movement serves only to restore to the boat its equilibrium on the sea of harmonious euphony. Modern men usually become excessively impatient when they meet such natures, who *will never be anything* in the world, only it is not allowable to say of them that they *are nothing.* But in certain moods the sight of them raises the unusual question: 'Why should there be melody at all? Why should it not suffice us when life mirrors itself peacefully in a deep lake?' The Middle Ages were richer in such natures than our times. How seldom one now meets with any one who can live on so peacefully and happily with himself even in the midst of the crowd, saying to himself, like Goethe, 'The best thing of all is the deep calm in which I live and grow in opposition to the world, and gain what it cannot take away from me with fire and sword.'

627

To live and experience – If we observe how some people can deal with their experiences – their unimportant, everyday experiences – so that these become soil which yields fruit thrice a year; whilst others – and how many! – are driven through the surf of the most exciting adventures, the most diversified movements of times and peoples, and yet always remain light, always remain on the surface, like cork; we are finally tempted to divide mankind into a minority (minimality) of those who know how to make much out of little, and a majority of those who know how to make little out of much; indeed, we even meet with the counter-sorcerers who, instead of making the world out of nothing, make a nothing out of the world.

628

Seriousness in play – In Genoa one evening, in the twilight, I heard from a tower a long chiming of bells; it was never like to end, and sounded as if insatiable above the noise of the streets, out into the evening sky and sea-air, so thrilling, and at the same time so childish and so sad. I then remembered the words of Plato, and suddenly felt the force of them in my heart: '*Human matters, one and all, are not worthy of great seriousness; nevertheless* . . .'

629

Conviction and justice – The requirement that a person must afterwards, when cool and sober, stand by what he says, promises, and resolves during passion, is one of the heaviest burdens that weigh upon mankind. To have to acknowledge for all future time the consequences of anger, of fiery revenge, of enthusiastic devotion, may lead to a bitterness against these feelings proportionate to the idolatry with which they are idolised, especially by artists. These cultivate to its full extent the *esteem of the passions*, and have always done so; to be sure, they also glorify the terrible satisfaction of the passions which a person affords himself, the outbreaks of vengeance, with death, mutilation, or voluntary banishment in their train, and the resignation of the broken heart. In any case they keep alive curiosity about the passions; it is as if they said: 'Without passions you have no experience whatever.' Because we have sworn fidelity (perhaps even to a purely fictitious being, such as a god), because we have surrendered our heart to a prince, a party, a woman, a priestly order, an artist, or a thinker, in a state of infatuated delusion that threw a charm over us and made those beings appear worthy of all veneration, and every sacrifice – are we, therefore, firmly and inevitably bound? Or did we not, after all, deceive ourselves then? Was there not a hypothetical promise, under the tacit presupposition that those beings to whom we consecrated ourselves were really the beings they seemed to be in our imagination? Are we under obligation to be faithful to our errors, even with the knowledge that by this fidelity we shall cause injury to our higher selves? No, there is no law, no obligation of that sort; we *must* become traitors, we must act unfaithfully and abandon our ideals again and again. We cannot advance from one period of life into another without causing these pains of treachery and also suffering from them. Might it be necessary to guard against the ebullitions of our feelings in order to escape these pains? Would not the world then become too arid, too ghost-like for us? Rather will we ask ourselves whether these pains are *necessary* on a change of convictions, or whether they do not depend on a *mistaken* opinion and estimate. Why do we admire a person who remains true to his convictions and despise him who changes them? I fear the answer must be, 'because every one takes for granted that such a change is caused only by motives of more general utility or of personal trouble.' That is to say, we believe at bottom that nobody alters his opinions as long as they are advantageous to him, or at least as long as they do not cause him any harm. If it is so, however, it furnishes a bad proof of the *intellectual* significance of all convictions. Let us once examine how convictions arise, and let us see whether their importance is not greatly over-estimated; it will thereby be seen that the change of convictions also is in all circumstances judged according to a false standard, that we have hitherto been accustomed to suffer too much from this change.

630

Conviction is belief in the possession of absolute truth on any matter of knowledge. This belief takes it for granted, therefore, that there are absolute truths; also, that perfect methods have been found for attaining to them; and finally, that every one who has convictions makes use of these perfect methods. All three notions show at once that the man of convictions is not the man of scientific thought; he seems to us still in the age of theoretical innocence, and is practically a child, however grown-up he may be. Whole centuries, however, have been lived under the influence of those childlike presuppositions, and out of them have flowed the mightiest sources of human strength. The countless numbers who sacrificed themselves for their convictions believed they were doing it for the sake of absolute truth. They were all wrong, however; probably no one has, ever sacrificed himself for Truth; at least, the dogmatic expression of the faith of any such person has been unscientific or only partly scientific. But really, people wanted to carry their point because they believed that they *must be* in the right. To allow their belief to be wrested from them probably meant calling in question their eternal salvation. In an affair of such extreme importance the 'will' was too audibly the prompter of the intellect. The presupposition of every believer of every shade of belief has been that he *could not* be confuted; if the counter-arguments happened to be very strong, it always remained for him to decry intellect generally, and, perhaps, even to set up the '*credo quia absurdum est*' as the standard of extreme fanaticism. It is not the struggle of opinions that has made history so turbulent; but the struggle of belief in opinions – that is to say, of convictions. If all those who thought so highly of their convictions, who made sacrifices of all kinds for them, and spared neither honour, body, nor life in their service, had only devoted half of their energy to examining their right to adhere to this or that conviction and by what road they arrived at it, how peaceable would the history of mankind now appear! How much more knowledge would there be! All the cruel scenes in connection with the persecution of heretics of all kinds would have been avoided, for two reasons: firstly, because the inquisitors would above all have inquired of themselves, and would have recognised the presumption of defending absolute truth; and secondly, because the heretics themselves would, after examination, have taken no more interest in such badly established doctrines as those of all religious sectarians and 'orthodox' believers.

631

From the ages in which it was customary to believe in the possession of absolute truth, people have inherited a profound *dislike* of all sceptical and relative attitudes with regard to questions of knowledge; they mostly prefer to acquiesce, for good or evil, in the convictions of those in authority (fathers, friends, teachers, princes), and they have a kind of remorse of conscience when they do not do so. This tendency is quite comprehensible, and its results furnish no ground for condemnation of the course of the development of human reason. The scientific spirit in man, however, has gradually to bring to maturity the virtue of *cautious forbearance*, the wise moderation, which is better known in practical than in theoretical life, and which, for instance, Goethe has represented in

Antonio, as an object of provocation for all Tassos – that is to say, for unscientific and at the same time inactive natures. The man of convictions has in himself the right not to comprehend the man of cautious thought, the theoretical Antonio; the scientific man, on the other hand, has no right to blame the former on that account, he takes no notice thereof, and knows, moreover, that in certain cases the former will yet cling to him, as Tasso finally clung to Antonio.

632

He who has not passed through different phases of conviction, but sticks to the faith in whose net he was first caught, is, under all circumstances, just on account of this unchangeableness, a representative of *atavistic* culture; in accordance with this lack of culture (which always presupposes plasticity for culture), he is severe, unintelligent, unteachable, without liberality, an ever suspicious person, an unscrupulous person who has recourse to all expedients for enforcing his opinions because he cannot conceive that there must be other opinions; he is, in such respects, perhaps a source of strength, and even wholesome in cultures that have become too emancipated and languid, but only because he strongly incites to opposition: for thereby the delicate organisation of the new culture, which is forced to struggle with him, becomes strong itself.

633

In essential respects we are still the same men as those of the time of the Reformation; how could it be otherwise? But the fact that we *no longer* allow ourselves certain means for promoting the triumph of our opinions distinguishes us from that age, and proves that we belong to a higher culture. He who still combats and overthrows opinions with calumnies and outbursts of rage, after the manner of the Reformation men, obviously betrays the fact that he would have burnt his adversaries had he lived in other times, and that he would have resorted to all the methods of the Inquisition if he had been an opponent of the Reformation. The Inquisition was rational at that time; for it represented nothing else than the universal application of martial law, which had to be proclaimed throughout the entire domain of the Church, and which, like all martial law, gave a right to the extremest methods, under the presupposition, of course, (which we now no longer share with those people) that the Church *possessed* truth and had to preserve it at all costs, and at any sacrifice, for the salvation of mankind. Now, however, one does not so readily concede to any one that he possesses the truth; strict methods of investigation have diffused enough of distrust and precaution, so that every one who violently advocates opinions in word and deed is looked upon as an enemy of our modern culture, or, at least, as an atavist. As a matter of fact the pathos that man possesses truth is now of very little consequence in comparison with the certainly milder and less noisy pathos of the search for truth, which is never weary of learning afresh and examining anew.

634

Moreover, the methodical search for truth is itself the outcome of those ages in which convictions were at war with each other. If the individual had not cared about *his* 'truth', that is to say, about carrying his point, there would have been no method of investigation; thus, however, by the eternal struggle of the claims of different individuals to absolute truth, people went on step by step to find irrefragable principles according to which the rights of the claims could be tested and the dispute settled. At first people decided according to authorities; later on they criticised one another's ways and means of finding the presumed truth; in the interval there was a period when people deduced the consequences of the adverse theory, and perhaps found them to be productive of injury and unhappiness; from which it was then to be inferred by every one that the conviction of the adversary involved an error. The *personal struggle of the thinker* at last so sharpened his methods that real truths could be discovered, and the mistakes of former methods exposed before the eyes of all.

635

On the whole, scientific methods are at least as important results of investigation as any other results, for the scientific spirit is based upon a knowledge of method, and if the methods were lost, all the results of science could not prevent the renewed prevalence of superstition and absurdity. Clever people may *learn* as much as they like of the results of science, but one still notices in their conversation, and especially in the hypotheses they make, that they lack the scientific spirit; they have not the instinctive distrust of the devious courses of thinking which, in consequence of long training, has taken root in the soul of every scientific man. It is enough for them to find any kind of hypothesis on a subject, they are then all on fire for it, and imagine the matter is thereby settled. To have an opinion is with them equivalent to immediately becoming fanatical for it, and finally taking it to heart as a conviction. In the case of an unexplained matter they become heated for the first idea that comes into their head which has any resemblance to an explanation – a course from which the worst results constantly follow, especially in the field of politics. On that account everybody should nowadays have become thoroughly acquainted with at least *one* science, for then surely he knows what is meant by method, and how necessary is the extremest carefulness. To women in particular this advice is to be given at present; as to those who are irretrievably the victims of all hypotheses, especially when these have the appearance of being witty, attractive, enlivening, and invigorating. Indeed, on close inspection one sees that by far the greater number of educated people still desire convictions from a thinker and nothing but *convictions*, and that only a small minority want *certainty*. The former want to be forcibly carried away in order thereby to obtain an increase of strength; the latter few have the real interest which disregards personal advantages and the increase of strength also. The former class, who greatly predominate, are always reckoned upon when the thinker comports himself and labels himself as a *genius*, and thus views himself as a higher being to whom authority belongs. In so far as genius of this kind upholds the ardour of convictions, and arouses distrust of the cautious and modest spirit of science, it is an enemy of truth, however much it may think itself the wooer thereof.

636

There is, certainly, also an entirely different species of genius, that of justice; and I cannot make up my mind to estimate it lower than any kind of philosophical, political, or artistic genius. Its peculiarity is to go, with heartfelt aversion, out of the way of everything that blinds and confuses people's judgment of things; it is consequently an *adversary of convictions*, for it wants to give their own to all, whether they be living or dead, real or imaginary – and for that purpose it must know thoroughly; it therefore places everything in the best light and goes around it with careful eyes. Finally, it will even give to its adversary the blind or short-sighted 'conviction' (as men call it – among women it is called 'faith'), what is due to conviction for the sake of truth.

637

Opinions evolve out of *passions*; *indolence of intellect* allows those to congeal into *convictions*. He, however, who is conscious of himself as a *free*, restless, lively spirit can prevent this congelation by constant change; and if he is altogether a thinking snowball, he will not have opinions in his head at all, but only certainties and properly estim- ated probabilities. But we, who are of a mixed nature, alternately inspired with ardour and chilled through and through by the intellect, want to kneel before justice, as the only goddess we acknowledge, The *fire* in us generally makes us unjust, and impure in the eyes of our goddess; in this condition we are not permitted to take her hand, and the serious smile of her approval never rests upon us. We reverence her as the veiled Isis of our life; with shame we offer her our pain as penance and sacrifice when the fire threatens to burn and consume us. It is the *intellect* that saves us from being utterly burnt and reduced to ashes; it occasionally drags us away from the sacrificial altar of justice or enwraps us in a garment of asbestos. Liberated from the fire, and impelled by the intellect, we then pass from opinion to opinion, through the change of parties, as noble *betrayers* of all things that can in any way be betrayed – and nevertheless without a feeling of guilt.

638

The wanderer – He who has attained intellectual emancipation to any extent cannot, for a long time, regard himself otherwise than as a wanderer on the face of the earth and not even as a traveller *towards* a final goal, for there is no such thing. But he certainly wants to observe and keep his eyes open to whatever actually happens in the world; therefore he cannot attach his heart too firmly to anything individual; he must have in himself something wandering that takes pleasure in change and transitoriness. To be sure such a man will have bad nights, when he is weary and finds the gates of the town that should offer him rest closed; perhaps he may also find that, as in the East, the desert reaches to the gates, that wild beasts howl far and near, that a strong wind arises, and that robbers take away his beasts of burden. Then the dreadful night closes over him like a second desert upon the desert, and his heart grows weary of wandering. Then when the morning sun rises upon him, glowing like a Deity of anger, when the town is opened, he sees perhaps in the faces of the dwellers therein still more desert, uncleanliness, deceit, and insecurity than outside the gates – and the day is almost worse than the night. Thus it may occasionally happen to the wanderer, but then there come as compensation the delightful mornings of other lands and days, when already in the grey of the dawn he sees the throng of muses dancing by, close to him, in the mist of the mountain; when afterwards, in the symmetry of his ante-meridian soul, he strolls silently under the trees, out of whose crests and leafy hiding-places all manner of good and bright things are flung to him, the gifts of all the free spirits who are at home in mountains, forests, and solitudes, and who, like himself, alternately merry and thoughtful, are wanderers and philosophers. Born of the secrets of the early dawn, they ponder the question how the day, between the hours of ten and twelve, can have such a pure, transparent, and gloriously cheerful countenance: they seek the *ante-meridian* philosophy.

An Epode
Among Friends
[translated by T. Common]

i.   Nice, when mute we lie a-dreaming,
Nicer still when we are laughing,
'Neath the sky heaven's chariot speeding,
On the moss the book a-reading,
Sweetly loud with friends all laughing
Joyous, with white teeth a-gleaming.

Do I well, we're mute and humble;
Do I ill – we'll laugh exceeding;
Make it worse and worse, unheeding,
Worse proceeding, more laughs needing,
Till into the grave we stumble.

Friends! Yea! so shall it obtain?
Amen! Till we meet again.

ii.   No excuses need be started!
Give, ye glad ones, open hearted,
To this foolish book before you
Ear and heart and lodging meet;
Trust me, 'twas not meant to bore you,
Though of folly I may treat!

What I find, seek, and am needing,
Was it e'er in book for reading?
Honour now fools in my name,
Learn from out this book by reading
How 'our sense' from reason came.

Thus, my friends, shall it obtain?
Amen! Till we meet again.

HUMAN, ALL-TOO-HUMAN
PART TWO

PREFACE

I

One should only speak where one cannot remain silent, and only speak of what one has *conquered* – the rest is all chatter, 'literature', bad breeding. My writings speak only of my conquests, 'I' am in them, with all that is hostile to me, *ego ipsissimus*, or, if a more haughty expression be permitted, *ego ipsissimum*. It may be guessed that I have many below me. . . . But first I always needed time, convalescence, distance, separation, before I felt the stirrings of a desire to flay, despoil, lay bare, 'represent' (or whatever one likes to call it) for the additional knowledge of the world, something that I had lived through and outlived, something done or suffered. Hence all my writings – with one exception, important, it is true – must be *ante-dated* – they always tell of a 'behind-me'. Some even, like the first three *Thoughts out of Season*, must be thrown back before the period of creation and experience of a previously published book (*The Birth of Tragedy* in the case cited, as anyone with subtle powers of observation and comparison could not fail to perceive). That wrathful outburst against the Germanism, smugness, and raggedness of speech of old David Strauss, the contents of the first *Thought out of Season*, gave a vent to feelings that had inspired me long before, as a student, in the midst of German culture and cultured Philistinism (I claim the paternity of the now much used and misused phrase 'cultured Philistinism'). What I said against the 'historical disease' I said as one who had slowly and laboriously recovered from that disease, and who was not at all disposed to renounce 'history' in the future because he had suffered from her in the past. When in the third *Thought out of Season* I gave expression to my reverence for my first and only teacher, the *great* Arthur Schopenhauer – I should now give it a far more personal and emphatic voice – I was for my part already in the throes of moral scepticism and dissolution, that is, as much concerned with the criticism as with the study of all pessimism down to the present day. I already did not believe in 'a blessed thing', as the people say, not even in Schopenhauer. It was at this very period that an unpublished essay of mine, 'On Truth and Falsehood in an Extra-Moral Sense', came into being. Even my ceremonial oration in honour of Richard Wagner, on the occasion of his triumphal celebration at Bayreuth in 1876 – Bayreuth signifies the greatest triumph that an artist has ever won – a work that bears the strongest stamp of 'individuality', was in the background an act of homage and gratitude to a bit of the past in me, to the fairest but most perilous calm of my sea-voyage . . . and as a matter of fact a severance and a farewell. (Was Richard Wagner mistaken on this point? I do not think so. So long as we still love, we do not paint such pictures, we do not yet 'examine', we do not place ourselves so far away as is essential for one who 'examines'. 'Examining needs at least a secret antagonism, that of an opposite point of view,' it is said on page 46 of the above-named work itself, with an insidious, melancholy application that was perhaps understood by few.) The composure that gave me the *power* to speak after many intervening years of solitude and abstinence, first came with the book, *Human, All-too Human*, to which this second preface and apologia is dedicated. As a book for 'free spirits' it shows some trace of that almost cheerful and inquisitive coldness of the psychologist, who has *behind* him many painful things that he keeps *under* him, and moreover establishes them for himself and fixes them firmly as with a needle-point. Is it to be wondered at that at such sharp, ticklish work blood flows now and again, that indeed the psychologist has blood on his fingers and not *only* on his fingers?

2

The *Miscellaneous Maxims and Opinions* were in the first place, like *The Wanderer and His Shadow*, published separately as continuations and appendices to the above-mentioned human, all-too human *Book for Free Spirits*: and at the same time, as a continuation and confirmation of an intellectual cure, consisting in a course of anti-romantic self-treatment, such as my instinct, which had always remained healthy, had itself discovered and prescribed against a temporary attack of the most dangerous form of romantics. After a

convalescence of six years I may well be permitted to collect these
same writings and publish them as a second volume of *Human, All-
too Human*. Perhaps, if surveyed together, they will more clearly
and effectively teach their lesson – a lesson of health that may be
recommended as a *disciplina voluntatis* to the more intellectual
natures of the rising generation. Here speaks a pessimist who has
often leaped out of his skin but has always returned into it, thus,
a pessimist with goodwill towards pessimism – at all events a
romanticist no longer. And has not a pessimist, who possesses this
serpentine knack of changing his skin, the right to read a lecture to
our pessimists of today, who are one and all still in the toils of
romanticism? Or at least to show them how it is – done?

3

It was then, in fact, high time to bid farewell, and I soon received
proof. Richard Wagner, who seemed all-conquering, but was in
reality only a decayed and despairing romantic, suddenly collapsed,
helpless and broken, before the Christian Cross. . . . Was there not
a single German with eyes in his head and sympathy in his heart for
this appalling spectacle? Was I the only one whom he caused –
suffering? In any case, the unexpected event illumined for me in
one lightning flash the place that I had abandoned, and also the
horror that is felt by everyone who is unconscious of a great
danger until he has passed through it. As I went forward alone, I
shuddered, and not long afterwards I was ill, or rather more than
ill – weary: weary from my ceaseless disappointment about all that
remained to make us modern men enthusiastic, at the thought of
the power, work, hope, youth, love, flung to all the winds: weary
from disgust at the effeminacy and undisciplined rhapsody of this
romanticism, at the whole tissue of idealistic lies and softening of
conscience, which here again had won the day over one of the
bravest of men: last, and not least, weary from the bitterness of an
inexorable suspicion – that after this disappointment I was doomed
to mistrust more thoroughly, to despise more thoroughly, to be
alone more thoroughly than ever before. My task – whither had it
flown? Did it not look now as if my task were retreating from me
and as if I should for a long future period have no more right to it?
What was I to do to endure this most terrible privation? – I began
by entirely forbidding myself all romantic music, that ambiguous,

pompous, stifling art, which robs the mind of its sternness and its joyousness and provides a fertile soil for every kind of vague yearning and spongy sensuality. '*Cave musicam*'* is even today my advice to all who are enough of men to cling to purity in matters of the intellect. Such music enervates, softens, feminises, its 'eternal feminine' draws us – *down*! My first suspicion, my most immediate precaution, was directed against romantic music. If I hoped for anything at all from music, it was in the expectation of the coming of a musician bold, subtle, malignant, southern, healthy enough to take an immortal revenge upon that other music.

4

Lonely now and miserably self-distrustful, I took sides, not without resentment, *against* myself and *for* everything that hurt me and was hard to me. Thus I once more found the way to that courageous pessimism that is the antithesis of all romantic fraud, and, as it seems to me today, the way to 'myself', to my task. That hidden masterful Something, for which we long have no name until at last it shows itself as our task – that tyrant in us exacts a terrible price for every attempt that we make to escape him or give him the slip, for every premature act of self-constraint, for every reconciliation with those to whom we do not belong, for every activity, however reputable, which turns us aside from our main purpose, yes, even for every virtue that would fain protect us from the cruelty of our most individual responsibility. 'Disease' is always the answer when we wish to have doubts of our rights to our own task, when we begin to make it easier for ourselves in any way. How strange and how terrible! It is our very alleviations for which we have to make the severest atonement! And if we want to return to health, we have no choice left – we must load ourselves *more heavily* than we were ever laden before.

5

It was then that I learnt the hermitical habit of speech acquired only by the most silent and suffering. I spoke without witnesses, or rather indifferent to the presence of witnesses, so as not to suffer from silence, I spoke of various things that did not concern me in a style that gave the impression that they did. Then, too, I learnt

---

* Beware music.

the art of showing myself cheerful, objective, inquisitive in the presence of all that is healthy and evil – is this, in an invalid, as it seems to me, his 'good taste'? Nevertheless, a more subtle eye and sympathy will not miss what perhaps gives a charm to these writings – the fact that here speaks one who has suffered and abstained in such a way as if he had never suffered or abstained. Here equipoise, composure, even gratitude towards life *shall* be maintained, here rules a stern, proud, ever vigilant, ever susceptible will, which has undertaken the task of defending life against pain and snapping off all conclusions that are wont to grow like poisonous fungi from pain, disappointment, satiety, isolation and other morasses. Perhaps this gives our pessimists a hint to self-examination? For it was then that I hit upon the aphorism, 'a sufferer has as yet no right to pessimism', and that I engaged in a tedious, patient campaign against the unscientific first principles of all romantic pessimism, which seeks to magnify and interpret individual, personal experiences into 'general judgments', universal condemnations – it was then, in short, that I sighted a new world. Optimism for the sake of restitution, in order at some time to have the right to become a pessimist – do you understand that? Just as a physician transfers his patient to totally strange surroundings, in order to displace him from his entire 'past', his troubles, friends, letters, duties, stupid mistakes and painful memories, and teaches him to stretch out hands and senses towards new nourishment, a new sun, a new future: so I, as physician and invalid in one, forced myself into an utterly different and untried zone of the soul, and particularly into an absorbing journey to a strange land, a strange atmosphere, into a curiosity for all that was strange. A long process of roaming, seeking, changing followed, a distaste for fixity of any kind – a dislike for clumsy affirmation and negation: and at the same time a dietary and discipline which aimed at making it as easy as possible for the soul to fly high, and above all constantly to fly away. In fact a minimum of life, an unfettering from all coarser forms of sensuality, an independence in the midst of all marks of outward disfavour, together with the pride in being able to live in the midst of all this disfavour: a little cynicism perhaps, a little of the 'tub of Diogenes', a good deal of whimsical happiness, whimsical gaiety, much calm, light, subtle folly, hidden enthusiasm – all this produced in the end a great spiritual strengthening, a growing joy and exuberance of health. Life itself rewards us for our tenacious will to life, for such a long war as I waged against the pessimistic weariness of life, even for every observant glance of our gratitude, glances that do not miss the smallest, most delicate, most fugitive gifts. . . . In the end we receive Life's great gifts, perhaps the greatest it can bestow – we regain *our* task.

6

Should my experience – the history of an illness and a convalescence, for it resulted in a convalescence – be only my personal experience? and merely just my 'Human, All-too-human'? Today I would fain believe the reverse, for I am becoming more and more confident that my books of travel were not penned for my sole benefit, as appeared for a time to be the case. May I, after six years of growing assurance, send them once more on a journey for an experiment? – May I commend them particularly to the ears and hearts of those who are afflicted with some sort of a 'past', and have enough intellect left to suffer even intellectually from their past? But above all would I commend them to you whose burden is heaviest, you choice spirits, most encompassed with perils, most intellectual, most courageous, who must be the *conscience* of the modern soul and as such be versed in its *science*: in whom is concentrated all of disease, poison or danger that can exist today: whose lot decrees that you must be more sick than any individual because you are not 'mere individuals': whose consolation it is to know and, ah! to walk the path to a new health, a health of to-morrow and the day after: you men of destiny, triumphant, conquerors of time, the healthiest and the strongest, you *good Europeans*!

7

To express finally in a single formula my opposition to the romantic pessimism of the abstinent, the unfortunate, the conquered: there is a will to the tragic and to pessimism, which is a sign as much of the severity as of the strength of the intellect (taste, emotion, conscience). With this will in our hearts we do not fear, but we investigate ourselves the terrible and the problematical elements characteristic of all existence. Behind such a will stand courage and pride and the desire for a really great enemy. That was *my* pessimistic outlook from the first – a new outlook, methinks, an outlook that even at this day is new and strange? To this moment I hold to it firmly and (if it will be believed) not only *for* myself but occasionally *against* myself. . . . You would prefer to have that proved first? Well, what else does all this long preface – prove?

SILS–MARIA, UPPER ENGADINE
September 1886

PART ONE

*Miscellaneous Maxims
and Opinions*

I

To the disillusioned in philosophy. If you hitherto believed in the highest value of life and now find yourselves disillusioned, must you immediately get rid of life at the lowest possible price?

2

Overnice. One can even become overnice as regards the clearness of concepts. How disgusted one is then at having truck with the half-clear, the hazy, the aspiring, the doubting! How ridiculous and yet not mirth-provoking is their eternal fluttering and straining without ever being able to fly or to grasp!

3

The wooers of reality. He who realises at last how long and how thoroughly he has been befooled, embraces out of spite even the ugliest reality. So that in the long run of the world's history the best men have always been wooers of reality, for the best have always been longest and most thoroughly deceived.

4

Advance of freethinking. The difference between past and present freethinking cannot better be characterised than by that aphorism for the recognition and expression of which all the fearlessness of the eighteenth century was needed, and which even then, if measured by our modern view, sinks into an unconscious naïveté. I mean Voltaire's aphorism, '*croyez-moi, mon ami, l'erreur aussi a son mérite.*' *

5

A hereditary sin of philosophers. Philosophers have at all times appropriated and *corrupted* the maxims of censors of men (moralists), by taking them over without qualification and trying to prove as

* 'Believe me, my friend, error has its merits, too.'

necessary what the moralists only meant as a rough indication or as a truth suited to their fellow-countrymen or fellow-townsmen for a single decade. Moreover, the philosophers thought that they were thereby raising themselves above the moralists! Thus it will be found that the celebrated teachings of Schopenhauer as to the supremacy of the will over the intellect, of the immutability of character, the negativity of pleasure – all errors, in the sense in which he understands them – rest upon principles of popular wisdom enunciated by the moralists. Take the very word 'will', which Schopenhauer twisted so as to become a common denotation of several human conditions and with which he filled a gap in the language (to his own great advantage, in so far as he was a moralist, for he became free to speak of the will as Pascal had spoken of it). In the hands of its creator, Schopenhauer's 'will', through the philosophic craze for generalisation, already turned out to be a bane to knowledge. For this will was made into a poetic metaphor, when it was held that all things in nature possess will. Finally, that it might be applied to all kinds of disordered mysticism, the word, by a fraudulent convention, was misused. So now all our fashionable philosophers repeat it and seem to be perfectly certain that all things have a will and are in fact One Will. According to the description generally given of this All-One-Will, this is much as if one should positively try to have the stupid Devil for one's God.

6

Against visionaries. The visionary denies the truth to himself, the liar only to others.

7

Enmity to light. If we make it clear to anyone that, strictly, he can never speak of truth, but only of probability and of its degrees, we generally discover, from the undisguised joy of our pupil, how greatly men prefer the uncertainty of their intellectual horizon, and how in their heart of hearts they hate truth because of its definiteness. Is this due to a secret fear felt by all that the light of truth may at some time be turned too brightly upon themselves? To their wish to be of some consequence, and accordingly their concealment from the world of what they are?

Or is it to be traced to their horror of the all-too-brilliant light, to which their crepuscular, easily dazzled, bat-like souls are not accustomed, so that hate it they must?

8

Christian scepticism. Pilate, with his question, 'What is Truth?' is now gleefully brought on the scene as an advocate of Christ, in order to cast suspicion on all that is known or knowable as being mere appearance, and to erect the Cross on the appalling background of the Impossibility of Knowledge.

9

'Natural Law', a phrase of superstition. When you talk so delightedly of Nature acting according to law, you must either assume that all things in Nature follow their law from a voluntary obedience imposed by themselves – in which case you admire the morality of Nature: or you are enchanted with the idea of a creative mechanician, who has made a most cunning watch with human beings as accessory ornaments. Necessity, through the expression 'conformity to law', then becomes more human and a coign of refuge in the last instance for mythological reveries.

10

Fallen forfeit to history. All misty philosophers and obscurers of the world, in other words all metaphysicians of coarse or refined texture are seized with eyeache, earache, and toothache when they begin to suspect that there is truth in the saying: 'All philosophy has from now fallen forfeit to history'. In view of their aches and pains we may pardon them for throwing stones and filth at him who talks like this, but this teaching may itself thereby become dirty and disreputable for a time and lose in effect.

11

The pessimist of the intellect. He whose intellect is really free will think freely about the intellect itself, and will not shut his eyes to certain terrible aspects of its source and tendency. For this reason others will perhaps designate him the bitterest opponent of free thought and give him that dreadful, abusive name of 'pessimist of the intellect': accustomed as they are to typify a man not by his strong point, his pre-eminent virtue, but by the quality that is most foreign to his nature.

12

The metaphysicians' knapsack. To all who talk so boastfully of the scientific basis of their metaphysics it is best to make no reply. It is enough to tug at the bundle that they rather shyly keep hidden behind their backs. If one succeeds in lifting it, the results of that 'scientific basis' come to light, to their great confusion: a dear little 'God', a genteel immortality, perhaps a little spiritualism, and in any case a complicated mass of poor-sinners'-misery and pharisee-arrogance.

13

Occasional harmfulness of knowledge. The utility involved in the unchecked investigation of knowledge is so constantly proved in a hundred different ways, that one must remember to include in the bargain the subtler and rarer damage which individuals must suffer on that account. The chemist cannot avoid occasionally being poisoned or burnt at his experiments. What applies to the chemist, is true of the whole of our culture. This, it may be added, clearly shows that knowledge should provide itself with healing balsam against burns and should always have antidotes ready against poisons.

14

The craving of the philistine. The philistine thinks that his most urgent need is a purple patch or turban of metaphysics, nor will he let it slip. Yet he would look less ridiculous without this adornment.

15

Enthusiasts. With all that enthusiasts say in favour of their gospel or their master they are defending themselves, however much they comport themselves as the judges and not the accused: because they are involuntarily reminded almost at every moment that they are exceptions and have to assert their legitimacy.

16

The good seduces to life. All good things, even all good books that are written against life, are strong means of attraction to life.

17

The happiness of the historian. 'When we hear the hair-splitting metaphysicians and prophets of the after-world speak, we others feel indeed that we are the "poor in spirit", but that ours is the heavenly kingdom of change, with spring and autumn, summer and winter, and theirs the afterworld, with its grey, everlasting frosts and shadows.' Thus soliloquised a man as he walked in the morning sunshine, a man who in his pursuit of history has constantly changed not only his mind but his heart. In contrast to the metaphysicians, he is happy to harbour in himself not an 'immortal soul' but many *mortal* souls.

18

Three varieties of thinkers. There are streaming, flowing, trickling mineral springs, and three corresponding varieties of thinkers. The layman values them by the volume of the water, the expert by the contents of the water – in other words, by the elements in them that are not water.

19

The picture of life. The task of painting the picture of life, often as it has been attempted by poets and philosophers, is nevertheless irrational. Even in the hands of the greatest artist-thinkers, pictures and miniatures of one life only – their own – have come into being, and indeed no other result is possible. While in the process of developing, a thing that develops cannot mirror itself as fixed and permanent, as a *definite object*.

20

Truth will have no gods before it. The belief in truth begins with the doubt of all truths in which one has previously believed.

21

Where silence is required. If we speak of freethinking as of a highly dangerous journey over glaciers and frozen seas, we find that those who do not care to travel on this track are offended, as if they had been reproached with cowardice and weak knees. The difficult, which we find to be beyond our powers, must not even be mentioned in our presence.

22

*Historia in nuce.** The most serious parody I ever heard was this: 'In the beginning was the nonsense, and the nonsense was with God, and the nonsense was God.'

23

Incurable. The idealist is incorrigible: if he be thrown out of his Heaven, he makes himself a suitable ideal out of Hell. Disillusion him, and lo! he will embrace disillusionment with no less ardour than he recently embraced hope. In so far as his impulse belongs to the great incurable impulses of human nature, he can bring about tragic destinies and later become a subject for tragedy himself, for such tragedies as deal with the incurable, implacable, inevitable in the lot and character of man.

24

Applause itself as the continuation of the play. Sparkling eyes and an amiable smile are the tributes of applause paid to all the great comedy of world and existence – but this applause is a comedy within a comedy, meant to tempt the other spectators to a *plaudite amici.*†

25

Courage for tedium. He who has not the courage to allow himself and his work to be considered tedious, is certainly no intellect of the first rank, whether in the arts or in the sciences. A scoffer, who happened for once in a way to be a thinker, might add, with

---

* History in a nutshell.
† '*Plaudite, amici, comoedia finita!*': 'Applaud, my friends, the comedy is over.' Reputedly said by Beethoven on his deathbed, after receiving the last rites.

a glance at the world and at history: 'God did not possess this courage, for he wanted to make and he made all things so interesting.'

26

From the most intimate experience of the thinker. Nothing is harder for a man than to conceive of an object impersonally, I mean to see in it an object and not a person. One may even ask whether it is possible for him to dispense for a single moment with the machinery of his instinct to create and construct a personality. After all, he associates with his thoughts, however abstract they may be, as with individuals, against whom he must fight or to whom he must attach himself, whom he must protect, support and nourish. Let us watch or listen to ourselves at the moment when we hear or discover a new idea. Perhaps it displeases us because it is so defiant and so autocratic, and we unconsciously ask ourselves whether we cannot place a contradiction of it by its side as an enemy, or fasten on to it a 'perhaps' or a 'sometimes': the mere little word 'probably' gives us a feeling of satisfaction, for it shatters the oppressive tyranny of the unconditional. If, on the other hand, the new idea enters in gentle shape, sweetly patient and humble, and falling at once into the arms of contradiction, we put our autocracy to the test in another way. Can we not come to the aid of this weak creature, stroke it and feed it, give it strength and fullness, and truth and even unconditionality? Is it possible for us to show ourselves parental or chivalrous or compassionate towards our idea? – Then again, we see here a judgment and there a judgment, sundered from each other, never looking at or making any movement towards each other. So we are tickled by the thought, whether it be not here feasible to make a match, to draw a *conclusion*, with the anticipation that if a consequence follows this conclusion it is not only the two judgments united in wedlock but the matchmakers that will gain honour. If, however, we cannot acquire a hold upon that thought either on the path of defiance and ill-will or on that of good-will (if we hold it to be true) – then we submit to it and do homage to it as a leader and a prince, give it a chair of honour, and speak not of it without a flourish of trumpets: for we are bright in its brightness. Woe to him who tries to dim this brightness! Perhaps we ourselves one day grow suspicious of our idea. Then we, the indefatigable 'king-makers' of the history of the intellect, cast it down from its throne and immediately exalt its adversary. Surely if this be considered and thought out a little further, no one will speak of an 'absolute impulse to knowledge'!

Why, then, does man prefer the true to the untrue, in this secret combat with thought-personalities, in this generally clandestine match-making of thoughts, constitution-founding of thoughts, child-rearing of thoughts, nursing and almsgiving of thoughts? For the same reason that he practises honesty in intercourse with real persons: *now* from habit, heredity, and training, *originally* because the true, like the fair and the just, is more expedient and more reputable than the untrue. For in the realm of thought it is difficult to assume a power and glory that are built on error or on falsehood. The feeling that such an edifice might at some time collapse is humiliating to the self-esteem of the architect — he is ashamed of the fragility of the material, and, as he considers himself more important than the rest of the world, he would fain construct nothing that is less durable than the rest of the world. In his longing for truth he embraces the belief in a personal immortality, the most arrogant and defiant idea that exists, closely allied as it is to the underlying thought, *pereat mundus, dum ego salvus sim!* * His work has become his 'ego', he transforms himself into the Imperishable with its universal challenge. It is his immeasurable pride that will only employ the best and hardest stones for the work — truths, or what he holds for such. Arrogance has always been justly called the 'vice of the sage'; yet without this vice, fruitful in impulses, Truth and her status on earth would be in a parlous plight. In our propensity to fear our thoughts, concepts and words, and yet to honour ourselves in them, unconsciously to ascribe to them the power of rewarding, despising, praising, and blaming us, and so to associate with them as with free intellectual personalities, as with independent powers, as with our equals — herein lie the roots of the remarkable phenomenon which I have called 'intellectual conscience'. Thus something of the highest moral species has bloomed from a black root.

---

* 'Let the world perish, so long as I am saved.'

27

The obscurantists. The essential feature of the black art of obscurantism is not its intention of clouding the brain, but its attempt to darken the picture of the world and cloud our idea of existence. It often employs the method of thwarting all illumination of the intellect, but at times it uses the very opposite means, seeking by the highest refinement of the intellect to induce a satiety of the intellect's fruits. Hair-splitting metaphysicians, who pave the way for scepticism and by their excessive acumen provoke a distrust of acumen, are excellent instruments of the more subtle form of obscurantism. Is it possible that even Kant may be applied to this purpose? Did he even *intend* something of the sort, for a time at least, to judge from his own notorious exposition: 'to clear the way for belief by setting limitations to knowledge'? – Certainly he did not succeed, nor did his followers, on the wolf and fox tracks of this highly refined and dangerous form of obscurantism – the most dangerous of all, for the black art here appears in the garb of light.

28

By what kind of philosophy art is corrupted. When the mists of a metaphysical-mystical philosophy succeed in making all aesthetic phenomena *opaque*, it follows that these phenomena cannot be comparatively valued, inasmuch as each becomes individually inexplicable. But when once they cannot be compared for the sake of valuation, there arises an entire absence-of-criticism, a blind indulgence. From this source springs a continual diminution of the enjoyment of art (which is only distinguished from the crude satisfaction of a need by the highest refinement of taste and appreciation). The more taste diminishes, the more does the desire for art change and revert to a vulgar hunger, which the artist henceforth seeks to appease by ever coarser fare.

29

On Gethsemane. The most painful thing a thinker can say to artists is: 'Could ye not *watch* with me one hour?'

30

At the loom. There are many (artists and women, for instance) who work against the few that take a pleasure in untying the knot of things and unravelling their woof. The former always want to weave the woof together again and entangle it and so turn the conceived into the un-conceived and if possible inconceivable. Whatever the result may be, the woof and knot always look rather untidy, because too many hands are working and tugging at them.

31

In the desert of science. As the man of science proceeds on his modest and toilsome wanderings, which must often enough be journeys in the desert, he is confronted with those brilliant mirages known as 'philosophic systems'. With magic powers of deception they show him that the solution of all riddles and the most refreshing draught of true water of life are close at hand. His weary heart rejoices, and he well-nigh touches with his lips the goal of all scientific endurance and hardship, so that almost unconsciously he presses forward. Other natures stand still, as if spellbound by the beautiful illusion: the desert swallows them up, they become lost to science. Other natures, again, that have often experienced these subjective consolations, become very disheartened and curse the salty taste which these mirages leave behind in the mouth and from which springs a raging thirst – without one's having come one step nearer to any sort of a spring.

32

The so-called 'real reality'. When the poet depicts the various callings – such as those of the warrior, the silk-weaver, the sailor – he feigns to know all these things thoroughly, to be an expert. Even in the exposition of human actions and destinies he behaves as if he had been present at the spinning of the whole web of existence. In so far he is an impostor. He practises his frauds on pure ignoramuses, and that is why he succeeds. They praise him for his deep, genuine knowledge, and lead him finally into the delusion that he really knows as much as the individual experts and creators, yes, even as the great world-spinners themselves. In the end, the im-postor becomes honest, and actually believes in his own sincerity. Emotional people say to his very face that he has the 'higher' truth and sincerity – for they are weary of reality for the time being, and accept the poetic dream as a pleasant relaxation and a night's rest for head and heart. The visions of the dream now appear to them of more value, because, as has been said, they find them more beneficial, and mankind has always held that what is apparently of more value is more true, more real. All that is generally called reality, the poets, conscious of this power, proceed with intention to disparage and to distort into the uncertain, the illusory, the spurious, the impure, the sinful, sorrowful, and deceitful. They make use of all doubts about the limits of knowledge, of all sceptical excesses, in order to spread over everything the rumpled veil of uncertainty. For they desire that when this darkening process is complete their wizardry and soul-magic may be accepted without hesitation as the path to 'true truth' and 'real reality'.

33

The wish to be just and the wish to be a judge. Schopenhauer, whose profound understanding of what is human and all-too-human and original sense for facts was not a little impaired by the bright leopard-skin of his metaphysic (the skin must first be pulled off him if one wants to find the real moralist genius beneath) – Schopenhauer makes this admirable distinction, wherein he comes far nearer the mark than he would himself dare to admit: 'Insight into the stern necessity of human actions is the boundary line that divides philosophic from other brains.' He worked against that wonderful insight of which he was sometimes capable by the prejudice that he had in common with the moral man (not the moralist), a prejudice that he expresses quite guilelessly and devoutly as follows: 'The ultimate and true explanation of the inner being of the entirety of things must of necessity be closely connected with that about the ethical significance of human actions.' This connection is not 'necessary' at all: such a connection must rather be rejected by that principle of the stern necessity of human actions, that is, the unconditioned non-freedom and non-responsibility of the will. Philosophic brains will accordingly be distinguished from others by their disbelief in the metaphysical significance of morality. This must create between the two kinds of brain a gulf of a depth and unbridgeableness of which the much-deplored gulf between 'cultured' and 'uncultured' scarcely gives a conception. It is true that many back doors, which the 'philosophic brains', like Schopenhauer's own, have left for themselves, must be recognised as useless. None leads into the open, into the fresh air of the free will, but every door through which people had slipped hitherto showed behind it once more the gleaming brass wall of fate. For we are in a prison, and can only dream of freedom, not make ourselves free. That the recognition of this fact cannot be resisted much longer is shown by the despairing and incredible postures and grimaces of those who still press against it and continue their wrestling-bout with it. Their attitude at present is something like this: 'So no one is responsible for his actions? And all is full of guilt and the consciousness of guilt? But someone *must* be the sinner. If it is no longer possible or permissible to accuse and sentence the individual, the one poor wave in the inevitable rough-and-tumble of the waves of development – well, then, let this stormy sea, this development itself, be the sinner. Here is free will: this totality can be accused and sentenced, can atone and expiate. *So let God be the sinner and man his redeemer.* Let the world's history be guilt, expiation, and self-murder. Let the evil-doer be his own judge, the judge his own hangman.' This Christianity strained to its limits – for what else is it? – is the last thrust in the fencing-match between the teaching of unconditioned morality and the teaching of un-conditioned non-freedom. It would be quite horrible if it were anything more than a logical pose, a hideous grimace of the underlying thought, perhaps the death-convulsion of the heart that seeks a remedy in its despair, the heart to which delirium whispers: 'Behold, thou art the lamb which taketh away the sin of God.' This error lies not only in the feeling, 'I am responsible', but just as much in the contradiction, 'I am not responsible, but some-one must be.' That is simply not true. Hence the philosopher must say, like Christ, 'Judge not', and the final distinction between the philosophic brains and the others would be that the former wish to be just and the latter wish to be judges.

34

Sacrifice. You hold that sacrifice is the hallmark of moral action? – Just consider whether in every action that is done with deliberation, in the best as in the worst, there be not a sacrifice.

35

Against the 'triers of the reins' of morality. One must know the best and the worst that a man is capable of in theory and in practice before one can judge how strong his moral nature is and can be. But this is an experiment that one can never carry out.

36

Serpent's tooth. Whether we have a serpent's tooth or not we cannot know before someone has set his heel upon our necks. A wife or a mother could say: until someone has put his heel upon the neck of our darling, our child. Our character is determined more by the absence of certain experiences than by the experiences we have undergone.

37

Deception in love. We forget and purposely banish from our minds a good deal of our past. In other words, we wish our picture, that beams at us from the past, to belie us, to flatter our vanity – we are constantly engaged in this self-deception. And you who talk and boast so much of 'self-oblivion in love', of the 'absorption of the ego in the other person' – you hold that this is something different? So you break the mirror, throw yourselves into another personality that you admire, and enjoy the new portrait of your ego, though calling it by the other person's name – and this whole proceeding is not to be thought self-deception, self-seeking, you marvellous beings? – It seems to me that those who hide something of themselves from themselves, or hide their whole selves from themselves, are alike committing a theft from the treasury of knowledge. It is clear, then, against what transgression the maxim 'Know thyself' is a warning.

38

To the denier of his vanity. He who denies his own vanity usually possesses it in so brutal a form that he instinctively shuts his eyes to avoid the necessity of despising himself.

39

Why the stupid so often become malignant. To those arguments of our adversary against which our head feels too weak our heart replies by throwing suspicion on the motives of his arguments.

40

The art of moral exceptions. An art that points out and glorifies the exceptional cases of morality – where the good becomes bad and the unjust just – should rarely be given a hearing: just as now and again we buy something from gipsies, with the fear that they are diverting to their own pockets much more than their mere profit from the purchase.

41

Enjoyment and non-enjoyment of poisons. The only decisive argument that has always deterred men from drinking a poison is not that it is deadly, but that it has an unpleasant taste.

42

The world without consciousness of sin. If men only committed such deeds as do not give rise to a bad conscience, the human world would still look bad and rascally enough, but not so sickly and pitiable as at present. Enough wicked men without conscience have existed at all times, and many good honest folk lack the feeling of pleasure in a good conscience.

43

The conscientious. It is more convenient to follow one's conscience than one's intelligence, for at every failure conscience finds an excuse and an encouragement in itself. That is why there are so many conscientious and so few intelligent people.

44

Opposite means of avoiding bitterness. One temperament finds it useful to be able to give vent to its disgust in words, being made sweeter by speech. Another reaches its full bitterness only by speaking out: it is more advisable for it to have to gulp down something – the restraint that men of this stamp place upon themselves in the presence of enemies and superiors improves their character and prevents it from becoming too acrid and sour.

45

Not to be too dejected. To get bed-sores is unpleasant, but no proof against the merits of the cure that prescribes that you should take to your bed. Men who have long lived outside themselves, and have at last devoted themselves to the inward philosophic life, know that one can also get sores of character and intellect. This, again, is on the whole no argument against the chosen way of life, but necessitates a few small exceptions and apparent relapses.

46

The human 'thing in itself'. The most vulnerable and yet most unconquerable of things is human vanity: nay, through being wounded its strength increases and can grow to giant proportions.

47

The farce of many industrious persons. By an excess of effort they win leisure for themselves, and then they can do nothing with it but count the hours until the tale is ended.

48

The possession of joy abounding. He that has joy abounding must be a good man, but perhaps he is not the cleverest of men, although he has reached the very goal towards which the cleverest man is striving with all his cleverness.

49

In the mirror of nature. Is not a man fairly well described, when we are told that he likes to walk between tall fields of golden corn: that he prefers the forest and flower colours of sere and chilly autumn to all others, because they point to something more beautiful than Nature has ever attained: that he feels as much at home under big broad-leaved walnut trees as among his nearest kinsfolk: that in the mountains his greatest joy is to come across those tiny distant lakes from which the very eyes of solitude seem to peer at him: that he loves that grey calm of the misty twilight that steals along the windows on autumn and early winter evenings and shuts out all soulless sounds as with velvet curtains: that in unhewn stones he recognises the last remaining traces of the primeval age, eager for speech, and honours them from childhood upwards: that, lastly, the sea with its shifting serpent skin and wild-beast beauty is, and remains to him, unfamiliar? – Yes, something of the man is described herewith, but the mirror of Nature does not say that the same man, with (and not even 'in spite of') all his idyllic sensibilities, might be disagreeable, stingy, and conceited. Horace, who was a good judge of such matters, in his famous *beatus ille qui procul negotiis** puts the tenderest feeling for country life into the mouth of a Roman money-lender.

50

Power without victory. The strongest cognition (that of the complete non-freedom of the human will) is yet the poorest in results, for it has always had the mightiest of opponents – human vanity.

51

Pleasure and error. A beneficial influence on friends is exerted by one man unconsciously, through his nature; by another consciously, through isolated actions. Although the former nature is held to be the higher, the latter alone is allied to good conscience and pleasure – the pleasure in justification by good works, which rests upon a belief in the volitional character of our good and evil doing – that is to say, upon a mistake.

52

The folly of committing injustice. The injustice we have inflicted ourselves is far harder to bear than the injustice inflicted upon us by others (not always from moral grounds, be it observed). After all, the doer is always the sufferer – that is, if he be capable of feeling the sting of conscience or of perceiving that by his action he has armed society against himself and cut himself off. For this reason we should beware still more of doing than of suffering injustice, for the sake of our own inward happiness – so as not to lose our feeling of well-being – quite apart from any consideration of the precepts of religion and morality. For in suffering injustice we have the consolation of a good

* 'Happy he who, far from business cares . . . '

conscience, of hope and of revenge, together with the sympathy and applause of the just, nay of the whole of society, which is afraid of the evil-doer. Not a few are skilled in the impure self-deception that enables them to transform every injustice of their own into an injustice inflicted upon them from without, and to reserve for their own acts the exceptional right to the plea of self-defence. Their object, of course, is to make their own burden lighter.

53

Envy with or without a mouthpiece. Ordinary envy is wont to cackle when the envied hen has laid an egg, thereby relieving itself and becoming milder. But there is a yet deeper envy that in such a case becomes dead silent, desiring that every mouth should be sealed and always more and more angry because this desire is not gratified. Silent envy grows in silence.

54

Anger as a spy. Anger exhausts the soul and brings its very dregs to light. Hence, if we know no other means of gaining certainty, we must understand how to arouse anger in our dependants and adversaries, in order to learn what is really done and thought to our detriment.

55

Defence morally more difficult than attack. The true heroic deed and masterpiece of the good man does not lie in attacking opinions and continuing to love their propounders, but in the far harder task of defending his own position without causing or intending to cause bitter heartburns to his opponent. The sword of attack is honest and broad, the sword of defence usually runs out to a needle point.

56

Honest towards honesty. One who is openly honest towards himself ends by being rather conceited about this honesty. He knows only too well why he is honest — for the same reason that another man prefers outward show and hypocrisy.

57

Coals of fire. The heaping of coals of fire on another's head is generally misunderstood and falls flat, because the other knows himself to be just as much in the right, and on his side too has thought of collecting coals.

58

Dangerous books. A man says: 'Judging from my own case, I find that this book is harmful.' Let him but wait, and perhaps one day he will confess that the book did him a great service by thrusting forward and bringing to light the hidden disease of his soul. Altered opinions alter not at all (or very little) the character of a man: but they illuminate individual facets of his personality, which hitherto, in another constellation of opinions, had remained dark and unrecognisable.

59

Simulated pity. We simulate pity when we wish to show ourselves superior to the feeling of animosity, but generally in vain. This point is not noticed without a considerable enhancement of that feeling of animosity.

60

Open contradiction often conciliatory. At the moment when a man openly makes known his difference of opinion from a well-known party leader, the whole world thinks that he must be angry with the latter. Sometimes, however, he is just on the point of ceasing to be angry with him. He ventures to put himself on the same plane as his opponent, and is free from the tortures of suppressed envy.

61

Seeing our light shining. In the darkest hour of depression, sickness, and guilt, we are still glad to see others taking a light from us and making use of us as of the disk of the moon. By this round-about route we derive some light from our own illuminating faculty.

62

Fellowship in joy. The snake that stings us means to hurt us and rejoices in so doing: the lowest animal can picture to itself the *pain* of others. But to picture to oneself the *joy* of others and to rejoice thereat is the highest privilege of the highest animals, and again, amongst them, is the property only of the most select specimens – accordingly a rare 'human thing'. Hence there have been philosophers who denied fellowship in joy.

63

Supplementary pregnancy. Those who have arrived at works and deeds are in an obscure way, they know not how, all the more pregnant with them, as if to prove supplementarily that these are their children and not those of chance.

64

Hard-hearted from vanity. Just as justice is so often a cloak for weakness, so men who are fairly intelligent, but weak, sometimes attempt dissimulation from ambitious motives and purposely show themselves unjust and hard, in order to leave behind them the impression of strength.

65

Humiliation. If in a large sack of profit we find a single grain of humiliation we still make a wry face even at our good luck.

66

*Extreme Herostratism.** There might be Herostratuses who set fire to their own temple, in which their images are honoured.

67

A world of diminutives. The fact that all that is weak and in need of help appeals to the heart induces in us the habit of designating by diminutive and softening terms all that appeals to our hearts – and accordingly *making* such things weak and clinging to our imaginations.

* Herostratus of Ephesus set fire to the temple of Diana because he could think of no other way of becoming famous.

68

The bad characteristic of sympathy. Sympathy has a peculiar impudence for its companion. For, wishing to help at all costs, sympathy is in no perplexity either as to the means of assistance or as to the nature and cause of the disease, and goes on courageously administering all its quack medicines to restore the health and reputation of the patient.

69

Importunacy. There is even an importunacy in relation to works, and the act of associating oneself from early youth on an intimate footing with the illustrious works of all times evinces an entire absence of shame. Others are only importunate from ignorance, not knowing with whom they have to do – for instance classical scholars young and old in relation to the works of the Greeks.

70

The will is ashamed of the intellect. In all coolness we make reasonable plans against our passions. But we make the most serious mistake in this connection in being often ashamed, when the design has to be carried out, of the coolness and calculation with which we conceived it. So we do just the unreasonable thing, from that sort of defiant magnanimity that every passion involves.

71

Why the sceptics offend morality. He who takes his morality solemnly and seriously is enraged against the sceptics in the domain of morals. For where he lavishes all his force, he wishes others to marvel but not to investigate and doubt. Then there are natures whose last shred of morality is just the belief in morals. They behave in the same way towards sceptics, if possible still more passionately.

72

Shyness. All moralists are shy, because they know they are confounded with spies and traitors, so soon as their penchant is noticed. Besides, they are generally conscious of being impotent in action, for in the midst of work the motives of their activity almost withdraw their attention from the work.

73

A danger to universal morality. People who are at the same time noble and honest come to deify every devilry that brings out their honesty, and to suspend for a time the balance of their moral judgment.

74

The saddest error. It is an unpardonable offence when one discovers that where one was convinced of being loved, one is only regarded as a household utensil and decoration, whereby the master of the house can find an outlet for his vanity before his guests.

75

Love and duality. What else is love but understanding and rejoicing that another lives, works, and feels in a different and opposite way to ourselves? That love may be able to bridge over the contrasts by joys, we must not remove or deny those contrasts. Even self-love presupposes an irreconcileable duality (or plurality) in one person.

76

Signs from dreams. What one sometimes does not know and feel accurately in waking hours – whether one has a good or a bad conscience as regards some person – is revealed completely and unambiguously by dreams.

77

Debauchery. Not joy but joylessness is the mother of debauchery.

78

Reward and punishment. No one accuses without an underlying notion of punishment and revenge, even when he accuses his fate or himself. All complaint is accusation, all self-congratulation is praise. Whether we do one or the other, we always make someone responsible.

79

Doubly unjust. We sometimes advance truth by a twofold injustice: when we see and represent consecutively the two sides of a case which we are not in a position to see together, but in such a way that every time we mistake or deny the other side, fancying that what we see is the whole truth.

80

Mistrust. Self-mistrust does not always proceed uncertainly and shyly, but sometimes in a furious rage, having worked itself into a frenzy in order not to tremble.

81

Philosophy of parvenus. If you want to be a personality you must even hold your shadow in honour.

82

Knowing how to wash oneself clean. We must know how to emerge cleaner from unclean conditions, and, if necessary, how to wash ourselves even with dirty water.

83

Letting yourself go. The more you let yourself go, the less others let you go.

84

The innocent rogue. There is a slow, gradual path to vice and rascality of every description. In the end, the traveller is quite abandoned by the insect-swarms of a bad conscience, and although a thorough scoundrel he walks in innocence.

85

Making plans. Making plans and conceiving projects involves many agreeable sentiments. He that had the strength to be nothing but a contriver of plans all his life would be a happy man. But one must occasionally have a rest from this activity by carrying a plan into execution, and then comes anger and sobriety.

86

Wherewith we see the ideal. Every efficient man is blocked by his efficiency and cannot look out freely from its prison. Had he not also a goodly share of imperfection, he could, by reason of his virtue, never arrive at an intellectual or moral freedom. Our shortcomings are the eyes with which we see the ideal.

87

Dishonest praise. Dishonest praise causes many more twinges of conscience than dishonest blame, probably only because we have exposed our capacity for judgment far more completely through excessive praise than through excessive and unjust blame.

88

How one dies is indifferent. The whole way in which a man thinks of death during the prime of his life and strength is very expressive and significant for what we call his character. But the hour of death itself, his behaviour on the death-bed, is almost indifferent. The exhaustion of waning life, especially when old people die, the irregular or insufficient nourishment of the brain during this last period, the occasionally violent pain, the novel and untried nature of the whole position, and only too often the ebb and flow of superstitious impressions and fears, as if dying were of much consequence and meant the crossing of bridges of the most terrible kind – all this forbids our using death as a testimony concerning the living. Nor is it true that the dying man is generally more honest than the living. On the contrary, through the solemn attitude of the bystanders, the repressed or flowing streams of tears and emotions, everyone is inveigled into a comedy of vanity, now conscious, now unconscious. The serious way in which every dying man is treated must have been to many a poor despised devil the highest joy of his whole life and a sort of compensation and repayment for many privations.

89

Morality and its sacrifice. The origin of morality may be traced to two ideas: 'The community is of more value than the individual', and 'The permanent interest is to be preferred to the temporary.'

The conclusion drawn is that the permanent interest of the community is unconditionally to be set above the temporary interest of the individual, especially his momentary well-being, but also his permanent interest and even the prolongation of his existence. Even if the individual suffers by an arrangement that suits the mass, even if he is depressed and ruined by it, morality must be maintained and the victim brought to the sacrifice. Such a trend of thought arises, however, only in those who are *not* the victims – for in the victim's case it enforces the claim that the individual might be worth more than the many, and that the present enjoyment, the 'moment in paradise', should perhaps be rated higher than a tame succession of untroubled or comfortable circumstances. But the philosophy of the sacrificial victim always finds voice too late, and so victory remains with morals and morality: which are really nothing more than the sentiment for the whole concept of morals under which one lives and has been reared – and reared not as an individual but as a member of the whole, as a cipher in a majority. Hence it constantly happens that the individual makes himself into a majority by means of his morality.

90

The good and the good conscience. You hold that all good things have at all times had a good conscience? Science, which is certainly a very good thing, has come into the world without such a conscience and quite free from all pathos, rather clandestinely, by roundabout ways, walking with shrouded or masked face like a sinner, and always with the feeling at least of being a smuggler. Good conscience has bad conscience for its stepping-stone, not for its opposite. For all that is good has at one time been new and consequently strange, anti-moral, immoral, and has gnawed like a worm at the heart of the fortunate discoverer.

91

Success sanctifies the intentions. We should not shrink from treading the road to a virtue, even when we see clearly that nothing but egotism, and accordingly utility, personal comfort, fear, considerations of health, reputation, or glory, are the impelling motives. These motives are styled ignoble and selfish. Very well, but if they stimulate us to some virtue – for example, self-denial, dutifulness, order, thrift, measure, and moderation – let us listen to them, whatever their epithets may be! For if we reach the goal to which they summon us, then the virtue we have attained, by means of the pure air it makes us breathe and the spiritual well-being it communicates, ennobles the remoter impulses of our action, and afterwards we no longer perform those actions from the same coarse motives that inspired us before. Education should therefore force the virtues on the pupil, as far as possible, according to his disposition. Then virtue, the sunshine and summer atmosphere of the soul, can contribute her own share of work and add mellowness and sweetness.

92

Dabblers in Christianity, not Christians. So that is your Christianity! – To annoy humanity you praise 'God and His Saints', and again when you want to praise humanity you go so far that God and His Saints must be annoyed. I wish you would at least learn Christian manners, as you are so deficient in the civility of the Christian heart.

93

The religious and irreligious impression of nature. A true believer must be to us an object of veneration, but the same holds good of a true, sincere, convinced unbeliever. With men of the latter stamp we are near to the high mountains where mighty rivers have their source, and with believers we are under vigorous, shady, restful trees.

94

Judicial murder. The two greatest judicial murders* in the world's history are, to speak without exaggeration, concealed and well-concealed suicide. In both cases a man *willed* to die, and in both cases he let his breast be pierced by the sword in the hand of human injustice.

95

'Love'. The finest artistic conception wherein Christianity had the advantage over other religious systems lay in one word – Love. Hence it became the *lyric* religion (whereas in its two other creations Semitism bestowed heroico-epical religions upon the

---

* The trials of Socrates and Jesus.

world). In the word 'love' there is so much meaning, so much that
stimulates and appeals to memory and hope, that even the meanest
intelligence and the coldest heart feel some glimmering of its sense.
The cleverest woman and the lowest man think of the comparatively unselfish moments of their whole life, even if with them
Eros never soared high: and the vast number of beings who *miss*
love from their parents or children or sweethearts, especially those
whose sexual instincts have been refined away, have found their
heart's desire in Christianity.

96

The fulfilment of Christianity. In Christianity there is also an Epicurean trend of thought, starting from the idea that God can only
demand of man, his creation and his image, what it is possible for
man to fulfil, and accordingly that Christian virtue and perfection
are attainable and often attained. Now, for instance, the belief in
loving one's enemies – even if it is only a belief or fancy, and by no
means a psychological reality (a real love) – gives unalloyed happiness, so long as it is genuinely believed. (As to the reason of this,
psychologist and Christian might well differ.) Hence earthly life,
through the belief, I mean the fancy, that it satisfies not only the
injunction to love our enemies, but all the other injunctions of
Christianity, and that it has really assimilated and embodied in itself
the Divine perfection according to the command, 'Be perfect as
your Father in heaven is perfect', might actually become a holy
life. Thus error can make Christ's promise come true.

97

Of the future of Christianity. We may be allowed to form a conjecture as to the disappearance of Christianity and as to the places
where it will be the slowest to retreat, if we consider where and for
what reasons Protestantism spread with such startling rapidity. As is
well known, Protestantism promised to do far more cheaply all
that the old Church did, without costly masses, pilgrimages, and
priestly pomp and circumstance. It spread particularly among the
Northern nations, which were not so deeply rooted as those of the
South in the old Church's symbolism and love of ritual. In the
South the more powerful pagan religion survived in Christianity,
whereas in the North Christianity meant an opposition to and a

break with the old-time creed, and hence was from the first more thoughtful and less sensual, but for that very reason, in times of peril, more fanatical and more obstinate. If from the standpoint of *thought* we succeed in uprooting Christianity, we can at once know the point where it will begin to disappear – the very point at which it will be most stubborn in defence. In other places it will bend but not break, lose its leaves but burst into leaf afresh, because the senses, and not thought, have gone over to its side. But it is the senses that maintain the belief that with all its expensive outlay the Church is more cheaply and conveniently managed than under the stern conditions of work and wages. Yet what does one hold leisure (or semi-idleness) to be worth, when once one has become accustomed to it? The senses plead against a dechristianised world, saying that there would be too much work to do in it and an insufficient supply of leisure. They take the part of magic – that is, they let God work himself (*oremus nos, Deus laboret*).*

98

Theatricality and honesty of unbelievers. There is no book that contains in such abundance or expresses so faithfully all that man occasionally finds salutary – ecstatic inward happiness, ready for sacrifice or death in the belief in and contemplation of *his* truth – as the book that tells of Christ. From that book a clever man may learn all the means whereby a book can be made into a world-book, a vade-mecum for all, and especially that master-means of representing everything as discovered, nothing as future and uncertain. All influential books try to leave the same impression, as if the widest intellectual horizon were circumscribed here and as if about the sun that shines here every constellation visible at present or in the future must revolve. Must not then all purely scientific books be poor in influence on the same grounds as such books are rich in influence? Is not the book fated to live humble and among humble folk, in order to be crucified in the end and never resurrected? In relation to what the religious inform us of their 'knowledge' and their 'holy spirit', are not all upright men of science 'poor in spirit'? Can any religion demand more self-denial and draw the selfish out of themselves more inexorably than science? – This and

---

* Let us pray, and let God do the work.

similar things we may say, in any case with a certain theatricality, when we have to defend ourselves against believers, for it is impossible to conduct a defence without a certain amount of theatricality. But between ourselves our language must be more honest, and we employ a freedom that those believers are not even allowed, in their own interests, to understand. Away, then, with the monastic cowl of self-denial, with the appearance of humility! Much more and much better – so rings our truth! If science were not linked with the pleasure of knowledge, the utility of the thing known, what should we care for science? If a little faith, love, and hope did not lead our souls to knowledge, what would attract us to science? And if in science the ego means nothing, still the inventive, happy ego, every upright and industrious ego, means a great deal in the republic of the men of science. The homage of those who pay homage, the joy of those whom we wish well or honour, in some cases glory and a fair share of immortality, is the personal reward for every suppression of personality: to say nothing here of meaner views and rewards, although it is just on this account that the majority have sworn and always continue to swear fidelity to the laws of the republic and of science. If we had not remained in some degree unscientific, what would science matter to us? Taking everything together and speaking in plain language: 'To a purely knowing being knowledge would be indifferent.' – Not the quality but the quantity of faith and devoutness distinguishes us from the pious, the believers. We are content with less. But should one of them cry out to us: 'Be content and show yourselves contented!' we could easily answer: 'As a matter of fact, we do not belong to the most discontented class. But you, if your faith makes you happy, show yourselves to be happy. Your faces have always done more harm to your faith than our reasons! If that glad message of your Bible were written in your faces, you would not need to demand belief in the authority of that book in such stiff-necked fashion. Your words, your actions should continually make the Bible superfluous – in fact, through you a new Bible should continually come into being. As it is, your apologia for Christianity is rooted in your unchristianity, and with your defence you write your own condemnation. If you, however, should wish to emerge from your dissatisfaction with Christianity, you should ponder over the experience of two thousand years, which, clothed in the modest form of a question, may be voiced as follows: 'If Christ really intended to redeem the world, may he not be said to have failed?'

99

The poet as guide to the future. All the surplus poetical force that still exists in modern humanity, but is not used under our conditions of life, should (without any deduction) be devoted to a definite goal – not to depicting the present nor to reviving and summarising the past, but to pointing the way to the future. Nor should this be so done as if the poet, like an imaginative political economist, had to anticipate a more favourable national and social state of things and picture their realisation. Rather will he, just as the earlier poets portrayed the images of the gods, portray the fair images of men. He will divine those cases where, in the midst of our modern world and reality (which will not be shirked or repudiated in the usual poetic fashion), a great, noble soul is still possible, where it may be embodied in harmonious, equable conditions, where it may become permanent, visible, and representative of a type, and so, by the stimulus to imitation and envy, help to create the future. The poems of such a poet would be distinguished by appearing secluded and protected from the heated atmosphere of the passions. The irremediable failure, the shattering of all the strings of the human instrument, the scornful laughter and gnashing of teeth, and all tragedy and comedy in the usual old sense, would appear by the side of this new art as mere archaic lumber, a blurring of the outlines of the world-picture. Strength, kindness, gentleness, purity, and an unsought, innate moderation in the personalities and their action: a levelled soil, giving rest and pleasure to the foot: a shining heaven mirrored in faces and events: science and art welded into a new unity: the mind living together with her sister, the soul, without arrogance or jealousy, and enticing from contrasts the grace of seriousness, not the impatience of discord – all this would be the general environment, the background on which the delicate differences of the embodied ideals would make the real picture, that of ever-growing human majesty. Many roads to this poetry of the future start from Goethe, but the quest needs good pathfinders and above all a far greater strength than is possessed by modern poets, who unscrupulously represent the half-animal and the immaturity and intemperance that are mistaken by them for power and naturalness.

100

*The Muse as Penthesilea.** 'Better to rot than to be a woman without charm.' When once the Muse thinks thus, the end of her art is again at hand. But it can be a tragic and also a comic finale.

101

The circuitous path to the beautiful. If the beautiful is to be identified with that which gives pleasure – and thus sang the Muses once – the useful is often the necessary circuitous path to the beautiful, and has a perfect right to spurn the short-sighted censure of men who live for the moment, who will not wait, and who think that they can reach all good things without ever taking a circuitous path.

102

An excuse for many a transgression. The ceaseless desire to create, the eternal looking outward of the artist, hinders him from becoming better and more beautiful as a personality: unless his craving for glory be great enough to compel him to exhibit in his relations with other men a growth corresponding to the growing beauty and greatness of his works. In any case he has but a limited measure of strength, and how could the proportion of strength that he spends on himself be of any benefit to his work – or *vice versa*?

103

Satisfying the best people. If we have satisfied the best people of our time with our art, it is a sign that we shall not satisfy the best people of the succeeding period. We have indeed 'lived for all time', and the applause of the best people ensures our fame.

104

Of one substance. If we are of one substance with a book or a work of art, we think in our heart of hearts that it must be excellent, and are offended if others find it ugly, over-spiced, or pretentious.

* Queen of the Amazons, killed by Achilles at Troy.

105

Speech and emotion. That speech is not given to us to communicate our emotions may be seen from the fact that all simple men are ashamed to seek for words to express their deeper feelings. These feelings are expressed only in actions, and even here such men blush if others seem to divine their motives. After all, among poets, to whom God generally denies this shame, the more noble are more monosyllabic in the language of emotion, and evince a certain constraint: whereas the real poets of emotion are for the most part shameless in practical life.

106

A mistake about a privation. He that has not for a long time been completely weaned from an art, and is still always at home in it, has no idea how small a privation it is to live without that art.

107

Three-quarter strength. A work that is meant to give an impression of health should be produced with three-quarters, at the most, of the strength of its creator. If he has gone to his farthest limit, the work excites the observer and disconcerts him by its tension. All good things have something lazy about them and lie like cows in the meadow.

108

Refusing to have hunger as a guest. As refined fare serves a hungry man as well as and no better than coarser food, the more pretentious artist will not dream of inviting the hungry man to his meal.

109

Living without art and wine. It is with works of art as with wine – it is better if one can do without both and keep to water, and if from the inner fire and inner sweetness of the soul the water spontaneously changes again into wine.

110

The pirate-genius. The pirate-genius in art, who even knows how to deceive subtle minds, arises when someone unscrupulously and from youth upwards regards all good things, that are not protected by law, as the property of a particular person, as his legitimate spoil. Now all the good things of past ages and masters lie free around us, hedged about and protected by the reverential awe of the few who know them. To these few our robber-genius, by the force of his impudence, bids defiance and accumulates for himself a wealth that once more calls forth homage and awe.

111

To the poets of great towns. In the gardens of modern poetry it will clearly be observed that the sewers of great towns are too near. With the fragrance of flowers is mingled something that betrays abomination and putrescence. With pain I ask: 'Must you poets always request wit and dirt to stand godfather, when an innocent and beautiful sensation has to be christened by you? Are you obliged to dress your noble goddess in a hood of devilry and caricature? But whence this necessity, this obligation?' The reason is – because you live too near the sewers.

112

Of the salt of speech. No one has ever explained why the Greek writers, having at command such an unparalleled wealth and power of language, made so sparing a use of their resources that every post-classical Greek book appears by comparison crude, over-coloured, and extravagant. It is said that towards the North Polar ice and in the hottest countries salt is becoming less and less used, whereas on the other hand the dwellers on the plains and by the coast in the more temperate zones use salt in great abundance. Is it possible that the Greeks from a twofold reason – because their intellect was colder and clearer but their fundamental passionate nature far more tropical than ours – did not need salt and spice to the same extent that we do?

113

The freest writer. In a book for free spirits one cannot avoid mention of Laurence Sterne, the man whom Goethe honoured as the freest spirit of his century. May he be satisfied with the honour of being called the freest writer of all times, in comparison with whom all others appear stiff, square-toed, intolerant, and downright boorish! In his case we should not speak of the clear and rounded but of 'the endless melody' – if by this phrase we arrive at a name for an artistic style in which the definite form is continually broken, thrust aside and transferred to the realm of the indefinite, so that it signifies one and the other at the same time. Sterne is the great master of *double entendre*, this phrase being naturally used in a far wider sense than is commonly done when one applies it to sexual relations. We may give up for lost the reader who always wants to know exactly what Sterne thinks about a matter, and whether he be making a serious or a smiling face (for he can do both with one wrinkling of his features; he can be and even wishes to be right and wrong at the same moment, to interweave profundity and farce). His digressions are at once continuations and further developments of the story, his maxims contain a satire on all that is sententious, his dislike of seriousness is bound up with a disposition to take no matter merely externally and on the surface. So in the proper reader he arouses a feeling of uncertainty whether he be walking, lying, or standing, a feeling most closely akin to that of floating in the air. He, the most versatile of writers, communicates something of this versatility to his reader. Yes, Sterne unexpectedly changes the parts, and is often as much reader as author, his book being like a play within a play, a theatre audience before another theatre audience. We must surrender at discretion to the mood of Sterne, although we can always expect it to be gracious. It is strangely instructive to see how so great a writer as Diderot has affected this *double entendre* of Sterne's – to be equally ambiguous throughout is just the Sternian super-humour. Did Diderot imitate, admire, ridicule, or parody Sterne in his *Jacques le Fataliste*? One cannot be exactly certain, and this uncertainty was perhaps intended by the author. This very doubt makes the French unjust to the work of one of their first masters, one who need not be ashamed of comparison with any of the ancients or moderns. For humour (and especially for this humorous attitude towards humour itself) the French are too serious. Is it necessary to add that of all great authors Sterne is the worst model, in fact the inimitable author, and that even Diderot had to pay for his daring? What the worthy Frenchmen and before them some Greeks and Romans aimed at and attained in prose is the very opposite of what Sterne aims at and attains. He raises himself as a masterly exception above all that artists in writing demand of themselves – propriety, reserve, character, steadfastness of purpose, comprehensiveness, perspicuity, good deportment in gait and feature. Unfortunately Sterne the man seems to have been only too closely related to Sterne the writer. His squirrel-soul sprang with insatiable unrest from branch to branch; he knew what lies between sublimity and rascality; he had sat on every seat, always with unabashed watery eyes and mobile play of feature. He was – if language does not revolt from such a combination – of a hard-hearted kindness, and in the midst of the joys of a grotesque and even corrupt imagination he showed the bashful grace of innocence. Such a carnal and spiritual hermaphroditism, such untrammelled wit penetrating into every vein and muscle, was perhaps never possessed by any other man.

114

A choice reality. Just as the good prose writer only takes words that belong to the language of daily intercourse, though not by a long way all its words – whence arises a choice style – so the good poet of the future will only represent the real and turn his eyes away from all fantastic, superstitious, half-voiced, forgotten stories, to which earlier poets devoted their powers. Only reality, though by a long way not every reality – but a choice reality.

115

Degenerate species of art. Side by side with the genuine species of art, those of great repose and great movement, there are degenerate species – weary, blasé art and excited art. Both would have their weakness taken for strength and wish to be confounded with the genuine species.

116

A hero impossible from lack of colour. The typical poets and artists of our age like to compose their pictures upon a background of shimmering red, green, grey, and gold, on the background of nervous sensuality – a condition well understood by the children of this century. The drawback comes when we do *not* look at these pictures with the eyes of our century. Then we see that the great figures painted by these artists have something flickering, tremulous and dizzy about them, and accordingly we do not ascribe to them heroic deeds, but at best mock-heroic, swaggering *mis*deeds.

117

Overladen style. The overladen style is a consequence of the impoverishment of the organising force together with a lavish stock of expedients and intentions. At the beginnings of art the very reverse conditions sometimes appear.

118

Pulchrum est paucorum hominum.* History and experience tell us that the significant grotesqueness that mysteriously excites the imagination and carries one beyond everyday reality, is older and grows more luxuriantly than the beautiful and reverence for the beautiful in art: and that it begins to flourish exceedingly when the sense for beauty is on the wane. For the vast majority of mankind this grotesque seems to be a higher need than the beautiful, presumably because it contains a coarser narcotic.

119

Origins of taste in works of art. If we consider the primary germs of the artistic sense, and ask ourselves what are the various kinds of joy produced by the firstlings of art – as, for example, among savage tribes – we find first of all the joy of understanding what another means. Art in this case is a sort of conundrum, which causes its solver pleasure in his own quick and keen perceptions. Then the roughest works of art remind us of the pleasant things we have actually experienced, and so give joy – as, for example, when

* Beauty belongs to the few.

the artist alludes to a chase, a victory, a wedding. Again, the representation may cause us to feel excited, touched, inflamed, as for instance in the glorification of revenge and danger. Here the enjoyment lies in the excitement itself, in the victory over tedium. The memory, too, of unpleasant things, so far as they have been overcome or make us appear interesting to the listener as subjects for art (as when the singer describes the mishaps of a daring seaman), can inspire great joy, the credit for which is given to art. A more subtle variety is the joy that arises at the sight of all that is regular and symmetrical in lines, points, and rhythms. For by a certain analogy is awakened the feeling for all that is orderly and regular in life, which one has to thank alone for all well-being. So in the cult of symmetry we unconsciously do homage to rule and proportion as the source of our previous happiness, and the joy in this case is a kind of hymn of thanksgiving. Only when a certain satiety of the last-mentioned joy arises does a more subtle feeling step in, that enjoyment might even lie in a violation of the symmetrical and regular. This feeling, for example, impels us to seek reason in apparent unreason, and the sort of aesthetic riddle-guessing that results is in a way the higher species of the first-named artistic joy. He who pursues this speculation still further will know what kind of hypotheses for the explanation of aesthetic phenomena are hereby fundamentally rejected.

120

Not too near. It is a disadvantage for good thoughts when they follow too closely on one another, for they hide the view from each other. That is why great artists and writers have made an abundant use of the mediocre.

121

Roughness and weakness. Artists of all periods have made the discovery that in roughness lies a certain strength, and that not everyone can be rough who wants to be: also that many varieties of weakness have a powerful effect on the emotions. From this source are derived many artistic substitutes, which not even the greatest and most conscientious artists can abstain from using.

122

Good memory. Many a man fails to become a thinker for the sole reason that his memory is too good.

123

Arousing instead of appeasing hunger. Great artists fancy that they have taken full possession of a soul. In reality, and often to their painful disappointment, that soul has only been made more capacious and insatiable, so that a dozen greater artists could plunge into its depths without filling it up.

124

Artists' anxiety. The anxiety lest people may not believe that their figures are *alive* can mislead many artists of declining taste to portray these figures so that they appear as if mad. From the same anxiety, on the other hand, Greek artists of the earliest ages gave even dead and sorely wounded men that smile which they knew as the most vivid sign of life — careless of the actual forms bestowed by nature on life at its last gasp.

125

The circle must be completed. He who follows a philosophy or a genre of art to the end of its career and beyond, understands from inner experience why the masters and disciples who come after have so often turned, with a depreciatory gesture, into a new groove. The circle must be described — but the individual, even the greatest, sits firm on his point of the circumference, with an inexorable look of obstinacy, as if the circle ought never to be completed.

126

The older art and the soul of the present. Since every art becomes more and more adapted to the expression of spiritual states, of the more lively, delicate, energetic, and passionate states, the later masters, spoilt by these means of expression, do not feel at their ease in the presence of the old-time works of art. They feel as if the ancients had merely been lacking in the means of making their souls speak clearly, also perhaps in some necessary technical preliminaries.

They think that they must render some assistance in this quarter, for they believe in the similarity or even unity of all souls. In truth, however, measure, symmetry, a contempt for graciousness and charm, an unconscious severity and morning chilliness, an evasion of passion, as if passion meant the death of art – such are the constituents of sentiment and morality in all old masters, who selected and arranged their means of expression not at random but in a necessary connection with their morality. Knowing this, are we to deny those that come after the right to animate the older works with their soul? No, for these works can only survive through our giving them our soul, and our blood alone enables them to speak to *us*. The real 'historic' discourse would talk ghostly speech to ghosts. We honour the great artists less by that barren timidity that allows every word, every note to remain intact than by energetic endeavours to aid them continually to a new life. True, if Beethoven were suddenly to come to life and hear one of his works performed with that modern animation and nervous refinement that bring glory to our masters of execution, he would probably be silent for a long while, uncertain whether he should raise his hand to curse or to bless, but perhaps say at last: 'Well, well! That is neither I nor not-I, but a third thing – it seems to me, too, something right, if not just *the* right thing. But you must know yourselves what to do, as in any case it is you who have to listen. As our Schiller says, "the living man is right." So have it your own way, and let me go down again.'

127

Against the disparagers of brevity. A brief dictum may be the fruit and harvest of long reflection. The reader, however, who is a novice in this field and has never considered the case in point, sees something embryonic in all brief dicta, not without a reproachful hint to the author, requesting him not to serve up such raw and ill-prepared food.

128

Against the short-sighted. Do you think it is piece-work because it is (and must be) offered you in pieces?

129

Readers of aphorisms. The worst readers of aphorisms are the friends of the author, if they make a point of referring the general to the particular instance to which the aphorism owes its origin. This namby-pamby attitude brings all the author's trouble to naught, and instead of a philosophic lesson and a philosophic frame of mind, they deservedly gain nothing but the satisfaction of a vulgar curiosity.

130

Readers' insults. The reader offers a twofold insult to the author by praising his second book at the expense of his first (or *vice versa*) and by expecting the author to be grateful to him on that account.

131

The exciting element in the history of art. We fall into a state of terrible tension when we follow the history of an art – as, for example, that of Greek oratory – and, passing from master to master, observe their increasing precautions to obey the old and the new laws and all these self-imposed limitations. We see that the bow *must* snap, and that the so-called 'loose' composition, with the wonderful means of expression smothered and concealed (in this particular case the florid style of Asianism), was once necessary and almost *beneficial.*

132

To the great in art. That enthusiasm for some object which you, O great man, introduce into this world causes the intelligence of the many to be stunted. The knowledge of this fact spells humiliation. But the enthusiast wears his hump with pride and pleasure, and you have the consolation of feeling that you have increased the world's happiness.

133

Conscienceless aesthetes. The real fanatics of an artistic school are perhaps those utterly inartistic natures that are not even grounded in the elements of artistic study and creation, but are impressed

with the strongest of all the elementary influences of an art. For
them there is no aesthetic conscience – hence nothing to hold
them back from fanaticism.

134

How the soul should be moved by the new music. The artistic purpose
followed by the new music, in what is now forcibly but none
too lucidly termed 'endless melody', can be understood by going into the sea, gradually losing one's firm tread on the bottom,
and finally surrendering unconditionally to the fluid element.
One has to *swim.* In the previous, older music one was forced,
with delicate or stately or impassioned movement, to *dance.*
The measure necessary for dancing, the observance of a distinct
balance of time and force in the soul of the hearer, imposed a
continual self-control. Through the counteraction of the cooler
draught of air which came from this caution and the warmer
breath of musical enthusiasm, that music exercised its spell.
Richard Wagner aimed at a different excitation of the soul, allied,
as above said, to swimming and floating. This is perhaps the
most essential of his innovations. His famous method, originating
from this aim and adapted to it – the 'endless melody' – strives
to break and sometimes even to despise all mathematical equilibrium of time and force. He is only too rich in the invention of
such effects, which sound to the old school like rhythmic paradoxes and blasphemies. He dreads petrifaction, crystallisation, the
development of music into the architectural. He accordingly sets
up a three-time rhythm in opposition to the double-time, not
infrequently introduces five-time and seven-time, immediately
repeats a phrase, but with a prolation, so that its time is again
doubled and trebled. From an easy-going imitation of such art
may arise a great danger to music, for by the side of the superabundance of rhythmic emotion demoralisation and decadence
lurk in ambush. The danger will become very great if such music
comes to associate itself more and more closely with a quite
naturalistic art of acting and pantomime, trained and dominated
by no higher plastic models; an art that knows no measure in itself
and can impart no measure to the kindred element, the all-too-
womanish nature of music.

135

Poet and reality. The Muse of the poet who is not in love with reality will not be reality, and will bear him children with hollow eyes and all too tender bones.

136

Means and end. In art the end does not justify the means, but holy means can justify the end.

137

The worst readers. The worst readers are those who act like plundering soldiers. They take out some things that they might use, cover the rest with filth and confusion, and blaspheme about the whole.

138

Signs of a good writer. Good writers have two things in common: they prefer being understood to being admired, and they do not write for the critical and over-shrewd reader.

139

The mixed species. The mixed species in art bear witness to their authors' distrust of their own strength. They seek auxiliary powers, advocates, hiding-places – such is the case with the poet who calls in philosophy, the musician who calls in the drama, and the thinker who calls in rhetoric to his aid.

140

Shutting one's mouth. When his book opens its mouth, the author must shut his.

141

Badges of rank. All poets and men of letters who are in love with the superlative want to do more than they can.

142

Cold books. The deep thinker reckons on readers who feel with him the happiness that lies in deep thinking. Hence a book that looks cold and sober, if seen in the right light, may seem bathed in the sunshine of spiritual cheerfulness and become a genuine soul-comforter.

143

A knack of the slow-witted. The slow-witted thinker generally allies himself with loquacity and ceremoniousness. By the former he thinks he is gaining mobility and fluency, by the latter he gives his peculiarity the appearance of being a result of free will and artistic purpose, with a view to dignity, which needs slow movement.

144

Le style Baroque. He who as thinker and writer is not born or trained to dialectic and the consecutive arrangement of ideas, will unconsciously turn to the rhetoric and dramatic forms. For, after all, his object is to make himself understood and to carry the day by force, and he is indifferent whether, as shepherd, he honestly guides to himself the hearts of his fellow-men, or, as robber, he captures them by surprise. This is true of the plastic arts as of music: where the feeling of insufficient dialectic or a deficiency in expression or narration, together with an urgent, over-powerful impulse to form, gives birth to that species of style known as 'baroque'. Only the ill-educated and the arrogant will at once find a depreciatory force in this word. The baroque style always arises at the time of decay of a great art, when the demands of art in classical expression have become too great. It is a natural phenomenon which will be observed with melancholy – for it is a forerunner of the night – but at the same time with admiration for its peculiar compensatory arts of expression and narration. To this style belongs, firstly, a choice of material and subjects of the highest dramatic tension, at which the heart trembles even when there is no art, because heaven and hell are all too near the emotions: then, the oratory of strong passion and gestures, of ugly sublimity, of great masses, in fact of absolute quantity *per se* (as is shown in Michael Angelo, the father or grandfather of the Italian baroque stylists): the lights of dusk, illumination and conflagration playing upon those strongly moulded forms: ever-new ventures in means and aims, strongly underscored by artists for artists, while the layman must fancy he sees an unconscious overflowing of all the horns of plenty of an original nature-art: all these characteristics that constitute the greatness of that style are neither possible nor permitted in the earlier ante-classical and classical periods of a branch of art. Such luxuries hang long on the tree like forbidden fruit. Just now, when music is passing into this last phase, we may learn to know the phenomenon of the baroque style in peculiar splendour, and, by comparison, find much that is instructive for earlier ages. For from Greek times onward there has often been a baroque style, in poetry, oratory, prose writing, sculpture, and, as is well known, in architecture. This style, though wanting in the highest nobility – the nobility of an innocent, unconscious, triumphant perfection – has nevertheless given pleasure to many of the best and most serious minds of their time. Hence, as aforesaid, it is presumptuous to depreciate it without reserve, however happy we may feel because our taste for it has not made us insensible to the purer and greater style.

145

The value of honest books. Honest books make the reader honest, at least by exciting his hatred and aversion, which otherwise cunning cleverness knows so well how to conceal. Against a book, however, we let ourselves go, however restrained we may be in our relations with men.

146

How art makes partisans. Individual fine passages, an exciting general tenor, a moving and absorbing finale – so much of a work of art is accessible even to most laymen. In an art period when it is desired to win over the great majority of the laymen to the side of the artists and to make a party perhaps for the very preservation of art, the creative artist will do well to offer nothing more than the above. Then he will not be a squanderer of his strength, in spheres where no one is grateful to him. For to perform the remaining functions, the imitation of Nature in her organic development and growth, would in that case be like sowing seeds in water.

147

Becoming great to the detriment of history. Every later master who leads the taste of art-lovers into his channel unconsciously gives rise to a selection and revaluation of the older masters and their works. Whatever in them is conformable and akin to him, and anticipates and foreshadows him, appears henceforth as the only important element in them and their works – a fruit in which a great error usually lies hidden like a worm.

148

How an epoch becomes lured to art. If we teach people by all the enchantments of artists and thinkers to feel reverence for their defects, their intellectual poverty, their absurd infatuations and passions (as it is quite possible to do); if we show them only the lofty side of crime and folly, only the touching and appealing element in weakness and flabbiness and blind devotion (that too has often enough been done) – we have employed the means for inspiring even an unphilosophical and inartistic age with an ecstatic love of philosophy and art (especially of thinkers and artists as personalities) and, in the worst case, perhaps with the only means of defending the existence of such tender and fragile beings.

149

Criticism and joy. Criticism, one-sided and unjust as well as intelligent criticism, gives so much pleasure to him who exercises it that the world is indebted to every work and every action that inspires much criticism and many critics. For criticism draws after it a glittering train of joyousness, wit, self-admiration, pride, instruction, designs of improvement. The god of joy created the bad and the mediocre for the same reason that he created the good.

150

Beyond his limits. When an artist wants to be more than an artist – for example, the moral awakener of his people – he at last falls in love, as a punishment, with a monster of moral substance. The Muse laughs, for, though a kind-hearted goddess, she can also be malignant from jealousy. Milton and Klopstock are cases in point.

151

A glass eye. The tendency of a talent towards moral subjects, characters, motives, towards the 'beautiful soul' of the work of art, is often only a glass eye put on by the artist who lacks a beautiful soul. It may result, though rarely, that his eye finally becomes living Nature, if indeed it be Nature with a somewhat troubled look. But the ordinary result is that the whole world thinks it sees Nature where there is only cold glass.

152

Writing and desire for victory. Writing should always indicate a victory, indeed a conquest of oneself which must be communicated to others for their behoof. There are, however, dyspeptic authors who only write when they cannot digest something, or when something has remained stuck in their teeth. Through their anger they try unconsciously to disgust the reader too, and to exercise violence upon him – that is, they desire victory, but victory over others.

153

A good book needs time. Every good book tastes bitter when it first comes out, for it has the defect of newness. Moreover, it suffers damage from its living author, if he is well known and much talked about. For all the world is accustomed to confuse the author with his work. Whatever of profundity, sweetness, and brilliance the work may contain must be developed as the years go by, under the care of growing, then old, and lastly traditional reverence. Many hours must pass, many a spider must have woven its web about the book. A book is made better by good readers and clearer by good opponents.

154

Extravagance as an artistic means. Artists well understand the idea of using extravagance as an artistic means in order to convey an impression of wealth. This is one of those innocent wiles of soul-seduction that the artist must know, for in his world, which has only appearance in view, the means to appearance need not necessarily be genuine.

155

The hidden barrel-organ. Genius, by virtue of its more ample drapery, knows better than talent how to hide its barrel-organ. Yet after all it too can only play its seven old pieces over and over again.

156

The name on the title-page. It is now a matter of custom and almost of duty for the author's name to appear on the book, and this is a main cause of the fact that books have so little influence. If they are good, they are worth more than the personalities of their authors, of which they are the quintessences. But as soon as the author makes himself known on the title-page, the quintessence, from the reader's point of view, becomes diluted with the personal, the most personal element, and the aim of the book is frustrated. It is the ambition of the intellect no longer to appear individual.

157

The most cutting criticism. We make the most cutting criticism of a man or a book when we indicate his or its ideal.

158

Little or no love. Every good book is written for a particular reader and men of his stamp, and for that very reason is looked upon unfavourably by all other readers, by the vast majority. Its reputation accordingly rests on a narrow basis and must be built up by degrees. The mediocre and bad book is mediocre and bad because it seeks to please, and does please, a great number.

159

Music and disease. The danger of the new music lies in the fact that it puts the cup of rapture and exaltation to the lips so invitingly, and with such a show of moral ecstasy, that even the noble and temperate man always drinks a drop too much. This minimum of intemperance, constantly repeated, can in the end bring about a deeper convulsion and destruction of mental health than any coarse excess could do. Hence nothing remains but some day to fly from the grotto of the nymph, and through perils and billowy seas to forge one's way to the smoke of Ithaca and the embraces of a simpler and more human spouse.

160

Advantage for opponents. A book full of intellect communicates something thereof even to its opponents.

161

Youth and criticism. To criticise a book means, for the young, not to let oneself be touched by a single productive thought therefrom, and to protect one's skin with hands and feet. The youngster lives in opposition to all novelty that he cannot love in the lump, in a position of self-defence, and in this connection he commits, as often as he can, a superfluous sin.

162

Effect of quantity. The greatest paradox in the history of poetic art lies in this: that in all that constitutes the greatness of the old poets a man may be a barbarian, faulty and deformed from top to toe, and still remain the greatest of poets. This is the case with Shakespeare, who, as compared with Sophocles, is like a mine of immeasurable wealth in gold, lead, and rubble, whereas Sophocles is not merely gold, but gold in its noblest form, one that almost makes us forget the money-value of the metal. But quantity in its highest intensity has the same effect as quality. That is a good thing for Shakespeare.

163

All beginning is dangerous. The poet can choose whether to raise emotion from one grade to another, and so finally to exalt it to a great height – or to try a surprise attack, and from the start to pull the bell-rope with might and main. Both processes have their danger – in the first case his hearer may run away from him through boredom, in the second through terror.

164

In favour of critics. Insects sting, not from malice, but because they too want to live. It is the same with our critics – they desire our blood, not our pain.

165

Success of aphorisms. The inexperienced, when an aphorism at once illuminates their minds with its naked truth, always think that it is old and well known. They look askance at the author, as if he had wanted to steal the common property of all, whereas they enjoy highly spiced half-truths, and give the author to understand as much. He knows how to appreciate the hint, and easily guesses thereby where he has succeeded and failed.

166

The desire for victory. An artist who exceeds the limit of his strength in all that he undertakes will end by carrying the multitude along with him, through the spectacle of violent wrestling that he affords. Success is not always the accompaniment only of victory, but also of the desire for victory.

167

Sibi scribere.* The sensible author writes for no other posterity than his own – that is, for his age – so as to be able even then to take pleasure in himself.

168

Praise of the aphorism. A good aphorism is too hard for the tooth of time, and is not worn away by all the centuries, although it serves as food for every epoch. Hence it is the greatest paradox in literature, the imperishable in the midst of change, the nourishment which always remains highly valued, as salt does, and never becomes stupid like salt.

169

The art-need of the second order. The people may have something of what can be called art-need, but it is small, and can be cheaply satisfied. On the whole, the remnant of art (it must be honestly confessed) suffices for this need. Let us consider, for example, the kind of melodies and songs in which the most vigorous, unspoiled, and true-hearted classes of the population find genuine delight; let us live among shepherds, cowherds, peasants, huntsmen, soldiers,

---

* Writing for oneself.

and sailors, and give ourselves the answer. And in the country town, just in the houses that are the homes of inherited civic virtue, is it not the worst music at present produced that is loved and, one might say, cherished? He who speaks of deeper needs and unsatisfied yearnings for art among the people, as it is, is a crank or an impostor. Be honest! Only in exceptional men is there now an art-need in the highest sense – because art is once more on the down-grade, and human powers and hopes are for the time being directed to other matters. Apart from this, outside the populace, there exists indeed, in the higher and highest strata of society, a broader and more comprehensive art-need, but *of the second order.* Here there is a sort of artistic commune, which possibly means to be sincere. But let us look at the elements! They are in general the more refined malcontents, who attain no genuine pleasure in themselves; the cultured, who have not become free enough to dispense with the consolations of religion, and yet do not find its incense sufficiently fragrant; the half-aristocratic, who are too weak to combat by a heroic conversion or renunciation the one fundamental error of their lives or the pernicious bent of their characters; the highly gifted, who think themselves too dignified to be of service by modest activity, and are too lazy for real, self-sacrificing work; girls who cannot create for themselves a satisfactory sphere of duties; women who have tied themselves by a light-hearted or nefarious marriage, and know that they are not tied securely enough; scholars, physicians, merchants, officials who specialised too early and never gave their lives a free enough scope – who do their work efficiently, it is true, but with a worm gnawing at their hearts; finally, all imperfect artists – these are nowadays the true needers of art! What do they really desire from art? Art is to drive away hours and moments of discomfort, boredom, half-bad conscience, and, if possible, transform the faults of their lives and characters into faults of world-destiny. Very different were the Greeks, who realised in their art the outflow and overflow of their own sense of well-being and health, and loved to see their perfection once more from a standpoint outside themselves. They were led to art by delight in themselves; our contemporaries – by disgust of themselves.

170

The Germans in the theatre. The real theatrical talent of the Germans
was Kotzebue. He and his Germans, those of higher as well as
those of middle-class society, were necessarily associated, and his
contemporaries should have said of him in all seriousness, 'in him
we live and move and have our being.' Here was nothing – no
constraint, pretence, or half-enjoyment: what he could and would
do was understood. Yes, until now the honest theatrical success on
the German stage has been in the hands of the shamefaced or
unashamed heirs of Kotzebue's methods and influence – that is, as
far as comedy still flourishes at all. The result is that much of the
Germanism of that age, sometimes far off from the great towns,
still survives. Good-natured; incontinent in small pleasures; always
ready for tears; with the desire, in the theatre at any rate, to be able
to get rid of their innate sobriety and strict attention to duty and
exercise; a smiling, nay, a laughing indulgence; confusing goodness and sympathy and welding them into one, as is the essential
characteristic of German sentimentality; exceedingly happy at
a noble, magnanimous action; for the rest, submissive towards
superiors, envious of each other, and yet in their heart of hearts
thoroughly self-satisfied – such were they and such was he. The
second dramatic talent was Schiller. He discovered a class of
hearers which had hitherto never been taken into consideration:
among the callow German youth of both sexes. His poetry
responded to their higher, nobler, more violent if more confused
emotions, their delight in the jingle of moral words (a delight that
begins to disappear when we reach the thirties). Thus he won for
himself, by virtue of the passionateness and partisanship of the
young, a success which gradually reacted with advantage upon
those of riper years. Generally speaking, Schiller rejuvenated the
Germans. Goethe stood and still stands above the Germans in
every respect. To them he will never belong. How could a nation
in well-being and well-wishing come up to the intellectuality of
Goethe? Beethoven composed and Schopenhauer philosophised
above the heads of the Germans, and it was above their heads, in
the same way, that Goethe wrote his *Tasso*, his *Iphigenie*. He was
followed by a small company of highly cultured persons, who
were educated by antiquity, life, and travel, and had grown out

of German ways of thought. He himself did not wish it to be otherwise. When the Romantics set up their well-conceived Goethe cult; when their amazing skill in appreciation was passed on to the disciples of Hegel, the real educators of the Germans of this century; when the awakening national ambition turned out advantageous to the fame of the German poets; when the real standard of the nation, as to whether it could honestly find enjoyment in anything, became inexorably subordinated to the judgment of individuals and to that national ambition – that is, when people began to enjoy by compulsion – then arose that false, spurious German culture which was ashamed of Kotzebue; which brought Sophocles, Calderon, and even the Second Part of Goethe's *Faust* on the stage; and which, on account of its foul tongue and congested stomach, no longer knows now what it likes and what it finds tedious. Happy are those who have taste, even if it be a bad taste! Only by this characteristic can one be wise as well as happy. Hence the Greeks, who were very refined in such matters, designated the sage by a word that means 'man of taste', and called wisdom, artistic as well as scientific, 'taste' (*sophia*).

171

Music as a latecomer in every culture. Among all the arts that are accustomed to grow on a definite culture-soil and under definite social and political conditions, music is the last plant to come up, arising in the autumn and fading-season of the culture to which it belongs. At the same time, the first signs and harbingers of a new spring are usually already noticeable, and sometimes music, like the language of a forgotten age, rings out into a new, astonished world, and comes too late. In the art of the Dutch and Flemish musicians the soul of the Christian middle ages at last found its fullest tone: their sound-architecture is the posthumous but legitimate and equal sister of Gothic. Not until Händel's music was the note of the best in the soul of Luther and his kin heard, the great Judaeoheroical impulse that created the whole Reformation movement. Mozart first expressed in golden melody the age of Louis XIV, and the art of Racine and Claude Lorrain. The eighteenth century – that century of rhapsody, of broken ideals and transitory happiness – only sang itself out in the music of Beethoven and Rossini. A lover of sentimental similes might say that all really important music was a swan-song. Music is, in fact, not a universal language for all time, as is so often said in its praise, but responds exactly to a particular period and warmth of emotion which involves a quite definite, individual culture, determined by time and place, as its inner law. The music of Palestrina would be quite unintelligible to a Greek; and again, what would the music of Rossini convey to Palestrina? – It may be that our most modern German music, with all its pre-eminence and desire of pre-eminence, will soon be no longer understood. For this music sprang from a culture that is undergoing a rapid decay, from the soil of that epoch of reaction and restoration in which a certain Catholicism of feeling, as well as a delight in all indigenous, national, primitive manners, burst into bloom and scattered a blended perfume over Europe. These two emotional tendencies, adopted in their greatest strength and carried to their farthest limits, found final expression in the music of Wagner. Wagner's predilection for the old native sagas, his free idealisation of their unfamiliar gods and heroes – who are really sovereign beasts of prey with occasional fits of thoughtfulness, magnanimity, and boredom – his re-animation of those figures, to which he gave in addition the medieval Christian thirst for ecstatic sensuality and spiritualisation – all this Wagnerian give-and-take with regard to materials, souls, figures, and words – would clearly express the spirit of his music, if it could not, like all music, speak quite unambiguously of itself. This spirit wages the last campaign of reaction against the spirit of illumination which passed into this century from the last, and also against the super-national ideas of French revolutionary romanticism and of English and American colourlessness in the reconstruction of state and society. But is it not evident that the spheres of thought and emotion apparently suppressed by Wagner and his school have long since acquired fresh strength, and that his late musical protest against them generally rings into ears that prefer to hear different and opposite notes; so that one day that high and wonderful art will suddenly become unintelligible and will be covered by the spider's web of oblivion? – In considering this state of affairs we must not let ourselves be led astray by those transitory fluctuations which arise like a reaction within a reaction, as a temporary sinking of the mountainous wave in the midst of the general upheaval. Thus, this decade of national war, ultramontane martyrdom, and socialistic unrest may, in its remoter after-effect, even aid the Wagnerian art to acquire a sudden halo, without guaranteeing that it 'has a future' or that it has *the* future. It is in the very nature of music that the fruits of its great culture-vintage should lose their taste and wither earlier than the fruits of the plastic arts or those that grow on the tree of knowledge. Among all the products of the human artistic sense ideas are the most solid and lasting.

172

The poet no longer a teacher. Strange as it may sound to our time, there were once poets and artists whose soul was above the passions with their delights and convulsions, and who therefore took their pleasure in purer materials, worthier men, more delicate complications and dénouements. If the artists of our day for the most part unfetter the will, and so are under certain circumstances for that very reason emancipators of life, those were tamers of the will, enchanters of animals, creators of men. In fact, they moulded, re-moulded, and new-moulded life, whereas the fame of poets of our day lies in unharnessing, unchaining, and shattering. The ancient Greeks demanded of the poet that he should be the teacher of grown men. How ashamed the poet would be now if this demand were made of him! He is not even a good student of himself, and so never himself becomes a good poem or a fine picture. Under the most favourable circumstances he remains the shy, attractive ruin of a temple, but at the same time a cavern of cravings, overgrown like a ruin with flowers, nettles, and poisonous weeds, inhabited and haunted by snakes, worms, spiders, and birds; an object for sad reflection as to why the noblest and most precious must grow up at once like a ruin, without the past and future of perfection.

173

Looking forward and backward. An art like that which streams out of Homer, Sophocles, Theocritus, Calderon, Racine, Goethe, as the superabundance of a wise and harmonious conduct of life – that is the true art, at which we grasp when we have ourselves become wiser and more harmonious. It is not that barbaric, if ever so delightful, outpouring of hot and highly coloured things from an undisciplined, chaotic soul, which is what we understood by 'art' in our youth. It is obvious from the nature of the case that for certain periods of life an art of overstrain, excitement, antipathy to the orderly, monotonous, simple, logical, is an inevitable need, to which artists must respond, lest the soul of such periods should unburden itself in other ways, through all kinds of disorder and impropriety. Hence youths as they generally are, full, fermenting, tortured above all things by boredom, and women who lack work that fully occupies their soul, require that art of delightful disorder. All the more violently on that account are they inflamed with a desire for satisfaction without change, happiness without stupor and intoxication.

174

Against the art of works of art. Art is above all and first of all meant to embellish life, to make us ourselves endurable and if possible agreeable in the eyes of others. With this task in view, art moderates us and holds us in restraint, creates forms of intercourse, binds over the uneducated to laws of decency, cleanliness, politeness, well-timed speech and silence. Hence art must conceal or transfigure everything that is ugly – the painful, terrible, and disgusting elements which in spite of every effort will always break out afresh in accordance with the very origin of human nature. Art has to perform this duty especially in regard to the passions and spiritual agonies and anxieties, and to cause the significant factor to shine through unavoidable or unconquerable ugliness. To this great, super-great task the so-called art proper, that of works of art, is a mere accessory. A man who feels within himself a surplus of such powers of embellishment, concealment, and transfiguration will finally seek to unburden himself of this surplus in works of art. The same holds good, under special circumstances, of a whole nation. But as a rule we nowadays begin art at the end, hang on to its tail, and think that works of art constitute art proper, and that life should be improved and transformed by this means – fools that we are! If we begin a dinner with dessert, and try sweet after sweet, small wonder that we ruin our digestions and even our appetites for the good, hearty, nourishing meal to which art invites us!

175

Continued existence of art. Why, really, does a creative art nowadays continue to exist? Because the majority who have hours of leisure (and such an art is for them only) think that they cannot fill up their time without music, theatres and picture-galleries, novels and poetry. Granted that one could keep them from this indulgence, either they would strive less eagerly for leisure, and the invidious sight of the rich would be less common (a great gain for the stability of society), or they would have leisure, but would learn to reflect on what can be learnt and unlearnt: on their work, for instance, their associations, the pleasure they could bestow. All the world, with the exception of the artist, would in both cases reap the advantage. Certainly, there are many vigorous, sensible readers who could take objection to this. Still, it must be said on behalf of the coarse and malignant that the author himself is concerned with this protest, and that there is in his book much to be read that is not actually written down therein.

176

The mouthpiece of the gods. The poet expresses the universal higher opinions of the nation, he is its mouthpiece and flute; but by virtue of metre and all other artistic means he so expresses them that the nation regards them as something quite new and wonderful, and believes in all seriousness that he is the mouthpiece of the gods. Yes, under the clouds of creation the poet himself forgets whence he derives all his intellectual wisdom – from father and mother, from teachers and books of all kinds, from the street and particularly from the priest. He is deceived by his own art, and really believes, in a naïve period, that a god is speaking through him, that he is creating in a state of religious inspiration. As a matter of fact, he is only saying what he has learnt, a medley of popular wisdom and popular foolishness. Hence, so far as a poet is really *vox populi* he is held to be *vox Dei.**

177

What all art wants to do and cannot. The last and hardest task of the artist is the presentment of what remains the same, reposes in itself,

* *Vox populi*: the voice of the people; *vox Dei*: the voice of God.

is lofty and simple and free from the bizarre. Hence the noblest forms of moral perfection are rejected as inartistic by weaker artists, because the sight of these fruits is too painful for their ambition. The fruit gleams at them from the topmost branches of art, but they lack the ladder, the courage, the grip to venture so high. In himself a Phidias is quite possible as a poet, but, if modern strength be taken into consideration, almost solely in the sense that to God nothing is impossible. The desire for a poetical Claude Lorrain is already an immodesty at present, however earnestly one man's heart may yearn for such a consummation. The presentment of the highest man, the most simple and at the same time the most complete, has hitherto been beyond the scope of all artists. Perhaps, however, the Greeks, in the ideal of Athene, saw farther than any men did before or after their time.

178

Art and restoration. The retrograde movements in history, the so-called periods of restoration, which try to revive intellectual and social conditions that existed before those immediately preceding – and seem really to succeed in giving them a brief resurrection – have the charm of sentimental recollection, ardent longing for what is almost lost, hasty embracing of a transitory happiness. It is on account of this strange trend towards seriousness that in such transient and almost dreamy periods art and poetry find a natural soil, just as the tenderest and rarest plants grow on mountain-slopes of steep declivity. Thus many a good artist is unwittingly impelled to a 'restoration' way of thinking in politics and society, for which, on his own account, he prepares a quiet little corner and garden. Here he collects about himself the human remains of the historical epoch that appeals to him, and plays his lyre to many who are dead, half-dead, and weary to death, perhaps with the above-mentioned result of a brief resurrection.

179

Happiness of the age. In two respects our age is to be accounted happy. With respect to the *past*, we enjoy all cultures and their productions, and nurture ourselves on the noblest blood of all periods. We stand sufficiently near to the magic of the forces from whose womb these periods are born to be able in passing to submit to their spell with pleasure and terror; whereas earlier cultures could only enjoy themselves, and never looked beyond themselves, but were rather overarched by a bell of broader or narrower dome, through which indeed light streamed down to them, but which their gaze could not pierce. With respect to the *future*, there opens out to us for the first time a mighty, comprehensive vista of human and economic purposes engirdling the whole inhabited globe. At the same time, we feel conscious of a power ourselves to take this new task in hand without presumption, without requiring supernatural aids. Yes, whatever the result of our enterprise, however much we may have overestimated our strength, at any rate we need render account to no one but ourselves, and mankind can henceforth begin to do with itself what it will. There are, it is true, peculiar human bees, who only know how to suck the bitterest and worst elements from the chalice of every flower. It is true that all flowers contain something that is not honey, but these bees may be allowed to feel in their own way about the happiness of our time, and continue to build up their hive of discomfort.

180

A vision. Hours of instruction and meditation for adults, even the most mature, and such institutions visited without compulsion but in accordance with the moral injunction of the whole community; the churches as the meeting-places most worthy and rich in memories for the purpose; at the same time daily festivals in honour of the reason that is attained and attainable by man; a newer and fuller budding and blooming of the ideal of the teacher, in which the clergyman, the artist and the physician, the man of science and the sage are blended, and their individual virtues should come to the fore as a collective virtue in their teaching itself, in their discourses, in their method – this is my ever-recurring vision, of which I firmly believe that it has raised a corner of the veil of the future.

181

Education a distortion. The extraordinary haphazardness of the whole system of education, which leads every adult to say nowadays that his sole educator was chance, and the weathercock-nature of educational methods and aims, may be explained as follows.

The oldest and the newest culture-powers, as in a turbulent mass-meeting, would rather be heard than understood, and wish to prove at all costs by their outcries and clamourings that they still exist or already exist. The poor teachers and educators are first dazed by this senseless noise, then become silent and finally apathetic, allowing anything to be done to them just as they in their turn allow anything to be done to their pupils. They are not trained themselves, so how are they to train others? They are themselves no straight-growing, vigorous, succulent trees, and he who wishes to attach himself to them must wind and bend himself and finally become distorted and deformed as they.

182

Philosophers and artists of the age. Rhapsody and frigidity, burning desires and waning of the heart's glow – this wretched medley is to be found in the picture of the highest European society of the present day. There the artist thinks that he is achieving a great deal when through his art he lights the torch of the heart as well as the torch of desire. The philosopher has the same notion, when in the chilliness of his heart, which he has in common with his age, he cools hot desires in himself and his following by his world-denying judgments.

183

Not to be a soldier of culture without necessity. At last people are learning what it costs us so dear not to know in our youth – that we must first do superior actions and secondly seek the superior wherever and under whatever names it is to be found; that we must at once go out of the way of all badness and mediocrity *without fighting it*; and that even doubt as to the excellence of a thing (such as quickly arises in one of practised taste) should rank as an argument against it and a reason for completely avoiding it. We must not shrink from the danger of occasionally making a mistake and confounding the less accessible good with the bad and imperfect. Only he who can do nothing better should attack the world's evils as the soldier of culture. But those who should support culture and spread its teachings ruin themselves if they go about armed, and by precautions, night-watches, and bad dreams turn the peace of their domestic and artistic life into sinister unrest.

184

How natural history should be expounded. Natural history, like the history of the war and victory of moral and intellectual forces in the campaign against anxiety, self-delusion, laziness, superstition, folly, should be so expounded that every reader or listener may be continually aroused to strive after mental and physical health and soundness, after the feeling of joy, and be awakened to the desire to be the heir and continuator of mankind, to an ever nobler adventurous impulse. Hitherto natural history has not found its true language, because the inventive and eloquent artists – who are needed for this purpose – never rid themselves of a secret mistrust of it, and above all never wish to learn from it a thorough lesson. Nevertheless it must be conceded to the English that their scientific manuals for the lower strata of the people have made admirable strides towards that ideal. But then such books are written by their foremost men of learning, full, complete, and inspiring natures, and not, as among us, by mediocre investigators.

185

Genius in humanity. If genius, according to Schopenhauer's observation, lies in the coherent and vivid recollection of our own experience, a striving towards genius in humanity collectively might be deduced from the striving towards knowledge of the whole historic past – which is beginning to mark off the modern age more and more as compared with earlier ages and has for the first time broken down the barriers between nature and spirit, men and animals, morality and physics. A perfectly conceived history would be cosmic self-consciousness.

186

The cult of culture. On great minds is bestowed the terrifying all-too-human of their natures, their blindnesses, deformities, and extravagances, so that their more powerful, easily all-too-powerful influence may be continually held within bounds through the distrust aroused by such qualities. For the sum-total of all that humanity needs for its continued existence is so comprehensive, and demands powers so diverse and so numerous, that for every one-sided predilection, whether in science or politics or art or commerce, to which such natures would persuade us, mankind as a whole has to pay a heavy price. It has always been a great disaster to culture when human beings are worshipped. In this sense we may understand the precept of Mosaic law which forbids us to have any other gods but God. Side by side with the cult of genius and violence we must always place, as its complement and remedy, the cult of culture. This cult can find an intelligent appreciation even for the material, the inferior, the mean, the misunderstood, the weak, the imperfect, the onesided, the incomplete, the untrue, the apparent, even the wicked and horrible, and can grant them the concession that *all this is necessary*. For the continued harmony of all things human, attained by amazing toil and strokes of luck, and just as much the work of Cyclopes and ants as of geniuses, shall never be lost. How, indeed, could we dispense with that deep, universal, and often uncanny bass, without which, after all, melody cannot be melody?

187

The antique world and pleasure. The man of the antique world understood better how to rejoice, we understand better how to grieve less. They continually found new motives for feeling happy, for celebrating festivals, being inventive with all their wealth of shrewdness and reflection. We, on the other hand, concentrate our intellect rather on the solving of problems which have in view painlessness and the removal of sources of discomfort. With regard to suffering existence, the ancients sought to forget or in some way to convert the sensation into a pleasant one, thus trying to supply palliatives. We attack the causes of suffering, and on the whole prefer to use prophylactics. Perhaps we are only building upon a foundation whereon a later age will once more set up the temple of joy.

188

The muses as liars. 'We know how to tell many lies,' so sang the Muses once, when they revealed themselves to Hesiod. The conception of the artist as deceiver, once grasped, leads to important discoveries.

189

How paradoxical Homer can be. Is there anything more desperate, more horrible, more incredible, shining over human destiny like a winter sun, than that idea of Homer's?

So the decree of the gods willed it, and doomed man to perish, that it might be a matter for song even to distant generations.

In other words, we suffer and perish so that poets may not lack material, and this is the dispensation of those very gods of Homer who seem much concerned about the joyousness of generations to come, but very little about us men of the present. To think that such ideas should ever have entered the head of a Greek!

190

Supplementary justification of existence. Many ideas have come into the world as errors and fancies but have turned out truths, because men have afterwards given them a genuine basis to rest upon.

191

Pro and con necessary. He who has not realised that every great man must not only be encouraged but also, for the sake of the common welfare, opposed, is certainly still a great child – or himself a great man.

192

Injustice of genius. Genius is most unjust towards geniuses, if they be contemporary. Either it thinks it has no need of them and considers them superfluous (for it can do without them), or their influence crosses the path of its electric current, in which case it even calls them pernicious.

193

The saddest destiny of a prophet. He has worked twenty years to convince his contemporaries, and succeeds at last, but in the meantime his adversaries have also succeeded – he is no longer convinced of himself.

194

Three thinkers like one spider. In every philosophical school three thinkers follow one another in this relation: the first produces from himself sap and seed, the second draws it out in threads and spins a cunning web, the third waits in this web for the victims who are caught in it – and tries to live upon this philosophy.

195

From association with authors. It is as bad a habit to go about with an author grasping him by the nose as grasping him by the horn (and every author has his horn).

196

A team of two. Vagueness of thought and outbursts of sentimentality are as often wedded to the reckless desire to have one's own way by hook or by crook, to make oneself alone of any consequence, as a genuinely helpful, gracious, and kindly spirit is wedded to the impulse towards clearness and purity of thought and towards emotional moderation and self-restraint.

197

Binding and separating forces. Surely it is in the heads of men that there arises the force that binds them – an understanding of their common interest or the reverse; and in their hearts the force that separates them – a blind choosing and groping in love and hate, a devotion to one at the expense of all, and a consequent contempt for the common utility.

198

Marksmen and thinkers. There are curious marksmen who miss their mark, but leave the shooting-gallery with secret pride in the fact that their bullet at any rate flew very far (beyond the mark, it is true), or that it did not hit the mark but hit something else. There are thinkers of the same stamp.

199

Attack from two sides. We act as enemies towards an intellectual tendency or movement when we are superior to it and disapprove of its aim, or when its aim is too high and unrecognisable to our eye – in other words, when it is superior to us. So the same party may be attacked from two sides, from above and from below. Not infrequently the assailants, from common hatred, form an alliance which is more repulsive than all that they hate.

200

Original. Original minds are distinguished not by being the first to see a new thing, but by seeing the old, well-known thing, which is seen and overlooked by everyone, as something new. The first discoverer is usually that quite ordinary and unintellectual visionary – chance.

201

Error of philosophers. The philosopher believes that the value of his philosophy lies in the whole, in the structure. Posterity finds it in the stone with which he built and with which, from that time forth, men will build oftener and better – in other words, in the fact that the structure may be destroyed and yet have value as material.

202

Wit. Wit is the epitaph of an emotion.

203

The moment before solution. In science it occurs every day and every hour that a man, immediately before the solution, remains stuck, being convinced that his efforts have been entirely in vain – like one who, in untying a noose, hesitates at the moment when it is nearest to coming loose, because at that very moment it looks most like a knot.

204

Among the visionaries. The thoughtful man, and he who is sure of his intelligence, may profitably consort with visionaries for a decade and abandon himself in their torrid zone to a moderate insanity. He will thus have travelled a good part of the road towards that cosmopolitanism of the intellect which can say without presumption, 'Nothing intellectual is alien to me.'

205

Keen air. The best and healthiest element in science as amid the
mountains is the keen air that plays about it. Intellectual molly-
coddles (such as artists) dread and abuse science on account of this
atmosphere.

206

Why savants are nobler than artists. Science requires nobler natures
than does poetry; natures that are more simple, less ambitious,
more restrained, calmer, that think less of posthumous fame and
can bury themselves in studies which, in the eye of the many,
scarcely seem worthy of such a sacrifice of personality. There is
another loss of which they are conscious. The nature of their
occupation, its continual exaction of the greatest sobriety, weakens
their will; the fire is not kept up so vigorously as on the hearths of
poetic minds. As such, they often lose their strength and prime
earlier than artists do – and, as has been said, they are aware of their
danger. Under all circumstances they seem less gifted because they
shine less, and thus they will always be rated below their value.

207

How far piety obscures. In later centuries the great man is credited
with all the great qualities and virtues of his century. Thus all
that is best is continually obscured by piety, which treats the
picture as a sacred one, to be surrounded with all manner of votive
offerings. In the end the picture is completely veiled and covered
by the offerings, and thenceforth is more an object of faith than
of contemplation.

208

Standing on one's head. If we make truth stand on its head, we
generally fail to notice that our own head, too, is not in its right
position.

209

Origin and utility of fashion. The obvious satisfaction of the individual with his own form excites imitation and gradually creates
the form of the many – that is, fashion. The many desire, and

indeed attain, that same comforting satisfaction with their own form. Consider how many reasons every man has for anxiety and shy self-concealment, and how, on this account, three-fourths of his energy and goodwill is crippled and may become unproductive! So we must be very grateful to fashion for unfettering that three-fourths and communicating self-confidence and the power of cheerful compromise to those who feel themselves bound to each other by its law. Even foolish laws give freedom and calm of the spirit, so long as many persons have submitted to their sway.

210

Looseners of tongues. The value of many men and books rests solely on their faculty for compelling all to speak out the most hidden and intimate things. They are looseners of tongues and crowbars to open the most stubborn teeth. Many events and misdeeds which are apparently only sent as a curse to mankind possess this value and utility.

211

Intellectual freedom of domicile. Who of us could dare to call himself a 'free spirit' if he could not render homage after his fashion, by taking on his own shoulders a portion of that burden of public dislike and abuse, to men to whom this name is attached as a reproach? We might as well call ourselves in all seriousness 'spirits free of domicile' (*Freizügig*) (and without that arrogant or high-spirited defiance) because we feel the impulse to freedom (*Zug zur Freiheit*) as the strongest instinct of our minds and, in contrast to fixed and limited minds, practically see our ideal in an intellectual nomadism – to use a modest and almost depreciatory expression.

212

Yes, the favour of the Muses! – What Homer says on this point goes right to our heart, so true, so terrible is it:

> The Muse loved him with all her heart and gave him good and evil, for she took away his eyes and vouchsafed him sweet song.

This is an endless text for thinking men: she gives good and evil, that is *her* manner of loving with all her heart and soul! And each man will interpret specially for himself why we poets and thinkers have to give up our eyes in her service.

213

Against the cultivation of music. The artistic training of the eye from childhood upwards by means of drawing, painting, landscape-sketching, figures, scenes, involves an estimable gain in life, making the eyesight keen, calm, and enduring in the observation of men and circumstances. No similar secondary advantage arises from the artistic cultivation of the ear, whence public schools will generally do well to give the art of the eye a preference over that of the ear.

214

The discoverers of trivialities. Subtle minds, from which nothing is farther than trivialities, often discover a triviality after taking all manner of circuitous routes and mountain paths, and, to the astonishment of the non-subtle, rejoice exceedingly.

215

Morals of savants. A regular and rapid advance in the sciences is only possible when the individual is compelled to be not so distrustful as to test every calculation and assertion of others, in fields which are remote from his own. A necessary condition, however, is that every man should have competitors in his own sphere, who are extremely distrustful and keep a sharp eye upon him. From this juxtaposition of 'not too distrustful' and 'extremely distrustful' arises sincerity in the republic of learning.

216

Reasons for sterility. There are highly gifted minds which are always sterile only because, from temperamental weakness, they are too impatient to wait for their pregnancy.

217

The perverted world of tears. The manifold discomforts which the demands of higher culture cause to man finally pervert his nature to such an extent that he usually keeps himself stoical and unbending. Thus he has tears in reserve only for rare occasions of happiness, so that many must weep even at the enjoyment of painlessness – only when happy does his heart still beat.

218

The Greeks as interpreters. When we speak of the Greeks we unwittingly speak of today and yesterday; their universally known history is a blank mirror, always reflecting something that is not in the mirror itself. We enjoy the freedom of speaking about them in order to have the right of being silent about others – so that these Greeks themselves may whisper something in the ear of the reflective reader. Thus the Greeks facilitate to modern men the communication of much that is debatable and hard to communicate.

219

Of the acquired character of the Greeks. We are easily led astray by the renowned Greek clearness, transparency, simplicity, and order, by their crystal-like naturalness and crystal-like art, into believing that all these gifts were bestowed on the Greeks – for instance, that they could not but write well, as Lichtenberg expressed it on one occasion. Yet no statement could be more hasty and more untenable. The history of prose from Gorgias to Demosthenes shows a course of toiling and wrestling towards light from the obscure, overloaded, and tasteless, reminding one of the labour of heroes who had to construct the first roads through forest and bog. The dialogue of tragedy was the real achievement of the dramatist, owing to its uncommon clearness and precision, whereas the national tendency was to riot in symbolism and allusion, a tendency expressly fostered by the great choral lyric. Similarly it was the achievement of Homer to liberate the Greeks from Asiatic pomp and gloom, and to have attained the clearness of architecture in details great and small. Nor was it by any means thought easy to say anything in a pure and illuminating style. How else should we account for the great admiration for the epigram of Simonides, which shows itself so simple, with no gilded points or arabesques of wit, but says all that it has to say plainly and with the calm of the sun, not with the straining after effect of the lightning. Since the struggle towards light from an almost native twilight is Greek, a thrill of jubilation runs through the people when they hear a laconic sentence, the language of elegy or the maxims of the Seven Wise Men. Hence they were so fond of giving precepts in verse, a practice that we find objectionable. This was the true Apolline task of the Hellenic spirit, with the aim of rising superior to the perils of metre and the obscurity which is otherwise characteristic of poetry. Simplicity, flexibility, and sobriety were wrestled for and not given by nature to this people. The danger of a relapse into Asianism constantly hovered over the Greeks, and really overtook them from time to time like a murky, overflowing tide of mystical impulses, primitive savagery and darkness. We see them plunge in; we see Europe, as it were, flooded, washed away – for Europe was very small then ; but they always emerge once more to the light, good swimmers and divers that they are, those fellow-countrymen of Odysseus.

220

The pagan characteristic. Perhaps there is nothing more astonishing to the observer of the Greek world than to discover that the Greeks from time to time held festivals, as it were, for all their passions and evil tendencies alike, and in fact even established a kind of series of festivals, by order of the State, for their 'all-too-human'. This is the pagan characteristic of their world, which Christianity has never understood and never can understand, and has always combated and despised. They accepted this all-too-human as unavoidable, and preferred, instead of railing at it, to give it a kind of secondary right by grafting it on to the usages of society and religion. All in man that has power they called divine, and wrote it on the walls of their heaven. They do not deny this natural instinct that expresses itself in evil characteristics, but regulate and limit it to definite cults and days, so as to turn those turbulent streams into as harmless a course as possible, after devising sufficient precautionary measures. That is the root of all the moral broad-mindedness of antiquity. To the wicked, the dubious, the backward, the animal element, as to the barbaric, pre-Hellenic and Asiatic, which still lived in the depths of Greek nature, they allowed a moderate outflow, and did not strive to destroy it utterly. The whole system was under the domain of the State, which was built up not on individuals or castes, but on common human qualities. In the structure of the State the Greeks show that wonderful sense for typical facts which later on enabled them to become investigators of Nature, historians, geographers, and philosophers. It was not a limited moral law of priests or castes, which had to decide about the constitution of the State and State worship, but the most comprehensive view of the reality of all that is human. Whence do the Greeks derive this freedom, this sense of reality? Perhaps from Homer and the poets who preceded him. For just those poets whose nature is generally not the most wise or just possess, in compensation, that delight in reality and activity of every kind, and prefer not to deny even evil. It suffices for them if evil moderates itself, does not kill or inwardly poison everything – in other words, they have similar ideas to those of the founders of Greek constitutions, and were their teachers and forerunners.

221

Exceptional Greeks. In Greece, deep, thorough, serious minds were the exception. The national instinct tended rather to regard the serious and thorough as a kind of grimace. To borrow forms from a foreign source, not to create but to transform into the fairest shapes – that is Greek. To imitate, not for utility but for artistic illusion, ever and anon to gain the mastery over forced seriousness, to arrange, beautify, simplify – that is the continual task from Homer to the Sophists of the third and fourth centuries of our era, who are all outward show, pompous speech, declamatory gestures, and address themselves to shallow souls that care only for appearance, sound, and effect. And now let us estimate the greatness of those exceptional Greeks, who created science! Whoever tells of them, tells the most heroic story of the human mind!

222

Simplicity not the first nor the last thing in point of time. In the history of religious ideas many errors about development and false gradations are made in matters which in reality are not consecutive outgrowths but contemporary yet separate phenomena. In particular, simplicity has still far too much the reputation of being the oldest, the initial thing. Much that is human arises by subtraction and division, and not merely by doubling, addition, and unification. For instance, men still believe in a gradual development of the idea of God from those unwieldy stones and blocks of wood

342 HUMAN, ALL-TOO-HUMAN PART TWO

up to the highest forms of anthropomorphism. Yet the fact is that
so long as divinity was attributed to and felt in trees, logs of wood,
stones, and beasts, people shrank from humanising their forms as
from an act of godlessness. First of all, poets, apart from all considerations of cult and the ban of religious shame, have had to
make the inner imagination of man accustomed and compliant to
this notion. Wherever more pious periods and phases of thought
gained the upper hand, this liberating influence of poets fell into
the background, and sanctity remained, after as before, on the side
of the monstrous, uncanny, quite peculiarly inhuman. And then,
much of what the inner imagination ventures to picture to itself
would exert a painful influence if externally and corporeally represented. The inner eye is far bolder and more shameless than the
outer (whence the well-known difficulty and, to some extent,
impossibility, of working epic material into dramatic form). The
religious imagination for a long time entirely refuses to believe in
the identity of God with an image: the image is meant to fix the
numen of the Deity, actually and specifically, although in a mysterious and not altogether intelligible way. The oldest image of the
gods is meant to shelter and at the same time to hide the god – to
indicate him but not to expose him to view. No Greek really
looked upon his Apollo as a pointed pillar of wood, his Eros as
a lump of stone. These were symbols, which were intended to
inspire dread of the manifestation of the god. It was the same with
those blocks of wood out of which individual limbs, generally in
excessive number, were fashioned with the scantiest of carving –
as, for instance, a Laconian Apollo with four hands and four ears.
In the incomplete, symbolical, or excessive lies a terrible sanctity,
which is meant to prevent us from thinking of anything human or
similar to humanity. It is not an embryonic stage of art in which
such things are made – as if they were not *able* to speak more
plainly and portray more sensibly in the age when such images
were honoured! Rather, men are afraid of just one thing – direct
speaking out. Just as the *cella* hides and conceals in a mysterious
twilight, yet not completely, the holy of holies, the real *numen* of
the Deity; just as, again, the peripteric temple hides the *cella*,
protecting it from indiscreet eyes as with a screen and a veil, yet
not completely – so it is with the image of the Deity, and at the
same time the concealment of the Deity. Only when outside the

cult, in the profane world of athletic contest, the joy in the victor
had risen so high that the ripples thus started reacted upon the lake
of religious emotion, was the statue of the victor set up before the
temple. Then the pious pilgrim had to accustom his eye and his
soul, whether he would or no, to the inevitable sight of human
beauty and super-strength, so that the worship of men and gods
melted into each other from physical and spiritual contact. Then
too for the first time the fear of really humanising the figures of the
gods is lost, and the mighty arena for great plastic art is opened –
even now with the limitation that wherever there is to be adoration the primitive form and ugliness are carefully preserved and
copied. But the Hellene, as he dedicates and makes offerings, may
now with religious sanction indulge in his delight in making god
become a man.

223

Whither we must travel. Immediate self-observation is not enough,
by a long way, to enable us to learn to know ourselves. We need
history, for the past continues to flow through us in a hundred
channels. We ourselves are, after all, nothing but our own sensation at every moment of this continued flow. Even here, when
we wish to step down into the stream of our apparently most
peculiar and personal development, Heraclitus' aphorism, 'You
cannot step twice into the same river', holds good. This is a piece
of wisdom which has, indeed, gradually become trite, but nevertheless has remained as strong and true as it ever was. It is the same
with the saying that, in order to understand history, we must
scrutinise the living remains of historical periods; that we must
travel, as old Herodotus travelled, to other nations, especially to
those so-called savage or half-savage races in regions where man
has doffed or not yet donned European garb. For they are ancient
and firmly established steps of culture on which we can stand.
There is, however, a more subtle art and aim in travelling, which
does not always necessitate our passing from place to place and
going thousands of miles away. Very probably the last three
centuries, in all their colourings and refractions of culture, survive
even in our vicinity, only they have to be discovered. In some
families, or even in individuals, the strata are still superimposed on
each other, beautifully and perceptibly; in other places there are

dispersions and displacements of the structure which are harder to understand. Certainly in remote districts, in less known mountain valleys, circumscribed communities have been able more easily to maintain an admirable pattern of a far older sentiment, a pattern that must here be investigated. On the other hand, it is improbable that such discoveries will be made in Berlin, where man comes into the world washed-out and sapless. He who after long practice of this art of travel has become a hundred-eyed Argus will accompany his Io – I mean his ego – everywhere, and in Egypt and Greece, Byzantium and Rome, France and Germany, in the age of wandering or settled races, in Renaissance or Reformation, at home and abroad, in sea, forest, plant, and mountain, will again light upon the travel-adventure of this ever-growing, ever-altered ego. Thus self-knowledge becomes universal knowledge as regards the entire past, and, by another chain of observation, which can only be indicated here, self-direction and self-training in the freest and most far-seeing spirits might become universal direction as regards all future humanity.

224

Balm and poison. We cannot ponder too deeply on this fact: Christianity is the religion of antiquity grown old; it presupposes degenerate old culture-stocks, and on them it had, and still has, power to work like balm. There are periods when ears and eyes are full of slime, so that they can no longer hear the voice of reason and philosophy or see the wisdom that walks in bodily shape, whether it bears the name of Epictetus or of Epicurus. Then, perhaps, the erection of the martyr's cross and the 'trumpet of the last judgment' may have the effect of still inspiring such races to end their lives decently. If we think of Juvenal's Rome, of that poisonous toad with the eyes of Venus, we understand what it means to make the sign of the Cross before the world, we honour the silent Christian community and are grateful for its having stifled the Graeco-Roman Empire. If, indeed, most men were then born in spiritual slavery, with the sensuality of old men, what a pleasure to meet beings who were more soul than body, and who seemed to realise the Greek idea of the shades of the underworld – shy, scurrying, chirping, kindly creatures, with a reversion on the 'better life', and therefore so unassuming, so secretly scornful, so proudly patient! – This Christianity, as the evening chime of the *good* antiquity, with cracked, weary and yet melodious bell, is balm in the ears even to one who only now traverses those centuries historically. What must it have been to those men themselves! – To young and fresh barbarian nations, on the other hand, Christianity is a poison. For to implant the teaching of sinfulness and damnation in the heroic, childlike, and animal soul of the old Germans is nothing but poisoning. An enormous chemical fermentation and decomposition, a medley of sentiments and judgments, a rank growth of adventurous legend, and hence in the long run a fundamental weakening of such barbarian peoples, was the inevitable result. True, without this weakening what should we have left of Greek culture, of the whole cultured past of the human race? For the barbarians untouched by Christianity knew very well how to make a clean sweep of old cultures, as was only too clearly shown by the heathen conquerors of Romanised Britain. Thus Christianity, against its will, was compelled to aid in making 'the antique world' immortal. There remains, however, a counter-question and the possibility of a counter-reckoning. Without this weakening through the poisoning referred to, would any of those fresh stocks – the Germans, for instance – have been in a position gradually to find by themselves a higher, a peculiar, a new culture, of which the most distant conception would therefore have been lost to humanity? – In this, as in every case, we do not know, Christianly speaking, whether God owes the devil or the devil God more thanks for everything having turned out as it has.

225

Faith makes holy and condemns. A Christian who happened upon forbidden paths of thought might well ask himself on some occasion whether it is really necessary that there should be a God, side by side with a representative Lamb, if faith in the existence of these beings suffices to produce the same influences? If they do exist after all, are they not superfluous beings? For all that is given by the Christian religion to the human soul, all that is beneficent, consoling, and edifying, just as much as all that depresses and crushes, emanates from that faith and not from the objects of that faith. It is here as in another well-known case – there were indeed no witches, but the terrible effects of the belief in witches were the same as if they really had existed. For all occasions where the Christian awaits the immediate intervention of a God, though in vain (for there is no God), his religion is inventive enough to find subterfuges and reasons for tranquillity. In so far Christianity is an ingenious religion. Faith, indeed, has up to the present not been able to move real mountains, although I do not know who assumed that it could. But it can put mountains where there are none.

226

The tragi-comedy of Regensburg. Here and there we see with terrible clearness the harlequinade of Fortune, how she fastens the rope, on which she wills that succeeding centuries should dance, on to a few days, one place, the condition and opinions of one brain. Thus the fate of modern German history lies in the days of that disputation at Regensburg: the peaceful settlement of ecclesiastical and moral affairs, without religious wars or a counter-reformation, and also the unity of the German nation, seemed assured: the deep, gentle spirit of Contarini hovered for one moment over the theological squabble, victorious, as representative of the riper Italian piety, reflecting the morning glory of intellectual freedom. But Luther's hard head, full of suspicions and strange misgivings, showed resistance. Because justification by grace appeared to him *his* greatest motto and discovery, he did not believe the phrase in the mouth of Italians; whereas, in point of fact, as is well known, they had invented it much earlier and spread it throughout Italy in deep silence. In this apparent agreement Luther saw the tricks of the devil, and hindered the work of peace as well as he could, thereby advancing to a great extent the aims of the Empire's foes. And now, in order to have a still stronger idea of the dreadful farcicality of it all, let us add that none of the principles about which men then disputed in Regensburg – neither that of original sin, nor that of redemption by proxy, nor that of justification by faith – is in any way true or even has any connection with truth: that they are now all recognised as incapable of being discussed. Yet on this account the world was set on fire – that is to say, by opinions which correspond to no things or realities; whereas as regards purely philological questions – as, for instance, that of the sacramental words in the Eucharist – discussion at any rate is permitted, because in this case the truth can be said. But 'where nothing is, even truth has lost her right.' – Lastly, it only remains to be said that it is true these principles give rise to sources of power so mighty that without them all the mills of the modern world could not be driven with such force. And it is primarily a matter of force, only secondarily of truth (and perhaps not even secondarily) – is it not so, my dear up-to-date friends?

227

Goethe's errors. Goethe is a signal exception among great artists in that he did not live within the limited confines of his real capacity, as if that must be the essential, the distinctive, the unconditional, and the last thing in him and for all the world. Twice he intended to possess something higher than he really possessed – and went astray in the second half of his life, where he seems quite convinced that he is one of the great scientific discoverers and illuminators. So too in the first half of his life he demanded of himself something higher than the poetic art seemed to him – and here already he made a mistake. That nature wished to make him a plastic artist – *this* was his inwardly glowing and scorching secret, which finally drove him to Italy, that he might give vent to his mania in this direction and make to it every possible sacrifice. At last, shrewd as he was, and honestly averse to any mental perversion in himself, he discovered that a tricksy elf of desire had attracted him to the belief in this calling, and that he must free himself of the greatest passion of his heart and bid it farewell. The painful conviction, tearing and gnawing at his vitals, that it was necessary to bid farewell, finds full expression in the character of Tasso. Over Tasso, that Werther intensified, hovers the premonition of something worse than death, as when one says: 'Now it is over, after this farewell: how shall I go on living without going mad?' These two fundamental errors of his life gave Goethe, in face of a purely literary attitude towards poetry (the only attitude then known to the world), such an unembarrassed and apparently almost arbitrary position. Not to speak of the period when Schiller (poor Schiller, who had no time himself and left no time to others) drove away his shy dread of poetry, his fear of all literary life and craftsmanship,

Goethe appears like a Greek who now and then visits his beloved, doubting whether she be not a goddess to whom he can give no proper name. In all his poetry one notices the inspiring neighbourhood of plastic art and Nature. The features of these figures that floated before him – and perhaps he always thought he was on the track of the metamorphoses of one goddess – became, without his will or knowledge, the features of all the children of his art. Without the extravagances of error he would not have been Goethe – that is, the only German artist in writing who has not yet become out of date – just because he desired as little to be a writer as a German by vocation.

228

Travellers and their grades. Among travellers we may distinguish five grades. The first and lowest grade is of those who travel and are seen – they become really travelled and are, as it were, blind. Next come those who really see the world. The third class experience the results of their seeing. The fourth weave their experience into their life and carry it with them henceforth. Lastly, there are some men of the highest strength who, as soon as they have returned home, must finally and necessarily work out in their lives and productions all the things seen that they have experienced and incorporated in themselves. Like these five species of travellers, all mankind goes through the whole pilgrimage of life, the lowest as purely passive, the highest as those who act and live out their lives without keeping back any residue of inner experiences.

229

In climbing higher. So soon as we climb higher than those who hitherto admired us, we appear to them as sunken and fallen. For they imagined that under all circumstances they were on the heights in our company (maybe also through our agency).

230

Measure and moderation. Of two quite lofty things, measure and moderation, it is best never to speak. A few know their force and significance, from the mysterious paths of inner experiences and conversions: they honour in them something quite godlike, and are afraid to speak aloud. All the rest hardly listen when they are spoken about, and think the subjects under discussion are tedium and mediocrity. We must perhaps except those who have once heard a warning note from that realm but have stopped their ears against the sound. The recollection of it makes them angry and exasperated.

231

Humanity of friendship and comradeship. 'If thou wilt take the left hand, then I will go to the right',* that feeling is the hall-mark of humanity in intimate intercourse, and without that feeling every friendship, every band of apostles or disciples, sooner or later becomes a fraud.

232

The profound. Men of profound thought appear to themselves in intercourse with others like comedians, for in order to be understood they must always simulate superficiality.

233

For the scorners of 'herd-humanity'. He who regards human beings as a herd, and flies from them as fast as he can, will certainly be caught up by them and gored upon their horns.

234

The main transgression against the vain. In society, he who gives another an opportunity of favourably setting forth his knowledge, sentiments, and experience sets himself above him. Unless he is felt by the other to be a superior being without limitation, he is guilty of an attack upon his vanity, while what he aimed at was the gratification of the other man's vanity.

235

Disappointment. When a long life of action distinguished by speeches and writings gives publicity to a man's personality, personal intercourse with him is generally disappointing on two grounds. Firstly, one expects too much from a brief period of intercourse (namely, all that the thousand and one opportunities of life can alone bring out). Secondly, no recognised person gives himself the trouble to

* Genesis xiii.9.

woo recognition in individual cases. He is too careless, and we are at too high a tension.

236

Two sources of kindness. To treat all men with equal good-humour, and to be kind without distinction of persons, may arise as much from a profound contempt for mankind as from an ingrained love of humanity.

237

The wanderer in the mountains to himself. There are certain signs that you have gone farther and higher. There is a freer, wider prospect before you, the air blows cooler yet milder in your face (you have unlearned the folly of confounding mildness with warmth), your gait is more firm and vigorous, courage and discretion have waxed together. On all these grounds your journey may now be more lonely and in any case more perilous than heretofore, if indeed not to the extent believed by those who from the misty valley see you, the roamer, striding on the mountains.

238

With the exception of our neighbour. I admit that my head is set wrong on my neck only, for every other man, as is well known, knows better than I what I should do or leave alone. The only one who cannot help me is myself, poor beggar! Are we not all like statues on which false heads have been placed? Eh, dear neighbour? – Ah no; you, just you, are the exception!

239

Caution. We must either not go about at all with people who are lacking in the reverence for personalities, or inexorably fetter them beforehand with the manacles of convention.

240

The wish to appear vain. In conversation with strangers or little-known acquaintances, to express only selected thoughts, to speak of one's famous acquaintances, and important experiences and travels, is a sign that one is not proud, or at least would not like to appear proud. Vanity is the polite mask of pride.

241

Good friendship. A good friendship arises when the one man deeply respects the other, more even than himself; loves him also, though not so much as himself; and finally, to facilitate intercourse, knows how to add the delicate bloom and veneer of intimacy, but at the same time wisely refrains from a true, real intimacy, from the confounding of *meum* and *tuum*.

242

Friends as ghosts. If we change ourselves vitally, our friends, who have not changed, become ghosts of our own past: their voice sounds shadowy and dreadful to us, as if we heard our own voice speaking, but younger, harder, less mellow.

243

One eye and two glances. The same people whose eyes naturally plead for favours and indulgences are accustomed, from their frequent humiliations and cravings for revenge, to assume a shameless glance as well.

244

The haze of distance. A child throughout life — that sounds very touching, but is only the verdict from the distance. Seen and known close at hand, he is always called 'puerile throughout life'.

245

Advantage and disadvantage in the same misunderstanding. The mute perplexity of the subtle brain is usually understood by the non-subtle as a silent superiority, and is much dreaded; whereas the perception of perplexity would produce good will.

246

The sage giving himself out to be a fool. The philanthropy of the sage sometimes makes him decide to pretend to be excited, enraged, or delighted, so that he may not hurt his surroundings by the coldness and rationality of his true nature.

247

Forcing oneself to attention. So soon as we note that anyone in intercourse and conversation with us has to force himself to attention, we have adequate evidence that he loves us not, or loves us no longer.

248

The way to a Christian virtue. Learning from one's enemies is the best way to love them, for it inspires us with a grateful mood towards them.

249

Stratagem of the importunate. The importunate man gives us gold coins as change for our convention coins, and thereby tries to force us afterwards to treat our convention as an oversight and him as an exception.

250

Reason for dislike. We become hostile to many an artist or writer, not because we notice in the end that he has duped us, but because he did not find more subtle means necessary to entrap us.

251

In parting. Not by the way one soul approaches another, but by the way it separates, do I recognise its relationship and homogeneity with the other.

252

Silentium. We must not speak about our friends, or we renounce the sentiment of friendship.

253

Impoliteness. Impoliteness is often the sign of a clumsy modesty, which when taken by surprise loses its head and would fain hide the fact by means of rudeness.

254

Honesty's miscalculation. Our newest acquaintances are sometimes the first to learn what we have hitherto kept dark. We have the foolish notion that our proof of confidence is the strongest fetter wherewith to hold them fast. But *they* do not know enough about us to feel so strongly the sacrifice involved in our speaking out, and betray our secrets to others without any idea of betrayal. Hereby we possibly lose our old friends.

255

In the ante-chamber of favour. All men whom we let stand long in the ante-chamber of our favour get into a state of fermentation or become bitter.

256

Warning to the despised. When we have sunk unmistakably in the estimation of mankind we should cling tooth and nail to modesty in intercourse, or we shall betray to others that we have sunk in our own estimation as well. Cynicism in intercourse is a sign that a man, when alone, treats himself too as a dog.

257

Ignorance often ennobles. With regard to the respect of those who pay respect, it is an advantage ostensibly not to understand certain things. Ignorance, too, confers privileges.

258

The opponent of grace. The impatient and arrogant man does not care for grace, feeling it to be a corporeal, visible reproach against himself. For grace is heartfelt toleration in movement and gesture.

259

On seeing again. When old friends see each other again after a long separation, it often happens that they affect an interest in matters to which they have long since become indifferent. Sometimes both remark this, but dare not raise the veil – from a mournful doubt. Hence arise conversations as in the realm of the dead.

260

Making friends only with the industrious. The man of leisure is dangerous to his friends, for, having nothing to do, he talks of what his friends are doing or not doing, interferes, and finally makes himself a nuisance. The clever man will only make friends with the industrious.

261

One weapon twice as much as two. It is an unequal combat when one man defends his cause with head and heart, the other with head alone. The first has sun and wind against him, as it were, and his two weapons interfere with each other: he loses the prize – in the eyes of truth. True, the victory of the second, with his one weapon, is seldom a victory after the hearts of all the other spectators, and makes him unpopular.

262

Depth and troubled waters. The public easily confounds him who fishes in troubled waters with him who pumps up from the depths.

263

Demonstrating one's vanity to friend and foe. Many a man, from vanity, maltreats even his friends, when in the presence of witnesses to whom he wishes to make his own preponderance clear. Others exaggerate the merits of their enemies, in order to point proudly to the fact that they are worthy of such foes.

264

Cooling off. The over-heating of the heart is generally allied with illness of the head and judgment. He who is concerned for a time with the health of his head must know what he has to cool, careless of the future of his heart. For if we are capable at all of giving warmth, we are sure to become warm again and then have our summer.

265

Mingled feelings. Towards science women and self-seeking artists entertain a feeling that is composed of envy and sentimentality.

266

Where danger is greatest. We seldom break our leg so long as life continues a toilsome upward climb. The danger comes when we begin to take things easily and choose the convenient paths.

267

Not too early. We must beware of becoming sharp too early, or we shall also become thin too early.

268

Joy in refractoriness. The good teacher knows cases where he is proud that his pupil remains true to himself in opposition to him – at times when the youth must not understand the man or would be harmed by understanding him.

269

The experiment of honesty. Young men, who wish to be more honest than they have been, seek as victim someone acknowledged to be honest, attacking him first with an attempt to reach his height by abuse – with the underlying notion that this first experiment at any rate is void of danger. For just such a one has no right to chastise the impudence of the honest man.

270

The eternal child. We think, short-sighted that we are, that fairy-tales and games belong to childhood. As if at any age we should care to live without fairy-tales and games! Our words and sentiments are indeed different, but the essential fact remains the same, as is proved by the child himself looking on games as his work and fairytales as his truth. The shortness of life ought to preserve us from a pedantic distinction between the different ages – as if every age brought something new – and a poet ought one day to portray a man of two hundred, who really lives without fairy-tales and games.

271

Every philosophy is the philosophy of a period of life. The period of life in which a philosopher finds his teaching is manifested by his teaching; he cannot avoid that, however elevated above time and hour he may feel himself. Thus, Schopenhauer's philosophy remains a mirror of his hot and melancholy youth – it is no mode of thought for older men. Plato's philosophy reminds one of the middle thirties, when a warm and a cold current generally rush together, so that spray and delicate clouds and, under favourable circumstances and glimpses of sunshine, enchanting rainbow-pictures result.

272

Of the intellect of women. The intellectual strength of a woman is best proved by the fact that she offers her own intellect as a sacrifice out of love for a man and his intellect, and that nevertheless in the new domain, which was previously foreign to her nature, a second intellect at once arises as an aftergrowth, to which the man's mind impels her.

273

Raising and lowering in the sexual domain. The storm of desire will sometimes carry a man up to a height where all desire is silenced, where he really loves and lives in a better state of being rather than in a better state of choice. On the other hand, a good woman, from true love, often climbs down to desire, and lowers herself in her own eyes. The latter action in particular is one of the most pathetic sensations which the idea of a good marriage can involve.

274

Man promises, woman fulfils. By woman Nature shows how far she has hitherto achieved her task of fashioning humanity, by man she shows what she has had to overcome and what she still proposes to do for humanity. The most perfect woman of every age is the holiday-task of the Creator on every seventh day of culture, the recreation of the artist from his work.

275

Transplanting. If we have spent our intellect in order to gain mastery over the intemperance of the passions, the sad result often follows that we transfer the intemperance to the intellect, and from that time forth are extravagant in thought and desire of knowledge.

276

Laughter as treachery. How and when a woman laughs is a sign of her culture, but in the ring of laughter her nature reveals itself, and in highly cultured women perhaps even the last insoluble residue of their nature. Hence the psychologist will say with Horace, though from different reasons: '*Ridete puellae.*' *

277

From the youthful soul. Youths varyingly show devotion and impudence towards the same person, because at bottom they only despise or admire themselves in that other person, and between the two feelings but stagger to and fro in themselves, so long as they have not found in experience the measure of their will and ability.

278

For the amelioration of the world. If we forbade the discontented, the sullen, and the atrabilious to propagate, we might transform the world into a garden of happiness. This aphorism belongs to a practical philosophy for the female sex.

279

Not to distrust your emotions. The feminine phrase 'Do not distrust your emotions' does not mean much more than 'Eat what tastes good to you.' This may also, especially for moderate natures, be a good everyday rule. But other natures must live according to another maxim: 'You must eat not only with your mouth but also with your brain, in order that the greediness of your mouth may not prove your undoing.'

* 'Laugh, girls.'

280

A cruel fancy of love. Every great love involves the cruel thought of killing the object of love, so that it may be removed once for all from the mischievous play of change. For love is more afraid of change than of destruction.

281

Doors. In everything that is learnt or experienced, the child, just like the man, sees doors; but for the former they are places to go *to*, for the latter to go *through*.

282

Sympathetic women. The sympathy of women, which is talkative, takes the sick-bed to market.

283

Early merit. He who acquires merit early in life tends to forget all reverence for age and old people, and accordingly, greatly to his disadvantage, excludes himself from the society of the mature, those who confer maturity. Thus in spite of his early merit he remains green, importunate, and boyish longer than others.

284

Souls all of a piece. Women and artists think that where we do not contradict them we cannot. Reverence on ten counts and silent disapproval on ten others appears to them an impossible combination, because their souls are all of a piece.

285

Young talents. With respect to young talents we must strictly follow Goethe's maxim, that we should often avoid harming error in order to avoid harming truth. Their condition is like the diseases of pregnancy, and involves strange appetites. These appetites should be satisfied and humoured as far as possible, for the sake of the fruit they may be expected to produce. It is true that, as nurse of these remarkable invalids, one must learn the difficult art of voluntary self-abasement.

286

Disgust with truth. Women are so constituted that all truth (in relation to men, love, children, society, aim of life) disgusts them – and that they try to be revenged on everyone who opens their eyes.

287

The source of great love. Whence arises the sudden passion of a man for a woman, a passion so deep, so vital? Least of all from sensuality only: but when a man finds weakness, need of help, and high spirits united in the same creature, he suffers a sort of overflowing of soul, and is touched and offended at the same moment. At this point arises the source of great love.

288

Cleanliness. In the child, the sense for cleanliness should be fanned into a passion, and then later on he will raise himself, in ever new phases, to almost every virtue, and will finally appear, in compensation for all talent, as a shining cloud of purity, temperance, gentleness, and character, happy in himself and spreading happiness around.

289

Of vain old men. Profundity of thought belongs to youth, clarity of thought to old age. When, in spite of this, old men sometimes speak and write in the manner of the profound, they do so from vanity, imagining that they thereby assume the charm of juvenility, enthusiasm, growth, apprehensiveness, hopefulness.

290

Enjoyment of novelty. Men use a new lesson or experience later on as a ploughshare or perhaps also as a weapon, women at once make it into an ornament.

291

How both sexes behave when in the right. If it is conceded to a woman that she is right, she cannot deny herself the triumph of setting her heel on the neck of the vanquished; she must taste her victory to the full. On the other hand, man towards man in such a case is ashamed of being right. But then man is accustomed to victory; with woman it is an exception.

292

Abnegation in the will to beauty. In order to become beautiful, a woman must not desire to be considered pretty. That is to say, in ninety-nine out of a hundred cases where she could please she must scorn and put aside all thoughts of pleasing. Only then can she ever reap the delight of him whose soul's portal is wide enough to admit the great.

293

Unintelligible, unendurable. A youth cannot understand that an old man has also had his delights, his dawns of feeling, his changings and soarings of thought. It offends him to think that such things have existed before. But it makes him very bitter to hear that, to become fruitful, he must lose those buds and dispense with their fragrance.

294

The party with the air of martyrdom. Every party that can assume an air of martyrdom wins good-natured souls over to its side and thereby itself acquires an air of good nature – greatly to its advantage.

295

Assertions surer than arguments. An assertion has, with the majority of men at any rate, more effect than an argument, for arguments provoke mistrust. Hence demagogues seek to strengthen the arguments of their party by assertions.

296

The best concealers. All regularly successful men are profoundly cunning in making their faults and weaknesses look like manifestations of strength. This proves that they must know their defects uncommonly well.

297

From time to time. He sat in the city gateway and said to one who passed through that this was the city gate. The latter replied that this was true, but that one must not be too much in the right if one expected to be thanked for it. 'Oh,' answered the other, 'I don't want thanks, but from time to time it is very pleasant not merely to be in the right but to remain in the right.'

298

Virtue was not invented by the Germans. Goethe's nobleness and free-dom from envy, Beethoven's fine hermitical resignation, Mozart's cheerfulness and grace of heart, Händel's unbending manliness and freedom under the law, Bach's confident and luminous inner life, such as does not even need to renounce glamour and success – are these qualities peculiarly German? If they are not, they at least prove to what goal Germans should strive and to what they can attain.

299

Pia fraus or something else. I hope I am mistaken, but I think that in Germany of today a twofold sort of hypocrisy is set up as the duty of the moment for everyone. From imperial–political misgivings Germanism is demanded, and from social apprehensions Christ-ianity – but both only in words and gestures, and particularly in ability to keep silent. It is the veneer that nowadays costs so much and is paid for so highly; and for the benefit of the spectators the face of the nation assumes German and Christian wrinkles.

300

How far even in the good the half may be more than the whole. In all things that are constructed to last and demand the service of many hands, much that is less good must be made a rule, although the organiser knows what is better and harder very well. He will calculate that there will never be a lack of persons who *can* correspond to the rule, and he knows that the middling good is the rule. The youth seldom sees this point, and as an innovator thinks how marvellously he is in the right and how strange is the blindness of others.

301

The partisan. The true partisan learns nothing more, he only ex-periences and judges. It is significant that Solon, who was never a partisan but pursued his aims above and apart from parties or even against them, was the father of that simple phrase wherein lies the secret of the health and vitality of Athens: 'I grow old, but I am always learning.'

302

What is German according to Goethe. They are really intolerable people of whom one cannot even accept the good, who have freedom of disposition but do not remark that they are lacking in freedom of taste and spirit. Yet just this, according to Goethe's well-weighed judgment, is German. His voice and his example indicate that the German should be more than a German if he wishes to be useful or even endurable to other nations – and which direction his striving should take, in order that he may rise above and beyond himself.

303

When it is necessary to remain stationary. When the masses begin to rage, and reason is under a cloud, it is a good thing, if the health of one's soul is not quite assured, to go under a doorway and look out to see what the weather is like.

304

The revolution-spirit and the possession-spirit. The only remedy against Socialism that still lies in your power is to avoid provoking Socialism – in other words, to live in moderation and contentment, to prevent as far as possible all lavish display, and to aid the State as far as possible in its taxing of all superfluities and luxuries. You do not like this remedy? Then, you rich bourgeois who call yourselves 'Liberals', confess that it is your own inclination that you find so terrible and menacing in Socialists, but allow to prevail in yourselves as unavoidable, as if with you it were something different. As you are constituted, if you had not your fortune and the cares of maintaining it, this bent of yours would make Socialists of you. Possession alone differentiates you from them. If you wish to conquer the assailants of your prosperity, you must first conquer yourselves. And if that prosperity only meant well-being, it would not be so external and provocative of envy; it would be more generous, more benevolent, more compensatory, more helpful. But the spurious, histrionic element in your pleasures, which lie more in the feeling of contrast (because others have them not, and feel envious) than in feelings of realised and heightened power – your houses, dresses, carriages, shops, the demands of your palates and your tables, your noisy operatic and musical enthusiasm; lastly your women, formed and fashioned but of base metal, gilded but without the ring of gold, chosen by you for show and considering themselves meant for show – these are the things that spread the poison of that national disease, which seizes the masses ever more and more as a Socialistic heart-itch, but has its origin and breeding-place in you. Who shall now arrest this epidemic?

305

Party tactics. When a party observes that a previous member has changed from an unqualified to a qualified adherent, it endures it so ill that it irritates and mortifies him in every possible way with the object of forcing him to a decisive break and making him an opponent. For the party suspects that the intention of finding a relative value in its faith, a value which admits of pro and con, of weighing and discarding, is more dangerous than downright opposition.

306

For the strengthening of parties. Whoever wishes to strengthen a party internally should give it an opportunity of being forcibly treated with obvious injustice. The party thus acquires a capital of good conscience, which hitherto it perhaps lacked.

307

To provide for one's past. As men after all only respect the old-established and slowly developed, he who would survive after his death must not only provide for posterity but still more for the past. Hence tyrants of every sort (including tyrannical artists and politicians) like to do violence to history, so that history may seem a preparation for and a ladder up to them.

308

Party writers. The beating of drums, which delights young writers who serve a party, sounds to him who does not belong to the party like a rattling of chains, and excites sympathy rather than admiration.

309

Taking sides against ourselves. Our followers never forgive us for taking sides against ourselves, for we seem in their eyes not only to be spurning their love but to be exposing them to the charge of lack of intelligence.

310

Danger in wealth. Only a man of intellect should hold property: otherwise property is dangerous to the community. For the owner, not knowing how to make use of the leisure which his possessions might secure to him, will continue to strive after more property. This strife will be his occupation, his strategy in the war with *ennui*. So in the end real wealth is produced from the moderate property that would be enough for an intellectual man. Such wealth, then, is the glittering outcrop of intellectual dependence and poverty, but it looks quite different from what its humble origin might lead one to expect, because it can mask itself with culture and art – it can, in fact, purchase the mask. Hence it excites envy in the poor and uncultured – who at bottom always envy culture and see no mask in the mask – and gradually paves the way for a social revolution. For a gilded coarseness and a histrionic blowing of trumpets in the pretended enjoyment of culture inspires that class with the thought, 'It is only a matter of money', whereas it is indeed to some extent a matter of money, but far more of intellect.

311

Joy in commanding and obeying. Commanding is a joy, like obeying; the former when it has not yet become a habit, the latter just when it has become a habit. Old servants under new masters advance each other mutually in giving pleasure.

312

Ambition for a forlorn hope. There is an ambition for a forlorn hope which forces a party to place itself at the post of extreme danger.

313

When asses are needed. We shall not move the crowd to cry 'Hosanna!' until we have ridden into the city upon an ass.

314

Party usage. Every party attempts to represent the important elements that have sprung up outside it as unimportant, and if it does not succeed, it attacks those elements the more bitterly, the more excellent they are.

315

Becoming empty. Of him who abandons himself to the course of events, a smaller and smaller residue is continually left. Great politicians may therefore become quite empty men, although they were once full and rich.

316

Welcome enemies. The Socialistic movements are nowadays becoming more and more agreeable rather than terrifying to the dynastic governments, because by these movements they are provided with a right and a weapon for making exceptional rules, and can thus attack their real bogies, democrats and anti-dynasts. Towards all that such governments professedly detest they feel a secret cordiality and inclination. But they are compelled to draw the veil over their soul.

317

Possession possesses. Only up to a certain point does possession make men feel freer and more independent; one step farther, and possession becomes lord, the possessor a slave. The latter must sacrifice his time, his thoughts to the former, and feels himself compelled to an intercourse, nailed to a spot, incorporated with the State – perhaps quite in conflict with his real and essential needs.

318

Of the mastery of them that know. It is easy, ridiculously easy, to set up a model for the choice of a legislative body. First of all the honest and reliable men of the nation, who at the same time are masters and experts in some one branch, have to become prominent by mutual scenting-out and recognition. From these, by a narrower process of selection, the learned and expert of the first rank in each individual branch must again be chosen, also by mutual recognition and guarantee. If the legislative body be com-posed of these, it will finally be necessary, in each individual case, that only the voices and judgments of the most specialised experts should decide; the honesty of all the rest should have become so great that it is simply a matter of decency to leave the voting also in the hands of these men. The result would be that the law, in the strictest sense, would emanate from the intelligence of the most intelligent. As things now are, voting is done by parties, and at every division there must be hundreds of uneasy consciences among the ill-taught, the incapable of judgment, among those who merely repeat, imitate, and go with the tide. Nothing lowers the dignity of a new law so much as this inherent shamefaced feeling of insincerity that necessarily results at every party division. But, as has been said, it is easy, ridiculously easy, to set up such a model: no power on earth is at present strong enough to realise such an ideal – unless the belief in the highest utility of knowledge, and of those that know, at last dawns even upon the most hostile minds and is preferred to the prevalent belief in majorities. In the sense of such a future may our watchword be: 'More reverence for them that know, and down with all parties!'

319

Of the 'nation of thinkers' (or Of bad thinking). The vague, vacill-ating, premonitory, elementary, intuitive elements – to choose obscure names for obscure things – that are attributed to the German nature would be, if they really still existed, a proof that our culture has remained several stages behind and is still surrounded by the spell and atmosphere of the Middle Ages. It is true that in this backwardness there are certain advantages: by these qualities the Germans (if, as has been said before, they still possess them) would possess the capacity, which other nations have now lost, for doing certain things and particularly for under-standing certain things. Much undoubtedly is lost if the lack of sense – which is just the common factor in all those qualities – is lost. Here too, however, there are no losses without the highest compensatory gains, so that no reason is left for lamenting, grant-ing that we do not, like children and gourmands, wish to enjoy at once the fruits of all seasons of the year.

320

Carrying coals to Newcastle. The governments of the great States
have two instruments for keeping the people dependent, in fear
and obedience: a coarser, the army; and a more refined, the
school. With the aid of the former they win over to their side the
ambition of the higher strata and the strength of the lower, so far
as both are characteristic of active and energetic men of moderate
or inferior gifts. With the aid of the latter they win over gifted
poverty, especially the intellectually pretentious semi-poverty of
the middle classes. Above all, they make teachers of all grades into
an intellectual court looking unconsciously 'towards the heights'.
By putting obstacle after obstacle in the way of private schools
and the wholly distasteful individual tuition they secure the disposal of a considerable number of educational posts, towards
which numerous hungry and submissive eyes are turned to an
extent five times as great as can ever be satisfied. These posts,
however, must support the holder but meagrely, so that he maintains a feverish thirst for promotion and becomes still more closely
attached to the views of the government. For it is always more
advantageous to foster moderate discontent than contentment, the
mother of courage, the grandmother of free thought and exuberance. By means of this physically and mentally bridled body of
teachers, the youth of the country is as far as possible raised to
a certain level of culture that is useful to the State and arranged on
a suitable sliding-scale. Above all, the immature and ambitious
minds of all classes are almost imperceptibly imbued with the idea
that only a career which is recognised and hall-marked by the State
can lead immediately to social distinction. The effect of this belief
in government examinations and titles goes so far that even men
who have remained independent and have risen by trade or
handicraft still feel a pang of discontent in their hearts until their
position too is marked and acknowledged by a gracious bestowal
of rank and orders from above – until one becomes a 'somebody'.
Finally the State connects all these hundreds of offices and posts in
its hands with the obligation of being trained and hallmarked in
these State schools if one ever wishes to enter this charmed circle.
Honour in society, daily bread, the possibility of a family, protection from above, the feeling of community in a common culture –

all this forms a network of hopes into which every young man walks: how should he feel the slightest breath of mistrust? In the end, perhaps, the obligation of being a soldier for one year has become with everyone, after the lapse of a few generations, an unreflecting habit, an understood thing, with an eye to which we construct the plan of our lives quite early. Then the State can venture on the master-stroke of weaving together school and army, talent, ambition and strength by means of common advantages – that is, by attracting the more highly gifted on favourable terms to the army and inspiring them with the military spirit of joyful obedience; so that finally, perhaps, they become attached permanently to the flag and endow it by their talents with an ever new and more brilliant lustre. Then nothing more is wanted but an opportunity for great wars. These are provided from professional reasons (and so in all innocence) by diplomats, aided by newspapers and Stock Exchanges. For 'the nation', as a nation of soldiers, need never be supplied with a good conscience in war – it has one already.

321

The press. If we consider how even today all great political transactions glide upon the stage secretly and stealthily; how they are hidden by unimportant events, and seem small when close at hand; how they only show their far-reaching effect, and leave the soil still quaking, long after they have taken place – what significance can we attach to the Press in its present position, with its daily expenditure of lung-power in order to bawl, to deafen, to excite, to terrify? Is it anything more than an everlasting false alarm, which tries to lead our ears and our wits into a false direction?

322

After a great event. A nation and a man whose soul has come to light through some great event generally feel the immediate need of some act of childishness or coarseness, as much from shame as for purposes of recreation.

323

To be a good German means to de-Germanise oneself. National differences consist, far more than has hitherto been observed, only in the differences of various grades of culture, and are only to a very small extent permanent (nor even that in a strict sense). For this reason all arguments based on national character are so little binding on one who aims at the alteration of convictions – in other words, at culture. If, for instance, we consider all that has already been German, we shall improve upon the hypothetical question, 'What is German?' by the counter-question, 'What is *now* German?' and every good German will answer it practically, by overcoming his German characteristics. For when a nation advances and grows, it bursts the girdle previously given to it by its national outlook. When it remains stationary or declines, its soul is surrounded by a fresh girdle, and the crust, as it becomes harder and harder, builds a prison around, with walls growing ever higher. Hence if a nation has much that is firmly established, this is a sign that it wishes to petrify and would like to become nothing but a monument. This happened, from a definite date, in the case of Egypt. So he who is well-disposed towards the Germans may for his part consider how he may more and more grow out of what is German. The tendency to be un-German has therefore always been a mark of efficient members of our nation.

324

Foreignisms. A foreigner who travelled in Germany found favour or the reverse by certain assertions of his, according to the districts in which he stayed. All intelligent Suabians, he used to say, are coquettish. The other Suabians still believed that Uhland was a poet and Goethe immoral. The best about German novels now in vogue was that one need not read them, for one knew already what they contained. The native of Berlin seemed more good-humoured than the South German, for he was all too fond of mocking, and so could endure mockery himself, which the South German could not. The intellect of the Germans was kept down by their beer and their newspapers: he recommended them tea and pamphlets, of course as a cure. He advised us to contemplate the different nations of worn-out Europe and see how well each displayed some particular quality of old age, to the delight of those who sit before the great spectacle: how the French successfully represent the cleverness and amiability of old age, the English the experience and reserve, the Italians the innocence and candour. Can the other masks of old age be wanting?

Where is the proud old man, the domineering old man, the covetous old man? – The most dangerous region in Germany was Saxony and Thuringia: nowhere else was there more mental nimbleness, more knowledge of men, side by side with freedom of thought; and all this was so modestly veiled by the ugly dialect and the zealous officiousness of the inhabitants that one hardly noticed that one here had to deal with the intellectual drill-sergeants of Germany, her teachers for good or evil. The arrogance of the North Germans was kept in check by their tendency to obey, that of the South Germans by their tendency – to make themselves comfortable. It appeared to him that in their women German men possessed awkward but self-opinionated housewives, who belauded themselves so perseveringly that they had almost persuaded the world, and at any rate their husbands, of their peculiarly German housewifely virtue. When the conversation turned on Germany's home and foreign policy, he used to say (he called it 'betray the secret') that Germany's greatest statesman did not believe in great statesmen. The future of Germany he found menaced and menacing, for Germans had forgotten how to enjoy themselves (an art that the Italians understood so well), but, by the great games of chance called wars and dynastic revolutions, had accustomed themselves to emotionalism, and consequently would one day have an *émeute*. For that is the strongest emotion that a nation can procure for itself. The German Socialist was all the more dangerous because impelled by no definite necessity: his trouble lay in not knowing what he wanted; so, even if he attained many of his objects, he would still pine away from desire in the midst of delights, just like Faust, but presumably like a very vulgar Faust. 'For the Faust-Devil,' he finally exclaimed, 'by whom cultured Germans were so much plagued, was exorcised by Bismarck; but now the Devil has entered into the swine, and is worse than ever!'

325

Opinions. Most men are nothing and count for nothing until they have arrayed themselves in universal convictions and public opinions. This is in accordance with the tailors' philosophy, 'The apparel makes the man.' Of exceptional men, however, it must be said, 'The wearer primarily makes the apparel.' Here opinions

cease to be public, and become something else than masks, ornament, and disguise.

326

Two kinds of sobriety. In order not to confound the sobriety arising
from mental exhaustion with that arising from moderation, one
must remark that the former is peevish, the latter cheerful.

327

Debasement of joy. To call a thing good not a day longer than it
appears to us good, and above all not a day earlier — that is the only
way to keep joy pure. Otherwise, joy all too easily becomes insipid
and rotten to the taste, and counts, for whole strata of the people,
among the adulterated foodstuffs.

328

The scapegoat of virtue. When a man does his very best, those who
mean well towards him, but are not capable of appreciating him,
speedily seek a scapegoat to immolate, thinking it is the scapegoat
of sin — but it is the scapegoat of virtue.

329

Sovereignty. To honour and acknowledge even the bad, when it
pleases one, and to have no conception of how one could be
ashamed of being pleased thereat, is the mark of sovereignty in
things great and small.

330

Influence a phantom, not a reality. The man of mark gradually learns
that so far as he has influence he is a phantom in other brains, and
perhaps he falls into a state of subtle vexation of soul, in which he
asks himself whether he must not maintain this phantom of himself
for the benefit of his fellow-men.

331

Giving and taking. When one takes away (or anticipates) the
smallest thing that another possesses, the latter is blind to the
fact that he has been given something greater, nay, even the
greatest thing.

332

Good ploughland. All rejection and negation betoken a deficiency in fertility. If we were good ploughland, we should allow nothing to be unused or lost, and in every thing, event, or person we should welcome manure, rain, or sunshine.

333

Intercourse as an enjoyment. If a man renounces the world and intentionally lives in solitude, he may come to regard intercourse with others, which he enjoys but seldom, as a special delicacy.

334

To know how to suffer in public. We must advertise our misfortunes and from time to time heave audible sighs and show visible marks of impatience. For if we could let others see how assured and happy we are in spite of pain and privation, how envious and ill-tempered they would become at the sight! – But we must take care not to corrupt our fellow-men; besides, if they knew the truth, they would levy a heavy toll upon us. At any rate our public misfortune is our private advantage.

335

Warmth on the heights. On the heights it is warmer than people in the valleys suppose, especially in winter. The thinker recognises the full import of this simile.

336

To will the good and be capable of the beautiful. It is not enough to practise the good, one must have willed it, and, as the poet says, include the Godhead in our will. But the beautiful we must not will, we must be capable of it, in innocence and blindness, without any psychical curiosity. He that lights his lantern to find perfect men should remember the token by which to know them. They are the men who always act for the sake of the good and in so doing always attain to the beautiful without thinking of the beautiful. Many better and nobler men, from impotence or from want of beauty in their souls, remain unrefreshing and ugly to behold, with all their good will and good works. They rebuff and injure even virtue through the repulsive garb in which their bad taste arrays her.

337

Danger of renunciation. We must beware of basing our lives on too narrow a foundation of appetite. For if we renounce all the joys involved in positions, honours, associations, revels, creature comforts, and arts, a day may come when we perceive that this repudiation has led us not to wisdom but to satiety of life.

338

Final opinion on opinions. Either we should hide our opinions or hide ourselves behind our opinions. Whoever does otherwise, does not know the way of the world, or belongs to the order of pious fire-eaters.

339

*'Gaudeamus igitur'.** Joy must contain edifying and healing forces for the moral nature of man. Otherwise, how comes it that our soul, as soon as it basks in the sunshine of joy, unconsciously vows to itself, 'I will be good!' 'I will become perfect!' and is at once seized by a premonition of perfection that is like a shudder of religious awe?

340

To one who is praised. So long as you are praised, believe that you are not yet on your own course but on that of another.

341

Loving the master. The apprentice and the master love the master in different ways.

342

All-too-beautiful and human. 'Nature is too beautiful for thee, poor mortal,' one often feels. But now and then, at a profound contemplation of all that is human, in its fullness, vigour, tenderness, and complexity, I have felt as if I must say, in all humility, 'Man also is too beautiful for the contemplation of man!' Nor did I mean the moral man alone, but everyone.

* Let us rejoice, therefore.

343

Real and personal estate. When life has treated us in true robber fashion, and has taken away all that it could of honour, joys, connections, health, and property of every kind, we perhaps discover in the end, after the first shock, that we are richer than before. For now we know for the first time what is so peculiarly ours that no robber hand can touch it, and perhaps, after all the plunder and devastation, we come forward with the airs of a mighty real estate owner.

344

Involuntarily idealised. The most painful feeling that exists is finding out that we are always taken for something higher than we really are. For we must thereby confess to ourselves, 'There is in you some element of fraud — your speech, your expression, your bearing, your eye, your dealings; and this deceitful something is as necessary as your usual honesty, but constantly destroys its effect and its value.

345

Idealist and liar. We must not let ourselves be tyrannised even by that finest faculty of idealising things: otherwise, truth will one day part company from us with the insulting remark: 'Thou arch-liar, what have I to do with thee?'

346

Being misunderstood. When one is misunderstood generally, it is impossible to remove a particular misunderstanding. This point must be recognised, to save superfluous expenditure of energy in self-defence.

347

The water-drinker speaks. Go on drinking your wine, which has refreshed you all your life — what affair is it of yours if I have to be a water-drinker? Are not wine and water peaceable, brotherly elements, that can live side by side without mutual recriminations?

348

From cannibal country. In solitude the lonely man is eaten up by himself, among crowds by the many. Choose which you prefer.

349

The freezing-point of the will. 'Some time the hour will come at last, the hour that will envelop you in the golden cloud of pain-lessness; when the soul enjoys its own weariness and, happy in patient playing with patience, resembles the waves of a lake, which on a quiet summer day, in the reflection of a many-hued evening sky, sip and sip at the shore and again are hushed – without end, without purpose, without satiety, without need – all calm rejoicing in change, all ebb and flow of Nature's pulse.' Such is the feeling and talk of all invalids, but if they attain that hour, a brief period of enjoyment is followed by *ennui*. But this is the thawing-wind of the frozen will, which awakes, stirs, and once more begets desire upon desire. Desire is a sign of con-valescence or recovery.

350

The disclaimed ideal. It happens sometimes by an exception that a man only reaches the highest when he disclaims his ideal. For this ideal previously drove him onward too violently, so that in the middle of the track he regularly got out of breath and had to rest.

351

A treacherous inclination. It should be regarded as a sign of an envious but aspiring man, when he feels himself attracted by the thought that with regard to the eminent there is but one salvation – love.

352

Staircase happiness. Just as the wit of many men does not keep pace with opportunity (so that opportunity has already passed through the door while wit still waits on the staircase outside), so others have a kind of staircase happiness, which walks too slowly to keep pace with swift-footed Time. The best that it can enjoy of an experience, of a whole span of life, falls to its share long afterwards, often only as a weak, spicy fragrance, giving rise to longing and sadness – as if 'it might have been possible' – some time or other – to drink one's fill of this element: but now it is too late.

353

Worms. The fact that an intellect contains a few worms does not detract from its ripeness.

354

The seat of victory. A good seat on horseback robs an opponent of his courage, the spectator of his heart – why attack such a man? Sit like one who has been victorious!

355

Danger in admiration. From excessive admiration for the virtues of others one can lose the sense of one's own, and finally, through lack of practice, lose these virtues themselves, without retaining the alien virtues as compensation.

356

Uses of sickliness. He who is often ill not only has a far greater pleasure in health, on account of his so often getting well, but acquires a very keen sense of what is healthy or sickly in actions and achievements, both his own and others'. Thus, for example, it is just the writers of uncertain health – among whom, unfortunately, nearly all great writers must be classed – who are wont to have a far more even and assured tone of health in their writings, because they are better versed than are the physically robust in the philosophy of psychical health and convalescence and in their teachers – morning, sunshine, forest, and fountain.

357

Disloyalty a condition of mastery. It cannot be helped – every master has but one pupil, and *he* becomes disloyal to him, for he also is destined for mastery.

358

Never in vain. In the mountains of truth you never climb in vain. Either you already reach a higher point today, or you exercise your strength in order to be able to climb higher to-morrow.

359

Through grey window-panes. Is what you see through this window of the world so beautiful that you do not wish to look through any other window – ay, and, even try to prevent others from so doing?

360

A sign of radical changes. When we dream of persons long forgotten or dead, it is a sign that we have suffered radical changes, and that the soil on which we live has been completely undermined. The dead rise again, and our antiquity becomes modernity.

361

Medicine of the soul. To lie still and think little is the cheapest medicine for all diseases of the soul, and, with the aid of good-will, becomes pleasanter every hour that it is used.

362

Intellectual order of precedence. You rank far below others when you try to establish the exception and they the rule.

363

The fatalist. You must believe in fate – science can compel you thereto. All that develops in you out of that belief – cowardice, devotion or loftiness, and uprightness – bears witness to the soil in which the grain was sown, but not to the grain itself, for from that seed anything and everything can grow.

364

The reason for much fretfulness. He that prefers the beautiful to the useful in life will undoubtedly, like children who prefer sweet-meats to bread, destroy his digestion and acquire a very fretful outlook on the world.

365

Excess as a remedy. We can make our own talent once more accept-able to ourselves by honouring and enjoying the opposite talent for some time to excess. Using excess as a remedy is one of the more refined devices in the art of life.

366

'*Will a self*'. Active, successful natures act, not according to the maxim, 'Know thyself', but as if always confronted with the command, 'Will a self, so you will become a self.' – Fate seems always to have left them a choice. Inactive, contemplative natures, on the other hand, reflect on how they have chosen their self 'once for all' at their entry into life.

367

To live as far as possible without a following. How small is the importance of followers we first grasp when we have ceased to be the followers of our followers.

368

Obscuring oneself. We must understand how to obscure ourselves in order to get rid of the gnat-swarms of pestering admirers.

369

Ennui. There is an *ennui* of the most subtle and cultured brains, to which the best that the world can offer has become stale. Accustomed to eat ever more and more recherché fare and to feel disgust at coarser diet, they are in danger of dying of hunger. For the very best exists but in small quantities, and has sometimes become inaccessible or hard as stone, so that even good teeth can no longer bite it.

370

The danger in admiration. The admiration of a quality or of an art may be so strong as to deter us from aspiring to possess that quality or art.

371

What is required of art. One man wants to enjoy himself by means of art, another for a time to get out of or above himself. To meet both requirements there exists a twofold species of artists.

372

Secessions. Whoever secedes from us offends not us, perhaps, but certainly our adherents.

373

After death. It is only long after the death of a man that we find it inconceivable that he should be missed – in the case of really great men, only after decades. Those who are honest usually think when anyone dies that he is not much missed, and that the pompous funeral oration is a piece of hypocrisy. Necessity first teaches the necessariness of an individual, and the proper epitaph is a belated sigh.

374

Leaving in Hades. We must leave many things in the Hades of half-conscious feeling, and not try to release them from their shadow-existence, or else they will become, as thoughts and words, our demoniacal tyrants, with cruel lust after our blood.

375

Near to beggary. Even the richest intellect sometimes mislays the key to the room in which his hoarded treasures repose. He is then like the poorest of the poor, who must beg to get a living.

376

Chain-thinkers. To him who has thought a great deal, every new thought that he hears or reads at once assumes the form of a chain.

377

Pity. In the gilded sheath of pity is sometimes hidden the dagger of envy.

378

What is genius? – To aspire to a lofty aim and to will the means to that aim.

379

Vanity of combatants. He who has no hope of victory in a combat, or who is obviously worsted, is all the more desirous that his style of fighting should be admired.

380

The philosophic life misinterpreted. At the moment when one is beginning to take philosophy seriously, the whole world fancies that one is doing the reverse.

381

Imitation. By imitation, the bad gains, the good loses credit – especially in art.

382

Final teaching of history. 'Oh that I had but lived in those times!' is the exclamation of foolish and frivolous men. At every period of history that we seriously review, even if it be the most belauded era of the past, we shall rather cry out at the end, 'Anything but a return to that! The spirit of that age would oppress you with the weight of a hundred atmospheres, the good and beautiful in it you would not enjoy, its evil you could not digest.' Depend upon it, posterity will pass the same verdict on our own epoch, and say that it was unbearable, that life under such conditions was intolerable. 'And yet everyone can endure his own times?' Yes, because the spirit of his age not only lies *upon* him but is *in* him. The spirit of the age offers resistance to itself and can bear itself.

383

Greatness as a mask. By greatness in our comportment we embitter our foes; by envy that we do not conceal we almost reconcile them to us. For envy levels and makes equal; it is an unconscious, plaintive variety of modesty. It may be indeed that here and there, for the sake of the above-named advantage, envy has been assumed as a mask by those who are not envious. Certainly, however, greatness in comportment is often used as the mask of envy by ambitious men who would rather suffer drawbacks and embitter their foes than let it be seen that they place them on an equal footing with themselves.

384

Unpardonable. You gave him an opportunity of displaying the greatness of his character, and he did not make use of the opportunity. He will never forgive you for that.

385

Contrasts. The most senile thought ever conceived about men lies in the famous saying, 'The ego is always hateful', the most childish in the still more famous saying, 'Love thy neighbour as thyself.' – With the one knowledge of men has ceased, with the other it has not yet begun.

386

A defective ear. 'We still belong to the mob so long as we always shift the blame on to others; we are on the track of wisdom when we always make ourselves alone responsible; but the wise man finds no one to blame, neither himself nor others.' – Who said that? Epictetus, eighteen hundred years ago. The world has heard but forgotten the saying. No, the world has not heard and not forgotten it: everything is not forgotten. But we had not the necessary ear, the ear of Epictetus. So he whispered it into his own ear? – Even so: wisdom is the whispering of the sage to himself in the crowded market-place.

387

A defect of standpoint, not of vision. We always stand a few paces too near ourselves and a few paces too far from our neighbour. Hence we judge him too much in the lump, and ourselves too much by individual, occasional, insignificant features and circumstances.

388

Ignorance about weapons. How little we care whether another knows a subject or not! – whereas he perhaps sweats blood at the bare idea that he may be considered ignorant on the point. Yes, there are exquisite fools, who always go about with a quiverful of mighty, excommunicatory utterances, ready to shoot down anyone who shows freely that there are matters in which their judgment is not taken into account.

389

At the drinking-table of experience. People whose innate moderation leads them to drink but the half of every glass, will not admit that everything in the world has its lees and sediment.

390

Singing-birds. The followers of a great man often put their own eyes out, so that they may be the better able to sing his praise.

391

Beyond our ken. The good generally displeases us when it is beyond our ken.

392

Rule as mother or as child. There is one condition that gives birth to rules, another to which rules give birth.

393

Comedy. We sometimes earn honour or love for actions and achievements which we have long since sloughed as the snake sloughs his skin. We are hereby easily seduced into becoming the comic actors of our own past, and into throwing the old skin once more about our shoulders – and that not merely from vanity, but from good-will towards our admirers.

394

A mistake of biographers. The small force that is required to launch a boat into the stream must not be confounded with the force of the stream that carries the boat along. Yet this mistake is made in nearly all biographies.

395

Not buying too dear. The things that we buy too dear we generally turn to bad use, because we have no love for them but only a painful recollection. Thus they involve a twofold drawback.

396

The philosophy that society always needs. The pillars of the social structure rest upon the fundamental fact that everyone cheerfully contemplates all that he is, does, and attempts, his sickness or health, his poverty or affluence, his honour or insignificance, and says to himself, 'After all, I would not change places with anyone!' –

Whoever wishes to add a stone to the social structure should always try to implant in mankind this cheerful philosophy of contentment and refusal to change places.

397
The mark of a noble soul. A noble soul is not that which is capable of the highest flights, but that which rises little and falls little, living always in a free and bright atmosphere and altitude

398
Greatness and its contemplator. The noblest effect of greatness is that it gives the contemplator a power of vision that magnifies and embellishes.

399
Being satisfied. We show that we have attained maturity of understanding when we no longer go where rare flowers lurk under the thorniest hedges of knowledge, but are satisfied with gardens, forests, meadows, and ploughlands, remembering that life is too short for the rare and uncommon.

400
Advantage in privation. He who always lives in the warmth and fullness of the heart, and, as it were, in the summer air of the soul, cannot form an idea of that fearful delight which seizes more wintry natures, who for once in a way are kissed by the rays of love and the milder breath of a sunny February day.

401
Recipe for the sufferer. You find the burden of life too heavy? Then you must increase the burden of your life. When the sufferer finally thirsts after and seeks the river of Lethe, then he must become a *hero* to be certain of finding it.

402
The judge. He who has seen another's ideal becomes his inexorable judge, and as it were his evil conscience.

403

The utility of great renunciation. The useful thing about great renunc-iation is that it invests us with that youthful pride through which we can thenceforth easily demand of ourselves small renunciations.

404

How duty acquires a glamour. You can change a brazen duty into gold in the eyes of all by always performing something more than you have promised.

405

Prayer to mankind. 'Forgive us our virtues' – so should we pray to mankind.

406

They that create and they that enjoy. Everyone who enjoys thinks that the principal thing to the tree is the fruit, but in point of fact the principal thing to it is the seed. Herein lies the difference between them that create and them that enjoy.

407

The glory of all great men. What is the use of genius, if it does not invest him who contemplates and reveres it with such freedom and loftiness of feeling that he no longer has need of genius? – To make themselves superfluous is the glory of all great men.

408

The journey to Hades. I too have been in the underworld, even as Odysseus, and I shall often be there again. Not sheep alone have I sacrificed that I might be able to converse with a few dead souls, but not even my own blood have I spared. There were four pairs who responded to me in my sacrifice: Epicurus and Montaigne, Goethe and Spinoza, Plato and Rousseau, Pascal and Schopenhauer. With them I have to come to terms. When I have long wandered alone, I will let them prove me right or wrong; to them will I listen, if they prove each other right or wrong. In all that I say, conclude, or think out for myself and others, I fasten my eyes on those eight and see their eyes fastened on mine. May the living forgive me if I look upon them at times as shadows, so pale and fretful, so restless and, alas! so eager for life. Those eight, on the other hand, seem to me so living that I feel as if even now, after their death, they could never become weary of life. But eternal vigour of life is the important point: what matters 'eternal life', or indeed life at all?

PART TWO

*The Wanderer
and his Shadow*

The Shadow: It is so long since I heard you speak that I should like to give you an opportunity of talking.

The Wanderer: I hear a voice — where? whose? I almost fancied that I heard myself speaking, but with a voice yet weaker than my own.

The Shadow [*after a pause*]: Are you not glad to have an opportunity of speaking?

The Wanderer: By God and everything else in which I disbelieve, it is my shadow that speaks. I hear it, but I do not believe it.

The Shadow: Let us assume that it exists, and think no more about it. In another hour all will be over.

The Wanderer: That is just what I thought when in a forest near Pisa I saw first two and then five camels.

The Shadow: It is all the better if we are both equally forbearing towards each other when for once our reason is silent. Thus we shall avoid losing our tempers in conversation, and shall not at once apply mutual thumbscrews in the event of any word sounding for once unintelligible to us. If one does not know exactly how to answer, it is enough to say *something*. Those are the reasonable terms on which I hold conversation with any person. During a long talk the wisest of men becomes a fool once and a simpleton thrice.

The Wanderer: Your moderation is not flattering to those to whom you confess it.

The Shadow: Am I, then, to flatter?

The Wanderer: I thought a man's shadow was his vanity. Surely vanity would never say, 'Am I, then, to flatter?'

The Shadow: Nor does human vanity, so far as I am acquainted with it, ask, as I have done twice, *whether* it may speak. It simply speaks.

The Wanderer: Now I see for the first time how rude I am to you, my beloved shadow. I have not said a word of my supreme *delight* in hearing and not merely seeing you. You must know that I love shadows even as I love light. For the existence of beauty of face, clearness of speech, kindliness and firmness of character, the shadow is as necessary as the light. They are not opponents – rather do they hold each other's hands like good friends; and when the light vanishes, the shadow glides after it.

The Shadow: Yes, and I hate the same thing that you hate – night. I love men because they are votaries of life. I rejoice in the gleam of their eyes when they recognise and discover, they who never weary of recognising and discovering. That shadow which all things cast when the sunshine of knowledge falls upon them – that shadow too am I.

The Wanderer: I think I understand you, although you have expressed yourself in somewhat shadowy terms. You are right. Good friends give to each other here and there, as a sign of mutual understanding, an obscure phrase which to any third party is meant to be a riddle. And we are good friends, you and I. So enough of preambles! Some few hundred questions oppress my soul, and the time for you to answer them is perchance but short. Let us see how we may come to an understanding as quickly and peaceably as possible.

The Shadow: But shadows are more shy than men. You will not reveal to any man the manner of our conversation?

The Wanderer: *The manner* of our conversation? Heaven preserve me from wire-drawn, literary dialogues! If Plato had found less pleasure in spinning them out, his readers would have found more pleasure in Plato. A dialogue that in real life is a source of delight, when turned into writing and read, is a picture with nothing but false perspectives. Everything is too long or too short. Yet perhaps I may reveal the *points on which* we have come to an understanding?

The Shadow: With that I am content. For everyone will only recognise your views once more, and no one will think of the shadow.

The Wanderer: Perhaps you are wrong, my friend! Hitherto they have observed in my views more of the shadow than of me.

The Shadow: More of the shadow than of the light? Is that possible?

The Wanderer: Be serious, dear fool! My very first question demands seriousness.

*   *   *

I

Of the tree of knowledge. Probability, but no truth; the semblance of freedom, but no freedom – these are the two fruits by virtue of which the tree of knowledge cannot be confounded with the tree of life.

2

The world's reason. That the world is *not* the abstract essence of an eternal reasonableness is sufficiently proved by the fact that that *bit of the world* which we know – I mean our human reason – is none too reasonable. And if *this* is not eternally and wholly wise and reasonable, the rest of the world will not be so either. Here the conclusion *a minori ad majus, a parte ad totum** holds good, and that with decisive force.

3

'In the beginning was'. To glorify the origin – that is the metaphysical after-shoot which sprouts again at the contemplation of history, and absolutely makes us imagine that *in the beginning* of things lies all that is most valuable and essential.

4

Standard for the value of truth. The difficulty of climbing mountains is no gauge of their height. Yet in the case of science it is different! – we are told by certain persons who wish to be considered 'the initiated' – the difficulty in finding truth is to determine the value of truth! This insane morality originates in the idea that 'truths' are really nothing more than gymnastic appliances, with which we have to exercise ourselves until we are thoroughly tired. It is a morality for the athletes and gymnasts of the intellect.

5

Use of words and reality. There exists a simulated contempt for all the things that mankind actually holds most important, for all

* From the lesser to the greater; from the part to the whole.

everyday matters. For instance, we say 'we only eat to live' – an abominable *lie*, like that which speaks of the procreation of children as the real purpose of all sexual pleasure. Conversely, the reverence for 'the most important things' is hardly ever quite genuine. The priests and metaphysicians have indeed accustomed us to a hypocritically exaggerated *use of words* regarding these matters, but they have not altered the feeling that these most important things are not so important as those despised 'everyday matters'. A fatal consequence of this twofold hypocrisy is that we never make these everyday matters (such as eating, housing, clothes, and intercourse) the object of a constant unprejudiced and *universal* reflection and revision, but, as such a process appears degrading, we divert from them our serious intellectual and artistic side. Hence in such matters habit and frivolity win an easy victory over the thoughtless, especially over inexperienced youth. On the other hand, our continual transgressions of the simplest laws of body and mind reduce us all, young and old, to a disgraceful state of dependence and servitude – I mean to that fundamentally superfluous dependence upon physicians, teachers and clergymen, whose dead weight still lies heavy upon the whole of society.

6

Earthly infirmities and their main cause. If we look about us, we are always coming across men who have eaten eggs all their lives without observing that the oblong-shaped taste the best; who do not know that a thunder-storm is beneficial to the stomach; that perfumes are most fragrant in cold, clear air; that our sense of taste varies in different parts of our mouths; that every meal at which we talk well or listen well does harm to the digestion. If we are not satisfied with these examples of defective powers of observation, we shall concede all the more readily that the everyday matters are very imperfectly seen and rarely observed by the majority. Is this a matter of indifference? – Let us remember, after all, that from this defect are derived *nearly all the bodily and spiritual infirmities* of the individual. Ignorance of what is good and bad for us, in the arrangement of our mode of life, the division of our day, the selection of our friends and the time we devote to them, in business and leisure, commanding and obeying, our feeling for nature and for art, our eating, sleeping, and meditation; ignorance and lack of keen perceptions *in the smallest and most ordinary details* – this it is that makes the world 'a vale of tears' for so many. Let us not say that here as everywhere the fault lies with human *unreason*. Of reason there is enough and to spare, but it is *wrongly directed* and *artificially diverted* from these little intimate things. Priests and teachers, and the sublime ambition of all idealists, coarser and subtler, din it even into the child's ears that the means of serving mankind at large depend upon altogether different *things* – upon the salvation of the soul, the service of the State, the advancement of science, or even upon social position and property; whereas the needs of the individual, his requirements great and small during the twenty-four hours of the day, are quite paltry or indifferent. Even Socrates attacked with all his might this arrogant neglect of the human for the benefit of humanity, and loved to indicate by a quotation from Homer the true sphere and conception of all anxiety and reflection: 'All that really matters,' he said, 'is the good and evil hap I find at home.'

7

Two means of consolation. Epicurus, the soul-comforter of later antiquity, said, with that marvellous insight which to this very day is so rarely to be found, that for the calming of the spirit the solution of the final and ultimate theoretical problems is by no means necessary. Hence, instead of raising a barren and remote discussion of the final question, whether the gods existed, it sufficed him to say to those who were tormented by 'fear of the gods': 'If there are gods, they do not concern themselves with us.' The latter position is far stronger and more favourable, for, by conceding a few points to the other, one makes him readier to listen and to take to heart. But as soon as he sets about proving the opposite (that the gods do concern themselves with us), into what thorny jungles of error must the poor man fall, quite of his own accord, and without any cunning on the part of his interlocutor! The latter must only have enough subtlety and humanity to conceal his sympathy with this tragedy. Finally, the other comes to feel disgust – the strongest argument against any proposition – disgust with his own hypothesis. He becomes cold, and goes away in the same frame of mind as the pure atheist who says, 'What do the gods matter to me? The devil take them!' – In other cases,

especially when a half-physical, half-moral assumption had cast a
gloom over his spirit, Epicurus did not refute the assumption. He
agreed that it might be true, but that there was *a second assumption*
to explain the same phenomenon, and that it could perhaps
be maintained in other ways. The plurality of hypotheses (for
example, that concerning the origin of conscientious scruples)
suffices even in our time to remove from the soul the shadows
that arise so easily from pondering over a hypothesis which is
isolated, merely visible, and hence overvalued a hundredfold.
Thus whoever wishes to console the unfortunate, the criminal,
the hypochondriac, the dy-ing, may call to mind the two soothing suggestions of Epicurus, which can be applied to a great
number of problems. In their simplest form they would run:
firstly, granted the thing is so, it does not concern us; secondly,
the thing may be so, but it may also be otherwise.

8

In the night. So soon as night begins to fall our sensations concerning everyday matters are altered. There is the wind, prowling
as if on forbidden paths, whispering as if in search of something,
fretting because he cannot find it. There is the lamplight, with its
dim red glow, its weary look, unwillingly fighting against night, a
sullen slave to wakeful man. There are the breathings of the
sleeper, with their terrible rhythm, to which an ever-recurring
care seems to blow the trumpet-melody – we do not hear it, but
when the sleeper's bosom heaves we feel our heart-strings tighten;
and when the breath sinks and almost dies away into a deathly
stillness, we say to ourselves, 'Rest awhile, poor troubled spirit!' All
living creatures bear so great a burden that we wish them an
eternal rest; night invites to death. If human beings were deprived
of the sun and resisted night by means of moonlight and oil-lamps,
what a philosophy would cast its veil over them! We already see
only too plainly how a shadow is thrown over the spiritual and
intellectual nature of man by that moiety of darkness and sunless-
ness that envelops life.

9

Origin of the doctrine of free will. Necessity sways one man in the
shape of his passions, another as a habit of hearing and obeying,

a third as a logical conscience, a fourth as a caprice and a mischievous delight in evasions. These four, however, seek the freedom of their will at the very point where they are most securely fettered. It is as if the silkworm sought freedom of will in spinning. What is the reason? Clearly this, that everyone thinks himself most free where his vitality is strongest; hence, as I have said, now in passion, now in duty, now in knowledge, now in caprice. A man unconsciously imagines that where he is strong, where he feels most thoroughly alive, the element of his freedom must lie. He thinks of dependence and apathy, independence and vivacity as forming inevitable pairs. Thus an experience that a man has undergone in the social and political sphere is wrongly transferred to the ultimate metaphysical sphere. There the strong man is also the free man, there the vivid feeling of joy and sorrow, the high hopes, the keen desires, the powerful hates are the attributes of the ruling, independent natures, while the thrall and the slave live in a state of dazed oppression. The doctrine of free will is an invention of the ruling classes.

10

Absence of feeling of new chains. So long as we do not feel that we are in some way dependent, we consider ourselves independent – a false conclusion that shows how proud man is, how eager for dominion. For he hereby assumes that he would always be sure to observe and recognise dependence so soon as he suffered it, the preliminary hypothesis being that he generally lives in independence, and that, should he lose that independence for once in a way, he would immediately detect a contrary sensation. Suppose, however, the reverse to be true – that he is always living in a complex state of dependence, but thinks himself free where, through long habit, he no longer feels the weight of the chain? He only suffers from new chains, and 'free will' really means nothing more than an absence of feeling of new chains.

11

Freedom of the will and the isolation of facts. Our ordinary inaccurate observation takes a group of phenomena as one and calls them a fact. Between this fact and another we imagine a vacuum, we isolate each fact. In reality, however, the sum of our actions and cognitions is no series of facts and intervening vacua, but a continuous stream. Now the belief in free will is incompatible with the idea of a continuous, uniform, undivided, indivisible flow. This belief presupposes that every single action is isolated and indivisible; it is an atomic theory as regards volition and cognition. We misunderstand facts as we misunderstand characters, speaking of similar characters and similar facts, whereas both are non-existent. Further, we bestow praise and blame only on this false hypothesis, that there are similar facts, that a graduated order of species of facts exists, corresponding to a graduated order of values. Thus we isolate not only the single fact, but the groups of apparently equal facts (good, evil, compassionate, envious actions, and so forth). In both cases we are wrong. The word and the concept are the most obvious reason for our belief in this isolation of groups of actions. We do not merely thereby designate the things; the thought at the back of our minds is that by the word and the concept we can grasp the essence of the actions. We are still constantly led astray by words and actions, and are induced to think of things as simpler than they are, as separate, indivisible, existing in the absolute. Language contains a hidden philosophical mythology, which, however careful we may be, breaks out afresh at every moment. The belief in free will – that is to say, in similar facts and isolated facts – finds in language its continual apostle and advocate.

12

The fundamental errors. A man cannot feel any psychical pleasure or pain unless he is swayed by one of two illusions. Either he believes in the identity of certain facts, certain sensations, and in that case finds spiritual pleasure and pain in comparing present with past conditions and in noting their similarity or difference (as is invariably the case with recollection); or he believes in the freedom of the will, perhaps when he reflects, 'I ought not to have done this', 'This might have turned out differently', and from these reflections likewise he derives pleasure and pain. Without the errors that are rife in every psychical pain and pleasure, humanity would never have developed. For the root idea of humanity is that man is free in a world of bondage – man, the eternal wonder-worker, whether his deeds be good or evil – man, the amazing exception, the super-beast, the quasi-god, the mind of creation, the indispensable, the key-word to the cosmic riddle, the mighty lord of nature and despiser of nature, the creature that calls *its* history 'the history of the world'! *Vanitas vanitatum homo.**

13

Repetition. It is an excellent thing to express a thing consecutively in two ways, and thus provide it with a right and a left foot. Truth can stand indeed on one leg, but with two she will walk and complete her journey.

14

Man as the comic actor of the world. It would require beings more intellectual than men to relish to the full the humorous side of man's view of himself as the goal of all existence and of his serious pronouncement that he is satisfied only with the prospect of fulfilling a world-mission. If a God created the world, he created man to be his ape, as a perpetual source of amusement in the midst of his rather tedious eternities. The music of the spheres surrounding the world would then presumably be the mocking laughter of all the other creatures around mankind. God in his boredom uses pain for the tickling of his favourite animal, in order to enjoy his proudly tragic gestures and expressions of suffering, and, in general, the intellectual inventiveness of the vainest of his creatures – as inventor of this inventor. For he who invented man as a joke had more intellect and more joy in intellect than has man. Even here, where our human nature is willing to humble itself, our vanity again plays us a trick, in that we men should like in this vanity at least to be quite marvellous and incomparable. Our uniqueness in the world! Oh, what an improbable thing it is! Astronomers, who occasionally acquire a horizon outside our world, give us to understand that the drop of life on the earth is without significance for the total character of the mighty ocean of birth and decay; that countless stars present conditions for the generation of life similar to those of the earth – and yet these are but a handful in comparison with the endless number that have never known, or have long been cured, of the eruption of life; that life on each of these stars, measured by the period of its existence, has been but an instant, a flicker, with long, long intervals afterwards – and thus in no way the aim and

---

* Vanity of vanities, that is man.

final purpose of their existence. Possibly the ant in the forest is quite as firmly convinced that it is the aim and purpose of the existence of the forest, as we are convinced in our imaginations (almost unconsciously) that the destruction of mankind involves the destruction of the world. It is even modesty on our part to go no farther than this, and not to arrange a universal twilight of the world and the gods as the funeral ceremony of the last man. Even to the eye of the most unbiased astronomer a lifeless world can scarcely appear otherwise than as a shining and swinging star wherein man lies buried.

15

The modesty of man. How little pleasure is enough for the majority to make them feel that life is good! How modest is man!

16

Where indifference is necessary. Nothing would be more perverse than to wait for the truths that science will finally establish concerning the first and last things, and until then to think (and especially to believe) in the traditional way, as one is so often advised to do. The impulse that bids us seek nothing but *certainties* in this domain is a religious offshoot, nothing better – a hidden and only apparently sceptical variety of the 'metaphysical need', the underlying idea being that for a long time no view of these ultimate certainties will be obtainable, and that until then the 'believer' has the right not to trouble himself about the whole subject. We have no need of these certainties about the farthermost horizons in order to live a full and efficient human life, any more than the ant needs them in order to be a good ant. Rather must we ascertain the origin of that troublesome significance that we have attached to these things for so long. For this we require the history of ethical and religious sentiments, since it is only under the influence of such sentiments that these most acute problems of knowledge have become so weighty and terrifying. Into the outermost regions to which the mental eye can penetrate (without ever penetrating *into* them), we have smuggled such concepts as guilt and punishment (everlasting punishment, too!). The darker those regions, the more careless we have been. For ages men have let their imaginations run riot where they could establish nothing, and have induced posterity to accept these fantasies as something serious and true, with this abominable lie as their final trump-card: that faith is worth more than knowledge. What we need now in regard to these ultimate things is not knowledge as against faith, but indifference as against faith and pretended knowledge in these matters! – Everything must lie nearer to us than what has hitherto been preached to us as the most important thing, I mean the questions: 'What end does man serve?' 'What is his fate after death?' 'How does he make his peace with God?' and all the rest of that bag of tricks. The problems of the dogmatic philosophers, be they idealists, materialists, or realists, concern us as little as do these religious questions. They all have the same object in view – to force us to a decision in matters where neither faith nor knowledge is needed. It is better even for the most ardent lover of knowledge that the territory open to investigation and to reason should be encircled by a belt of fog-laden, treacherous marshland, a strip of ever watery, impenetrable, and indeterminable country. It is just by the comparison with the realm of darkness on the edge of the world of knowledge that the bright, accessible region of that world rises in value. We must once more become good friends of the 'everyday matters', and not, as hitherto, despise them and look beyond them at clouds and monsters of the night. In forests and caverns, in marshy tracts and under dull skies, on the lowest rungs of the ladder of culture, man has lived for aeons, and lived in poverty. There he has learnt to despise the present, his neighbours, his life, and himself, and we, the inhabitants of the brighter fields of Nature and mind, still inherit in our blood some taint of this contempt for everyday matters.

17

Profound interpretations. He who has interpreted a passage in an author 'more profoundly' than was intended, has not interpreted the author but has obscured him. Our metaphysicians are in the same relation, or even in a worse relation, to the text of Nature. For, to apply their profound interpretations, they often alter the text to suit their purpose – or, in other words, corrupt the text. A curious example of the corruption and obscuration of an author's text is furnished by the ideas of Schopenhauer on the pregnancy of women. 'The sign of a continuous will to life in

time,' he says, 'is copulation; the sign of the light of knowledge
which is associated anew with this will and holds the possibility of
a deliverance, and that too in the highest degree of clearness, is
the renewed incarnation of the will to life. This incarnation is
betokened by pregnancy, which is therefore frank and open, and
even proud, whereas copulation hides itself like a criminal.' He
declares that every woman, if surprised in the sexual act, would
be likely to die of shame, but 'displays her pregnancy without a
trace of shame, nay even with a sort of pride.' Now, firstly, this
condition cannot easily be displayed more aggressively than it
displays itself, and when Schopenhauer gives prominence only to
the intentional character of the display, he is fashioning his text to
suit the interpretation. Moreover, his statement of the universality
of the phenomenon is not true. He speaks of 'every woman'.
Many women, especially the younger, often appear painfully
ashamed of their condition, even in the presence of their nearest kinsfolk. And when women of riper years, especially in the
humbler classes, do actually appear proud of their condition, it is
because they would give us to understand that they are still
desirable to their husbands. That a neighbour on seeing them or a
passing stranger should say or think 'Can it be possible?' – this is an
alms always acceptable to the vanity of women of low mental
capacity. In the reverse instance, to conclude from Schopenhauer's
proposition, the cleverest and most intelligent women would tend
more than any to exult openly in their condition. For they have
the best prospect of giving birth to an intellectual prodigy, in
whom 'the will' can once more 'negative' itself for the universal
good. Stupid women, on the other hand, would have every reason
to hide their pregnancy more modestly than anything they hide. It
cannot be said that this view corresponds to reality. Granted,
however, that Schopenhauer was right on the general principle
that women show more self-satisfaction when pregnant than at any
other time, a better explanation than this lies to hand. One might
imagine the clucking of a hen even before she lays an egg, saying,
'Look! look! I shall lay an egg! I shall lay an egg!'

18

The modern Diogenes. Before we look for man, we must have found
the lantern. Will it have to be the Cynic's lantern?

19

Immoralists. Moralists must now put up with being rated as immoralists, because they dissect morals. He, however, who would dissect must kill, but only in order that we may know more, judge better, live better, not in order that all the world may dissect. Unfortunately, men still think that every moralist in his every action must be a pattern for others to imitate. They confound him with the preacher of morality. The older moralists did not dissect enough and preached too often, whence that confusion and the unpleasant consequences for our latter-day moralists are derived.

20

A caution against confusion. There are moralists who treat the strong, noble, self-denying attitude of such beings as the heroes of Plutarch, or the pure, enlightened, warmth-giving state of soul peculiar to truly good men and women, as difficult scientific problems. They investigate the origin of such phenomena, indicating the complex element in the apparent simplicity, and directing their gaze to the tangled skein of motives, the delicate web of conceptual illusions, and the sentiments of individuals or of groups, that are a legacy of ancient days gradually increased. Such moralists are very different from those with whom they are most commonly confounded, from those petty minds that do not believe at all in these modes of thought and states of soul, and imagine their own poverty to be hidden somewhere behind the glamour of greatness and purity. The moralists say, 'Here are problems', and these pitiable creatures say, 'Here are impostors and deceptions.' Thus the latter deny the existence of the very things which the former are at pains to explain.

21

Man as the measurer. Perhaps all human morality had its origin in the tremendous excitement that seized primitive man when he discovered measure and measuring, scales and weighing (for the word *Mensch* [man] means 'the measurer' – he wished to *name* himself after his greatest discovery!). With these ideas they mounted into regions that are quite beyond all measuring and weighing, but did not appear to be so in the beginning.

22

The principle of equilibrium. The robber and the man of power who promises to protect a community from robbers are perhaps at bottom beings of the same mould, save that the latter attains his ends by other means than the former – that is to say, through regular imposts paid to him by the community, and no longer through forced contributions. (The same relation exists between merchant and pirate, who for a long period are one and the same person: where the one function appears to them inadvisable, they exercise the other. Even today mercantile morality is really nothing but a refinement on piratical morality – buying in the cheapest market, at prime cost if possible, and selling in the dearest.) The essential point is that the man of power promises to maintain the equilibrium against the robber, and herein the weak find a possibility of living. For either they must group themselves into an equivalent power, or they must subject themselves to someone of equivalent power (i.e. render service in return for his efforts). The latter course is generally preferred, because it really keeps two dangerous beings in check – the robber through the man of power, and the man of power through the standpoint of advantage; for the latter profits by treating his subjects with graciousness and tolerance, in order that they may support not only themselves but their ruler. As a matter of fact, conditions may still be hard and cruel enough, yet in comparison with the complete annihilation that was formerly always a possibility, men breathe freely. The community is at first the organisation of the weak to counterbalance menacing forces. An organisation to outweigh those forces would be more advisable, if its members grew strong enough to destroy the adverse power: and when it is a question of one mighty oppressor, the *attempt* will certainly be made. But if the one man is the head of a clan, or if he has a large following, a rapid and decisive annihilation is improbable, and a long or permanent feud is only to be expected. This feud, however, involves the least desirable condition for the community, for it thereby loses the time to provide for its means of subsistence with the necessary regularity, and sees the product of all work hourly threatened. Hence the community prefers to raise its power of attack and defence to the exact plane on which the power of its dangerous neighbour stands, and to give him to understand that an equal weight now lies in its own side of the scales – so why not be good friends? – Thus equilibrium is a most important conception for the understanding of the ancient doctrines of law and morals. Equilibrium is, in fact, the basis of jüstice. When justice in ruder ages says, 'An eye for an eye, a tooth for a tooth', it presupposes the attainment of this equilibrium and tries to maintain it by means of this compensation; so that, when crime is committed, the injured party will not take the revenge of blind anger. By means of the *jus talionis* the equilibrium of the disturbed relations of power is restored, for in such primitive times an eye or an arm more means a bit more power, more weight. In a community where all consider themselves equal, disgrace and punishment await crime – that is, violations of the principle of equilibrium. Disgrace is thrown into the scale as a counter-weight against the encroaching individual, who has gained profit by his encroachment, and now suffers losses (through disgrace) which annul and outweigh the previous profits. Punishment, in the same way, sets up a far greater counterweight against the preponderance which every criminal hopes to obtain – imprisonment as against a deed of violence, restitution and fines as against theft. Thus the sinner is reminded that his action has excluded him from the community and from its moral advantages, since the community treats him as an inferior, a weaker brother, an outsider. For this reason punishment is not merely retaliation, but has something more, something of the cruelty of the state of nature, and of this it would serve as a reminder.

23

Whether the adherents of the doctrine of free will have a right to punish? Men whose vocation it is to judge and punish try to establish in every case whether an evil-doer is really responsible for his act, whether he was able to apply his reasoning powers, whether he acted with motives and not unconsciously or under constraint. If he is punished, it is because he preferred the worse to the better motives, which he must consequently have known. Where this knowledge is wanting, man is, according to the prevailing view, not responsible – unless his ignorance, e.g. his *ignorantia legis*, be the consequence of an intentional neglect to learn what he ought:

in that case he already preferred the worse to the better motives at the time when he refused to learn, and must now pay the penalty of his unwise choice. If, on the other hand, perhaps through stupidity or shortsightedness, he has never seen the better motives, he is generally not punished, for people say that he made a wrong choice, he acted like a brute beast. The intentional rejection of the better reason is now needed before we treat the offender as fit to be punished. But how can anyone be intentionally more unreasonable than he ought to be? Whence comes the decision, if the scales are loaded with good and bad motives? So the origin is not error or blindness, not an internal or external constraint? (It should furthermore be remembered that every so-called 'external constraint' is nothing more than the internal constraint of fear and pain.) Whence? is the repeated question. So reason is not to be the cause of action, because reason cannot decide against the better motives? Thus we call 'free will' to our aid. Absolute discretion is to decide, and a moment is to intervene when no motive exercises an influence, when the deed is done as a miracle, resulting from nothing. This assumed discretion is punished in a case where no discretion should rule. Reason, which knows law, prohibition, and command, should have left no choice, they say, and should have acted as a constraint and a higher power. Hence the offender is punished because he makes use of 'free will' – in other words, has acted without motive where he should have been guided by motives. But why did he do it? This question must not even be asked; the deed was done without a 'Why?', without motive, without origin, being a thing purposeless, unreasoned. However, according to the above-named preliminary condition of punishability, such a deed should not be punished at all! Moreover, even this reason for punishing should not hold good, that in this case something had *not* been done, had been omitted, that reason had not been used at all: for at any rate the omission was unintentional, and only intentional omission is considered punishable. The offender has indeed preferred the worse to the better motives, but without motive and purpose: he has indeed failed to apply his reason, but not exactly with the object of not applying it. The very assumption made in the case of punishable crime, that the criminal intentionally renounced his reason, is removed by the hypothesis of 'free will'. According to your own principles, you must not punish, you adherents of the doctrine of free will! – These principles are, however, nothing but a very marvellous conceptual mythology, and the hen that hatched them has brooded on her eggs far away from all reality.

24

Judging the criminal and his judge. The criminal, who knows the whole concatenation of circumstances, does not consider his act so far beyond the bounds of order and comprehension as does his judge. His punishment, however, is measured by the degree of astonishment that seizes the judge when he finds the crime incomprehensible. If the defending counsel's knowledge of the case and its previous history extends far enough, the so-called extenuating circumstances which he duly pleads must end by absolving his client from all guilt. Or, to put it more plainly, the advocate will, step by step, tone down and finally remove the astonishment of the judge, by forcing every honest listener to the tacit avowal, 'He was bound to act as he did, and if we punished, we should be punishing eternal Necessity.' – Measuring the punishment by the degree of knowledge we possess or can obtain of the previous history of the crime – is that not in conflict with all equity?

25

Exchange and equity. In an exchange, the only just and honest course would be for either party to demand only so much as he considers his commodity to be worth, allowance being made for trouble in acquisition, scarcity, time spent and so forth, besides the subjective value. As soon as you make your price bear a relation to the other's need, you become a refined sort of robber and extortioner. If money is the sole medium of exchange, we must remember that a shilling is by no means the same thing in the hands of a rich heir, a farm labourer, a merchant, and a university student. It would be equitable for everyone to receive much or little for his money, according as he has done much or little to earn it. In practice, as we all know, the reverse is the case. In the world of high finance the shilling of the idle rich man can buy more than that of the poor, industrious man.

26

Legal conditions as means. Law, where it rests upon contracts between equals, holds good so long as the power of the parties to the contract remains equal or similar. Wisdom created law to end all feuds and useless expenditure among men on an equal footing. Quite as definite an end is put to this waste, however, when one party has become decidedly weaker than the other. Subjection enters and law ceases, but the result is the same as that attained by law. For now it is the wisdom of the superior which advises to spare the inferior and not uselessly to squander his strength. Thus the position of the inferior is often more favourable than that of the equal. Hence legal conditions are temporary *means* counselled by wisdom, and not ends.

27

Explanation of malicious joy. Malicious joy arises when a man consciously finds himself in evil plight and feels anxiety or remorse or pain. The misfortune that overtakes B makes him equal to A, and A is reconciled and no longer envious. If A is prosperous, he still hoards up in his memory B's misfortune as a capital, so as to throw it in the scale as a counterweight when he himself suffers adversity. In this case too he feels 'malicious joy' [*Schadenfreude*]. The sentiment of equality thus applies its standard to the domain of luck and chance. Malicious joy is the commonest expression of victory and restoration of equality, even in a higher state of civilisation. This emotion has only been in existence since the time when man learnt to look upon another as his equal – in other words, since the foundation of society.

28

The arbitrary element in the award of punishment. To most criminals punishment comes just as illegitimate children come to women. They have done the same thing a hundred times without any bad consequences. Suddenly comes discovery, and with discovery punishment. Yet habit should make the deed for which the criminal is punished appear more excusable, for he has developed a propensity that is hard to resist. Instead of this, the criminal is punished more severely if the suspicion of habitual crime rests on him, and habit is made a valid reason against all extenuation. On the other hand, a model life, wherein crime shows up in more terrible contrast, should make the guilt appear more heavy! But here the custom is to soften the punishment. Everything is measured not from the standpoint of the criminal but from that of society and its losses and dangers. The previous utility of an individual is weighed against his one nefarious action, his previous criminality is added to that recently discovered, and punishment is thus meted out as highly as possible. But if we thus punish or reward a man's past (for in the former case the diminution of punishment is a reward) we ought to go farther back and punish and reward the cause of his past – I mean parents, teachers, society. In many instances we shall then find the *judges* somehow or other sharing in the guilt. It is arbitrary to stop at the criminal himself when we punish his past: if we will not grant the absolute excusability of every crime, we should stop at each individual case and probe no farther into the past – in other words, isolate guilt and not connect it with previous actions. Otherwise we sin against logic. The teachers of free will should draw the inevitable conclusion from their doctrine of 'free will' and boldly decree: 'No action has a past.'

29

Envy and her nobler sister. Where equality is really recognised and permanently established, we see the rise of that propensity that is generally considered immoral, and would scarcely be conceivable in a state of nature – envy. The envious man is susceptible to every sign of individual superiority to the common herd, and wishes to depress everyone once more to the level – or raise himself to the superior plane. Hence arise two different modes of action, which Hesiod designated good and bad Eris. In the same way, in a condition of equality there arises indignation if A is prosperous above and B unfortunate beneath their deserts and equality. These latter, however, are emotions of nobler natures. They feel the want of justice and equity in things that are independent of the arbitrary choice of men – or, in other words, they desire the equality recognised by man to be recognised as well by Nature and chance. They are angry that men of equal merits should not have equal fortune.

30

The envy of the gods. 'The envy of the gods' arises when a despised person sets himself on an equality with his superior (like Ajax), or is made equal with him by the favour of fortune (like Niobe, the too-favoured mother). In the social class system this envy demands that no one shall have merits above his station, that his prosperity shall be on a level with his position, and especially that his self-consciousness shall not outgrow the limits of his rank. Often the victorious general, or the pupil who achieves a masterpiece, has experienced 'the envy of the gods'.

31

Vanity as an anti-social aftergrowth. As men, for the sake of security, have made themselves equal in order to found communities, but as also this conception is imposed by a sort of constraint and is entirely opposed to the instincts of the individual, so, the more universal security is guaranteed, the more do new offshoots of the old instinct for predominance appear. Such offshoots appear in the setting-up of class distinctions, in the demand for professional dignities and privileges, and, generally speaking, in vanity (manners, dress, speech, and so forth). So soon as danger to the community is apparent, the majority, who were unable to assert their preponderance in a time of universal peace, once more bring about the condition of equality, and for the time being the absurd privileges and vanities disappear. If the community, however, collapses utterly and anarchy reigns supreme, there arises the state of nature: an absolutely ruthless inequality as recounted by Thucydides in the case of Corcyra. Neither a natural justice nor a natural injustice exists.

32

Equity. Equity is a development of justice, and arises among such as do not come into conflict with the communal equality. This more subtle recognition of the principle of equilibrium is applied to cases where nothing is prescribed by law. Equity looks forwards and backwards, its maxim being, 'Do unto others as you would that they should do unto you.' *Aequum* means: 'This principle is conformable to our equality; it tones down even our small differences to an appearance of equality, and expects us to be indulgent in cases where we are not compelled to pardon.'

33

Elements of revenge. The word 'revenge' is spoken so quickly that it almost seems as if it could not contain more than one conceptual and emotional root. Hence we are still at pains to find this root. Our economists, in the same way, have never wearied of scenting a similar unity in the word 'value', and of hunting after the primitive root idea of value. As if all words were not pockets, into which this or that or several things have been stuffed at once! So 'revenge' is now one thing, now another, and sometimes more composite. Let us first distinguish that defensive counter-blow, which we strike, almost unconsciously, even at inanimate objects (such as machinery in motion) that have hurt us. The notion is to set a check to the object that has hurt us, by bringing the machine to a stop. Sometimes the force of this counter-blow, in order to attain its object, will have to be strong enough to shatter the machine. If the machine be too strong to be disorganised by one man, the latter will all the same strike the most violent blow he can – as a sort of last attempt. We behave similarly towards persons who hurt us, at the immediate sensation of the hurt. If we like to call this an act of revenge, well and good: but we must remember that here self-preservation alone has set its cog-wheels of reason in motion, and that after all we do not think of the doer of the injury but only of ourselves. We act without any idea of doing injury in return, only with a view to getting away safe and sound. It needs time to pass in thought from oneself to one's adversary and ask oneself at what point he is most vulnerable. This is done in the second variety of revenge, the preliminary idea of which is to consider the vulnerability and susceptibility of the other. The intention then is to give pain. On the other hand, the idea of securing himself against further injury is in this case so entirely outside the avenger's horizon, that he almost regularly brings about his own further injury and often foresees it in cold blood. If in the first sort of revenge it was the fear of a second blow that made the counter-blow as strong as possible, in this case there is an almost complete indifference to what one's adversary will do: the strength of the counter-blow is only determined by what he has *already* done to us. Then what has he done? What profit is it to us if he is now suffering, after we have suffered through him? This is a case of readjustment, whereas the first act of revenge only serves the purpose of self-preservation. It may be that through our adversary we have lost property, rank, friends, children – these losses are not recovered by revenge, the readjustment only concerns a subsidiary loss which is added to all the other losses. The revenge of readjustment does not preserve one from further injury, it does not make good the injury already suffered – except in one case. If our honour has suffered through our adversary, revenge can restore it. But in any case honour *has* suffered an injury if intentional harm has been done us, because our adversary proved thereby that he was not afraid of us. By revenge we prove that we are not afraid of him either, and herein lies the settlement, the readjustment. (The intention of showing their complete lack of fear goes so far in some people that the dangers of revenge – loss of health or life or other losses – are in their eyes an indispensable condition of every vengeful act. Hence they practise the duel, although the law also offers them aid in obtaining satisfaction for what they have suffered. They are not satisfied with a safe means of recovering their honour, because this would not prove their fearlessness.) – In the first-named variety of revenge it is just fear that strikes the counter-blow; in the second case it is the absence of fear, which, as has been said, wishes to manifest itself in the counter-blow. Thus nothing appears more different than the motives of the two courses of action which are designated by the one word 'revenge'. Yet it often happens that the avenger is not precisely certain as to what really prompted his deed: perhaps he struck the counter-blow from fear and the instinct of self-preservation, but in the background, when he has time to reflect upon the standpoint of wounded honour, he imagines that he has avenged himself for the sake of his honour – this motive is in any case more *reputable* than the other. An essential point is whether he sees his honour injured in the eyes of others (the world) or only in the eyes of his offenders: in the latter case he will prefer secret, in the former open revenge. Accordingly, as he enters strongly or feebly into the soul of the doer and the spectator, his revenge will be more bitter or more tame. If he is entirely lacking in this sort of imagination, he will not think at all of revenge, as the feeling of 'honour' is not present in him, and accordingly cannot be wounded. In the same way, he will not think of revenge if he despises the offender and the spectator; because as objects of his contempt they cannot give him honour, and accordingly cannot rob him of honour. Finally, he will forego revenge in the not uncommon case of his loving the offender. It is true that he then suffers loss of honour in the other's eyes, and will perhaps become less worthy of having his love returned. But even to renounce all requital of love is a sacrifice that love is ready to make when its only object is to avoid hurting the beloved object: this would mean hurting oneself more than one is hurt by the sacrifice. Accordingly, everyone will avenge himself, unless he be bereft of honour or inspired by contempt or by love for the offender. Even if he turns to the law-courts, he desires revenge as a private individual; but also, as a thoughtful, prudent man of society, he desires the revenge of society upon one who does not respect it. Thus by legal punishment private honour as well as that of society is restored – that is to say, punishment is revenge. Punishment undoubtedly contains the first-mentioned element of revenge, in as far as by its means society helps to preserve itself, and strikes a counter-blow in self-defence. Punishment desires to prevent further injury, to scare other offenders. In this way the two elements of revenge, different as they are, are united in punishment, and this may perhaps tend most of all to maintain the above-mentioned confusion of ideas, thanks to which the individual avenger generally does not know what he really wants.

34

The virtues that damage us. As members of communities we think we have no right to exercise certain virtues which afford us great honour and some pleasure as private individuals (for example, indulgence and favour towards miscreants of all kinds) – in short, every mode of action whereby the advantage of society would suffer through our virtue. No bench of judges, face to face with its conscience, may permit itself to be gracious. This privilege is reserved for the king as an individual, and we are glad when he makes use of it, proving that we should like to be gracious individually, but not collectively. Society recognises only the virtues profitable to her, or at least not injurious to her –

virtues like justice, which are exercised without loss, or, in fact, at compound interest. The virtues that damage us cannot have originated in society, because even now opposition to them arises in every small society that is in the making. Such virtues are therefore those of men of unequal standing, invented by the superior individuals; they are the virtues of rulers, and the idea underlying them is: 'I am mighty enough to put up with an obvious loss; that is a proof of my power.' Thus they are virtues closely akin to pride.

35

The casuistry of advantage. There would be no moral casuistry if there were no casuistry of advantage. The most free and refined intelligence is often incapable of choosing between two alternatives in such a way that his choice necessarily involves the greater advantage. In such cases we choose because we must, and afterwards often feel a kind of emotional seasickness.

36

Turning hypocrite. Every beggar turns hypocrite, like everyone who makes his living out of indigence, be it personal or public. The beggar does not feel want nearly so keenly as he must make others feel it, if he wishes to make a living by mendicancy.

37

A sort of cult of the passions. You hypochondriacs, you philosophic blind-worms talk of the formidable nature of human passions, in order to inveigh against the dread character of the whole world-structure. As if the passions were always and everywhere formidable! As if this sort of terror must always exist in the world! — Through a carelessness in small matters, through a deficiency in observation of self and of the rising generation, you have yourselves allowed your passions to develop into such unruly monsters that you are frightened now at the mere mention of the word 'passion'! It rests with you and it rests with us to divest the passions of their formidable features and so to dam them that they do not become devastating floods. We must not exalt our errors into eternal fatalities. Rather shall we honestly endeavour to convert all the passions of humanity into sources of joy.

38

The sting of conscience. The sting of conscience, like the gnawing of a dog at a stone, is mere foolishness.

39

Origin of rights. Rights may be traced to traditions, traditions to momentary agreements. At some time or other men were mutually content with the consequences of making an agreement, and, again, too indolent formally to renew it. Thus they went on living as if it had constantly been renewed, and gradually, when oblivion cast its veil over the origin, they thought they possessed a sacred, unalterable foundation on which every generation would be compelled to build. Tradition was now a constraint, even if it no more involved the profit originally derived from making the agreement. Here the weak have always found their strong fortress. They are inclined to immortalise the momentary agreement, the single act of favour shown towards them.

40

The significance of oblivion in moral sentiment. The same actions that in primitive society first aimed at the common advantage were later on performed from other motives: from fear or reverence of those who demanded and recommended them; or from habit, because men had seen them done about them from childhood upwards; or from kindness, because the practising of them caused delight and approving looks on all sides; or from vanity, because they were praised. Such actions, in which the fundamental motive, that of utility, has been *forgotten*, are then called moral; not, indeed, because they are done from those other motives, but because they are not done with a conscious purpose of utility. Whence the hatred of utility that suddenly manifests itself here, and by which all praiseworthy actions formally exclude all actions for the sake of utility? – Clearly society, the rallying-point of all morality and of all maxims in praise of moral action, has had to battle too long and too fiercely with the selfishness and obstinacy of the individual not to rate every motive morally higher than utility. Hence it looks as if morals had not sprung from utility, whereas in fact morals are originally the public utility, which had great difficulty in prevailing over the interests of the unit and securing a loftier reputation.

41

The heirs to the wealth of morality. Even in the domain of morals there is an inherited wealth, which is owned by the gentle, the good-tempered, the compassionate, the indulgent. They have inherited from their forefathers their gentle mode of action, but not common sense (the source of that mode of action). The pleasant thing about this wealth is that one must always bestow and communicate a portion of it, if its presence is to be felt at all. Thus this wealth unconsciously aims at bridging the gulf between the morally rich and the morally poor, and, what is its best and most remarkable feature, not for the sake of a future mean between rich and poor, but for the sake of a universal prosperity and superfluity. Such may be the prevailing view of inherited moral wealth, but it seems to me that this view is maintained more *in majorem gloriam* of morality than in honour of truth. Experience at least establishes a maxim which must serve, if not as a refutation, at any rate as an important check upon that generalisation. Without the most ex- quisite intelligence, says experience, without the most refined capacity for choice and a strong propensity to observe the mean, the morally rich will become spendthrifts of morality. For by abandoning themselves without restraint to their compassionate, gentle, conciliatory, harmonising instincts, they make all about them more careless, more covetous, and more sentimental. The children of these highly moral spendthrifts easily and (sad to relate) at best become pleasant but futile wasters.

42

The judge and extenuating circumstances. 'One should behave as a man of honour even towards the devil and pay his debts,' said an old soldier, when the story of Faust had been related to him in rather fuller detail. 'Hell is the right place for Faust!' 'You are terrible, you men!' cried his wife; 'how can that be? After all, his only fault was having no ink in his ink-stand! It is indeed a sin to write with blood, but surely for that such a handsome man ought not to burn in Hell-fire?'

43

Problem of the duty of truth. Duty is an imperious sentiment that forces us to action. We call it good, and consider it outside the pale of discussion. The origin, limits, and justification of duty we will not debate or allow to be debated. But the thinker considers everything an evolution and every evolution a subject for discussion, and is accordingly without duty so long as he is merely a thinker. As such, he would not recognise the duty of seeing and speaking the truth; he would not *feel* the sentiment at all. He asks, whence comes it and whither will it go? But even this questioning appears to him questionable. Surely, however, the consequence would be that the thinker's machinery would no longer work properly if he could really feel himself unencumbered by duty in the search for knowledge? It would appear, then, that for fuel the same element is necessary as must be investigated by means of the machine. Perhaps the formula will be: granted there were a duty of recognising truth, what is then the truth in regard to every other kind of duty? – But is not a hypothetical sense of duty a contradiction in terms?

44

Grades of morals. Morality is primarily a means of preserving the community and saving it from destruction. Next it is a means of maintaining the community on a certain plane and in a certain degree of benevolence. Its motives are fear and hope, and these in a more coarse, rough, and powerful form, the more the propensity towards the perverse, one-sided, and personal still persists. The most terrible means of intimidation must be brought into play so long as milder forms have no effect and that twofold species of preservation cannot be attained. (The strongest intimidation, by the way, is the invention of a hereafter with a hell everlasting.) For this purpose we must have racks and torturers of the soul. Further grades of morality, and accordingly means to the end referred to, are the commandments of a God (as in the Mosaic law). Still further and higher are the commandments of an absolute sense of duty with a 'Thou shalt' – all rather roughly hewn yet *broad* steps, because on the finer, narrower steps men cannot yet set their feet. Then comes a morality of inclination, of taste, finally of insight –

which is beyond all the illusory motives of morality, but has convinced itself that humanity for long periods could be allowed no other.

45

The morality of pity in the mouths of the intemperate. All those who are not sufficiently masters of themselves and do not know morality as a self-control and self-conquest continuously exercised in things great and small, unconsciously come to glorify the good, compassionate, benevolent impulses of that instinctive morality which has no head, but seems merely to consist of a heart and helpful hands. It is to their interest even to cast suspicion upon a morality of reason and to set up the other as the sole morality.

46

Sewers of the soul. Even the soul must have its definite sewers, through which it can allow its filth to flow off: for this purpose it may use persons, relations, social classes, its native country, or the world, or finally – for the wholly arrogant (I mean our modern 'pessimists') – *le bon Dieu.*

47

A kind of rest and contemplation. Beware lest your rest and contemplation resemble that of a dog before a butcher's stall, prevented by fear from advancing and by greed from retiring, and opening its eyes wide as though they were mouths.

48

Prohibitions without reasons. A prohibition, the reason of which we do not understand or admit, is almost a command, not only for the stiff-necked but for the thirster after knowledge. We at once make an experiment in order to learn *why* the prohibition was made. Moral prohibitions, like those of the Decalogue, are only suited to ages when reason lies vanquished. Nowadays a prohibition like 'Thou shalt not kill', 'Thou shalt not commit adultery', laid down without reasons, would have an injurious rather than a beneficial effect.

49

Character portrait. What sort of a man is it that can say of himself: 'I despise very easily, but never hate. I at once find out in every man something which can be honoured and for which I honour him: the so-called amiable qualities attract me but little'?

50

Pity and contempt. The expression of pity is regarded as a sign of contempt, because one has clearly ceased to be an object of *fear* as soon as one becomes an object of pity. One has sunk below the level of the equilibrium. For this equilibrium does not satisfy human vanity, which is only satisfied by the feeling that one is imposing respect and awe. Hence it is difficult to explain why pity is so highly prized, just as we need to explain why the unselfish man, who is originally despised or feared as being artful, is praised.

51

The capacity for being small. We must be as near to flowers, grasses, and butterflies as a child, that is, not much bigger than they. We adults have grown up beyond them and have to stoop to them. I think the grasses hate us when we confess our love for them. He who would have a share in all good things must understand at times how to be small.

52

The sum-total of conscience. The sum-total of our conscience is all that has regularly been demanded of us, without reason, in the days of our childhood, by people whom we respected or feared. From conscience comes that feeling of obligation ('This I must do, this omit') which does not ask, Why must I? – In all cases where a thing is done with 'because' and 'why', man acts without conscience, but not necessarily on that account *against* conscience. The belief in authority is the source of conscience; which is therefore not the voice of God in the heart of man, but the voice of some men in man.

53

Conquest of the passions. The man who has overcome his passions has entered into possession of the most fruitful soil, like the colonist who has become lord over bogs and forests. To sow the seed of spiritual good works on the soil of the vanquished passions is the next and most urgent task. The conquest itself is a means, not an end: if it be not so regarded, all kind of weeds and devil's crop quickly spring up upon the fertile soil that has been cleared, and soon the growth is all wilder and more luxuriant than before.

54

Skill in service. All so-called practical men have skill in service, whether it be serving others or themselves; this is what makes them practical. Robinson owned a servant even better than Friday – his name was Crusoe.

55

Danger in speech to intellectual freedom. Every word is a preconceived judgment.

56

Intellect and boredom. The proverb, 'The Hungarian is far too lazy to feel bored', gives food for thought. Only the highest and most active animals are capable of being bored. The boredom of God on the seventh day of Creation would be a subject for a great poet.

57

Intercourse with animals. The origin of our morality may still be observed in our relations with animals. Where advantage or the reverse do not come into play, we have a feeling of complete irresponsibility. For example, we kill or wound insects or let them live, and as a rule think no more about it. We are so clumsy that even our gracious acts towards flowers and small animals are almost always murderous: this does not in the least detract from our pleasure in them. Today is the festival of the small animals, the most sultry day of the year. There is a swarming and crawling around us, and we, without intention, but also without reflection, crush here and there a little fly or winged beetle. If animals do us harm, we strive to *annihilate* them in every possible way. The means are often cruel enough, even without our really intending them to be so – it is the cruelty of thoughtlessness. If they are useful, we turn them to advantage, until a more refined wisdom teaches us that certain animals amply reward a different mode of treatment, that of tending and breeding. Here responsibility first arises. Torturing is avoided in the case of the domestic animal. One man is indignant if another is cruel to his cow, quite in accordance with the primitive communal morality, which sees the commonwealth in danger whenever an individual does wrong. He who perceives any transgression in the community fears indirect harm to himself. Thus we fear in this case for the quality of meat, agriculture, and means of communication if we see the domestic animals ill-treated. Moreover, he who is harsh to animals awakens a suspicion that he is also harsh to men who are weak, inferior, and incapable of revenge. He is held to be ignoble and deficient in the finer form of pride. Thus arises a foundation of moral judgments and sentiments, but the greatest contribution is made by superstition. Many animals incite men by glances, tones, and gestures to transfer themselves into them in imagination, and some religions teach us, under certain circumstances, to see in animals the dwelling-place of human and divine souls: whence they recommend a nobler caution or even a reverential awe in intercourse with animals. Even after the disappearance of this superstition the sentiments awakened by it continue to exercise their influence, to ripen and to blossom. Christianity, as is well known, has shown itself in this respect a poor and retrograde religion.

58

New actors. Among human beings there is no greater banality than death. Second in order, because it is possible to die without being born, comes birth, and next comes marriage. But these hackneyed little tragi-comedies are always presented, at each of their unnumbered and innumerable performances, by new actors, and accordingly do not cease to find interested spectators: whereas we might well believe that the whole audience of the world-theatre had long since hanged themselves to every tree from sheer boredom at these performances. So much depends on new actors, so little on the piece.

59

What is 'being obstinate'? The shortest way is not the straightest possible, but that wherein favourable winds swell our sails. So says the wisdom of seamen. Not to follow his course is obstinate, firmness of character being then adulterated by stupidity.

60

The word 'vanity'. It is annoying that certain words, with which we moralists positively cannot dispense, involve in themselves a kind of censorship of morals, dating from the times when the most ordinary and natural impulses were denounced. Thus that fundamental conviction that on the waves of society we either find navigable waters or suffer shipwreck far more through what we appear than through what we are (a conviction that must act as guiding principle of all action in relation to society) is branded with the general word 'vanity'. In other words, one of the most weighty and significant of qualities is branded with an expression which denotes it as essentially empty and negative: a great thing is designated by a diminutive, ay, even slandered by the strokes of caricature. There is no help for it; we must use such words, but then we must shut our ears to the insinuations of ancient habits.

61

The fatalism of the Turk. The fatalism of the Turk has this fundamental defect, that it contrasts man and fate as two distinct things. Man, says this doctrine, may struggle against fate and try to baffle it, but in the end fate will always gain the victory. Hence the most rational course is to resign oneself or to live as one pleases. As a matter of fact, every man is himself a piece of fate. When he thinks that he is struggling against fate in this way, fate is accomplishing its ends even in that struggle. The combat is a fantasy, but so is the resignation in fate – all these fantasies are included in fate. The fear felt by most people of the doctrine that denies the freedom of the will is a fear of the fatalism of the Turk. They imagine that man will become weakly resigned and will stand before the future with folded hands, because he cannot alter anything of the future. Or that he will give a free rein to his caprices, because the predestined cannot be made worse by that course. The follies of men are as much a piece of fate as are his wise actions, and even that fear of belief in fate is a fatality. You yourself, you poor timid creature, are that indomitable *Moira*, which rules even the gods; whatever may happen, you are a curse or a blessing, and in any case the fetters wherein the strongest lies bound: in you the whole future of the human world is predestined, and it is no use for you to be frightened of yourself.

62

The advocate of the devil. 'Only by our own suffering do we become wise, only by others' suffering do we become good' – so runs that strange philosophy which derives all morality from pity and all intellectuality from the isolation of the individual. Herein this philosophy is the unconscious pleader for all human deterioration. For pity needs suffering, and isolation contempt of others.

63

The moral character-masks. In ages when the character-masks of different classes are definitely fixed, like the classes themselves, moralists will be seduced into holding the moral character-masks, too, as absolute, and in delineating them accordingly. Thus Molière is intelligible as the contemporary of the society of Louis XIV: in our society of transitions and intermediate stages he would seem an inspired pedant.

64

The most noble virtue. In the first era of the higher humanity courage is accounted the most noble virtue, in the next justice, in the third temperance, in the fourth wisdom. In which era do *we* live? In which do *you* live?

65

A necessary preliminary. A man who will not become master of his irritability, his venomous and vengeful feelings, and his lust, and attempts to become master in anything else, is as stupid as the farmer who lays out his field beside a torrent without guarding against that torrent.

66

What is truth? – *Schwarzert* [Melanchthon]: We often preach our faith when we have lost it, and leave not a stone unturned to find it – and then we often do not preach worst!

Luther: Brother, you are really speaking like an angel today.

Schwarzert: But that is the idea of your enemies, and they apply it to you.

Luther: Then it would be a lie from the devil's hind-quarters.

67

The habit of contrasts. Superficial, inexact observation sees contrasts everywhere in nature (for instance, 'hot and cold'), where there are no contrasts, only differences of degree. This bad habit has induced us to try to understand and interpret even the inner nature, the intellectual and moral world, in accordance with such contrasts. An infinite amount of cruelty, arrogance, harshness, estrangement, and coldness has entered into human emotion, because men imagined they saw contrasts where there were only transitions.

68

Can we forgive? – How can we forgive them at all, if they know not what they do? We have nothing to forgive. But does a man ever fully know what he is doing? And if this point at least remains always debatable, men never have anything to forgive each other, and indulgence is for the reasonable man an impossible thing. Finally, if the evil-doers had really known what they did, we should still only have a right to forgive if we had a right to accuse and to punish. But we have not that right.

69

Habitual shame. Why do we feel shame when some virtue or merit is attributed to us which, as the saying goes, 'we have not deserved'? Because we appear to have intruded upon a territory to which we do not belong, from which we should be excluded, as from a holy place or holy of holies, which ought not to be trodden by our foot. Through the errors of others we have, nevertheless, penetrated to it, and we are now swayed partly by fear, partly by reverence, partly by surprise; we do not know whether we ought to fly or to enjoy the blissful moment with all its gracious advantages. In all shame there is a mystery, which seems desecrated or in danger of desecration through us. All *favour* begets shame. But if it be remembered that we have never really 'deserved' anything, this feeling of shame, provided that we surrender ourselves to this point of view in a spirit of Christian contemplation, becomes habitual, because upon such a one God seems continually to be conferring his blessing and his favours. Apart from this Christian interpretation, the state of habitual shame will be possible even to the entirely godless sage, who clings firmly to the basic non-responsibility and non-meritoriousness of all action and being. If he be treated as if he had deserved this or that, he will seem to have won his way into a higher order of beings, who do actually deserve something, who are free and can really bear the burden of responsibility for their own volition and capacity. Whoever says to him, 'You have deserved it', appears to cry out to him, 'You are not a human being, but a god.'

70

The most unskilful teacher. In one man all his real virtues are implanted on the soil of his spirit of contradiction, in another on his incapacity to say 'no' — in other words, on his spirit of acquiescence. A third has made all his morality grow out of his pride as a solitary, a fourth from his strong social instinct. Now, supposing that the seeds of the virtues in these four cases, owing to mischance or unskilful teachers, were not sown on the soil of their nature, which provides them with the richest and most abundant mould, they would become weak, unsatisfactory men (devoid of morality). And who would have been the most unskilful of teachers, the evil genius of these men? The moral fanatic, who thinks that the good can only grow out of the good and on the soil of the good.

71

The cautious style. A. But if this were known to *all*, it would be injurious to the *majority*. You yourself call your opinions dangerous to those in danger, and yet you make them public?

B. I write so that neither the mob, nor the *populi*, nor the parties of all kinds can read me. So my opinions will never be 'public opinions'.

A. How do you write, then?

B. Neither usefully nor pleasantly – for the three classes I have mentioned.

72

Divine missionaries. Even Socrates feels himself to be a divine missionary, but I am not sure whether we should not here detect a tincture of that Attic irony and fondness for jesting whereby this odious, arrogant conception would be toned down. He talks of the fact without unction – his images of the gadfly and the horse are simple and not sacerdotal. The real religious task which he has set himself – to *test* god in a hundred ways and see whether he spoke the truth – betrays a bold and free attitude, in which the missionary walked by the side of his god. This testing of god is one of the most subtle compromises between piety and free-thinking that has ever been devised. Nowadays we do not even need this compromise any longer.

73

Honesty in painting. Raphael, who cared a great deal for the Church (so far as she could pay him), but, like the best men of his time, cared little for the objects of the Church's belief, did not advance one step to meet the exacting, ecstatic piety of many of his patrons. He remained honest even in that exceptional picture which was originally intended for a banner in a procession – the Sistine Madonna. Here for once he wished to paint a vision, but such a vision as even noble youths without 'faith' may and will have – the vision of the future wife, a wise, high-souled, silent, and very beautiful woman, carrying her first-born in her arms. Let men of an older generation, accustomed to prayer and devotion, find here, like the worthy elder on the left, something superhuman to revere. We younger men (so Raphael seems to call to us) are occupied with the beautiful maiden on the right, who says to the spectator of the picture, with her challenging and by no means devout look, 'The mother and her child – is not that a pleasant, inviting sight?' The face and the look are reflected in the joy in the faces of the beholders. The artist who devised all this enjoys himself in this way, and adds his own delight to the delight of the art-lover. As regards the 'messianic' expression in the face of the child, Raphael, honest man, who would not paint any state of soul in which he did not believe, has amiably cheated his religious admirers. He painted that freak of nature which is very often found, the man's eye in the child's face, and that, too, the eye of a brave, helpful man who sees distress. This eye should be accompanied by a beard. The fact that a beard is wanting, and that two different ages are seen in one countenance, is the pleasing paradox which believers have interpreted in accordance with their faith in miracles. The artist could only expect as much from their art of exposition and interpretation.

74

Prayer. On two hypotheses alone is there any sense in prayer, that not quite extinct custom of olden times. It would have to be possible either to fix or alter the will of the godhead, and the devotee would have to know best himself what he needs and should really desire. Both hypotheses, axiomatic and traditional in all other religions, are denied by Christianity. If Christianity nevertheless maintained prayer side by side with its belief in the all-wise and all-provident divine reason (a belief that makes prayer really senseless and even blasphemous), it showed here once more its admirable 'wisdom of the serpent'. For an outspoken command, 'Thou shalt not pray', would have led Christians by way of boredom to the denial of Christianity. In the Christian *ora et labora, ora* plays the rôle of pleasure. Without *ora* what could those unlucky saints who renounced *labora* have done? But to have a chat with God, to ask him for all kinds of pleasant things, to feel a slight amusement at one's own folly in still having any wishes at all, in spite of so excellent a father – all that was an admirable invention for saints.

75

A holy lie. The lie that was on Arria's lips when she died (*Paete, non dolet*)* obscures all the truths that have ever been uttered by the

---

* 'It doesn't hurt, Paetus.' Spoken by the wife of the Stoic Thrasea Paetus, during their suicide pact following the emperor Nero's discovery of their complicity in a conspiracy against him.

dying. It is the only holy *lie* that has become famous, whereas elsewhere the odour of sanctity has clung only to *errors*.

76
The most necessary apostle. Among twelve apostles one must always be hard as stone, in order that upon him the new church may be built.

77
Which is more transitory, the body or the spirit? – In legal, moral, and religious institutions the external and concrete elements – in other words, rites, gestures, and ceremonies – are the most permanent. They are the body to which a new spirit is constantly being superadded. The cult, like an unchangeable text, is ever interpreted anew. Concepts and emotions are fluid, customs are solid.

78
The belief in disease qua disease. Christianity first painted the devil on the wall of the world. Christianity first brought the idea of sin into the world. The belief in the remedies, which is offered as an antidote, has gradually been shaken to its very foundations. But the belief in the disease, which Christianity has taught and propagated, still exists.

79
Speech and writings of religious men. If the priest's style and general expression, both in speaking and writing, do not clearly betray the religious man, we need no longer take his views upon religion and his pleading for religion seriously. These opinions have become powerless for him if, judging by his style, he has at command irony, arrogance, malice, hatred, and all the changing eddies of mood, just like the most irreligious of men – how far more powerless will they be for his hearers and readers! In short, he will serve to make the latter still more irreligious.

80
The danger in personality. The more God has been regarded as a personality in himself, the less loyal have we been to him. Men are far more attached to their thought-images than to their best

beloved. That is why they sacrifice themselves for State, Church, and even for God – so far as he remains *their* creation, their thought, and is not too much looked upon as a personality. In the latter case they almost always quarrel with him. After all, it was the most pious of men who let slip that bitter cry: 'My God, why hast thou forsaken me?'

81

Worldly justice. It is possible to unhinge worldly justice with the doctrine of the complete non-responsibility and innocence of every man. An attempt has been made in the same direction on the basis of the opposite doctrine of the full responsibility and guilt of every man. It was the founder of Christianity who wished to abolish worldly justice and banish judgment and punishment from the world. For he understood all guilt as 'sin' – that is, an outrage against God and not against the world. On the other hand, he considered every man in a broad sense, and almost in every sense, a sinner. The guilty, however, are not to be the judges of their peers – so his rules of equity decided. Thus all dispensers of worldly justice were in his eyes as culpable as those they condemned, and their air of guiltlessness appeared to him hypocritical and pharisaical. Moreover, he looked to the motives and not to the results of actions, and thought that only one was keen-sighted enough to give a verdict on motives – himself or, as he expressed it, God.

82

An affectation in parting. He who wishes to sever his connection with a party or a creed thinks it necessary for him to refute it. This is a most arrogant notion. The only thing necessary is that he should clearly see what tentacles hitherto held him to this party or creed and no longer hold him, what views impelled him to it and now impel him in some other directions. We have not joined the party or creed on strict grounds of knowledge. We should not affect this attitude on parting from it either.

83

Saviour and physician. In his knowledge of the human soul the founder of Christianity was, as is natural, not without many great deficiencies and prejudices, and, as physician of the soul, was addicted to that disreputable, laical belief in a universal medicine. In his methods he sometimes resembles that dentist who wishes to heal all pain by extracting the tooth. Thus, for example, he assails sensuality with the advice: 'If thine eye offend thee, pluck it out.' – Yet there still remains the distinction that the dentist at least attains his object – painlessness for the patient – although in so clumsy a fashion that he becomes ridiculous; whereas the Christian who follows that advice and thinks he has killed his sensuality, is wrong, for his sensuality still lives in an uncanny, vampire form, and torments him in hideous disguises.

84

Prisoners. One morning the prisoners entered the yard for work, but the warder was not there. Some, as their manner was, set to work at once; others stood idle and gazed defiantly around. Then one of them strode forward and cried, 'Work as much as you will or do nothing, it all comes to the same. Your secret machinations have come to light; the warder has been keeping his eye on you of late, and will cause a terrible judgment to be passed upon you in a few days' time. You know him – he is of a cruel and resentful disposition. But now, listen: you have mistaken me hitherto. I am not what I seem, but far more – I am the son of the warder, and can get anything I like out of him. I can save you – nay, I will save you. But remember this: I will only save those of you who *believe* that I am the son of the prison warder. The rest may reap the fruits of their unbelief.' 'Well,' said an old prisoner after an interval of silence, 'what can it matter to you whether we believe you or not? If you are really the son, and can do what you say, then put in a good word for us all. That would be a real kindness on your part. But have done with all talk of belief and unbelief!' 'What is more,' cried a younger man, 'I don't believe him: he has only got a bee in his bonnet. I'll wager that in a week's time we shall find ourselves in the same place as we are today, and the warder will know nothing.' 'And if the warder ever knew anything, he knows it no longer,' said the last of the prisoners, coming down into the yard at that moment, 'for he has just died suddenly.' 'Ah ha!' cried several in confusion, 'ah ha! Sir Son, Sir Son, how stands it now with your title? Are we by any chance *your* prisoners now?' 'I told you,' answered the man gently, 'I will set free all who believe in me, as surely as my father still lives.' – The prisoners did not laugh, but shrugged their shoulders and left him to himself.

85

The persecutors of God. Paul conceived and Calvin followed up the idea that countless creatures have been predestined to damnation from time immemorial, and that this fair world was made in order that the glory of God might be manifested therein. So heaven and hell and mankind merely exist to satisfy the vanity of God! What a cruel, insatiable vanity must have smouldered in the soul of the first or second thinker of such a thought! – Paul, then, after all, remained Saul – the persecutor of God.

86

Socrates. If all goes well, the time will come when, in order to advance themselves on the path of moral reason, men will rather take up the *Memorabilia* of Socrates than the Bible, and when Montaigne and Horace will be used as pioneers and guides for the understanding of Socrates, the simplest and most enduring of interpretative sages. In him converge the roads of the most different philosophic modes of life, which are in truth the modes of the different temperaments, crystallised by reason and habit and all ultimately directed towards the delight in life and in self. The apparent conclusion is that the most peculiar thing about Socrates was his share in all the temperaments. Socrates excels the founder of Christianity by virtue of his merry style of seriousness and by that wisdom of sheer roguish pranks which constitutes the best state of soul in a man. Moreover, he had a superior intelligence.

87

Learning to write well. The age of good speaking is over, because the age of city-state culture is over. The limit allowed by Aristotle to the great city – in which the town-crier must be able to make himself heard by the whole assembled community – troubles us as little as do any city-communities, us who even wish to be understood beyond the boundaries of nations. Therefore everyone who is of a good European turn of mind must learn to *write* well, and to write better and better. He cannot help himself, he must learn that:

even if he was born in Germany, where bad writing is looked upon as a national privilege. Better writing means better thinking; always to discover matter more worthy of communication; to be able to communicate it properly; to be translateable into the tongues of neighbouring nations; to make oneself comprehensible to foreigners who learn our language; to work with the view of making all that is good common property, and of giving free access everywhere to the free; finally, to pave the way for that still remote state of things, when the great task shall come for good Europeans – guidance and guardianship of the universal world-culture. Whoever preaches the opposite doctrine of not troubling about good writing and good reading (both virtues grow together and decline together) is really showing the peoples a way of becoming more and more *national*. He is intensifying the malady of this century, and is a foe to good Europeans, a foe to free spirits.

88

The theory of the best style. The theory of the best style may at one time be the theory of finding the expression by which we transfer every mood of ours to the reader and the listener. At another, it may be the theory of finding expressions for the more desirable human moods, the communication and transference of which one desires most – for the mood of a man moved from the depth of his heart, intellectually cheerful, bright, and sincere, who has conquered his passions. This will be the theory of the best style, a theory that corresponds to the good man.

89

Paying attention to movement. The movement of the sentences shows whether the author be tired. Individual expressions may nevertheless be still strong and good, because they were invented earlier and for their own sake, when the thought first flashed across the author's mind. This is frequently the case with Goethe, who too often dictated when he was tired.

90

'Already' and 'still' – A. German prose is still very young. Goethe declares that Wieland is its father.

B. So young and already so ugly!

C. But, so far as I am aware, Bishop Ulfilas already wrote German prose, which must therefore be fifteen hundred years old.

B. So old and still so ugly!

91

Original German. German prose, which is really not fashioned on any pattern and must be considered an original creation of German taste, should give the eager advocate of a future original German culture an indication of how real German dress, German society, German furniture, German meals would look without the imitation of models. Someone who had long reflected on these vistas finally cried in great horror, 'But, Heaven help us, perhaps we already have that original culture – only we don't like to talk about it!'

92

Forbidden books. One should never read anything written by those arrogant wiseacres and puzzle-brains who have the detestable vice of logical paradox. They apply *logical* formulae just where everything is really improvised at random and built in the air. ('Therefore' with them means, 'You idiot of a reader, this "therefore" does not exist for you, but only for me.' The answer to this is: 'You idiot of a writer, then why do you write?')

93

Displaying one's wit. Everyone who wishes to display his wit thereby proclaims that he has also a plentiful lack of wit. That vice which clever Frenchmen have of adding a touch of *dédain* to their best ideas arises from a desire to be considered richer than they really are. They wish to be carelessly generous, as if weary of continual spending from overfull treasuries.

94

French and German literature. The misfortune of the French and German literature of the last hundred years is that the Germans ran away too early from the French school, and the French, later on, went too early to the German school.

95

Our prose. None of the present-day cultured nations has so bad a prose as the German. When clever, *blasé* Frenchmen say, 'There is no German prose', we ought really not to be angry, for this criticism is more polite than we deserve. If we look for reasons, we come at last to the strange phenomenon that the German knows only improvised prose and has no conception of any other. He simply cannot understand the Italian, who says that prose is as much harder than poetry as the representation of naked beauty is harder to the sculptor than that of draped beauty. Verse, images, rhythm, and rhyme need honest effort – that even the German realises, and he is not inclined to set a very high value on extempore poetry. But the notion of working at a page of prose as at a statue sounds to him like a tale from fairyland.

96

The grand style. The grand style comes into being when the beautiful wins a victory over the monstrous.

97

Dodging. We do not realise, in the case of distinguished minds, wherein lies the excellence of their expression, their turn of phrase, until we can say what word every mediocre writer would inevitably have hit upon in expressing the same idea. All great artists, in steering their car, show themselves prone to dodge and leave the track, but never to fall over.

98

Something like bread. Bread neutralises and takes out the taste of other food, and is therefore necessary to every long meal. In all works of art there must be something like bread, in order that they may produce divers effects. If these effects followed one another without occasional pauses and intervals, they would soon make us weary and provoke disgust – in fact, a long meal of art would then be impossible.

99

Jean Paul. Jean Paul knew a great deal, but had no science; understood all manner of tricks of art, but had no art; found almost everything enjoyable, but had no taste; possessed feeling and seriousness, but in dispensing them poured over them a nauseous sauce of tears; had even wit, but, unfortunately for his ardent desire for it, far too little – whence he drives the reader to despair by his very lack of wit. In short, he was the bright, rank-smelling weed that shot up overnight in the fair pleasaunces of Schiller and Goethe. He was a good, comfortable man, and yet a destiny, a destiny in a dressing-gown.

100

Palate for opposites. In order to enjoy a work of the past as its contemporaries enjoyed it, one must have a palate for the prevailing taste of the age which it attacked.

101

Spirits-of-wine authors. Many writers are neither spirit nor wine, but spirits of wine. They can flare up, and then they give warmth.

102

The interpretative sense. The sense of taste, as the true interpretative sense, often talks the other senses over to its point of view and imposes upon them its laws and customs. At table one can receive disclosures about the most subtle secrets of the arts ; it suffices to observe what tastes good and when and after what and how long it tastes good.

103

Lessing. Lessing had a genuine French talent, and, as writer, went most assiduously to the French school. He knows well how to arrange and display his wares in his shop-window. Without this true art his thoughts, like the objects of them, would have remained rather in the dark, nor would the general loss be great. His art, however, has taught many (especially the last generation of German scholars) and has given enjoyment to a countless number. It is true his disciples had no need to learn from him, as they often did, his unpleasant tone with its mingling of petulance and candour. Opinion is now unanimous on Lessing as 'lyric poet', and will some day be unanimous on Lessing as 'dramatic poet'.

104

Undesirable readers. How an author is vexed by those stolid, awkward readers who always fall at every place where they stumble, and always hurt themselves when they fall!

105

Poets' thoughts. Real thoughts of real poets always go about with a veil on, like Egyptian women; only the deep *eye* of thought looks out freely through the veil. Poets' thoughts are as a rule not of such value as is supposed. We have to pay for the veil and for our own curiosity into the bargain.

106

Write simply and usefully. Transitions, details, colour in depicting the passions – we make a present of all these to the author because we bring them with us and set them down to the credit of his book, provided he makes us some compensation.

107

Wieland. Wieland wrote German better than anyone else, and had the genuine adequacies and inadequacies of the master. His translations of the letters of Cicero and Lucian are the best in the language. His ideas, however, add nothing to our store of thought. We can endure his cheerful moralities as little as his cheerful immoralities, for both are very closely connected. The men who enjoyed them were at bottom better men than we are, but also a good deal heavier. They *needed* an author of this sort. The Germans did not need Goethe, and therefore cannot make proper use of him. We have only to consider the best of our statesmen and artists in this light. None of them had or *could* have had Goethe as their teacher.

108

Rare festivals. Pithy conciseness, repose, and maturity – where you find these qualities in an author, cry halt and celebrate a great festival in the desert. It will be long before you have such a treat again.

109

The treasure of German prose. Apart from Goethe's writings and especially Goethe's conversations with Eckermann (the best German book in existence), what German prose literature remains that is worth reading over and over again? Lichtenberg's *Aphorisms*, the first book of Jung-Stilling's *Story of My Life*, Adalbert Stifter's *St Martin's Summer* and Gottfried Keller's *People of Seldwyla* – and there, for the time being, it comes to an end.

110

Literary and colloquial style. The art of writing demands, first and foremost, substitutions for the means of expression which speech alone possesses – in other words, for gestures, accent, intonation, and look. Hence literary style is quite different from colloquial style, and far more difficult, because it has to make itself as intelligible as the latter with fewer accessories. Demosthenes delivered his speeches otherwise than we read them; he worked them up for reading purposes. Cicero's speeches ought to be 'demosthenised' with the same object, for at present they contain more of the Roman Forum than we can endure.

111

Caution in quotation. Young authors do not know that a good expression or idea only looks well among its peers; that an excellent quotation may spoil whole pages, nay the whole book; for it seems to cry warningly to the reader, 'Mark you, I am the precious stone, and round about me is lead – pale, worthless lead!' Every word, every idea only desires to live in its own company – that is the moral of a choice style.

112

How should errors be enunciated? – We may dispute whether it be more injurious for errors to be enunciated badly or as well as the best truths. It is certain that in the former case they are doubly harmful to the brain and are less easily removed from it. But, on the other hand, they are not so certain of effect as in the latter case. They are, in fact, less contagious.

113

Limiting and widening. Homer limited and diminished the horizon of his subject, but allowed individual scenes to expand and blossom out. Later, the tragedians are constantly renewing this process. Each takes his material in ever smaller and smaller fragments than his predecessor did, but each attains a greater wealth of blooms within the narrow hedges of these sequestered garden enclosures.

114

Literature and morality mutually explanatory. We can show from Greek literature by what forces the Greek spirit developed, how it entered upon different channels, and where it became enfeebled. All this also depicts to us how Greek morality proceeded, and how all morality will proceed: how it was at first a constraint and displayed cruelty, then became gradually milder; how a pleasure in certain actions, in certain forms and conventions arose, and from this again a propensity for solitary exercise, for solitary possession; how the track becomes crowded and overcrowded with competitors; how satiety enters in, new objects of struggle and ambition are sought, and forgotten aims are awakened to life; how the drama is repeated, and the spectators become altogether weary of looking on, because the whole gamut seems to have been run through – and then comes a stoppage, an expiration, and the rivulets are lost in the sand. The end, or at any rate *an* end, has come.

115

What landscapes give permanent delight. Such and such a landscape has features eminently suited for painting, but I cannot find the formula for it; it remains beyond my grasp as a whole. I notice that all landscapes which please me permanently have a simple geometrical scheme of lines underneath all their complexity. Without such a mathematical substratum no scenery becomes artistically pleasing. Perhaps this rule may be applied symbolically to human beings.

116

Reading aloud. The ability to read aloud involves of necessity the ability to declaim. Everywhere we must apply pale tints, but we must determine the degree of pallor in close relation to the richly and deeply coloured background, that always hovers before our eyes and acts as our guide – in other words, in accordance with the way in which we should *declaim* the same passages. That is why we must be able to declaim.

117

The dramatic sense. He who has not the four subtler senses of art tries to understand everything with the fifth sense, which is the coarsest of all – the dramatic sense.

118

Herder. Herder fails to be all that he made people think he was and himself wished to think he was. He was no great thinker or discoverer, no newly fertile soil with the unexhausted strength of a virgin forest. But he possessed in the highest degree the power of scenting the future, he saw and picked the first-fruits of the seasons earlier than all others, and they then believed that he had made them grow. Between darkness and light, youth and age, his mind was like a hunter on the watch, looking everywhere for transitions, depressions, convulsions, the outward and visible signs of internal growth. The unrest of spring drove him to and fro, but he was himself not the spring. At times, indeed, he had some inkling of this, and yet would fain not have believed it – he, the ambitious priest, who would have so gladly been the intellectual pope of his epoch! This is his despair. He seems to have lived long as a pretender to several kingdoms or even to a universal monarchy. He had his following which believed in him, among others the young Goethe. But whenever crowns were really distributed, he was passed over. Kant, Goethe, and then the first true German historians and scholars robbed him of what he thought he had reserved for himself (although in silence and secret he often thought the reverse). Just when he doubted in himself, he gladly clothed himself in dignity and enthusiasm: these were often in him mere garments, which had to hide a great deal and also to deceive and comfort him. He really had fire and enthusiasm, but his ambition was far greater! It blew impatiently at the fire, which flickered, crackled, and smoked – his *style* flickers, crackles, and smokes – but he yearned for the great flame which never broke out. He did not sit at the table of the genuine creators, and his

ambition did not admit of his sitting modestly among those
who simply enjoy. Thus he was a restless spirit, the taster of all
intellectual dishes, which were collected by the Germans from
every quarter and every age in the course of half a century. Never
really happy and satisfied, Herder was also too often ill, and then at
times envy sat by his bed, and hypocrisy paid her visit as well. He
always had an air of being scarred and crippled, and he lacked
simple, stalwart manliness more completely than any of the so-
called 'classical writers'.

119

Scent of words. Every word has its scent; there is a harmony and
discord of scents, and so too of words.

120

The far-fetched style. The natural style is an offence to the lover of
the far-fetched style.

121

A vow. I will never again read an author of whom one can suspect
that he *wanted* to make a book, but only those writers whose
thoughts unexpectedly became a book.

122

The artistic convention. Three-fourths of Homer is convention, and
the same is the case with all the Greek artists, who had no reason
for falling into the modern craze for originality. They had no fear
of convention, for after all convention was a link between them
and their public. Conventions are the artistic means *acquired* for
the understanding of the hearer; the common speech, learnt with
much toil, whereby the artist can really communicate his ideas.
All the more when he wishes, like the Greek poets and musicians,
to conquer at once with each of his works (since he is accustomed
to compete publicly with one or two rivals), the first condition is
that he must be understood at once, and this is only possible by
means of convention. What the artist devises beyond convention
he offers of his own free will and takes a risk, his success at best
resulting in the setting-up of a new convention. As a rule originality is marvelled at, sometimes even worshipped, but seldom

understood. A stubborn avoidance of convention means a desire not to be understood. What, then, is the object of the modern craze for originality?

123

Artists' affectation of scientific method. Schiller, like other German artists, fancied that if a man had intellect he was entitled to improvise even with the pen on all difficult subjects. So there we see his prose essays – in every way a model of how *not* to attack scientific questions of aesthetics and ethics, and a danger for young readers who, in their admiration for Schiller the poet, have not the courage to think meanly of Schiller the thinker and author. The temptation to traverse for once the forbidden paths, and to have his say in science as well, is easy and pardonable in the artist. For even the ablest artist from time to time finds his handicraft and his workshop unendurable. This temptation is so strong that it makes the artist show all the world what no one wishes to see, that his little chamber of thought is cramped and untidy. Why not, indeed? He does not live there. He proceeds to show that the storeroom of his knowledge is partly empty, partly filled with lumber. Why not, indeed? This condition does not really become the artist-child badly. In particular, the artist shows that for the very easiest exercises of scientific method, which are accessible even to beginners, his joints are too stiff and untrained. Even of that he need not really be ashamed! On the other hand, he often develops no mean art in imitating all the mistakes, vices, and base pedantries that are practised in the scientific community, in the belief that these belong to the appearance of the thing, if not to the thing itself. This is the very point that is so amusing in artists' writing, that the artist involuntarily acts as his vocation demands: he parodies the scientific and inartistic natures. Towards science he should show no attitude but that of parody, in so far as he is an artist and only an artist.

124

The Faust-idea. A little sempstress is seduced and plunged into despair: a great scholar of all the four Faculties is the evil-doer. That cannot have happened in the ordinary course, surely? No, certainly not! Without the aid of the devil incarnate, the great scholar would never have achieved the deed. Is this really destined to be the greatest German 'tragic idea', as one hears it said among Germans? – But for Goethe even this idea was too terrible. His kind heart could not avoid placing the little sempstress, 'the good soul that forgot itself but once', near to the saints, after her involuntary death. Even the great scholar, 'the good man' with 'the dark impulse', is brought into heaven in the nick of time, by a trick which is played upon the devil at the decisive moment. In heaven the lovers find themselves again. Goethe once said that his nature was too conciliatory for really tragic subjects.

125

Are there 'German classics'? – Sainte-Beuve observes somewhere that the word 'classic' does not suit the genius of certain literatures. For instance, nobody could talk seriously of 'German classics'. – What do our German publishers, who are about to add fifty more to the fifty German classics we are told to accept, say to that? Does it not almost seem as if one need only have been dead for the last thirty years, and lie a lawful prey to the public, in order to hear suddenly and unexpectedly the trumpet of resurrection as a 'Classic'? And this in an age and a nation where at least five out of the six great fathers of its literature are undoubtedly antiquated or becoming antiquated – without there being any need for the age or the nation to be ashamed of this. For those writers have given way before the strength of our time – let that be considered in all fairness! – Goethe, as I have indicated, I do not include. He belongs to a higher species than 'national literatures': hence life, revival, and decay do not enter into the reckoning in his relations with his countrymen. He lived and now lives but for the few; for the majority he is nothing but a flourish of vanity which is trumpeted from time to time across the border into foreign ears. Goethe, not merely a great and good man, but a *culture*, is in German history an interlude without a sequel. Who, for instance, would be able to point to any trace of Goethe's influence in German politics of the last seventy years (whereas the influence, certainly of Schiller, and perhaps of Lessing, can be traced in the political world)? But what of those five others? Klopstock, in a most honourable way, became out of date even in his own lifetime, and so completely that the meditative book of his later years, *The Republic of Learning*, has never been taken seriously from that day to this. Herder's misfortune was that his writings were always either new or antiquated. Thus for stronger and more subtle minds (like Lichtenberg) even Herder's masterpiece, his *Ideas for the History of Mankind*, was in a way antiquated at the very moment of its appearance. Wieland, who lived to the full and made others live likewise, was clever enough to anticipate by death the waning of his influence. Lessing, perhaps, still lives today – but among a young and ever younger band of scholars. Schiller has fallen from the hands of young men into those of boys, of all German boys. It is a well-known sign of obsolescence when a book descends to people of less and less mature age. Well, what is it that has thrust these five into the background, so that well-educated men of affairs no longer read them? A better taste, a riper knowledge, a higher reverence for the real and the true: in other words, the very virtues which these five (and ten or twenty others of lesser repute) first re-planted in Germany, and which now, like a mighty forest, cast over their graves not only the shadow of awe, but something of the shadow of oblivion. But classical writers are not planters of intellectual and literary virtues. They bring those virtues to perfection and are their highest luminous peaks, and being brighter, freer, and purer than all that surrounds them, they remain shining above the nations when the nations themselves perish. There may come an elevated stage of humanity, in which the Europe of the peoples is a dark, forgotten thing, but Europe lives on in thirty books, very old but never antiquated – in the classics.

126

Interesting, but not beautiful. This countryside conceals its meaning, but it has one that we should like to guess. Everywhere that I look, I read words and hints of words, but I do not know where begins the sentence that solves the riddle of all these hints. So I get a stiff neck in trying to discover whether I should start reading from this or that point.

127

Against innovators in language. The use of neologisms or archaisms, the preference for the rare and the bizarre, the attempt to enrich rather than to limit the vocabulary, are always signs either of an immature or of a corrupted taste. A noble poverty but a masterly freedom within the limits of that modest wealth distinguishes the Greek artists in oratory. They wish to have less than the people has – for the people is richest in old and new – but they wish to have that little *better*. The reckoning up of their archaic and exotic forms is soon done, but we never cease marvelling if we have an eye for their light and delicate manner in handling the commonplace and apparently long outworn elements in word and phrase.

128

Gloomy and serious authors. He who commits his sufferings to paper becomes a gloomy author, but he becomes a serious one if he tells us what he *has* suffered and why he is now enjoying a pleasurable repose.

129

Healthiness of taste. How is it that health is less contagious than disease – generally, and particularly in matters of taste? Or are there epidemics of health?

130

A resolution. Never again to read a book that is born and christened (with ink) at the same moment.

131

Improving our ideas. Improving our style means improving our ideas, and nothing else. He who does not at once concede this can never be convinced of the point.

132

Classical books. The weakest point in every classical book is that it is written too much in the mother tongue of its author.

133

Bad books. The book should demand pen, ink, and desk, but usually it is pen, ink, and desk that demand the book. That is why books are of so little account at present.

134

Presence of sense. When the public reflects on paintings, it becomes a poet; when on poems, an investigator. At the moment when the artist summons it it is always lacking in the right sense, and accordingly in presence of sense, not in presence of mind.

135

Choice ideas. The choice style of a momentous period does not only select its words but its ideas – and both from the customary and prevailing usage. Venturesome ideas, that smell too fresh, are to the maturer taste no less repugnant than new and reckless images and phrases. Later on both choice ideas and choice words soon smack of mediocrity, because the scent of the choice vanishes quickly, and then nothing but the customary and commonplace element is tasted.

136

Main reason for corruption of style. The desire to display more sentiment than one really feels for a thing corrupts style, in language and in all art. All great art shows rather the opposite tendency. Like every man of moral significance, it loves to check emotion on its way and not let it run its course to the very end. This modesty of letting emotion but half appear is most clearly to be observed, for example, in Sophocles. The features of sentiment seem to become beautified when sentiment feigns to be more shy than it really is.

137

An hxcuse for the heavy style. The lightly uttered phrase seldom falls on the ear with the full weight of the subject. This is, however, due to the bad training of the ear, which by education must pass from what has hitherto been called music to the school of the higher harmony – in other words, to conversation.

138

Bird's-eye views. Here torrents rush from every side into a ravine: their movement is so swift and stormy, and carries the eye along so quickly, that the bare or wooded mountain slopes around seem not to sink down but to fly down. We are in an agonised tension at the sight, as if behind all this were hidden some hostile element, before which all must fly, and against which the abyss alone gave protection. This landscape cannot be painted, unless we hover above it like a bird in the open air. Here for once the so-called bird's-eye view is not an artistic caprice, but the sole possibility.

139

Rash comparisons. If rash comparisons are not proofs of the wantonness of the writer, they are proofs of the exhaustion of his imagination. In any case they bear witness to his bad taste.

140

Dancing in chains. In the case of every Greek artist, poet, or writer we must ask: What is the new constraint which he imposes upon himself and makes attractive to his contemporaries, so as to find imitators? For the thing called 'invention' (in metre, for example) is always a self-imposed fetter of this kind. 'Dancing in chains' – to make that hard for themselves and then to spread a false notion that it is easy – that is the trick that they wish to show us. Even in Homer we may perceive a wealth of inherited formulae and laws of epic narration, within the circle of which he had to dance, and he himself created new conventions for them that came after. This was the discipline of the Greek poets: first to impose upon themselves a manifold constraint by means of the earlier poets; then to invent in addition a new constraint, to impose it upon themselves and cheerfully to overcome it, so that constraint and victory are perceived and admired.

141

Author's copiousness. The last quality that a good author acquires is copiousness: whoever has it to begin with will never become a good author. The noblest racehorses are lean until they are permitted to rest from their victories.

142

Wheezing heroes. Poets and artists who suffer from a narrow chest of the emotions generally make their heroes wheeze. They do not know what easy breathing means.

143

The short-sighted. The short-sighted are the deadly foes of all authors who let themselves go. These authors should know the wrath with which such people shut the book in which they observe that its creator needs fifty pages to express five ideas. And the cause of their wrath is that they have endangered what remains of their vision almost without compensation. A short-sighted person said, 'All authors let themselves go.' 'Even the Holy Ghost?' 'Even the Holy Ghost.' But he had a right to, for he wrote for those who had lost their sight altogether.

144

The style of immortality. Thucydides and Tacitus both imagined immortal life for their works when they executed them. That might be guessed (if not known otherwise) from their style. The one thought to give permanence to his ideas by salting them, the other by boiling them down; and neither, it seems, made a miscalculation.

145

Against images and similes. By images and similes we convince, but we do not prove. That is why science has such a horror of images and similes. Science does not want to convince or make plausible, and rather seeks to provoke cold distrust by its mode of expression, by the bareness of its walls. For distrust is the touchstone for the gold of certainty.

146

Caution. In Germany, he who lacks thorough knowledge should beware of writing. The good German does not say in that case 'he is ignorant', but 'he is of doubtful character'. – This hasty conclusion, by the way, does great credit to the Germans.

147

Painted skeletons. Painted skeletons are those authors who try to make up for their want of flesh by artistic colourings.

148

The grand style and something better. It is easier to learn how to write the grand style than how to write easily and simply. The reasons for this are inextricably bound up with morality.

149

Sebastian Bach. In so far as we do not hear Bach's music as perfect and experienced connoisseurs of counterpoint and all the varieties of the fugal style (and accordingly must dispense with real artistic enjoyment), we shall feel in listening to his music – in Goethe's magnificent phrase – as if 'we were present at God's creation of the world.' In other words, we feel here that something great is in the making but not yet made – our mighty modern music, which by conquering nationalities, the Church, and counterpoint has conquered the world. In Bach there is still too much crude Christianity, crude Germanism, crude scholasticism. He stands on the threshold of modern European music, but turns from thence to look at the Middle Ages.

150

Händel. Händel, who in the invention of his music was bold, original, truthful, powerful, inclined to and akin to all the heroism of which a *nation* is capable, often proved stiff, cold, nay even weary of himself in composition. He applied a few well-tried methods of execution, wrote copiously and quickly, and was glad when he had finished – but that joy was not the joy of God and other creators in the eventide of their working day.

151

Haydn. So far as genius can exist in a man who is merely *good*, Haydn had genius. He went just as far as the limit which morality sets to intellect, and only wrote music that has 'no past'.

152

Beethoven and Mozart. Beethoven's music often appears like a deeply emotional meditation on unexpectedly hearing once more a piece long thought to be forgotten, 'Tonal Innocence': it is music about music. In the song of the beggar and child in the street, in the monotonous airs of vagrant Italians, in the dance of the village inn or in carnival nights he discovers his melodies. He stores them together like a bee, snatching here and there some notes or a short phrase. To him these are hallowed memories of 'the better world', like the ideas of Plato. Mozart stands in quite a different relation to his melodies. He finds his inspiration not in hearing music but in gazing at life, at the most stirring life of southern lands. He was always dreaming of Italy, when he was not there.

153

Recitative. Formerly recitative was dry, but now we live in the age of moist recitative. It has fallen into the water, and the waves carry it whithersoever they list.

154

'Cheerful' music. If for a long time we have heard no music, it then goes like a heavy southern wine all too quickly into the blood and leaves behind it a soul dazed with narcotics, half-awake, longing for sleep. This is particularly the case with cheerful music, which inspires in us bitterness and pain, satiety and homesickness together, and forces us to sip again and again as at a sweetened draught of poison. The hall of gay, noisy merriment then seems to grow narrow, the light to lose its brightness and become browner. At last we feel as if this music were penetrating to a prison where a poor wretch cannot sleep for home-sickness.

155

Franz Schubert. Franz Schubert, inferior as an artist to the other great musicians, had nevertheless the largest share of inherited musical wealth. He spent it with a free hand and a kind heart, so that for a few centuries musicians will continue to *nibble* at his ideas and inspirations. In his works we find a store of *unused* inventions; the greatness of others will lie in making use of those inventions. If Beethoven may be called the ideal listener for a troubadour, Schubert has a right to be called the ideal troubadour.

156

Modern musical execution. Great tragic or dramatic execution of music acquires its character by imitating the gesture of the great sinner, such as Christianity conceives and desires him: the slow-stepping, passionately brooding man, distracted by the agonies of conscience, now flying in terror, now clutching with delight, now standing still in despair – and all the other marks of great sinfulness. Only on the Christian assumption that all men are great sinners and do nothing but sin could we justify the application of this style of execution to *all* music. So far, music would be the reflection of all the actions and impulses of man, and would continually have to express by gestures the language of the great sinner. At such a performance, a listener who was not enough of a Christian to understand this logic might indeed cry out in horror, 'For the love of Heaven, how did sin find its way into music?'

157

Felix Mendelssohn. Felix Mendelssohn's music is the music of the good taste that enjoys all the good things that have ever existed. It always points behind. How could it have much 'in front', much of a future? – But did he want it to have a future? He possessed a virtue rare among artists, that of gratitude without *arrière-pensée*. This virtue, too, always points behind.

158

A mother of arts. In our sceptical age, real devotion requires almost a brutal heroism of ambition. Fanatical shutting of the eyes and bending of the knee no longer suffice. Would it not be possible for ambition – in its eagerness to be the last devotee of all the ages – to become the begetter of a final church music, as it has been the begetter of the final church architecture? (They call it the Jesuit style.)

159

Freedom in fetters – a princely freedom. Chopin, the last of the modern musicians, who gazed at and worshipped beauty, like Leopardi; Chopin, the Pole, the inimitable (none that came before or after him has a right to this name) – Chopin had the same princely punctilio in convention that Raphael shows in the use of the simplest traditional colours. The only difference is that Chopin applies them not to colour but to melodic and rhythmic traditions. He admitted the validity of these traditions because he was born under the sway of etiquette. But in these fetters he plays and dances as the freest and daintiest of spirits, and, be it observed, he does not spurn the chain.

160

Chopin's barcarolle. Almost all states and modes of life have a moment of rapture, and good artists know how to discover that moment. Such a moment there is even in life by the seashore – that dreary, sordid, unhealthy existence, dragged out in the neighbourhood of a noisy and covetous rabble. This moment of rapture Chopin in his barcarolle expressed in sound so supremely that gods themselves, when they heard it, might yearn to lie long summer evenings in a boat.

161

Robert Schumann. 'The Stripling', as the romantic songsters of Germany and France of the first three decades of this century imagined him – this stripling was completely translated into song and melody by Robert Schumann, the eternal youth, so long as he felt himself in full possession of his powers. There are indeed moments when his music reminds one of the eternal 'old maid'.

162

Dramatic singers. 'Why does this beggar sing?' 'Probably he does not know how to wail.' 'Then he does right.' But our dramatic singers, who wail because they do not know how to sing – are they also in the right?

163

Dramatic music. For him who does not see what is happening on the stage, dramatic music is a monstrosity, just as the running commentary to a lost text is a monstrosity. Such music requires us to have ears where our eyes are. This, however, is doing violence to Euterpe, who, poor Muse, wants to have her eyes and ears where the other Muses have theirs.

164

Victory and reasonableness. Unfortunately in the aesthetic wars, which artists provoke by their works and apologias for their works, just as is the case in real war, it is might and not reason that decides. All the world now assumes as a historical fact that, in his dispute with Piccini, Gluck was in the right. At any rate, he was victorious, and had might on his side.

165

Of the principle of musical execution. Do the modern musical performers really believe that the supreme law of their art is to give every piece as much high-relief as is possible, and to make it speak at all costs a dramatic language? Is not this principle, when applied for example to Mozart, a veritable sin against the spirit – the gay, sunny, airy, delicate spirit – of Mozart, whose seriousness was of a kindly and not awe-inspiring order, whose pictures do not try to leap from the wall and drive away the beholder in panic? Or do you think that all Mozart's music is identical with the statue-music in *Don Juan*? And not only Mozart's, but all music? – You reply that the advantage of your principle lies in its greater *effect*. You would be right if there did not remain the counter-question, '*On whom* has the effect operated, and *on whom* should an artist of the first rank desire to produce his effect?' Never on the populace! Never on the immature! Never on the morbidly sensitive! Never on the diseased! And above all – never on the *blasé*!

166

The music of today. This ultra-modern music, with its strong lungs and weak nerves, is frightened above all things of itself.

167

Where music is at home. Music reaches its high-water mark only among men who have not the ability or the right to argue. Accordingly, its chief promoters are princes, whose aim is that there should be not much criticism nor even much thought in their neighbourhood. Next come societies which, under some pressure or other (political or religious), are forced to become habituated to silence, and so feel all the greater need of spells to charm away emotional *ennui* – these spells being generally eternal love-making and eternal music. Thirdly, we must reckon whole nations in which there is no 'society', but all the greater number of individuals with a bent towards solitude, mystical thinking, and a reverence for all that is inexpressible; these are the genuine 'musical souls'. The Greeks, as a nation delighting in talking and argument, accordingly put up with music only as an *hors d'oeuvre* to those arts which really admit of discussion and dispute. About music one can hardly even *think* clearly. The Pythagoreans, who in so many respects were exceptional Greeks, are said to have been great musicians. This was the school that invented a five-years' silence, but did not invent a dialectic.

168

Sentimentality in music. We may be ever so much in sympathy with serious and profound music, yet nevertheless, or perhaps all the more for that reason, we shall at occasional moments be over-powered, entranced, and almost melted away by its opposite – I mean, by those simple Italian operatic airs which, in spite of all their monotony of rhythm and childishness of harmony, seem at times to sing to us like the very soul of music. Admit this or not as you please, you Pharisees of good taste, it is so, and it is my present task to propound the riddle that it is so, and to nibble a little myself at the solution. In childhood's days we tasted the honey of many things for the first time. Never was honey so good as then; it seduced us to life, into abundant life, in the guise of the first spring, the first flower, the first butterfly, the first friendship. Then – perhaps in our ninth year or so – we heard our first music, and this was the first that we understood; thus the simplest and most childish tunes, that were not much more than a sequel to the nurse's lullaby and the strolling fiddler's tune, were our first experience. (For even the most trifling 'revelations' of art need preparation and study; there is no 'immediate' effect of art, what-ever charming fables the philosophers may tell.) Our sensation on hearing these Italian airs is associated with those first musical raptures, the strongest of our lives. The bliss of childhood and its flight, the feeling that our most precious possession can never be brought back, all this moves the chords of the soul more strongly than the most serious and profound music can move them. This mingling of aesthetic pleasure with moral pain, which nowadays it is customary to call (rather too haughtily, I think) 'sentimentality' – it is the mood of Faust at the end of the first scene – this 'senti-mentality' of the listener is all to the advantage of Italian music. It is a feeling which the experienced connoisseurs in art, the pure 'aesthetes', like to ignore. Moreover, almost all music has a magical effect only when we hear it speak the language of our own *past*. Accordingly, it seems to the layman that all the old music is continually growing better, and that all the latest is of little value. For the latter arouses no 'sentimentality', that most essential element of happiness, as aforesaid, for every man who cannot approach this art with pure aesthetic enjoyment.

169

As friends of music. Ultimately we are and remain good friends with music, as we are with the light of the moon. Neither, after all, tries to supplant the sun: they only want to illumine our nights to the best of their powers. Yet we may jest and laugh at them, may we not? Just a little, at least, and from time to time? At the man in the moon, at the woman in music?

170

Art in an age of work. We have the conscience of an industrious epoch. This debars us from devoting our best hours and the best part of our days to art, even though that art be the greatest and worthiest. Art is for us a matter of leisure, of recreation, and we consecrate to it the *residue* of our time and strength. This is the cardinal fact that has altered the relation of art to life. When art makes its great demands of time and strength upon its recipients, it has to battle against the conscience of the industrious and efficient, it is relegated to the idle and conscienceless, who, by their very nature, are not exactly suited to great art, and consider its claims arrogant. It might, therefore, be all over with art, since it lacks air and the power to breathe. But perhaps great art attempts, by a sort of coarsening and disguising, to make itself at home in that other atmosphere, or at least to put up with it – an atmosphere which is really a natural element only for petty art, the art of recreation, of pleasant distraction. This happens nowadays almost everywhere. Even the exponents of great art promise recreation and distraction; even they address themselves to the exhausted; even they demand from him the evening hours of his working-day – just like the artists of the entertaining school, who are content to smooth the furrowed brow and brighten the lack-lustre eye.

What, then, are the devices of their mightier brethren? These have in their medicine-chests the most powerful excitants, which might give a shock even to a man half-dead: they can deafen you, intoxicate you, make you shudder, or bring tears to your eyes. By this means they overpower the exhausted man and stimulate him for one night to an over-lively condition, to an ecstasy of terror and delight. This great art, as it now lives in opera, tragedy, and music – have we a right to be angry with it, because of its perilous fascination, as we should be angry with a cunning courtesan? Certainly not. It would far rather live in the pure element of morning calm, and would far rather make its appeal to the fresh, expectant, vigorous morning-soul of the beholder or listener. Let us be thankful that it prefers living thus to vanishing altogether. But let us also confess that an era that once more introduces free and complete high-days and holidays into life will have no use for *our* great art.

171

The employees of science and the others. Really efficient and successful men of science might be collectively called 'The Employees'. If in youth their acumen is sufficiently practised, their memory is full, and hand and eye have acquired sureness, they are appointed by an older fellow-craftsman to a scientific position where their qualities may prove useful. Later on, when they have themselves gained an eye for the gaps and defects in their science, they place themselves in whatever position they are needed. These persons all exist for the sake of science. But there are rarer spirits, spirits that seldom succeed or fully mature – 'for whose sake science exists' – at least, in their view. They are often unpleasant, conceited, or cross-grained men, but almost always prodigies to a certain extent. They are neither employees nor employers; they make use of what those others have worked out and established, with a certain princely carelessness and with little and rare praise – just as if the others belonged to a lower order of beings. Yet they possess the same qualities as their fellow-workers, and that sometimes in a less developed form. Moreover, they have a peculiar limitation, from which the others are free; this makes it impossible to put them into a place and to see in them useful tools. They can only live in their own air and on their own soil. This limitation suggests to them what elements of a science 'are theirs' – in other words, what they can carry home into their house and atmosphere: they think that they are always collecting their scattered 'property'. If they are prevented from building at their own nest, they perish like shelterless birds. The loss of freedom causes them to wilt away. If they show, like their colleagues, a fondness for certain regions of science, it is always only regions where the fruits and seeds necessary to them can thrive. What do they care whether science, taken as a whole, has untilled or badly tilled regions? They lack all impersonal interest in a scientific problem. As they are themselves personal through and through, all their knowledge and ideas are remoulded into a person, into a living complexity, with its parts interdependent, overlapping, jointly nurtured, and with a peculiar atmosphere and scent as a whole. Such natures, with their system of personal knowledge, produce the illusion that a science (or even the whole of philosophy) is finished and has reached its goal. The life in their system works this magic, which at times has been fatal to science and deceptive to the really efficient workers above described, and at other times, when drought and exhaustion prevailed, has acted as a kind of restorative, as if it were the air of a cool, refreshing resting-place. These men are usually called *philosophers*.

172

Recognition of talent. As I went through the village of S, a boy began to crack his whip with all his might – he had made great progress in this art, and he knew it. I threw him a look of recognition – in reality it hurt me cruelly. We do the same in our recognition of many of the talents. We do good to them when they hurt us.

173

Laughing and smiling. The more joyful and assured the mind becomes, the more man loses the habit of loud laughter. In compensation, there is an intellectual smile continually bubbling up in him, a sign of his astonishment at the innumerable concealed delights of a good existence.

174

The talk of invalids. Just as in spiritual grief we tear our hair, strike our foreheads, lacerate our cheeks or even (like Oedipus) gouge our eyes out, so against violent physical pain we call to our aid a bitter, violent emotion, through the recollection of slanderous and malignant people, through the denigration of our future, through the sword-pricks and acts of malice which we mentally direct against the absent. And at times it is true that one devil drives out another – but then we have the other. Hence a different sort of talk, tending to alleviate pain, should be recommended invalids: reflections upon the kindnesses and courtesies that can be performed towards friend and foe.

175
Mediocrity as a mask. Mediocrity is the happiest mask which the superior mind can wear, because it does not lead the great majority – that is, the mediocre – to think that there is any disguise. Yet the superior mind assumes the mask just for their sake – so as not to irritate them, nay, often from a feeling of pity and kindness.

176
The patient. The pine tree seems to listen, the fir tree to wait, and both without impatience. They do not give a thought to the petty human being below who is consumed by his impatience and his curiosity.

177
The best joker. My favourite joke is the one that takes the place of a heavy and rather hesitating idea, and that at once beckons with its finger and winks its eye.

178
The accessories of all reverence. Wherever the past is revered, the over-cleanly and overtidy people should not be admitted. Piety does not feel content without a little dust, dirt, and dross.

179
The great danger of savants. It is just the most thorough and profound savants who are in peril of seeing their life's goal set ever lower and lower, and, with a feeling of this in their minds, of becoming ever more discouraged and more unendurable in the latter half of their lives. At first they plunge into their science with spacious hopes and set themselves daring tasks, the ends of which are already

anticipated by their imaginations. Then there are moments as in the lives of the great maritime discoverers – knowledge, presentiment, and power raise each other higher and higher, until a new shore first dawns upon the eye in the far distance. But now the stern man recognises more and more how important it is that the individual task of the enquirer should be limited as far as possible, so that it may be entirely accomplished and the intolerable waste of force from which earlier periods of science suffered may be avoided. In those days everything was done ten times over, and then the eleventh always had the last and best word. Yet the more the savant learns and practises this art of solving riddles in their entirety, the more pleasure he finds in so doing. But at the same time his demands upon what is here called 'entirety' grow more exacting. He sets aside everything that must remain in this sense incomplete, he acquires a disgust and an acute scent for the half-soluble – for all that can only give a kind of certainty in a general and indefinite form. His youthful plans crumble away before his eyes. There remains scarcely anything but a few little knots, in untying which the master now takes his pleasure and shows his strength. Then, in the midst of all this useful, restless activity, he, now grown old, is suddenly then often overcome by a deep misgiving, a sort of torment of conscience. He looks upon himself as one changed, as if he were diminished, humbled, transformed into a dexterous *dwarf*; he grows anxious as to whether mastery in small matters be not a convenience, an escape from the summons to greatness in life and form. But he cannot pass *beyond* any longer – the time for that has gone by.

180

Teachers in the age of books. Now that self-education and mutual education are becoming more widespread, the teacher in his usual form must become almost unnecessary. Friends eager to learn, who wish to master some branch of knowledge together, find in our age of books a shorter and more natural way than 'school' and 'teachers'.

181

Vanity as the greatest utility. Originally the strong individual uses not only Nature but even societies and weaker individuals as objects of rapine. He exploits them, so far as he can, and then passes on. As he lives from hand to mouth, alternating between hunger and superfluity, he kills more animals than he can eat, and robs and maltreats men more than is necessary. His manifestation of power is at the same time one of revenge against his cramped and worried existence. Furthermore, he wishes to be held more powerful than he is, and thus misuses opportunities; the accretion of fear that he begets being an accretion of power. He soon observes that he stands or falls not by what he *is* but by what he is *thought* to be. Herein lies the origin of vanity. The man of power seeks by every means to increase others' faith in his power. The thralls who tremble before him and serve him know, for their part, that they are worth just so much as they appear to him to be worth, and so they work with an eye to this valuation rather than to their own self-satisfaction. We know vanity only in its most weakened forms, in its idealisations and its small doses, because we live in a late and very emasculated state of society. Originally vanity is the great utility, the strongest means of preservation. And indeed vanity will be greater, the cleverer the individual, because an increase in the belief in power is easier than an increase in the power itself, but only for him who has intellect or (as must be the case under primitive conditions) who is cunning and crafty.

182

Weather-signs of culture. There are so few decisive weather-signs of culture that we must be glad to have at least one unfailing sign at hand for use in house and garden. To test whether a man belongs to us (I mean to the free spirits) or not, we must test his sentiments regarding Christianity. If he looks upon Christianity with other than a critical eye, we turn our backs to him, for he brings us impure air and bad weather. It is no longer our task to teach such men what a sirocco wind is. They have Moses and the prophets of weather and of enlightenment. If they will not listen to these, then –

183

There is a proper time for wrath and punishment. Wrath and punishment are our inheritance from the animals. Man does not become of age until he has restored to the animals this gift of the cradle.

Herein lies buried one of the mightiest ideas that men can have, the idea of a progress of all progresses. Let us go forward together a few millenniums, my friends! There is still reserved for mankind a great deal of joy, the very scent of which has not yet been wafted to the men of our day! Indeed, we may promise ourselves this joy, nay summon and conjure it up as a necessary thing, so long as the development of human reason does not stand still. Some day we shall no longer be reconciled to the logical sin that lurks in all wrath and punishment, whether exercised by the individual or by society – some day, when head and heart have learnt to live as near together as they now are far apart. That they no longer stand so far apart as they did originally is fairly palpable from a glance at the whole course of humanity. The individual who can review a life of introspective work will become conscious of the *rapprochement* arrived at, with a proud delight at the distance he has bridged, in order that he may thereupon venture upon more ample hopes.

184

Origin of pessimists. A snack of good food often decides whether we are to look to the future with hollow eye or in hopeful mood. The same influence extends to the very highest and most intellectual states. Discontent and reviling of the world are for the present generation an inheritance from starveling ancestors. Even in our artists and poets we often notice that, however exuberant their life, they are not of good birth, and have often, from oppressed and ill-nourished ancestors, inherited in their blood and brain much that comes out as the subject and even the conscious colouring of their work. The culture of the Greeks is a culture of men of wealth, in fact, inherited wealth. For a few centuries they lived better than we do (better in every sense, in particular far more simply in food and drink). Then the brain finally became so well-stored and subtle, and the blood flowed so quickly, like a joyous, clear wine, that the best in them came to light no longer as gloomy, distorted, and violent, but full of beauty and sunshine.

185

Of reasonable death. Which is more reasonable, to stop the machine when the works have done the task demanded of them, or to let it run on until it stands still of its own accord – in other words, is destroyed? Is not the latter a waste of the cost of upkeep, a misuse of the strength and care of those who serve? Are men not here throwing away that which would be sorely needed elsewhere? Is it not a kind of contempt of the machines propagated, in that many of them are so uselessly tended and kept up? – I am speaking of involuntary (natural) and voluntary (reasonable) death. Natural death is independent of all reason and is really an irrational death, in which the pitiable substance of the shell determines how long the kernel is to exist or not; in which, accordingly, the stunted, diseased and dull-witted jailer is lord, and indicates the moment at which his distinguished prisoner shall die. Natural death is the suicide of nature – in other words, the annihilation of the most rational being through the most irrational element that is attached thereto. Only through religious illumination can the reverse appear; for then, as is equitable, the higher reason (God) issues its orders, which the lower reason has to obey. Outside religious thought natural death is not worth glorifying. The wise dispensation and disposal of death belongs to that now quite incomprehensible and immoral-sounding morality of the future, the dawn of which it will be an ineffable delight to behold.

186

Retrograde influences. All criminals force society back to earlier stages of culture than that in which they are placed for the time being. Their influence is retrograde. Let us consider the tools that society must forge and maintain for its defence: the cunning detectives, the jailers, the hangmen. Nor should we forget the public counsel for prosecution and defence. Finally we may ask ourselves whether the judge himself and punishment and the whole legal procedure are not oppressive rather than elevating in their reaction upon all who are not law-breakers. For we shall never succeed in arraying self-defence and revenge in the garb of innocence, and so long as men are used and sacrificed as a means to the end of society, all loftier humanity will deplore this necessity.

187

War as a remedy. For nations that are growing weak and contempt-ible war may be prescribed as a remedy, if indeed they really want to go on living. National consumption as well as individual admits of a brutal cure. The eternal will to live and inability to die is, however, in itself already a sign of senility of emotion. The more fully and thoroughly we live, the more ready we are to sacrifice life for a single pleasurable emotion. A people that lives and feels in this wise has no need of war.

188

Intellectual and physical transplantation as remedies. The different cultures are so many intellectual climates, every one of which is peculiarly harmful or beneficial to this or that organism. History as a whole, as the knowledge of different cultures, is the science of remedies, but not the science of the healing art itself. We still need a physician who can make use of these remedies, in order to send everyone – temporarily or permanently – to the climate that just suits him. To live in the present, within the limits of a single culture, is insufficient as a universal remedy: too many highly useful kinds of men, who cannot breathe freely in this atmosphere, would perish. With the aid of history we must give them air and try to preserve them: even men of lower cultures have their value. Add to this cure of intellects that humanity, on considerations of bodily health, must strive to discover by means of a medical geography what kinds of degeneration and disease are caused by each region of the earth, and conversely, what ingredients of health the earth affords: and then, gradually, nations, families, and individuals must be transplanted long and permanently enough for them to become masters of their inherited physical infirmities. The whole world will finally be a series of sanatoria.

189

Reason and the tree of mankind. What you all fear in your senile short-sightedness, regarding the over-population of the world, gives the more hopeful a mighty task. Man is some day to become a tree overshadowing the whole earth, with millions upon millions of buds that shall all grow to fruits side by side, and the earth itself shall be prepared for the nourishment of this tree. That the shoot, tiny as yet, may increase in sap and strength; that the sap may flow in countless channels for the nutrition of the whole and the parts – from these and similar tasks we must derive our standard for measuring whether a man of today is useful or worthless. The task is unspeakably great and adventurous: let us all contribute our share to prevent the tree from rotting before its time! The historically trained mind will no doubt succeed in calling up the human activities of all the ages before its eyes, as the community of ants with its cunningly wrought mounds stands before our eyes. Superficially judged, mankind as a whole, like ant-kind, might admit of our speaking of 'instinct'. On a closer examination we observe how whole nations, nay whole centuries, take pains to discover and test new means of benefiting the great mass of humanity, and thus finally the great common fruit-tree of the world. Whatever injury the individual nations or periods may suffer in this testing process, they have each become wise through this injury, and from them the tide of wisdom slowly pours over the principles of whole races and whole epochs. Ants too go astray and make blunders. Through the folly of its remedies, mankind may well go to rack and ruin before the proper time. There is no sure guiding instinct for the former or the latter. Rather must we boldly face the great task of preparing the earth for a plant of the most ample and joyous fruitfulness – a task set by reason to reason!

190

The praise of disinterestedness and its origin. Between two neighbouring chieftains there was a long-standing quarrel: they laid waste each other's territories, stole cattle, and burnt down houses, with an indecisive result on the whole, because their power was fairly equal. A third, who from the distant situation of his property was able to keep aloof from these feuds, yet had reason to dread the day when one of the two neighbours should gain a decisive preponderance, at last intervened between the combatants with ceremonial goodwill. Secretly he lent a heavy weight to his peace proposal by giving either to understand that he would henceforth join forces with the other against the one who strove to break the peace. They met in his presence, they hesitatingly placed into his hand the hands that had hitherto been the tools and only too often the causes of hatred – and then they really and seriously tried to keep the peace. Either saw with astonishment how suddenly his prosperity and his comfort increased; how he now had as neighbour a dealer ready to buy and sell instead of a treacherous or openly scornful evil-doer; how even in unforeseen troubles, they could reciprocally save each other from distress, instead of, as before, making capital out of this distress of his neighbour and enhancing it to the highest degree. It even seemed as if the human type had improved in both countries, for the eyes had become brighter, the forehead had lost its wrinkles; all now felt confidence in the future – and nothing is more advantageous for the souls and bodies of men than this confidence. They saw each other every year on the anniversary of the alliance, the chieftains as well as their retinue, and indeed before the eyes of the mediator, whose mode of action they admired and revered more and more, the greater the profit that they owed to him became. Then his mode of action was called *disinterested*. They had looked far too fixedly at the profit they had reaped themselves hitherto to see anything more of their neighbour's method of dealing than that his condition in consequence of this had not altered so much as their own; he had rather remained the same: and thus it appeared that the former had not had his profit in view. For the first time people said to themselves that disinterestedness was a virtue. It is true that in minor private matters similar circumstances had arisen, but men only had eyes for this virtue when it was depicted on the walls in a large script that was legible to the whole community. Moral qualities are not recognised as virtues, endowed with names, held in esteem, and recommended as worthy of acquisition until the moment when they have *visibly* decided the happiness and destiny of whole societies. For then the loftiness of sentiment and the excitation of the inner creative forces is in many so great, that offerings are brought to this quality, offerings from the best of what each possesses. At its feet the serious man lays his seriousness, the dignified man his dignity, women their gentleness, the young all the wealth of hope and futurity that in them lies; the poet lends it words and names, sets it marching in the procession of similar beings, gives it a pedigree, and finally, as is the way of artists, adores the picture of his fancy as a new godhead – he even teaches others to adore. Thus in the end, with the co-operation of universal love and gratitude, a virtue becomes, like a statue, a repository of all that is good and honourable, a sort of temple and divine personage combined. It appears thenceforward as an individual virtue, as an absolute entity, which it was not before, and exercises the power and privileges of a sanctified super-humanity. In the later days of

Greece the cities were full of such deified human abstractions (if one may so call them). The nation, in its own fashion, had set up a Platonic 'Heaven of Ideas' on earth, and I do not think that its inhabitants were felt to be less alive than any of the old Homeric divinities.

191

Days of darkness. 'Days of Darkness' is the name given in Norway to the period when the sun remains below the horizon the whole day long. The temperature then falls slowly but continually. A fine simile for all thinkers for whom the sun of the human future is temporarily eclipsed.

192

The philosophy of luxury. A garden, figs, a little cheese, and three or four good friends – that was the luxury of Epicurus.

193

The epochs of life. The real epochs of life are those brief periods of cessation midway between the rise and decline of a dominating idea or emotion. Here once again there is satisfaction: all the rest is hunger and thirst – or satiety.

194

Dreams. Our dreams, if for once in a way they succeed and are complete – generally a dream is a bungled piece of work – are symbolic concatenations of scenes and images in place of a narrative poetical language. They paraphrase our experiences or expectations or relations with poetic boldness and definiteness, so that in the morning we are always astonished at ourselves when we remember the nature of our dream. In dreams we use up too much artistry – and hence are often too poor in artistry in the daytime.

195

Nature and science. As in nature, so in science the worse and less fertile soils are first cultivated – because the means that science in its early stages has at command are fairly sufficient for this purpose. The working of the most fertile soils requires an enormous, carefully developed, persevering method, tangible individual results, and an organised body of well-trained workers. All these are found together only at a late stage. Impatience and ambition often grasp too early at these most fertile soils, but the results are then from the first null and void. In nature such losses would usually be avenged by the starvation of the settlers.

196

The simple life. A simple mode of life is nowadays difficult, requiring as it does far more reflection and gift for invention than even very clever people possess. The most honourable will perhaps still say, 'I have not the time for such lengthy reflection. The simple life is for me too lofty a goal: I will wait till those wiser than I have discovered it.'

197

Peaks and needle-points. The poor fertility, the frequent celibacy, and in general the sexual coldness of the highest and most cultivated spirits, as that of the classes to which they belong, is essential in human economy. Intelligence recognises and makes use of the fact that at an acme of intellectual development the danger of a neurotic offspring is very great. Such men are the peaks of mankind – they ought no longer to run out into needle-points.

198

*Natura non facit saltum.** However strongly man may develop upwards and seem to leap from one contradiction to another, a close observation will reveal the dovetails where the new building grows out of the old. This is the biographer's task: he must reflect upon his subject on the principle that nature takes no jumps.

199

Clean, but – He who clothes himself with rags washed clean dresses cleanly, to be sure, but is still ragged.

200

The solitary speaks. In compensation for much disgust, disheartenment, boredom – such as a lonely life without friends, books,

* Nature takes no jumps.

duties, and passions must involve – we enjoy those short spans of deep communion with ourselves and with Nature. He who fortifies himself completely against boredom fortifies himself against himself too. He will never drink the most powerful elixir from his own innermost spring.

201

False renown. I hate those so-called natural beauties which really have significance only through science, especially geographical science, but are insignificant in an aesthetic sense: for example, the view of Mont Blanc from Geneva. This is an insignificant thing without the auxiliary mental joy of science: the nearer mountains are all more beautiful and fuller of expression, but 'not nearly so high', adds that absurd depreciatory science. The eye here contradicts science: how can it truly rejoice in the contradiction?

202

Those that travel for pleasure. Like animals, stupid and perspiring, they climb mountains: people forgot to tell them that there were fine views on the way.

203

Too much and too little. Men nowadays live too much and think too little. They have hunger and dyspepsia together, and become thinner and thinner, however much they eat. He who now says 'Nothing has happened to me' is a blockhead.

204

End and goal. Not every end is the goal. The end of a melody is not its goal, and yet if a melody has not reached its end, it has also not reached its goal. A parable.

205

Neutrality of nature on a grand scale. The neutrality of Nature on a grand scale (in mountain, sea, forest, and desert) is pleasing, but only for a brief space. Afterwards we become impatient. 'Have they all nothing to say to *us*? Do *we* not exist so far as they are concerned?' There arises a feeling that a *lèse-majesté* is committed against humanity.

206

Forgetting our purpose. In a journey we commonly forget its goal. Almost every vocation is chosen and entered upon as means to an end, but is continued as the ultimate end. Forgetting our purpose is the most frequent form of folly.

207

Solar orbit of an idea. When an idea is just rising on the horizon, the soul's temperature is usually very low. Gradually the idea develops in warmth, and is hottest (that is to say, exerts its greatest influence) when belief in the idea is already on the wane.

208

How to have every man against you. If someone now dared to say, 'He that is not for me is against me', he would at once have all against him. This sentiment does credit to our era

209

Being ashamed of wealth. Our age endures only a single species of rich men – those who are ashamed of their wealth. If we hear it said of anyone that he is very rich, we at once feel a similar sentiment to that experienced at the sight of a repulsively swollen invalid, one suffering from diabetes or dropsy. We must with an effort remember our humanity, in order to go about with this rich man in such a way that he does not notice our feeling of disgust. But as soon as he prides himself at all on his wealth, our feelings are mingled with an almost compassionate surprise at such a high degree of human unreason. We would fain raise our hands to heaven and cry, 'Poor deformed and overburdened creature, fettered a hundredfold, to whom every hour brings or may bring something unpleasant, in whose frame twitches every event that occurs in scores of countries, how can you make us believe that you feel at ease in your position? If you appear anywhere in public, we know that it is a sort of running the gauntlet amid countless glances that have for you only cold hate or importunity or silent scorn. You may earn more easily than others, but it is only a superfluous earning, which brings little joy, and the guarding of what you have earned is now, at any rate, a more troublesome business than any toilsome process of earning. You are continually suffering, because you are continually losing. What avails it you that they are always injecting you with fresh artificial blood? That does not relieve the pain of those cupping-glasses that are fixed, for ever fixed, on your neck! – But, to be quite fair to you, it is difficult or perhaps impossible for you *not* to be rich. You *must* guard, you *must* earn more; the inherited bent of your character is the yoke fastened upon you. But do not on that account deceive us – be honestly and visibly ashamed of the yoke you wear, as in your soul you are weary and unwilling to wear it. This shame is no disgrace.'

210

Extravagant presumptions. There are men so presumptuous that they can only praise a greatness which they publicly admire by representing it as steps and bridges that lead to themselves.

211

On the soil of insult. He who wishes to deprive men of a conception is generally not satisfied with refuting it and drawing out of it the illogical worm that resides within. Rather, when the worm has been killed, does he throw the whole fruit as well into the mire, in order to make it ignoble in men's sight and to inspire disgust. Thus he thinks that he has found a means of making the usual 'third-day resurrection' of conceptions an impossibility. He is wrong, for on the very soil of insult, in the midst of the filth, the kernel of the conception soon produces new seeds. The right thing then, is not to scorn and bespatter what one wishes finally to remove, but to lay it tenderly on ice again and again, having regard to the fact that conceptions are very tenacious of life. Here we must act according to the maxim: 'One refutation is no refutation.'

212

The lot of morality. Since spiritual bondage is being relaxed, morality (the inherited, traditional, instinctive mode of action in accordance with moral sentiments) is surely also on the decline. This, however, is not the case with the individual virtues, moderation, justice, repose; for the greatest freedom of the conscious intellect leads at some time, even unconsciously, back to these virtues, and then enjoins their practice as expedient.

213

The fanatic of distrust and his surety. The Elder: You wish to make the tremendous venture and instruct mankind in the great things? What is your surety?

Pyrrho: It is this: I intend to warn men against myself; I intend to confess all the defects of my character quite openly, and reveal to the world my hasty conclusions, my contradictions, and my foolish blunders. 'Do not listen to me,' I will say to them, 'until I have become equal to the meanest among you, nay am even less than he. Struggle against truth as long as you can, from your disgust with her advocate. I shall be your seducer and betrayer if you find in me the slightest glimmering of respectability and dignity.'

The Elder: You promise too much; you cannot bear this burden.

Pyrrho: Then I will tell men even that, and say that I am too weak, and cannot keep my promise. The greater my unworthiness, the more will they mistrust the truth, when it passes through my lips.

The Elder: You propose to teach distrust of truth?

Pyrrho: Yes; distrust as it never was yet on earth, distrust of anything and everything. This is the only road to truth. The right eye must not trust the left eye, and for some time light must be called darkness: this is the path that you must tread. Do not imagine that it will lead you to fruit trees and fair pastures. You will find on this road little hard grains — these are truths. For years and years you will have to swallow handfuls of lies, so as not to die of hunger, although you know that they are lies. But those grains will be sown and planted, and perhaps, perhaps some day will come the harvest. No one may *promise* that day, unless he be a fanatic.

The Elder: Friend, friend! Your words too are those of a fanatic!

Pyrrho: You are right! I will be distrustful of all words.

The Elder: Then you will have to be silent.

Pyrrho: I shall tell men that I have to be silent, and that they are to mistrust my silence.

The Elder: So you draw back from your undertaking?

Pyrrho: On the contrary – you have shown me the door through which I must pass.

The Elder: I don't know whether we yet completely understand each other?

Pyrrho: Probably not.

The Elder: If only you understand yourself!

[*Pyrrho turns round and laughs*]

The Elder: Ah, friend! Silence and laughter – is that now your whole philosophy?

Pyrrho: There might be a worse.

214

European books. In reading Montaigne, La Rochefoucauld, La Bruyère, Fontenelle (especially the *Dialogues des Morts*), Vauvenargues, and Chamfort we are nearer to antiquity than in any group of six authors of other nations. Through these six the spirit of the last centuries before Christ has once more come into being, and they collectively form an important link in the great and still continuous chain of the Renaissance. Their books are raised above all changes of national taste and philosophical nuances from which as a rule every book takes and must take its hue in order to become famous. They contain more real ideas than all the books of German philosophers put together: ideas of the sort that breed ideas – I am at a loss how to define to the end: enough to say that they appear to me writers who wrote neither for children nor for visionaries, neither for virgins nor for Christians, neither for Germans nor for – I am again at a loss how to finish my list. To praise them in plain terms, I may say that had they been written in Greek, they would have been understood by Greeks. How much, on the other hand, would even a Plato have understood of the writings of our best German thinkers – Goethe and Schopenhauer, for instance – to say nothing of the repugnance that he would have felt to their style, particularly to its obscure, exaggerated, and occasionally dry-as-dust elements? And these are defects from which these two among German thinkers suffer least and yet far too much (Goethe as thinker was fonder than he should have been of embracing the cloud, and Schopenhauer almost constantly wanders, not with impunity, among symbols of objects rather than among the objects themselves). On the other hand, what clearness and graceful precision there is in these Frenchmen! The Greeks, whose ears were most refined, could not but have approved of this art, and one quality they would even have admired and reverenced – the French verbal wit: they were extremely fond of this quality, without being particularly strong in it themselves.

215

Fashion and modernity. Wherever ignorance, uncleanness, and superstition are still rife, where communication is backward, agriculture poor, and the priesthood powerful, national costumes are still worn. Fashion, on the other hand, rules where the opposite conditions prevail. Fashion is accordingly to be found next to the virtues in modern Europe. Are we to call it their seamy side? – Masculine dress that is fashionable and no longer national proclaims of its wearer: firstly, that he does not wish to appear as an individual or as member of a class or race; that he has made an intentional suppression of these kinds of vanity a law unto himself: secondly, that he is a worker, and has little time for dressing and self-adornment, and moreover regards anything expensive or luxurious in material and cut as out of harmony with his work: lastly, that by his clothes he indicates the more learned and intellectual callings as those to which he stands or would like to stand nearest as a European – whereas such national costumes as still exist would exhibit the occupations of brigand, shepherd, and soldier as the most desirable and distinguished. Within this general character of masculine fashion exist the slight fluctuations demanded by the vanity of young men, the dandies and dawdlers of our great cities – in other words, Europeans who have not yet reached maturity. European women are as yet far less mature, and for this reason the fluctuations with them are much greater. They also will not have the national costume, and hate to be recognised by their dress as German, French, or Russian. They are, however, very desirous of creating an impression as individuals. Then, too, their dress must leave no one in doubt that they belong to one of the more reputable classes of society (to 'good' or 'high' or 'great' society), and on this score their pretensions are all the greater if they belong scarcely or not at all to that class. Above all, the young woman does not want to wear what an older woman wears, because she thinks she loses her market value if she is suspected of being somewhat advanced in years. The older woman, on the other hand, would like to deceive the world as long as possible by a youthful garb. From this competition must continually arise temporary fashions, in which the youthful element is unmistakably and inimitably apparent. But after the inventive genius of the young female artists has run riot for some time in such indiscreet revelations of youth (or rather, after the inventive genius of older, courtly civilisations and of still existing peoples – in fact, of the whole world of dress – has been pressed into the service, and, say, the Spaniards, Turks, and ancient Greeks have been yoked together for the glorification of fair flesh), then they at last discover, time and again, that they have not been good judges of their own interest; that if they wish to have power over men the game of hide-and-seek with the beautiful body is more likely to win than naked or half-naked honesty. And then the wheel of taste and vanity turns once more in an opposite direction. The rather older young women find that their kingdom has come, and the competition of the dear, absurd creatures rages again from the beginning. But the more women advance mentally, and no longer among themselves concede the pre-eminence to an unripe age, the smaller their fluctuations of costume grow and the less elaborate their adornment. A just verdict in this respect must not be based on ancient models – in other words, not on the standard of the dress of women who dwell on the shores of the Mediterranean – but must have an eye to the climatic conditions of the central and northern regions, where the intellectual and creative spirit of Europe now finds its most natural home. Generally speaking, therefore, it is not change that will be the characteristic mark of fashion and modernity, for change is retrograde, and betokens the still unripened men and women of Europe; but rather the repudiation of national, social, and individual vanity. Accordingly, it is commendable, because involving a saving of time and strength, if certain cities and districts of Europe think and invent for all the rest in the matter of dress, in view of the fact that a sense of form does not seem to have been bestowed upon all. Nor is it really an excessive ambition, so long as these fluctuations still exist, for Paris, for example, to claim to be the sole inventor and innovator in this sphere. If a German, from hatred of these claims on the part of a French city, wishes to dress differently – as, for example, in the Dürer style – let him reflect that he then has a costume which the Germans of olden times wore, but which the Germans have not in the slightest degree invented. For there has never been a style of dress that characterised the German as a German. Moreover, let him observe how he looks in his costume, and whether his altogether modern face, with all its hues and wrinkles, does not raise a protest against a Dürer fashion of dress. Here, where the concepts 'modern' and 'European' are almost identical, we understand by 'Europe' a far wider region than is embraced by the Europe of geography, the little peninsula of Asia. In particular, we must include America, in so far as America is the daughter of our civilisation. On the other hand, not all Europe falls under the heading of cultured 'Europe', but only those nations and divisions of nations which have their common past in Greece, Rome, Judaism, and Christianity.

216

'German virtue'. There is no denying that from the end of the eighteenth century a current of moral awakening flowed through Europe. Then only Virtue found again the power of speech. She learnt to discover the unrestrained gestures of exaltation and emotion, she was no longer ashamed of herself, and she created philosophies and poems for her own glorification. If we look for the sources of this current, we come upon Rousseau, but the mythical Rousseau, the phantom formed from the impression left by his writings (one might almost say again, his mythically inter-preted writings) and by the indications that he provided himself. He and his public constantly worked at the fashioning of this ideal figure. The other origin lies in the resurrection of the Stoical side of Rome's greatness, whereby the French so nobly carried on the task of the Renaissance. With striking success they proceeded from the reproduction of antique forms to the reproduction of antique characters. Thus they may always claim a title to the highest honours, as the nation which has hitherto given the modern world its best books and its best men. How this twofold archetype, the mythical Rousseau and the resurrected spirit of Rome, affected France's weaker neighbours, is particularly noticeable in Germany, which, in consequence of her novel and quite unwonted impulse to seriousness and loftiness in will and self-control, finally came to feel astonishment at her own new-found virtue, and launched into the world the concept 'German virtue', as if this were the most

original and hereditary of her possessions. The first great men who transfused into their own blood that French impulse towards greatness and consciousness of the moral will were more honest, and more grateful. Whence comes the moralism of Kant? He is continually reminding us: from Rousseau and the revival of Stoic Rome. The moralism of Schiller has the same source and the same glorification of the source. The moralism of Beethoven in notes is a continual song in praise of Rousseau, the antique French, and Schiller. 'Young Germany' was the first to forget its gratitude, because in the meantime people had listened to the preachers of hatred of the French. The 'young German' came to the fore with more consciousness than is generally allowed to youths. When he investigated his paternity, he might well think of the proximity of Schiller, Schleiermacher, and Fichte. But he should have looked for his grandfathers in Paris and Geneva, and it was very short-sighted of him to believe what he believed: that virtue was not more than thirty years old. People became used to demanding that the word 'German' should connote 'virtue', and this process has not been wholly forgotten to this day. Be it observed further that this moral awakening, as may almost be guessed, has resulted only in drawbacks and obstacles to the *recognition* of moral phenomena. What is the entire German philosophy, starting from Kant, with all its French, English, and Italian offshoots and by-products? A semi-theological attack upon Helvetius, a rejection of the slowly and laboriously acquired views and signposts of the right road, which in the end he collected and expressed so well. To this day Helvetius is the best-abused of all good moralists and good men in Germany.

217

Classic and Romantic. Both classically and romantically minded spirits – two species that always exist – cherish a vision of the future; but the former derive their vision from the strength of their time, the latter from its weakness.

218

The machine as teacher. Machinery teaches in itself the dovetailed working of masses of men, in activities where each has but one thing to do. It is the model of party organisations and of warfare.

On the other hand, it does not teach individual self-glorification, for it makes of the many a machine, and of each individual a tool for one purpose. Its most general effect is to teach the advantage of centralisation.

219

Unable to settle. One likes to live in a small town. But from time to time just this small town drives us out into bare and lonely Nature, especially when we think we know it too well. Finally, in order to refresh ourselves from Nature, we go to the big town. A few draughts from this cup and we see its dregs, and the circle begins afresh, with the small town as starting-point. So the moderns live; they are in all things rather too thorough to be able to settle like the men of other days.

220

Reaction against the civilisation of machinery. The machine, itself a product of the highest mental powers, sets in motion hardly any but the lower, unthinking forces of the men who serve it. True, it unfetters a vast quantity of force which would otherwise lie dormant. But it does not communicate the impulse to climb higher, to improve, to become artistic. It creates activity and monotony, but this in the long run produces a counter-effect, a despairing *ennui* of the soul, which through machinery has learnt to hanker after the variety of leisure.

221

The danger of enlightenment. All the half-insane, theatrical, bestially cruel, licentious, and especially sentimental and self-intoxicating elements which go to form the true revolutionary substance, and became flesh and spirit, before the revolution, in Rousseau – all this composite being, with factitious enthusiasm, finally set even 'enlightenment' upon its fanatical head, which thereby began itself to shine as in an illuminating halo. Yet, enlightenment is essentially foreign to that phenomenon, and, if left to itself, would have pierced silently through the clouds like a shaft of light, long content to transfigure individuals alone, and thus only slowly transfiguring national customs and institutions as well. But now, bound hand and foot to a violent and abrupt monster, enlightenment itself became violent and abrupt. Its danger has therefore become almost greater than its useful quality of liberation and illumination, which it introduced into the great revolutionary movement. Whoever grasps this will also know from what confusion it has to be extricated, from what impurities to be cleansed, in order that it may then by itself continue the work of enlightenment and also nip the revolution in the bud and nullify its effects.

222

Passion in the Middle Ages. The Middle Ages are the period of great passions. Neither antiquity nor our modern age possesses this widening of the soul. Never was the capacity of the soul greater or measured by larger standards. The physical, primeval sensuality of the barbarian races and the over-soulful, over-vigilant, over-brilliant eyes of Christian mystics, the most childish and youthful and the most over-ripe and world-weary, the savageness of the beast of prey and the effeminacy and excessive refinement of the late antique spirit – all these elements were then not seldom united in one and the same person. Thus, if a man was seized by a passion, the rapidity of the torrent must have been greater, the whirl more confused, the fall deeper than ever before. We modern men may be content to feel that we have suffered a loss here.

223

Robbing and saving. All intellectual movements whereby the great may hope to rob and the small to save are sure to prosper. That is why, for instance, the German Reformation made progress.

224

Gladsome souls. When even a remote hint of drink, drunkenness, and an evil-smelling kind of jocularity was given, the souls of the old Germans waxed gladsome. Otherwise they were depressed, but here they found something they really understood.

225

Debauchery at Athens. Even when the fish-market of Athens acquired its thinkers and poets, Greek debauchery had a more idyllic and refined appearance than Roman or German debauchery ever had.

The voice of Juvenal would have sounded there like a hollow trumpet, and would have been answered by a good-natured and almost childish outburst of laughter.

226

Cleverness of the Greek. As the desire for victory and pre-eminence is an ineradicable trait of human nature, older and more primitive than any respect of or joy in equality, the Greek State sanctioned gymnastic and artistic competitions among equals. In other words, it marked out an arena where this impulse to conquer would find a vent without jeopardising the political order. With the final decline of gymnastic and artistic contests the Greek State fell into a condition of profound unrest and dissolution.

227

The 'eternal Epicurus'. Epicurus has lived in all periods, and lives yet, unbeknown to those who called and still call themselves Epicureans, and without repute among philosophers. He has himself even forgotten his own name – that was the heaviest luggage that he ever cast off.

228

The style of superiority. 'University slang', the speech of the German students, has its origin among the students who do not study. The latter know how to acquire a preponderance over their more serious fellows by exposing all the farcical elements of culture, respectability, erudition, order, and moderation, and by having words taken from these realms always on their lips, like the better and more learned students, but with malice in their glance and an accompanying grimace. This language of superiority – the only one that is original in Germany – is nowadays unconsciously used by statesmen and newspaper critics as well. It is a continual process of ironical quotation, a restless, cantankerous squinting of the eye right and left, a language of inverted commas and grimaces.

229

The recluse. We retire into seclusion, but not from personal misgivings, as if the political and social conditions of the day did not satisfy us; rather because by our retirement we try to save and collect forces which will some day be urgently needed by culture, the more this present is *this present,* and, as such, fulfils its task. We form a capital and try to make it secure, but, as in times of real danger, our method is to bury our hoard.

230

Tyrants of the intellect. In our times, anyone who expressed a single moral trait so thoroughly as the characters of Theophrastus and Molière do, would be considered ill, and be spoken of as possessing 'a fixed idea'. The Athens of the third century, if we could visit it, would appear to us populated by fools. Nowadays the democracy of ideas rules in every brain – there the multitude collectively is lord. A single idea that tried to be lord is now called, as above stated, 'a fixed idea'. This is our method of murdering tyrants – we hint at the madhouse.

231

A most dangerous emigration. In Russia there is an emigration of the intelligence. People cross the frontier in order to read and write good books. Thus, however, they are working towards turning their country, abandoned by the intellect, into a gaping Asiatic maw, which would fain swallow our little Europe.

232

Political fools. The almost religious love of the king was transferred by the Greeks, when the monarchy was abolished, to the *polis.* An idea can be loved more than a person, and does not thwart the lover so often as a beloved human being (for the more men know themselves to be loved, the less considerate they usually become, until they are no longer worthy of love, and a rift really arises). Hence the reverence for State and *polis* was greater than the reverence for princes had ever been. The Greeks are the political fools of ancient history – today other nations boast that distinction.

233

Against neglect of the eyes. Might one not find among the cultured classes of England, who read the *Times*, a decline in their powers of sight every ten years?

234

Great works and great faith. One man had great works, but his comrade had great faith in these works. They were inseparable, but obviously the former was entirely dependent upon the latter.

235

The sociable man. 'I don't get on well with myself', said someone in explanation of his fondness for society. 'Society has a stronger digestion than I have, and can put up with me.'

236

Shutting the mind's eyes. If we are practised and accustomed to reflect upon our actions, we must nevertheless close the inner eye while performing an action (be this even only writing letters or eating or drinking). Even in conversation with average people we must know how to obscure our own mental vision in order to attain and grasp average thinking. This shutting of the eyes is a conscious act and can be achieved by the will.

237

The most terrible revenge. If we wish to take a thorough revenge upon an opponent, we must wait until we have our hand quite full of truths and equities, and can calmly use the whole lot against him. Hence the exercise of revenge may be identified with the exercise of equity. It is the most terrible kind of revenge, for there is no higher court to which an appeal can be made. Thus did Voltaire revenge himself on Piron, with five lines that sum up Piron's whole life, work, and character: every word is a truth. So too he revenged himself upon Frederick the Great in a letter to him from Ferney.

238

Taxes of luxury. In shops we buy the most necessary and urgent things, and have to pay very dear, because we pay as well for what is also to be had there cheap, but seldom finds a customer – articles of luxury that minister to pleasure. Thus luxury lays a constant tax upon the man of simple life who does without luxuries.

239

Why beggars still live. If all alms were given only out of compassion, the whole tribe of beggars would long since have died of starvation.

240

Why beggars still live. The greatest of almsgivers is cowardice.

241

How the thinker makes use of a conversation. Without being eavesdroppers, we can hear a good deal if we are able to see well, and at the same time to let ourselves occasionally get out of our own sight. But people do not know how to make use of a conversation. They pay far too much attention to what *they* want to say and reply, whereas the true listener is often contented to make a provisional answer and to say something merely as a payment on account of politeness, but on the other hand, with his memory lurking in ambush, carries away with him all that the other said, together with his tones and gestures in speaking. In ordinary conversation everyone thinks *he* is the leader, just as if two ships, sailing side by side and giving each other a slight push here and there, were each firmly convinced that the other ship was following or even being towed.

242

The art of excusing oneself. If someone excuses himself to us, he has to make out a very good case, otherwise we readily come to feel ourselves the culprits, and experience an unpleasant emotion.

243

Impossible intercourse. The ship of your thoughts goes too deep for you to be able to travel with it in the waters of these friendly, decorous, obliging people. There are too many shallows and sandbanks: you would have to tack and turn, and would find yourself continually at your wits' end, and they would soon also be in perplexity as to *your* perplexity, the reason for which they cannot divine.

244

The fox of foxes. A true fox not only calls sour the grapes he cannot reach, but also those he has reached and snatched from the grasp of others.

245

In intimate intercourse. However closely men are connected, there are still all the four quarters of the heavens in their common horizon, and at times they become aware of this fact.

246

The silence of disgust. Behold! someone undergoes a thorough and painful transformation as thinker and human being, and makes a public avowal of the change. And those who hear him see nothing, and still believe he is the same as before! This common experience has already disgusted many writers. They had rated the intellectuality of mankind too highly, and made a vow to be silent as soon as they became aware of their mistake.

247

Business seriousness. The business of many rich and eminent men is their form of recreation from too long periods of habitual leisure. They then become as serious and impassioned as other people do in their rare moments of leisure and amusement.

248

The eye's double sense. Just as a sudden scaly ripple runs over the waters at your feet, so there are similar sudden uncertainties and ambiguities in the human eye. They lead to the question: is it a shudder, or a smile, or both?

249

Positive and negative. This thinker needs no one to refute him – he is quite capable of doing that himself.

250

The revenge of the empty nets. Above all we should beware of those who have the bitter feeling of the fisherman who after a hard day's work comes home in the evening with nets empty.

251

Non-assertion of our rights. The exertion of power is laborious and demands courage. That is why so many do not assert their most valid rights, because their rights are a kind of power, and they are too lazy or too cowardly to exercise them. *Indulgence* and *patience* are the names given to the virtues that cloak these faults.

252

Bearers of light. In society there would be no sunshine if the born flatterers (I mean the so-called amiable people) did not bring some in with them.

253

When most benevolent. When a man has been highly honoured and has eaten a little, he is most benevolent.

254

To the light. Men press forward to the light not in order to see better but to shine better. The person before whom we shine we gladly allow to be called a light.

255

The hypochondriac. The hypochondriac is a man who has just enough intellect and pleasure in the intellect to take his sorrows, his losses, and his mistakes seriously. But the field on which he grazes is too small: he crops it so close that in the end he has to look for single stalks. Thus he finally becomes envious and avaricious – and only then is he unbearable.

256

Giving in return. Hesiod advises us to give the neighbour who has helped us good measure and, if possible, fuller measure in return, as soon as we have the power. For this is where the neighbour's pleasure comes in, since his former benevolence brings him interest. Moreover, he who gives in return also has his pleasure, inasmuch as, by giving a little more than he got, he redeems the slight humiliation of being compelled to seek aid.

257

More subtle than is necessary. Our sense of observation for how far others perceive our weaknesses is much more subtle than our sense of observation for the weaknesses of others. It follows that the first-named sense is more subtle than is necessary.

258

A kind of bright shadows. Close to the nocturnal type of man we almost regularly find, as if bound up with him, a bright soul. This is, as it were, the negative shadow cast by the former.

259

Not to take revenge. There are so many subtle sorts of revenge that one who has occasion to take revenge can really do or omit to do what he likes. In any case, the whole world will agree, after a time, that he *has* avenged himself. Hence the avoidance of revenge is hardly within man's power. He must not even so much as say that he does not *want* to do so, since the contempt for revenge is interpreted and felt as a sublime and exquisite form of revenge. It follows that we must do nothing superfluous.

260

The mistake of those who pay homage. Everyone thinks he is paying a most agreeable compliment to a thinker when he says that he himself hit upon exactly the same idea and even upon the same expression. The thinker, however, is seldom delighted at hearing such news, nay, rather, he often becomes distrustful of his own thoughts and expressions. He silently resolves to revise both some day. If we wish to pay homage to anyone, we must beware of expressing our agreement, for this puts us on the same level. Often it is a matter of social tact to listen to an opinion as if it were not ours or even travelled beyond the limits of our own horizon – as, for example, when an old man once in a while opens the store-house of his acquired knowledge.

261

Letters. A letter is an unannounced visit, and the postman is the intermediary of impolite surprises. Every week we ought to have one hour for receiving letters, and then go and take a bath.

262

Prejudiced. Someone said: I have been prejudiced against myself from childhood upwards, and hence I find some truth in every censure and some absurdity in every eulogy. Praise I generally value too low and blame too high.

263

The path to equality. A few hours of mountain-climbing make a blackguard and a saint two rather similar creatures. Weariness is the shortest path to equality and fraternity – and finally liberty is bestowed by sleep.

264

Calumny. If we begin to trace to its source a real scandalous misrepresentation, we shall rarely look for its origin in our honourable and straightforward enemies; for if they invented anything of the sort about us, they, as being our enemies, would gain no credence. Those, however, to whom for a time we have been most useful, but who, from some reason or other, may be secretly sure that they will obtain no more from us – such persons are in a position to start the ball of slander rolling.. They gain credence, firstly, because it is assumed that they would invent nothing likely to do them damage; secondly, because they have learnt to know us intimately. As a consolation, the much-slandered man may say to himself: calumnies are diseases of others that break out in your body. They prove that society is a (moral) organism, so that you can prescribe to *yourself* the cure that will in the end be useful to others.

265

The child's kingdom of heaven. The happiness of a child is as much of a myth as the happiness of the Hyperboreans of whom the Greeks fabled. The Greeks supposed that, if indeed happiness dwells anywhere on our earth, it must certainly dwell as far as possible from us, perhaps over yonder at the edge of the world. Old people have the same thought – if man is at all capable of being happy, he must be happy as far as possible from our age, at the frontiers and beginnings of life. For many a man the sight of children, through the veil of this myth, is the greatest happiness that he can feel. He enters himself into the forecourt of heaven when he says, 'Suffer the little children to come unto me, for of them is the kingdom of heaven.' The myth of the child's kingdom of heaven holds good, in some way or other, wherever in the modern world some sentimentality exists.

266

The impatient. It is just the growing man who does not want things in the growing stage. He is too impatient for that. The youth will not wait until, after long study, suffering, and privation, his picture of men and things is complete. Accordingly, he confidently accepts another picture that lies ready to his hand and is recommended to him, and pins his faith to that, as if it must give him at once the lines and colours of his own painting. He presses a philosopher or a poet to his bosom, and must from that time forth perform long stretches of forced labour and renounce his own self. He learns much in the process, but he often forgets what is most worth learning and knowing – his self. He remains all his life a partisan. Ah, a vast amount of tedious work has to be done before you find your own colours, your own brush, your own canvas! – Even then you are very far from being a master in the art of life, but at least you are the boss in your own workshop.

267

There are no teachers. As thinkers we ought only to speak of self-teaching. The instruction of the young by others is either an experiment performed upon something as yet unknown and unknowable, or else a thorough levelling process, in order to make the new member of society conform to the customs and manners that prevail for the time being. In both cases the result is accordingly unworthy of a thinker – the handiwork of parents and teachers, whom some valiantly honest person has called '*nos ennemis naturels*'.* One day, when, as the world thinks, we have long since finished our education, we *discover ourselves*. Then begins the task of the thinker, and then is the time to summon him to our aid – not as a teacher, but as a self-taught man who has experience.

* Stendhal: 'our natural enemies'.

268

Sympathy with youth. We are sorry when we hear that someone who is still young is losing his teeth or growing blind. If we knew all the irrevocable and hopeless feelings hidden in his whole being, how great our sorrow would be! Why do we really suffer on this account? Because youth has to continue the work we have undertaken, and every flaw and failing in its strength is likely to injure *our* work, that will fall into its hands. It is the sorrow at the imperfect guarantee of our immortality: or, if we only feel ourselves as executors of the human mission, it is the sorrow that this mission must pass to weaker hands than ours.

269

The ages of life. The comparison of the four ages of life with the four seasons of the year is a venerable piece of folly. Neither the first twenty nor the last twenty years of a life correspond to a season of the year, assuming that we are not satisfied with drawing a parallel between white hair and snow and similar colour-analogies. The first twenty years are a preparation for life in general, for the whole year of life, a sort of long New Year's Day. The last twenty review, assimilate, bring into union and harmony all that has been experienced till then: as, in a small degree, we do on every New Year's Eve with the whole past year. But in between there really lies an interval which suggests a comparison with the seasons – the time from the twentieth to the fiftieth year (to speak here of decades in the lump, while it is an understood thing that everyone must refine for himself these rough outlines). Those three decades correspond to three seasons – summer, spring, and autumn. Winter human life has none, unless we like to call the (unfortunately) often intervening hard, cold, lonely, hopeless, unfruitful periods of disease the winters of man. The twenties, hot, oppressive, stormy, impetuous, exhausting years, when we praise the day in the evening, when it is over, as we wipe the sweat from our foreheads – years in which work seems to us cruel but necessary – these twenties are the summer of life. The thirties, on the other hand, are its spring-time, with the air now too warm, now too cold, ever restless and stimulating, bubbling sap, bloom of leaves, fragrance of buds everywhere, many delightful mornings and evenings, work to which the song of birds awakens us, a true work of the heart, a kind of joy in our own robustness, strengthened by the savour of hopeful anticipation. Lastly the forties, mysterious like all that is stationary, like a high, broad plateau, traversed by a fresh breeze, with a clear, cloudless sky above it, which always has the same gentle look all day and half the night – the time of harvest and cordial gaiety – that is the autumn of life.

270

Women's intellect in modern society. What women nowadays think of men's intellect may be divined from the fact that in their art of adornment they think of anything but of emphasising the intellectual side of their faces or their single intellectual features. On the contrary, they conceal such traits, and understand, for example by an arrangement of their hair over their forehead, how to give themselves an appearance of vivid, eager sensuality and materialism, just when they but slightly possess those qualities. Their conviction that intellect in women frightens men goes so far that they even gladly deny the keenness of the most intellectual sense and purposely invite the reputation of short-sightedness. They think they will thereby make men more confiding. It is as if a soft, attractive twilight were spreading itself around them.

271

Great and transitory. What moves the observer to tears is the rapturous look of happiness with which a fair young bride gazes upon her husband. We feel all the melancholy of autumn in thinking of the greatness and of the transitoriness of human happiness.

272

Sense and sacrifice. Many a woman has the *intelletto del sacrifizio*,* and no longer enjoys life when her husband refuses to sacrifice her. With all her wit, she then no longer knows – whither? and without perceiving it, is changed from sacrificial victim to sacrificial priest.

273

The unfeminine. 'Stupid as a man,' say the women; 'Cowardly as a woman,' say the men. Stupidity in a woman is unfeminine.

* cf. the Jesuit maxim '*sacrifizio dell' intelletto*'.

274

Masculine and feminine temperament and mortality. That the male sex
has a worse temperament than the female follows from the fact that
male children have a greater mortality than female, clearly because
they 'leap out of their skins' more easily. Their wildness and
unbearableness soon make all the bad stuff in them deadly.

275

The age of Cyclopean building. The democratisation of Europe is a
resistless force. Even he who would stem the tide uses those very
means that democratic thought first put into men's hands, and he
makes these means more handy and workable. The most inveterate enemies of democracy (I mean the spirits of upheaval) seem
only to exist in order, by the fear that they inspire, to drive forward
the different parties faster and faster on the democratic course.
Now we may well feel sorry for those who are working consciously and honourably for this future. There is something dreary
and monotonous in their faces, and the grey dust seems to have
been wafted into their very brains. Nevertheless, posterity may
possibly some day laugh at our anxiety, and see in the democratic
work of several generations what we see in the building of stone
dams and walls – an activity that necessarily covers clothes and
face with a great deal of dust, and perhaps unavoidably makes the
workmen, too, a little dull-witted; but who would on that account
desire such work undone? It seems that the democratisation of
Europe is a link in the chain of those mighty prophylactic principles which are the thought of the modern era, and whereby we
rise up in revolt against the Middle Ages. Now, and now only, is
the age of Cyclopean building! A final security in the foundations,
that the future may build on them without danger! Henceforth, an
impossibility of the orchards of culture being once more destroyed
overnight by wild, senseless mountain torrents! Dams and walls
against barbarians, against plagues, against physical and spiritual
serfdom! And all this understood at first roughly and literally, but
gradually in an ever higher and more spiritual sense, so that all the
principles here indicated may appear as the intellectual preparation
of the highest artist in horticulture, who can only apply himself to
his own task when the other is fully accomplished! – True, if we

consider the long intervals of time that here lie between means and end, the great, supreme labour, straining the powers and brains of centuries, that is necessary in order to create or to provide each individual means, we must not bear too hardly upon the workers of the present when they loudly proclaim that the wall and the fence are already the end and the final goal. After all, no one yet sees the gardener and the fruit, for whose sake the fence exists.

276

The right of universal suffrage. The people has not granted itself universal suffrage but, wherever this is now in force, it has received and accepted it as a temporary measure. But in any case the people has the right to restore the gift, if it does not satisfy its anticipations. This dissatisfaction seems universal nowadays, for when, at any occasion where the vote is exercised, scarce two-thirds, nay perhaps not even the majority of all voters, go to the polls, that very fact is a vote against the whole suffrage system. On this point, in fact, we must pronounce a much sterner verdict. A law that enacts that the majority shall decide as to the welfare of all cannot be built up on the foundation that it alone has provided, for it is bound to require a far broader foundation, namely the unanimity of all. Universal suffrage must not only be the expression of the will of a majority, but of the whole country. Thus the dissent of a very small minority is already enough to set aside the system as impracticable; and the abstention from voting is in fact a dissent of this kind, which ruins the whole institution. The 'absolute veto' of the individual, or – not to be too minute – the veto of a few thousands, hangs over the system as the consequence of justice. On every occasion when it is employed, the system must, according to the variety of the division, first prove that it has still a right to exist.

277

False conclusions. What false conclusions are drawn in spheres where we are not at home, even by those of us who are accustomed as men of science to draw right conclusions! It is humiliating! Now it is clear that in the great turmoil of worldly doings, in political affairs, in all sudden and urgent matters such as almost every day brings up, these false conclusions must decide. For no one feels at home with novelties that have sprung up in the night. All political work, even with great statesmen, is an improvisation that trusts to luck.

278

Premises of the age of machinery. The press, the machine, the railway, the telegraph are premises of which no one has yet dared to draw the conclusions that will follow in a thousand years.

279

A drag upon culture. When we are told that here men have no time for productive occupations, because military manœuvres and processions take up their days, and the rest of the population must feed and clothe them, their dress, however, being striking, often gay and full of absurdities; that there only a few distinguished qualities are recognised, individuals resemble each other more than elsewhere, or at any rate are treated as equals, yet obedience is exacted and yielded without reasoning, for men command and make no attempt to convince; that here punishments are few, but these few cruel and likely to become the final and most terrible; that there treason ranks as the capital offence, and even the criticism of evils is only ventured on by the most audacious; that there, again, human life is cheap, and ambition often takes the form of setting life in danger – when we hear all this, we at once say, 'This is a picture of a barbarous society that rests on a hazardous footing.' One man perhaps will add, 'It is a portrait of Sparta.' But another will become meditative and declare that this is a description of our modern military system, as it exists in the midst of our altogether different culture and society, a living anachronism, the picture, as above said, of a community resting on a hazardous footing; a posthumous work of the past, which can only act as a drag upon the wheels of the present. Yet at times even a drag upon culture is vitally necessary – that is to say, when culture is advancing too rapidly downhill or (as perhaps in this case) *uphill*.

280

More reverence for them that know. In the competition of production and sale the public is made judge of the product. But the public has no special knowledge, and judges by the appearance of the wares. In consequence, the art of appearance (and perhaps the taste for it) must increase under the dominance of competition, while on the other hand the quality of every product must deteriorate. The result will be – so far as reason does not fall in value – that one day an end will be put to that competition, and a new principle will win the day. Only the master of the craft should pronounce a verdict on the work, and the public should be dependent on the belief in the personality of the judge and his honesty. Accordingly, no anonymous work! At least an expert should be there as guarantor and pledge his name if the name of the creator is lacking or is unknown. The cheapness of an article is for the layman another kind of illusion and deceit, since only durability can decide that a thing is cheap and to what an extent. But it is difficult, and for a layman impossible, to judge of its durability. Hence that which produces an effect on the eye and costs little at present gains the advantage – this being naturally machine-made work. Again, machinery – that is to say, the cause of the greatest rapidity and facility in production – favours the most saleable kind of article. Otherwise it involves no tangible profit; it would be too little used and too often stand idle. But as to what is most saleable, the public, as above said, decides: it must be the most exchangeable – in other words, the thing that appears good and also appears cheap. Thus in the domain of labour our motto must also hold good: 'More respect for them that know!'

281

The danger of kings. Democracy has it in its power, without any violent means, and only by a lawful pressure steadily exerted, to make kingship and emperorship hollow, until only a zero remains, perhaps with the significance of every zero in that, while nothing in itself, it multiplies a number ten-fold if placed on the right side. Kingship and emperorship would remain a gorgeous ornament upon the simple and appropriate dress of democracy, a beautiful superfluity that democracy allows itself, a relic of all the historically venerable, primitive ornaments, nay the symbol of history itself, and in this unique position a highly effective thing if, as above said, it does not stand alone, but is put on the right side. In order to avoid the danger of this nullification, kings hold by their teeth to their dignity as war-lords. To this end they need wars, or in other words exceptional circumstances, in which that slow, lawful pressure of the democratic forces is relaxed.

282

The teacher a necessary evil. Let us have as few people as possible between the productive minds and the hungry and recipient minds! The middlemen almost unconsciously adulterate the food which they supply. For their work as middlemen they want too high a fee for themselves, and this is drawn from the original, productive spirits – namely, interest, admiration, leisure, money, and other advantages. Accordingly, we should always look upon the teacher as a necessary evil, just like the merchant; as an evil that we should make as small as possible. Perhaps the prevailing distress in Germany has its main cause in the fact that too many wish to live and live well by trade (in other words, desiring as far as possible to diminish prices for the producer and raise prices for the consumer, and thus to profit by the greatest possible loss to both). In the same way, we may certainly trace a main cause of the prevailing intellectual poverty in the superabundance of teachers. It is because of teachers that so little is learnt, and that so badly.

283

The tax of homage. Him whom we know and honour – be he physician, artist, or artisan – who does and produces something for us, we gladly pay as highly as we can, often a fee beyond our means. On the other hand, we pay the unknown as low a price as possible; here is a contest in which everyone struggles and makes others struggle for a foot's breadth of land. In the work of the known there is something that cannot be bought, the sentiment and ingenuity put into his work for our own sake. We think we cannot better express our sense of obligation than by a sort of sacrifice on our part. The heaviest tax is the tax of homage. The more competition prevails, the more we buy for the unknown and work for the unknown, the lower does this tax become, whereas it is really the standard for the loftiness of man's spiritual intercourse.

284

The means towards genuine peace. No government will nowadays admit that it maintains an army in order to satisfy occasionally its passion for conquest. The army is said to serve only defensive purposes. This morality, which justifies self-defence, is called in as the government's advocate. This means, however, reserving morality for ourselves and immorality for our neighbour, because he must be thought eager for attack and conquest if our state is forced to consider means of self-defence. At the same time, by our explanation of our need of an army (because he denies the lust of attack just as our state does, and ostensibly also maintains his army for defensive reasons), we proclaim him a hypocrite and cunning criminal, who would fain seize by surprise, without any fighting, a harmless and unwary victim. In this attitude all states face each other today. They presuppose evil intentions on their neighbour's part and good intentions on their own. This hypothesis, however, is an *inhuman* notion, as bad as and worse than war. Nay, at bottom it is a challenge and motive to war, foisting as it does upon the neighbouring state the charge of immorality, and thus provoking hostile intentions and acts. The doctrine of the army as a means of self-defence must be abjured as completely as the lust of conquest. Perhaps a memorable day will come when a nation renowned in wars and victories, distinguished by the highest development of military order and intelligence, and accustomed to make the heaviest sacrifice to these objects, will voluntarily exclaim, 'We will break our swords', and will destroy its whole military system, lock, stock, and barrel. Making ourselves defenceless (after having been the most strongly defended) from a loftiness of sentiment – that is the means towards genuine peace, which must always rest upon a pacific disposition. The so-called armed peace that prevails at present in all countries is a sign of a bellicose disposition, of a disposition that trusts neither itself nor its neighbour, and, partly from hate, partly from fear, refuses to lay down its weapons. Better to perish than to hate and fear, and twice as far better to perish than to make oneself hated and feared – this must some day become the supreme maxim of every political community! – Our liberal representatives of the people, as is well known, have not the time for reflection on the nature of humanity, or else they would know that they are working in vain when they work for 'a gradual diminution of the military burdens'. On the contrary, when the distress of these burdens is greatest, the sort of God who alone can help here will be nearest. The tree of military glory can only be destroyed at one swoop, with one stroke of lightning. But, as you know, lightning comes from the cloud and from above.

285

Whether property can be squared with justice. When the injustice of property is strongly felt (and the hand of the great clock is once more at this place), we formulate two methods of relieving this injustice: either an equal distribution, or an abolition of private possession and a return to State ownership. The latter method is especially dear to the hearts of our Socialists, who are angry with that primitive Jew for saying, 'Thou shalt not steal.' In their view the eighth commandment should rather run, 'Thou shalt not possess.' – The former method was frequently tried in antiquity, always indeed on a small scale, and yet with poor success. From this failure we too may learn. 'Equal plots of land' is easily enough said, but how much bitterness is aroused by the necessary division and separation, by the loss of time-honoured possessions, how much piety is wounded and sacrificed! We uproot the foundation of morality when we uproot boundary-stones. Again, how much fresh bitterness among the new owners, how much envy and looking askance! For there have never been two really equal plots of land, and if there were, man's envy of his neighbour would prevent him from believing in their equality. And how long would this equality, unhealthy and poisoned at the very roots, endure? In a few generations, by inheritance, here one plot would come to five owners, there five plots to one. Even supposing that men acquiesced in such abuses through the enactment of stern laws of inheritance, the same equal plots would indeed exist, but there would also be needy malcontents, owning nothing but dislike of their kinsmen and neighbours, and longing for a general upheaval. If, however, by the second method we try to restore ownership to the community and make the individual but a temporary tenant, we interfere with agriculture. For man is opposed to all that is only a transitory possession, unblessed with his own care and sacrifice. With such property he behaves in freebooter fashion, as robber or as worthless spendthrift. When Plato declares that self-seeking would be removed with the abolition of property, we may answer him that, if self-seeking be taken away, man will no longer possess the four cardinal virtues either; as we must say that the most deadly plague could not injure mankind so terribly as if vanity were one day to disappear. Without vanity and self-seeking what are human virtues? By this I am far from meaning that these virtues are but varied names and masks for these two qualities. Plato's Utopian refrain, which is still sung by Socialists, rests upon a deficient knowledge of men. He lacked the historical science of moral emotions, the insight into the origin of the good and useful characteristics of the human soul. He believed, like all antiquity, in good and evil as in black and white – that is to say, in a radical difference between good and bad men and good and bad qualities. In order that property may henceforth inspire more confidence and become more moral, we should keep open all the paths of work for small fortunes, but should prevent the effortless and sudden acquisition of wealth. Accordingly, we should take all the branches of transport and trade which favour the accumulation of large fortunes – especially, therefore, the money market – out of the hands of private persons or private companies, and look upon those who own too much, just as upon those who own nothing, as types fraught with danger to the community.

286

The value of labour. If we try to determine the value of labour by the amount of time, industry, good or bad will, constraint, inventiveness or laziness, honesty or make-believe bestowed upon it, the valuation can never be a just one. For the whole personality would have to be thrown into the scale, and this is impossible. Here the motto is, 'Judge not!' But after all the cry for justice is the cry we now hear from those who are dissatisfied with the present valuation of labour. If we reflect further we find every person non-responsible for his product, the labour; hence merit can never be derived therefrom, and every labour is as good or as bad as it must be through this or that necessary concatenation of forces and weaknesses, abilities and desires. The worker is not at liberty to say whether he shall work or not, or to decide how he shall work. Only the standpoints of usefulness, wider and narrower, have created the valuation of labour. What we at present call justice does very well in this sphere as a highly refined utility, which does not only consider the moment and exploit the immediate opportunity, but looks to the permanence of all conditions, and thus also keeps in view the well-being of the worker, his physical and spiritual contentment, in order that he and his posterity may work well for our posterity and become trustworthy for longer periods than the individual span of human life. The *exploitation* of the worker was, as we now understand, a piece of folly, a robbery at the expense of the future, a jeopardisation of society. We almost have the war now, and in any case the expense of maintaining peace, of concluding treaties and winning confidence, will henceforth be very great, because the folly of the exploiters was very great and long-lasting.

287

Of the study of the social body. The worst drawback for the modern student of economics and political science in Europe, and especially in Germany, is that the actual conditions, instead of exemplifying rules, illustrate exceptions or stages of transition and extinction. We must therefore learn to look beyond actually existing conditions and, for example, turn our eyes to distant North America, where we can still contemplate and investigate, if we will, the initial and normal movement of the social body. In Germany such a study requires arduous and historical research, or, as I have suggested, a telescope.

288

How far machinery humiliates. Machinery is impersonal; it robs the piece of work of its pride, of the individual merits and defects that cling to all work that is not machine-made – in other words, of its bit of humanity. Formerly, all buying from handicraftsmen meant a mark of distinction for their personalities, with whose productions people surrounded themselves. Furniture and dress accordingly became the symbols of mutual valuation and personal connection. Nowadays, on the other hand, we seem to live in the midst of anonymous and impersonal serfdom. We must not buy the facilitation of labour too dear.

289

Century-old quarantine. Democratic institutions are centres of quarantine against the old plague of tyrannical desires. As such they are extremely useful and extremely tedious.

290

The most dangerous partisan. The most dangerous partisan is he whose defection would involve the ruin of the whole party – in other words, the best partisan.

291

Destiny and the stomach. A piece more or less of bread and butter in the jockey's body is occasionally the decisive factor in races and bets, and thus in the good and bad luck of thousands. So long as the destiny of nations depends upon diplomats, the stomachs of diplomats will always be the object of patriotic misgivings. *Quousque tandem.**

292

The victory of democracy. All political powers nowadays attempt to exploit the fear of Socialism for their own strengthening. Yet in the long run democracy alone gains the advantage, for *all* parties are now compelled to flatter 'the masses' and grant them facilities and liberties of all kinds, with the result that the masses finally become omnipotent. The masses are as far as possible removed from Socialism as a doctrine of altering the acquisition of property. If once they get the steering-wheel into their hands, through great majorities in their Parliaments, they will attack with progressive taxation the whole dominant system of capitalists, merchants, and financiers, and will in fact slowly create a middle class which may forget Socialism like a disease that has been overcome. The practical result of this increasing democratisation will next be a European league of nations, in which each individual nation, delimited by the proper geographical frontiers, has the position of a canton with its separate rights. Small account will be taken of the historic

---

* The opening words of Cicero's first speech against Catiline: '*Quousque tandem abutere, Catilina, patientia nostra?*' – 'How much longer, Catiline, are you going to abuse our patience?'

memories of previously existing nations, because the pious affection for these memories will be gradually uprooted under the democratic régime, with all its craze for novelty and experiment. The corrections of frontiers that will prove necessary will be so carried out as to serve the interests of the great cantons and at the same time that of the whole federation, but not that of any venerable memories. To find the standpoints for these corrections will be the task of future diplomats, who will have to be at the same time students of civilisation, agriculturists, and commercial experts, with no armies but motives and utilities at their back. Then only will foreign and home politics be inseparably connected, whereas today the latter follows its haughty dictator, and gleans in sorry baskets the stubble that is left over from the harvest of the former.

293

Goal and means of democracy. Democracy tries to create and guarantee independence for as many as possible in their opinions, way of life, and occupation. For this purpose democracy must withhold the political suffrage both from those who have nothing and from those who are really rich, as being the two intolerable classes of men. At the removal of these classes it must always work, because they are continually calling its task in question. In the same way democracy must prevent all measures that seem to aim at party organisation. For the three great foes of independence, in that threefold sense, are the have-nots, the rich, and the parties. I speak of democracy as of a thing to come. What at present goes by that name is distinguished from older forms of government only by the fact that it drives with new horses; the roads and the wheels are the same as of yore. Has the danger really become less with *these* conveyances of the commonwealth?

294

Discretion and success. That great quality of discretion, which is fundamentally the virtue of virtues, their ancestress and queen, has in common life by no means always success on its side. The wooer would find himself deceived if he had wooed that virtue only for the sake of success. For it is rated by practical people as suspicious, and is confused with cunning and hypocrisy: he who obviously lacks discretion, the man who quickly grasps and sometimes misses his grasp, has prejudice on his side – he is an honest, trustworthy fellow. Practical people, accordingly, do not like the prudent man, thinking he is to them a danger. Moreover, we often assume the prudent man to be anxious, preoccupied, pedantic – unpractical, butterfly people find him uncomfortable, because he does not live in their happy-go-lucky way, without thinking of actions and duties; he appears among them as their embodied conscience, and the bright day is dimmed to their eyes before his gaze. Thus when success and popularity fail him, he may often say by way of private consolation, 'So high are the taxes you have to pay for the possession of the most precious of human commodities – still it is worth the price!'

295

Et in Arcadia ego. I looked down, over waves of hills, to a milky-green lake, through firs and pines austere with age; rocky crags of all shapes about me, the soil gay with flowers and grasses. A herd of cattle moved, stretched, and expanded itself before me; single cows and groups in the distance, in the clearest evening light, hard by the forest of pines; others nearer and darker; all in calm and eventide contentment. My watch pointed to half-past six. The bull of the herd had stepped into the white foaming brook, and went forward slowly, now striving against, now giving way to his tempestuous course; thus, no doubt, he took his sort of fierce pleasure. Two dark brown beings, of Bergamasque origin, tended the herd, the girl dressed almost like a boy. On the left, overhanging cliffs and fields of snow above broad belts of woodland; to the right, two enormous ice-covered peaks, high above me, shimmering in the veil of the sunny haze – all large, silent, and bright. The beauty of the whole was awe-inspiring and conducive to a mute worship of the moment and its revelation. Unconsciously, as if nothing could be more natural, you peopled this pure, clear world of light (which had no trace of yearning, of expectancy, of looking forward or backward) with Greek heroes. You felt it all as Poussin and his school felt it – at once heroic and idyllic. So individual men too have lived, constantly feeling themselves in the world and the world in themselves, and among them one of the greatest men, the inventor of a heroico-idyllic form of philosophy – Epicurus.

296

Counting and measuring. The art of seeing many things, of weighing one with another, of reckoning one thing with another and constructing from them a rapid conclusion, a fairly correct sum – that goes to make a great politician or general or merchant. This quality is, in fact, a power of speedy mental calculation. The art of seeing *one* thing alone, of finding therein the sole motive for action, the guiding principle of all other action, goes to make the hero and also the fanatic. This quality means a dexterity in measuring with one scale.

297

Not to see too soon. As long as we undergo some experience, we must give ourselves up to the experience and shut our eyes – in other words, not become observers of what we are undergoing. For to observe would disturb good digestion of the experience, and instead of wisdom we should gain nothing but dyspepsia.

298

From the practice of the wise. To become wise we must *will* to undergo certain experiences, and accordingly leap into their jaws. This, it is true, is very dangerous. Many a 'sage' has been eaten up in the process.

299

Exhaustion of the intellect. Our occasional coldness and indifference towards people, which is imputed to us as hardness and defect of character, is often only an exhaustion of the intellect. In this state other men are to us, as we are to ourselves, tedious or immaterial.

300

'The one thing needful'. If we are clever, the one thing we need is to have joy in our hearts. 'Ah,' adds someone, 'if we are clever, the best thing we can do is to be wise.'

301

A sign of love. Someone said, 'There are two persons about whom I have never thought deeply. That is a sign of my love for them.'

302

How we seek to improve bad arguments. Many a man adds a bit of his personality to his bad arguments, as if they would thus go better and change into straight and good arguments. In the same way, players at skittles, even after a throw, try to give a direction to the ball by turns and gestures.

303

Honesty. It is but a small thing to be a pattern sort of man with regard to rights and property – for instance (to name trifling points, which of course give a better proof of this sort of pattern nature than great examples), if as a boy one never steals fruit from another's orchard, and as a man never walks on unmown fields. It is but little; you are then still only a 'law-abiding person', with just that degree of morality of which a 'society', a group of human beings, is capable.

304

'Man!' – What is the vanity of the vainest individual as compared with the vanity which the most modest person feels when he thinks of his position in nature and in the world as 'Man!'

305

The most necessary gymnastic. Through deficiency in self-control in small matters a similar deficiency on great occasions slowly arises. Every day on which we have not at least once denied ourselves some *trifle* is turned to bad use and a danger to the next day. This gymnastic is indispensable if we wish to maintain the joy of being our own master.

306

Losing ourselves. When we have first found ourselves, we must understand how from time to time to *lose* ourselves and then to find ourselves again. This is true on the assumption that we are thinkers. A thinker finds it a drawback always to be tied to one person.

307

When it is necessary to part. You must, for a time at least, part from that which you want to know and measure. Only when you have left a city do you see how high its towers rise above its houses.

308

At noontide. He to whom an active and stormy morning of life is allotted, at the noontide of life feels his soul overcome by a strange longing for a rest that may last for months and years. All grows silent around him, voices sound farther and farther in the distance, the sun shines straight down upon him. On a hidden woodland sward he sees the great god Pan sleeping, and with Pan Nature seems to him to have gone to sleep with an expression of eternity on their faces. He wants nothing, he troubles about nothing; his heart stands still, only his eye lives. It is a death with waking eyes. Then man sees much that he never saw before, and, so far as his eye can reach, all is woven into and as it were buried in a net of light. He feels happy, but it is a heavy, very heavy kind of happiness. Then at last the wind stirs in the trees, noontide is over, life carries him away again, life with its blind eyes, and its tempestuous retinue behind it – desire, illusion, oblivion, enjoyment, destruction, decay. And so comes evening, more stormy and more active than was even the morning. To the really active man these prolonged phases of cognition seem almost uncanny and morbid, but not unpleasant.

309

To beware of one's portrait-painter. A great painter, who in a portrait has revealed and put on canvas the fullest expression and look of which a man is capable, will almost always think, when he sees the man later in real life, that he is only looking at a caricature.

310

The two principles of the new life. First principle: to arrange one's life on the most secure and tangible basis, not as hitherto upon the most distant, undetermined, and cloudy foundation. *Second principle:* to establish the rank of the nearest and nearer things, and of the more and less secure, before one arranges one's life and directs it to a final end.

311

Dangerous irritability. Talented men who are at the same time *idle* will always appear somewhat irritated when one of their friends has accomplished a thorough piece of work. Their jealousy is awakened, they are ashamed of their own laziness, or rather, they fear that their active friend will now despise them even more than before. In such a mood they criticise the new achievement, and, to the utter astonishment of the author, their criticism becomes a revenge.

312

Destructions of illusions. Illusions are certainly expensive amusements; but the destruction of illusions is still more expensive, if looked upon as an amusement, as it undoubtedly is by some people.

313

The monotone of the 'sage'. – Cows sometimes have a look of wondering which stops short on the path to questioning. In the eye of the higher intelligence, on the other hand, the *nil admirari* is spread out like the monotony of the cloudless sky.

314

Not to be ill too long. We should beware of being ill too long. The lookers-on become impatient of their customary duty of showing sympathy, because they find it too much trouble to maintain the appearance of this emotion for any length of time. Then they immediately pass to suspicion of our character, with the conclusion: 'You deserve to be ill, and we need no longer be at pains to show our sympathy.'

315

A hint to enthusiasts. He who likes to be carried away, and would fain be carried on high, must beware lest he become too heavy. For instance, he must not learn much, and especially not let himself be crammed with science. Science makes men ponderous – take care, ye enthusiasts!

316

Knowledge of how to surprise oneself. He who would see himself as he is, must know how to *surprise* himself, torch in hand. For with the mind it is as with the body: whoever is accustomed to look at himself in the glass forgets his ugliness, and only recognises it again by means of the portrait-painter. Yet he even grows used to the picture and forgets his ugliness all over again. Herein we see the universal law that man cannot endure unalterable ugliness, unless for a moment. He forgets or denies it in all cases. The moralists must reckon upon that 'moment' for bringing forward their truths.

317

Opinions and fish. We are possessors of our opinions as of fish – that is, in so far as we are possessors of a fish pond. We must go fishing and have luck – then we have *our* fish, *our* opinions. I speak here of live opinions, of live fish. Others are content to possess a cabinet of fossils – and, in their head, 'convictions'.

318

Signs of freedom and servitude. To satisfy one's needs so far as possible oneself, even if imperfectly, is the path towards freedom in mind and personality. To satisfy many even superfluous needs, and that as fully as possible, is a training for servitude. The sophist Hippias, who himself earned and made all that he wore within and without, is the representative of the highest freedom of mind and personality. It does not matter whether all is done equally well and perfectly – pride can repair the damaged places.

319

Belief in oneself. In our times we mistrust everyone who believes in himself. Formerly this was enough to make people believe in one. The recipe for finding faith now runs: 'Spare not thyself! In order to set thy opinion in a credible light, thou must first set fire to thy own hut!'

320

At once richer and poorer. I know a man who accustomed himself even in childhood to think well of the intellectuality of mankind –

in other words, of their real devotion as regards things of the intellect, their unselfish preference for that which is recognised as true – but who had at the same time a modest or even depreciatory view of his own brain (judgment, memory, presence of mind, imagination). He set no value on himself when he compared himself with others. Now in the course of years he was compelled, first once and then in a hundred ways, to revise this verdict. One would have thought he would be thoroughly satisfied and delighted. Such, in fact, was to some extent the case, but, as he once said, 'Yet a bitterness of the deepest dye is mingled with my feeling, such as I did not know in earlier life; for since I learnt to value men and myself more correctly, my intellect seems to me of less use. I scarcely think I can now do any good at all with it, because the minds of others cannot understand the good. I now always see before me the frightful gulf between those who could give help and those who need help. So I am troubled by the misfortune of having my intellect to myself and of being forced to enjoy it alone so far as it can give any enjoyment. But to give is more blessed than to possess, and what is the richest man in the solitude of a desert?'

321

How we should attack. The reasons for which men believe or do not believe are in very few people as strong as they might be. As a rule, in order to shake a belief it is far from necessary to use the heaviest weapon of attack. Many attain their object by merely making the attack with some noise – in fact, pop-guns are often enough. In dealing with very vain persons, the semblance of a strong attack is enough. They think they are being taken quite seriously, and readily give way.

322

Death. Through the certain prospect of death a precious, fragrant drop of frivolity might be mixed with every life – and now, you singular druggist-souls, you have made of death a drop of poison, unpleasant to taste, which makes the whole of life hideous.

323

Repentance. Never allow repentance free play, but say at once to yourself, 'That would be adding a second piece of folly to the first.'

If you have worked evil, you must bethink yourself of doing good. If you are punished for your actions, submit to the punishment with the feeling that by this very submission you are somehow doing good, in that you are deterring others from falling into the same error. Every malefactor who is punished has a right to consider himself a benefactor to mankind.

324

Becoming a thinker. How can anyone become a thinker if he does not spend at least a third part of the day without passions, men, and books?

325

The best remedy. A little health on and off is the best remedy for the invalid.

326

Don't touch. There are dreadful people who, instead of solving a problem, complicate it for those who deal with it and make it harder to solve. Whoever does not know how to hit the nail on the head should be entreated not to hit the nail at all.

327

Forgetting Nature. We speak of Nature, and, in doing so, forget ourselves: we ourselves are Nature, *quand même*. Consequently, Nature is something quite different from what we feel on hearing her name pronounced.

328

Profundity and ennui. In the case of profound men, as of deep wells, it takes a long time before anything that is thrown into them reaches the bottom. The spectators, who generally do not wait long enough, too readily look upon such a man as callous and hard – or even as boring.

329

When it is time to vow fidelity to oneself. We sometimes go astray in an intellectual direction which does not correspond to our talents. For a time we struggle heroically against wind and tide, really against ourselves; but finally we become weary and we pant. What we accomplish gives us no real pleasure, since we think that we have paid too heavy a price for these successes. We even despair of our productivity, of our future, perhaps in the midst of victory. Finally, finally we turn back – and then the wind swells our sails and bears us into our smooth water. What bliss! How certain of victory we feel! Only now do we know what we are and what we intend, and now we vow fidelity to ourselves, and have a right to do so – as men that know.

330

Weather prophets. Just as the clouds reveal to us the direction of the wind high above our heads, so the lightest and freest spirits give signs of future weather by their course. The wind in the valley and the market-place opinions of today have no significance for the future, but only for the past.

331

Continual acceleration. Those who begin slowly and find it hard to become familiar with a subject, sometimes acquire afterwards the quality of continual acceleration – so that in the end no one knows where the current will take them.

332

The three good things. Greatness, calm, sunlight – these three embrace all that a thinker desires and also demands of himself: his hopes and duties, his claims in the intellectual and moral sphere, nay even in his daily manner of life and the scenic background of his residence. Corresponding to these three things are, firstly thoughts that exalt, secondly thoughts that soothe, and thirdly thoughts that illuminate – but, fourthly, thoughts that share in all these three qualities, in which all earthly things are transfigured. This is the kingdom of the great *trinity of joy*.

333

Dying for 'truth'. We should not let ourselves be burnt for our opinions – we are not so certain of them as all that. But we might let ourselves be burnt for the right of possessing and changing our opinions.

334

Market value. If we wish to pass exactly for what we are, we must be something that has its market value. As, however, only objects in common use have a market value, this desire is the consequence either of shrewd modesty or of stupid immodesty.

335

Moral for builders. We must remove the scaffolding when the house has been built.

336

Sophocleanism. Who poured more water into wine than the Greeks? Sobriety and grace combined – that was the aristocratic privilege of the Athenian in the time of Sophocles and after. Imitate that whoever can! In life and in work!

337

Heroism. The heroic consists in doing something great (or in nobly *not* doing something) without feeling oneself to be in competition *with* or *before* others. The hero carries with him, wherever he goes, the wilderness and the holy land with inviolable precincts.

338

Finding our 'double' in Nature. In some country places we rediscover ourselves, with a delightful shudder: it is the pleasantest way of finding our 'double'. – How happy must he be who has that feeling just here, in this perpetually sunny October air, in this happy elfin play of the wind from morn till eve, in this clearest of atmospheres and mildest of temperatures, in all the serious yet cheerful landscape of hill, lake, and forest on this plateau, which has encamped fearlessly next to the terrors of eternal snow: here, where Italy and Finland have joined hands, and where the home of all the silver colour-tones of Nature seems to be established. How happy must he be who can say, 'True, there are many grander and finer pieces of scenery, but this is so familiar and intimate to me, related by blood, nay even more to me!'

339

Affability of the sage. The sage will unconsciously be affable in his intercourse with other men, as a prince would be, and will readily treat them as equals, in spite of all differences of talent, rank, and character. For this characteristic, however, so soon as people notice it, he is most heavily censured.

340

Gold. All that is gold does not glitter. A soft sheen characterises the most precious metal.

341

Wheel and drag. The wheel and the drag have different duties, but also one in common – that of hurting each other.

342

Disturbances of the thinker. All that interrupts the thinker in his thoughts (disturbs him, as people say) must be regarded by him calmly, as a new model who comes in by the door to offer himself to the artist. Interruptions are the ravens which bring food to the recluse.

343

Being very clever. Being very clever keeps men young, but they must put up with being considered, for that very reason, older than they are. For men read the handwriting of the intellect as signs of *experience* – that is, of having lived much and evilly, of suffering, error, and repentance. Hence, if we are very clever and show it, we appear to them older and wickeder than we are.

344

How we must conquer. We ought not to desire victory if we only have the prospect of overcoming our opponent by a hair's breadth. A good victory makes the vanquished rejoice, and must have about it something divine which spares *humiliation*.

345

An illusion of superior minds. Superior minds find it difficult to free themselves from an illusion; for they imagine that they excite envy among the mediocre and are looked upon as exceptions. As a matter of fact, however, they are looked upon as superfluous, as something that would not be missed if it did not exist.

346
Demanded by cleanliness. Changing opinions is in some natures as much demanded by cleanliness as changing clothes. In the case of other natures it is only demanded by vanity.

347
Also worthy of a hero. Here is a hero who did nothing but shake the tree as soon as the fruits were ripe. Do you think that too small a thing? Well, just look at the tree that he shook.

348
A gauge for wisdom. The growth of wisdom may be gauged exactly by the diminution of ill-temper.

349
Expressing an error disagreeably. It is not to everyone's taste to hear truth pleasantly expressed. But let no one at least believe that error will become truth if it is disagreeably expressed.

350
The golden maxim. Man has been bound with many chains, in order that he may forget to comport himself like an animal. And indeed he has become more gentle, more intellectual, more joyous, more meditative than any animal. But now he still suffers from having carried his chains so long, from having been so long without pure air and free movement – these chains, however, are, as I repeat again and again, the ponderous and significant errors of moral, religious, and metaphysical ideas. Only when the disease of chains is overcome is the first great goal reached – the separation of man from the brute. At present we stand in the midst of our work of removing the chains, and in doing so we need the strictest precautions. Only the ennobled man may be granted freedom of spirit; to him alone comes the alleviation of life and heals his wounds; he is the first who can say that he lives for the sake of joy, with no other aim; in any other mouth,

his motto of 'Peace around me and goodwill towards all the most familiar things', would be dangerous. In this motto for single individuals he is thinking of an ancient saying, magnificent and pathetic, which applied to all, and has remained standing above all mankind, as a motto and a beacon whereby shall perish all who adorn their banner too early – the rock on which Christianity foundered. It is not even yet time, it seems, for *all men* to have the lot of those shepherds who saw the heavens lit up above them and heard the words: 'Peace on earth and goodwill to one another among men.' – It is still the age of the individual.

* * *

The Shadow: Of all that you have enunciated, nothing pleased me more than one promise: 'Ye want again to be good neighbours to the most familiar things.' This will be to the advantage of us poor shadows too. For do but confess that you have hitherto been only too fond of reviling us.

The Wanderer: Reviling? But why did you never defend yourselves? After all, you were very close to our ears.

The Shadow: It seemed to us that we were too near you to have a right to talk of ourselves.

The Wanderer: What delicacy! Ah, you shadows are 'better men' than we, I can see that.

The Shadow: And yet you called us 'importunate' – us, who know one thing at least extremely well: how to be silent and to wait – no Englishman knows it better. It is true we are very, very often in the retinue of men, but never as their bondsmen. When man shuns light, we shun man – so far, at least, we are free.

The Wanderer: Ah, light shuns man far oftener, and then also you abandon him.

The Shadow: It has often pained me to leave you. I am eager for knowledge, and much in man has remained obscure to me, because I cannot always be in his company. At the price of complete knowledge of man I would gladly be your slave.

The Wanderer: Do you know, do I know, whether you would not then unwittingly become master instead of slave? Or would remain a slave indeed, but would lead a life of humiliation and disgust because you despised your master? Let us both be content with freedom such as you have enjoyed up to now — you and I! For the sight of a being not free would embitter my greatest joys; all that is best would be repugnant to me if anyone had to share it with me — I will not hear of any slaves about me. That is why I do not care for the dog, that lazy, tail-wagging parasite, who first became 'doggish' as the slave of man, and of whom they still say that he is loyal to his master and follows him like —

The Shadow: Like his shadow, they say. Perhaps I have already followed you too long today? It has been the longest day, but we are nearing the end; be patient a little more! The grass is damp; I am feeling chilly.

The Wanderer: Oh, is it already time to part? And I had to hurt you in the end — I saw you became darker.

The Shadow: I blushed the only colour I have at command. I remembered that I had often lain at your feet like a dog, and that you then —

The Wanderer: Can I not with all speed do something to please you? Have you no wish?

The Shadow: None, except perhaps the wish that the philosophic 'dog'* expressed to Alexander the Great — just move a little out of my light; I feel cold.

The Wanderer: What am I to do?

The Shadow: Walk under those fir-trees and look around you towards the mountains; the sun is sinking.

The Wanderer: Where are you? Where are you?

---

* Diogenes, founder of the Cynic school of philosophy.

BEYOND GOOD AND EVIL

PREFACE

Supposing that Truth is a woman – what then? Is there not ground for suspecting that all philosophers, in so far as they have been dogmatists, have failed to understand women – that the terrible seriousness and clumsy importunity with which they have usually paid their addresses to Truth, have been unskilled and unseemly methods for winning a woman? Certainly she has never allowed herself to be won; and at present every kind of dogma stands with sad and discouraged mien – *if*, indeed, it stands at all! For there are scoffers who maintain that it has fallen, that all dogma lies on the ground – nay more, that it is at its last gasp. But to speak seriously, there are good grounds for hoping that all dogmatising in philosophy, whatever solemn, whatever conclusive and decided airs it has assumed, may have been only a noble puerilism and tyronism; and probably the time is at hand when it will be once and again understood *what* has actually sufficed for the basis of such imposing and absolute philosophical edifices as the dogmatists have hitherto reared: perhaps some popular superstition of immemorial time (such as the soul-superstition, which, in the form of subject- and ego-superstition, has not yet ceased doing mischief); perhaps some play upon words, a deception on the part of grammar, or an audacious generalisation of very restricted, very personal, very human – all-too-human – facts. The philosophy of the dogmatists, it is to be hoped, was only a promise for thousands of years afterwards, as was astrology in still earlier times, in the service of which probably more labour, gold, acuteness, and patience have been spent than on any actual science hitherto: we owe to it, and to its 'super-terrestrial' pretensions in Asia and Egypt, the grand style of architecture. It seems that in order to inscribe themselves upon the heart of humanity with ever-lasting claims, all great things have first to wander about the earth as enormous and awe-inspiring caricatures: dogmatic philosophy has been a caricature of this kind – for instance, the Vedanta doctrine in Asia, and Platonism in Europe. Let us not be ungrateful to it, although it must certainly be confessed that the worst, the most tiresome, and the most dangerous of errors hitherto has been a dogmatist error – namely, Plato's invention of Pure Spirit and the Good in Itself. But now when it has been surmounted, when Europe, rid of this nightmare, can again draw breath freely and at least enjoy a healthier – sleep, we, *whose duty is wakefulness itself*, are the heirs of all the strength which the struggle against this error has fostered. It amounted to the very inversion of truth, and the denial of the *perspective* – the fundamental condition – of life, to speak of Spirit and the Good as Plato spoke of them; indeed one might ask, as a physician: 'How did such a malady attack that finest product of antiquity, Plato? Had the wicked Socrates really corrupted him? Was Socrates after all a corrupter of youths, and deserved his hemlock?' But the struggle against Plato, or – to speak plainer, and for the 'people' – the struggle against the ecclesiastical oppression of millennia of Christianity (for Christianity is Platonism for the 'people'), produced in Europe a magnificent tension of soul, such as had not existed anywhere previously; with such a tensely-strained bow one can now aim at the furthest goals. As a matter of fact, the European feels this tension as a state of distress, and twice attempts have been made in grand style to unbend the bow: once by means of Jesuitism, and the second time by means of democratic enlightenment – which, with the aid of liberty of the press and newspaper-reading, might, in fact, bring it about that the spirit would not so easily find itself in 'distress'! (The Germans invented gunpowder – all credit to them! – but they again made things square – they invented printing.) But we, who are neither Jesuits, nor democrats, nor even sufficiently Germans, we *good Europeans*, and free, *very* free spirits – we have it still, all the distress of spirit and all the tension of its bow! And perhaps also the arrow, the duty, and, who knows? *the goal to aim at. . . .*

SILS–MARIA, UPPER ENGADINE
June 1885

BEYOND GOOD AND EVIL

First Chapter: *Prejudices of Philosophers*

I

The Will to Truth, which is to tempt us to many a hazardous enterprise, the famous Truthfulness of which all philosophers have hitherto spoken with respect, what questions has this Will to Truth not laid before us! What strange, perplexing, questionable questions! It is already a long story; yet it seems as if it were hardly commenced. Is it any wonder if we at last grow distrustful, lose patience, and turn impatiently away? That this Sphinx teaches us at last to ask questions ourselves? *Who* is it really that puts questions to us here? *What* really is this 'Will to Truth' in us? In fact we made a long halt at the question as to the origin of this Will – until at last we came to an absolute standstill before a yet more fundamental question. We enquired about the *value* of this Will. Granted that we want the truth: *why not rather* untruth? And uncertainty? Even ignorance? The problem of the value of truth presented itself before us – or was it we who presented ourselves before the problem? Which of us is the Oedipus here? Which the Sphinx? It would seem to be a rendezvous of questions and notes of interrogation. And could it be believed that it at last seems to us as if the problem had never been propounded before, as if we were the first to discern it, get a sight of it, and *risk raising* it? For there is risk in raising it, perhaps there is no greater risk.

2

'*How could* anything originate out of its opposite? For example, truth out of error? Or the Will to Truth out of the will to deception? Or the generous deed out of selfishness? Or the pure sun-bright vision of the wise man out of covetousness? Such genesis is impossible; whoever dreams of it is a fool, nay, worse than a fool; things of the highest value must have a different origin, an origin of *their own* – in this transitory, seductive, illusory, paltry world, in this turmoil of delusion and cupidity, they cannot have their source. But rather in the lap of Being, in the intransitory, in the concealed God, in the 'Thing-in-itself' – *there* must be their source, and nowhere else!' – This mode of reasoning discloses the typical prejudice by which metaphysicians of all times can be recognised, this mode of valuation is at the back of all their logical procedure; through this 'belief' of theirs, they exert themselves for their 'knowledge', for something that is in the end solemnly christened 'the Truth'. The fundamental belief of metaphysicians is *the belief in antitheses of values*. It never occurred even to the wariest of them to doubt here on the very threshold (where doubt, however, was most necessary); though they had made a solemn vow, '*de omnibus dubitandum*.' * For it may be doubted, firstly, whether antitheses exist at all; and secondly, whether the popular valuations and antitheses of value upon which metaphysicians have set their seal, are not perhaps merely superficial estimates, merely provisional perspectives, besides being probably made from some corner, perhaps from below – 'frog perspectives', as it were, to borrow an expression current among painters. In spite of all the value which may belong to the true, the positive, and the unselfish, it might be possible that a higher and more fundamental value for life generally should be assigned to pretence, to the will to delusion, to selfishness, and cupidity. It might even be possible that *what* constitutes the value of those good and respected things, consists precisely in their being insidiously related, knotted, and crocheted to these evil and apparently opposed things – perhaps even in being essentially identical with them. Perhaps! But who wishes to concern himself with such dangerous 'Perhapses'! For that investigation one must await the advent of a new order of philosophers, such as will have other tastes and inclinations, the reverse of those hitherto prevalent – philosophers of the dangerous 'Perhaps' in every sense of the term. And to speak in all seriousness, I see such new philosophers beginning to appear.

* Everything is open to question.

3

Having kept a sharp eye on philosophers, and having read between their lines long enough, I now say to myself that the greater part of conscious thinking must be counted amongst the instinctive functions, and it is so even in the case of philosophical thinking; one has here to learn anew, as one learned anew about heredity and 'innateness'. As little as the act of birth comes into consideration in the whole process and procedure of heredity, just as little is 'being-conscious' *opposed* to the instinctive in any decisive sense; the greater part of the conscious thinking of a philosopher is secretly influenced by his instincts, and forced into definite channels. And behind all logic and its seeming sovereignty of movement, there are valuations, or to speak more plainly, physiological demands, for the maintenance of a definite mode of life. For example, that the certain is worth more than the uncertain, that illusion is less valuable than 'truth': such valuations, in spite of their regulative importance for *us*, might notwithstanding be only superficial valuations, special kinds of *niaiserie*, such as may be necessary for the maintenance of beings such as ourselves. Supposing, in effect, that man is not just the 'measure of things' . . .

4

The falseness of an opinion is not for us any objection to it: it is here, perhaps, that our new language sounds most strangely. The question is, how far an opinion is life-furthering, life-preserving, species-preserving, perhaps species-rearing; and we are fundamentally inclined to maintain that the falsest opinions (to which the synthetic judgments *a priori* belong) are the most indispensable to us; that without a recognition of logical fictions, without a comparison of reality with the purely *imagined* world of the absolute and immutable, without a constant counterfeiting of the world by means of numbers, man could not live – that the renunciation of false opinions would be a renunciation of life, a negation of life. *To recognise untruth as a condition of life*: that is certainly to impugn the traditional ideas of value in a dangerous manner, and a philosophy which ventures to do so, has thereby alone placed itself beyond good and evil.

5

That which causes philosophers to be regarded half-distrustfully
and half-mockingly, is not the oft-repeated discovery how innocent they are – how often and easily they make mistakes and lose
their way, in short, how childish and childlike they are – but that
there is not enough honest dealing with them, whereas they all raise
a loud and virtuous outcry when the problem of truthfulness is even
hinted at in the remotest manner. They all pose as though their
real opinions had been discovered and attained through the self-
evolving of a cold, pure, divinely indifferent dialectic (in contrast to
all sorts of mystics, who, fairer and foolisher, talk of 'inspiration');
whereas, in fact, a prejudiced proposition, idea, or 'suggestion',
which is generally their hearts desire abstracted and refined, is
defended by them with arguments sought out after the event. They
are all advocates who do not wish to be regarded as such, generally
astute defenders, also, of their prejudices, which they dub 'truths' –
and *very* far from having the conscience which bravely admits this
to itself; very far from having the good taste of the courage which
goes so far as to let this be understood, perhaps to warn friend or
foe, or in cheerful confidence and self-ridicule. The spectacle of
the Tartuffery of old Kant, equally stiff and decent, with which
he entices us into the dialectic by-ways that lead (more correctly
mislead) to his 'categorical imperative' – makes us fastidious ones
smile, we who find no small amusement in spying out the subtle
tricks of old moralists and ethical preachers. Or, still more so, the
hocus-pocus in mathematical form, by means of which Spinoza has
as it were clad his philosophy in mail and mask – in fact, the 'love of
his wisdom', to translate the term fairly and squarely – in order
thereby to strike terror at once into the heart of the assailant who
should dare to cast a glance on that invincible maiden, that Pallas
Athene – how much of personal timidity and vulnerability does this
masquerade of a sickly recluse betray!

6

It has gradually become clear to me what every great philosophy up
till now has consisted of – namely, the confession of its originator,
and a species of involuntary and unconscious autobiography; and
moreover that the moral (or immoral) purpose in every philosophy

has constituted the true vital germ out of which the entire plant
has always grown. Indeed, to understand how the abstrusest metaphysical assertions of a philosopher have been arrived at, it is always
well (and wise) to first ask oneself: 'What morality do they (or does
he) aim at?' Accordingly, I do not believe that an 'impulse to
knowledge' is the father of philosophy; but that another impulse,
here as elsewhere, has only made use of knowledge (and mistaken
knowledge!) as an instrument. But whoever considers the fundamental impulses of man with a view to determining how far they
may have here acted as *inspiring* genii (or as demons and cobolds),
will find that they have all practised philosophy at one time or
another, and that each one of them would have been only too
glad to look upon itself as the ultimate end of existence and the
legitimate *lord* over all the other impulses. For every impulse is
imperious, and *as such*, attempts to philosophise. To be sure, in the
case of scholars, in the case of really scientific men, it may be
otherwise – 'better', if you will; there there may really be such a
thing as an 'impulse to knowledge', some kind of small, independent clockwork, which, when well wound up, works away indust-
riously to that end, *without* the rest of the scholarly impulses taking
any material part therein. The actual 'interests' of the scholar,
therefore, are generally in quite another direction – in the family,
perhaps, or in money-making, or in politics; it is, in fact, almost
indifferent at what point of research his little machine is placed, and
whether the hopeful young worker becomes a good philologist, a
mushroom specialist, or a chemist; he is not *characterised* by becoming this or that. In the philosopher, on the contrary, there is
absolutely nothing impersonal; and above all, his morality furnishes
a decided and decisive testimony as to *who he is* – that is to say, in
what order the deepest impulses of his nature stand to each other.

7

How malicious philosophers can be! I know of nothing more
stinging than the joke Epicurus took the liberty of making on
Plato and the Platonists: he called them *Dionysiokolakes*. In its
original sense, and on the face of it, the word signifies 'Flatterers
of Dionysius' – consequently, tyrants' accessories and lick-spittles;
besides this, however, it is as much as to say, 'They are all *actors*,
there is nothing genuine about them' (for *Dionysiokolax* was a

popular name for an actor). And the latter is really the malignant reproach that Epicurus cast upon Plato: he was annoyed by the grandiose manner, the *mise en scène* style of which Plato and his scholars were masters – of which Epicurus was not a master! He, the old school-teacher of Samos, who sat concealed in his little garden at Athens and wrote three hundred books, perhaps out of rage and ambitious envy of Plato, who knows! Greece took a hundred years to find out who the garden-god Epicurus really was. Did she ever find out?

8

There is a point in every philosophy at which the 'conviction' of the philosopher appears on the scene; or, to put it in the words of an ancient mystery:

> *Adventavit asinus,*
> *Pulcher et fortissimus.**

9

You desire to *live* 'according to Nature'? Oh, you noble Stoics, what fraud of words! Imagine to yourselves a being like Nature, boundlessly extravagant, boundlessly indifferent, without purpose or consideration, without pity or justice, at once fruitful and barren and uncertain: imagine to yourselves *indifference* as a power – how *could* you live in accordance with such indifference? To live – is not that just endeavouring to be otherwise than this Nature? Is not living valuing, preferring, being unjust, being limited, endeavouring to be different? And granted that your imperative, 'living according to Nature', means actually the same as 'living according to life' – how could you do *differently?* Why should you make a principle out of what you yourselves are, and must be? In reality, however, it is quite otherwise with you: while you pretend to read with rapture the canon of your law in Nature, you want something quite the contrary, you extraordinary stage-players and self-deluders! In your pride you wish to dictate your morals and ideals to Nature, to Nature herself, and to incorporate them therein; you insist that it shall be Nature 'according to the Stoa', and would like everything to be made after your own image, as a vast, eternal

---

* [From the East] the donkey came,
  Stout and strong as twenty men.   [medieval song]

glorification and generalisation of Stoicism! With all your love for truth, you have forced yourselves so long, so persistently, and with such hypnotic rigidity to see Nature *falsely*, that is to say, Stoically, that you are no longer able to see it otherwise – and to crown all, some unfathomable superciliousness gives you the Bedlamite hope that *because* you are able to tyrannise over yourselves – Stoicism is self-tyranny – Nature will also allow herself to be tyrannised over: is not the Stoic a *part* of Nature? . . . But this is an old and everlasting story: what happened in old times with the Stoics still happens today, as soon as ever a philosophy begins to believe in itself. It always creates the world in its own image; it cannot do otherwise; philosophy is this tyrannical impulse itself, the most spiritual Will to Power, the will to 'creation of the world', the will to the *causa prima*.

10

The eagerness and subtlety, I should even say craftiness, with which the problem of 'the real and the apparent world' is dealt with at present throughout Europe, furnishes food for thought and attention; and he who hears only a 'Will to Truth' in the background, and nothing else, cannot certainly boast of the sharpest ears. In rare and isolated cases, it may really have happened that such a Will to Truth – a certain extravagant and adventurous pluck, a metaphysician's ambition of the forlorn hope – has participated therein: that which in the end always prefers a handful of 'certainty' to a whole cartload of beautiful possibilities; there may even be puritanical fanatics of conscience, who prefer to put their last trust in a sure nothing, rather than in an uncertain something. But that is Nihilism, and the sign of a despairing, mortally wearied soul, notwithstanding the courageous bearing such a virtue may display. It seems, however, to be otherwise with stronger and livelier thinkers who are still eager for life. In that they side *against* appearance, and speak superciliously of 'perspective', in that they rank the credibility of their own bodies about as low as the credibility of the ocular evidence that 'the earth stands still', and thus, apparently, allowing with complacency their securest possession to escape (for what does one at present believe in more firmly than in one's body?) – who knows if they are not really trying to win back something which was formerly an even *securer* possession, something of the old domain of the faith of former times, perhaps the 'immortal soul', perhaps 'the old God', in short, ideas by which they could live better, that is to say, more vigorously and more joyously, than by 'modern ideas'? There is *distrust* of these modern ideas in this mode of looking at things, a disbelief in all that has been constructed yesterday and today; there is perhaps some slight admixture of satiety and scorn, which can no longer endure the *bric-à-brac* of ideas of the most varied origin, such as so-called Positivism at present throws on the market; a disgust of the more refined taste at the village-fair motleyness and patchiness of all these reality-philosophasters, in whom there is nothing either new or true, except this motleyness. Therein it seems to me that we should agree with those sceptical anti-realists and knowledge-microscopists of the present day; their instinct, which repels them from *modern* reality, is unrefuted . . . what do their retrograde by-paths concern us! The main thing about them is *not* that they wish to go 'back', but that they wish to get *away* therefrom. A little *more* strength, swing, courage, and artistic power, and they would be *off* – and not back!

II

It seems to me that there is everywhere an attempt at present to divert attention from the actual influence which Kant exercised on German philosophy, and especially to ignore prudently the value which he set upon himself. Kant was first and foremost proud of his Table of Categories; with it in his hand he said: 'This is the most difficult thing that could ever be undertaken on behalf of metaphysics.' Let us only understand this 'could be'! He was proud of having *discovered* a new faculty in man, the faculty of synthetic judgment *a priori*. Granting that he deceived himself in this matter; the development and rapid flourishing of German philosophy depended nevertheless on his pride, and on the eager rivalry of the younger generation to discover if possible something – at all events 'new faculties' – of which to be still prouder!' – But let us reflect for a moment – it is high time to do so. 'How are synthetic judgments *a priori possible*?' Kant asks himself – and what is really his answer? '*By means of a means* (faculty)' – but unfortunately not in five words, but so circumstantially, imposingly, and with such display of German profundity and verbal flourishes, that one altogether loses sight of the comical *niaiserie allemande* involved in such an answer. People were beside themselves with delight over this new faculty, and the jubilation reached its climax when Kant further discovered a moral faculty in man – for at that time Germans were still moral, not yet dabbling in the 'politics of hard fact'. Then came the honeymoon of German philosophy. All the young theologians of the Tübingen institution went immediately into the groves – all seeking for 'faculties'. And what did they not find – in that innocent, rich, and still youthful period of the German spirit, to which Romanticism, the malicious fairy, piped and sang, when one could not yet distinguish between 'finding' and 'inventing'! Above all a faculty for the 'transcendental'; Schelling christened it, intellectual intuition, and thereby gratified the most earnest longings of the naturally pious-inclined Germans. One can do no greater wrong to the whole of this exuberant and eccentric movement (which was really youthfulness, notwithstanding that it disguised itself so boldly in hoary and senile conceptions) than to take it seriously, or even treat it with moral indignation. Enough, however – the world grew older, and the dream vanished. A time came when people rubbed their foreheads, and they still rub them today. People had been dreaming, and first and foremost – old Kant. 'By means of a means (faculty)' – he had said, or at least meant to say. But, is that – an answer? An explanation? Or is it not rather merely a repetition of the question? How does opium induce sleep? 'By means of a means (faculty)', namely the *virtus dormitiva*, replies the doctor in Molière,

> *Quia est in eo virtus dormitiva,*
> *Cujus est natura sensus assoupire.**

But such replies belong to the realm of comedy, and it is high time to replace the Kantian question, 'How are synthetic judgments *a priori* possible?' by another question, 'Why is belief in such judgments *necessary*?' – in effect, it is high time that we should understand that such judgments must be *believed* to be true, for the sake of the preservation of creatures like ourselves; though they still might naturally be *false* judgments! Or, more plainly spoken, and roughly and readily – synthetic judgments *a priori* should not 'be

---

* Because there is in it a virtue of sleep,
  Whose nature it is to make the senses drowsy.

possible' at all; we have no right to them; in our mouths they are nothing but false judgments. Only, of course, the belief in their truth is necessary, as plausible belief and ocular evidence belonging to the perspective view of life. And finally, to call to mind the enormous influence which 'German philosophy' – I hope you understand its right to inverted commas (goosefeet)? – has exercised throughout the whole of Europe, there is no doubt that a certain *virtus dormitiva* had a share in it; thanks to German philosophy, it was a delight to the noble idlers, the virtuous, the mystics, the artists, the three-fourths Christians, and the political obscurantists of all nations, to find an antidote to the still overwhelming sensualism which overflowed from the last century into this, in short – *'sensus assoupire'* . . .

12

As regards materialistic atomism, it is one of the best refuted theories that have been advanced, and in Europe there is now perhaps no one in the learned world so unscholarly as to attach serious signification to it, except for convenient everyday use (as an abbreviation of the means of expression) – thanks chiefly to the Pole Boscovich: he and the Pole Copernicus have hitherto been the greatest and most successful opponents of ocular evidence. For whilst Copernicus has persuaded us to believe, contrary to all the senses, that the earth does *not* stand fast, Boscovich has taught us to abjure the belief in the last thing that 'stood fast' of the earth – the belief in 'substance', in 'matter', in the earth-residuum, and particle-atom: it is the greatest triumph over the senses that has hitherto been gained on earth. One must, however, go still further, and also declare war, relentless war to the knife, against the 'atomistic requirements' which still lead a dangerous after-life in places where no one suspects them, like the more celebrated 'metaphysical requirements': one must also above all give the finishing stroke to that other and more portentous atomism which Christianity has taught best and longest, the *soul-atomism*. Let it be permitted to designate by this expression the belief which regards the soul as something indestructible, eternal, indivisible, as a monad, as an *atomon: this* belief ought to be expelled from science! Between ourselves, it is not at all necessary to get rid of 'the soul' thereby, and thus renounce one of the oldest and most venerated hypotheses – as happens frequently to the clumsiness of naturalists, who can hardly touch on the soul without immediately losing it. But the way is open for new acceptations and refinements of the soul-hypothesis; and such conceptions as 'mortal soul', and 'soul as subjective multiplicity', and 'soul as social structure of the instincts and passions', want henceforth to have legitimate rights in science. In that the *new* psychologist is about to put an end to the superstitions which have hitherto flourished with almost tropical luxuriance around the idea of the soul, he is really, as it were, thrusting himself into a new desert and a new distrust – it is possible that the older psychologists had a merrier and more comfortable time of it; eventually, however, he finds that precisely thereby he is also condemned to *invent* – and, who knows? perhaps to *discover* the new.

13

Psychologists should bethink themselves before putting down the instinct of self-preservation as the cardinal instinct of an organic being. A living thing seeks above all to *discharge* its strength – life itself is *Will to Power*; self-preservation is only one of the indirect and most frequent *results* thereof. In short, here, as everywhere else, let us beware of *superfluous* teleological principles! – one of which is the instinct of self-preservation (we owe it to Spinoza's inconsistency). It is thus, in effect, that method ordains, which must be essentially economy of principles.

14

It is perhaps just dawning on five or six minds that natural philosophy is only a world-exposition and world-arrangement (according to us, if I may say so!) and *not* a world-explanation; but in so far as it is based on belief in the senses, it is regarded as more, and for a long time to come must be regarded as more – namely, as an explanation. It has eyes and fingers of its own, it has ocular evidence and palpableness of its own: this operates fascinatingly, persuasively, and *convincingly* upon an age with fundamentally plebeian tastes – in fact, it follows instinctively the canon of truth of eternal popular sensualism. What is clear, what is 'explained'? Only that which can be seen and felt – one must pursue every problem thus far. Obversely, however, the charm of the Platonic mode of thought, which was an *aristocratic* mode, consisted precisely in *resistance to* obvious sense-evidence – perhaps among men who enjoyed even stronger and more fastidious senses than our contemporaries, but who knew how to find a higher triumph in remaining masters of them: and this by means of pale, cold, grey conceptional networks which they threw over the motley whirl of the senses – the mob of the senses, as Plato said. In this overcoming of the world, and interpreting of the world in the manner of Plato, there was an *enjoyment* different from that which the physicists of today offer us – and likewise the Darwinists and antiteleologists among the physiological workers, with their principle of the 'smallest possible effort', and the greatest possible blunder. 'Where there is nothing more to see or to grasp, there is also nothing more for men to do' – that is certainly an imperative different from the Platonic one, but it may notwithstanding be the right imperative for a hardy, laborious race of machinists and bridge-builders of the future, who have nothing but *rough* work to perform.

15

To study physiology with a clear conscience, one must insist on the fact that the sense-organs are *not* phenomena in the sense of the idealistic philosophy; as such they certainly could not be causes! Sensualism, therefore, at least as regulative hypothesis, if not as heuristic principle. What? And others say even that the external world is the work of our organs? But then our body, as a part of this external world, would be the work of our organs! But then our organs themselves would be the work of our organs! It seems to me that this is a complete *reductio ad absurdum*, if the conception *causa sui* is something fundamentally absurd. Consequently, the external world is *not* the work of our organs – ?

16

There are still harmless self-observers who believe that there are 'immediate certainties'; for instance, 'I think', or as the superstition of Schopenhauer puts it, 'I will'; as though cognition here got hold of its object purely and simply as 'the thing in itself', without any falsification taking place either on the part of the subject or the object. I would repeat it, however, a hundred times, that 'immediate certainty', as well as 'absolute knowledge' and the 'thing in

itself', involve a *contradictio in adjecto*; we really ought to free ourselves from the misleading significance of words! The people on
their part may think that cognition is knowing all about things, but
the philosopher must say to himself: 'When I analyse the process
that is expressed in the sentence, "I think", I find a whole series of
daring assertions, the argumentative proof of which would be
difficult, perhaps impossible: for instance, that it is *I* who think,
that there must necessarily be something that thinks, that thinking
is an activity and operation on the part of a being who is thought
of as a cause, that there is an "ego", and finally, that it is already
determined what is to be designated by thinking – that I *know*
what thinking is. For if I had not already decided within myself
what it is, by what standard could I determine whether that
which is just happening is not perhaps "willing" or "feeling"?
In short, the assertion "I think", assumes that I *compare* my state at
the present moment with other states of myself which I know, in
order to determine what it is; on account of this retrospective
connection with further "knowledge", it has at any rate no
immediate certainty for me.' – In place of the 'immediate certainty' in which the people may believe in the special case, the
philosopher thus finds a series of metaphysical questions presented to him, veritable conscience questions of the intellect, to
wit: 'From whence did I get the notion of "thinking"? Why do I
believe in cause and effect? What gives me the right to speak of an
"ego," and even of an "ego" as cause, and finally of an "ego" as
cause of thought?' He who ventures to answer these metaphysical
questions at once by an appeal to a sort of *intuitive* perception, like
the person who says, 'I think, and know that this, at least, is true,
actual, and certain' – will encounter a smile and two notes of
interrogation in a philosopher nowadays. 'Sir,' the philosopher
will perhaps give him to understand, 'it is improbable that you are
not mistaken, but why should it be the truth?'

17

With regard to the superstitions of logicians, I shall never tire of
emphasising a small, terse fact, which is unwillingly recognised by
these credulous minds – namely, that a thought comes when 'it'
wishes, and not when 'I' wish; so that it is a *perversion* of the facts of
the case to say that the subject 'I' is the condition of the predicate

'think'. *One* thinks; but that this 'one' is precisely the famous old 'ego', is, to put it mildly, only a supposition, an assertion, and assuredly not an 'immediate certainty'. After all, one has even gone too far with this 'one thinks' – even the 'one' contains an *interpretation* of the process, and does not belong to the process itself. One infers here according to the usual grammatical formula – 'To think is an activity; every activity requires an agency that is active; consequently' . . . It was pretty much on the same lines that the older atomism sought, besides the operating 'power', the material particle wherein it resides and out of which it operates – the atom. More rigorous minds, however, learnt at last to get along without this 'earth-residuum', and perhaps some day we shall accustom ourselves, even from the logician's point of view, to get along without the little 'one' (to which the worthy old 'ego' has refined itself).

18

It is certainly not the least charm of a theory that it is refutable; it is precisely thereby that it attracts the more subtle minds. It seems that the hundred-times-refuted theory of the 'free will' owes its persistence to this charm alone; someone is always appearing who feels himself strong enough to refute it.

19

Philosophers are accustomed to speak of the will as though it were the best-known thing in the world; indeed, Schopenhauer has given us to understand that the will alone is really known to us, absolutely and completely known, without deduction or addition. But it again and again seems to me that in this case Schopenhauer also only did what philosophers are in the habit of doing – he seems to have adopted a *popular prejudice* and exaggerated it. Willing – seems to me to be above all something *complicated*, something that is a unity only in name – and it is precisely in a name that popular prejudice lurks, which has got the mastery over the inadequate precautions of philosophers in all ages. So let us for once be more cautious, let us be 'unphilosophical' : let us say that in all willing there is firstly a plurality of sensations, namely, the sensation of the condition '*away from which* we go', the sensation of the condition '*towards which* we go', the sensation of this '*from*' and

'*towards*' itself, and then besides, an accompanying muscular sensation, which, even without our putting in motion 'arms and legs',
commences its action by force of habit, directly we 'will' anything.
Therefore, just as sensations (and indeed many kinds of sensations)
are to be recognised as ingredients of the will, so, in the second
place, thinking is also to be recognised; in every act of the will
there is a ruling thought – and let us not imagine it possible to
sever this thought from the 'willing', as if the will would then
remain over! In the third place, the will is not only a complex of
sensation and thinking, but it is above all an *emotion*, and in fact the
emotion of the command. That which is termed 'freedom of the
will' is essentially the emotion of supremacy in respect to him who
must obey: 'I am free, "he" must obey' – this consciousness is
inherent in every will; and equally so the straining of the attention,
the straight look which fixes itself exclusively on one thing, the
unconditional judgment that 'this and nothing else is necessary
now', the inward certainty that obedience will be rendered – and
whatever else pertains to the position of the commander. A man
who *wills* commands something within himself which renders
obedience, or which he believes renders obedience. But now let
us notice what is the strangest thing about the will – this affair so
extremely complex, for which the people have only one name.
Inasmuch as in the given circumstances we are at the same time the
commanding *and* the obeying parties, and as the obeying party we
know the sensations of constraint, impulsion, pressure, resistance,
and motion, which usually commence immediately after the act
of will; inasmuch as, on the other hand, we are accustomed to
disregard this duality, and to deceive ourselves about it by means of
the synthetic term 'I': a whole series of erroneous conclusions, and
consequently of false judgments about the will itself, has become
attached to the act of willing – to such a degree that he who wills
believes firmly that willing *suffices* for action. Since in the majority
of cases there has only been exercise of will when the effect of the
command – consequently obedience, and therefore action – was
to be *expected*, the *appearance* has translated itself into the sentiment,
as if there were there a *necessity of effect*; in a word, he who wills
believes with a fair amount of certainty that will and action are
somehow one; he ascribes the success, the carrying out of the
willing, to the will itself, and thereby enjoys an increase of the

sensation of power which accompanies all success. 'Freedom of Will' – that is the expression for the complex state of delight of the person exercising volition, who commands and at the same time identifies himself with the executor of the order – who, as such, enjoys also the triumph over obstacles, but thinks within himself that it was really his own will that overcame them. In this way the person exercising volition adds the feelings of delight of his successful executive instruments, the useful 'underwills' or under-souls – indeed, our body is but a social structure composed of many souls – to his feelings of delight as commander. *L'effet c'est moi*: what happens here is what happens in every well-constructed and happy commonwealth, namely, that the governing class ident-ifies itself with the successes of the commonwealth. In all willing it is absolutely a question of commanding and obeying, on the basis, as already said, of a social structure composed of many 'souls'; on which account a philosopher should claim the right to include willing-as-such within the sphere of morals – regarded as the doctrine of the relations of supremacy under which the phen-omenon of 'life' manifests itself.

20

That the separate philosophical ideas are not anything optional or autonomously evolving, but grow up in connection and relation-ship with each other; that, however suddenly and arbitrarily they seem to appear in the history of thought, they nevertheless belong just as much to a system as the collective members of the fauna of a continent – is betrayed in the end by the circumstance: how unfailingly the most diverse philosophers always fill in again a definite fundamental scheme of *possible* philosophies. Under an invisible spell, they always revolve once more in the same orbit; however independent of each other they may feel themselves with their critical or systematic wills, something within them leads them, something impels them in definite order the one after the other – to wit, the innate methodology and relationship of their ideas. Their thinking is in fact far less a discovery than a re-recognising, a remembering, a return and a home-coming to a far-off, ancient common-household of the soul, out of which those ideas formerly grew: philosophising is so far a kind of atavism of the highest order. The wonderful family resemblance of all Indian,

Greek, and German philosophising is easily enough explained. In fact, where there is affinity of language, owing to the common philosophy of grammar – I mean owing to the unconscious domination and guidance of similar grammatical functions – it cannot but be that everything is prepared at the outset for a similar development and succession of philosophical systems; just as the way seems barred against certain other possibilities of world-interpretation. It is highly probable that philosophers within the domain of the Ural-Altaic languages (where the conception of the subject is least developed) look otherwise 'into the world', and will be found on paths of thought different from those of the Indo-Germans and Mussulmans, the spell of certain grammatical functions is ultimately also the spell of *physiological* valuations and racial conditions. – So much by way of rejecting Locke's superficiality with regard to the origin of ideas.

21

The *causa sui* is the best self-contradiction that has yet been conceived, it is a sort of logical violation and unnaturalness ; but the extravagant pride of man has managed to entangle itself profoundly and frightfully with this very folly. The desire for 'freedom of will' in the superlative, metaphysical sense, such as still holds sway, unfortunately, in the minds of the half-educated, the desire to bear the entire and ultimate responsibility for one's actions oneself, and to absolve God, the world, ancestors, chance, and society therefrom, involves nothing less than to be precisely this *causa sui,* and, with more than Munchausen daring, to pull oneself up into existence by the hair, out of the slough of nothingness. If anyone should find out in this manner the crass stupidity of the celebrated conception of 'free will' and put it out of his head altogether, I beg of him to carry his 'enlightenment' a step further, and also put out of his head the contrary of this monstrous conception of 'free will' : I mean 'non-free will', which is tantamount to a misuse of cause and effect. One should not wrongly *materialise* 'cause' and 'effect', as the natural philosophers do (and whoever like them naturalise in thinking at present), according to the prevailing mechanical doltishness which makes the cause press and push until it 'effects' its end; one should use 'cause' and 'effect' only as pure *conceptions*, that is to say, as conventional fictions for the purpose of designation and mutual understanding – *not* for explanation. In 'being-in-itself' there is nothing of 'causal-connection', of 'necessity', or of 'psychological non-freedom'; there the effect does *not* follow the cause, there 'law' does not obtain. It is *we* alone who have devised cause, sequence, reciprocity, relativity, constraint, number, law, freedom, motive, and purpose; and when we interpret and inter-mix this symbol-world, as 'being in itself', with things, we act once more as we have always acted – *mythologically*. The 'non-free will' is mythology; in real life it is only a question of *strong* and *weak* wills. – It is almost always a symptom of what is lacking in himself, when a thinker, in every 'causal-connection' and 'psycho-logical necessity', manifests something of compulsion, indigence, obsequiousness, oppression, and non-freedom; it is suspicious to have such feelings – the person betrays himself. And in general, if I have observed correctly, the 'non-freedom of the will' is regarded as a problem from two entirely opposite stand-points, but always in a profoundly *personal* manner: some will not give up their 'responsibility', their belief in *themselves*, the personal right to *their* merits, at any price (the vain races belong to this class); others on the contrary, do not wish to be answerable for any-thing, or blamed for anything, and owing to an inward self-contempt, seek *to get out of the business*, no matter how. The latter, when they write books, are in the habit at present of taking the side of criminals; a sort of socialistic sympathy is their favourite disguise. And as a matter of fact, the fatalism of the weak-willed embellishes itself surprisingly when it can pose as '*la religion de la souffrance humaine*'; that is *its* 'good taste'.

22

Let me be pardoned, as an old philologist who cannot desist from the mischief of putting his finger on bad modes of interpretation, but 'Nature's conformity to law', of which you physicists talk so proudly, as though – why, it exists only owing to your inter-pretation and bad 'philology'. It is no matter of fact, no 'text', but rather just a naïvely humanitarian adjustment and perversion of meaning, with which you make abundant concessions to the democratic instincts of the modern soul! 'Everywhere equality before the law – Nature is not different in that respect, nor better than we': a fine instance of secret motive, in which the vulgar antagonism to everything privileged and autocratic – likewise a second and more refined atheism – is once more disguised. '*Ni dieu, ni maître*' * – that, also, is what you want; and therefore 'Cheers for natural law!' – is it not so? But, as has been said, that is interpretation, not text; and somebody might come along, who, with opposite intentions and modes of interpretation, could read out of the same 'Nature', and with regard to the same phenomena, just the tyrannically inconsiderate and relentless enforcement of the claims of power – an interpreter who should so place the unexceptionalness and unconditionalness of all 'Will to Power' before your eyes, that almost every word, and the word 'tyranny' itself, would eventually seem unsuitable, or like a weakening and softening metaphor – as being too human; and who should, nevertheless, end by asserting the same about this world as you do, namely, that it has a 'necessary' and 'calculable' course, *not*, however, because laws obtain in it, but because they are absolutely *lacking*, and every power effects its ultimate consequences every moment. Granted that this also is only interpretation – and you will be eager enough to make this objection? – well, so much the better.

23

All psychology hitherto has run aground on moral prejudices and timidities, it has not dared to launch out into the depths. In so far as it is allowable to recognise in that which has hitherto been written, evidence of that which has hitherto been kept silent, it seems as if nobody had yet harboured the notion of psychology as the morphology and *development-doctrine of the Will to Power*, as I conceive of it. The power of moral prejudices has penetrated deeply into the most intellectual world, the world apparently most indifferent and unprejudiced, and has obviously operated in an injurious, obstructive, blinding, and distorting manner. A proper physio-psychology has to contend with unconscious antagonism in the heart of the investigator, it has 'the heart' against it: even a doctrine of the reciprocal conditionalness of the 'good' and the 'bad' impulses, causes (as refined immorality) distress and aversion in a still strong and manly conscience – still more so, a doctrine of the derivation of all good impulses from bad ones. If, however, a

* 'Neither god, nor master.'

person should regard even the emotions of hatred, envy, covetous-ness, and imperiousness as life-conditioning emotions, as factors which must be present, fundamentally and essentially, in the general economy of life (which must, therefore, be further devel-oped if life is to be further developed), he will suffer from such a view of things as from sea-sickness. And yet this hypothesis is far from being the strangest and most painful in this immense and almost new domain of dangerous knowledge; and there are in fact a hundred good reasons why everyone should keep away from it who *can* do so! On the other hand, if one has once drifted hither with one's bark, well! very good! now let us set our teeth firmly! let us open our eyes and keep our hand fast on the helm! We sail away right *over* morality, we crush out, we destroy perhaps the remains of our own morality by daring to make our voyage thither – but what do *we* matter! Never yet did a *profounder* world of insight reveal itself to daring travellers and adventurers, and the psychologist who thus 'makes a sacrifice' – it is *not* the *sacrifizio dell' intelletto,* on the contrary! – will at least be entitled to demand in return that psychology shall once more be recognised as the queen of the sciences, for whose service and equipment the other sciences exist. For psychology is once more the path to the fundamental problems.

Second Chapter: *The Free Spirit*

24

O sancta simplicitas! In what strange simplification and falsification man lives! One can never cease wondering when once one has got eyes for beholding this marvel! How we have made everything around us clear and free and easy and simple! How we have been able to give our senses a passport to everything superficial, our thoughts a godlike desire for wanton pranks and wrong inferences! – How from the beginning, we have contrived to retain our ignorance in order to enjoy an almost inconceivable freedom, thoughtlessness, imprudence, heartiness, and gaiety – in order to enjoy life! And only on this solidified, granite-like foundation of ignorance could knowledge rear itself hitherto, the will to knowledge on the foundation of a far more powerful will, the will to ignorance, to the uncertain, to the untrue! Not as its opposite, but – as its refinement! It is to be hoped, indeed, that *language*, here as elsewhere, will not get over its awkwardness, and that it will continue to talk of opposites where there are only degrees and many refinements of gradation; it is equally to be hoped that the incarnated Tartuffery of morals, which now belongs to our unconquerable 'flesh and blood', will turn the words round in the mouths of us discerning ones. Here and there we understand it, and laugh at the way in which precisely the best knowledge seeks most to retain us in this *simplified*, thoroughly artificial, suitably imagined and suitably falsified world: at the way in which, whether it will or not, it loves error, because, as living itself, it loves life!

25

After such a cheerful commencement, a serious word would fain be heard; it appeals to the most serious minds. Take care, ye philosophers and friends of knowledge, and beware of martyrdom!

Of suffering 'for the truth's sake'! even in your own defence! It spoils all the innocence and fine neutrality of your conscience; it makes you headstrong against objections and red rags; it stupefies, animalises, and brutalises, when in the struggle with danger, slander, suspicion, expulsion, and even worse consequences of enmity, ye have at last to play your last card as protectors of truth upon earth — as though 'the Truth' were such an innocent and incompetent creature as to require protectors! And you of all people, ye knights of the sorrowful countenance, Messrs Loafers and Cobweb-spinners of the spirit! Finally, ye know sufficiently well that it cannot be of any consequence if *ye* just carry your point; ye know that hitherto no philosopher has carried his point, and that there might be a more laudable truthfulness in every little interrogative mark which you place after your special words and favourite doctrines (and occasionally after yourselves) than in all the solemn pantomime and trumping games before accusers and law-courts! Rather go out of the way! Flee into concealment! And have your masks and your ruses, that ye may be mistaken for what you are, or somewhat feared! And pray, don't forget the garden, the garden with golden trellis-work! And have people around you who are as a garden — or as music on the waters at eventide, when already the day becomes a memory. Choose the *good* solitude, the free, wanton, lightsome solitude, which also gives you the right still to remain good in any sense whatsoever! How poisonous, how crafty, how bad, does every long war make one, which cannot be waged openly by means of force! How *personal* does a long fear make one, a long watching of enemies, of possible enemies! These pariahs of society, these long-pursued, badly-persecuted ones — also the compulsory recluses, the Spinozas or Giordano Brunos — always become in the end, even under the most intellectual masquerade, and perhaps without being themselves aware of it, refined vengeance-seekers and poison-brewers (just lay bare the foundation of Spinoza's ethics and theology!), not to speak of the stupidity of moral indignation, which is the unfailing sign in a philosopher that the sense of philosophical humour has left him. The martyrdom of the philosopher, his 'sacrifice for the sake of truth', forces into the light whatever of the agitator and actor lurks in him; and if one has hitherto contemplated him only with artistic curiosity, with regard to many a philosopher it is easy to understand the dangerous desire to see him also in his deterioration (deteriorated into a 'martyr', into a stage- and tribune-bawler). Only, that it is necessary with such a desire to be clear *what* spectacle one will see in any case – merely a satyric play, merely an epilogue farce, merely the continued proof that the long, real tragedy *is at an end*, supposing that every philosophy has been a long tragedy in its origin.

26

Every select man strives instinctively for a citadel and a privacy, where he is *free* from the crowd, the many, the majority – where he may forget 'men who are the rule', as their exception – exclusive only of the case in which he is pushed straight to such men by a still stronger instinct, as a discerner in the great and exceptional sense. Whoever, in intercourse with men, does not occasionally glisten in all the green and grey colours of distress, owing to disgust, satiety, sympathy, gloominess and solitariness, is assuredly not a man of elevated tastes; supposing, however, that he does not voluntarily take all this burden and disgust upon himself, that he persistently avoids it, and remains, as I said, quietly and proudly hidden in his citadel, one thing is then certain: he was not made, he was not predestined for knowledge. For as such, he would one day have to say to himself: 'The devil take my good taste! but "the rule" is more interesting than the exception – than myself, the exception!' And he would go *down*, and above all, he would go 'inside'. The long and serious study of the *average* man – and consequently much disguise, self-overcoming, familiarity, and bad intercourse (all intercourse is bad intercourse except with one's equals): – that constitutes a necessary part of the life-history of every philosopher; perhaps the most disagreeable, odious, and disappointing part. If he is fortunate, however, as a favourite child of knowledge should be, he will meet with suitable auxiliaries who will shorten and lighten his task; I mean so-called cynics, those who simply recognise the animal, the commonplace and 'the rule' in themselves, and at the same time have so much spirituality and ticklishness as to make them talk of themselves and their like *before witnesses* – sometimes they wallow, even in books, as on their own dung-hill. Cynicism is the only form in which base souls approach what is called honesty; and the higher man must open his ears to all the coarser or finer cynicism, and congratulate himself when the clown becomes shameless right before him, or the scientific satyr speaks out. There are even cases where enchantment mixes with the disgust – namely, where by a freak of nature, genius is bound to some such indiscreet billy-goat and ape, as in the case of the Abbé Galiani, the profoundest, acutest, and perhaps also filthiest man of his century – he was far profounder than Voltaire, and consequently also, a good deal more silent. It happens more frequently, as has been hinted, that a scientific head is placed on an ape's body, a fine exceptional understanding in a base soul, an occurrence by no means rare, especially amongst doctors and moral physiologists. And whenever anyone speaks without bitterness, or rather quite innocently, of man as a belly with two requirements, and a head with one; whenever anyone sees, seeks and *wants* to see only hunger, sexual instinct, and vanity as the real and only motives of human actions; in short, when anyone speaks 'badly' – and not even 'ill' – of man, then ought the lover of knowledge to hearken attentively and diligently; he ought, in general, to have an open ear wherever there is talk without indignation. For the indignant man, and he who perpetually tears and lacerates himself with his own teeth (or, in place of himself, the world, God, or society), may indeed, morally speaking, stand higher than the laughing and self-satisfied satyr, but in every other sense he is the more ordinary, more indifferent, and less instructive case. And no one is such a *liar* as the indignant man.

27

It is difficult to be understood, especially when one thinks and lives *gangasrotogati** among those only who think and live otherwise – namely, *kurmagati*,[†] or at best 'froglike', *mandeikagati* [‡] (I do everything to be 'difficultly understood' myself!) – and one should be heartily grateful for the good will to some refinement of interpretation. As regards 'the good friends', however, who are always too easy-going, and think that as friends they have a right to ease, one does well at the very first to grant them a playground and romping-place for misunderstanding – one can

---

* Like the river Ganges: *presto*.
† Like the tortoise: *lento*.
‡ Like the frog: *staccato*.

thus laugh still; or get rid of them altogether, these good friends –
and laugh then also!

28

What is most difficult to render from one language into another
is the *tempo* of its style, which has its basis in the character of
the race, or to speak more physiologically, in the average *tempo*
of the assimilation of its nutriment. There are honestly meant
translations, which, as involuntary vulgarisations, are almost falsifications of the original, merely because its lively and merry *tempo*
(which overleaps and obviates all dangers in word and expression)
could not also be rendered. A German is almost incapacitated for
presto in his language; consequently also, as may be reasonably
inferred, for many of the most delightful and daring *nuances* of free,
free-spirited thought. And just as the buffoon and satyr are foreign
to him in body and conscience, so Aristophanes and Petronius are
untranslatable for him. Everything ponderous, viscous, and pompously clumsy, all long-winded and wearying species of style, are
developed in profuse variety among Germans – pardon me for
stating the fact that even Goethe's prose, in its mixture of stiffness
and elegance, is no exception, as a reflection of the 'good old time'
to which it belongs, and as an expression of German taste at a time
when there was still a 'German taste', which was a rococo-taste *in
moribus et artibus.** Lessing is an exception, owing to his histrionic
nature, which understood much, and was versed in many things;
he who was not the translator of Bayle to no purpose, who took
refuge willingly in the shadow of Diderot and Voltaire, and still
more willingly among the Roman comedy-writers – Lessing loved
also free-spiritism in the *tempo*, and flight out of Germany. But
how could the German language, even in the prose of Lessing,
imitate the *tempo* of Machiavelli, who in his *Principe* makes us
breathe the dry, fine air of Florence, and cannot help presenting
the most serious events in a boisterous *allegrissimo*, perhaps not
without a malicious artistic sense of the contrast he ventures to
present – long, heavy, difficult, dangerous thoughts, and a *tempo* of
the gallop, and of the best, wantonest humour? Finally, who
would venture on a German translation of Petronius, who, more

---

* In morals and the arts.

than any great musician hitherto, was a master of *presto* in invention, ideas, and words? What matter in the end about the swamps of the sick, evil world, or of the 'ancient world', when like him, one has the feet of a wind, the rush, the breath, the emancipating scorn of a wind, which makes everything healthy, by making everything *run*! And with regard to Aristophanes – that transfiguring, complementary genius, for whose sake one *pardons* all Hellenism for having existed, provided one has understood in its full profundity *all* that there requires pardon and transfiguration; there is nothing that has caused me to meditate more on *Plato's* secrecy and sphinx-like nature, than the happily preserved *petit fait* that under the pillow of his death-bed there was found no 'Bible', nor anything Egyptian, Pythagorean, or Platonic – but a book of Aristophanes. How could even a Plato have endured life – a Greek life which he repudiated – without an Aristophanes!

29

It is the business of the very few to be independent; it is a privilege of the strong. And whoever attempts it, even with the best right, but without being *obliged* to do so, proves that he is probably not only strong, but also daring beyond measure. He enters into a labyrinth, he multiplies a thousandfold the dangers which life in itself already brings with it; not the least of which is that no one can see how and where he loses his way, becomes isolated, and is torn piecemeal by some minotaur of conscience. Supposing such a one comes to grief, it is so far from the comprehension of men that they neither feel it, nor sympathise with it. And he cannot any longer go back! He cannot even go back again to the sympathy of men!

30

Our deepest insights must – and should – appear as follies, and under certain circumstances as crimes, when they come unauthorisedly to the ears of those who are not disposed and predestined for them. The exoteric and the esoteric, as they were formerly distinguished by philosophers – among the Indians, as among the Greeks, Persians, and Mussulmans, in short, wherever people believed in gradations of rank and *not* in equality and equal rights – are not so much in contradistinction to one another in respect to the exoteric

2. THE FREE SPIRIT

class, standing without, and viewing, estimating, measuring, and judging from the outside, and not from the inside; the more essential distinction is that the class in question views things from below upwards – while the esoteric class views things *from above downwards*. There are heights of the soul from which tragedy itself no longer appears to operate tragically; and if all the woe in the world were taken together, who would dare to decide whether the sight of it would *necessarily* seduce and constrain to sympathy, and thus to a doubling of the woe? . . . That which serves the higher class of men for nourishment or refreshment, must be almost poison to an entirely different and lower order of human beings. The virtues of the common man would perhaps mean vice and weaknesses in a philosopher; it might be possible for a highly developed man, supposing him to degenerate and go to ruin, to acquire qualities thereby alone, for the sake of which he would have to be honoured as a saint in the lower world into which he had sunk. There are books which have an inverse value for the soul and the health according as the inferior soul and the lower vitality, or the higher and more powerful, make use of them. In the former case they are dangerous, disturbing, unsettling books, in the latter case they are herald-calls which summon the bravest to *their* bravery. Books for the general reader are always ill-smelling books, the odour of paltry people clings to them. Where the populace eat and drink, and even where they reverence, it is accustomed to stink. One should not go into churches if one wishes to breathe *pure* air.

31

In our youthful years we still venerate and despise without the art of *nuance*, which is the best gain of life, and we have rightly to do hard penance for having fallen upon men and things with Yea and Nay. Everything is so arranged that the worst of all tastes, *the taste for the unconditional*, is cruelly befooled and abused, until a man learns to introduce a little art into his sentiments, and prefers to try conclusions with the artificial, as do the real artists of life. The angry and reverent spirit peculiar to youth appears to allow itself no peace, until it has suitably falsified men and things, to be able to vent its passion upon them: youth in itself even, is something falsifying and deceptive. Later on, when the young soul, tortured

by continual disillusions, finally turns suspiciously against itself –
still ardent and savage even in its suspicion and remorse of conscience: how it upbraids itself, how impatiently it tears itself, how
it revenges itself for its long self-blinding, as though it had been a
voluntary blindness! In this transition one punishes oneself by
distrust of one's sentiments; one tortures one's enthusiasm with
doubt, one feels even the good conscience to be a danger, as if it
were the self-concealment and lassitude of a more refined uprightness; and above all, one espouses upon principle the cause *against*
'youth'. – A decade later, and one comprehends that all this also
was still – youth!

32

Throughout the longest period of human history – one calls it the
prehistoric period – the value or non-value of an action was inferred from its *consequences*; the action in itself was not taken into
consideration, any more than its origin; but pretty much as in
China at present, where the distinction or disgrace of a child
redounds to its parents, the retro-operating power of success or
failure was what induced men to think well or ill of an action. Let
us call this period the *pre-moral* period of mankind; the imperative,
'know thyself!' was then still unknown. – In the last ten thousand
years, on the other hand, on certain large portions of the earth,
one has gradually got so far, that one no longer lets the consequences of an action, but its origin, decide with regard to its
worth: a great achievement as a whole, an important refinement
of vision and of criterion, the unconscious effect of the supremacy of aristocratic values and of the belief in 'origin', the mark
of a period which may be designated in the narrower sense as the
moral one: the first attempt at self-knowledge is thereby made.
Instead of the consequences, the origin – what an inversion of
perspective! And assuredly an inversion effected only after long
struggle and wavering! To be sure, an ominous new superstition,
a peculiar narrowness of interpretation, attained supremacy precisely thereby: the origin of an action was interpreted in the most
definite sense possible, as origin out of an *intention*; people were
agreed in the belief that the value of an action lay in the value of
its intention. The intention as the sole origin and antecedent
history of an action: under the influence of this prejudice moral

praise and blame have been bestowed, and men have judged and even philosophised almost up to the present day. – Is it not possible, however, that the necessity may now have arisen of again making up our minds with regard to the reversing and fundamental shifting of values, owing to a new self-consciousness and acuteness in man – is it not possible that we may be standing on the threshold of a period which to begin with, would be distinguished negatively as *ultra-moral*: nowadays when, at least amongst us immoralists, the suspicion arises that the decisive value of an action lies precisely in that which is *not intentional*, and that all its intentionalness, all that is seen, sensible, or 'sensed' in it, belongs to its surface or skin – which, like every skin, betrays something, but *conceals* still more? In short, we believe that the intention is only a sign or symptom, which first requires an explanation – a sign, moreover, which has too many interpretations, and consequently hardly any meaning in itself alone: that morality, in the sense in which it has been understood hitherto, as intention-morality, has been a prejudice, perhaps a prematureness or preliminariness, probably something of the same rank as astrology and alchemy, but in any case something which must be surmounted. The surmounting of morality, in a certain sense even the self-surmounting of morality – let that be the name for the long secret labour which has been reserved for the most refined, the most upright, and also the most wicked consciences of today, as the living touchstones of the soul.

33

It cannot be helped: the sentiment of surrender, of sacrifice for one's neighbour, and all self-renunciation-morality, must be mercilessly called to account, and brought to judgment; just as the aesthetics of 'disinterested contemplation', under which the emasculation of art nowadays seeks insidiously enough to create itself a good conscience. There is far too much witchery and sugar in the sentiments 'for others' and '*not* for myself', for one not needing to be doubly distrustful here, and for one asking promptly: 'Are they not perhaps – *deceptions*?' – That they *please* – him who has them, and him who enjoys their fruit, and also the mere spectator – that is still no argument in their *favour*, but just calls for caution. Let us therefore be cautious!

34

At whatever standpoint of philosophy one may place oneself now-adays, seen from every position, the *erroneousness* of the world in which we think we live is the surest and most certain thing our eyes can light upon: we find proof after proof thereof, which would fain allure us into surmises concerning a deceptive principle in the 'nature of things'. He, however, who makes thinking itself, and consequently 'the spirit', responsible for the falseness of the world – an honourable exit, which every conscious or unconscious *advocatus dei* avails himself of – he who regards this world, including space, time, form, and movement, as falsely *deduced*, would have at least good reason in the end to become distrustful also of all thinking; has it not hitherto been playing upon us the worst of scurvy tricks? And what guarantee would it give that it would not continue to do what it has always been doing? In all seriousness, the innocence of thinkers has something touching and respect-inspiring in it, which even nowadays permits them to wait upon consciousness with the request that it will give them *honest* answers: for example, whether it be 'real' or not, and why it keeps the outer world so resolutely at a distance, and other questions of the same description. The belief in 'immediate certainties' is a *moral naïveté* which does honour to us philosophers; but – we have now to cease being '*merely* moral' men! Apart from morality, such belief is a folly which does little honour to us! If in middle-class life an ever-ready distrust is regarded as the sign of a 'bad character', and consequently as an imprudence, here amongst us, beyond the middle-class world and its Yeas and Nays, what should prevent us being imprudent and saying: the philo-sopher has at length a *right* to 'bad character', as the being who has hitherto been most befooled on earth – he is now under *obligation* to distrustfulness, to the wickedest squinting out of every abyss of suspicion. – Forgive me the joke of this gloomy grimace and turn of expression; for I myself have long ago learned to think and estimate differently with regard to deceiving and being deceived, and I keep at least a couple of pokes in the ribs ready for the blind rage with which philosophers struggle against being deceived. Why *not*? It is nothing more than a moral prejudice that truth is worth more than semblance; it is, in fact, the worst proved supposition in the world. *So* much must be conceded: there could have been no life at all except upon the basis of perspective estimates and semblances; and if, with the virtuous enthusiasm and stupidity of many philosophers, one wished to do away altogether with the 'seeming world' – well, granted that you *could* do that – at least nothing of your 'truth' would thereby remain! Indeed, what is it that forces us in general to the supposition that there is an essential opposition of 'true' and 'false'? Is it not enough to suppose degrees of seemingness, and as it were lighter and darker shades and tones of semblance – different *valeurs*, as the painters say? Why might not the world *which concerns us* – be a fiction? And to anyone who suggested: 'But to a fiction belongs an originator?' – might it not be bluntly replied: *Why*? May not this 'belong' also belong to the fiction? Is it not at length permitted to be a little ironical towards the subject, just as towards the predicate and object? Might not the philosopher elevate himself above faith in grammar? All respect to governesses, but is it not time that philosophy should renounce governess-faith?

35

O Voltaire! O humanity! O idiocy! There is something ticklish in 'the truth', and in the *search* for the truth; and if man goes about it too humanely – '*il ne cherche le vrai que pour faire le bien*' * – I wager he finds nothing!

36

Supposing that nothing else is 'given' as real but our world of desires and passions, that we cannot sink or rise to any other 'reality' but just that of our impulses – for thinking is only a relation of these impulses to one another – are we not permitted to make the attempt and to ask the question whether this which is 'given' does not *suffice*, by means of our counterparts, for the understanding even of the so-called mechanical (or 'material') world? I do not mean as an illusion, a 'semblance', a 'represent-ation' (in the Berkeleyan and Schopenhauerian sense), but as possessing the same degree of reality as our emotions themselves – as a more primitive form of the world of emotions, in which everything still lies locked in a mighty unity, which afterwards branches off and develops itself in organic processes (naturally also, refines and debilitates) – as a kind of instinctive life in which all

---

* 'He seeks truth only in order to do good.'

organic functions, including self-regulation, assimilation, nutrition, secretion, and change of matter, are still synthetically united with one another – as a *primary form* of life? – In the end, it is not only permitted to make this attempt, it is commanded by the conscience of *logical method*. Not to assume several kinds of causality, so long as the attempt to get along with a single one has not been pushed to its furthest extent (to absurdity, if I may be allowed to say so): that is a morality of method which one may not repudiate nowadays – it follows 'from its definition', as mathematicians say. The question is ultimately whether we really recognise the will as *operating*, whether we believe in the causality of the will; if we do so – and fundamentally our belief *in this* is just our belief in causality itself – we *must* make the attempt to posit hypothetically the causality of the will as the only causality. 'Will' can naturally only operate on 'will' – and not on 'matter' (not on 'nerves', for instance): in short, the hypothesis must be hazarded, whether will does not operate on will wherever 'effects' are recognised – and whether all mechanical action, inasmuch as a power operates therein, is not just the power of will, the effect of will. Granted, finally, that we succeeded in explaining our entire instinctive life as the development and ramification of one fundamental form of will – namely, the Will to Power, as *my* thesis puts it; granted that all organic functions could be traced back to this Will to Power, and that the solution of the problem of generation and nutrition – it is one problem – could also be found therein: one would thus have acquired the right to define *all* active force unequivocally as *Will to Power*. The world seen from within, the world defined and designated according to its 'intelligible character' – it would simply be 'Will to Power', and nothing else.

37

'What? Does not that mean in popular language: God is disproved, but not the devil?' – On the contrary! On the contrary, my friends! And who the devil also compels you to speak popularly!

38

As happened finally in all the enlightenment of modern times with the French Revolution (that terrible farce, quite superfluous when judged close at hand, into which, however, the noble and visionary spectators of all Europe have interpreted from a distance their own indignation and enthusiasm so long and passionately, *until the text has disappeared under the interpretation*), so a noble posterity might once more misunderstand the whole of the past, and perhaps only thereby make *its* aspect endurable. – Or rather, has not this already happened? Have not we ourselves been – that 'noble posterity'? And, in so far as we now comprehend this, is it not – thereby already past?

39

Nobody will very readily regard a doctrine as true merely because it makes people happy or virtuous – excepting perhaps the amiable 'Idealists', who are enthusiastic about the good, true, and beautiful, and let all kinds of motley, coarse, and good-natured desirabilities swim about promiscuously in their pond. Happiness and virtue are no arguments. It is willingly forgotten, however, even on the part of thoughtful minds, that to make unhappy and to make bad are just as little counter-arguments. A thing could be *true*, although it were in the highest degree injurious and dangerous; indeed, the fundamental constitution of existence might be such that one succumbed by a full knowledge of it – so that the strength of a mind might be measured by the amount of 'truth' it could endure – or to speak more plainly, by the extent to which it *required* truth attenuated, veiled, sweetened, damped, and falsified. But there is no doubt that for the discovery of certain *portions* of truth the wicked and unfortunate are more favourably situated and have a greater likelihood of success; not to speak of the wicked who are happy – a species about whom moralists are silent. Perhaps severity and craft are more favourable conditions for the development of strong, independent spirits and philosophers than the gentle, refined, yielding good-nature, and habit of taking things easily, which are prized, and rightly prized in a learned man. Presupposing always, to begin with, that the term 'philosopher' be not confined to the philosopher who writes books, or even introduces *his* philosophy into books! – Stendhal furnishes a last feature of the portrait of the free-spirited philosopher, which for the sake of German taste I will not omit to underline – for it is *opposed* to German taste. '*Pour être bon philosophe,*' says this last great psychologist, '*il faut être sec, clair, sans illusion. Un banquier, qui a fait* *fortune, a une partie du caractère requis pour faire des découvertes en philosophie, c'est-à-dire pour voir clair dans ce qui est.'* *

40

Everything that is profound loves the mask; the profoundest things have a hatred even of figure and likeness. Should not the *contrary* only be the right disguise for the shame of a god to go about in? A question worth asking! – it would be strange if some mystic has not already ventured on the same kind of thing. There are proceedings of such a delicate nature that it is well to overwhelm them with coarseness and make them unrecognisable; there are actions of love and of an extravagant magnanimity after which nothing can be wiser than to take a stick and thrash the witness soundly: one thereby obscures his recollection. Many a one is able to obscure and abuse his own memory, in order at least to have vengeance on this sole party in the secret: shame is inventive. They are not the worst things of which one is most ashamed: there is not only deceit behind a mask – there is so much goodness in craft. I could imagine that a man with something costly and fragile to conceal, would roll through life clumsily and rotundly like an old, green, heavily-hooped wine-cask: the refinement of his shame requiring it to be so. A man who has depths in his shame meets his destiny and his delicate decisions upon paths which few ever reach, and with regard to the existence of which his nearest and most intimate friends may be ignorant; his mortal danger conceals itself from their eyes, and equally so his regained security. Such a hidden nature, which instinctively employs speech for silence and concealment, and is inexhaustible in evasion of communication, *desires* and insists that a mask of himself shall occupy his place in the hearts and heads of his friends; and supposing he does not desire it, his eyes will some day be opened to the fact that there is nevertheless a mask of him there – and that it is well to be so. Every profound spirit needs a mask; nay, more, around every profound spirit there continually grows a mask, owing to the constantly false, that is to say, *superficial* interpretation of every word he utters, every step he takes, every sign of life he manifests.

* To be a good philosopher, one must be dry, clear, without illusions. A banker who has made a fortune, has one part of the character require for making discoveries in philosophy – that is to say, for seeing clearly into what is.

41

One must subject oneself to one's own tests that one is destined for independence and command, and do so at the right time. One must not avoid one's tests, although they constitute perhaps the most dangerous game one can play, and are in the end tests made only before ourselves and before no other judge. Not to cleave to any person, be it even the dearest – every person is a prison and also a recess. Not to cleave to a fatherland, be it even the most suffering and necessitous – it is even less difficult to detach one's heart from a victorious fatherland. Not to cleave to a sympathy, be it even for higher men, into whose peculiar torture and helplessness chance has given us an insight. Not to cleave to a science, though it tempt one with the most valuable discoveries, apparently specially reserved for *us*. Not to cleave to one's own liberation, to the voluptuous distance and remoteness of the bird, which always flies further aloft in order always to see more under it – the danger of the flier. Not to cleave to our own virtues, nor become as a whole a victim to any of our specialities, to our 'hospitality' for instance, which is the danger of dangers for highly developed and wealthy souls, who deal prodigally, almost indifferently with themselves, and push the virtue of liberality so far that it becomes a vice. One must know how *to conserve oneself* – the best test of independence.

42

A new order of philosophers is appearing; I shall venture to baptize them by a name not without danger. As far as I understand them, as far as they allow themselves to be understood – for it is their nature to *wish* to remain something of a puzzle – these philosophers of the future might rightly, perhaps also wrongly, claim to be designated as *'tempters'*. This name itself is after all only an attempt, or, if it be preferred, a temptation.

43

Will they be new friends of 'truth', these coming philosophers? Very probably, for all philosophers hitherto have loved their truths. But assuredly they will not be dogmatists. It must be contrary to their pride, and also contrary to their taste, that their truth should still be truth for everyone – that which has hitherto been the secret wish and ultimate purpose of all dogmatic efforts. 'My opinion is *my* opinion: another person has not easily a right to it' – such a philosopher of the future will say, perhaps. One must renounce the bad taste of wishing to agree with many people. 'Good' is no longer good when one's neighbour takes it into his mouth. And how could there be a 'common good'! The expression contradicts itself; that which can be common is always of small value. In the end things must be as they are and have always been – the great things remain for the great, the abysses for the profound, the delicacies and thrills for the refined, and, to sum up shortly, everything rare for the rare.

44

Need I say expressly after all this that they will be free, *very* free spirits, these philosophers of the future – as certainly also they will not be merely free spirits, but something more, higher, greater, and fundamentally different, which does not wish to be misunderstood and mistaken? But while I say this, I feel under *obligation* almost as much to them as to ourselves (we free spirits who are their heralds and forerunners), to sweep away from ourselves altogether a stupid old prejudice and misunderstanding, which, like a fog, has too long made the conception of 'free spirit' obscure. In every country of Europe, and the same in America, there is at present something which makes an abuse of this name: a very narrow, prepossessed, enchained class of spirits, who desire almost the opposite of what our intentions and instincts prompt – not to mention that in respect to the *new* philosophers who are appearing, they must still more be closed windows and bolted doors. Briefly and regrettably, they belong to the *levellers*, these wrongly named 'free spirits' – as glib-tongued and scribe-fingered slaves of the democratic taste and its 'modern ideas': all of them men without solitude, without personal solitude, blunt honest fellows to whom neither courage nor honourable conduct ought to be denied; only, they are not free, and are ludicrously superficial, especially in their innate partiality for seeing the cause of almost *all* human misery and failure in the old forms in which society has hitherto existed – a notion which happily inverts the truth entirely! What they would fain attain with all their strength, is the universal, green-meadow happiness of the herd, together with security, safety, comfort, and alleviation of life for everyone; their two most frequently chanted songs and doctrines are called 'Equality of Rights' and 'Sympathy with all Sufferers' – and suffering itself is looked upon by them as something which must be *done away with*. We opposite ones, however, who have opened our eye and conscience to the question how and where the plant 'man' has hitherto grown most vigorously, believe that this has always taken place under the opposite conditions, that for this end the dangerousness of his situation had to be increased enormously, his inventive faculty and dissembling power (his 'spirit') had to develop into subtlety and daring under long oppression and compulsion, and his Will to Life had to be increased to the unconditioned Will to Power – we believe that severity, violence, slavery, danger in the street and in the heart, secrecy, stoicism, tempter's art and develry of every kind – that everything wicked, terrible, tyrannical, predatory, and serpentine in man, serves as well for the elevation of the human species as its opposite: – we do not even say enough when we only say *this much*; and in any case we find ourselves here, both with our speech and our silence, at the *other* extreme of all modern ideology and gregarious desirability, as their antipodes perhaps? What wonder that we 'free spirits' are not exactly the most communicative spirits? that we do not wish to betray in every respect *what* a spirit can free itself from, and *where* perhaps it will then be driven? And as to the import of the dangerous formula, 'Beyond Good and Evil', with which we at least avoid confusion, we *are* something else than '*libres-penseurs*', '*liberi pensatori*', 'free-thinkers', and whatever these honest advocates of 'modern ideas' like to call themselves. Having been at home, or at least guests, in many realms of the spirit; having escaped again and again from the gloomy, agreeable nooks in which preferences and prejudices, youth, origin, the accident of men and books, or even the weariness of travel seemed to confine us; full of malice against the seductions of dependency which lie concealed in honours, money, positions, or exaltation of the senses; grateful even for distress and the vicissitudes of illness, because they always free us from some rule, and its 'prejudice', grateful to the god, devil, sheep, and worm in us; inquisitive to a fault, investigators to the point of cruelty, with unhesitating fingers for the intangible, with teeth and stomachs for the most indigestible, ready for any business that requires sagacity and acute senses, ready for every adventure, owing to an excess of 'free will'; with anterior and posterior souls, into the ultimate intentions of which it is difficult to pry, with foregrounds and backgrounds to the end of which no foot may run; hidden ones under the mantles of light, appropriators, although we resemble heirs and spendthrifts, arrangers and collectors from morning till night, misers of our wealth and our full-crammed drawers, economical in learning and forgetting, inventive in scheming; sometimes proud of tables of categories, sometimes pedants, sometimes night-owls of work even in full day; yea, if necessary, even scarecrows – and it is necessary nowadays, that is to say, inasmuch as we are the born, sworn, jealous friends of *solitude*, of our own profoundest midnight and midday solitude – such kind of men are we, we free spirits! And perhaps *ye* are also something of the same kind, ye coming ones? ye *new* philosophers?

Third Chapter: *The Religious Mood*

The human soul and its limits, the range of man's inner experiences hitherto attained, the heights, depths and distances of these
experiences, the entire history of the soul *up to the present time*, and
its still unexhausted possibilities: this is the preordained hunting-
domain for a born psychologist and lover of a 'big hunt'. But how
often must he say despairingly to himself: 'A single individual!
alas, only a single individual! and this great forest, this virgin
forest!' So he would like to have some hundreds of hunting
assistants, and fine trained hounds, that he could send into the
history of the human soul, to drive *his* game together. In vain:
again and again he experiences, profoundly and bitterly, how
difficult it is to find assistants and dogs for all the things that
directly excite his curiosity. The evil of sending scholars into new
and dangerous hunting-domains, where courage, sagacity, and
subtlety in every sense are required, is that they are no longer
serviceable just when the '*big* hunt', and also the great danger
commences – it is precisely then that they lose their keen eye and
nose. In order, for instance, to divine and determine what sort of
history the problem of *knowledge and conscience* has hitherto had
in the souls of *homines religiosi*, a person would perhaps himself
have to possess as profound, as bruised, as immense an experience
as the intellectual conscience of Pascal; and then he would still
require that wide-spread heaven of clear, wicked spirituality,
which, from above, would be able to oversee, arrange, and
effectively formulise this mass of dangerous and painful experiences. – But who could do me this service! And who would have
time to wait for such servants! – They evidently appear too rarely,
they are so improbable at all times! Eventually one must do
everything *oneself* in order to know something; which means that
one has *much* to do! – But a curiosity like mine is once for all the

most agreeable of vices – pardon me! I mean to say that the love of truth has its reward in heaven, and already upon earth.

46

Faith, such as early Christianity desired, and not infrequently achieved in the midst of a sceptical and southernly free-spirited world, which had centuries of struggle between philosophical schools behind it and in it, counting besides the education in tolerance which the *imperium Romanum* gave – this faith is *not* that sincere, austere slave-faith by which perhaps a Luther or a Cromwell, or some other northern barbarian of the spirit remained attached to his God and Christianity; it is much rather the faith of Pascal, which resembles in a terrible manner a continuous suicide of reason – a tough, long-lived, wormlike reason, which is not to be slain at once and with a single blow. The Christian faith from the beginning, is sacrifice: the sacrifice of all freedom, all pride, all self-confidence of spirit; it is at the same time subjection, self-derision, and self-mutilation. There is cruelty and religious Phoenicianism in this faith, which is adapted to a tender, many-sided, and very fastidious conscience; it takes for granted that the subjection of the spirit is indescribably *painful*, that all the past and all the habits of such a spirit resist the *absurdissimum*, in the form of which 'faith' comes to it. Modern men, with their obtuseness as regards all Christian nomenclature, have no longer the sense for the terribly superlative conception which was implied to an antique taste by the paradox of the formula, 'God on the Cross'. Hitherto there had never and nowhere been such boldness in inversion, nor anything at once so dreadful, questioning, and questionable as this formula: it promised a transvaluation of all ancient values. – It was the Orient, the *profound* Orient, it was the Oriental slave who thus took revenge on Rome and its noble, light-minded toleration, on the Roman 'Catholicism' of non-faith; and it was always, not the faith, but the freedom from the faith, the half-stoical and smiling indifference to the seriousness of the faith, which made the slaves indignant at their masters and revolt against them. 'Enlightenment' causes revolt: for the slave desires the unconditioned, he understands nothing but the tyrannous, even in morals; he loves as he hates, without *nuance*, to the very depths, to the point of pain, to the point of sickness – his many *hidden* sufferings make him revolt against the noble taste which seems to *deny* suffering. The scepticism with regard to suffering, fundamentally only an attitude of aristocratic morality, was not the least of the causes, also, of the last great slave-insurrection which began with the French Revolution.

47

Wherever the religious neurosis has appeared on the earth so far, we find it connected with three dangerous prescriptions as to regimen: solitude, fasting, and sexual abstinence – but without it being possible to determine with certainty which is cause and which is effect, or *if* any relation at all of cause and effect exists there. This latter doubt is justified by the fact that one of the most regular symptoms among savage as well as among civilised peoples is the most sudden and excessive sensuality; which then with equal suddenness transforms into penitential paroxysms, world-renunciation, and will-renunciation: both symptoms perhaps explainable as disguised epilepsy? But nowhere is it *more* obligatory to put aside explanations: around no other type has there grown such a mass of absurdity and superstition, no other type seems to have been more interesting to men and even to philosophers – perhaps it is time to become just a little indifferent here, to learn caution, or, better still, to look away, *to go away*. – Yet in the background of the most recent philosophy, that of Schopenhauer, we find almost as the problem in itself, this terrible note of interrogation of the religious crisis and awakening. How is the negation of will *possible*? How is the saint possible? – That seems to have been the very question with which Schopenhauer made a start and became a philosopher. And thus it was a genuine Schopenhauerian consequence, that his most convinced adherent (perhaps also his last, as far as Germany is concerned), namely, Richard Wagner, should bring his own life-work to an end just here, and should finally put that terrible and eternal type upon the stage as Kundry, *type vécu*, and as it loved and lived, at the very time that the mad-doctors in almost all European countries had an opportunity to study the type close at hand, wherever the religious neurosis – or as I call it, 'the religious mood' – made its latest epidemical outbreak and display as the 'Salvation Army'. – If it be a question, however, as to what has been so extremely interesting to men of all sorts in all ages, and even to philosophers, in the whole phenomenon of the saint, it is undoubtedly the appearance of the miraculous therein – namely, the immediate *succession of opposites*, of states of the soul regarded as morally antithetical: it was believed here to be self-evident that a 'bad man' was all at once turned into a 'saint', a good man. The hitherto existing psychology was wrecked at this point; is it not possible it may have happened principally because psychology had placed itself under the dominion of morals, because it *believed* in oppositions of moral values, and saw, read, and *interpreted* these oppositions into the text and facts of the case? What? 'Miracle' only an error of interpretation? A lack of philology?

48

It seems that the Latin races are far more deeply attached to their Catholicism than we Northerners are to Christianity generally, and that consequently unbelief in Catholic countries means something quite different from what it does among Protestants – namely, a sort of revolt against the spirit of the race, while with us it is rather a return to the spirit (or non-spirit) of the race. We Northerners undoubtedly derive our origin from barbarous races, even as regards our talents for religion – we have *poor* talents for it. One may make an exception in the case of the Celts, who have therefore furnished also the best soil for the Christian infection in the north: the Christian ideal blossomed forth in France as much as ever the pale sun of the north would allow it. How strangely pious for our taste are still these later French sceptics, whenever there is any Celtic blood in their origin! How Catholic, how un-German does Auguste Comte's Sociology seem to us, with the Roman logic of its instincts! How Jesuitical, that amiable and shrewd cicerone of Port-Royal, Sainte-Beuve, in spite of all his hostility to Jesuits! And even Ernest Renan: how inaccessible to us Northerners does the language of such a Renan appear, in whom every instant the merest touch of religious thrill throws his refinedly voluptuous and comfortably couching soul off its balance! Let us repeat after him these fine sentences – and what wickedness and haughtiness is immediately aroused by way of answer in our probably less beautiful but harder souls, that is to say, in our more German souls! – '*Disons donc hardiment que la religion est un produit de l'homme normal, que l'homme est le plus dans le vrai quand il est le plus religieux et le plus assuré d'une destinée infinie. . . . C'est quand il est bon qu'il veut que la virtu corresponde à un order éternel, c'est quand il contemple les choses d'une manière désintéressée qu'il trouve la mort révoltante et absurde. Comment ne pas supposer que c'est dans ces moments-là, que l'homme voit le mieux?'* * . . .* These sentences are so extremely *antipodal* to my ears and habits of thought, that in my first impulse of rage on finding them, I wrote on the margin, '*la niaiserie religieuse par excellence!*' † – until in my later rage I even took a fancy to them, these sentences with their truth absolutely inverted! It is so nice and such a distinction to have one's own antipodes!

49

That which is so astonishing in the religious life of the ancient Greeks is the irrestrainable stream of *gratitude* which it pours forth – it is a very superior kind of man who takes *such* an attitude towards nature and life. – Later on, when the populace got the upper hand in Greece, *fear* became rampant also in religion; and Christianity was preparing itself.

50

The passion for God: there are churlish, honest-hearted, and importunate kinds of it, like that of Luther – the whole of Protestantism lacks the southern *delicatezza*. There is an Oriental exaltation of the mind in it, like that of an undeservedly favoured or elevated slave, as in the case of St Augustine, for instance, who lacks in an offensive manner, all nobility in bearing and desires. There is a feminine tenderness and sensuality in it, which modestly and unconsciously longs for a *unio mystica et physica*, as in the case of Madame de Guyon. In many cases it appears, curiously enough, as the disguise of a girl's or youth's puberty; here and there even as the hysteria of an old maid, also as her last ambition. The Church has frequently canonised the woman in such a case.

---

* 'Let us say boldly, then, that religion is a product of the normal man, that man is most in the right when he is most religious and most assured of an everlasting destiny . . . It is when he is good that he wants virtue to correspond to an eternal order, it is when he contemplates things in a disinterested fashion that he finds death revolting and absurd. How can we avoid imagining that it is in those moments that man sees most clearly?'
† 'Religious folly of the highest order.'

51

The mightiest men have hitherto always bowed reverently before
the saint, as the enigma of self-subjugation and utter voluntary
privation – why did they thus bow? They divined in him – and
as it were behind the questionableness of his frail and wretched
appearance – the superior force which wished to test itself by such
a subjugation; the strength of will, in which they recognised their
own strength and love of power, and knew how to honour it: they
honoured something in themselves when they honoured the saint.
In addition to this, the contemplation of the saint suggested to
them a suspicion: such an enormity of self-negation and anti-
naturalness will not have been coveted for nothing, they have said,
enquiringly. There is perhaps a reason for it, some very great
danger, about which the ascetic might wish to be more accurately
informed through his secret interlocutors and visitors? In a word,
the mighty ones of the world learned to have a new fear before him,
they divined a new power, a strange, still unconquered enemy: it
was the 'Will to Power' which obliged them to halt before the
saint. They had to question him.

52

In the Jewish Old Testament, the book of divine justice, there are
men, things, and sayings on such an immense scale, that Greek
and Indian literature has nothing to compare with it. One stands
with fear and reverence before those stupendous remains of what
man was formerly, and one has sad thoughts about old Asia and its
little out-pushed peninsula Europe, which would like, by all
means, to figure before Asia as the 'Progress of Mankind'. To
be sure, he who is himself only a slender, tame house-animal, and
knows only the wants of a house-animal (like our cultured people
of today, including the Christians of 'cultured' Christianity), need
neither be amazed nor even sad amid those ruins – the taste for
the Old Testament is a touchstone with respect to 'great' and
'small': perhaps he will find that the New Testament, the book of
grace, still appeals more to his heart (there is much of the odour
of the genuine, tender, stupid beadsman and petty soul in it). To
have bound up this New Testament (a kind of *rococo* of taste in
every respect) along with the Old Testament into one book, as

the 'Bible', as 'The Book in Itself', is perhaps the greatest audacity and 'sin against the Spirit' which literary Europe has upon its conscience.

53

Why Atheism nowadays? 'The father' in God is thoroughly refuted; equally so 'the judge', 'the rewarder'. Also his 'free will': he does not hear – and even if he did, he would not know how to help. The worst is that he seems incapable of communicating himself clearly; is he uncertain? – This is what I have made out (by questioning, and listening at a variety of conversations) to be the cause of the decline of European theism; it appears to me that though the religious instinct is in vigorous growth – it rejects the theistic satisfaction with profound distrust.

54

What does all modern philosophy mainly do? Since Descartes – and indeed more in defiance of him than on the basis of his procedure – an *attentat* has been made on the part of all philosophers on the old conception of the soul, under the guise of a criticism of the subject and predicate conception – that is to say, an *attentat* on the fundamental presupposition of Christian doctrine. Modern philosophy, as epistemological scepticism, is secretly or openly *anti-Christian*, although (for keener ears, be it said) by no means anti-religious. Formerly, in effect, one believed in 'the soul' as one believed in grammar and the grammatical subject: one said, 'I' is the condition, 'think' is the predicate and is conditioned – to think is an activity for which one *must* suppose a subject as cause. The attempt was then made, with marvellous tenacity and subtlety, to see if one could not get out of this net – to see if the opposite was not perhaps true: 'think' the condition, and 'I' the conditioned; 'I', therefore, only a synthesis which has been *made* by thinking itself. *Kant* really wished to prove that, starting from the subject, the subject could not be proved – nor the object either: the possibility of an *apparent existence* of the subject, and therefore of 'the soul', may not always have been strange to him – the thought which once had an immense power on earth as the Vedanta philosophy.

55

There is a great ladder of religious cruelty, with many rounds; but three of these are the most important. Once on a time men sacrificed human beings to their god, and perhaps just those they loved the best – to this category belong the firstling sacrifices of all primitive religions, and also the sacrifice of the Emperor Tiberius in the Mithra-Grotto on the Island of Capri, that most terrible of all Roman anachronisms. Then, during the moral epoch of mankind, they sacrificed to their God the strongest instincts they possessed, their 'nature'; *this* festal joy shines in the cruel glances of ascetics and 'anti-natural' fanatics. Finally, what still remained to be sacrificed? Was it not necessary in the end for men to sacrifice everything comforting, holy, healing, all hope, all faith in hidden harmonies, in future blessedness and justice? Was it not necessary to sacrifice God himself, and out of cruelty to themselves to worship stone, stupidity, gravity, fate, nothingness? To sacrifice God for nothingness – this paradoxical mystery of the ultimate cruelty has been reserved for the rising generation; we all know something thereof already.

56

Whoever, like myself, prompted by some enigmatical desire, has long endeavoured to go to the bottom of the question of pessimism and free it from the half-Christian, half-German narrowness and stupidity in which it has finally presented itself to this century, namely, in the form of Schopenhauer's philosophy; whoever, with an Asiatic and super-Asiatic eye, has actually looked inside, and into the most world-renouncing of all possible modes of thought – beyond good and evil, and no longer like Buddha and Schopenhauer, under the dominion and delusion of morality – whoever has done this, has perhaps just thereby, without really desiring it, opened his eyes to behold the opposite ideal: the ideal of the most world-approving, exuberant and vivacious man, who has not only learnt to compromise and arrange with that which was and is, but wishes to have it again *as it was and is*, for all eternity, insatiably calling out *da capo*, not only to himself, but to the whole piece and play; and not only to the play, but actually to him who requires the play – and makes it necessary; because he always requires himself anew – and makes himself necessary. – What? And this would not be – *circulus vitiosus deus?* *

57

The distance, and as it were the space around man, grows with the strength of his intellectual vision and insight: his world becomes profounder; new stars, new enigmas, and notions are ever coming into view. Perhaps everything on which the intellectual eye has exercised its acuteness and profundity has just been an occasion for its exercise, something of a game, something for children and childish minds. Perhaps the most solemn conceptions that have caused the most fighting and suffering, the conceptions 'God' and 'sin', will one day seem to us of no more importance than a child's plaything or a child's pain seems to an old man – and perhaps another plaything and another pain will then be necessary once more for 'the old man' – always childish enough, an eternal child!

58

Has it been observed to what extent outward idleness, or semi-idleness, is necessary to a real religious life (alike for its favourite microscopic labour of self-examination, and for its soft placidity called 'prayer', the state of perpetual readiness for the 'coming of God'), I mean the idleness with a good conscience, the idleness of olden times and of blood, to which the aristocratic sentiment that work is *dishonouring* – that it vulgarises body and soul – is not quite unfamiliar? And that consequently the modern, noisy, time-engrossing, conceited, foolishly proud laboriousness educates and prepares for 'unbelief' more than anything else? Amongst these, for instance, who are at present living apart from religion in Germany, I find 'free-thinkers' of diversified species and origin, but above all a majority of those in whom laboriousness from generation to generation has dissolved the religious instincts; so that they no longer know what purpose religions serve, and only note their existence in the world with a kind of dull astonishment. They feel themselves already fully occupied, these good people, be it by their business or by their pleasures, not to mention the 'Fatherland', and the newspapers, and their 'family duties'; it seems that they have no time whatever left for religion; and above all, it

* God as a vicious circle.

is not obvious to them whether it is a question of a new business or a new pleasure – for it is impossible, they say to themselves, that people should go to church merely to spoil their tempers. They are by no means enemies of religious customs; should certain circumstances, State affairs perhaps, require their participation in such customs, they do what is required, as so many things are done – with a patient and unassuming seriousness, and without much curiosity or discomfort; – they live too much apart and outside to feel even the necessity for a *for* or *against* in such matters. Among those indifferent persons may be reckoned nowadays the majority of German Protestants of the middle classes, especially in the great laborious centres of trade and commerce; also the majority of laborious scholars, and the entire University personnel (with the exception of the theologians, whose existence and possibility there always gives psychologists new and more subtle puzzles to solve). On the part of pious, or merely church-going people, there is seldom any idea of *how much* goodwill, one might say arbitrary will, is now necessary for a German scholar to take the problem of religion seriously; his whole profession (and as I have said, his whole workmanlike laboriousness, to which he is compelled by his modern conscience) inclines him to a lofty and almost charitable serenity as regards religion, with which is occasionally mingled a slight disdain for the 'uncleanliness' of spirit which he takes for granted wherever any one still professes to belong to the Church. It is only with the help of history (*not* through his own personal experience, therefore) that the scholar succeeds in bringing himself to a respectful seriousness, and to a certain timid deference in presence of religions; but even when his sentiments have reached the stage of gratitude towards them, he has not personally advanced one step nearer to that which still maintains itself as Church or as piety; perhaps even the contrary. The practical indifference to religious matters in the midst of which he has been born and brought up, usually sublimates itself in his case into circumspection and cleanliness, which shuns contact with religious men and things; and it may be just the depth of his tolerance and humanity which prompts him to avoid the delicate trouble which tolerance itself brings with it. – Every age has its own divine type of naïveté, for the discovery of which other ages may envy it: and how much naïveté – adorable, childlike, and boundlessly foolish naïveté – is involved in this belief of the scholar in his superiority, in the good conscience of his tolerance, in the unsuspecting, simple certainty with which his instinct treats the religious man as a lower and less valuable type, beyond, before, and *above* which he himself has developed – he, the little arrogant dwarf and mob-man, the sedulously alert, head-and-hand drudge of 'ideas', of 'modern ideas'!

59

Whoever has seen deeply into the world has doubtless divined what wisdom there is in the fact that men are superficial. It is their preservative instinct which teaches them to be flighty, lightsome, and false. Here and there one finds a passionate and exaggerated adoration of 'pure forms' in philosophers as well as in artists: it is not to be doubted that whoever has *need* of the cult of the superficial to that extent, has at one time or another made an unlucky dive *beneath* it. Perhaps there is even an order of rank with respect to those burnt children, the born artists who find the enjoyment of life only in trying to *falsify* its image (as if taking wearisome revenge on it); one might guess to what degree life has disgusted them, by the extent to which they wish to see its image falsified, attenuated, ultrified, and deified – one might reckon the *homines religiosi* amongst the artists, as their *highest* rank. It is the profound, suspicious fear of an incurable pessimism which compels whole centuries to fasten their teeth into a religious interpretation of existence: the fear of the instinct which divines that truth might be attained *too soon*, before man has become strong enough, hard enough, artist enough . . . Piety, the 'Life in God', regarded in this light, would appear as the most elaborate and ultimate product of the *fear* of truth, as artist-adoration and artist-intoxication in presence of the most logical of all falsifications, as the will to the inversion of truth, to untruth at any price. Perhaps there has hitherto been no more effective means of beautifying man than piety; by means of it man can become so artful, so superficial, so iridescent, and so good, that his appearance no longer offends.

60

To love mankind *for God's sake* – this has so far been the noblest and remotest sentiment to which mankind has attained. That love to mankind, without any redeeming intention in the background, is only an *additional* folly and brutishness, that the inclination to this love has first to get its proportion, its delicacy, its grain of salt and sprinkling of ambergris from a higher inclination – whoever first perceived and 'experienced' this, however his tongue may have stammered as it attempted to express such a delicate matter, let him for all time be holy and respected, as the man who has so far flown highest and gone astray in the finest fashion!

61

The philosopher, as *we* free spirits understand him – as the man of the greatest responsibility, who has the conscience for the general development of mankind – will use religion for his disciplining and educating work, just as he will use the contemporary political and economic conditions. The selecting and disciplining influence – destructive, as well as creative and fashioning – which can be exercised by means of religion is manifold and varied, according to the sort of people placed under its spell and protection. For those who are strong and independent, destined and trained to command, in whom the judgment and skill of a ruling race is incorporated, religion is an additional means for overcoming resistance in the exercise of authority – as a bond which binds rulers and subjects in common, betraying and surrendering to the former the conscience of the latter, their inmost heart, which would fain escape obedience. And in the case of the unique natures of noble origin, if by virtue of superior spirituality they should incline to a more retired and contemplative life, reserving to themselves only the more refined forms of government (over chosen disciples or members of an order), religion itself may be used as a means for obtaining peace from the noise and trouble of managing *grosser* affairs, and for securing immunity from the *unavoidable* filth of all political agitation. The Brahmins, for instance, understood this fact. With the help of a religious organisation, they secured to themselves the power of nominating kings for the people, while their sentiments prompted them to keep apart and outside, as men with a higher and super-regal mission. At the same time religion gives inducement and opportunity to some of the subjects to qualify themselves for future ruling and commanding: the slowly ascending ranks and classes, in which, through fortunate marriage customs, volitional power and delight in self-control are on the increase. To them religion offers sufficient incentives and temptations to aspire to higher intellectuality, and to experience the sentiments of authoritative self-control, of silence, and of solitude. Asceticism and Puritanism are almost indispensable means of educating and ennobling a race which seeks to rise above its hereditary baseness and work itself upward to future supremacy. And finally, to ordinary men, to the majority of the people, who exist for service and general utility, and are only so far entitled to exist, religion gives invaluable contentedness with their lot and condition, peace of heart, ennoblement of obedience, additional social happiness and sympathy, with something of transfiguration and embellishment, something of justification of all the commonplaceness, all the meanness, all the semi-animal poverty of their souls. Religion, together with the religious significance of life, sheds sunshine over such perpetually harassed men, and makes even their own aspect endurable to them; it operates upon them as the Epicurean philosophy usually operates upon sufferers of a higher order, in a refreshing and refining manner, almost *turning* suffering *to account*, and in the end even hallowing and vindicating it. There is perhaps nothing so admirable in Christianity and Buddhism as their art of teaching even the lowest to elevate themselves by piety to a seemingly higher order of things, and thereby to retain their satisfaction with the actual world in which they find it difficult enough to live – this very difficulty being necessary.

62

To be sure – to make also the bad counter-reckoning against such religions, and to bring to light their secret dangers – the cost is always excessive and terrible when religions do *not* operate as an educational and disciplinary medium in the hands of the philosopher, but rule voluntarily and *paramountly*, when they wish to be the final end, and not a means along with other means. Among men, as among all other animals, there is a surplus of defective, diseased, degenerating, infirm, and necessarily suffering individuals; the successful cases, among men also, are always the exception; and in view of the fact that man is *the animal not yet properly adapted to his environment*, the rare exception. But worse still. The higher the type a man represents, the greater is the

improbability that he will *succeed;* the accidental, the law of irrationality in the general constitution of mankind, manifests itself most
terribly in its destructive effect on the higher orders of men, the
conditions of whose lives are delicate, diverse, and difficult to
determine. What, then, is the attitude of the two greatest religions
above-mentioned to the *surplus* of failures in life? They endeavour
to preserve and keep alive whatever can be preserved; in fact, as
the religions *for sufferers*, they take the part of these upon principle;
they are always in favour of those who suffer from life as from a
disease, and they would fain treat every other experience of life as
false and impossible. However highly we may esteem this indulgent and preservative care (inasmuch as in applying to others, it
has applied, and applies also to the highest and usually the most
suffering type of man), the hitherto *paramount* religions – to give a
general appreciation of them – are among the principal causes
which have kept the type of 'man' upon a lower level – they have
preserved too much *that which should have perished*. One has to
thank them for invaluable services; and who is sufficiently rich in
gratitude not to feel poor at the contemplation of all that the
'spiritual men' of Christianity have done for Europe hitherto! But
when they had given comfort to the sufferers, courage to the
oppressed and despairing, a staff and support to the helpless, and
when they had allured from society into convents and spiritual
penitentiaries the broken-hearted and distracted: what else had
they to do in order to work systematically in that fashion, and with
a good conscience, for the preservation of all the sick and suffering,
which means, in deed and in truth, to work for *the deterioration of
the European race*? To *reverse* all estimates of value – *that* is what they
had to do! And to shatter the strong, to spoil great hopes, to cast
suspicion on the delight in beauty, to break down everything autonomous, manly, conquering, and imperious – all instincts which
are natural to the highest and most successful type of 'man' – into
uncertainty, distress of conscience, and self-destruction; forsooth,
to invert all love of the earthly and of supremacy over the earth,
into hatred of the earth and earthly things – *that* is the task the
Church imposed on itself, and was obliged to impose, until,
according to its standard of value, 'unworldliness', 'unsensuous-
ness', and 'higher man' fused into one sentiment. If one could
observe the strangely painful, equally coarse and refined comedy

3. THE RELIGIOUS MOOD 569

of European Christianity with the derisive and impartial eye of an Epicurean god, I should think one would never cease marvelling and laughing; does it not actually seem that some single will has ruled over Europe for eighteen centuries in order to make a *sublime abortion* of man? He, however, who, with opposite requirements (no longer Epicurean) and with some divine hammer in his hand, could approach this almost voluntary degeneration and stunting of mankind, as exemplified in the European Christian (Pascal, for instance), would he not have to cry aloud with rage, pity, and horror: 'Oh, you bunglers, presumptuous pitiful bunglers, what have you done! Was that a work for your hands? How you have hacked and botched my finest stone! What have *you* presumed to do!' – I should say that Christianity has hitherto been the most portentous of presumptions. Men, not great enough, nor hard enough, to be entitled as artists to take part in fashioning *man*; men, not sufficiently strong and far-sighted to *allow*, with sublime self-constraint, the obvious law of the thousandfold failures and perishings to prevail; men, not sufficiently noble to see the radically different grades of rank and intervals of rank that separate man from man – *such* men, with their 'equality before God', have hitherto swayed the destiny of Europe; until at last a dwarfed, almost ludicrous species has been produced, a gregarious animal, something obliging, sickly, mediocre, the European of the present day.

Fourth Chapter: *Apophthegms and Interludes*

63

He who is a thorough teacher takes things seriously – and even himself – only in relation to his pupils.

64

'Knowledge for its own sake' – that is the last snare laid by morality: we are thereby completely entangled in morals once more.

65

The charm of knowledge would be small, were it not that so much shame has to be overcome on the way to it.

65a

We are most dishonourable towards our God: he is not *permitted* to sin.

66

The tendency of a person to allow himself to be degraded, robbed, deceived, and exploited might be the diffidence of a god amongst men.

67

Love to one only is a barbarity, for it is exercised at the expense of all others. Love to God also!

68

'I did that,' says my memory. 'I could not have done that,' says my pride, and remains inexorable. Eventually – the memory yields.

69

One has regarded life carelessly, if one has failed to see the hand that – kills with leniency.

70

If a man has character, he has also his typical experience, which always recurs.

71

The sage as astronomer. – So long as thou feelest the stars as an 'above thee', thou lackest the eye of the discerning one.

72

It is not the strength, but the duration of great sentiments that makes great men.

73

He who attains his ideal, precisely thereby surpasses it.

73a

Many a peacock hides his tail from every eye – and calls it his pride.

74

A man of genius is unbearable, unless he possess at least two things besides: gratitude and purity.

75

The degree and nature of a man's sensuality extends to the highest altitudes of his spirit.

76

Under peaceful conditions the militant man attacks himself.

77

With his principles a man seeks either to dominate, or justify, or honour, or reproach, or conceal his habits: two men with the same principles probably seek fundamentally different ends there with.

78

He who despises himself, nevertheless esteems himself thereby, as a despiser.

79

A soul which knows that it is loved, but does not itself love, betrays its sediment: its dregs come up.

80

A thing that is explained ceases to concern us. – What did the god mean who gave the advice, 'Know thyself!' Did it perhaps imply: 'Cease to be concerned about thyself! Become objective!' – And Socrates? – And the 'scientific man'?

81

It is terrible to die of thirst at sea. Is it necessary that you should so salt your truth that it will no longer – quench thirst?

82

'Sympathy for all' – would be harshness and tyranny for *thee*, my good neighbour!

83

Instinct. – When the house is on fire one forgets even the dinner. – Yes, but one recovers it from amongst the ashes.

84

Woman learns how to hate in proportion as she – forgets how to charm.

85

The same emotions are in man and woman, but in different *tempo;* on that account man and woman never cease to misunderstand each other.

86

In the background of all their personal vanity, women themselves have still their impersonal scorn – for 'woman'.

87

Fettered heart, free spirit. – When one firmly fetters one's heart and keeps it prisoner, one can allow one's spirit many liberties: I said this once before. But people do not believe it when I say so, unless they know it already.

88

One begins to distrust very clever persons when they become embarrassed.

89

Dreadful experiences raise the question whether he who experiences them is not something dreadful also.

90

Heavy, melancholy men turn lighter, and come temporarily to their surface, precisely by that which makes others heavy — by hatred and love.

91

So cold, so icy, that one burns one's finger at the touch of him! Every hand that lays hold of him shrinks back! — And for that very reason many think him red-hot.

92

Who has not, at one time or another — sacrificed himself for the sake of his good name?

93

In affability there is no hatred of men, but precisely on that account a great deal too much contempt of men.

94

The maturity of man — that means, to have reacquired the seriousness that one had as a child at play.

95

To be ashamed of one's immorality is a step on the ladder at the end of which one is ashamed also of one's morality.

96

One should part from life as Ulysses parted from Nausicaa — blessing it rather than in love with it.

97

What? A great man? I always see merely the play-actor of his own ideal.

98

When one trains one's conscience, it kisses one while it bites.

99

The disappointed one speaks. – 'I listened for the echo and I heard only praise.'

100

We all feign to ourselves that we are simpler than we are; we thus relax ourselves away from our fellows.

101

A discerning one might easily regard himself at present as the animalisation of God.

102

Discovering reciprocal love should really disenchant the lover with regard to the beloved. 'What! *She* is modest enough to love even you? Or stupid enough? Or – or – '

103

The danger in happiness. – 'Everything now turns out best for me, I now love every fate – who would like to be my fate?'

104

Not their love of humanity, but the impotence of their love, prevents the Christians of today – burning us.

105

The *pia fraus* is still more repugnant to the taste (*the 'piety'*) of the free spirit (the 'pious man of knowledge') than the *impia fraus*.* Hence the profound lack of judgment, in comparison with the church, characteristic of the type 'free spirit' – as *its* non-freedom.

* *Pia Fraus*: holy deception; *impia fraus*: unholy deception.

106

By means of music the very passions enjoy themselves.

107

A sign of strong character, when once the resolution has been taken, to shut the ear even to the best counter-arguments. Occasionally, therefore, a will to stupidity.

108

There is no such thing as moral phenomena, but only a moral interpretation of phenomena.

109

The criminal is often enough not equal to his deed: he extenuates and maligns it.

110

The advocates of a criminal are seldom artists enough to turn the beautiful terribleness of the deed to the advantage of the doer.

111

Our vanity is most difficult to wound just when our pride has been wounded.

112

To him who feels himself preordained to contemplation and not to belief, all believers are too noisy and obtrusive; he guards against them.

113

'You want to prepossess him in your favour? Then you must be embarrassed before him.'

114

The immense expectation with regard to sexual love, and the coyness in this expectation, spoils all the perspectives of women at the outset.

115

Where there is neither love nor hatred in the game, woman's play is mediocre.

116

The great epochs of our life are at the points when we gain courage to rebaptize our badness as the best in us.

117

The will to overcome an emotion, is ultimately only the will of another, or of several other, emotions.

118

There is an innocence of admiration: it is possessed by him to whom it has not yet occurred that he himself may be admired some day.

119

Our loathing of dirt may be so great as to prevent us cleaning ourselves — 'justifying' ourselves.

120

Sensuality often forces the growth of love too much, so that its root remains weak, and is easily torn up.

121

It is a curious thing that God learned Greek when he wished to turn author — and that he did not learn it better.

122

To rejoice on account of praise is in many cases merely politeness of heart — and the very opposite of vanity of spirit.

123

Even concubinage has been corrupted — by marriage.

124

He who exults at the stake, does not triumph over pain, but because of the fact that he does not feel pain where he expected it. A parable.

125

When we have to change an opinion about anyone, we charge heavily to his account the inconvenience he thereby causes us.

126

A nation is a detour of nature to arrive at six or seven great men. – Yes, and then to get round them.

127

In the eyes of all true women science is hostile to the sense of shame. They feel as if one wished to peep under their skin with it – or worse still! under their dress and finery.

128

The more abstract the truth you wish to teach, the more must you allure the senses to it.

129

The devil has the most extensive perspectives for God; on that account he keeps so far away from him – the devil, in effect, as the oldest friend of knowledge.

130

What a person *is* begins to betray itself when his talent decreases – when he ceases to show what he *can do*. Talent is also an adornment; an adornment is also a concealment.

131

The sexes deceive themselves about each other: the reason is that in reality they honour and love only themselves (or their own ideal, to express it more agreeably). Thus man wishes woman to be peaceable: but in fact woman is *essentially* unpeaceable, like the cat, however well she may have assumed the peaceable demeanour.

132

One is punished best for one's virtues.

133

He who cannot find the way to his ideal, lives more frivolously and shamelessly than the man without an ideal.

134

From the senses originate all trustworthiness, all good conscience, all evidence of truth.

135

Pharisaism is not a deterioration of the good man; a considerable part of it is rather an essential condition of being good.

136

The one seeks an *accoucheur* for his thoughts, the other seeks someone whom he can assist: a good conversation thus originates.

137

In intercourse with scholars and artists one readily makes mistakes of opposite kinds: in a remarkable scholar one not infrequently finds a mediocre man; and often even in a mediocre artist, one finds a very remarkable man.

138

We do the same when awake as when dreaming: we only invent and imagine him with whom we have intercourse – and forget it immediately.

139

In revenge and in love woman is more barbarous than man.

140

Advice as a riddle. – 'If the band is not to break, bite it first – secure to make!'

141

The belly is the reason why man does not so readily take himself for a god.

142

The chastest utterance I ever heard: '*Dans le véritable amour c'est l'âme qui enveloppe le corps.*'*

143

Our vanity would like what we do best to pass precisely for what is most difficult to us. – Concerning the origin of many systems of morals.

144

When a woman has scholarly inclinations there is generally something wrong with her sexual nature. Barrenness itself conduces to a certain virility of taste; man, indeed, if I may say so, is 'the barren animal'.

145

Comparing man and woman generally, one may say that woman would not have the genius for adornment, if she had not the instinct for the *secondary* rôle.

146

He who fights with monsters should be careful lest he thereby become a monster. And if thou gaze long into an abyss, the abyss will also gaze into thee.

147

From old Florentine novels – moreover, from life: *Buona femmina e mala femmina vuol bastone.*† – Sacchetti, Nov. 86.

148

To seduce their neighbour to a favourable opinion, and afterwards to believe implicitly in this opinion of their neighbour – who can do this conjuring trick so well as women?

149

That which an age considers evil is usually an unseasonable echo of what was formerly considered good – the atavism of an old ideal.

---

* 'In true love it is the soul that encloses the body.'
† 'A good woman, and a bad woman, wants a stick.'

150

Around the hero everything becomes a tragedy; around the demi-god everything becomes a satyrplay; and around God everything becomes – what? Perhaps a 'world'?

151

It is not enough to possess a talent: one must also have your permission to possess it – eh, my friends?

152

'Where there is the tree of knowledge, there is always Paradise': so say the most ancient and the most modern serpents.

153

What is done out of love always takes place beyond good and evil.

154

Objection, evasion, joyous distrust, and love of irony are signs of health; everything absolute belongs to pathology.

155

The sense of the tragic increases and declines with sensuousness.

156

Insanity in individuals is something rare – but in groups, parties, nations, and epochs it is the rule.

157

The thought of suicide is a great consolation: by means of it one gets successfully through many a bad night.

158

Not only our reason, but also our conscience, truckles to our strongest impulse – the tyrant in us.

159

One *must* repay good and ill; but why just to the person who did us good or ill?

160

One no longer loves one's knowledge sufficiently after one has communicated it.

161

Poets act shamelessly towards their experiences: they exploit them.

162

'Our fellow-creature is not our neighbour, but our neighbour's neighbour' – so thinks every nation.

163

Love brings to light the noble and hidden qualities of a lover – his rare and exceptional traits: it is thus liable to be deceptive as to his normal character.

164

Jesus said to his Jews: 'The law was for servants – love God as I love him, as his Son! What have we Sons of God to do with morals!'

165

In sight of every party. – A shepherd has always need of a bell-wether – or he has himself to be a wether occasionally.

166

One may indeed lie with the mouth; but with the accompanying grimace one nevertheless tells the truth.

167

To vigorous men intimacy is a matter of shame – and something precious.

168

Christianity gave Eros poison to drink; he did not die of it, certainly, but degenerated to Vice.

169

To talk much about oneself may also be a means of concealing oneself.

170

In praise there is more obtrusiveness than in blame.

171

Pity has an almost ludicrous effect on a man of knowledge, like tender hands on a Cyclops.

172

One occasionally embraces someone or other, out of love to mankind (because one cannot embrace all); but this is what one must never confess to the individual.

173

One does not hate as long as one disesteems, but only when one esteems equal or superior.

174

Ye Utilitarians – ye, too, love the *utile* only as a *vehicle* for your inclinations – ye, too, really find the noise of its wheels insupportable!

175

One loves ultimately one's desires, not the thing desired.

176

The vanity of others is only counter to our taste when it is counter to our vanity.

177

With regard to what 'truthfulness' is, perhaps nobody has ever been sufficiently truthful.

178

One does not believe in the follies of clever men: what a forfeiture of the rights of man!

179

The consequences of our actions seize us by the forelock, very indifferent to the fact that we have meanwhile 'reformed'.

180

There is an innocence in lying which is the sign of good faith in a cause.

181

It is inhuman to bless when one is being cursed.

182

The familiarity of superiors embitters one, because it may not be returned.

183

'I am affected, not because you have deceived me, but because I can no longer believe in you.'

184

There is a haughtiness of kindness which has the appearance of wickedness.

185

'I dislike him.' – Why? – 'I am not a match for him.' – Did any one ever answer so?

186

The moral sentiment in Europe at present is perhaps as subtle, belated, diverse, sensitive, and refined, as the 'Science of Morals' belonging thereto is recent, initial, awkward, and coarse-fingered – an interesting contrast, which sometimes becomes incarnate and obvious in the very person of a moralist. Indeed, the expression 'Science of Morals' is, in respect to what is designated thereby, far too presumptuous and counter to *good* taste – which is always a foretaste of more modest expressions. One ought to avow with the utmost fairness *what* is still necessary here for a long time, *what* is alone proper for the present: namely, the collection of material, the comprehensive survey and classification of an immense domain of delicate sentiments of worth, and distinctions of worth, which live, grow, propagate, and perish – and perhaps attempts to give a clear idea of the recurring and more common forms of these living crystallisations – as preparation for a *theory of types* of morality. To be sure, people have not hitherto been so modest. All the philosophers, with a pedantic and ridiculous seriousness, demanded of themselves something very much higher, more pretentious, and ceremonious, when they concerned themselves with morality as a science: they wanted to *give a basis* to morality – and every philosopher hitherto has believed that he has given it a basis; morality itself, however, has been regarded as something 'given'. How far from their awkward pride was the seemingly insignificant problem – left in dust and decay – of a description of forms of morality, notwithstanding that the finest hands and senses could hardly be fine enough for it! It was precisely owing to moral philosophers knowing the moral facts imperfectly, in an arbitrary epitome, or an accidental abridgment – perhaps as the morality of their environment, their position, their church, their *Zeitgeist*, their climate and zone – it was precisely because they were badly instructed with regard to nations, eras, and past ages, and were by no means eager to know about these matters, that they did not even come in sight of the real problems of morals – problems which only disclose themselves by a comparison of *many* kinds of morality. In every 'Science of Morals' hitherto, strange as it may sound, the problem of morality itself has been *omitted*; there has been no suspicion that there was anything problematic there! That which philosophers called 'giving a basis to morality', and endeavoured to realise, has, when seen in a right light, proved merely a learned form of good *faith* in prevailing morality, a new means of its *expression*, consequently just a matter-of-fact within the sphere of a definite morality, yea, in its ultimate motive, a sort of denial that it is *lawful* for this morality to be called in question – and in any case the reverse of the testing, analysing, doubting, and vivisecting of this very faith. Hear, for instance, with what innocence – almost worthy of honour – Schopenhauer represents his own task, and draw your conclusions concerning the scientificalness of a 'Science' whose latest master still talks in the strain of children and old wives: 'The principle,' he says (page 136 of the *Grundprobleme der Ethik*), 'the axiom about the purport of which all moralists are *practically* agreed: *neminem laede, immo omnes quantum potes juva** – is *really* the proposition which all moral teachers strive to establish, . . . the *real* basis of ethics which has been sought, like the philosopher's stone, for centuries.' – The difficulty of establishing the proposition referred to may indeed be great – it is well known that Schopenhauer also was unsuccessful in his efforts; and whoever has thoroughly realised how absurdly false and sentimental this proposition is, in a world whose essence is Will to Power, may be reminded that Schopenhauer, although a pessimist, *actually* – played the flute . . . daily after dinner: one may read about the matter in his biography. A question by the way: a pessimist, a repudiator of God and of the world, who *makes a halt* at morality – who assents to morality, and plays the flute to *laede-neminem* morals . . . what, is that really – a pessimist?

187

Apart from the value of such assertions as 'there is a categorical imperative in us', one can always ask: What does such an assertion indicate about him who makes it? There are systems of morals

* 'Injure no one, rather help everyone to the best of your ability.'

which are meant to justify their author in the eyes of other people; other systems of morals are meant to tranquillise him, and make him self-satisfied; with other systems he wants to crucify and humble himself; with others he wishes to take revenge; with others to conceal himself; with others to glorify himself and gain superiority and distinction; – this system of morals helps its author to forget, that system makes him, or something of him, forgotten; many a moralist would like to exercise power and creative arbitrariness over mankind; many another, perhaps, Kant especially, gives us to understand by his morals that 'what is estimable in me, is that I know how to obey – and with you it *shall* not be otherwise than with me!' In short, systems of morals are only a *sign-language of the emotions*.

188

In contrast to *laisser-aller*, every system of morals is a sort of tyranny against 'nature' and also against 'reason'; that is, however, no objection, unless one should again decree by some system of morals, that all kinds of tyranny and unreasonableness are unlawful. What is essential and invaluable in every system of morals, is that it is a long constraint. In order to understand Stoicism, or Port-Royal, or Puritanism, one should remember the constraint under which every language has attained to strength and freedom – the metrical constraint, the tyranny of rhyme and rhythm. How much trouble have the poets and orators of every nation given themselves! – not excepting some of the prose writers of today, in whose ear dwells an inexorable conscientiousness – 'for the sake of a folly', as utilitarian bunglers say, and thereby deem themselves wise – 'from submission to arbitrary laws', as the anarchists say, and thereby fancy themselves 'free', even free-spirited. The singular fact remains, however, that everything of the nature of freedom, elegance, boldness, dance, and masterly certainty, which exists or has existed, whether it be in thought itself, or in administration, or in speaking and persuading, in art just as in conduct, has only developed by means of the tyranny of such arbitrary law; and in all seriousness, it is not at all improbable that precisely this is 'nature' and 'natural' – and *not laisser-aller*! Every artist knows how different from the state of letting himself go, is his 'most natural' condition, the free arranging, locating, disposing, and constructing in the moments of 'inspiration' – and how strictly and delicately he then obeys a thousand laws, which, by their very rigidness and precision, defy all formulation by means of ideas (even the most stable idea has, in comparison therewith, something floating, manifold, and ambiguous in it). The essential thing 'in heaven and in earth' is, apparently (to repeat it once more), that there should be long *obedience* in the same direction; there thereby results, and has always resulted in the long run, something which has made life worth living; for instance, virtue, art, music, dancing, reason, spirituality – anything whatever that is transfiguring, refined, foolish, or divine. The long bondage of the spirit, the distrustful constraint in the communicability of ideas, the discipline which the thinker imposed on himself to think in accordance with the rules of a church or a court, or conformable to Aristotelian premises, the persistent spiritual will to interpret everything that happened according to a Christian scheme, and in every occurrence to rediscover and justify the Christian God – all this violence, arbitrariness, severity, dreadfulness, and unreasonableness, has proved itself the disciplinary means whereby the European spirit has attained its strength, its remorseless curiosity and subtle mobility; granted also that much irrecoverable strength and spirit had to be stifled, suffocated, and spoilt in the process (for here, as everywhere, 'nature' shows herself as she is, in all her extravagant and *indifferent* magnificence, which is shocking, but nevertheless noble). That for centuries European thinkers only thought in order to prove something – nowadays, on the contrary, we are suspicious of every thinker who 'wishes to prove something' – that it was always settled beforehand what *was to be* the result of their strictest thinking, as it was perhaps in the Asiatic astrology of former times, or as it is still at the present day in the innocent, Christian-moral explanation of immediate personal events 'for the glory of God', or 'for the good of the soul' – this tyranny, this arbitrariness, this severe and magnificent stupidity, has *educated* the spirit; slavery, both in the coarser and the finer sense, is apparently an indispensable means even of spiritual education and discipline. One may look at every system of morals in this light: it is 'nature' therein which teaches to hate the *laisser-aller*, the too great freedom, and implants the need for limited horizons, for immediate duties – it teaches the *narrowing of perspectives*, and thus, in a certain sense, that stupidity is a condition of life and development. 'Thou must obey someone, and for a long time; *otherwise* thou wilt come to grief, and lose all respect for thyself' – this seems to me to be the moral imperative of nature, which is certainly neither 'categorical', as old Kant wished (consequently the 'otherwise'), nor does it address itself to the individual (what does nature care for the individual!), but to nations, races, ages, and ranks, above all, however, to the animal 'man' generally, to *mankind*.

189

Industrious races find it a great hardship to be idle: it was a master stroke of *English* instinct to hallow and begloom Sunday to such an extent that the Englishman unconsciously hankers for his week- and work-day again – as a kind of cleverly devised, cleverly inter- calated *fast*, such as is also frequently found in the ancient world (although, as is appropriate in southern nations, not precisely with respect to work). Many kinds of fasts are necessary; and wherever powerful impulses and habits prevail, legislators have to see that intercalary days are appointed, on which such impulses are fettered, and learn to hunger anew. Viewed from a higher standpoint, whole generations and epochs, when they show themselves in- fected with any moral fanaticism, seem like those intercalated periods of restraint and fasting, during which an impulse learns to humble and submit itself – at the same time also to *purify* and *sharpen* itself; certain philosophical sects likewise admit of a similar interpretation (for instance, the Stoa, in the midst of Hellenic culture, with the atmosphere rank and overcharged with Aphro- disiacal odours). – Here also is a hint for the explanation of the paradox, why it was precisely in the most Christian period of Eur- opean history, and in general only under the pressure of Christian sentiments, that the sexual impulse sublimated into love (*amour- passion*).

190

There is something in the morality of Plato which does not really belong to Plato, but which only appears in his philosophy, one might say, in spite of him: namely, Socratism, for which he himself was too noble. 'No one desires to injure himself, hence all evil is done unwittingly. The evil man inflicts injury on himself; he would not do so, however, if he knew that evil is evil. The evil man, therefore, is only evil through error; if one free him from error one will necessarily make him — good.' — This mode of reasoning savours of the *populace*, who perceive only the unpleasant consequences of evil-doing, and practically judge that 'it is *stupid* to do wrong'; while they accept 'good' as identical with 'useful and pleasant', without further thought. As regards every system of utilitarianism, one may at once assume that it has the same origin, and follow the scent: one will seldom err. — Plato did all he could to interpret something refined and noble into the tenets of his teacher, and above all to interpret himself into them — he, the most daring of all interpreters, who lifted the entire Socrates out of the street, as a popular theme and song, to exhibit him in endless and impossible modifications — namely, in all his own disguises and multiplicities. In jest, and in Homeric language as well, what is the Platonic Socrates, if not —

*prosthe Platon opithen te Platon messê te Ximaira.**

191

The old theological problem of 'Faith' and 'Knowledge', or more plainly, of instinct and reason — the question whether, in respect to the valuation of things, instinct deserves more authority than rationality, which wants to appreciate and act according to motives, according to a 'Why', that is to say, in conformity to purpose and utility — it is always the old moral problem that first appeared in the person of Socrates, and had divided men's minds long before Christianity. Socrates himself, following, of course, the taste of his talent — that of a surpassing dialectician — took first the side of reason; and, in fact, what did he do all his life but laugh at the awkward incapacity of the noble Athenians, who were men of instinct, like all noble men, and could never give satisfactory answers concerning the motives of their actions? In the end, however, though silently and secretly, he laughed also at himself: with his finer conscience and introspection, he found in himself the same difficulty and incapacity. 'But why' — he said to himself — 'should one on that account separate oneself from the instincts! One must set them right, and the reason *also* — one must follow the instincts, but at the same time persuade the reason to support them

* Plato in front, Plato behind, and a Chimera in between'.

with good arguments.' This was the real *falseness* of that great and mysterious ironist; he brought his conscience up to the point that he was satisfied with a kind of self-outwitting: in fact, he perceived the irrationality in the moral judgment. – Plato, more innocent in such matters, and without the craftiness of the plebeian, wished to prove to himself, at the expenditure of all his strength – the greatest strength a philosopher had ever expended – that reason and instinct lead spontaneously to one goal, to the good, to 'God'; and since Plato, all theologians and philosophers have followed the same path – which means that in matters of morality, instinct (or as Christians call it, 'Faith', or as I call it, 'the herd') has hitherto triumphed. Unless one should make an exception in the case of Descartes, the father of rationalism (and consequently the grandfather of the Revolution), who recognised only the authority of reason: but reason is only a tool, and Descartes was superficial.

192

Whoever has followed the history of a single science, finds in its development a clue to the understanding of the oldest and commonest processes of all 'knowledge and cognisance': there, as here, the premature hypotheses, the fictions, the good stupid will to 'belief', and the lack of distrust and patience are first developed – our senses learn late, and never learn completely, to be subtle, reliable, and cautious organs of knowledge. Our eyes find it easier on a given occasion to produce a picture already often produced, than to seize upon the divergence and novelty of an impression: the latter requires more force, more 'morality'. It is difficult and painful for the ear to listen to anything new; we hear strange music badly. When we hear another language spoken, we involuntarily attempt to form the sounds into words with which we are more familiar and conversant – it was thus, for example, that the Germans modified the spoken word *arcubalista* into *armbrust* (crossbow). Our senses are also hostile and averse to the new; and generally, even in the 'simplest' processes of sensation, the emotions *dominate* – such as fear, love, hatred, and the passive emotion of indolence. – As little as a reader nowadays reads all the single words (not to speak of syllables) of a page – he rather takes about five out of every twenty words at random, and 'guesses' the probably appropriate sense to them – just as little do we see a tree correctly and completely in respect to its leaves, branches, colour, and shape; we find it so much easier to fancy the chance of a tree. Even in the midst of the most remarkable experiences, we still do just the same; we fabricate the greater part of the experience, and can hardly be made to contemplate any event, *except* as 'inventors' thereof. All this goes to prove that from our fundamental nature and from remote ages we have been – *accustomed to lying*. Or, to express it more politely and hypocritically, in short, more pleasantly – one is much more of an artist than one is aware of. – In an animated conversation, I often see the face of the person with whom I am speaking so clearly and sharply defined before me, according to the thought he expresses, or which I believe to be evoked in his mind, that the degree of distinctness far exceeds the *strength* of my visual faculty – the delicacy of the play of the muscles and of the expression of the eyes *must* therefore be imagined by me. Probably the person put on quite a different expression, or none at all.

193

Quidquid luce fuit, tenebris agit:* but also contrariwise. What we experience in dreams, provided we experience it often, pertains at last just as much to the general belongings of our soul as anything 'actually' experienced; by virtue thereof we are richer or poorer, we have a requirement more or less, and finally, in broad daylight, and even in the brightest moments of our waking life, we are ruled to some extent by the nature of our dreams. Supposing that someone has often flown in his dreams, and that at last, as soon as he dreams, he is conscious of the power and art of flying as his privilege and his peculiarly enviable happiness; such a person, who believes that on the slightest impulse, he can actualise all sorts of curves and angles, who knows the sensation of a certain divine levity, an 'upwards' without effort or constraint, a 'downwards' without descending or lowering – without *trouble*! – how could the man with such dream-experiences and dream-habits fail to find 'happiness' differently coloured and defined, even in his waking hours! How could he fail – to long *differently* for happiness? 'Flight', such as is described by poets, must, when compared with his own 'flying', be far too earthly, muscular, violent, far too 'troublesome' for him.

* 'Whatever has occurred in daylight, acts in darkness..'

194

The difference among men does not manifest itself only in the difference of their lists of desirable things – in their regarding different good things as worth striving for, and being disagreed as to the greater or less value, the order of rank, of the commonly recognised desirable things – it manifests itself much more in what they regard as actually *having* and *possessing* a desirable thing. As regards a woman, for instance, the control over her body and her sexual gratification serves as an amply sufficient sign of ownership and possession to the more modest man; another with a more suspicious and ambitious thirst for possession, sees the 'questionableness', the mere apparentness of such ownership, and wishes to have finer tests in order to know especially whether the woman not only gives herself to him, but also gives up for his sake what she has or would like to have – only *then* does he look upon her as 'possessed'. A third, however, has not even here got to the limit of his distrust and his desire for possession: he asks himself whether the woman, when she gives up everything for him, does not perhaps do so for a phantom of him; he wishes first to be thoroughly, indeed, profoundly well known; in order to be loved at all he ventures to let himself be found out. Only then does he feel the beloved one fully in his possession, when she no longer deceives herself about him, when she loves him just as much for the sake of his devilry and concealed insatiability, as for his goodness, patience, and spirituality. One man would like to possess a nation, and he finds all the higher arts of Cagliostro and Catalina suitable for his purpose. Another, with a more refined thirst for possession, says to himself: 'One may not deceive where one desires to possess' – he is irritated and impatient at the idea that a mask of him should rule in the hearts of the people: 'I must, therefore, *make* myself known, and first of all learn to know myself!' Amongst helpful and charitable people, one almost always finds the awkward craftiness which first gets up suitably him who has to be helped, as though, for instance, he should 'merit' help, seek just *their* help, and would show himself deeply grateful, attached, and subservient to them for all help. With these conceits, they take control of the needy as a property, just as in general they are charitable and helpful out of a desire for property. One finds them jealous when they are crossed or forestalled in their charity. Parents involuntarily make something like themselves out of their children – they call that 'education'; no mother doubts at the bottom of her heart that the child she has born is thereby her property, no father hesitates about his right to subject it to *his own* ideas and notions of worth. Indeed, in former times fathers deemed it right to use their discretion concerning the life or death of the newly born (as amongst the ancient Germans). And like the father, so also do the teacher, the class, the priest, and the prince still see in every new individual an unobjectionable opportunity for a new possession. The consequence is . . .

195

The Jews – a people 'born for slavery', as Tacitus and the whole ancient world say of them; 'the chosen people among the nations', as they themselves say and believe – the Jews performed the miracle of the inversion of valuations, by means of which life on earth obtained a new and dangerous charm for a couple of millennia. Their prophets fused into one the expressions 'rich', 'godless', 'wicked', 'violent', 'sensual', and for the first time coined the word 'world' as a term of reproach. In this inversion of valuations (in which is also included the use of the word 'poor' as synonymous with 'saint' and 'friend') the significance of the Jewish people is to be found; it is with *them* that the *slave-insurrection in morals* commences.

196

It is to be *inferred* that there are countless dark bodies near the sun – such as we shall never see. Amongst ourselves, this is an allegory; and the psychologist of morals reads the whole star-writing merely as an allegorical and symbolic language in which much may be unexpressed.

197

The beast of prey and the man of prey (for instance, Caesar Borgia) are fundamentally misunderstood, 'nature' is misunderstood, so long as one seeks a 'morbidness' in the constitution of these healthiest of all tropical monsters and growths, or even an innate 'hell' in them – as almost all moralists have done hitherto. Does it not seem that there is a hatred of the virgin forest and of the tropics among moralists? And that the 'tropical man' must be discredited at all costs, whether as disease and deterioration of mankind, or as his own hell and self-torture? And why? In favour of the 'temperate zones'? In favour of the temperate men? The 'moral'? The mediocre? – This for the chapter: 'Morals as Timidity'.

198

All the systems of morals which address themselves to individuals with a view to their 'happiness', as it is called – what else are they but suggestions for behaviour adapted to the degree of *danger* from themselves in which the individuals live; recipes for their passions, their good and bad propensities, in so far as such have the Will to Power and would like to play the master; small and great expediencies and elaborations, permeated with the musty odour of old family medicines and old-wife wisdom; all of them grotesque and absurd in their form – because they address themselves to 'all', because they generalise where generalisation is not authorised; all of them speaking unconditionally, and taking themselves unconditionally; all of them flavoured not merely with one grain of salt, but rather endurable only, and sometimes even seductive, when they are over-spiced and begin to smell dangerously, especially of 'the other world'. That is all of little value when estimated intellectually, and is far from being 'science', much less 'wisdom'; but, repeated once more, and three times repeated, it is expediency, expediency, expediency, mixed with stupidity, stupidity, stupidity – whether it be the indifference and statuesque coldness towards the heated folly of the emotions, which the Stoics advised and fostered; or the no-more-laughing and no-more-weeping of Spinoza, the destruction of the emotions by their analysis and vivisection, which he recommended so naively; or the lowering of the emotions to an innocent mean at which they may be satisfied, the Aristotelianism of morals; or even morality as the enjoyment of the emotions in a voluntary attenuation and spiritualisation by the symbolism of art, perhaps as music, or as love of God, and of mankind for God's sake – for in religion the passions are once more enfranchised, provided that . . . ; or, finally, even the complaisant and wanton surrender to the emotions, as has been taught by Hafis and Goethe, the bold letting-go of the reins, the spiritual and corporeal *licentia morum* in the exceptional cases of wise old codgers and drunkards, with whom it 'no longer has much danger'. – This also for the chapter: 'Morals as Timidity'.

199

Inasmuch as in all ages, as long as mankind has existed, there have also been human herds (family alliances, communities, tribes, peoples, states, churches), and always a great number who obey in proportion to the small number who command – in view, therefore, of the fact that obedience has been most practised and fostered among mankind hitherto, one may reasonably suppose that, generally speaking, the need thereof is now innate in everyone, as a kind of *formal conscience* which gives the command: 'Thou shalt unconditionally do something, unconditionally refrain from something'; in short, 'Thou shalt'. This need tries to satisfy itself and to fill its form with a content; according to its strength, impatience, and eagerness, it at once seizes as an omnivorous appetite with little selection, and accepts whatever is shouted into its ear by all sorts of commanders – parents, teachers, laws, class prejudices, or public opinion. The extraordinary limitation of human development, the hesitation, protractedness, frequent retrogression, and turning thereof, is attributable to the fact that the herd-instinct of obedience is transmitted best, and at the cost of the art of command. If one imagine this instinct increasing to its greatest extent, commanders and independent individuals will finally be lacking altogether; or they will suffer inwardly from a bad conscience, and will have to impose a deception on themselves in the first place in order to be able to command: just as if they also were only obeying. This condition of things actually exists in Europe at present – I call it the moral hypocrisy of the commanding class. They know no other way of protecting themselves from their bad conscience than by playing the rôle of executors of older and higher orders (of predecessors, of the constitution, of justice, of the law, or of God himself), or they even justify themselves by maxims from the current opinions of the herd, as 'first servants of their people', or 'instruments of the public weal'. On the other hand, the gregarious European man nowadays assumes an air as if he were the only kind of man that is allowable; he glorifies his qualities, such as public spirit, kindness, deference, industry, temperance, modesty, indulgence, sympathy, by virtue of which he is gentle, endurable, and useful to the herd, as the peculiarly human virtues. In cases, however, where it is believed that the leader and bell-wether cannot be dispensed with, attempt after attempt is made nowadays to replace commanders by the summing together of clever gregarious men: all representative constitutions, for example, are of this origin. In spite of all, what a blessing, what a deliverance from a weight becoming unendurable, is the appearance of an absolute ruler for these gregarious Europeans – of this fact the effect of the appearance of Napoleon was the last great proof: the history of the influence of Napoleon is almost the history of the higher happiness to which the entire century has attained in its worthiest individuals and periods.

200

The man of an age of dissolution which mixes the races with one another, who has the inheritance of a diversified descent in his body – that is to say, contrary, and often not only contrary, instincts and standards of value, which struggle with one another and are seldom at peace – such a man of late culture and broken lights, will, on an average, be a weak man. His fundamental desire is that the war which is *in him* should come to an end; happiness appears to him in the character of a soothing medicine and mode of thought (for instance, Epicurean or Christian); it is above all things the happiness of repose, of undisturbedness, of repletion, of final unity – it is the 'Sabbath of Sabbaths', to use the expression of the holy rhetorician, St Augustine, who was himself such a man. – Should, however, the contrariety and conflict in such natures operate as an *additional* incentive and stimulus to life – and if, on the other hand, in addition to their powerful and irreconcilable instincts, they have also inherited and indoctrinated into them a proper mastery and subtlety for carrying on the conflict with themselves (that is to say, the faculty of self-control and self-deception), there then arise those marvellously incomprehensible, and inexplicable beings, those enigmatical men, predestined for conquering and circumventing others, the finest examples of which are Alcibiades and Caesar (with whom I should like to associate the *first* of Europeans according to my taste, the Hohenstaufen, Frederick the Second), and amongst artists, perhaps

Lionardo da Vinci. They appear precisely in the same periods when that weaker type, with its longing for repose, comes to the front; the two types are complementary to each other, and spring from the same causes.

201

As long as the utility which determines moral estimates is only gregarious utility, as long as the preservation of the community is only kept in view, and the immoral is sought precisely and exclusively in what seems dangerous to the maintenance of the community, there can be no 'morality of love to one's neighbour'. Granted even that there is already a little constant exercise of consideration, sympathy, fairness, gentleness, and mutual assistance, granted that even in this condition of society all those instincts are already active which are latterly distinguished by honourable names as 'virtues', and eventually almost coincide with the conception 'morality': in that period they do not as yet belong to the domain of moral valuations – they are still *ultra-moral*. A sympathetic action, for instance, is neither called good nor bad, moral nor immoral, in the best period of the Romans; and should it be praised, a sort of resentful disdain is compatible with this praise, even at the best, directly the sympathetic action is compared with one which contributes to the welfare of the whole, to the *res publica*. After all, 'love to our neighbour' is always a secondary matter, partly conventional and arbitrarily manifested in relation to our *fear of our neighbour*. After the fabric of society seems on the whole established and secured against external dangers, it is this fear of our neighbour which again creates new perspectives of moral valuation. Certain strong and dangerous instincts, such as the love of enterprise, foolhardiness, revengefulness, astuteness, rapacity, and love of power, which up till then had not only to be honoured from the point of view of general utility – under other names, of course, than those here given – but had to be fostered and cultivated (because they were perpetually required in the common danger against the common enemies), are now felt in their dangerousness to be doubly strong – when the outlets for them are lacking – and are gradually branded as immoral and given over to calumny. The contrary instincts and inclinations now attain to moral honour; the gregarious instinct gradually draws its conclusions. How much or how little dangerousness to the community or to equality is contained in an opinion, a condition, an emotion, a disposition, or an endowment – that is now the moral perspective; here again fear is the mother of morals. It is by the loftiest and strongest instincts, when they break out passionately and carry the individual far above and beyond the average, and the low level of the gregarious conscience, that the self-reliance of the community is destroyed; its belief in itself, its backbone, as it were, breaks; consequently these very instincts will be most branded and defamed. The lofty independent spirituality, the will to stand alone, and even the cogent reason, are felt to be dangers; everything that elevates the individual above the herd, and is a source of fear to the neighbour, is henceforth called *evil*; the tolerant, unassuming, self-adapting, self-equalising disposition, the *mediocrity* of desires, attains to moral distinction and honour. Finally, under very peaceful circumstances, there is always less opportunity and necessity for training the feelings to severity and rigour; and now every form of severity, even in justice, begins to disturb the conscience; a lofty and rigorous nobleness and self-responsibility almost offends, and awakens distrust, 'the lamb', and still more 'the sheep', wins respect. There is a point of diseased mellowness and effeminacy in the history of society, at which society itself takes the part of him who injures it, the part of the *criminal*, and does so, in fact, seriously and honestly. To punish, appears to it to be somehow unfair – it is certain that the idea of 'punishment' and 'the obligation to punish' are then painful and alarming to people. 'Is it not sufficient if the criminal be rendered *harmless*? Why should we still punish? Punishment itself is terrible!' – with these questions gregarious morality, the morality of fear, draws its ultimate conclusion. If one could at all do away with danger, the cause of fear, one would have done away with this morality at the same time, it would no longer be necessary, it *would not consider itself* any longer necessary! – Whoever examines the conscience of the present-day European, will always elicit the same imperative from its thousand moral folds and hidden recesses, the imperative of the timidity of the herd: 'we wish that some time or other there may be *nothing more to fear*!' Some time or other – the will and the way *thereto* is nowadays called 'progress' all over Europe.

202

Let us at once say again what we have already said a hundred times, for people's ears nowadays are unwilling to hear such truths – *our* truths. We know well enough how offensively it sounds when anyone plainly, and without metaphor, counts man amongst the animals; but it will be accounted to us almost a *crime*, that it is precisely in respect to men of 'modern ideas' that we have constantly applied the terms 'herd', 'herd-instincts', and such like expressions. What avail is it? We cannot do otherwise, for it is precisely here that our new insight is. We have found that in all the principal moral judgments Europe has become unanimous, including likewise the countries where European influence prevails: in Europe people evidently *know* what Socrates thought he did not know, and what the famous serpent of old once promised to teach – they 'know' today what is good and evil. It must then sound hard and be distasteful to the ear, when we always insist that that which here thinks it knows, that which here glorifies itself with praise and blame, and calls itself good, is the instinct of the herding human animal: the instinct which has come and is ever coming more and more to the front, to preponderance and supremacy over other instincts, according to the increasing physiological approximation and resemblance of which it is the symptom. *Morality in Europe at present is herding-animal morality;* and therefore, as we understand the matter, only one kind of human morality, beside which, before which, and after which many other moralities, and above all *higher* moralities, are or should be possible. Against such a 'possibility', against such a 'should be', however, this morality defends itself with all its strength; it says obstinately and inexorably: 'I am morality itself and nothing else is morality!' Indeed, with the help of a religion which has humoured and flattered the sublimest desires of the herding-animal, things have reached such a point that we always find a more visible expression of this morality even in political and social arrangements: the *democratic* movement is the inheritance of the Christian movement. That its *tempo*, however, is much too slow and sleepy for the more impatient ones, for those who are sick and distracted by the herding-instinct, is indicated by the increasingly furious howling, and always less disguised teeth-gnashing of the anarchist dogs, who are now roving through the highways of European culture. Apparently in opposition to the peacefully industrious democrats and Revolution-ideologues, and still more so to the awkward philosophasters and fraternity-visionaries who call themselves Socialists and want a 'free society', those are really at one with them all in their thorough and instinctive hostility to every form of society other than that of the *autonomous* herd (to the extent even of repudiating the notions 'master' and 'servant' – *ni dieu ni maître*,* says a socialist formula); at one in their tenacious opposition to every special claim, every special right and privilege (this means ultimately opposition to *every* right, for when all are equal, no one needs 'rights' any longer); at one in their distrust of punitive justice (as though it were a violation of the weak, unfair to the *necessary* consequences of all former society); but equally at one in their religion of sympathy, in their compassion for all that feels, lives, and suffers (down to the very animals, up even to 'God' – the extravagance of 'sympathy for God' belongs to a democratic age); altogether at one in the cry and impatience of their sympathy, in their deadly hatred of suffering generally, in their almost feminine incapacity for witnessing it or *allowing* it; at one in their involuntary beglooming and heart-softening, under the spell of which Europe seems to be threatened with a new Buddhism; at one in their belief in the morality of *mutual* sympathy, as though it were morality in itself, the climax, the *attained* climax of mankind, the sole hope of the future, the consolation of the present, the great discharge from all the obligations of the past; altogether at one in their belief in the community as the *deliverer*, in the herd, and therefore in 'themselves'.

203

We, who hold a different belief – we, who regard the democratic movement, not only as a degenerating form of political organisation, but as equivalent to a degenerating, a waning type of man, as involving his mediocrising and depreciation: where have *we* to fix our hopes? In *new philosophers* – there is no other alternative: in minds strong and original enough to initiate opposite estimates of value, to transvalue and invert 'eternal valuations'; in forerunners, in men of the future, who in the present shall fix the

* 'Neither god nor master'.

constraints and fasten the knots which will compel millennia to take *new* paths. To teach man the future of humanity as his *will*, as depending on human will, and to make preparation for vast hazardous enterprises and collective attempts in rearing and educating, in order thereby to put an end to the frightful rule of folly and chance which has hitherto gone by the name of 'history' (the folly of the 'greatest number' is only its last form) – for that purpose a new type of philosophers and commanders will some time or other be needed, at the very idea of which everything that has existed in the way of occult, terrible, and benevolent beings might look pale and dwarfed. The image of such leaders hovers before *our* eyes – is it lawful for me to say it aloud, ye free spirits? The conditions which one would partly have to create and partly utilise for their genesis; the presumptive methods and tests by virtue of which a soul should grow up to such an elevation and power as to feel a *constraint* to these tasks; a transvaluation of values, under the new pressure and hammer of which a conscience should be steeled and a heart transformed into brass, so as to bear the weight of such responsibility; and on the other hand the necessity for such leaders, the dreadful danger that they might be lacking, or miscarry and degenerate – these are *our* real anxieties and glooms, ye know it well, ye free spirits! these are the heavy distant thoughts and storms which sweep across the heaven of *our* life. There are few pains so grievous as to have seen, divined, or experienced how an exceptional man has missed his way and deteriorated; but he who has the rare eye for the universal danger of 'man' himself *deteriorating*, he who like us has recognised the extraordinary fortuitousness which has hitherto played its game in respect to the future of mankind – a game in which neither the hand, nor even a 'finger of God' has participated! – he who divines the fate that is hidden under the idiotic unwariness and blind confidence of 'modern ideas', and still more under the whole of Christo-European morality – suffers from an anguish with which no other is to be compared. He sees at a glance all that could still *be made out of man* through a favourable accumulation and augmentation of human powers and arrangements; he knows with all the knowledge of his conviction how unexhausted man still is for the greatest possibilities, and how often in the past the type man has stood in presence of mysterious decisions and new paths – he knows still better from his painfullest recollections on what wretched obstacles promising developments of the highest rank have hitherto usually gone to pieces, broken down, sunk, and become contemptible. The *universal degeneracy of mankind* to the level of the 'man of the future' – as idealised by the socialistic fools and shallow-pates – this degeneracy and dwarfing of man to an absolutely gregarious animal (or as they call it, to a man of 'free society'), this brutalising of man into a pigmy with equal rights and claims, is undoubtedly *possible*! He who has thought out this possibility to its ultimate conclusion knows *another* loathing unknown to the rest of mankind – and perhaps also a new *mission*!

Sixth Chapter: *We Scholars*

204

At the risk that moralising may also reveal itself here as that which it has always been – namely, resolutely *montrer ses plaies*,* according to Balzac – I would venture to protest against an improper and injurious alteration of rank, which quite unnoticed, and as if with the best conscience, threatens nowadays to establish itself in the relations of science and philosophy. I mean to say that one must have the right out of one's own *experience* – experience, as it seems to me, always implies unfortunate experience? – to treat of such an important question of rank, so as not to speak of colour like the blind, or *against* science like women and artists ('Ah! this dreadful science!' sigh their instinct and their shame, 'it always *finds things out!*'). The declaration of independence of the scientific man, his emancipation from philosophy, is one of the subtler after-effects of democratic organisation and disorganisation: the self-glorification and self-conceitedness of the learned man is now everywhere in full bloom, and in its best springtime – which does not mean to imply that in this case self-praise smells sweetly. Here also the instinct of the populace cries, 'Freedom from all masters!' and after science has, with the happiest results, resisted theology, whose 'handmaid' it had been too long, it now proposes in its wantonness and indiscretion to lay down laws for philosophy, and in its turn to play the 'master' – what am I saying! to play the *philosopher* on its own account. My memory – the memory of a scientific man, if you please! – teems with the naïvetés of insolence which I have heard about philosophy and philosophers from young naturalists and old physicians (not to mention the most cultured and most conceited of all learned men, the philologists and schoolmasters, who are both the one and the other by profession). On one occasion it was the specialist and the Jack Horner who instinctively

* Showing one's wounds.

stood on the defensive against all synthetic tasks and capabilities; at another time it was the industrious worker who had got a scent of *otium* and refined luxuriousness in the internal economy of the philosopher, and felt himself aggrieved and belittled thereby. On another occasion it was the colour-blindness of the utilitarian, who sees nothing in philosophy but a series of *refuted* systems, and an extravagant expenditure which 'does nobody any good'. At another time the fear of disguised mysticism and of the boundary-adjustment of knowledge became conspicuous, at another time the disregard of individual philosophers, which had involuntarily extended to disregard of philosophy generally. In fine, I found most frequently, behind the proud disdain of philosophy in young scholars, the evil after-effect of some particular philosopher, to whom on the whole obedience had been foresworn, without, however, the spell of his scornful estimates of other philosophers having been got rid of – the result being a general ill-will to all philosophy. (Such seems to me, for instance, the after-effect of Schopenhauer on the most modern Germany: by his unintell-igent rage against Hegel, he has succeeded in severing the whole of the last generation of Germans from its connection with German culture, which culture, all things considered, has been an elevation and a divining refinement of the *historical sense*; but precisely at this point Schopenhauer himself was poor, irreceptive, and un-German to the extent of ingeniousness). On the whole, speaking generally, it may just have been the humanness, all-too-humanness of the modern philosophers themselves, in short, their contemptibleness, which has injured most radically the reverence for philosophy and opened the doors to the instinct of the populace. Let it but be acknowledged to what an extent our modern world diverges from the whole style of the world of Heraclitus, Plato, Empedocles, and whatever else all the royal and magnificent anchorites of the spirit were called; and with what justice an honest man of science *may* feel himself of a better family and origin, in view of such representatives of philosophy, who, owing to the fashion of the present day, are just as much aloft as they are down below – in Germany, for instance, the two lions of Berlin, the anarchist Eugen Dühring and the amalgamist Eduard von Hartmann. It is especially the sight of those hotch-potch philosophers, who call themselves 'realists', or 'positivists', which is calculated to implant a dangerous distrust in the soul of a young and ambitious scholar: those philosophers, at the best, are themselves but scholars and specialists, that is very evident! All of them are persons who have been vanquished and *brought back again* under the dominion of science, who at one time or another claimed more from themselves, without having a right to the 'more' and its responsibility – and who now, creditably, rancorously and vindictively, represent in word and deed, *disbelief* in the master-task and supremacy of philosophy. After all, how could it be otherwise? Science flourishes nowadays and has the good conscience clearly visible on its countenance; while that to which the entire modern philosophy has gradually sunk, the remnant of philosophy of the present day, excites distrust and displeasure, if not scorn and pity. Philosophy reduced to a 'theory of knowledge', no more in fact than a diffident science of epochs and doctrine of forbearance: a philosophy that never even gets beyond the threshold, and rigorously *denies* itself the right to enter – that is philosophy in its last throes, an end, an agony, something that awakens pity. How could such a philosophy – *rule*!

205

The dangers that beset the evolution of the philosopher are, in fact, so manifold nowadays, that one might doubt whether this fruit could still come to maturity. The extent and towering structure of the sciences have increased enormously, and therewith also the probability that the philosopher will grow tired even as a learner, or will attach himself somewhere and 'specialise': so that he will no longer attain to his elevation, that is to say, to his superspection, his circumspection, and his *despection*. Or he gets aloft too late, when the best of his maturity and strength is past; or when he is impaired, coarsened, and deteriorated, so that his view, his general estimate of things, is no longer of much importance. It is perhaps just the refinement of his intellectual conscience that makes him hesitate and linger on the way; he dreads the temptation to become a dilettante, a millipede, a milleantenna; he knows too well that as a discerner, one who has lost his self-respect no longer commands, no longer *leads*; unless he should aspire to become a great play-actor, a philosophical Cagliostro and spiritual rat-catcher – in short, a misleader. This is in the last instance a question of taste, if it has not really been a question of conscience.

To double once more the philosopher's difficulties, there is also the fact that he demands from himself a verdict, a Yea or Nay, not concerning science, but concerning life and the worth of life – he learns unwillingly to believe that it is his right and even his duty to obtain this verdict, and he has to seek his way to the right and the belief only through the most extensive (perhaps disturbing and destroying) experiences, often hesitating, doubting, and dumb-founded. In fact, the philosopher has long been mistaken and confused by the multitude, either with the scientific man and ideal scholar, or with the religiously elevated, desensualised, desecularised visionary and God-intoxicated man; and even yet when one hears anybody praised, because he lives 'wisely', or 'as a philosopher', it hardly means anything more than 'prudently and apart'. Wisdom: that seems to the populace to be a kind of flight, a means and artifice for withdrawing successfully from a bad game; but the *genuine* philosopher – does it not seem so to *us*, my friends? – lives 'un-philosophically' and 'unwisely', above all, *imprudently*, and feels the obligation and burden of a hundred attempts and temptations of life – he risks *himself* constantly, he plays *this* bad game.

206

In relation to the genius, that is to say, a being who either *engenders* or *produces* – both words understood in their fullest sense – the man of learning, the scientific average man, has always something of the old maid about him; for, like her, he is not conversant with the two principal functions of man. To both, of course, to the scholar and to the old maid, one concedes respectability, as if by way of indemnification – in these cases one emphasises the respectability – and yet, in the compulsion of this concession, one has the same admixture of vexation. Let us examine more closely: what is the scientific man? Firstly, a commonplace type of man, with com-monplace virtues: that is to say, a non-ruling, non-authoritative, and non-self-sufficient type of man; he possesses industry, patient adaptableness to rank and file, equability and moderation in cap-acity and requirement; he has the instinct for people like himself, and for that which they require – for instance: the portion of independence and green meadow without which there is no rest from labour, the claim to honour and consideration (which first and foremost presupposes recognition and recognisability), the sunshine of a good name, the perpetual ratification of his value and usefulness, with which the inward *distrust* which lies at the bottom of the heart of all dependent men and gregarious animals, has again and again to be overcome. The learned man, as is appropriate, has also maladies and faults of an ignoble kind: he is full of petty envy, and has a lynx-eye for the weak points in those natures to whose elevations he cannot attain. He is confiding, yet only as one who lets himself go, but does not *flow*; and precisely before the man of the great current he stands all the colder and more reserved – his eye is then like a smooth and irresponsive lake, which is no longer moved by rapture or sympathy. The worst and most dangerous thing of which a scholar is capable results from the instinct of mediocrity of his type, from the Jesuitism of mediocrity, which labours instinctively for the destruction of the exceptional man, and endeavours to break – or still better, to relax – every bent bow. To relax, of course, with consideration, and naturally with an indulgent hand – to *relax* with confiding sympathy: that is the real art of Jesuitism, which has always understood how to introduce itself as the religion of sympathy.

207

However gratefully one may welcome the *objective* spirit – and who has not been sick to death of all subjectivity and its confounded *ipsissimosity*! – in the end, however, one must learn caution even with regard to one's gratitude, and put a stop to the exaggeration with which the unselfing and depersonalising of the spirit has recently been celebrated, as if it were the goal in itself, as if it were salvation and glorification – as is especially accustomed to happen in the pessimist school, which has also in its turn good reasons for paying the highest honours to 'disinterested knowledge'. The objective man, who no longer curses and scolds like the pessimist, the *ideal* man of learning in whom the scientific instinct blossoms forth fully after a thousand complete and partial failures, is assuredly one of the most costly instruments that exist, but his place is in the hand of one who is more powerful. He is only an instrument; we may say, he is a *mirror* – he is no 'purpose in himself'. The objective man is in truth a mirror: accustomed to prostration before everything that wants to be known, with such desires only as knowing or 'reflecting' imply – he waits until something comes, and then expands himself sensitively, so that even the light footsteps and gliding past of spiritual beings may not be lost on his surface and film. Whatever 'personality' he still possesses seems to him accidental, arbitrary, or still oftener, disturbing; so much has he come to regard himself as the passage and reflection of outside forms and events. He calls up the recollection of 'himself' with an effort, and not infrequently wrongly; he readily confounds himself with other persons, he makes mistakes with regard to his own needs, and here only is he unrefined and negligent. Perhaps he is troubled about the health, or the pettiness and confined atmosphere of wife and friend, or the lack of companions and society – indeed, he sets himself to reflect on his suffering, but in vain! His thoughts already rove away to the *more general* case, and to-morrow he knows as little as he knew yesterday how to help himself. He does not now take himself seriously and devote time to himself: he is serene, *not* from lack of trouble, but from lack of capacity for grasping and dealing with *his* trouble. The habitual complaisance with respect to all objects and experiences, the radiant and impartial hospitality with which he receives everything that comes his way, his habit of inconsiderate goodnature, of dangerous indifference as to Yea and Nay: alas! there are enough of cases in which he has to atone for these virtues of his! – and as man generally, he becomes far too easily the *caput mortuum* of such virtues. Should one wish love or hatred from him – I mean love and hatred as God, woman, and animal understand them – he will do what he can, and furnish what he can. But one must not be surprised if it should not be much – if he should show himself just at this point to be false, fragile, questionable, and deteriorated. His love is constrained, his hatred is artificial, and rather *un tour de force,* a slight ostentation and exaggeration. He is only genuine so far as he can be objective; only in his serene totality is he still 'nature' and 'natural'. His mirroring and eternally self-polishing soul no longer knows how to affirm, no longer how to deny; he does not command; neither does he destroy. *'Je ne méprise presque rien'* * – he says, with Leibnitz: let us not overlook nor undervalue the *presque*! Neither is he a model man; he does not go in advance of any one, nor after either; he places himself generally too far off to have any reason for espousing the cause of either good or evil. If he has

* I despise virtually nothing.

been so long confounded with the *philosopher,* with the Caesar-
ean trainer and dictator of civilisation, he has had far too much
honour, and what is most essential in him has been overlooked –
he is an instrument, something of a slave, though certainly the
sublimest sort of slave, but nothing in himself – *presque rien!* The
objective man is an instrument, a costly, easily injured, easily
tarnished, measuring instrument and mirroring apparatus, which is
to be taken care of and respected; but he is no goal, no outgoing
nor upgoing, no complementary man in whom the *rest* of existence justifies itself, no termination – and still less a commencement,
an engendering, or primary cause, nothing hardy, powerful, self-
centred, that wants to be master; but rather only a soft, inflated,
delicate, movable potter's-form, that must wait for some kind of
content and frame to 'shape' itself thereto – for the most part a man
without frame and content, a 'selfless' man. Consequently, also,
nothing for women, *in parenthesi.*

208

When a philosopher nowadays makes known that he is not a
sceptic – I hope that has been gathered from the foregoing
description of the objective spirit? – people all hear it impatiently;
they regard him on that account with some apprehension, they
would like to ask so many, many questions . . . indeed among
timid hearers, of whom there are now so many, he is henceforth said to be dangerous. With his repudiation of scepticism,
it seems to them as if they heard some evil-threatening sound in
the distance, as if a new kind of explosive were being tried
somewhere, a dynamite of the spirit, perhaps a newly discovered
Russian *nihiline,* a pessimism *bonae voluntatis,** that not only denies,
means denial, but – dreadful thought! *practises* denial. Against
this kind of 'good will' – a will to the veritable, actual negation
of life – there is, as is generally acknowledged nowadays, no
better soporific and sedative than scepticism, the mild, pleasing,
lulling poppy of scepticism; and Hamlet himself is now prescribed
by the doctors of the day as an antidote to the 'spirit', and its
underground noises. 'Are not our ears already full of bad sounds?'
say the sceptics, as lovers of repose, and almost as a kind of safety
police, 'this subterranean Nay is terrible! Be still, ye pessimistic

---

* Of the good will.

moles!' The sceptic, in effect, that delicate creature, is far too easily frightened; his conscience is schooled so as to start at every Nay, and even at every sharp, decided Yea, and feels something like a bite thereby. Yea! and Nay! – they seem to him opposed to morality; he loves, on the contrary, to make a festival to his virtue by a noble aloofness, while perhaps he says with Montaigne: 'What do I know?' Or with Socrates: 'I know that I know nothing.' Or: 'Here I do not trust myself, no door is open to me.' Or: 'Even if the door were open, why should I enter immediately?' Or: 'What is the use of any hasty hypotheses? It might quite well be in good taste to make no hypotheses at all. Are you absolutely obliged to straighten at once what is crooked? to stuff every hole with some kind of oakum? Is there not time enough for that? Has not the time leisure? Oh, ye demons, can ye not at all *wait*? The uncertain also has its charms, the Sphinx, too, is a Circe, and Circe, too, was a philosopher' – Thus does a sceptic console himself; and in truth he needs some consolation. For scepticism is the most spiritual expression of a certain many-sided physiological temperament, which in ordinary language is called nervous debility and sickliness; it arises whenever races or classes which have been long separated, decisively and suddenly blend with one another. In the new generation, which has inherited as it were different standards and valuations in its blood, everything is disquiet, derangement, doubt, and tentative; the best powers operate restrictively, the very virtues prevent each other growing and becoming strong, equilibrium, ballast, and perpendicular stability are lacking in body and soul. That, however, which is most diseased and degenerated in such nondescripts is the *will*; they are no longer familiar with independence of decision, or the courageous feeling of pleasure in willing – they are doubtful of the 'freedom of the will' even in their dreams. Our present-day Europe, the scene of a senseless, precipitate attempt at a radical blending of classes, and *consequently* of races, is therefore sceptical in all its heights and depths, sometimes exhibiting the mobile scepticism which springs impatiently and wantonly from branch to branch, sometimes with gloomy aspect, like a cloud overcharged with interrogative signs – and often sick unto death of its will! Paralysis of will; where do we not find this cripple sitting nowadays! And yet how bedecked oftentimes!

How seductively ornamented! There are the finest gala dresses
and disguises for this disease; and that, for instance, most of
what places itself nowadays in the show-cases as 'objectiveness',
'the scientific spirit', *l'art pour l'art*,* and 'pure voluntary knowledge', is only decked-out scepticism and paralysis of will – I
am ready to answer for this diagnosis of the European disease. –
The disease of the will is diffused unequally over Europe; it is
worst and most varied where civilisation has longest prevailed; it
decreases according as 'the barbarian' still – or again – asserts his
claims under the loose drapery of Western culture. It is therefore
in the France of today, as can be readily disclosed and comprehended, that the will is most infirm; and France, which has
always had a masterly aptitude for converting even the portentous
crises of its spirit into something charming and seductive, now
manifests emphatically its intellectual ascendency over Europe,
by being the school and exhibition of all the charms of scepticism.
The power to will and to persist, moreover, in a resolution, is
already somewhat stronger in Germany, and again in the North
of Germany it is stronger than in Central Germany; it is considerably stronger in England, Spain, and Corsica, associated with
phlegm in the former and with hard skulls in the latter – not
to mention Italy, which is too young yet to know what it wants,
and must first show whether it can exercise will; but it is strongest and most surprising of all in that immense middle empire
where Europe as it were flows back to Asia – namely, in Russia.
There the power to will has been long stored up and accumulated,
there the will – uncertain whether to be negative or affirmative –
waits threateningly to be discharged (to borrow their pet phrase
from our physicists). Perhaps not only Indian wars and complications in Asia would be necessary to free Europe from its greatest
danger, but also internal subversion, the shattering of the empire
into small states, and above all the introduction of parliamentary
imbecility, together with the obligation of everyone to read his
newspaper at breakfast. I do not say this as one who desires it; in
my heart I should rather prefer the contrary – I mean such an
increase in the threatening attitude of Russia, that Europe would
have to make up its mind to become equally threatening – namely,
to acquire one will, by means of a new caste to rule over the

* 'Art for art's sake'.

Continent, a persistent, dreadful will of its own, that can set its aims thousands of years ahead; so that the long spun-out comedy of its petty-stateism, and its dynastic as well as its democratic many-willed-ness, might finally be brought to a close. The time for petty politics is past; the next century will bring the struggle for the dominion of the world – the *compulsion* to great politics.

209

As to how far the new warlike age on which we Europeans have evidently entered may perhaps favour the growth of another and stronger kind of scepticism, I should like to express myself preliminarily merely by a parable, which the lovers of German history will already understand. That unscrupulous enthusiast for big, handsome grenadiers (who, as King of Prussia, brought into being a military and sceptical genius – and therewith, in reality, the new and now triumphantly emerged type of German), the problematic, crazy father of Frederick the Great, had on one point the very knack and lucky grasp of the genius: he knew what was then lacking in Germany, the want of which was a hundred times more alarming and serious than any lack of culture and social form – his ill-will to the young Frederick resulted from the anxiety of a profound instinct. *Men were lacking*; and he suspected, to his bitterest regret, that his own son was not man enough. There, however, he deceived himself; but who would not have deceived himself in his place? He saw his son lapsed to atheism, to the *esprit*, to the pleasant frivolity of clever Frenchmen – he saw in the background the great bloodsucker, the spider scepticism; he suspected the incurable wretchedness of a heart no longer hard enough either for evil or good, and of a broken will that no longer commands, is no longer *able* to command. Meanwhile, however, there grew up in his son that new kind of harder and more dangerous scepticism – who knows *to what extent* it was encouraged just by his father's hatred and the icy melancholy of a will condemned to solitude? – the scepticism of daring manliness, which is closely related to the genius for war and conquest, and made its first entrance into Germany in the person of the great Frederick. This scepticism despises and nevertheless grasps; it undermines and takes possession; it does not believe, but it does not thereby lose itself; it gives the spirit a dangerous liberty, but it keeps strict guard over the heart. It is the *German* form of scepticism, which, as a continued Fredericianism, risen to the highest spirituality, has kept Europe for a considerable time under the dominion of the German spirit and its critical and historical distrust. Owing to the insuperably strong and tough masculine character of the great German philologists and historical critics (who, rightly estimated, were also all of them artists of destruction and dissolution), a *new* conception of the German spirit gradually established itself – in spite of all Romanticism in music and philosophy – in which the leaning towards masculine scepticism was decidedly prominent: whether, for instance, as fearlessness of gaze, as courage and sternness of the dissecting hand, or as resolute will to dangerous voyages of discovery, to spiritualised North Pole expeditions under barren and dangerous skies. There may be good grounds for it when warm-blooded and superficial humanitarians cross themselves before this spirit, *cet esprit fataliste, ironique, méphistophélique*, as Michelet calls it, not without a shudder. But if one would realise how characteristic is this fear of the 'man' in the German spirit which awakened Europe out of its 'dogmatic slumber', let us call to mind the former conception which had to be overcome by this new one – and that it is not so very long ago that a masculinised woman could dare, with unbridled presumption, to recommend the Germans to the interest of Europe as gentle, good-hearted, weak-willed, and poetical fools. Finally, let us only understand profoundly enough Napoleon's astonishment when he saw Goethe: it reveals what had been regarded for centuries as the 'German spirit'. '*Voilà un homme!*' – that was as much as to say: 'But this is a *man*! And I only expected to see a German!'

210

Supposing, then, that in the picture of the philosophers of the future, some trait suggests the question whether they must not perhaps be sceptics in the last-mentioned sense, something in them would only be designated thereby – and *not* they themselves. With equal right they might call themselves critics; and assuredly they will be men of experiments. By the name with which I ventured to baptize them, I have already expressly emphasised their attempting and their love of attempting: is this because, as critics in body and soul, they will love to make use of experiments in a new, and perhaps wider and more dangerous sense? In their passion for knowledge, will they have to go further in daring and painful attempts than the sensitive and pampered taste of a democratic century can approve of? — There is no doubt: these coming ones will be least able to dispense with the serious and not unscrupulous qualities which distinguish the critic from the sceptic: I mean the certainty as to standards of worth, the conscious employment of a unity of method, the wary courage, the standing-alone, and the capacity for self-responsibility; indeed, they will avow among themselves a *delight* in denial and dissection, and a certain considerate cruelty, which knows how to handle the knife surely and deftly, even when the heart bleeds. They will be *sterner* (and perhaps not always towards themselves only) than humane people may desire, they will not deal with the 'truth' in order that it may 'please' them, or 'elevate' and 'inspire' them — they will rather have little faith in '*truth*' bringing with it such revels for the feelings. They will smile, those rigorous spirits, when any one says in their presence: 'that thought elevates me, why should it not be true?' or: 'that work enchants me, why should it not be beautiful?' or: 'that artist enlarges me, why should he not be great?' Perhaps they will not only have a smile, but a genuine disgust for all that is thus rapturous, idealistic, feminine, and hermaphroditic; and if anyone could look into their inmost heart, he would not easily find therein the intention to reconcile 'Christian sentiments' with 'antique taste', or even with 'modern parliamentarism' (the kind of reconciliation necessarily found even amongst philosophers in our very uncertain and consequently very conciliatory century). Critical discipline, and every habit that conduces to purity and rigour in intellectual matters, will not only be demanded from themselves by these philosophers of the future; they may even make a display thereof as their special adornment — nevertheless they will not want to be called critics on that account. It will seem to them no small indignity to philosophy to have it decreed, as is so welcome nowadays, that 'philosophy itself is criticism and critical science — and nothing else whatever!' Though this estimate of philosophy may enjoy the approval of all the Positivists of France and Germany (and possibly it even flattered the heart and taste of *Kant*: let us call to mind the titles of his principal works), our new

philosophers will say, notwithstanding, that critics are instruments
of the philosopher, and just on that account, as instruments, they
are far from being philosophers themselves! Even the great China-
man of Königsberg was only a great critic.

211

I insist upon it that people finally cease confounding philosophical
workers, and in general scientific men, with philosophers – that
precisely here one should strictly give 'each his own', and not
give those far too much, these far too little. It may be necessary
for the education of the real philosopher that he himself should
have once stood upon all those steps upon which his servants,
the scientific workers of philosophy, remain standing, and *must*
remain standing: he himself must perhaps have been critic, and
dogmatist, and historian, and besides, poet, and collector, and
traveller, and riddle-reader, and moralist, and seer, and 'free
spirit', and almost everything, in order to traverse the whole
range of human values and estimations, and that he may *be able*
with a variety of eyes and consciences to look from a height to
any distance, from a depth up to any height, from a nook into any
expanse. But all these are only preliminary conditions for his task;
this task itself demands something else – it requires him *to create
values*. The philosophical workers, after the excellent pattern of
Kant and Hegel, have to fix and formalise some great existing
body of valuations – that is to say, former *determinations of value*,
creations of value, which have become prevalent, and are for a
time called 'truths' – whether in the domain of the *logical*, the
political (moral), or the *artistic*. It is for these investigators to make
whatever has happened and been esteemed hitherto, conspicuous,
conceivable, intelligible, and manageable, to shorten everything
long, even 'time' itself, and to *subjugate* the entire past: an
immense and wonderful task, in the carrying out of which all
refined pride, all tenacious will, can surely find satisfaction. *The
real philosophers, however, are commanders and law-givers*; they say:
'Thus *shall* it be!' They determine first the Whither and the Why
of mankind, and thereby set aside the previous labour of all
philosophical workers, and all subjugators of the past – they grasp
at the future with a creative hand, and whatever is and was,
becomes for them thereby a means, an instrument, and a hammer.

Their 'knowing' is *creating*, their creating is a law-giving, their will to truth is — *Will to Power*. — Are there at present such philosophers? Have there ever been such philosophers? *Must* there not be such philosophers some day? . . .

212

It is ever more obvious to me that the philosopher, as a man *indispensable* for the morrow and the day after the morrow, has always found himself, and *has been obliged* to find himself, in contradiction to the day in which he lives; his enemy has always been the ideal of his day. Hitherto all those extraordinary furtherers of humanity whom one calls philosophers — who rarely regarded themselves as lovers of wisdom, but rather as disagreeable fools and dangerous interrogators — have found their mission, their hard, involuntary, imperative mission (in the end however the greatness of their mission), in being the bad conscience of their age. In putting the vivisector's knife to the breast of the very *virtues of their age*, they have betrayed their own secret; it has been for the sake of a *new* greatness of man, a new untrodden path to his aggrandisement. They have always disclosed how much hypocrisy, indolence, self-indulgence, and self-neglect, how much falsehood was concealed under the most venerated types of contemporary morality, how much virtue was *outlived*; they have always said: 'We must remove hence to where *you* are least at home.' In face of a world of 'modern ideas', which would like to confine everyone in a corner, in a 'specialty', a philosopher, if there could be philosophers nowadays, would be compelled to place the greatness of man, the conception of 'greatness', precisely in his comprehensiveness and multifariousness, in his all-roundness; he would even determine worth and rank according to the amount and variety of that which a man could bear and take upon himself, according to the *extent* to which a man could stretch his responsibility. Nowadays the taste and virtue of the age weaken and attenuate the will; nothing is so adapted to the spirit of the age as weakness of will: consequently, in the ideal of the philosopher, strength of will, sternness and capacity for prolonged resolution, must specially be included in the conception of 'greatness'; with as good a right as the opposite doctrine, with its ideal of a silly, renouncing, humble, selfless humanity, was suited to an opposite age – such as the sixteenth century, which suffered from its accumulated energy of will, and from the wildest torrents and floods of selfishness. In the time of Socrates, among men only of worn-out instincts, old conservative Athenians who let themselves go – 'for the sake of happiness', as they said; for the sake of pleasure, as their conduct indicated – and who had continually on their lips the old pompous words to which they had long forfeited the right by the life they led, *irony* was perhaps necessary for greatness of soul, the wicked Socratic assurance of the old physician and plebeian, who cut ruthlessly into his own flesh, as into the flesh and heart of the 'noble', with a look that said plainly enough: 'Do not dissemble before me! Here – we are equal!' At present, on the contrary, when throughout Europe the herding animal alone attains to honours, and dispenses honours, when 'equality of right' can too readily be transformed into equality in wrong: I mean to say into general war against everything rare, strange, and privileged, against the higher man, the higher soul, the higher duty, the higher responsibility, the creative plenipotence and lordliness – at present it belongs to the conception of 'greatness' to be noble, to wish to be apart, to be capable of being different, to stand alone, to have to live by personal initiative; and the philosopher will betray something of his own ideal when he asserts: 'He shall be the greatest who can be the most solitary, the most concealed, the most divergent, the man beyond good and evil, the master of his virtues, and of superabundance of will; precisely this shall be called *greatness*: as diversified as can be entire, as ample as can be full.' And to ask once more the question: Is greatness *possible* – nowadays?

213

It is difficult to learn what a philosopher is, because it cannot be taught: one must 'know' it by experience – or one should have the pride *not* to know it. The fact that at present people all talk of things of which they *cannot* have any experience, is true more especially and unfortunately as concerns the philosopher and philosophical matters – the very few know them, are permitted to know them, and all popular ideas about them are false. Thus, for instance, the truly philosophical combination of a bold, exuberant spirituality which runs at *presto* pace, and a dialectic rigour and necessity which makes no false step, is unknown to most thinkers and scholars from their own experience, and therefore, should anyone speak of it in their presence, it is incredible to them. They conceive of every necessity as troublesome, as a painful compulsory obedience and state of constraint; thinking itself is regarded by them as something slow and hesitating, almost as a trouble, and often enough as 'worthy of the *sweat* of the noble' – but not at all as something easy and divine, closely related to dancing and exuberance! 'To think' and to take a matter 'seriously', 'arduously' – that is one and the same thing to them; such only has been their 'experience'. – Artists have here perhaps a finer intuition; they who know only too well that precisely when they no longer do anything 'arbitrarily', and everything of necessity, their feeling of freedom, of subtlety, of power, of creatively fixing, disposing, and shaping, reaches its climax – in short, that necessity and 'freedom of will' are then the same thing with them. There is, in fine, a gradation of rank in psychical states, to which the gradation of rank in the problems corresponds; and the highest problems repel ruthlessly everyone who ventures too near them, without being predestined for their solution by the loftiness and power of his spirituality. Of what use is it for nimble, everyday intellects, or clumsy, honest mechanics and empiricists to press, in their plebeian ambition, close to such problems, and as it were into this 'holy of holies' – as so often happens nowadays! But coarse feet must never tread upon such carpets: this is provided for in the primary law of things; the doors remain closed to those intruders, though they may dash and break their heads thereon! People have always to be born to a high station, or, more definitely, they have to be *bred* for it: a person has only a right to philosophy – taking the word in its higher significance – in virtue of his descent; the ancestors, the 'blood', decide here also. Many generations must have prepared the way for the coming of the philosopher; each of his virtues must have been separately acquired, nurtured, transmitted, and embodied; not only the bold, easy, delicate course and current of his thoughts, but above all the readiness for great responsibilities, the majesty of ruling glance and contemning look, the feeling of separation from the multitude with their duties and virtues, the kindly patronage and defence of whatever is misunderstood and calumniated, be it God or devil, the delight and practice of supreme justice, the art of commanding, the amplitude of will, the lingering eye which rarely admires, rarely looks up, rarely loves . . .

Seventh Chapter: *Our Virtues*

214

Our Virtues? – It is probable that we too have still our virtues, although naturally they are not those sincere and massive virtues on account of which we hold our grandfathers in esteem and also at a little distance from us. We Europeans of the day after tomorrow, we firstlings of the twentieth century – with all our dangerous curiosity, our multifariousness and art of disguising, our mellow and seemingly sweetened cruelty in sense and spirit – we shall presumably, *if* we must have virtues, have those only which have come to agreement with our most secret and heartfelt inclinations, with our most ardent requirements : well, then, let us look for them in our labyrinths! – where, as we know, so many things lose themselves, so many things get quite lost! And is there anything finer than to *search* for one's own virtues? Is it not almost to *believe* in one's own virtues? But this 'believing in one's own virtues' – is it not practically the same as what was formerly called one's 'good conscience', that long, respectable pigtail of an idea, which our grandfathers used to hang behind their heads, and often enough also behind their understandings? It seems, therefore, that however little we may imagine ourselves to be old-fashioned and grandfatherly respectable in other respects, in one thing we are nevertheless the worthy grandchildren of our grandfathers, we last Europeans with good consciences: we also still wear their pigtail. – Ah! if you only knew how soon, so very soon – it will be different!

215

As in the stellar firmament there are sometimes two suns which determine the path of one planet, and in certain cases suns of different colours shine around a single planet, now with red light, now with green, and then simultaneously illumine and flood it with motley colours: so we modern men, owing to the complicated

mechanism of our 'firmament', are determined by *different* moralities; our actions shine alternately in different colours, and are
seldom unequivocal — and there are often cases, also, in which our
actions are *motley-coloured*.

216

To love one's enemies? I think that has been well learnt: it takes
place thousands of times at present on a large and small scale;
indeed, at times the higher and sublimer thing takes place — we
learn to *despise* when we love, and precisely when we love best; all
of it, however, unconsciously, without noise, without ostentation,
with the shame and secrecy of goodness, which forbids the utterance of the pompous word and the formula of virtue. Morality as
attitude — is opposed to our taste nowadays. This is *also* an advance,
as it was an advance in our fathers that religion as an attitude finally
became opposed to their taste, including the enmity and Vol-
tairean bitterness against religion (and all that formerly belonged
to freethinker-pantomime). It is the music in our conscience, the
dance in our spirit, to which Puritan litanies, moral sermons, and
goody-goodness won't chime.

217

Let us be careful in dealing with those who attach great importance to being credited with moral tact and subtlety in moral
discernment! They never forgive us if they have once made a mistake *before* us (or even *with regard to* us) — they inevitably become
our instinctive calumniators and detractors, even when they still
remain our 'friends'. — Blessed are the forgetful: for they 'get the
better' even of their blunders.

218

The psychologists of France — and where else are there still psychologists nowadays? — have never yet exhausted their bitter and
manifold enjoyment of the *bêtise bourgeoise*, just as though . . . in
short, they betray something thereby. Flaubert, for instance, the
honest citizen of Rouen, neither saw, heard, nor tasted anything else
in the end; it was his mode of self-torment and refined cruelty. As
this is growing wearisome, I would now recommend for a change
something else for a pleasure — namely, the unconscious astuteness

with which good, fat, honest mediocrity always behaves towards loftier spirits and the tasks they have to perform, the subtle, barbed, Jesuitical astuteness, which is a thousand times subtler than the taste and understanding of the middle-class in its best moments – subtler even than the understanding of its victims – a repeated proof that 'instinct' is the most intelligent of all kinds of intelligence which have hitherto been discovered. In short, you psychologists, study the philosophy of the 'rule' in its struggle with the 'exception': there you have a spectacle fit for gods and godlike malignity! Or, in plainer words, practise vivisection on 'good people', on the 'homo bonae voluntatis' * . . . on yourselves!

219

The practice of judging and condemning morally, is the favourite revenge of the intellectually shallow on those who are less so; it is also a kind of indemnity for them being badly endowed by nature; and finally, it is an opportunity for acquiring spirit and becoming subtle – malice spiritualises. They are glad in their inmost heart that there is a standard according to which those who are overendowed with intellectual goods and privileges, are equal to them; they contend for the 'equality of all before God' and almost need the belief in God for this purpose. It is among them that the most powerful antagonists of atheism are found. If any one were to say to them: 'a lofty spirituality is beyond all comparison with the honesty and respectability of a merely moral man' – it would make them furious; I shall take care not to say so. I would rather flatter them with my theory that lofty spirituality itself exists only as the ultimate product of moral qualities; that it is a synthesis of all qualities attributed to the 'merely moral' man, after they have been acquired singly through long training and practice, perhaps during a whole series of generations; that lofty spirituality is precisely the spiritualising of justice, and the beneficent severity which knows that it is authorised to maintain gradations of rank in the world, even among things – and not only among men.

220

Now that the praise of the 'disinterested person' is so popular, one must – probably not without some danger – get an idea of

* The man of good will.

what people actually take an interest in, and what are the things generally which fundamentally and profoundly concern ordinary men – including the cultured, even the learned, and perhaps philosophers also, if appearances do not deceive. The fact thereby becomes obvious that the greater part of what interests and charms higher natures, and more refined and fastidious tastes, seems absolutely 'uninteresting' to the average man – if, notwithstanding, he perceive devotion to these interests, he calls it *désintéressé*, and wonders how it is possible to act 'disinterestedly'. There have been philosophers who could give this popular astonishment a seductive and mystical, other-world expression (perhaps because they did not know the higher nature by experience?), instead of stating the naked and candidly reasonable truth that 'disinterested' action is very interesting and 'interested' action, provided that . . . 'And love?' – What! Even an action for love's sake shall be 'unegoistic'? But you fools – ! 'And the praise of the self-sacrificer?' – But whoever has really offered sacrifice knows that he wanted and obtained something for it – perhaps something from himself for something from himself; that he relinquished here in order to have more there, perhaps in general to be more, or even feel himself 'more'. But this is a realm of questions and answers in which a more fastidious spirit does not like to stay: for here truth has to stifle her yawns so much when she is obliged to answer. And after all, truth is a woman; one must not use force with her.

221

'It sometimes happens,' said a moralistic pedant and trifle-retailer, 'that I honour and respect an unselfish man: not, however, because he is unselfish, but because I think he has a right to be useful to another man at his own expense. In short, the question is always who *he* is, and who *the other* is. For instance, in a person created and destined for command, self-denial and modest retirement, instead of being virtues would be the waste of virtues: so it seems to me. Every system of unegoistic morality which takes itself unconditionally and appeals to everyone, not only sins against good taste, but is also an incentive to sins of omission, an *additional* seduction under the mask of philanthropy – and precisely a seduction and injury to the higher, rarer, and more privileged types of men. Moral systems must be compelled first of all to bow before

the *gradations of rank*; their presumption must be driven home to
their conscience – until they thoroughly understand at last that it is
immoral to say that 'what is right for one is proper for another'. – So
said my moralistic pedant and *bonhomme*. Did he perhaps deserve
to be laughed at when he thus exhorted systems of morals to
practise morality? But one should not be too much in the right if
one wishes to have the laughers on *one's own* side; a grain of wrong
pertains even to good taste.

222

Wherever sympathy (fellow-suffering) is preached nowadays –
and, if I gather rightly, no other religion is any longer preached –
let the psychologist have his ears open: through all the vanity,
through all the noise which is natural to these preachers (as to all
preachers), he will hear a hoarse, groaning, genuine note of *self-
contempt*. It belongs to the overshadowing and uglifying of Europe,
which has been on the increase for a century (the first symptoms of
which are already specified documentarily in a thoughtful letter of
Galiani to Madame d'Epinay) – *if it is not really the cause thereof*! The
man of 'modern ideas', the conceited ape, is excessively dissatisfied
with himself – this is perfectly certain. He suffers, and his vanity
wants him only 'to suffer with his fellows'.

223

The hybrid European – a tolerably ugly plebeian, taken all in all –
absolutely requires a costume: he needs history as a storeroom of
costumes. To be sure, he notices that none of the costumes fit him
properly – he changes and changes. Let us look at the nineteenth
century with respect to these hasty preferences and changes in its
masquerades of style, and also with respect to its moments of
desperation on account of 'nothing suiting' us. It is in vain to get
ourselves up as romantic, or classical, or Christian, or Florentine,
or *barocco*, or 'national', *in moribus et artibus*:* it does not 'clothe
us'! But the 'spirit', especially the 'historical spirit', profits even
by this desperation: once and again a new sample of the past or of
the foreign is tested, put on, taken off, packed up, and above all
studied – we are the first studious age *in puncto* of 'costumes', I
mean as concerns morals, articles of belief, artistic tastes, and

* 'In morals and the arts' [or, 'morality and aesthetics'].

religions; we are prepared as no other age has ever been for a carnival in the grand style, for the most spiritual festival-laughter and -arrogance, for the transcendental height of supreme folly and Aristophanic ridicule of the world. Perhaps we are still discovering the domain of our *invention* just here, the domain where even we can still be original, probably as parodists of the world's history and as God's Merry-Andrews – perhaps, though nothing else of the present have a future, our *laughter* itself may have a future!

224

The *historical sense* (or the capacity for divining quickly the order of rank of the valuations according to which a people, a community, or an individual has lived, the 'divining instinct' for the relationships of these valuations, for the relation of the authority of the valuations to the authority of the operating forces) – this historical sense, which we Europeans claim as our speciality, has come to us in the train of the enchanting and mad *semi-barbarity* into which Europe has been plunged by the democratic mingling of classes and races – it is only the nineteenth century that has recognised this faculty as its sixth sense. Owing to this mingling, the past of every form and mode of life, and of cultures which were formerly closely contiguous and superimposed on one another, flows forth into us 'modern souls'; our instincts now run back in all directions, we ourselves are a kind of chaos: in the end, as we have said, the spirit perceives its advantage therein. By means of our semi-barbarity in body and in desire, we have secret access everywhere, such as a noble age never had; we have access above all to the labyrinth of imperfect civilisations, and to every form of semi-barbarity that has at any time existed on earth; and in so far as the most considerable part of human civilisation hitherto has just been semi-barbarity, the 'historical sense' implies almost the sense and instinct for everything, the taste and tongue for everything: whereby it immediately proves itself to be an *ignoble* sense. For instance, we enjoy Homer once more: it is perhaps our happiest acquisition that we know how to appreciate Homer, whom men of distinguished culture (as the French of the seventeenth century, like Saint-Evremond, who reproached him for his *esprit vaste*, and even Voltaire, the last echo of the century) cannot and could not so easily appropriate – whom they scarcely permitted themselves

to enjoy. The very decided Yea and Nay of their palate, their
promptly ready disgust, their hesitating reluctance with regard to
everything strange, their horror of the bad taste even of lively
curiosity, and in general the averseness of every distinguished and
self-sufficing culture to avow a new desire, a dissatisfaction with
its own condition, or an admiration of what is strange: all this
determines and disposes them unfavourably even towards the best
things of the world which are not their property or *could not*
become their prey – and no faculty is more unintelligible to such
men than just this historical sense, with its truckling, plebeian
curiosity. The case is not different with Shakespeare, that marvellous Spanish-Moorish-Saxon synthesis of taste, over whom an
ancient Athenian of the circle of Aeschylus would have half-killed
himself with laughter or irritation: but we – accept precisely this
wild motleyness, this medley of the most delicate, the most coarse,
and the most artificial, with a secret confidence and cordiality; we
enjoy it as a refinement of art reserved expressly for us, and allow
ourselves to be as little disturbed by the repulsive fumes and the
proximity of the English populace in which Shakespeare's art and
taste lives, as perhaps on the Chiaja of Naples, where, with all
our senses awake, we go our way, enchanted and voluntarily, in
spite of the drain-odour of the lower quarters of the town. That as
men of the 'historical sense' we have our virtues, is not to be
disputed – we are unpretentious, unselfish, modest, brave, habituated to self-control and self-renunciation, very grateful, very
patient, very complaisant – but with all this we are perhaps not
very 'tasteful'. Let us finally confess it, that what is most difficult
for us men of the 'historical sense' to grasp, feel, taste, and love,
what finds us fundamentally prejudiced and almost hostile, is precisely the perfection and ultimate maturity in every culture and
art, the essentially noble in works and men, their moment of
smooth sea and halcyon self-sufficiency, the goldenness and coldness which all things show that have perfected themselves. Perhaps
our great virtue of the historical sense is in necessary contrast to
good taste, at least to the very best taste; and we can only evoke in
ourselves imperfectly, hesitatingly, and with compulsion the small,
short, and happy godsends and glorifications of human life as they
shine here and there; those moments and marvellous experiences,
when a great power has voluntarily come to a halt before the

boundless and infinite – when a superabundance of refined delight has been enjoyed by a sudden checking and petrifying, by standing firmly and planting oneself fixedly on still trembling ground. *Proportionateness* is strange to us, let us confess it to ourselves; our itching is really the itching for the infinite, the immeasurable. Like the rider on his forward panting horse, we let the reins fall before the infinite, we modern men, we semi-barbarians – and are only in *our* highest bliss when we – *are in most danger*.

225

Whether it be hedonism, pessimism, utilitarianism, or eudaemonism, all those modes of thinking which measure the worth of things according to *pleasure* and *pain*, that is, according to accompanying circumstances and secondary considerations, are plausible modes of thought and naïvetés, which everyone conscious of *creative* powers and an artist's conscience will look down upon with scorn, though not without sympathy. Sympathy for *you*! – to be sure, that is not sympathy as you understand it: it is not sympathy for social 'distress', for 'society' with its sick and misfortuned, for the hereditarily vicious and defective who lie on the ground around us; still less is it sympathy for the grumbling, vexed, revolutionary slave-classes who strive after power – they call it 'freedom'. *Our* sympathy is a loftier and further-sighted sympathy: – we see how *man* dwarfs himself, how *you* dwarf him! and there are moments when we view *your* sympathy with an indescribable anguish, when we resist it – when we regard your seriousness as more dangerous than any kind of levity. You want, if possible – and there is not a more foolish 'if possible' – *to do away with suffering*; and we? – It really seems that *we* would rather have it increased and made worse than it has ever been! Well-being, as you understand it – is certainly not a goal; it seems to us an *end*; a condition which at once renders man ludicrous and contemptible – and makes his destruction *desirable*! The discipline of suffering, of *great* suffering – know ye not that it is only *this* discipline that has produced all the elevations of humanity hitherto? The tension of soul in misfortune which communicates to it its energy, its shuddering in view of rack and ruin, its inventiveness and bravery in undergoing, enduring, interpreting, and exploiting misfortune, and whatever depth, mystery, disguise, spirit, artifice, or greatness has been bestowed upon the soul – has it not been bestowed through suffering, through the discipline of great suffering? In man *creature* and *creator* are united: in man there is not only matter, shred, excess, clay, mire, folly, chaos; but there is also the creator, the sculptor, the hardness of the hammer, the divinity of the spectator, and the seventh day – do ye understand this contrast? And that *your* sympathy for the 'creature in man' applies to that which has to be fashioned, bruised, forged, stretched, roasted, annealed, refined – to that which must necessarily *suffer*, and *is meant* to suffer? And *our* sympathy – do ye not understand what our *reverse* sympathy applies to, when it resists your sympathy as the worst of all pampering and enervation? – So it is sympathy *against* sympathy! – But to repeat it once more, there are higher problems than the problems of pleasure and pain and sympathy; and all systems of philosophy which deal only with these are naïvetés.

226

We immoralists. – This world with which *we* are concerned, in which *we* have to fear and love, this almost invisible, inaudible world of delicate command and delicate obedience, a world of 'almost' in every respect, captious, insidious, sharp, and tender – yes, it is well protected from clumsy spectators and familiar curiosity! We are woven into a strong net and garment of duties, and *cannot* disengage ourselves – precisely here, we are 'men of duty', even we! Occasionally, it is true, we dance in our 'chains' and betwixt our 'swords'; it is none the less true that more often we gnash our teeth under the circumstances, and are impatient at the secret hardship of our lot. But do what we will, fools and appearances say of us: 'these are men *without* duty' – we have always fools and appearances against us!

227

Honesty, granting that it is the virtue from which we cannot rid ourselves, we free spirits – well, we will labour at it with all our perversity and love, and not tire of 'perfecting' ourselves in *our* virtue, which alone remains: may its glance some day overspread like a gilded, blue, mocking twilight this ageing civilisation with its dull gloomy seriousness! And if, nevertheless, our honesty should one day grow weary, and sigh, and stretch its limbs, and find us too hard, and would fain have it pleasanter, easier, and gentler, like an agreeable vice, let us remain *hard*, we latest Stoics, and let us send to its help whatever devilry we have in us – our disgust at the clumsy and undefined, our '*nitimur in vetitum*',* our love of ad-venture, our sharpened and fastidious curiosity, our most subtle, disguised, intellectual Will to Power and universal conquest, which rambles and roves avidiously around all the realms of the future – let us go with all our 'devils' to the help of our 'God'! It is probable that people will misunderstand and mistake us on that account: what does it matter! They will say: 'Their "honesty" – that is their devilry, and nothing else!' What does it matter! And even if they were right – have not all gods hitherto been such sanctified, re-baptized devils? And after all, what do we know of ourselves? And what the spirit that leads us wants *to be called*? (It is a question of names.) And how many spirits we harbour? Our honesty, we free spirits – let us be careful lest it become our vanity, our ornament and ostentation, our limitation, our stupidity! Every virtue inclines to stupidity, every stupidity to virtue; 'stupid to the point of sanctity', they say in Russia – let us be careful lest out of pure honesty we do not eventually become saints and bores! Is not life a hundred times too short for us – to bore ourselves? One would have to believe in eternal life in order to . . .

228

I hope to be forgiven for discovering that all moral philosophy hitherto has been tedious and has belonged to the soporific appliances – and that 'virtue', in my opinion, has been *more* injured by the *tediousness* of its advocates than by anything else; at the same time, however, I would not wish to overlook their general usefulness. It is desirable that as few people as possible should reflect upon morals, and consequently it is *very* desirable that morals should not some day become interesting! But let us not be afraid! Things still remain today as they have always been: I see no one in Europe who has (or *discloses*) an idea of the fact that philosophising concerning morals might be conducted in a dangerous, captious, and ensnaring manner – that *calamity* might be involved therein. Observe, for example, the indefatigable, inevitable Eng-

* 'Our striving for the forbidden'.

lish utilitarians: how ponderously and respectably they stalk on,
stalk along (a Homeric metaphor expresses it better) in the footsteps of Bentham, just as he had already stalked in the footsteps
of the respectable Helvétius! (no, he was not a dangerous man,
Helvétius, *ce sénateur Pococurante*, to use an expression of Galiani).
No new thought, nothing of the nature of a finer turning or better
expression of an old thought, not even a proper history of what has
been previously thought on the subject: an *impossible* literature,
taking it all in all, unless one knows how to leaven it with some
mischief. In effect, the old English vice called *cant*, which is *moral
Tartuffism*, has insinuated itself also into these moralists (whom one
must certainly read with an eye to their motives if one *must* read
them), concealed this time under the new form of the scientific
spirit; moreover, there is not absent from them a secret struggle
with the pangs of conscience, from which a race of former Puritans
must naturally suffer, in all their scientific tinkering with morals.
(Is not a moralist the opposite of a Puritan? That is to say, as a
thinker who regards morality as questionable, as worthy of interrogation, in short, as a problem? Is moralising not – immoral?) In
the end, they all want *English* morality to be recognised as authoritative, inasmuch as mankind, or the 'general utility', or 'the
happiness of the greatest number' – no! the happiness of *England*,
will be best served thereby. They would like, by all means, to
convince themselves that the striving after *English* happiness, I
mean after *comfort* and *fashion* (and in the highest instance, a seat
in Parliament), is at the same time the true path of virtue; in fact,
that in so far as there has been virtue in the world hitherto, it has
just consisted in such striving. Not one of those ponderous,
conscience-stricken herding-animals (who undertake to advocate
the cause of egoism as conducive to the general welfare) wants
to have any knowledge or inkling of the facts that the 'general
welfare' is no ideal, no goal, no notion that can be at all grasped,
but is only a nostrum – that what is fair to one *may not* at all be fair
to another, that the requirement of one morality for all is really a
detriment to higher men, in short, that there is a *distinction of rank*
between man and man, and consequently between morality and
morality. They are an unassuming and fundamentally mediocre
species of men, these utilitarian Englishmen, and, as already
remarked, in so far as they are tedious, one cannot think highly

enough of their utility. One ought even to *encourage* them, as has been partially attempted in the following rhymes –

> Hail, ye worthies, barrow-wheeling,
> 'Longer – better', aye revealing,
>   Stiffer aye in head and knee;
> Unenraptured, never jesting,
> Mediocre everlasting,
>   *Sans génie et sans esprit*!

229

In these later ages, which may be proud of their humanity, there still remains so much fear, so much *superstition* of the fear, of the 'cruel wild beast', the mastering of which constitutes the very pride of these humaner ages – that even obvious truths, as if by the agreement of centuries, have long remained unuttered, because they have the appearance of helping the finally slain wild beast back to life again. I perhaps risk something when I allow such a truth to escape; let others capture it again and give it so much 'milk of pious sentiment' to drink, that it will lie down quiet and forgotten, in its old corner. – One ought to learn anew about cruelty, and open one's eyes; one ought at last to learn impatience, in order that such immodest gross errors – as, for instance, have been fostered by ancient and modern philosophers with regard to tragedy – may no longer wander about virtuously and boldly. Almost everything that we call 'higher culture' is based upon the spiritualising and intensifying of *cruelty* – this is my thesis; the 'wild beast' has not been slain at all, it lives, it flourishes, it has only been – transfigured. That which constitutes the painful delight of tragedy is cruelty; that which operates agreeably in so-called tragic sympathy, and at the basis even of everything sublime, up to the highest and most delicate thrills of metaphysics, obtains its sweetness solely from the intermingled ingredient of cruelty. What the Roman enjoys in the arena, the Christian in the ecstasies of the cross, the Spaniard at the sight of the faggot and stake, or of the bull-fight, the present-day Japanese who presses his way to the tragedy, the workman of the Parisian suburbs who has a home-sickness for bloody revolutions, the Wagnerienne who, with un-hinged will, 'undergoes' the performance of *Tristan and Isolde* –

what all these enjoy, and strive with mysterious ardour to drink in, is the philtre of the great Circe 'cruelty'. Here, to be sure, we must put aside entirely the blundering psychology of former times, which could only teach with regard to cruelty that it originated at the sight of the suffering of *others:* there is an abundant, superabundant enjoyment even in one's own suffering, in causing one's own suffering – and wherever man has allowed himself to be persuaded to self-denial in the *religious* sense, or to self-mutilation, as among the Phoenicians and ascetics, or in general, to desensualisation, decarnalisation, and contrition, to Puritanical repentance-spasms, to vivisection of conscience and to Pascal-like *sacrifizio dell' intelletto*, he is secretly allured and impelled forwards by his cruelty, by the dangerous thrill of cruelty *towards himself.* – Finally, let us consider that even the seeker of knowledge operates as an artist and glorifier of cruelty, in that he compels his spirit to perceive *against* its own inclination, and often enough against the wishes of his heart – he forces it to say Nay, where he would like to affirm, love, and adore; indeed, every instance of taking a thing profoundly and fundamentally, is a violation, an intentional injuring of the fundamental will of the spirit, which instinctively aims at appearance and superficiality – even in every desire for knowledge there is a drop of cruelty.

230

Perhaps what I have here said about a 'fundamental will of the spirit' may not be understood without further details; I may be allowed a word of explanation. – That imperious something which is popularly called 'the spirit', wishes to be master internally and externally, and to feel itself master: it has the will of a multiplicity for a simplicity, a binding, taming, imperious, and essentially ruling will. Its requirements and capacities here, are the same as those assigned by physiologists to everything that lives, grows, and multiplies. The power of the spirit to appropriate foreign elements reveals itself in a strong tendency to assimilate the new to the old, to simplify the manifold, to overlook or repudiate the absolutely contradictory; just as it arbitrarily re-underlines, makes prominent, and falsifies for itself certain traits and lines in the foreign elements, in every portion of the 'outside world'. Its object thereby is the incorporation of new 'experiences', the assortment of new things in the old arrangements – in short, growth, or more properly, the *feeling* of growth, the feeling of increased power – is its object. This same will has at its service an apparently opposed impulse of the spirit, a suddenly adopted preference of ignorance, of arbitrary shutting out, a closing of windows, an inner denial of this or that, a prohibition to approach, a sort of defensive attitude against much that is knowable, a contentment with obscurity, with the shutting-in horizon, an acceptance and approval of ignorance: as that which is all necessary according to the degree of its appropriating power, its 'digestive power', to speak figuratively (and in fact 'the spirit' resembles a stomach more than anything else). Here also belong an occasional propensity of the spirit to let itself be deceived (perhaps with a waggish suspicion that it is *not* so and so, but is only allowed to pass as such), a delight in uncertainty and ambiguity, an exulting enjoyment of arbitrary, out-of-the-way narrowness and mystery, of the too-near, of the foreground, of the magnified, the diminished, the misshapen, the beautified – an enjoyment of the arbitrariness of all these manifestations of power. Finally, in this connection, there is the not unscrupulous readiness of the spirit to deceive other spirits and dissemble before them – the constant pressing and straining of a creating, shaping, changeable power: the spirit enjoys therein its craftiness and its variety of disguises, it enjoys also its feeling of security therein – it is precisely by its Protean arts that it is best protected and concealed! – *Counter to this* propensity for appearance, for simplification, for a disguise, for a cloak, in short, for an outside – for every outside is a cloak – there operates the sublime tendency of the man of knowledge, which takes, and *insists* on taking things profoundly, variously, and thoroughly; as a kind of cruelty of the intellectual conscience and taste, which every courageous thinker will acknowledge in himself, provided, as it ought to be, that he has sharpened and hardened his eye sufficiently long for introspection, and is accustomed to severe discipline and even severe words. He will say: 'There is something cruel in the tendency of my spirit': let the virtuous and amiable try to convince him that it is not so! In fact, it would sound nicer, if, instead of our cruelty, perhaps our 'extravagant honesty' were talked about, whispered about and glorified – we free, *very* free spirits – and some day perhaps *such* will actually be our – posthumous glory!

Meanwhile – for there is plenty of time until then – we should be least inclined to deck ourselves out in such florid and fringed moral verbiage; our whole former work has just made us sick of this taste and its sprightly exuberance. They are beautiful, glistening, jingling, festive words: honesty, love of truth, love of wisdom, sacrifice for knowledge, heroism of the truthful – there is something in them that makes one's heart swell with pride. But we anchorites and marmots have long ago persuaded ourselves in all the secrecy of an anchorite's conscience, that this worthy parade of verbiage also belongs to the old false adornment, frippery, and gold-dust of unconscious human vanity, and that even under such flattering colour and repainting, the terrible original text *homo natura* must again be recognised. In effect, to translate man back again into nature; to master the many vain and visionary interpretations and subordinate meanings which have hitherto been scratched and daubed over the eternal original text, *homo natura*; to bring it about that man shall henceforth stand before man as he now, hardened by the discipline of science, stands before the *other* forms of nature, with fearless Oedipus-eyes, and stopped Ulysses-ears, deaf to the enticements of old metaphysical bird-catchers, who have piped to him far too long: 'Thou art more! Thou art higher! Thou hast a different origin!' – this may be a strange and foolish task, but that it is a *task*, who can deny! Why did we choose it, this foolish task? Or, to put the question differently: 'Why knowledge at all?' Everyone will ask us about this. And thus pressed, we, who have asked ourselves the question a hundred times, have not found, and cannot find any better answer . . .

231

Learning alters us, it does what all nourishment does that does not merely 'conserve' – as the physiologist knows. But at the bottom of our souls, quite 'down below', there is certainly something unteachable, a granite of spiritual fate, of predetermined decision and answer to predetermined, chosen questions. In each cardinal problem there speaks an unchangeable 'I am this'; a thinker cannot learn anew about man and woman, for instance, but can only learn fully – he can only follow to the end what is 'fixed' about them in himself. Occasionally we find certain solutions of problems which make strong beliefs for *us*; perhaps they are henceforth called 'convictions'. Later on – one sees in them only footsteps to self-knowledge, guide-posts to the problem which we ourselves *are* – or more correctly to the great stupidity which we embody, our spiritual fate, the *unteachable* in us, quite 'down below'. – In view of this liberal compliment which I have just paid myself, permission will perhaps be more readily allowed me to utter some truths about 'woman as she is', provided that it is known at the outset how literally they are merely – *my* truths.

232

Woman wishes to be independent, and therefore she begins to enlighten men about 'woman as she is' – *this* is one of the worst developments of the general *uglifying* of Europe. For what must these clumsy attempts of feminine scientificality and self-exposure bring to light! Woman has so much cause for shame; in woman there is so much pedantry, superficiality, schoolmasterliness, petty presumption, unbridledness, and indiscretion concealed – study only woman's behaviour towards children! – which has really been best restrained and dominated hitherto by the *fear* of man. Alas, if ever the 'eternally tedious in woman' – she has plenty of it! – is allowed to venture forth! If she begins radically and on principle to unlearn her wisdom and art – of charming, of playing, of frightening-away-sorrow, of alleviating and taking-easily; if she forgets her delicate aptitude for agreeable desires! Female voices are already raised, which, by Saint Aristophanes! make one afraid – with medical explicitness it is stated in a threatening manner what woman first and last *requires* from man. Is it not in the very worst taste that woman thus sets herself up to be scientific? Enlightenment hitherto has fortunately been men's affair, men's gift – we remained therewith 'among ourselves'; and in the end, in view of all that women write about 'woman', we may well have considerable doubt as to whether woman really *desires* enlightenment about herself – and *can* desire it. If woman does not thereby seek a new *ornament* for herself – I believe ornamentation belongs to the eternally feminine? – why, then, she wishes to make herself feared: perhaps she thereby wishes to get the mastery. But she does not *want* truth – what does woman care for truth! From the very first nothing is more foreign, more repugnant, or more hostile to woman than truth – her great art is falsehood, her chief concern is appearance and beauty. Let us confess it, we men: we honour and love *this* very art and *this* very instinct in woman: we who have the hard task, and for our recreation gladly seek the company of beings under whose hands, glances, and delicate follies, our seriousness, our gravity, and profundity appear almost like follies to us. Finally, I ask the question: Did a woman herself ever acknowledge profundity in a woman's mind, or justice in a woman's heart? And is it not true that on the whole 'woman' has hitherto been most despised by woman herself, and not at all by us? – We men desire that woman should not continue to compromise herself by enlightening us; just as it was man's care and the consideration for woman, when the church decreed: *mulier taceat in ecclesia*. It was to the benefit of woman when Napoleon gave the too eloquent Madame de Staël to understand: *mulier taceat in politicis*! – and in my opinion, he is a true friend of woman who calls out to women today: *mulier taceat de muliere*!*

233

It betrays corruption of the instincts – apart from the fact that it betrays bad taste – when a woman refers to Madame Roland, or Madame de Staël, or Monsieur George Sand, as though something were proved thereby in *favour* of 'woman as she is'. Among men, these are the three *comical* women as they are – nothing more! – and just the best involuntary *counter-arguments* against feminine emancipation and autonomy.

234

Stupidity in the kitchen; woman as cook; the terrible thoughtlessness with which the feeding of the family and the master of the house is managed! Woman does not understand what food *means*, and she insists on being cook! If woman had been a thinking creature, she should certainly, as cook for thousands of years, have discovered the most important physiological facts, and should likewise have got possession of the healing art! Through bad female cooks – through the entire lack of reason in the kitchen – the development of mankind has been longest retarded and most

* *mulier taceat in ecclesia*: let woman keep silent in church; *mulier taceat in polticis*: let woman keep silent in politics; *mulier taceat de muliere*: let woman keep silent about woman.

interfered with; even today matters are very little better. – A word
to High School girls.

235

There are turns and casts of fancy, there are sentences, little
handfuls of words, in which a whole culture, a whole society
suddenly crystallises itself. Among these is the incidental remark
of Madame de Lambert to her son: '*Mon ami, ne vous permettez
jamais que des folies, qui vous feront grand plaisir*' * – the motherliest
and wisest remark, by the way, that was ever addressed to a son.

236

I have no doubt that every noble woman will oppose what Dante
and Goethe believed about woman – the former when he sang,
'*ella guardava suso, ed io in lei*',† and the latter when he interpreted
it, 'the eternally feminine draws us *aloft*'; for *this* is just what she
believes of the eternally masculine.

237

Seven Apophthegms for Women:

> How the longest *ennui* flees,
> When a man comes to our knees!

> Age, alas! and science staid,
> Furnish even weak virtue aid.

> Sombre garb and silence meet:
> Dress for every dame – discreet.

> Whom I thank when in my bliss?
> God! – and my good tailoress!

> Young, a flower-decked cavern home;
> Old, a dragon thence doth roam.

> Noble title, leg that's fine,
> Man as well: Oh, were *he* mine!

> Speech in brief and sense in mass –
> Slippery for the jenny-ass!

---

* 'My dear, allow yourself only those follies which will bring you great pleasure.'
† *Paradiso*, Canto 2: *Beatrice in suso, e io in lei guardava* – Beatrice upward gazed,
and I on her.

237a

Woman has hitherto been treated by men like birds, which, losing their way, have come down among them from an elevation: as something delicate, fragile, wild, strange, sweet, and animating – but as something also which must be cooped up to prevent it flying away.

238

To be mistaken in the fundamental problem of 'man and woman', to deny here the profoundest antagonism and the necessity for an eternally hostile tension, to dream here perhaps of equal rights, equal training, equal claims and obligations: that is a *typical* sign of shallow-mindedness; and a thinker who has proved himself shallow at this dangerous spot – shallow in instinct! – may generally be regarded as suspicious, nay more, as betrayed, as discovered; he will probably prove too 'short' for all fundamental questions of life, future as well as present, and will be unable to descend into *any* of the depths. On the other hand, a man who has depth of spirit as well as of desires, and has also the depth of benevolence which is capable of severity and harshness, and easily confounded with them, can only think of woman as *Orientals* do: he must conceive of her as a possession, as confinable property, as a being predestined for service and accomplishing her mission therein – he must take his stand in this matter upon the immense rationality of Asia, upon the superiority of the instinct of Asia, as the Greeks did formerly; those best heirs and scholars of Asia – who, as is well known, with their *increasing* culture and amplitude of power, from Homer to the time of Pericles, became gradually *stricter* towards woman, in short, more oriental. *How* necessary, *how* logical, even *how* humanely desirable this was, let us consider for ourselves!

239

The weaker sex has in no previous age been treated with so much respect by men as at present – this belongs to the tendency and fundamental taste of democracy, in the same way as disrespectfulness to old age – what wonder is it that abuse should be immediately made of this respect? They want more, they learn to make claims, the tribute of respect is at last felt to be well-nigh galling; rivalry for rights, indeed actual strife itself, would be preferred: in a word, woman is losing modesty. And let us immediately add that she is also losing taste. She is unlearning to *fear* man: but the woman who 'unlearns to fear' sacrifices her most womanly instincts. That woman should venture forward when the fear-inspiring quality in man – or more definitely, the *man* in man – is no longer either desired or fully developed, is reasonable enough and also intelligible enough; what is more difficult to understand is that precisely thereby – woman deteriorates. This is what is happening nowadays: let us not deceive ourselves about it! Wherever the industrial spirit has triumphed over the military and aristocratic spirit, woman strives for the economic and legal independence of a clerk: 'woman as clerkess' is inscribed on the portal of the modern society which is in course of formation. While she thus appropriates new rights, aspires to be 'master', and inscribes 'progress' of woman on her flags and banners, the very opposite realises itself with terrible obviousness: *woman retrogrades*. Since the French Revolution the influence of woman in Europe has *declined* in proportion as she has increased her rights and claims; and the 'emancipation of woman', in so far as it is desired and demanded by women themselves (and not only by masculine shallow-pates), thus proves to be a remarkable symptom of the increased weakening and deadening of the most womanly instincts. There is *stupidity* in this movement, an almost masculine stupidity, of which a well-reared woman – who is always a sensible woman – might be heartily ashamed. To lose the intuition as to the ground upon which she can most surely achieve victory; to neglect exercise in the use of her proper weapons; to let-herself-go before man, perhaps even 'to the book', where formerly she kept herself in control and in refined, artful humility; to neutralise with her virtuous audacity man's faith in a *veiled*, fundamentally different ideal in woman, something eternally, necessarily feminine; to emphatically and loquaciously dissuade man from the idea that woman must be preserved, cared for, protected, and indulged, like some delicate, strangely wild, and often pleasant domestic animal; the clumsy and indignant collection of everything of the nature of servitude and bondage which the position of woman in the hitherto existing order of society has entailed and still entails (as though slavery were a counter-argument, and not rather a con-

dition of every higher culture, of every elevation of culture) –
what does all this betoken, if not a disintegration of womanly
instincts, a de-feminising? Certainly, there are enough of idiotic
friends and corrupters of woman amongst the learned asses of the
masculine sex, who advise woman to de-feminise herself in this
manner, and to imitate all the stupidities from which 'man' in
Europe, European 'manliness', suffers – who would like to lower
woman to 'general culture', indeed even to newspaper reading and
meddling with politics. Here and there they wish even to make
women into free spirits and literary workers: as though a woman
without piety would not be something perfectly obnoxious or
ludicrous to a profound and godless man – almost everywhere her
nerves are being ruined by the most morbid and dangerous kind
of music (our latest German music), and she is daily being made
more hysterical and more incapable of fulfilling her first and last
function, that of bearing robust children. They wish to 'cultivate'
her in general still more, and intend, as they say, to make the
'weaker sex' *strong* by culture: as if history did not teach in the
most emphatic manner that the 'cultivating' of mankind and his
weakening – that is to say, the weakening, dissipating, and lang-
uishing of his *force of will* – have always kept pace with one another,
and that the most powerful and influential women in the world
(and lastly, the mother of Napoleon) had just to thank their force
of will – and not their school-masters! – for their power and
ascendency over men. That which inspires respect in woman, and
often enough fear also, is her *nature*, which is more 'natural' than
that of man, her genuine, carnivora-like, cunning flexibility, her
tiger-claws beneath the glove, her *naïveté* in egoism, her untrain-
ableness and innate wildness, the incomprehensibleness, extent,
and deviation of her desires and virtues . . . That which, in spite of
fear, excites one's sympathy for the dangerous and beautiful cat,
'woman', is that she seems more afflicted, more vulnerable, more
necessitous of love and more condemned to disillusionment than
any other creature. Fear and sympathy: it is with these feelings that
man has hitherto stood in presence of woman, always with one
foot already in tragedy, which rends while it delights. – What?
And all that is now to be at an end? And the *disenchantment* of
woman is in progress? The tediousness of woman is slowly evolving? Oh Europe! Europe! We know the horned animal which

was always most attractive to thee, from which danger is ever again threatening thee! Thy old fable might once more become 'history' – an immense stupidity might once again overmaster thee and carry thee away! And no God concealed beneath it – no! only an 'idea', a 'modern idea'!. . . .

Eighth Chapter: *Peoples and Countries*

240

I heard, once again for the first time, Richard Wagner's overture to *The Mastersingers:* it is a piece of magnificent, gorgeous, heavy, latter-day art, which has the pride to presuppose two centuries of music as still living, in order that it may be understood – it is an honour to Germans that such a pride did not miscalculate! What flavours and forces, what seasons and climes do we not find mingled in it! It impresses us at one time as ancient, at another time as foreign, bitter, and too modern, it is as arbitrary as it is pompously traditional, it is not infrequently roguish, still oftener rough and coarse – it has fire and courage, and at the same time the loose, dun-coloured skin of fruits which ripen too late. It flows broad and full: and suddenly there is a moment of inexplicable hesitation, like a gap that opens between cause and effect, an oppression that makes us dream, almost a nightmare; but already it broadens and widens anew, the old stream of delight – the most manifold delight – of old and new happiness; including *especially* the joy of the artist in himself, which he refuses to conceal, his astonished, happy cognisance of his mastery of the expedients here employed, the new, newly acquired, imperfectly tested expedients of art which he apparently betrays to us. All in all, however, no beauty, no South, nothing of the delicate southern clearness of the sky, nothing of grace, no dance, hardly a will to logic; a certain clumsiness even, which is also emphasised, as though the artist wished to say to us: 'It is part of my intention'; a cumbersome drapery, something arbitrarily barbaric and ceremonious, a flirring of learned and venerable conceits and witticisms; something German in the best and worst sense of the word, something in the German style, manifold, formless, and inexhaustible; a certain German potency and super-plenitude of soul, which is not afraid to hide itself under the *raffinements* of decadence – which, perhaps, feels itself most at ease there; a real, genuine token of the German soul, which is at the same time young and aged, too ripe and yet still too rich in futurity. This kind of music expresses best what I think of the Germans: they belong to the day before yesterday and the day after tomorrow – *they have as yet no today*.

241

We 'good Europeans', we also have hours when we allow ourselves a warm-hearted patriotism, a plunge and relapse into old loves and narrow views – I have just given an example of it – hours of national excitement, of patriotic anguish, and all other sorts of old-fashioned floods of sentiment. Duller spirits may perhaps only get done with what confines its operations in us to hours and plays itself out in hours – in a considerable time: some in half a year, others in half a lifetime, according to the speed and strength with which they digest and 'change their material'. Indeed, I could think of sluggish, hesitating races, which, even in our rapidly moving Europe, would require half a century ere they could surmount such atavistic attacks of patriotism and soil-attachment, and return once more to reason, that is to say, to 'good Europeanism'. And while digressing on this possibility, I happen to become an ear-witness of a conversation between two old patriots – they were evidently both hard of hearing and consequently spoke all the louder. '*He* has as much, and knows as much, philosophy as a peasant or a corps-student,' said the one – 'he is still innocent. But what does that matter nowadays! It is the age of the masses: they lie on their belly before everything that is massive. And so also *in politicis*. A statesman who rears up for them a new Tower of Babel, some monstrosity of empire and power, they call "great" – what does it matter that we more prudent and conservative ones do not meanwhile give up the old belief that it is only the great thought that gives greatness to an action or affair. Supposing a statesman were to bring his people into the position of being obliged henceforth to practise "high politics", for which they were by nature badly endowed and prepared, so that they would have to sacrifice their old and reliable virtues, out of love to a new and doubtful mediocrity – supposing a statesman were to condemn his people generally to "practise politics", when they have hitherto had something better to do and think about, and when in the depths of their souls they have been unable to free themselves from a prudent loathing of the restlessness, emptiness, and noisy wranglings of the essentially politics-practising nations – supposing such a statesman were to stimulate the slumbering passions and avidities of his people, were to make a stigma out of their former diffidence and delight in aloofness, an offence out of their exoticism and hidden permanency, were to depreciate their most radical proclivities, subvert their consciences, make their minds narrow, and their tastes "national" – what! a statesman who should do all this, which his people would have to do penance for throughout their whole future, if they had a future, such a statesman would be *great*, would he?' – 'Undoubtedly!' replied the other old patriot vehemently; 'otherwise he *could not* have done it! It was mad perhaps to wish such a thing! But perhaps everything great has just been mad at its commencement!' – 'Misuse of words!' cried his interlocutor, contradictorily – 'Strong! Strong! Strong and mad! *Not* great!' – The old men had obviously become heated as they thus shouted their 'truths' in each other's faces; but I, in my happiness and apartness, considered how soon a stronger one may become master of the strong; and also that there is a compensation for the intellectual superficialising of a nation – namely, in the deepening of another.

242

Whether we call it 'civilisation', or 'humanising', or 'progress', which now distinguishes the European; whether we call it simply, without praise or blame, by the political formula: the *democratic* movement in Europe – behind all the moral and political foregrounds pointed to by such formulas, an immense *physiological* process goes on, which is ever extending: the process of the assimilation of Europeans; their increasing detachment from the conditions under which, climatically and hereditarily, united races originate; their increasing independence of every definite *milieu*, that for centuries would fain inscribe itself with equal demands on soul and body – that is to say, the slow emergence of an essentially *super-national* and nomadic species of man, who possesses, physiologically speaking, a maximum of the art and power of adaptation as his typical distinction. This process of the *evolving European*, which can be retarded in its *tempo* by great relapses, but will perhaps just gain and grow thereby in vehemence and depth – the still raging storm and stress of 'national sentiment' pertains to it, and also the anarchism which is appearing at present – this process will probably arrive at results on which its naïve propagators and panegyrists, the apostles of 'modern ideas', would least care to reckon. The same new conditions under which on an average a levelling and mediocrising of man will take place – a useful, industrious, variously serviceable and clever gregarious man – are in the highest degree suitable to give rise to exceptional men of the most dangerous and attractive qualities. For, while the capacity for adaptation, which is ever trying changing conditions, and begins a new work with every generation, almost with every decade, makes the *powerfulness* of the type impossible; while the collective impression of such future Europeans will probably be that of numerous, talkative, weak-willed, and very handy workmen who *require* a master, a commander, as they require their daily bread; while, therefore, the democratising of Europe will tend to the production of a type prepared for *slavery* in the most subtle sense of the term: the *strong* man will necessarily in individual and exceptional cases, become stronger and richer than he has perhaps ever been before – owing to the unprejudicedness of his schooling, owing to the immense variety of practice, art, and disguise. I meant to say that the democratising of Europe is at the same time an involuntary arrangement for the rearing of *tyrants* – taking the word in all its meanings, even in its most spiritual sense.

243

I hear with pleasure that our sun is moving rapidly towards the constellation *Hercules*: and I hope that the men on this earth will do like the sun. And we foremost, we good Europeans!

244

There was a time when it was customary to call Germans 'deep', by way of distinction; but now that the most successful type of new Germanism is covetous of quite other honours, and perhaps misses 'smartness' in all that has depth, it is almost opportune and patriotic to doubt whether we did not formerly deceive ourselves with that commendation: in short, whether German depth is not at bottom something different and worse – and something from which, thank God, we are on the point of successfully ridding ourselves. Let us try, then, to relearn with regard to German depth; the only thing necessary for the purpose is a little vivisection of the German soul. – The German soul is above all manifold, varied in its source, aggregated and superimposed, rather than actually built: this is owing to its origin. A German who would embolden himself to assert: 'Two souls, alas, dwell in my breast', would make a bad guess at the truth, or, more correctly, he would come far short of the truth about the number of souls. As a people made up of the most extraordinary mixing and mingling of races, perhaps even with a preponderance of the pre-Aryan element, as the 'people of the centre' in every sense of the term, the Germans are more intangible, more ample, more contradictory, more unknown, more incalculable, more surprising, and even more terrifying than other peoples are to themselves – they escape *definition*, and are thereby alone the despair of the French. It is characteristic of the Germans that the question: 'What is German?' never dies out among them. Kotzebue certainly knew his Germans well enough: 'we are known,' they cried jubilantly to him – but Sand also thought he knew them. Jean Paul knew what he was doing when he declared himself incensed at Fichte's lying but patriotic flatteries and exaggerations – but it is probable that Goethe thought differently about Germans from Jean Paul, even though he acknowledged him to be right with regard to Fichte. It is a question what Goethe really thought about the Germans? – But about many things around him he never spoke explicitly, and all his life he knew how to keep an astute silence – probably he had good reason for it. It is certain that it was not the 'Wars of Independence' that made him look up more joyfully, any more than it was the French Revolution – the event on account of which he *reconstructed* his *Faust*, and indeed the whole problem of 'man', was the appearance of Napoleon. There are words of Goethe in which he condemns with impatient severity, as from a foreign land, that which Germans take a pride in: he once defined the famous German turn of mind as 'indulgence towards its own and others' weaknesses'. Was he wrong? it is characteristic of Germans that one is seldom entirely wrong about them. The German soul has passages and galleries in it, there are caves, hiding-places, and dungeons therein; its disorder has much of the charm of the mysterious; the German is well acquainted with the by-paths to chaos. And as everything loves its symbol, so the German loves the clouds and all that is obscure, evolving, crepuscular, damp, and shrouded: it seems to him that everything uncertain, undeveloped, self-displacing, and growing is 'deep'. The German himself does not *exist*: he is *becoming*, he is 'developing himself'. 'Development' is therefore the essentially German discovery and hit in the great domain of philosophical formulas – a ruling idea, which, together with German beer and German music, is labouring to Germanise all Europe. Foreigners are astonished and attracted by the riddles which the conflicting nature at the basis of the German soul propounds to them (riddles which Hegel systematised and Richard Wagner has in the end set to music). 'Good-natured and spiteful' – such a juxtaposition, preposterous in the case of every other people, is unfortunately only too often justified in Germany: one has only to live for a while among Swabians to know this! The clumsiness of the German scholar and his social distastefulness agree alarmingly well with his psychical rope-dancing and nimble boldness, of which all the gods have learnt to be afraid. If any one wishes to see the 'German soul' demonstrated *ad oculos,* let him only look at German taste, at German arts and manners: what boorish indifference to 'taste'! How the noblest and the commonest stand there in juxtaposition! How disorderly and how rich is the whole constitution of this soul! The German *drags* at his soul, he drags at everything he experiences. He digests his events badly; he never gets 'done' with them; and German depth is often only a difficult, hesitating 'digestion'. And just as all chronic invalids, all dyspeptics, like what is convenient, so the German loves 'frankness' and 'honesty'; it is so *convenient* to be frank and honest! – This confidingness, this complaisance, this showing-the-cards of German *honesty,* is probably the most dangerous and most successful disguise which the German is up to nowadays: it is his proper Mephistophelean art; with this he can 'still achieve much'! The German lets himself go, and thereby gazes with faithful, blue, empty German eyes – and other countries immediately confound him with his dressing-gown! – I meant to say that, let 'German depth' be what it will – among ourselves alone we perhaps take the liberty to laugh at it – we shall do well to continue henceforth to honour its appearance and good name, and not barter away too

cheaply our old reputation as a people of depth for Prussian
'smartness', and Berlin wit and sand. It is wise for a people to
pose, and *let* itself be regarded, as profound, clumsy, good-natured,
honest, and foolish: it might even be – profound to do so! Finally,
we should do honour to our name – we are not called the *'tiusche
Volk'* (deceptive people) for nothing. . . .

245

The 'good old' time is past, it sang itself out in Mozart – how
happy are *we* that his *rococo* still speaks to us, that his 'good company', his tender enthusiasm, his childish delight in the Chinese
and in flourishes, his courtesy of heart, his longing for the elegant,
the amorous, the tripping, the tearful, and his belief in the South,
can still appeal to *something left* in us! Ah, some time or other it will
be over with it! – but who can doubt that it will be over still
sooner with the intelligence and taste for Beethoven! For he was
only the last echo of a break and transition in style, and *not*, like
Mozart, the last echo of a great European taste which had existed
for centuries. Beethoven is the intermediate event between an old
mellow soul that is constantly breaking down, and a future over-
young soul that is always *coming*; there is spread over his music the
twilight of eternal loss and eternal extravagant hope – the same
light in which Europe was bathed when it dreamed with Rousseau, when it danced round the Tree of Liberty of the Revolution,
and finally almost fell down in adoration before Napoleon. But
how rapidly does *this* very sentiment now pale, how difficult
nowadays is even the *apprehension* of this sentiment, how strangely
does the language of Rousseau, Schiller, Shelley, and Byron sound
to our ear, in whom *collectively* the same fate of Europe was able to
speak, which knew how to *sing* in Beethoven! – Whatever German
music came afterwards, belongs to Romanticism, that is to say, to a
movement which, historically considered, was still shorter, more
fleeting, and more superficial than that great interlude, the transition of Europe from Rousseau to Napoleon, and to the rise of
democracy. Weber – but what do *we* care nowadays for *Freischütz*
and *Oberon*! Or Marschner's *Hans Heiling* and *Vampyre*! Or even
Wagner's *Tannhäuser*! That is extinct, although not yet forgotten
music. This whole music of Romanticism, besides, was not noble
enough, was not musical enough, to maintain its position anywhere

but in the theatre and before the masses; from the beginning it was second-rate music, which was little thought of by genuine musicians. It was different with Felix Mendelssohn, that halcyon master, who, on account of his lighter, purer, happier soul, quickly acquired admiration, and was equally quickly forgotten: as the beautiful *episode* of German music. But with regard to Robert Schumann, who took things seriously, and has been taken seriously from the first – he was the last that founded a school – do we not now regard it as a satisfaction, a relief, a deliverance, that this very Romanticism of Schumann's has been surmounted? Schumann, fleeing into the 'Saxon Switzerland' of his soul, with a half Werther-like, half Jean-Paul-like nature (assuredly not like Beethoven! Assuredly not like Byron!) – his *Manfred* music is a mistake and a misunderstanding to the extent of injustice; Schumann, with his taste, which was fundamentally a *petty* taste (that is to say, a dangerous propensity – doubly dangerous among Germans – for quiet lyricism and intoxication of the feelings), going constantly apart, timidly withdrawing and retiring, a noble weakling who revelled in nothing but anonymous joy and sorrow, from the beginning a sort of girl and *noli me tangere* * – this Schumann was already merely a *German* event in music, and no longer a European event, as Beethoven had been, as in a still greater degree Mozart had been; with Schumann German music was threatened with its greatest danger, that of *losing the voice for the soul of Europe* and sinking into a merely national affair.

246

What a torture are books written in German to a reader who has a *third* ear! How indignantly he stands beside the slowly turning swamp of sounds without tune and rhythms without dance, which Germans call a 'book'! And even the German who *reads* books! How lazily, how reluctantly, how badly he reads! How many Germans know, and consider it obligatory to know, that there is *art* in every good sentence – art which must be divined, if the sentence is to be understood! If there is a misunderstanding about its *tempo*, for instance, the sentence itself is misunderstood! That one must not be doubtful about the rhythm-determining syllables, that one should feel the breaking of the too-rigid symmetry as intentional and as a

* Touch me not.

charm, that one should lend a fine and patient ear to every *staccato* and every *rubato*, that one should divine the sense in the sequence of the vowels and diphthongs, and how delicately and richly they can be tinted and retinted in the order of their arrangement – who among book-reading Germans is complaisant enough to recognise such duties and requirements, and to listen to so much art and intention in language? After all, one just 'has no ear for it'; and so the most marked contrasts of style are not heard, and the most delicate artistry is as it were *squandered* on the deaf. – These were my thoughts when I noticed how clumsily and unintuitively two masters in the art of prose-writing have been confounded: one, whose words drop down hesitatingly and coldly, as from the roof of a damp cave – he counts on their dull sound and echo; and another who manipulates his language like a flexible sword, and from his arm down into his toes feels the dangerous bliss of the quivering, over-sharp blade, which wishes to bite, hiss, and cut.

247

How little the German style has to do with harmony and with the ear, is shown by the fact that precisely our good musicians themselves write badly. The German does not read aloud, he does not read for the ear, but only with his eyes; he has put his ears away in the drawer for the time. In antiquity when a man read – which was seldom enough – he read something to himself, and in a loud voice; they were surprised when any one read silently, and sought secretly the reason of it. In a loud voice: that is to say, with all the swellings, inflections, and variations of key and changes of *tempo*, in which the ancient *public* world took delight. The laws of the written style were then the same as those of the spoken style; and these laws depended partly on the surprising development and refined requirements of the ear and larynx; partly on the strength, endurance, and power of the ancient lungs. In the ancient sense, a period is above all a physiological whole, inasmuch as it is comprised in one breath. Such periods as occur in Demosthenes and Cicero, swelling twice and sinking twice, and all in one breath, were pleasures to the men of *antiquity*, who knew by their own schooling how to appreciate the virtue therein, the rareness and the difficulty in the deliverance of such a period – *we* have really no right to the *big* period, we modern men, who are short of breath in every sense! Those ancients, indeed, were all of them dilettanti in speaking, consequently connoisseurs, consequently critics – they thus brought their orators to the highest pitch; in the same manner as in the last century, when all Italian ladies and gentlemen knew how to sing, the virtuosoship of song (and with it also the art of melody) reached its elevation. In Germany, however (until quite recently when a kind of platform eloquence began shyly and awkwardly enough to flutter its young wings), there was properly speaking only one kind of public and *approximately* artistical discourse – that delivered from the pulpit. The preacher was the only one in Germany who knew the weight of a syllable or a word, in what manner a sentence strikes, springs, rushes, flows, and comes to a close; he alone had a conscience in his ears, often enough a bad conscience: for reasons are not lacking why proficiency in oratory should be especially seldom attained by a German, or almost always too late. The masterpiece of German prose is therefore with good reason the masterpiece of its greatest preacher: the *Bible* has hitherto been the best German book. Compared with Luther's Bible, almost everything else is merely 'literature' – something which has not grown in Germany, and therefore has not taken and does not take root in German hearts, as the Bible has done.

248

There are two kinds of geniuses: one which above all engenders and seeks to engender, and another which willingly lets itself be fructified and brings forth. And similarly, among the gifted nations, there are those on whom the woman's problem of pregnancy has devolved, and the secret task of forming, maturing, and perfecting – the Greeks, for instance, were a nation of this kind, and so are the French; and others which have to fructify and become the cause of new modes of life – like the Jews, the Romans, and, in all modesty be it asked: like the Germans? – nations tortured and enraptured by unknown fevers and irresistibly forced out of themselves, amorous and longing for foreign races (for such as 'let themselves be fructified'), and withal imperious, like everything conscious of being full of generative force, and consequently empowered 'by the grace of God'. These two kinds of geniuses seek each other like man and woman; but they also misunderstand each other – like man and woman.

249

Every nation has its own 'Tartuffery', and calls that its virtue. – One does not know – cannot know, the best that is in one.

250

What Europe owes to the Jews? – Many things, good and bad, and above all one thing of the nature both of the best and the worst: the grand style in morality, the fearfulness and majesty of infinite demands, of infinite significations, the whole Romanticism and sublimity of moral questionableness – and consequently just the most attractive, ensnaring, and exquisite element in those irid- escences and allurements to life, in the aftersheen of which the sky of our European culture, its evening sky, now glows – perhaps glows out. For this, we artists among the spectators and philo- sophers, are – grateful to the Jews.

251

It must be taken into the bargain, if various clouds and disturb- ances – in short, slight attacks of stupidity – pass over the spirit of a people that suffers and *wants* to suffer from national nervous fever and political ambition: for instance, among present-day Germans there is alternately the anti-French folly, the anti-Semitic folly, the anti-Polish folly, the Christian-romantic folly, the Wagnerian folly, the Teutonic folly, the Prussian folly (just look at those poor historians, the Sybels and Treitschkes, and their closely bandaged heads), and whatever else these little obscurations of the German spirit and conscience may be called. May it be forgiven me that I, too, when on a short daring sojourn on very infected ground, did not remain wholly exempt from the disease, but like every- one else, began to entertain thoughts about matters which did not concern me – the first symptom of political infection. About the Jews, for instance, listen to the following: I have never yet met a German who was favourably inclined to the Jews; and however decided the repudiation of actual anti-Semitism may be on the part of all prudent and political men, this prudence and policy is not perhaps directed against the nature of the sentiment itself, but only against its dangerous excess, and especially against the distasteful and infamous expression of this excess of sentiment – on this point we must not deceive ourselves. That Germany has amply *sufficient* Jews, that the German stomach, the German blood, has difficulty (and will long have difficulty) in disposing only of this quantity of 'Jew' – as the Italian, the Frenchman, and the Englishman have done by means of a stronger digestion – that is the unmistakable declaration and language of a general instinct, to which one must listen and according to which one must act. 'Let no more Jews come in! And shut the doors, especially towards the East (also towards Austria)!' – thus commands the instinct of a people whose nature is still feeble and uncertain, so that it could be easily wiped out, easily extinguished, by a stronger race. The Jews, however, are beyond all doubt the strongest, toughest, and purest race at present living in Europe; they know how to succeed even under the worst conditions (in fact better than under favourable ones), by means of virtues of some sort, which one would like nowadays to label as vices – owing above all to a resolute faith which does not need to be ashamed before 'modern ideas'; they alter only, *when* they do alter, in the same way that the Russian Empire makes its conquest – as an empire that has plenty of time and is not of yesterday – namely, according to the principle, 'as slowly as possible'! A thinker who has the future of Europe at heart, will, in all his perspectives concerning the future, calculate upon the Jews, as he will calculate upon the Russians, as above all the surest and likeliest factors in the great play and battle of forces. That which is at present called a 'nation' in Europe, and is really rather a *res facta***** than *nata* (indeed, sometimes confusingly similar to a *res ficta et picta*), is in every case something evolving, young, easily displaced, and not yet a race, much less such a race *aere perennius*, as the Jews are: such 'nations' should most carefully avoid all hot-headed rivalry and hostility! It is certain that the Jews, if they desired – or if they were driven to it, as the anti-Semites seem to wish – *could* now have the ascendency, nay, literally the supremacy, over Europe; that they are *not* working and planning for that end is equally certain. Meanwhile, they rather wish and desire, even somewhat importunately, to be insorbed and absorbed by Europe; they long to be finally settled, authorised, and respected some-where, and wish to put an end to the nomadic life, to the

---

* *Res facta*: a thing made; *res nata*: a thing born; *res ficta et picta*: a thing invented and painted; *aere perennius*: more enduring than brass.

'wandering Jew' – and one should certainly take account of this impulse and tendency, and *make advances* to it (it possibly betokens a mitigation of the Jewish instincts): for which purpose it would perhaps be useful and fair to banish the anti-Semitic bawlers out of the country. One should make advances with all prudence, and with selection; pretty much as the English nobility do. It stands to reason that the more powerful and strongly marked types of new Germanism could enter into relation with the Jews with the least hesitation, for instance, the nobleman officer from the Prussian border: it would be interesting in many ways to see whether the genius for money and patience (and especially some intellect and intellectuality – sadly lacking in the place referred to) could not in addition be annexed and trained to the hereditary art of commanding and obeying – for both of which the country in question has now a classic reputation. But here it is expedient to break off my festal discourse and my sprightly Teutonomania: for I have already reached my *serious topic*, the 'European problem', as I understand it, the rearing of a new ruling caste for Europe.

252

They are not a philosophical race – the English: Bacon represents an *attack* on the philosophical spirit generally, Hobbes, Hume, and Locke, an abasement, and a depreciation of the idea of a 'philosopher' for more than a century. It was *against* Hume that Kant uprose and raised himself; it was Locke of whom Schelling rightly said, '*Je méprise Locke*'; in the struggle against the English mechanical stultification of the world, Hegel and Schopenhauer (along with Goethe) were of one accord; the two hostile brother-geniuses in philosophy, who pushed in different directions towards the opposite poles of German thought, and thereby wronged each other as only brothers will do. – What is lacking in England, and has always been lacking, that half-actor and rhetorician knew well enough, the absurd muddle-head, Carlyle, who sought to conceal under passionate grimaces what he knew about himself: namely, what was *lacking* in Carlyle – real *power* of intellect, real *depth* of intellectual perception, in short, philosophy. It is characteristic of such an unphilosophical race to hold on firmly to Christianity – they *need* its discipline for 'moralising' and humanising. The Englishman, more gloomy, sensual, headstrong, and brutal than the

German – is for that very reason, as the baser of the two, also the most pious: he has all the *more need* of Christianity. To finer nostrils, this English Christianity itself has still a characteristic English taint of spleen and alcoholic excess, for which, owing to good reasons, it is used as an antidote – the finer poison to neutralise the coarser: a finer form of poisoning is in fact a step in advance with coarse-mannered people, a step towards spiritualisation. The English coarseness and rustic demureness is still most satisfactorily disguised by Christian pantomime, and by praying and psalm-singing (or, more correctly, it is thereby explained and differently expressed); and for the herd of drunkards and rakes who formerly learned moral grunting under the influence of Methodism (and more recently as the 'Salvation Army'), a penitential fit may really be the relatively highest manifestation of 'humanity' to which they can be elevated: so much may reasonably be admitted. That, however, which offends even in the humanest Englishman is his lack of music, to speak figuratively (and also literally): he has neither rhythm nor dance in the movements of his soul and body; indeed, not even the desire for rhythm and dance, for 'music'. Listen to him speaking; look at the most beautiful Englishwomen *walking* – in no country on earth are there more beautiful doves and swans; finally, listen to them singing! But I ask too much. . . .

253

There are truths which are best recognised by mediocre minds, because they are best adapted for them, there are truths which only possess charms and seductive power for mediocre spirits – one is pushed to this probably unpleasant conclusion, now that the influence of respectable but mediocre Englishmen – I may mention Darwin, John Stuart Mill, and Herbert Spencer – begins to gain the ascendency in the middle-class region of European taste. Indeed, who could doubt that it is a useful thing for *such* minds to have the ascendency for a time? It would be an error to consider the highly developed and independently soaring minds as specially qualified for determining and collecting many little common facts, and deducing conclusions from them; as exceptions, they are rather from the first in no very favourable position towards those who are 'the rules'. After all, they have more to do than merely to perceive – in effect, they have to *be* something new, they have to *signify* something new, they have to *represent* new values! The gulf between knowledge and capacity is perhaps greater, and also more mysterious, than one thinks: the capable man in the grand style, the creator, will possibly have to be an ignorant person – while on the other hand, for scientific discoveries like those of Darwin, a certain narrowness, aridity, and industrious carefulness (in short something English) may not be unfavourable for arriving at them. – Finally, let it not be forgotten that the English, with their profound mediocrity, brought about once before a general depression of European intelligence. What is called 'modern ideas', or 'the ideas of the eighteenth century', or 'French ideas' – that, consequently, against which the *German* mind rose up with profound disgust – is of English origin, there is no doubt about it. The French were only the apes and actors of these ideas, their best soldiers, and likewise, alas! their first and profoundest *victims*; for owing to the diabolical Anglomania of 'modern ideas', the *âme français* has in the end become so thin and emaciated, that at present one recalls its sixteenth and seventeenth centuries, its profound, passionate strength, its inventive excellency, almost with disbelief. One must, however, maintain this verdict of historical justice in a determined manner, and defend it against present prejudices and appearances: the European *noblesse* – of sentiment, taste, and manners, taking the word in every high sense – is the work and invention of *France*; the European ignobleness, the plebeianism of modern ideas – is *England's* work and invention.

254

Even at present France is still the seat of the most intellectual and refined culture of Europe, it is still the high school of taste; but one must know how to find this 'France of taste'. He who belongs to it keeps himself well concealed – they may be a small number in whom it lives and is embodied, besides perhaps being men who do not stand upon the strongest legs, in part fatalists, hypochondriacs, invalids, in part persons over-indulged, over-refined, such as have the *ambition* to conceal themselves. They have all something in common: they keep their ears closed in presence of the delirious folly and noisy spouting of the democratic *bourgeois*. In fact, a besotted and brutalised France at present sprawls in the foreground – it recently celebrated a veritable orgy of bad taste, and at the same time of self-admiration, at the funeral of Victor Hugo. There is also something else common to them: a predilection to resist intellectual Germanising – and a still greater inability to do so! In this France of intellect, which is also a France of pessimism, Schopenhauer has perhaps become more at home, and more indigenous than he has ever been in Germany; not to speak of Heinrich Heine, who has long ago been re-incarnated in the more refined and fastidious lyrists of Paris; or of Hegel, who at present, in the form of Taine – the *first* of living historians – exercises an almost tyrannical influence. As regards Richard Wagner, however, the more French music learns to adapt itself to the actual needs of the *âme moderne*, the more will it 'Wagnerise'; one can safely predict that beforehand – it is already taking place sufficiently! There are, however, three things which the French can still boast of with pride as their heritage and possession, and as indelible tokens of their ancient intellectual superiority in Europe, in spite of all voluntary or involuntary Germanising and vulgarising of taste. *Firstly*, the capacity for artistic emotion, for devotion to 'form', for which the expression, *l'art pour l'art*, along with numerous others, has been invented – such capacity has not been lacking in France for three centuries; and owing to its reverence for the 'small number', it has again and again made a sort of chamber music of literature possible, which is sought for in vain elsewhere in Europe. – The *second* thing whereby the French can lay claim to a superiority over Europe is their ancient, many-sided, *moralistic* culture, owing to which one finds on an average, even in the petty *romanciers* of the newspapers and chance *boulevardiers de Paris*, a psychological sensitiveness and curiosity, of which, for example, one has no conception (to say nothing of the thing itself!) in Germany. The Germans lack a couple of centuries of the moralistic work requisite thereto, which, as we have said, France has not grudged: those who call the Germans 'naïve' on that account give them commendation for a defect. (As the opposite of the German inexperience and innocence *in voluptate psychologica*, which is not too remotely associated with the tediousness of German intercourse – and as the most successful expression of genuine French curiosity and inventive talent in this domain of delicate thrills, Henri Beyle may be noted; that remarkable anticipatory and forerunning man, who, with a Napoleonic *tempo*, traversed *his*

Europe, in fact, several centuries of the European soul, as a sur-
veyor and discoverer thereof – it has required two generations
to *overtake* him one way or other, to divine long afterwards some
of the riddles that perplexed and enraptured him – this strange
Epicurean and man of interrogation, the last great psychologist of
France). – There is yet a *third* claim to superiority: in the French
character there is a successful half-way synthesis of the North and
South, which makes them comprehend many things, and enjoins
upon them other things, which an Englishman can never comprehend. Their temperament, turned alternately to and from the
South, in which from time to time the Provençal and Ligurian
blood froths over, preserves them from the dreadful, northern
grey-in-grey, from sunless conceptual-spectrism and from poverty
of blood – our *German* infirmity of taste, for the excessive prevalence of which at the present moment, blood and iron, that is to say
'high politics', has with great resolution been prescribed (according to a dangerous healing art, which bids me wait and wait, but
not yet hope). – There is also still in France a pre-understanding
and ready welcome for those rarer and rarely gratified men, who
are too comprehensive to find satisfaction in any kind of father-
landism, and know how to love the South when in the North and
the North when in the South – the born Midlanders, the 'good
Europeans'. For them *Bizet* has made music, this latest genius, who
has seen a new beauty and seduction – who has discovered a piece
of the *South in music.*

255

I hold that many precautions should be taken against German
music. Suppose a person loves the South as I love it – as a great
school of recovery for the most spiritual and the most sensuous ills,
as a boundless solar profusion and effulgence which o'erspreads a
sovereign existence believing in itself – well, such a person will
learn to be somewhat on his guard against German music, because,
in injuring his taste anew, it will also injure his health anew. Such
a Southerner, a Southerner not by origin but by *belief*, if he should
dream of the future of music, must also dream of it being freed
from the influence of the North; and must have in his ears the
prelude to a deeper, mightier, and perhaps more perverse and
mysterious music, a super-German music, which does not fade,

pale, and die away, as all German music does, at the sight of the blue, wanton sea and the Mediterranean clearness of sky – a super-European music, which holds its own even in presence of the brown sunsets of the desert, whose soul is akin to the palm-tree, and can be at home and can roam with big, beautiful, lonely beasts of prey. . . . I could imagine a music of which the rarest charm would be that it knew nothing more of good and evil; only that here and there perhaps some sailor's home-sickness, some golden shadows and tender weaknesses might sweep lightly over it; an art which, from the far distance, would see the colours of a sinking and almost incomprehensible *moral* world fleeing towards it, and would be hospitable enough and profound enough to receive such belated fugitives.

256

Owing to the morbid estrangement which the nationality-craze has induced and still induces among the nations of Europe, owing also to the short-sighted and hasty-handed politicians, who with the help of this craze, are at present in power, and do not suspect to what extent the disintegrating policy they pursue must necessarily be only an interlude policy – owing to all this, and much else that is altogether unmentionable at present, the most unmistakable signs that *Europe wishes to be one*, are now overlooked, or arbitrarily and falsely misinterpreted. With all the more profound and large-minded men of this century, the real general tendency of the mysterious labour of their souls was to prepare the way for that new *synthesis*, and tentatively to anticipate the European of the future; only in their simulations, or in their weaker moments, in old age perhaps, did they belong to the 'fatherlands' – they only rested from themselves when they became 'patriots'. I think of such men as Napoleon, Goethe, Beethoven, Stendhal, Heinrich Heine, Schopenhauer: it must not be taken amiss if I also count Richard Wagner among them, about whom one must not let oneself be deceived by his own misunderstandings (geniuses like him have seldom the right to understand themselves), still less, of course, by the unseemly noise with which he is now resisted and opposed in France: the fact remains, nevertheless, that Richard Wagner and the *later French Romanticism* of the forties, are most closely and intimately related to one another. They are akin,

fundamentally akin, in all the heights and depths of their requirements; it is Europe, the *one* Europe, whose soul presses urgently
and longingly, outwards and upwards, in their multifarious and
boisterous art – whither? Into a new light? Towards a new sun? But
who would attempt to express accurately what all these masters of
new modes of speech could not express distinctly? It is certain that
the same storm and stress tormented them, that they *sought* in the
same manner, these last great seekers! All of them steeped in
literature to their eyes and ears – the first artists of universal literary
culture – for the most part even themselves writers, poets, intermediaries and blenders of the arts and the senses (Wagner, as
musician is reckoned among painters, as poet among musicians, as
artist generally among actors); all of them fanatics for *expression* 'at
any cost' – I specially mention Delacroix, the nearest related to
Wagner; all of them great discoverers in the realm of the sublime,
also of the loathsome and dreadful, still greater discoverers in
effect, in display, in the art of the show-shop; all of them talented
far beyond their genius, out and out *virtuosi*, with mysterious
accesses to all that seduces, allures, constrains, and upsets; born
enemies of logic and of the straight line, hankering after the
strange, the exotic, the monstrous, the crooked, and the self-
contradictory; as men, Tantaluses of the will, plebeian parvenus,
who knew themselves to be incapable of a noble *tempo* or of a *lento*
in life and action – think of Balzac, for instance – unrestrained
workers, almost destroying themselves by work; antinomians and
rebels in manners, ambitious and insatiable, without equilibrium
and enjoyment; all of them finally shattering and sinking down at
the Christian cross (and with right and reason, for who of them
would have been sufficiently profound and sufficiently original
for an *Antichristian* philosophy?) – on the whole, a boldly daring,
splendidly overbearing, high-flying, and aloft-up-dragging class of
higher men, who had first to teach their century – and it is the
century of the *masses* – the conception 'higher man' . . . Let the
German friends of Richard Wagner advise together as to whether
there is anything purely German in the Wagnerian art, or whether
its distinction does not consist precisely in coming from *super-
German* sources and impulses: in which connection it may not be
underrated how indispensable Paris was to the development of his
type, which the strength of his instincts made him long to visit at

the most decisive time — and how the whole style of his proceedings, of his self-apostolate, could only perfect itself in sight of
the French socialistic original. On a more subtle comparison it will
perhaps be found, to the honour of Richard Wagner's German
nature, that he has acted in everything with more strength, daring,
severity, and elevation than a nineteenth-century Frenchman could
have done — owing to the circumstance that we Germans are as
yet nearer to barbarism than the French — perhaps even the most
remarkable creation of Richard Wagner is not only at present, but
for ever inaccessible, incomprehensible, and inimitable to the
whole latter-day Latin race: the figure of Siegfried, that *very free*
man, who is probably far too free, too hard, too cheerful, too
healthy, too *anti-Catholic* for the taste of old and mellow civilised
nations. He may even have been a sin against Romanticism, this
anti-Latin Siegfried: well, Wagner atoned amply for this sin in his
old sad days, when — anticipating a taste which has meanwhile
passed into politics — he began, with the religious vehemence
peculiar to him, to preach, at least, *the way to Rome*, if not to walk
therein. — That these last words may not be misunderstood, I will
call to my aid a few powerful rhymes, which will even betray to
less delicate ears what I mean — what I mean *counter to* the 'last
Wagner' and his *Parsifal* music —

> — Is this our mode? —
> From German heart came this vexed ululating?
> From German body, this self-lacerating?
> Is ours this priestly hand-dilation,
> This incense-fuming exaltation?
> Is ours this faltering, falling, shambling,
> This quite uncertain ding-dong-dangling?
> This sly nun-ogling, *Ave*-hour-bell ringing,
> This wholly false enraptured heaven-o'erspringing?
> — Is this our mode? —
> Think well! — ye still wait for admission —
> For what ye hear is *Rome — Rome's faith by intuition*!

Ninth Chapter: *What is Noble?*

257

Every elevation of the type 'man', has hitherto been the work of an aristocratic society – and so will it always be – a society believing in a long scale of gradations of rank and differences of worth among human beings, and requiring slavery in some form or other. Without the *pathos of distance*, such as grows out of the incarnated difference of classes, out of the constant outlooking and downlooking of the ruling caste on subordinates and instruments, and out of their equally constant practice of obeying and commanding, of keeping down and keeping at a distance – that other more mysterious pathos could never have arisen, the longing for an ever new widening of distance within the soul itself, the formation of ever higher, rarer, further, more extended, more comprehensive states, in short, just the elevation of the type 'man', the continued 'self-surmounting of man', to use a moral formula in a supermoral sense. To be sure, one must not resign oneself to any humanitarian illusions about the history of the origin of an aristocratic society (that is to say, of the preliminary condition for the elevation of the type 'man'): the truth is hard. Let us acknowledge unprejudicedly how every higher civilisation hitherto has *originated*! Men with a still natural nature, barbarians in every terrible sense of the word, men of prey, still in possession of unbroken strength of will and desire for power, threw themselves upon weaker, more moral, more peaceful races (perhaps trading or cattle-rearing communities), or upon old mellow civilisations in which the final vital force was flickering out in brilliant fireworks of wit and depravity. At the commencement, the noble caste was always the barbarian caste: their superiority did not consist first of all in their physical, but in their psychical power – they were more *complete* men (which at every point also implies the same as 'more complete beasts').

258

Corruption – as the indication that anarchy threatens to break out among the instincts, and that the foundation of the emotions, called 'life', is convulsed – is something radically different according to the organisation in which it manifests itself. When, for instance, an aristocracy like that of France at the beginning of the Revolution, flung away its privileges with sublime disgust and sacrificed itself to an excess of its moral sentiments, it was corruption – it was really only the closing act of the corruption which had existed for centuries, by virtue of which that aristocracy had abdicated step by step its lordly prerogatives and lowered itself to a *function* of royalty (in the end even to its decoration and paradedress). The essential thing, however, in a good and healthy aristocracy is that it should *not* regard itself as a function either of the kingship or the commonwealth, but as the *significance* and highest justification thereof – that it should therefore accept with a good conscience the sacrifice of a legion of individuals, who, *for its sake*, must be suppressed and reduced to imperfect men, to slaves and instruments. Its fundamental belief must be precisely that society is *not* allowed to exist for its own sake, but only as a foundation and scaffolding, by means of which a select class of beings may be able to elevate themselves to their higher duties, and in general to a higher *existence:* like those sun-seeking climbing plants in Java – they are called *Sipo Matador* – which encircle an oak so long and so often with their arms, until at last, high above it, but supported by it, they can unfold their tops in the open light, and exhibit their happiness.

259

To refrain mutually from injury, from violence, from exploitation, and put one's will on a par with that of others: this may result in a certain rough sense in good conduct among individuals when the necessary conditions are given (namely, the actual similarity of the individuals in amount of force and degree of worth, and their co-relation within one organisation). As soon, however, as one wished to take this principle more generally, and if possible even as *the fundamental principle of society*, it would immediately disclose what it really is – namely, a Will to the *denial* of life, a principle of dissolution and decay. Here one must think profoundly to the very basis and resist all sentimental weakness: life itself is *essent-ially* appropriation, injury, conquest of the strange and weak, suppression, severity, obtrusion of peculiar forms, incorporation, and at the least, putting it mildest, exploitation – but why should one for ever use precisely these words on which for ages a disparaging purpose has been stamped? Even the organisation within which, as was previously supposed, the individuals treat each other as equal – it takes place in every healthy aristocracy – must itself, if it be a living and not a dying organisation, do all that towards other bodies, which the individuals within it refrain from doing to each other: it will have to be the incarnated Will to Power, it will endeavour to grow, to gain ground, attract to itself and acquire ascendency – not owing to any morality or immorality, but because it *lives*, and because life *is* precisely Will to Power. On no point, however, is the ordinary consciousness of Europeans more unwilling to be corrected than on this matter; people now rave everywhere, even under the guise of science, about coming conditions of society in which 'the exploiting character' is to be absent – that sounds to my ears as if they promised to invent a mode of life which should refrain from all organic functions. 'Exploitation' does not belong to a depraved, or imperfect and primitive society: it belongs to the *nature* of the living being as a primary organic function; it is a consequence of the intrinsic Will to Power, which is precisely the Will to Life. – Granting that as a theory this is a novelty – as a reality it is the *fundamental fact* of all history: let us be so far honest towards ourselves!

260

In a tour through the many finer and coarser moralities which have hitherto prevailed or still prevail on the earth, I found certain traits recurring regularly together and connected with one another, until finally two primary types revealed themselves to me, and a radical distinction was brought to light. There is *master-morality* and *slave-morality*; – I would at once add, however, that in all higher and mixed civilisations, there are also attempts at the reconciliation of the two moralities; but one finds still oftener the confusion and mutual misunderstanding of them, indeed, sometimes their close juxtaposition – even in the same man, within one soul. The distinctions of moral values have either originated in a ruling caste, pleasantly conscious of being different from the ruled – or among the ruled class, the slaves and dependents of all sorts. In the first case, when it is the rulers who determine the conception 'good', it is the exalted, proud disposition which is regarded as the distinguishing feature, and that which determines the order of rank. The noble type of man separates from himself the beings in whom the opposite of this exalted, proud disposition displays itself: he despises them. Let it at once be noted that in this first kind of morality the antithesis 'good' and 'bad' means practically the same as 'noble' and 'despicable'; – the antithesis 'good' and '*evil*' is of a different origin. The cowardly, the timid, the insignificant, and those thinking merely of narrow utility are despised; moreover, also, the distrustful, with their constrained glances, the self-abasing, the dog-like kind of men who let themselves be abused, the mendicant flatterers, and above all the liars – it is a fundamental belief of all aristocrats that the common people are untruthful. 'We truthful ones' – the nobility in ancient Greece called themselves. It is obvious that everywhere the designations of moral value were at first applied to *men*, and were only derivatively and at a later period applied to *actions*; it is a gross mistake, therefore, when historians of morals start with questions like, 'Why have sympathetic actions been praised?' The noble type of man regards *himself* as a determiner of values; he does not require to be approved of; he passes the judgment: 'What is injurious to me is injurious in itself'; he knows that it is he himself only who confers honour on things; he is a *creator of values*. He honours whatever he recognises in himself: such morality is self-glorification. In the foreground there is the feeling of plenitude, of power, which seeks to overflow, the happiness of high tension, the consciousness of a wealth which would fain give and bestow: the noble man also helps the unfortunate, but not – or scarcely – out of pity, but rather from an impulse generated by the super-abundance of power. The noble man honours in himself the powerful one, him also who has power over himself, who knows how to speak and how to keep silence, who takes pleasure in subjecting himself to severity and hardness, and has reverence for all that is severe and hard. 'Wotan placed a hard heart in my breast,' says an old Scandinavian Saga: it is thus rightly expressed from the soul of a proud Viking. Such a type of man is even proud of *not* being made for sympathy; the hero of the Saga therefore adds warningly: 'He who has not a hard heart when young, will never have one.' The noble and brave who think thus are the furthest removed from the morality which sees precisely in sympathy, or in acting for the good of others, or in *désintéressement*, the characteristic of the moral; faith in oneself, pride in oneself, a radical enmity and irony towards 'selflessness', belong as definitely to noble morality, as do a careless scorn and precaution in presence of sympathy and the 'warm heart'. – It is the powerful who *know* how to honour, it is their art, their domain for invention. The profound reverence for age and for tradition – all law rests on this double reverence – the belief and prejudice in favour of ancestors and unfavourable to newcomers, is typical in the morality of the powerful; and if, reversely, men of 'modern ideas' believe almost instinctively in 'progress' and the 'future', and are more and more lacking in respect for old age, the ignoble origin of these 'ideas' has complacently betrayed itself thereby. A morality of the ruling class, however, is more especially foreign and irritating to present-day taste in the sternness of its principle that one has duties only to one's equals; that one may act towards beings of a lower rank, towards all that is foreign, just as seems good to one, or 'as the heart desires', and in any case 'beyond good and evil': it is here that sympathy and similar sentiments can have a place. The ability and obligation to exercise prolonged gratitude and prolonged revenge – both only within the circle of equals – artfulness in retaliation, *raffinement* of the idea in friendship, a certain necessity to have enemies (as outlets for the emotions of envy, quarrelsomeness, arrogance – in fact, in order to be a good *friend*): all these are typical characteristics of the noble morality, which, as has been pointed out, is not the morality of 'modern ideas', and is therefore at present difficult to realise, and also to unearth and disclose. – It is otherwise with the second type of morality, *slave-morality*. Supposing that the abused, the oppressed, the suffering, the unemancipated, the weary, and those uncertain of themselves, should moralise, what will be the common element in their moral estimates? Probably a pessimistic suspicion with regard to the entire situation of man will find expression, perhaps a condemnation of man, together with his situation. The slave has an unfavourable eye for the virtues of the powerful; he has a scepticism and distrust, a *refinement* of distrust of everything 'good' that is there honoured – he would fain persuade himself that the very happiness there is not genuine. On the other hand, *those* qualities which serve to alleviate the existence of sufferers are brought into prominence and flooded with light; it is here that sympathy, the kind, helping hand, the warm heart, patience, diligence, humility, and friendliness attain to honour; for here these are the most useful qualities, and almost the only means of supporting the burden of existence. Slave-morality is essentially the morality of utility. Here is the seat of the origin of the famous antithesis 'good' and '*evil*' – power and dangerousness are assumed to reside in the evil, a certain dreadfulness, subtlety, and strength, which do not admit of being despised. According to slave morality, therefore, the 'evil' man arouses fear; according to master-morality, it is precisely the 'good' man who arouses fear and seeks to arouse it, while the bad man is regarded as the despicable being. The contrast attains its maximum when, in accordance with the logical consequences of slave-morality, a shade of depreciation – it may be slight and well-intentioned – at last attaches itself even to the 'good' man of this morality; because, according to the servile mode of thought, the good man must in any case be the *safe* man: he is good-natured, easily deceived, perhaps a little stupid, *un bonhomme*. Everywhere that slave-morality gains the ascendency, language shows a tendency to approximate the significations of the words 'good' and 'stupid'. – A last fundamental difference: the desire for *freedom*, the instinct for happiness and the refinements of the feeling of liberty belong as necessarily to slave-morals and morality, as artifice and enthusiasm in reverence and devotion are the regular symptoms of an aristocratic mode of thinking and estimating. – Hence we can understand without further detail why love *as a passion* – it is our European speciality – must absolutely be of noble origin; as is well known, its invention is due to the Provençal poet-cavaliers, those brilliant ingenious men of the '*gai saber*', to whom Europe owes so much, and almost owes itself.

261

Vanity is one of the things which are perhaps most difficult for a noble man to understand: he will be tempted to deny it, where another kind of man thinks he sees it self-evidently. The problem for him is to represent to his mind beings who seek to arouse a good opinion of themselves which they themselves do not possess – and consequently also do not 'deserve' – and who yet *believe* in this good opinion afterwards. This seems to him on the one hand such bad taste and so self-disrespectful, and on the other hand so grotesquely unreasonable, that he would like to consider vanity an exception, and is doubtful about it in most cases when it is spoken of. He will say, for instance: 'I may be mistaken about my value, and on the other hand may nevertheless demand that my value should be acknowledged by others precisely as I rate it – that, however, is not vanity (but self-conceit, or, in most cases, that which is called "humility", and also "modesty").' Or he will even say: 'For many reasons I can delight in the good opinion of others, perhaps because I love and honour them, and rejoice in all their joys, perhaps also because their good opinion endorses and strengthens my belief in my own good opinion, perhaps because the good opinion of others, even in cases where I do not share it, is useful to me, or gives promise of usefulness – all this, however, is not vanity.' The man of noble character must first bring it home forcibly to his mind, especially with the aid of history, that, from time immemorial, in all social strata in any way dependent, the ordinary man *was* only that which he *passed for* – not being at all accustomed to fix values, he did not assign even to himself any other value than that which his master assigned to him (it is the peculiar *right of masters* to create values). It may be looked upon as the result of an extraordinary atavism, that the ordinary man, even at present, is still always *waiting* for an opinion about himself, and then instinctively submitting himself to it; yet by no means only to a 'good' opinion, but also to a bad and unjust one (think, for instance, of the greater part of the self-appreciations and self-depreciations which believing women learn from their confessors, and which in general the believing Christian learns from his Church). In fact, conformably to the slow rise of the democratic social order (and its cause, the blending of the blood of masters and slaves), the originally noble and rare impulse of the masters to assign a value to themselves and to 'think well' of themselves, will now be more and more encouraged and extended; but it has at all times an older, ampler, and more radically ingrained propensity opposed to it – and in the phenomenon of 'vanity' this older propensity overmasters the younger. The vain person rejoices over *every* good opinion which he hears about himself (quite apart from the point of view of its usefulness, and equally regardless of its truth or falsehood), just as he suffers from every bad opinion: for he subjects himself to both, he *feels* himself subjected to both, by that oldest instinct of subjection which breaks forth in him. – It is 'the slave' in the vain man's blood, the remains of the slave's craftiness – and how much of the 'slave' is still left in woman, for instance! – which seeks to *seduce* to good opinions of itself; it is the slave, too, who immediately afterwards falls prostrate himself before these opinions, as though he had not called them forth. – And to repeat it again: vanity is an atavism.

262

A *species* originates, and a type becomes established and strong in the long struggle with essentially constant *unfavourable* conditions. On the other hand, it is known by the experience of breeders that species which receive superabundant nourishment, and in general a surplus of protection and care, immediately tend in the most marked way to develop variations, and are fertile in prodigies and monstrosities (also in monstrous vices). Now look at an aristocratic commonwealth, say an ancient Greek *polis*, or Venice, as a voluntary or involuntary contrivance for the purpose of *rearing* human beings; there are there men beside one another, thrown upon their own resources, who want to make their species prevail, chiefly because they *must* prevail, or else run the terrible danger of being exterminated. The favour, the superabundance, the protection are there lacking under which variations are fostered; the species needs itself as species, as something which, precisely by virtue of its hardness, its uniformity, and simplicity of structure, can in general prevail and make itself permanent in constant struggle with its neighbours, or with rebellious or rebellion-threatening vassals. The most varied experience teaches it what are the qualities to which it principally owes the fact that it still exists, in spite of all gods and men, and has hitherto been victorious: these qualities it calls virtues, and these virtues alone it develops to maturity. It does so with severity, indeed it desires severity; every aristocratic morality is intolerant in the education of youth, in the control of women, in the marriage customs, in the relations of old and

young, in the penal laws (which have an eye only for the degenerating): it counts intolerance itself among the virtues, under the
name of 'justice'. A type with few, but very marked features, a
species of severe, warlike, wisely silent, reserved and reticent men
(and as such, with the most delicate sensibility for the charm and
nuances of society) is thus established, unaffected by the vicissitudes
of generations; the constant struggle with uniform *unfavourable*
conditions is, as already remarked, the cause of a type becoming
stable and hard. Finally, however, a happy state of things results,
the enormous tension is relaxed; there are perhaps no more
enemies among the neighbouring peoples, and the means of life,
even of the enjoyment of life, are present in superabundance. With
one stroke the bond and constraint of the old discipline severs: it
is no longer regarded as necessary, as a condition of existence –
if it would continue, it can only do so as a form of *luxury*, as
an archaïsing *taste*. Variations, whether they be deviations (into
the higher, finer, and rarer), or deteriorations and monstrosities,
appear suddenly on the scene in the greatest exuberance and
splendour; the individual dares to be individual and detach himself. At this turning-point of history there manifest themselves,
side by side, and often mixed and entangled together, a magnificent, manifold, virgin-forest-like upgrowth and up-striving, a
kind of *tropical tempo* in the rivalry of growth, and an extraordinary
decay and self-destruction, owing to the savagely opposing and
seemingly exploding egoisms, which strive with one another 'for
sun and light', and can no longer assign any limit, restraint, or
forbearance for themselves by means of the hitherto existing
morality. It was this morality itself which piled up the strength so
enormously, which bent the bow in so threatening a manner –
it is now 'out of date', it is getting 'out of date'. The dangerous
and disquieting point has been reached when the greater, more
manifold, more comprehensive life *is lived beyond* the old morality;
the 'individual' stands out, and is obliged to have recourse to his
own law-giving, his own arts and artifices for self-preservation,
self-elevation, and self-deliverance. Nothing but new 'Whys',
nothing but new 'Hows', no common formulas any longer, misunderstanding and disregard in league with each other, decay,
deterioration, and the loftiest desires frightfully entangled, the
genius of the race overflowing from all the cornucopias of good

and bad, a portentous simultaneousness of Spring and Autumn, full of new charms and mysteries peculiar to the fresh, still inexhausted, still unwearied corruption. Danger is again present, the mother of morality, great danger; this time shifted into the individual, into the neighbour and friend, into the street, into the own child, into their own heart, into all the most personal and secret recesses of their desires and volitions. What will the moral philosophers who appear at this time have to preach? They discover, these sharp onlookers and loafers, that the end is quickly approaching, that everything around them decays and produces decay, that nothing will endure until the day after to-morrow, except one species of man, the incurably *mediocre*. The mediocre alone have a prospect of continuing and propagating themselves – they will be the men of the future, the sole survivors. 'Be like them! Become mediocre!' is now the only morality which has still a significance, which still obtains a hearing. – But it is difficult to preach this morality of mediocrity! It can never avow what it is and what it desires! It has to talk of moderation and dignity and duty and brotherly love – it will have difficulty *in concealing its irony*!

263

There is an *instinct for rank*, which more than anything else is already the sign of a *high* rank; there is a *delight* in the *nuances* of reverence which leads one to infer noble origin and habits. The refinement, goodness, and loftiness of a soul are put to a perilous test when something passes by that is of the highest rank, but is not yet protected by the awe of authority from obtrusive touches and incivilities: something that goes its way like a living touchstone, undistinguished, undiscovered, and tentative, perhaps voluntarily veiled and disguised. He whose task and practice it is to investigate souls, will avail himself of many varieties of this very art to determine the ultimate value of a soul, the unalterable, innate order of rank to which it belongs: he will test it by its *instinct for reverence*. *Différence engendre haine*:* the vulgarity of many a nature spurts up suddenly like dirty water, when any holy vessel, any jewel from closed shrines, any book bearing the marks of great destiny, is brought before it; while on the other hand, there is an involuntary silence, a hesitation of the eye, a cessation of all

---

* Difference breeds hatred.

gestures, by which it is indicated that a soul *feels* the nearness of what is worthiest of respect. The way in which, on the whole, the reverence for the *Bible* has hitherto been maintained in Europe, is perhaps the best example of discipline and refinement of manners which Europe owes to Christianity: books of such profoundness and supreme significance require for their protection an external tyranny of authority, in order to acquire the *period* of thousands of years which is necessary to exhaust and unriddle them. Much has been achieved when the sentiment has been at last instilled into the masses (the shallowpates and the boobies of every kind) that they are not allowed to touch everything, that there are holy experiences before which they must take off their shoes and keep away the unclean hand – it is almost their highest advance towards humanity. On the contrary, in the so-called cultured classes, the believers in 'modern ideas', nothing is perhaps so repulsive as their lack of shame, the easy insolence of eye and hand with which they touch, taste, and finger everything; and it is possible that even yet there is more *relative* nobility of taste, and more tact for reverence among the people, among the lower classes of the people, especially among peasants, than among the newspaper-reading *demi-monde* of intellect, the cultured class.

264

It cannot be effaced from a man's soul what his ancestors have preferably and most constantly done: whether they were perhaps diligent economisers attached to a desk and a cash-box, modest and citizen-like in their desires, modest also in their virtues; or whether they were accustomed to commanding from morning till night, fond of rude pleasures and probably of still ruder duties and responsibilities; or whether, finally, at one time or another, they have sacrificed old privileges of birth and possession, in order to live wholly for their faith – for their 'God' – as men of an inexorable and sensitive conscience, which blushes at every compromise. It is quite impossible for a man *not* to have the qualities and predilections of his parents and ancestors in his constitution, whatever appearances may suggest to the contrary. This is the problem of race. Granted that one knows something of the parents, it is admissible to draw a conclusion about the child: any kind of offensive incontinence, any kind of sordid envy, or of clumsy self-vaunting – the three things which together have constituted the genuine plebeian type in all times – such must pass over to the child, as surely as bad blood; and with the help of the best education and culture one will only succeed in *deceiving* with regard to such heredity. – And what else does education and culture try to do nowadays! In our very democratic, or rather, very plebeian age, 'education' and 'culture' *must* be essentially the art of deceiving – deceiving with regard to origin, with regard to the inherited plebeianism in body and soul. An educator who nowadays preached truthfulness above everything else, and called out constantly to his pupils: 'Be true! Be natural! Show yourselves as you are!' – even such a virtuous and sincere ass would learn in a short time to have recourse to the *furca* of Horace, *naturam expellere:* with what results? 'Plebeianism' *usque recurret.**

265

At the risk of displeasing innocent ears, I submit that egoism belongs to the essence of a noble soul; I mean the unalterable belief that to a being such as 'we', other beings must naturally be in subjection, and have to sacrifice themselves. The noble soul accepts the fact of his egoism without question, and also without consciousness of harshness, constraint, or arbitrariness therein, but rather as something that may have its basis in the primary law of things – if he sought a designation for it he would say: 'It is justice itself.' He acknowledges under certain circumstances, which made him hesitate at first, that there are other equally privileged ones; as soon as he has settled this question of rank, he moves among those equals and equally privileged ones with the same assurance, as regards modesty and delicate respect, which he enjoys in intercourse with himself – in accordance with an innate heavenly mechanism which all the stars understand. It is an *additional* instance of his egoism, this artfulness and self-limitation in intercourse with his equals – every star is a similar egoist; he honours *himself* in them, and in the rights which he concedes to them, he has no doubt that the exchange of honours and rights, as the *essence* of all intercourse, belongs also to the natural condition of things. The noble soul gives as he takes, prompted by the passionate and

* Horace, *Epistles* i. x. 24: 'Naturam expellas furca, tamen usque recurrret.' – 'You may expel Nature with a fork, yet she will always come running back.'

sensitive instinct of requital, which is at the root of his nature. The notion of 'favour' has, *inter pares*, neither significance nor good repute; there may be a sublime way of letting gifts as it were light upon one from above, and of drinking them thirstily like dewdrops; but for those arts and displays the noble soul has no aptitude. His egoism hinders him here: in general, he looks 'aloft' unwillingly – he looks either *forward*, horizontally and deliberately, or downwards – *he knows that he is on a height.*

266

'One can only truly esteem him who does not *look out for* himself.' – Goethe to Rath Schlosser.

267

The Chinese have a proverb which mothers even teach their children: '*Siao-sin*' ('make thy heart *small*'). This is the essentially fundamental tendency in latter-day civilisations. I have no doubt that an ancient Greek, also, would first of all remark the self-dwarfing in us Europeans of today – in this respect alone we should immediately be 'distasteful' to him.

268

What, after all, is ignobleness? – Words are vocal symbols for ideas; ideas, however, are more or less definite mental symbols for frequently returning and concurring sensations, for groups of sensations. It is not sufficient to use the same words in order to understand one another: we must also employ the same words for the same kind of internal experiences, we must in the end have experiences *in common*. On this account the people of one nation understand one another better than those belonging to different nations, even when they use the same language; or rather, when people have lived long together under similar conditions (of climate, soil, danger, requirement, toil) there *originates* therefrom an entity that 'understands itself' – namely, a nation. In all souls a like number of frequently recurring experiences have gained the upper hand over those occurring more rarely: about these matters people understand one another rapidly and always more rapidly – the history of language is the history of a process of abbreviation; on the basis of this quick comprehension people always unite closer and closer. The greater the danger, the greater is the need of agreeing quickly and readily about what is necessary; not to misunderstand one another in danger – that is what cannot at all be dispensed with in intercourse. Also in all loves and friendships one has the experience that nothing of the kind continues when the discovery has been made that in using the same words, one of the two parties has feelings, thoughts, intuitions, wishes, or fears different from those of the other. (The fear of the 'eternal mis-understanding': that is the good genius which so often keeps persons of different sexes from too hasty attachments, to which sense and heart prompt them – and *not* some Schopenhauerian 'genius of the species'!). Whichever groups of sensations within a soul awaken most readily, begin to speak, and give the word of command – these decide as to the general order of rank of its values, and determine ultimately its list of desirable things. A man's estimates of value betray something of the *structure* of his soul, and wherein it sees its conditions of life, its intrinsic needs. Supposing now that necessity has from all time drawn together only such men as could express similar requirements and similar experiences by similar symbols, it results on the whole that the easy *communicability* of need, which implies ultimately the undergoing only of average and *common* experiences, must have been the most potent of all the forces which have hitherto operated upon mankind. The more similar, the more ordinary people, have always had and are still having the advantage; the more select, more refined, more unique, and difficultly comprehensible, are liable to stand alone; they succumb to accidents in their isolation, and seldom propagate themselves. One must appeal to immense opposing forces, in order to thwart this natural, all-too-natural *progressus in simile*, the evolution of man to the similar, the ordinary, the average, the gregarious – to the *ignoble*!

269

The more a psychologist – a born, an unavoidable psychologist and soul-diviner – turns his attention to the more select cases and individuals, the greater is his danger of being suffocated by sympathy: he *needs* sternness and cheerfulness more than any other man. For the corruption, the ruination of higher men, of the more unusually constituted souls, is in fact, the rule: it is dreadful to have such a rule always before one's eyes. The manifold torment of the psychologist who has discovered this ruination, who discovers once, and then discovers *almost* repeatedly throughout all history, this universal inner 'desperateness' of higher men, this eternal 'too late!' in every sense – may perhaps one day be the cause of his turning with bitterness against his own lot, and of his making an attempt at self-destruction – of his 'going to ruin' himself. One may perceive in almost every psychologist a tell-tale inclination for delightful intercourse with commonplace and well-ordered men: the fact is thereby disclosed that he always requires healing, that he needs a sort of flight and forgetfulness, away from what his insight and incisiveness – from what his 'business' – has laid upon his conscience. The fear of his memory is peculiar to him. He is easily silenced by the judgment of others; he hears with unmoved countenance how people honour, admire, love, and glorify, where he has *perceived* – or he even conceals his silence by expressly assenting to some plausible opinion. Perhaps the paradox of his situation becomes so dreadful that, precisely where he has learnt *great sympathy*, together with *great contempt*, the multitude, the educated, and the visionaries, have on their part learnt great reverence – reverence for 'great men' and marvellous animals, for the sake of whom one blesses and honours the fatherland, the earth, the dignity of mankind, and one's own self, to whom one points the young, and in view of whom one educates them. And who knows but in all great instances hitherto just the same happened: that the multitude worshipped a god, and that the 'god' was only a poor sacrificial animal! *Success* has always been the greatest liar – and the 'work' itself is a success; the great statesman, the conqueror, the discoverer, are disguised in their creations until they are unrecognisable; the 'work' of the artist, of the philosopher, only invents him who has created it, is *reputed* to have created it; the 'great men', as they are reverenced, are poor little fictions composed afterwards; in the world of historical values spurious coinage *prevails*. Those great poets, for example, such as Byron, Musset, Poe, Leopardi, Kleist, Gogol (I do not venture to mention much greater names, but I have them in my mind), as they now appear, and were perhaps obliged to be: men of the moment, enthusiastic, sensuous, and childish, light-minded and impulsive in their trust and distrust; with souls in which usually some flaw has to be concealed; often taking revenge with their works for an internal defilement, often seeking forgetfulness in their soaring from a too true memory, often lost in the mud and almost in love with it, until they become like the will-o'-the-wisps around the swamps, and *pretend to be* stars – the people then call them idealists – often struggling with protracted disgust, with an ever-reappearing phantom of disbelief, which makes them cold, and obliges them to languish for *gloria* and devour 'faith as it is' out of the hands of intoxicated adulators – what a *torment* these great artists are and the so-called higher men in general, to him who has once found them out! It is thus conceivable that it is just from woman – who is clairvoyant in the world of suffering, and also unfortunately eager to help and save to an extent far beyond her powers – that *they* have learnt so readily those outbreaks of boundless devoted *sympathy*, which the multitude, above all the reverent multitude, do not understand, and overwhelm with prying and self-gratifying interpretations. This sympathising invariably deceives itself as to its power; woman would like to believe that love can do *everything* – it is the *superstition* peculiar to her. Alas, he who knows the heart finds out how poor, helpless, pretentious, and blundering even the best and deepest love is – he finds that it rather *destroys* than saves! – It is possible that under the holy fable and travesty of the life of Jesus there is hidden one of the most painful cases of the martyrdom of *knowledge about love*: the martyrdom of the most innocent and most craving heart, that never had enough of any human love, that *demanded* love, that demanded inexorably and frantically to be loved and nothing else, with terrible outbursts against those who refused him their love; the story of a poor soul insatiated and insatiable in love, that had to invent hell to send thither those who *would not* love him – and that at last, enlightened about human love, had to invent a God who is entire love, entire *capacity* for love – who takes pity on human love, because it is so paltry, so ignorant! He who has such sentiments, he who has such *knowledge* about love – *seeks* for death! – But why should one deal with such painful matters? Provided, of course, that one is not obliged to do so.

270

The intellectual haughtiness and loathing of every man who has suffered deeply – it almost determines the order of rank *how* deeply men can suffer – the chilling certainty, with which he is thoroughly imbued and coloured, that by virtue of his suffering he *knows more* than the shrewdest and wisest can ever know, that he has been familiar with, and 'at home' in, many distant, dreadful worlds of which '*you* know nothing'! – this silent intellectual haughtiness of the sufferer, this pride of the elect of knowledge, of the 'initiated', of the almost sacrificed, finds all forms of disguise necessary to protect itself from contact with officious and sympathising hands, and in general from all that is not its equal in suffering. Profound suffering makes noble; it separates. – One of the most refined forms of disguise is Epicurism, along with a certain ostentatious boldness of taste, which takes suffering lightly, and puts itself on the defensive against all that is sorrowful and profound. There are 'gay men' who make use of gaiety, because they are misunderstood on account of it – they *wish* to be misunderstood. There are 'scientific minds' who make use of science, because it gives a gay appearance, and because scientificalness leads to the conclusion that a person is superficial – they *wish* to mislead to a false conclusion. There are free insolent minds which would fain conceal and deny that they are broken, proud, incurable hearts (the cynicism of Hamlet – the case of Galiani); and occasionally folly itself is the mask of an unfortunate *over-assured* knowledge. – From which it follows that it is the part of a more refined humanity to have reverence 'for the mask', and not to make use of psychology and curiosity in the wrong place.

271

That which separates two men most profoundly is a different sense and grade of purity. What does it matter about all their honesty and reciprocal usefulness, what does it matter about all their mutual good-will: the fact still remains – they 'cannot smell each other!' The highest instinct for purity places him who is affected with it in the most extraordinary and dangerous isolation, as a saint: for it is just holiness – the highest spiritualisation of the instinct in question. Any kind of cognisance of an indescribable excess in the joy of the bath, any kind of ardour or thirst which perpetually impels the soul out of night into the morning, and out of gloom, out of 'affliction' into clearness, brightness, depth, and refinement – just as much as such a tendency *distinguishes* – it is a noble tendency – it also *separates*. – The pity of the saint is pity for the *filth* of the human, all-too-human. And there are grades and heights where pity itself is regarded by him as impurity, as filth.

272

Signs of nobility: never to think of lowering our duties to the rank of duties for everybody; to be unwilling to renounce or to share our responsibilities; to count our prerogatives, and the exercise of them, among our *duties*.

273

A man who strives after great things, looks upon everyone whom he encounters on his way either as a means of advance, or a delay and hindrance – or as a temporary resting-place. His peculiar lofty *bounty* to his fellow-men is only possible when he attains his elevation and dominates. Impatience, and the consciousness of being always condemned to comedy up to that time – for even strife is a comedy, and conceals the end, as every means does – spoil all intercourse for him; this kind of man is acquainted with solitude, and what is most poisonous in it.

274

The Problem of those who Wait. – Happy chances are necessary, and many incalculable elements, in order that a higher man in whom the solution of a problem is dormant, may yet take action, or 'break forth', as one might say – at the right moment. On an average it *does not* happen; and in all corners of the earth there are waiting ones sitting, who hardly know to what extent they are waiting, and still less that they wait in vain. Occasionally, too, the waking call comes too late – the chance which gives 'permission' to take action – when their best youth, and strength for action have been used up in sitting still; and how many a one, just as he 'sprang up', has found with horror that his limbs are benumbed and his spirits are now too heavy! 'It is too late,' he has said to himself – and has become self-distrustful and henceforth for ever useless. – In the domain of genius, may not the 'Raphael without hands' (taking the expression in its widest sense) perhaps not be the exception, but the rule? – Perhaps genius is by no means so rare: but rather the five hundred *hands* which it requires in order to tyrannise over the *kairos*, 'the right time' – in order to take chance by the forelock!

275

He who does not *wish* to see the height of a man, looks all the more sharply at what is low in him, and in the foreground – and thereby betrays himself.

276

In all kinds of injury and loss the lower and coarser soul is better off than the nobler soul: the dangers of the latter must be greater, the probability that it will come to grief and perish is in fact immense, considering the multiplicity of the conditions of its existence. – In a lizard a finger grows again which has been lost; not so in man. –

277

It is too bad! Always the old story! When a man has finished building his house, he finds that he has learnt unawares something which he *ought* absolutely to have known before he – began to build. The eternal, fatal 'Too late!' The melancholia of everything *completed*! –

278

– Wanderer, who art thou? I see thee follow thy path without scorn, without love, with unfathomable eyes, wet and sad as a plummet which has returned to the light insatiated out of every depth – what did it seek down there? – with a bosom that never sighs, with lips that conceal their loathing, with a hand which only slowly grasps: who art thou? What hast thou done? Rest thee here: this place has hospitality for everyone – refresh thyself! And whoever thou art, what is it that now pleases thee? What will serve to refresh thee? Only name it, whatever I have I offer thee! 'To refresh me? To refresh me? Oh, thou prying one, what sayest thou! But give me, I pray thee – ' What? What? Speak out! 'Another mask! A second mask!'

279

Men of profound sadness betray themselves when they are happy: they have a mode of seizing upon happiness as though they would choke and strangle it, out of jealousy – ah, they know only too well that it will flee from them!

280

'Bad! Bad! What? Does he not – go back?' Yes! But you misunderstand him when you complain about it. He goes back like everyone who is about to make a great spring.

281

– 'Will people believe it of me? But I insist that they believe it of me: I have always thought very unsatisfactorily of myself and about myself, only in very rare cases, only compulsorily, always without delight in "the subject", ready to digress from "myself", and always without faith in the result, owing to an unconquerable distrust of the *possibility* of self-knowledge, which has led me so far as to feel a *contradictio in adjecto** even in the idea of 'direct knowledge' which theorists allow themselves: – this matter of fact is almost the most certain thing I know about myself. There must be a sort of repugnance in me to *believe* anything definite about myself. – Is there perhaps some enigma therein? Probably; but fortunately nothing for my own teeth. – Perhaps it betrays the species to which I belong? – but not to myself, as is sufficiently agreeable to me.'

282

– 'But what has happened to you?' – 'I do not know,' he said, hesitatingly; 'perhaps the Harpies have flown over my table.' – It sometimes happens nowadays that a gentle, sober, retiring man becomes suddenly mad, breaks the plates, upsets the table, shrieks, raves, and shocks everybody – and finally withdraws, ashamed, and raging at himself – whither? For what purpose? To famish apart? To suffocate with his memories? – To him who has the desires of a lofty and dainty soul, and only seldom finds his table laid and his food prepared, the danger will always be great – nowadays, how-

---

* Contradiction in terms.

ever, it is extraordinarily so. Thrown into the midst of a noisy and plebeian age, with which he does not like to eat out of the same dish, he may readily perish of hunger and thirst – or, should he nevertheless finally 'fall to', of sudden nausea. – We have probably all sat at tables to which we did not belong; and precisely the most spiritual of us, who are most difficult to nourish, know the dangerous *dyspepsia* which originates from a sudden insight and disillusionment about our food and our messmates – the *after-dinner nausea*.

283

If one wishes to praise at all, it is a delicate and at the same time a noble self-control, to praise only where one *does not* agree – otherwise in fact one would praise oneself, which is contrary to good taste – a self-control, to be sure, which offers excellent opportunity and provocation to constant *misunderstanding*. To be able to allow oneself this veritable luxury of taste and morality, one must not live among intellectual imbeciles, but rather among men whose misunderstandings and mistakes amuse by their refinement – or one will have to pay dearly for it! – 'He praises me, *therefore* he acknowledges me to be right' – this asinine method of inference spoils half of the life of us recluses, for it brings the asses into our neighbourhood and friendship.

284

To live in a vast and proud tranquillity; always beyond . . . To have, or not to have, one's emotions, one's For and Against, according to choice; to lower oneself to them for hours; to *seat* oneself on them as upon horses, and often as upon asses – for one must know how to make use of their stupidity as well as of their fire. To conserve one's three hundred foregrounds; also one's black spectacles: for there are circumstances when nobody must look into our eyes, still less into our 'motives'. And to choose for company that roguish and cheerful vice, politeness. And to remain master of one's four virtues, courage, insight, sympathy, and solitude. For solitude is a virtue with us, as a sublime bent and bias to purity, which divines that in the contact of man and man – 'in society' – it must be unavoidably impure. All society makes one somehow, somewhere, or sometime – 'commonplace'.

285

The greatest events and thoughts – the greatest thoughts, however, are the greatest events – are longest in being comprehended: the generations which are contemporary with them do not *experience* such events – they live past them. Something happens there as in the realm of the stars. The light of the furthest stars is longest in reaching man; and before it has arrived man *denies* – that there are stars there. 'How many centuries does a mind require to be understood?' – that is also a standard, one also makes a gradation of rank and an etiquette therewith, such as is necessary for mind and for star.

286

'Here is the prospect free, the mind exalted.' – But there is a reverse kind of man, who is also upon a height, and has also a free prospect – but looks *downwards*.

287

– What is noble? What does the word 'noble' still mean for us nowadays? How does the noble man betray himself, how is he recognised under this heavy overcast sky of the commencing plebeianism, by which everything is rendered opaque and leaden? – It is not his actions which establish his claim – actions are always ambiguous, always inscrutable; neither is it his 'works'. One finds nowadays among artists and scholars plenty of those who betray by their works that a profound longing for nobleness impels them; but this very *need of* nobleness is radically different from the needs of the noble soul itself, and is in fact the eloquent and dangerous sign of the lack thereof. It is not the works, but the *belief* which is here decisive and determines the order of rank – to employ once more an old religious formula with a new and deeper meaning – it is some fundamental certainty which a noble soul has about itself, something which is not to be sought, is not to be found, and perhaps, also, is not to be lost. – *The noble soul has reverence for itself.*

288

There are men who are unavoidably intellectual, let them turn and twist themselves as they will, and hold their hands before their treacherous eyes – as though the hand were not a betrayer; it always comes out at last that they have something which they hide – namely, intellect. One of the subtlest means of deceiving, at least as long as possible, and of successfully representing oneself to be stupider than one really is – which in everyday life is often as desirable as an umbrella – is called *enthusiasm*, including what belongs to it, for instance, virtue. For as Galiani said, who was obliged to know it: *vertu est enthousiasme*.

289

In the writings of a recluse one always hears something of the echo of the wilderness, something of the murmuring tones and timid vigilance of solitude; in his strongest words, even in his cry itself, there sounds a new and more dangerous kind of silence, of concealment. He who has sat day and night, from year's end to year's end, alone with his soul in familiar discord and discourse, he who has become a cave-bear, or a treasure-seeker, or a treasure-guardian and dragon in his cave – it may be a labyrinth, but can also be a gold-mine – his ideas themselves eventually acquire a twilight-colour of their own, and an odour, as much of the depth as of the mould, something uncommunicative and repulsive, which blows chilly upon every passer-by. The recluse does not believe that a philosopher – supposing that a philosopher has always in the first place been a recluse – ever expressed his actual and ultimate opinions in books: are not books written precisely to hide what is in us? – indeed, he will doubt whether a philosopher *can* have 'ultimate and actual' opinions at all; whether behind every cave in him there is not, and must necessarily be, a still deeper cave: an ampler, stranger, richer world beyond the surface, an abyss behind every bottom, beneath every 'foundation'. Every philosophy is a foreground philosophy – this is a recluse's verdict: 'There is something arbitrary in the fact that the *philosopher* came to a stand here, took a retrospect and looked around; that he *here* laid his spade aside and did not dig any deeper — there is also something suspicious in it.' Every philosophy also *conceals* a philosophy; every opinion is also a *lurking-place*, every word is also a *mask*.

290

Every deep thinker is more afraid of being understood than of being misunderstood. The latter perhaps wounds his vanity; but the former wounds his heart, his sympathy, which always says: 'Ah, why would *you* also have as hard a time of it as I have?'

291

Man, a *complex*, mendacious, artful, and inscrutable animal, uncanny to the other animals by his artifice and sagacity, rather than by his strength, has invented the good conscience in order finally to enjoy his soul as something *simple*; and the whole of morality is a long, audacious falsification, by virtue of which generally enjoyment at the sight of the soul becomes possible. From this point of view there is perhaps much more in the conception of 'art' than is generally believed.

292

A philosopher: that is, a man who constantly experiences, sees, hears, suspects, hopes, and dreams extraordinary things; who is struck by his own thoughts as if they came from the outside, from above and below, as a species of events and lightning-flashes *peculiar to him*; who is perhaps himself a storm pregnant with new lightnings; a portentous man, around whom there is always rumbling and mumbling and gaping and something uncanny going on. A philosopher: alas, a being who often runs away from himself, is often afraid of himself — but whose curiosity always makes him 'come to himself' again.

293

A man who says: 'I like that, I take it for my own, and mean to guard and protect it from everyone'; a man who can conduct a case, carry out a resolution, remain true to an opinion, keep hold of a woman, punish and overthrow insolence; a man who has his indignation and his sword, and to whom the weak, the suffering, the oppressed, and even the animals willingly submit and naturally belong; in short, a man who is a *master* by nature – when such a man has sympathy, well! *that* sympathy has value! But of what account is the sympathy of those who suffer! Or of those even who preach sympathy! There is nowadays, throughout almost the whole of Europe, a sickly irritability and sensitiveness towards pain, and also a repulsive irrestrainableness in complaining, an effeminising, which, with the aid of religion and philosophical nonsense, seeks to deck itself out as something superior – there is a regular cult of suffering. The *unmanliness* of that which is called 'sympathy' by such groups of visionaries, is always, I believe, the first thing that strikes the eye. – One must resolutely and radically taboo this latest form of bad taste; and finally I wish people to put the good amulet, *'gai saber'* ('gay science', in ordinary language), on heart and neck, as a protection against it.

294

The Olympian Vice. – Despite the philosopher who, as a genuine Englishman, tried to bring laughter into bad repute in all thinking minds – 'Laughing is a bad infirmity of human nature, which every thinking mind will strive to overcome' (Hobbes) – I would even allow myself to rank philosophers according to the quality of their laughing – up to those who are capable of *golden* laughter. And supposing that gods also philosophise, which I am strongly inclined to believe, owing to many reasons – I have no doubt that they also know how to laugh thereby in an overman-like and new fashion – and at the expense of all serious things! Gods are fond of ridicule: it seems that they cannot refrain from laughter even in holy matters.

295

The genius of the heart, as that great mysterious one possesses it, the tempter-god and born rat-catcher of consciences, whose voice can descend into the nether-world of every soul, who neither speaks a word nor casts a glance in which there may not be some motive or touch of allurement, to whose perfection it pertains that he knows how to appear – not as he is, but in a guise which acts as an *additional* constraint on his followers to press ever closer to him, to follow him more cordially and thoroughly – the genius of the heart, which imposes silence and attention on everything loud and self-conceited, which smooths rough souls and makes them taste a new longing – to lie placid as a mirror, that the deep heavens may be reflected in them – the genius of the heart, which teaches the clumsy and too hasty hand to hesitate, and to grasp more delicately; which scents the hidden and forgotten treasure, the drop of goodness and sweet spirituality under thick dark ice, and is a divining-rod for every grain of gold, long buried and imprisoned in mud and sand; the genius of the heart, from contact with which everyone goes away richer; not favoured or surprised, not as though gratified and oppressed by the good things of others; but richer in himself, newer than before, broken up, blown upon, and sounded by a thawing wind; more uncertain perhaps, more delicate, more fragile, more bruised, but full of hopes which as yet lack names, full of a new will and current, full of a new ill-will and counter-current . . . but what am I doing, my friends? Of whom am I talking to you? Have I forgotten myself so far that I have not even told you his name? Unless it be that you have already divined of your own accord who this questionable god and spirit is, that wishes to be *praised* in such a manner? For, as it happens to everyone who from childhood onward has always been on his legs, and in foreign lands, I have also encountered on my path many strange and dangerous spirits; above all, however, and again and again, the one of whom I have just spoken: in fact, no less a personage than the god *Dionysus*, the great equivocator and tempter, to whom, as you know, I once offered in all secrecy and reverence my first-fruits – the last, as it seems to me, who has offered a *sacrifice* to him, for I have found no one who could understand what I was then doing. In the meantime, however, I have learned much, far too much, about the philosophy of this god, and, as I said, from mouth to mouth – I, the last disciple and initiate of the god Dionysus: and perhaps I might at last begin to give you, my friends, as far as I am allowed, a little taste of this philosophy? In a hushed voice, as is but seemly: for it has to do with much that is secret, new, strange, wonderful, and uncanny. The very fact that Dionysus is a philosopher, and that therefore gods also philosophise, seems to me a novelty which is not unensnaring, and might perhaps arouse suspicion precisely amongst philosophers – amongst you, my friends, there is less to be said against it, except that it comes too late and not at the right time; for, as it has been disclosed to me, you are loth nowadays to believe in God and gods. It may happen, too, that in the frankness of my story I must go further than is agreeable to the strict usages of your ears? Certainly the god in question went further, very much further, in such dialogues, and was always many paces ahead of me. . . . Indeed, if it were allowed, I should have to give him, according to human usage, fine ceremonious titles of lustre and merit, I should have to extol his courage as investigator and discoverer, his fearless honesty, truthfulness, and love of wisdom. But such a god does not know what to do with all that respectable trumpery and pomp. 'Keep that,' he would say, 'for thyself and those like thee, and whoever else require it! I – have no reason to cover my nakedness!' One suspects that this kind of divinity and philosopher perhaps lacks shame? – He once said: 'Under certain circumstances I love mankind' – and referred thereby to Ariadne, who was present; 'in my opinion man is an agreeable, brave, inventive animal, that has not his equal upon earth, he makes his way even through all labyrinths. I like man, and often think how I can still further advance him, and make him stronger, more evil, and more profound.' – 'Stronger, more evil, and more profound?' I asked in horror. 'Yes,' he said again, 'stronger, more evil, and more profound; also more beautiful' – and thereby the tempter-god smiled with his halcyon smile, as though he had just paid some charming compliment. One here sees at once that it is not only shame that this divinity lacks – and in general there are good grounds for supposing that in some things the gods could all of them come to us men for instruction. We men are – more human.

296

Alas! what are you, after all, my written and painted thoughts! Not long ago you were so variegated, young, and malicious, so full of thorns and secret spices, that you made me sneeze and laugh – and now? You have already doffed your novelty, and some of you, I fear, are ready to become truths, so immortal do they look, so pathetically honest, so tedious! And was it ever otherwise? What then do we write and paint, we mandarins with Chinese brush, we immortalisers of things which *lend* themselves to writing, what are we alone capable of painting? Alas, only that which is just about to fade and begins to lose its odour! Alas, only exhausted and departing storms and belated yellow sentiments! Alas, only birds strayed and fatigued by flight, which now let themselves be captured with the hand – with *our* hand! We immortalise what cannot live and fly much longer, things only which are exhausted and mellow! And it is only for your *afternoon*, you, my written and painted thoughts, for which alone I have colours, many colours perhaps, many variegated softenings, and fifty yellows and browns and greens and reds – but nobody will divine thereby how ye looked in your morning, you sudden sparks and marvels of my solitude, you, my old, beloved – *evil* thoughts!

FROM THE HEIGHTS

by F. W. Nietzsche

[*translated by L. A. Magnus*]

1

Midday of Life! Oh, season of delight!
My summer's park!
Uneaseful joy to look, to lurk, to hark –
I peer for friends, am ready day and night –
Where linger ye, my friends? The time is right!

2

Is not the glacier's grey today for you
Rose-garlanded?
The brooklet seeks you; wind, cloud, with longing thread
And thrust themselves yet higher to the blue,
To spy for you from farthest eagle's view.

3

My table was spread out for you on high –
Who dwelleth so
Star-near, so near the grisly pit below? –
My realm – what realm hath wider boundary?
My honey – who hath sipped its fragrancy?

4

Friends, ye are there! Woe me – yet I am not
He whom ye seek?
Ye stare and stop – better your wrath could speak!
I am not I? Hand, gait, face, changed? And what
I am, to you my friends, now am I not?

5

Am I an other? Strange am I to Me?
　　　　Yet from Me sprung?
A wrestler, by himself too oft self-wrung?
Hindering too oft my own self's potency,
Wounded and hampered by self-victory?

6

I sought where-so the winds blow keenest. There
　　　　I learned to dwell
Where no man dwells, on lonesome ice-lorn fell,
And unlearned Man and God and curse and prayer?
Became a ghost haunting the glaciers bare?

7

Ye, my old friends! Look! ye turn pale, filled o'er
　　　　With love and fear!
Go! yet not in wrath. Ye could ne'er live here.
Here in the farthest realm of ice and scaur,
A huntsman must one be, like chamois soar.

8

An evil huntsman was I? See how taut
　　　　My bow was bent!
Strongest was he by whom such bolt were sent –
Woe now! that arrow is with peril fraught,
Perilous as none. – Have yon safe home ye sought!

9

Ye go! Thou didst endure enough, O heart –
　　　　Strong was thy hope;
Unto new friends thy portals widely ope,
Let old ones be. Bid memory depart!
Wast thou young then, now – better young thou art!

10

What linked us once together, one hope's tie –
　　　　(Who now doth con
Those lines, now fading, Love once wrote thereon?) –
Is like a parchment, which the hand is shy
To touch – like crackling leaves, all seared, all dry.

11

Oh! Friends no more! They are — what name for those? —
               Friends' phantom-flight
Knocking at my heart's window-pane at night,
Gazing on me, that speaks 'We were' and goes —
Oh, withered words, once fragrant as the rose!

12

Pinings of youth that might not understand!
               For which I pined,
Which I deemed changed with me, kin of my kind:
But they grew old, and thus were doomed and banned:
None but new kith are native of my land!

13

Midday of life! My second youth's delight!
               My summer's park!
Unrestful joy to long, to lurk, to hark!
I peer for friends! — am ready day and night,
For my new friends. Come! Come! The time is right!

*   *   *

14

This song is done — the sweet sad cry of rue
               Sang out its end;
A wizard wrought it, he the timely friend,
The midday-friend — no, do not ask me who;
At midday 'twas, when one became as two.

15

We keep our Feast of Feasts, sure of our bourne,
               Our aims self-same:
The Guest of Guests, friend Zarathustra, came!
The world now laughs, the grisly veil was torn,
And Light and Dark were one that wedding-morn.

WORDSWORTH CLASSICS
OF WORLD LITERATURE

General Editor: Tom Griffith

HUMAN, ALL-TOO-HUMAN
BEYOND GOOD AND EVIL